LUTHER AND WORLD MISSION

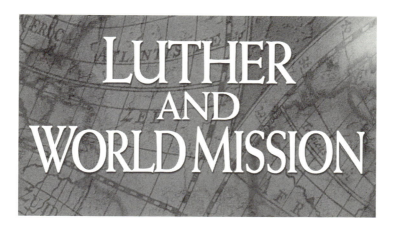

A HISTORICAL AND SYSTEMATIC STUDY
WITH SPECIAL REFERENCE
TO LUTHER'S BIBLE EXPOSITION

INGEMAR ÖBERG

TRANSLATED BY DEAN APEL

Originally published as *Luther och världsmissionen: Historisk-Systematiska studier med särskild hänsyn till bibelutläggningen*, Studier utgivna av Institutionen för systematisk teologi vid Åbo Akademi 23, Institute of Systematic Theology, Åbo Academy-University, Finland

CONCORDIA PUBLISHING HOUSE · SAINT LOUIS

English translation © 2007 Concordia Publishing House
3558 S. Jefferson Avenue, St. Louis, MO 63118-3968
1-800-325-3040 • www.cph.org

Manufactured in the United States of America

Library of Congress Cataloging-in-Publication Data

Öberg, Ingemar, 1930–2005
  [Luther och vårldsmissionen. English]
  Luther and world mission : a historical and systematic study with special reference to Luther's Bible exposition / Ingemar Öberg ; translated by Dean Apel.
    p. cm.
  Includes bibliographical references and index.
  ISBN-13: 978-0-570-03322-6
  ISBN-10: 0-570-03322-5
  1. Luther, Martin, 1483–1546. 2. Missions—Theory. 3. Bible—Criticism, interpretation, etc. I. Title.
  BR333.5.M57O2413 2007
  266'.41092—dc22
                                                                2006036789

1 2 3 4 5 6 7 8 9 10   16 15 14 13 12 11 10 09 08 07

CONTENTS

FOREWORD

GERMAN EVANGELICAL LACK OF ENTHUSIASM AND COMMITMENT for mission to those outside the faith profoundly disturbed the founder of the academic discipline of missiology, Gustav Warneck (1834–1910). He tried to deal with this phenomenon by shoving at least some of the blame for nineteenth-century indifference to spreading the Gospel onto Martin Luther.[1] Living more than three hundred years before the invention of the designation "Great Commission" for Matthew 28:18–20, Luther proved to be unable to provide precisely those citations for modern arguments and cases for Christian witness needed in Warneck's time. Since he recorded his regrets about Luther, a lot of ink has been spilled trying to assess how Luther fits into modern concepts of the mission on which God sends his church.

Warneck's frustration may have been the result of his genuine zeal for bringing the lost out of darkness into the light of Christ. However, in one sense such a concern is not terribly important. God called Luther to serve his church and world in the sixteenth century, in Germany, in a society that had relatively little contact with unbaptized people. Luther met fewer than two dozen unbaptized individuals in his entire life. The princely and municipal governments that were committed to Luther's reform made no imperialistic forays into the unexplored lands beyond Europe's borders. (When some did so decades later, they sent missionaries along with merchants to trading outposts.) The recultivation of the Christian faith in Europe was mission enough. If Luther did not share our perspectives on what God would have us do, we should concentrate on the needs of our time with the same dedication and spirit of self-sacrifice that he exhibited in

---

1 For example, in his *Abriss einer Geschichte der protestantischen Missionen: Von der Reformation bis auf die Gegenwart* (Berlin: M. Warneck, 1910), 6–23.

meeting the needs God set before him. The regret that Luther was not more "mission-minded" need not plague us.

In fact, we need only to look more closely at Luther's writings and we shall see the wealth of insights that he places at our disposal for sound mission thinking at the beginning of the twenty-first century. That is what Swedish missiologist Ingemar Öberg has done in this study. That Warneck's impression is false has been argued by several twentieth-century scholars. But the appearance of this classical study by Professor Öberg adds new insights and information by mining a wide variety of sources within Luther's writings with great care and acumen. Especially through his focused analysis of Luther's writings on the Jews and the Turks (chapter 4), Öberg demonstrates that Luther was concerned with Gospel proclamation.

Öberg's research focused on how Luther conveyed the biblical message directly from the text to his students and parishioners. With the lectures and sermons of the reformer at hand, Öberg builds upon and at the same time goes beyond previous valuable studies that assessed elements of Luther's thought for their significance for understanding how God's mission in this world can and should function in our day. This book is not so much concerned with an anachronistic saving of Luther's "honor," rather it demonstrates how the entire structure of Luther's thinking flows naturally into Christian witness and outreach to the lost.

No "mere" historical study, Öberg's argument reveals that the dynamic of Luther's thought impels every Christian to confess Jesus Christ and to strive to cultivate saving faith in other people. The reformer anchored his use of God's Word in his understanding of its nature as the instrument and power to deliver salvation and to convey the benefits of Christ to the lost. Öberg grounds his assessment in the reformer's confession of God and his Word. Öberg also builds his discussion on a perceptive analysis of Luther's teaching on what it means to be human and how God uses the creatures he created as his human agents and servants, responsible for carrying out his care and concern for his world. Öberg's use of commentaries and sermons is particularly helpful, for he shows how the reformer based his understanding of Christian witness firmly on Scripture and how he anticipated this understanding should be communicated to the people of God and to the future pastors who would shepherd them.

Professor Öberg was convinced that Luther's understanding of the Gospel of Christ provides a firm basis for effective witness in our time. As a guest in his home in Stavangar, on the Norwegian coast, nearly twenty years ago, I was impressed by his sensitivity to the need for and challenges of Christian witness in the homelands of the Lutheran confession, as well as in the other continents and cultures of God's world. His firm commitment to Luther's way of thinking was also evident in our conversation, and his insights into the potential for Lutheran contributions to modern missiology made a lasting and profound impression on me.

It is true that one cannot be a "confessional" Lutheran without actively confessing the faith for the edification of the congregation of God's people, for ecumenical testimony to the whole household of faith, and in evangelistic witness to those outside the faith. Several elements of Luther's thought are of great help for shaping a theological framework for God's mission in and through his church in the twenty-first century. This framework rests, first, on Luther's intensely personal understanding of God as Creator and Savior, as a God of community and conversation, a Creator who desires communication and communion with his human creatures. Although it is false to see Luther's theology as anything but utterly trinitarian, some of his most powerful preaching focuses on the incarnation and, above all, the death and resurrection of our Lord Jesus Christ. His ways of bringing Christ to his students and parishioners offer models and stimulation for thinking through how best to convey the heart of the Gospel to the nations in our day. At the same time, we dare never forget how fully and intensely trinitarian Luther's thought was. From him we gain a deep appreciation for the presence of the sustaining and providing Creator in his world and for the activity of the Holy Spirit in the lives of Christians, particularly as they bring God's Word to others.

Luther's explanation of God's use of his Word, in all its forms, to create and to re-create enables us to formulate our conception of how God wants us to bring people to faith and unite them with the congregation of the faithful. That his Word is an effective, living, acting instrument of his will assists our development of methods of witnessing in daily life. God's Word comes to end the identity of the sinner as sinner and to re-create that sinner as a newborn child of God. This insight into the nature of God's Word determines and shapes our testimony to God's mercy in Christ and the methods that we employ to make this testimony. Luther's definition of the whole life of the Christian as a life of repentance helps us think through how Law and Gospel actually function as God's tool of killing and making alive once again. Luther's understanding of the proper uses of the Creator's gifts in creation assists Christians in evaluating how the various gifts of God in each culture may be placed at the service of Christ's mission.

These and other insights and analyses of Ingemar Öberg in this volume lay a solid foundation for exploration of these and other aspects of the reformer's understanding of who God is, what he has done for us, a confession of who we are as his human creatures, and what he expects of us. May this volume serve as a challenge and stimulus for formulating missiological thinking for the twenty-first century.

Robert Kolb
Concordia Seminary, Saint Louis
First Sunday in Advent 2006

Translator's Preface

I FIRST MET PROFESSOR INGEMAR ÖBERG at Matongo Lutheran Theological College in Western Kenya in the spring of 1992. As a pastoral intern from the Lutheran School of Theology at Chicago, I was teaching at Matongo. Professor Öberg had just published the Swedish version of the book in your hands and had been invited to an international Lutheran confessional conference to lecture on some of its contents. Profound interest in both Luther and world mission made the lectures fascinating for me. I had rarely, if ever, been in the presence of anyone with such a detailed grasp of Luther's writings. Rarer still was the combination of that knowledge of the reformer with a keen understanding and a burning heart for world mission. After the conference, Charles Lindquist, at the time the personnel director for World Mission Prayer League, and I mused on the importance of Professor Öberg's ideas for wider dissemination. Would he consider an English version of his book? If so, who could translate the material? I did not know Swedish at the time.

Also during the spring of 1992, I developed a relationship with Anki (Ann-Christin) Smetana, a missionary from Västerbotten in northern Sweden. From 1993 to 1995, I lived in Sweden, learning the language and culture of my beloved. (In 1996, I became her husband.) After acquiring enough Swedish to read it, I purchased Professor Öberg's book in the bookstore of the Swedish Lutheran Evangelical Association in Vasa, Finland. I began translating bits and pieces that interested me. Then in June 1995, Anki suggested that I translate the entire book from beginning to end. After some more contact with Professor Öberg and Åbo Academy (which published the Swedish version of the book), I began the search for an interested publisher and have been grateful ever since for Concordia Publishing House's interest in the project.

After spending a couple years as an ordained minister in northern Kansas, Anki and I returned to mission work in Kenya in 1997. I continued work on the translation with the permission and blessing of the Evangelical Lutheran Church in Kenya and the theological faculty at Matongo.

I only met Professor Öberg once more face-to-face. In January 1997, as Anki and I stopped on our way to Kenya, Professor Öberg came to teach at the Fridhem Mission Center, which my father-in-law, Rolf Smetana, had founded. We exchanged a few ideas at the time and clarified some translation issues. We continued to communicate via letters until the initial translation was complete. Unfortunately Professor Öberg passed away in 2005 before the English translation was published. I hope he was not disappointed about the publishing delay. I am sure he is not now. I believe he would have been pleased, not that his book might get a wider readership nor that more people might be able to learn important details about Luther's theology, but that more people might hear God's Word and be directed and empowered by it to communicate the Gospel to the ends of the earth. May this translation serve that purpose.

As for acknowledgments, all those named above (and many others) deserve my thanks for advice, encouragement, and technical assistance.

I dedicate my work on this edition to the memory of Professor Öberg and to the honor of my beloved wife, Ann-Christin. Without her, it is unlikely that I ever would have bothered to learn Swedish, and she has, together with our children, had to tolerate many hours and days of my work at the computer and in the library to finish this translation.

Dean M. Apel
New Year's Eve 2006

PREFACE

AFTER SURVEYING THE WEIMAR EDITION of Luther's Works for many years, I have gradually come to realize that the mission literature and a majority of those who are interested in world mission have painted a far too negative picture of the reformer's views. After reporting my findings in essays and public lectures, including those at the Mission College in Stavanger (Norway), and after more careful study, I have gathered the results of my research in this book. I wish to explain the most important aspects of Luther's understanding of mission and what he thought about the church's commission to take the Gospel to non-Christian peoples.

When I use the terms *mission*, mission *concept*, mission *motif*, or *world mission*, keep in mind that Luther does not use the words *Weltmission* or *mission* as specific terms for the universal preaching of the Gospel. He does, however, use *senden/Sendung* and *mittere/missio*, as well as a collection of other phrases and metaphors, when he speaks about the Gospel's way to the people. The terms *world mission* and *mission* first became common several hundred years after Luther's death. My work would have been much easier if Luther had published programmatic writings about mission, but he almost never did. Had he spent part of his career organizing and managing a mission in a non-Christian land, my task would have been easier, but one has little to go on. This does not mean, however, that Luther considered the missionary task unimportant.

Above all, Luther is a Bible expositor and a reformer of the church. His work with the Bible gave birth to his reformation impulses and insights. Clearly, Luther's Bible exposition and preaching is often directed toward German and European problems. That does not mean Luther lacked a sense for mission or a zeal for bringing the saving Gospel to the whole world. Indeed, the opposite is true. Through decades of persistent study of the biblical texts and the problems of the church, Luther often spoke about the mission perspective in the Old and the

New Testaments. Only after thorough study of Luther's commentaries and sermons on biblical texts can one form an accurate picture of his mission thinking. Whether his views should then be labeled "missiology" is a question of judgment. Missiology today involves an interplay of theory and practice, mutually correcting and enriching each other.[1] Because Luther did not benefit from extensive practical experience in non-Christian contexts, his missiology has significant gaps. He has much to say about the theology of mission and theory, but he obviously does not have much to say about the everyday practice of cross-cultural mission.

The historical-systematic studies presented here summarize my findings about mission in Luther's writing and in significant elements of his thinking. (For the sake of the reader, many passages are quoted in translation.) This study presents Luther more as a mission theoretician than as a mission practitioner. He is a German reformer and not primarily a man of mission, though he said and thought much about world mission. Indeed, Luther sometimes almost bursts out in an appeal for mission and almost engages in cross-cultural mission himself.

I wish to thank secretary Aarno Alli of the theology faculty in Åbo (Finland) for faithfully typing my manuscript. Finally, I thank Norway's General Research Council in Oslo, the Mission College in Stavanger, and the theological faculty at the Åbo Academy, which, especially during my sabbatical years (1985–1986), gave me financial support and the opportunity to complete this study.

Ingemar Öberg
Stavanger, Norway, 1991

---

1 See discussion in *Luther and World Mission*, chapter 2. *Mission* may be defined as God's task of reconciling the fallen world to himself. This is a universal undertaking because God is the creator of all and loves his creation. God accomplished this reconciliation by sending his Son to die and rise for sinful humans, by sending the Spirit through the Son, and by sending the church through the Son and the Spirit to labor for the conversion of sinners to faith in himself. *Missiology* is the study of that mission in terms of its basis in scriptural revelation, its manifestation in historical dimension, its challenges in facing cultural and theological contexts, and its implementation in terms of practical issues facing those involved in (or training for) the mission task.

Abbreviations

AC	Augsburg Confession
Ap	Apology of the Augsburg Confession
BSLK	*Die Bekenntnisschriften der evangelisch-lutherischen Kirche*. 11th ed. Göttingen: Vandenhoeck & Ruprecht, 1992.
K-W	Kolb, Robert, and Timothy J. Wengert, eds. *The Book of Concord: The Confessions of the Evangelical Lutheran Church*. Translated by Charles Arand et al. Minneapolis: Fortress, 2000.
LC	Large Catechism
LW	Luther, Martin. *Luther's Works*. American Edition. General editors Jaroslav Pelikan and Helmut T. Lehmann. 56 vols. St. Louis: Concordia, and Philadelphia and Minneapolis: Muhlenberg and Fortress. 1955–86.
SA	Smalcald Articles
SC	Small Catechism
WA	Luther, Martin. *D. Martin Luthers Werke. Kritische Gesamtausgabe. Schriften*. 68 vols. Weimar: Herman Böhlaus Nachfolger, 1883–1999.
WABr	Luther, Martin. *D. Martin Luthers Werke. Kritische Gesamtausgabe. Briefwechsel*. 18 vols. Weimar: Herman Böhlaus Nachfolger, 1930–85.
WADB	Luther, Martin. *D. Martin Luthers Werke. Kritische Gesamtausgabe. Die Deutsche Bibel*. 12 vols. in 15. Weimar: Herman Böhlaus Nachfolger, 1906–61.
WATr	Luther, Martin. *D. Martin Luthers Werke. Kritische Gesamtausgabe. Tischreden*. 6 vols. Weimar: Herman Böhlaus Nachfolger, 1912–21.

LUTHER AND WORLD MISSION

Chapter One

LUTHER RESEARCH
AND THE APPROACH OF THIS STUDY

LUTHER AND WORLD MISSION

Older historians, as well as some recent writers, have painted a remarkably negative picture of Martin Luther's interest in mission, claiming the reformer had no
vision for evangelism in non-Christian lands. Such was the judgment of the
noted mission historian Gustav Warneck at the turn of the century. His successors—J. Richter, H. W. Schomerus, E. Schick, the Dane L. Bergman, and many
more—followed his line of thinking until Kenneth Scott Latourette's somewhat
more careful interpretations in our own time (1980).[1] As a result, in churchly and

---

1 Warneck, *Abriss einer Geschichte der protestantischen Missionen*, 6ff. (The first edition
appeared in 1882, but references in this book are made to the 1910 edition.) Warneck
suggests that the Protestant churches lacked direct contact with the heathen world and
were completely occupied with the reformation of a depraved Christianity. He is
acquainted with the political obstacles and the abundance of work at home, but he
finds that no one in Reformation lands complained that investment in foreign missions must wait. In his concept of mission, Warneck emphasizes the movement to foreign lands and the organization of missions. He feels the reformers lacked a vision for
the continuing mission task and the duty of mission. According to Warneck, Luther
(pp. 8ff.) had, of course, considered the Gospel as mission-preaching for later generations, but he personally would have thought about mission as Christianization of the
Turks, the Jews, the heathen, and the false Christians, all of whom were spread
throughout Christendom. Luther lacked the sense and the vision for mission among
foreign (that is, geographically removed) heathen. The Gospel and Christianity were

missiological contexts, the assumption has usually been that Luther had no positive views of mission. The above-named scholars seem to believe that Luther showed no interest in the practical organization of foreign mission or in sending missionaries to foreign lands. If Luther had a heart for mission, they argue, he would have sent missionaries. Thus Luther's reputation is doomed from the start.

In Warneck and Bergman, missionary organization is inextricably bound with the geographic factor. When the Swedish state church attempted to Christianize the Sami from 1559 until the present, that, in the eyes of Warneck and Bergman, is not a question of mission. But when the Moravians traveled to Greenland to do the same thing, that is mission, according to Warneck. Such conclusions indicate that mission has been incorrectly defined. Warneck also believes that Luther's accent on the eschatological in his thinking about God's reign prevents the development of his mission interest. Both Warneck and Bergman feel that Luther's teaching on the bondage of the will and on predestination reveals problems in the teaching of justification. That, they argue, has produced fatal consequences for aggressive mission thinking. Warneck and Bergman should have asked themselves why Luther's views on eschatology and predestination did not keep him from attempting to reform the church in Germany.

Explanations and excuses for the reformer's supposed negative stance toward foreign mission have included the geographic location of the nuclear lands of

---

universal, but the clear appeal for world mission is missing in the reformer's thought. Warneck explains away some of Luther's writings that speak about preaching to the heathen. Warneck presumes that Luther thought the universal preaching of the Gospel had been completed with the apostles. The organized sending of Christians to foreign lands had been replaced by occasional preaching and testimony among non-Christians in the home environment or among the heathen one might meet during captivity—for example, to the Turks. Warneck believes Luther's negative stance to organized foreign mission is a consequence of his teaching about predestination (God had already condemned the Turks and the Jews), as well as his view about Christ's imminent return. These ideas were later promoted further by J. Richter, H. W. Schomerus, and E. Schick, among others.

In Scandinavia, mission historians argued that Luther neither expressly emphasized the remaining responsibility for evangelization nor the organized sending of missionaries to foreign lands (the geographic aspect). Note especially Bergman, *Den lutherske Reformation og Missionen*, 2ff., 44ff. Cf. Bergman's "Reformationen og Hedningemisjonen," 13–34, 59–82, 113–41, 189–217. Bergman has nuanced slightly Warneck's ideas and those of others, but he has without a doubt contributed to the negative opinion about Luther's view of mission. According to Bergman, the reformer's teachings, especially about God's providence and predestination, reaped catastrophic consequences for Luther's views on mission (*Den lutherske Reformation og Missionen*, 71ff.). Even Latourette's monumental *History of the Expansion of Christianity* has a rather negative evaluation of Luther's place in mission history (3:25ff.).

the Reformation, the political conditions of the time, and Luther's preoccupation with the Reformation in Germany and the bordering countries. True, these factors contribute to Luther's understanding of mission. Nevertheless, on the basis of clear statements in Luther's own texts, I will later prove false the view that Luther's alleged passivity toward foreign mission grew from his expectation of the imminent return of Christ or his belief that the commission of universal mission had been fulfilled in the days of the apostles.

A more careful, source-oriented research has partially succeeded in correcting the false conclusions mentioned above, but the research has provided only summary data. Therefore the widely held view still prevails and questions remain. However, the research of Karl Holl, Werner Elert, E. Danbolt, Wilhelm Maurer, Walter Holsten, J. Aagaard, James A. Scherer, Juhani Forsberg, Eugene W. Bunkowske, Volker Stolle, P. Peters, and others published since 1930 has opened the eyes of many. Although these are often short essays and collections of texts, they make it no longer simple to draw the old, cliché-ridden picture of Luther's lack of interest in mission. Luther had a mission perspective and directly encouraged mission. Luther's view was not distorted by the expectation of the imminence of Christ's parousia, by his doctrine of predestination, nor by an assumption that the mission of the apostles was completed. Especially important is how the reformer (in a way strange to his "slanderers") focused mission on the meaning of God's/Christ's church-building work through the Word and the Sacraments, not primarily through organized mission nor the interest of modern mission for mission investments and technique. The most recently named scholars argue that the reformer identifies or integrates church and mission.[2]

---

2 The interpretation of Luther on mission changed only slightly in Drews, "Die Anschauungen reformatorischer Theologen über die Heidenmission," 1ff., 193ff., 289ff. Luther emphasized that mission is God's work (*missio Dei*); therefore it needed no organized mission activity to the heathen. Instead, the Christianization of the non-Christian world would come about as Christians dispersed among the people were persecuted and as Christians in captivity or in business traveled in non-Christian lands. Drews emphasizes that the doctrine of predestination in Luther becomes a hindrance for a truly foreign mission.

·Luther expert Karl Holl definitively corrected Warneck's suppostions as presented above. See Holl, "Luther und die Mission," 234–43. Holl feels the text material in Luther reveals that the reformer had a vision for the mission task. In a difficult, nearly impossible, political context, Luther suggests that certain regions ought to be fields for missionary activity. Holl helpfully emphasizes that the reformer's ecclesiology has important significance for his mission views. The priesthood of all believers must become involved in mission.

Werner Elert (*Morphologie des Luthertums*, 1:336–51) attacks the views of Warneck and others. Elert says sarcastically that the focus on concrete mission activity and organi-

Before reviewing my approach to this subject, here are some reasons for the misunderstandings and mistakes in the studies that have led to such a negative picture of Luther's relation to world mission. Many researchers have displayed an anachronistic blindness, not realizing how difficult—not to say impossible—it

---

zation belongs to the business department at the university, not to the theological department. The fixation on mission outreach and organization makes some scholars blind to Luther's theology of mission. In Luther's thinking, it is not human power but God's and the Gospel's power that are central. In everything that Luther thinks and writes about the Gospel, there is a sense for mission. Elert finds in Luther a clear yes that the Gospel must go out to all who have not yet heard it. The Gospel is always on the move, and the apostolic age had by no means completed the mission task. Luther does not limit obedience to the Great Commission to journeys over land and sea. Instead, he integrates the work of the church at home and the work of mission abroad. The Reformation itself was mission in the sense that it helped the Gospel find its way to people. Indeed, wherever non-Christianity has the advantage, there is a mission task.

In his essay "Misjon—evangeliets frie løp," Danbolt has chosen to highlight the difference between mission thinking and concrete mission investments. He holds that the Great Commission is a universal commission to all Christians, not only to professional missionaries. Mission exists both on the home front and among the heathen. Among the heathen, the testimony of both the individual Christian and the professional missionary is mission. It is the Gospel itself—not primarily people—that carries mission (243ff.). With these presuppositions, Danbolt finds evangelism well-established in Luther. Luther taught that the Gospel must continue to go out into every corner of the world. Because the non-Christian world and secularization are universal, the Gospel and mission must be the universal thrust as long as the world exists.

Wingren ("Lutherische Theologie und Weltmission," 73–78) and Dörries ("Luther und die Heidenpredigt," 327ff.) emphasized that the Gospel is becoming passé among the neo-heathens at home and abroad. They emphasize that God still calls through the Gospel itself, though one can never escape human factors.

Among the important contributors are the following: Holsten, "Reformation und Mission," 1–32; Maurer, "Reformation und Mission," 20–41; Genischen, "Missionsgeschichte der neueren Zeit," 5–10; Scherer, *Mission and Unity in Lutheranism*, 7ff.; and Scherer, *That the Gospel May Be Sincerely Preached*, 4–15. These books emphasize that, in Luther, mission is *missio Dei* and God's reign is universal. As for human factors in evangelism, the church as a whole (ordained and laity) ought to take the Gospel to everyone—to unbelievers abroad and at home. Luther does not speak about a special mission office.

Cf. also Peters, "Luthers weltweiter Missionssinn," 162–75. This article is well-anchored in Luther's commentaries and among other things suggests that the expansion of God's reign is the work of God/Christ. Luther had a vision for the responsibility of mission. Through his books, he has influenced Lutheran missions to the present. Eugene W. Bunkowske notes the mission theme, the continued relevance of the Great Commission for Luther, and how important Luther's writings have been to centuries of mission work ("Was Luther a Missionary?" 161–79).

would have been for Luther and his followers to start a foreign mission. Because of the expansion of Islam, Christianity had become in effect a provincial European religion rather than a world religion. Moreover, Luther's Reformation was tied to central Europe and could expand only northward. To the west, south, and east lay a belt of the Roman Catholic Church's sphere of power. Behind the powerful Muslim iron curtain, the death penalty was imposed on missionaries. The Atlantic Ocean and Islamic territories separated Reformation Germany from the Americas, Africa, and Asia. Before the defeat of the Spanish Armada in 1588, only Spanish and Portuguese ships could sail the world's oceans. Luther did not have the same opportunities as the later Protestant missions, especially those occurring during the last two centuries. He did not have the protection of the "Protestant" empires nor the benefit of public laws providing religious freedom in mission lands. It is surprising that it should be so difficult to understand that for an upstart like Luther it would be nearly impossible during the first part of the sixteenth century to send foreign missionaries from the Saxony of Frederick the Wise. Luther was working in a princedom that had no colonies or non-Christian regions. According to the generally accepted pattern of European religious politics, the religion of the ruler determined the religious affiliation of his subjects (*cuius regio, eius religio*).[3] Such a practice also determined the limits of mission outreach.

Several other short and mostly Scandinavian contributions with positive evaluations of the mission theme in Luther are: Aagaard, "Luthers syn på mission I–II," 121–40, 195–200; Aagaard, "Luthers Missionssyn," 114–20; and Aagaard, "Kap. Missionstheologie," 225–49. See also J. Heubach, ed., *Lutherische Beiträge zur Missio Dei*, Veröffentlichungen der Luther-Akademie Ratzeburg 3 (Erlangen: Martin Luther Verlag, 1982), especially the following essays: Öberg, "Mission und Heilsgeschichte bei Luther und in den Bekenntnisschriften" (pp. 25–42); Beisser, "Mission und Reich Gottes" (pp. 43–56); and Forsberg, "Abraham als Paradigma der Mission in der Theologie Luthers" (pp. 113–20). See also *Ekumenisk Orientering* 38 (1984) with the following articles: J. Aagaard, "The Lutheran Tradition and Missionary Theology" (pp. 3–10); Hallencreutz, "Luther och Olaus Petri om 'missionsbefallningen'" (pp. 11–22); Pörsti, "Luthers syn på evangelisation" (pp. 23–26); and Becker, ". . . like a traveling rain shower . . ." (pp. 27–43). See also Stolle, *Kirche aus allen Völkern*.

3 Aagaard, "Luthers syn på kirkens sendelse," 123. See especially Aagaard, "Luthers syn på mission I–II," 131ff.: "For Luther eksisterade der således i praksis ingen mulighed for at komme i forbindelse med den icke-kristne verden" ("Therefore, practically speaking, it was impossible for Luther to have any contact with the non-Christian world"). Aagaard sketches clearly how the Lutherans were locked in behind the Catholic sphere of influence and the Muslim iron curtain. Compare Holsten's discussion ("Reformation und Mission," 4f.) with E. Schick and H. Frick. Aagaard notes that the sociological structure with which the church lived in the nuclear regions of the Lutheran Reformation meant that mission and the ruling authorities (along with the colonial administrations) unavoidably had to be coupled with mission in foreign lands. Scherer

It is not enough merely to note that only the Roman Catholic mission could invest in the Americas, Africa, and Asia, but such a perspective helps to explain the restrictions Luther and the Lutherans faced. For example, Luther could not open missions in areas the 1493–1494 Padroado Document earmarked for the important Catholic kingdoms—Spain and Portugal—and their rulers. Moreover, Luther was banned and held in contempt by the empire from 1521 until his death. The pope, the emperor, and the Spanish and Portuguese princes could, with effective and simple means, prevent every attempt at foreign mission by the hated Wittenberger and his followers. As the mission literature shows, a Calvinist mission attempt in Brazil in 1557 ended with three martyrs and a journey home. They were hindered and opposed by pro-Catholic colonists.

However, one should not believe that Luther did not reckon with sacrifice and martyrdom in the work of God's reign. The Lutheran Reformation had its own martyrs in Brussels in the early 1520s, and Luther thanked God for the power of the Gospel and the strength of the martyrs' faith. During most of his career, Luther lived under threat of execution. If Luther, who saw himself first as a reformer, had at some time considered foreign missions, he would have recognized immediately how impossible such action would be. Ruling authorities were capable of placing many obstacles in the way of mission activity. It can be helpful to ask why the well-organized missionaries of our time do not attempt mission work in China and Iran. The answer is simple: They are neither allowed nor able to do so. For the moment these avenues are closed.

Luther saw as wholly decisive his call and task to reform and to renew the Christian faith in Germany and its borderlands. According to Luther, one ought first to fulfill his or her own call. Publicly called as a doctor of the church, he invested all his energy in reform at home. Among the ways he could have worked to further God's reign, reform at home became his priority. Luther believed that a new unbelief and a law-religion had infiltrated Western Christendom. He believed the tasks of reformation and foreign mission to non-Christian cultures were integral to Christ's purposes and the church's movement to all people. That means most of what the reformer asserts in his Bible commentaries is relevant for both

---

writes: "Whatever God in his sovereign freedom might be doing to advance the kingdom by spreading the gospel throughout the earth by various anonymous agents, in German territories evangelical preaching and teaching was confined to the lands of the Reformation where the *ius reformandi* applied. Under the privilege known as *cuius regio, eius religio*, each ruler had the right to determine the religious allegiance of his subjects. Evangelical churches existed in the form of territorial or regional bodies established by law, defended by military might, and practicing religious conformity. Personal religious freedom, as a corollary of justification by faith could not be implemented until two centuries later when the Enlightenment made the persecution of dissenters no longer tolerable" (*That the Gospel May Be Sincerely Preached*, 15).

domestic and foreign mission. Luther's sermons, lectures, thematic writings, and letters fill many volumes in the Weimar Edition. It is a lifelong task to plow through this vast, comprehensive material. It must have been an even greater task to write all these materials amid the dramatic events of the Reformation. Luther simply had enough to do with the Reformation itself. Therefore to the previously named concrete hindrances to mission must be added that, for Luther, reformation had to be of primary importance. Foreign evangelism (using the narrower definition) could exist only in the background. Luther did not demand that everyone do everything in the same way. His call as doctor and professor provided him with quite enough to do as a reformer in Wittenberg and Saxony. We shall see that Luther, in his exegetical study of the Bible and in preaching, did not consider world mission to be of secondary importance to reform. Luther was neither hesitant nor halfhearted about Jesus' Great Commission or the Christianization of unbelievers.

Luther research is a strenuous enterprise. It depends on the amount of material, the number of points of view, and the usefulness of the source material. Instead of developing a theme logically, Luther often let his exegesis of the biblical text determine the direction of discussion. Suddenly in the middle of lectures, biblical exegesis, or sermons, Luther, the exegete, clarifies by means of questions. With his exegesis, he injects his own verbose comments on the issues of his day. He never discussed world mission at length. His tract *That Christ Was Born a Jew* (1523) and some letters do address the issue more directly. But as a rule, Luther's comments about mission are dropped here and there into exegetical writing, Bible commentaries, and sermons. The work of finding, analyzing, and making available substantive comments on mission calls for perseverance and a command of the source material. A superficial grasp of Luther's writing explains the negative conclusion that Luther felt no responsibility for evangelism, that mission was not important to him. Scholars such as Warneck and Latourette have often expressed an opinion without penetrating and objectively analyzing the primary sources: Luther's exegesis of the Old and New Testaments, his many writings, and his sermons. Lack of familiarity with the original sources is the only way to explain the unfounded conclusions of such scholars. Assertions by Warneck and Bergman have led other scholars to their own negative evaluations. The first built on loose sand. The second, in turn, have followed. Such questionable use of the sources violates the most elementary rules of theological research.

Several theological obstacles have led to confusion. I noted previously that scholars often reduced the concept of mission to organized mission projects and geographic movement. Some have come to the mission topic with an evangelical or revivalistic orientation that does not harmonize with Luther's thinking. In the last two centuries, Pietism, the Baptist movement, and the large folk movements within various denominations have dominated mission thinking. These movements, which deserve admiration for their success in spreading the Gospel, dwelt on the special office of missionary, the charismatic mission call, fellowship, and mission organization. The message of these movements tended to focus on Second and Third Article concerns. Conversion, faith, and life with Jesus stood in the center. Hence scholars with this background usually have not discovered much interest in mission in Luther.

The reformer considered some of those same themes to be extremely important, but his understanding grew from a different base: creation theology, the inherent power of the Gospel, the doctrine of justification through faith, and that God personally builds his reign throughout the world. Note that many Lutheran missions did emerge from a genuine evangelical-Lutheran theology. Mission was often considered a tool, calling for loyalty to the church and its ordinances. One must also be wary of overgeneralizing about evangelical-revival mission thinking.[4] More than Luther, evangelical-revival thinking stressed the role of the missionary and showed much enthusiasm for the development of missions. Because the established churches were often lukewarm toward foreign mission, mission movements were often esteemed as something specific and separate from the status quo-mindedness of the churches in sending lands.

In chapter 2, we will review some of the doctrines and theological premises most important for Luther's mission perspective: his understanding of creation and the Law as related to the mission message and how Christ should be preached. For Luther, Christ and righteousness through faith made the preaching of the Gospel a necessity. That doctrine, in an almost tiresome manner, became the center for the reformer's ecclesiology and missiology. Without those two pillars, the whole superstructure of Luther's theology would be lost. Luther's writings show that he integrated church and mission, considering the whole apostolic church as

---

4 Holsten ("Reformation und Mission," 1ff.) has pointed out how Luther's understanding of mission is often judged by the standard of nineteenth-century pietistic-evangelical mission thinking. This scholar (compare the even more balanced Elert, *Morphologie des Luthertums*, 1:340ff.) has, however, a far too stereotypical negative judgment of nineteenth-century missions. I wish that Holsten would have dealt with the ecclesiology and missiology of the first Norwegian missionaries in South Africa from 1850 onward. This is genuine Lutheranism in which mission work is not seen anthropocentrically but theocentrically as a work of the Gospel and as a mission of the church. See also the clarifying study about nineteenth-century missions (both free and state church) and mission as the task of the church in Myklebust, *Misjonskunnskap*, 101–11. Even here the concept of congregation and ecclesiology are understood in connection with mission. Mission belongs to the societies and to the church, and the church works through the societies.

being sent and sending. Not the mission apparatus but the Gospel itself is central, reaching a land—often in several waves—like a rain shower.

Luther's view of how the Gospel reached people (that is, *mission*, to use later terminology) is developed from the Bible and its description of how the Gospel would be proclaimed for both Jews and Gentiles. Some problems in the evangelical-revival camp have developed from the denial of this essential unity of domestic and foreign preaching of the Gospel. As a result, for a long time we have talked about Western Christendom's established churches and Christianity as something completely different from foreign missions. Luther certainly saw the important and the unique in foreign mission, as this study will show. At the same time, he holds together or integrates the church's expansion of the Gospel in the West and on the front lines with non-Christians. The reformer starts from the basic premise that Jews and Gentiles are the audience for the Gospel and develops a mission universalism in which the Reformation's home front and the foreign front are held together. Mission happens on both fronts based on the same commission and sending of Christ. According to Luther, we have in principle one battle with two battle lines. His thinking harmonizes well with the contemporary understanding of home and foreign missions in which the sending by means of the Gospel is the same in both instances.[5]

---

5 Among other things, the studies of Holl, Elert, Danbolt, and, more recently, Aagaard and Scherer have such an enduring value precisely because they powerfully emphasize that Luther's ecclesiology and missiology are so integrated. The decisive factor in both church and mission is that God, through the dynamic and church-creating Gospel, is building his reign among the peoples. If mission is important at all, it must be important in and for the church itself. In mission, the Word has priority at the same time that Christianization cannot occur without concrete human activity. We shall see later that Luther is not preoccupied with the more or less dramatic personal calls of missionaries. What is important for Luther is that God in his Word says that the peoples will be invited to salvation through the Spirit of the new covenant and the Gospel. Becker has some well-formulated sentences about how Luther unites evangelization and mission as one war against the devil's work in people's hearts and lives: "Because the kingdom of Christ is always in *opposition* to the kingdom of the devil and because no Christian is secure against apostasy, the boundaries between what is usually described today as 'evangelization' (i.e. the awakening of sleeping and inactive Christians) and 'mission' (as the summons into the Church) are relatively fluctuating. God himself is at work with the Gospel in the world and in human hearts" (". . . like a traveling rain shower . . ." 24). Cf. Scherer, who writes how Luther considers his own task as a reformer in sixteenth-century Europe to be mission: "Since the gospel had fallen into oblivion in Christendom—Luther's Gentiles being those who had never heard the pure word of God preached in Germany—missionary obedience could only mean preaching the gospel anew. And since the distortion of the gospel message had led to the degeneration of mission into ecclesiastical propaganda, forced conversions,

The reformer also seeks to ensure the Gospel-centered character of church and mission when he powerfully underlines that it is God—Father, Son, and Spirit—who is the driving power in the work of God's reign. This does not mean that Luther could ignore the church's ordinances, gifts of grace, ministries, and types of leadership. God's mission through the Gospel has a human factor also. Although totally involved in the concrete problems of the Reformation, Luther developed his ecclesiology and missiology from Scripture and from the church's first mission epoch. He knew well that the Gospel does not, as the proverbial fart in the wind, make a sound by itself. The reformer could never ally himself with a docetic ecclesiology or missiology. But he delineates a necessary hierarchy: first, the work of Father, Son, and Holy Spirit; then the Word and the Sacraments as the tools of the Trinity; and finally the indispensable human agents.[6] Because Luther never technically founded a foreign mission—he considered mission to be inseparable from the church's fundamental purpose—it is interesting to see how far Luther reaches in his statements about the formation of concrete mission work among the people.

THE TASK, METHOD, AND PLAN OF THIS STUDY

The task and goal of the present study is to answer the simple question *Is Luther interested in foreign mission?* It should not be impossible to determine Luther's position on mission to non-Christians. In the broader definition of *mission*, we also will consider what Luther has to say about reformation and domestic mission in German and European Christendom. But to avoid becoming completely lost in the enormous amount of material, we must narrow this study to Luther's thinking about foreign mission, concentrating on the primary elements of his missiology. The main theological and ecclesiological premises in Luther's view of mission are important. Did Luther's missiology develop? Or are there only a few signs of a position on missiology? How does Luther's mission perspective relate to his theology in general? Finally, what did Luther say about mission practice?

---

crusades and nonevangelical methods, Luther's obedience to the mission command meant re-establishing the church on its own true foundation in Jesus Christ and the gospel. For Luther, mission was the essential task of the church in every age, but only a church itself grounded in the gospel could do mission" (That the Gospel May Be Sincerely Preached, 6). Cf. Aagaard, "Luthers syn på kirkens sendelse," 123f., and "Kap. Missionstheologie," 227f. See also Dörries, "Luther und die Heidenpredigt," 329ff., about how Luther speaks of "Christian heathen," thus expanding the concept of mission.

6 For the reformer's view of the priesthood of all believers, the gifts of grace, and calls or vocations, see *Luther and World Mission*, 88–95.

To find answers to these basic questions, I have used a historical-systematic method. By historical, I mean making a rather thorough inventory and analysis of Luther's writings in the Weimar Edition. I focus especially on the place and content of the mission motif in Luther's exegesis of texts in the Old and New Testaments, in his commentaries, and in his sermons. As stated, Luther's missiology cannot be found in programmatic writings on foreign mission, but it can be traced in his thirty-two years of work with the biblical texts. Luther is, after all, a biblical theologian, and the Scriptures lead him unfailingly into the problems of world mission.

The historical-descriptive examination is complemented by a comprehensive systematic side. This important element fills large sections in chapters 2 and 3 (see especially in chapter 3 the discussion of Luther's interpretation of the Epistles). Describing Luther's understanding of mission on the basis of his exegesis already covers much of the systematic aspect. Nevertheless a brief systematic analysis that sets Luther's missiology in the context of his larger theology is included. However, this analysis will not be systematic in the sense that it takes into account the entire biblical witness, the Lutheran Confessions, and contemporary theology. Luther's understanding of mission does not change substantially after 1519. Therefore I have not considered it necessary to analyze the history of its development, though when necessary, I do discuss its development.

The plan of this work is as follows: In this introductory chapter, we have reviewed the research and literature about Luther and world mission and discussed the goal and method of the study. Chapter 2 covers the most important theological premises and contexts for Luther's views on mission: Luther's ideas about God as Creator and Sustainer, natural law, and human responsibility for earthly vocations. This provides important background for understanding the primary work and mission of the church. God as Creator, Renewer, and Sustainer is an important part of the mission message. Chapter 2 places Luther's ecclesiology and missiology in its trinitarian context. The second chapter also includes a lengthy section on Luther's view of natural religion among unbelievers, a definition of natural religion, and how Luther relates natural religion to the wisdom that we have through Christ, to the Gospel, and to faith. Luther's commentary on the prologue to the Gospel of John summarizes his views on natural religion and on God's saving revelation through the Scriptures and preaching. Chapter 2 also has a sketch of relevant elements in Luther's view of the church and of ministry.

Chapter 3 is the core of my research and focuses on mission themes in Luther's work with the Bible. Luther integrates domestic and foreign mission, but the chapter dwells on the latter to avoid becoming lost in the mass of material and complicated problems. Luther arrives at his views on mission after years of persistent exegesis of the Old and New Testaments. Like Justin Martyr and

Irenaeus, Luther interprets the Old Testament in the light of the events and the basic message of the New Testament and the new covenant. The first section of chapter 3 tracks the mission perspective in Luther's commentaries on Genesis, the Psalms, Isaiah, and Zechariah. Luther uses the texts of the Old Testament that tell how the people come to Jerusalem to worship the true God (the centripetal mission perspective). Luther also treats the Old Testament texts that refer to going out with the message of salvation to unbelievers (the centrifugal mission perspective).

The second section of chapter 3 shows how Luther develops his mission motif and his mission theology in his exegesis, explanations, and sermons on the texts of the four Gospels, for example, Jesus' concern for the lost sheep of Israel (Matthew 15:21ff.; 10:15ff.) and how his concern is expanded (John 4:21, 23). Luther's worldwide mission drive is expressed in the commentaries on the parables of God's reign (Matthew 13), the petition "Thy kingdom come" (Matthew 6:10), and the parables of the wedding of the king's son and the great feast (Matthew 22:1ff.; Luke 14:16ff.). Of special interest are Luther's comments on Jesus' explicit commands to evangelize the world (Matthew 28:18ff.; Mark 16:15f.; Luke 24:25ff.). Special attention is devoted to the Gospel of John because of its late date and, therefore, its direct connection to the first mission epoch of the church. Especially illuminating are Luther's comments on the texts in which Jesus speaks of his enthronement next to the Father and the sending of the Spirit (John 14:23ff.; 16:5ff.). The commission in the Gospel of John is highlighted (John 20:19–23).

The third section of chapter 3 maps Luther's mission perspective on the basis of the Acts of the Apostles and the letters of the New Testament, especially Paul's letters. Luther's commentaries on these portions of Scripture describe mission as occurring at the leading of the ascended Christ as the Spirit creates the church through the Word and Sacraments. The second portion of this section expands on doctrines that are important for God's reign: the Law, the Gospel, and parenesis, among others.

Chapter 4 poses the question whether Luther had concrete proposals or took concrete measures to carry out foreign mission. This last question in this study— and the main point of the critiques of Luther offered by Warneck and Bergman— completes the circle. Concluding positively, chapter 4 highlights the place of apologetics and the mission motif in Luther's meeting with Central European Jews and in how Luther dealt with apologetics and mission when the Muslims (especially after 1529) threatened Western Europe and Germany.

Above all, Luther is a reformer of the church in Western Europe, but he had more than a theoretical vision for the Christianization of all peoples. On the other hand, Luther showed a certain discontinuity or imbalance between his comprehensive mission vision and his more sporadic suggestions for mission practice.

Only many years later did Lutheranism develop a missiology in which both theory and practice combined and in which both theory and practice could enrich and correct the other.

CHAPTER TWO

DOCTRINES AND THEOLOGICAL PREMISES IMPORTANT FOR LUTHER'S MISSION THEOLOGY

THIS CHAPTER SKETCHES DOCTRINES and theological premises that are decisive for Luther's mission thinking. We explore first Luther's doctrine about the Creator, the world, and fallen (so-called "natural") people; the law written in human hearts; and the earthly vocations of people. In addition, I examine the reformer's view of the natural knowledge of God and of natural religion, explaining their relationship to God's revelation in Christ and the Gospel of the church. Finally, we review the reformer's ecclesiology and understanding of ministry.

THE CREATOR, THE WORLD, AND HUMANITY

Luther structures his theology in a trinitarian and Christocentric manner. He emphasizes the Second Article and faith in Christ, but he does not overlook creation and the First Article, as is characteristic of many contemporary evangelical-Lutheran theologians—not to mention pietistic, evangelical-revival, and Barthian theologians.[1] Luther organizes his theology and preaching according to the works

---

1 See Wingren, *Skapelsen och lagen*, 13ff., 20ff.; and Wingren, *Luther frigiven*, especially 64ff., 72ff., 90ff. Wingren incisively comes to terms with the Christological totalitarianism of Karl Barth and Oscar Cullmann (and to a certain degree Anders Nygren and T. Bohlin). Wingren shows that the church, until Protestant orthodoxy, read the Old and New Testaments together and that theology, confession, and liturgy gave creation a central place. Later, a general isolation of the New Testament from the Old

that God has done and continues to do, the works to which the Old and New Testaments witness. Just as the Apostles' and Nicene Creeds confess and praise God's works in three sections, so the reformer speaks of God as Creator and Sustainer and as provident in creation; of Jesus Christ's incarnation, suffering, death, and resurrection; and of the Spirit and the church, the forgiveness of sins, the resurrection, and the judgment of the dead. However much the Gospel and faith stand in the center, Luther never forgets that God is the Creator and Sustainer who cares for all life and employs human beings in his care of creation.

Luther's view of creation and humanity is absolutely crucial as the context in which the specific Gospel about Christ ought to be proclaimed. More than that, preaching about the First Article and the material connected with it is intrinsic to the total message of church and mission. If the reformer actually had sent out Lutheran missionaries, the summaries concerning Christian creation theology found in the catechisms would have been by no means insignificant in that work. According to Luther, the fall and depravity of humanity make life in creation problematic. But God is the Creator and Sustainer, even of fallen humanity and fallen creation. Creation theology gives breadth to Luther's theology and makes it relevant for all people and for all that will occur. The hand, power, and care of the Creator reach out to the evil and to the good, to heathen, Jew, and Christian.

HUMANITY: ORIGINALLY AND AFTER THE FALL

Even if fallen human beings cannot fully understand the situation and the conditions of their original state, Luther says they need not speculate. Scripture illuminates the original state of humanity and of all God's creation.[2] God created humanity good, sustained humanity by his grace and power, and communicated with humanity through the Word that commanded/forbade and announced his goodwill toward humanity.[3] The reformer emphasizes that the first humans were

---

Testament occurred; thereby the Old Testament's message about God as the Creator was neglected. Cullmann, for example, has forgotten that the Old Testament was the ancient church's holy book and that in it creation theology is absolutely central. Barth's thesis is that the natural human knows absolutely nothing about God. Therefore Barth's theology begins with the incarnation, giving the Gospel priority over the Law. Luther, like the early church, structures his theology in a trinitarian manner. See Öberg, "Mission und Heilsgeschichte," 25ff.

2 For Luther's description of creation's original state, see especially Olsson, *Schöpfung, Vernunft und Gesetz in Luthers Theologie*, 211ff., 221ff., 256ff. See also the brief essays in Harnack, *Luthers Theologie*, 2:152f.; Köstlin, *Luthers Theologie*, 1:355ff., 2:355f.; Ljunggren, *Synd och skuld i Luthers teologi*, 100ff., 460ff.; and Althaus, *Die Theologie Martin Luthers*, 99ff.

3 Olsson (*Schöpfung, Vernunft und Gesetz in Luthers Theologie*, 214ff.) has shown how,

filled with divine life. Humanity was wholly absorbed by God in faith, love, and righteousness. Without desire for evil and without sin, humanity was characterized by perfect faith and spontaneous obedience. Further, Luther emphasizes that humanity possessed dominion (*dominium*) over everything created (Genesis 1:28ff.) and was creative in the world (Genesis 2:8). Humanity was God's image (*imago Dei*). Humanity reflected God in its full devotion to God, in its faith in God, and in its stewardship of creation and nature.[4]

Few theologians have written as emphatically as Luther about humanity's dominion over and stewardship of creation. The original, righteous human being had a knowledge of things that is inconceivable for us. Humanity was God's fellow worker (*cooperator Dei*), exercising dominion over and development of natural resources. Luther emphasizes this motif even as it impinges on the status of humanity changed by the fall.

For mission, how the reformer regards the natural and spiritual resources of humanity after the fall is important. Luther follows Genesis 3 and the tradition of the church concerning the fall into sin and its consequences. Humanity can never fully understand the fall nor how God could allow it to occur. One must be satisfied that humanity was created with the possibility to fall. But God can never be considered the cause of sin (*causa peccati*). Even if Luther carefully reasons how the fall could occur,[5] he believes the fall neither can be nor ought to be completely understood.

Genesis 3:1 is absolutely decisive for Luther's understanding of the fall and its catastrophic consequences for Adam and all the children of Adam—all human beings. Herbert Olsson has shown that Luther considered the immortality of humanity's original state to be sustained by the Word and faith. At creation, humanity could not fully comprehend God's inner being. Nor at the end of time will we be able to do so. God and his Word were at least partially hidden (Genesis 2:17). Therefore Adam could remain in faith or fall from it. The tempter exploited the ambiguity of God's command about "the tree of the knowledge of good and evil," promising Adam (unrealistically) the chance to observe the secrets of God. Adam listened to Satan: "Did God really say . . . ? You will not surely die . . . you will be like God, knowing good and evil" (Genesis 3:1, 4–5). So humanity fell from

---

according to Luther, the word that is given to humanity in Genesis 2:17 is formally a commandment (*praeceptum*). But this word at the same time is Gospel and assumes faith and trust in God. Therefore the fear that fills humanity after the fall does not arise from this commandment. According to Luther, Genesis 2:17 means that even humanity, which is absorbed by God, ought to exercise a piety borne by faith and a willing service. Humanity ought to be active and creative.

4 See Olsson, *Schöpfung, Vernunft und Gesetz in Luthers Theologie*, 256ff., 270ff.

5 Cf. Althaus, *Die Theologie Martin Luthers,* 142, and the Luther material he adduces.

God, the Word, faith, and spontaneous love/obedience. Luther often notes that the pattern for all sin and for all history of fallen humanity exists in the original fall. The sin in all sins is the fall from the Word and faith, the transformation of the will, and evil desire (*conscupiscentia*). All the sinful works of Adam's children are generated from this basic and original evil at the fall.[6]

From a missio-theological perspective, it is important to check how seriously a theologian considers the fall and the damage it has inflicted on humanity. Luther considers Adam's fall a catastrophe with the most negative consequences for all people. The dismal picture that Luther sketches has thoroughgoing consequences for his view of mission and evangelism. There is nothing positive in humanity to which the Word/Gospel can attach. According to Luther, humanity is ruled by unbelief and sin both in relation to God and in relation to creation. Unbelief and sin characterize all spiritual life and psychological/physical humanity. Humanity is in conflict with God. Sin characterizes especially our most important resources: reason and will. Luther often emphasized this perspective against Roman Catholic theology. All humanity is clothed in original sin (*Ersbünde*) or personal sin (*Personsünde*). All humanity is in rebellion against God, a basic depravity (*Natursünde*) that places every person under God's wrath (Genesis 2:17), under guilt, and under death.[7] No human being in this world is righteous in himself or herself. No one can stand before God.

Scholars have thoroughly examined Luther on the consequences of the fall:

1. After the fall, everything human in relation to God (*vita spiritualis*) is saturated with the primary sin of unbelief and of rebellion against God's will. This takes the form of pride or despair, disobedience toward God's will/command, and unrighteous living. Yet a typical response is that we seek to win God's favor through meritorious works. No longer filled with divine life, or born of God's grace and absorbed by God, we now seek ourselves by self-righteous efforts and are curved in on ourselves (*incurvatus in se*). In its relationship to God, humanity does not seek what God wants but is God's enemy. Humanity does not serve God the way it did before the fall when everyone trusted in God and spontaneously obeyed him. After the fall, everyone lives under God's wrath and judgment.[8]

---

6 See the thorough investigation of Luther's view of the fall and its consequences in Olsson, *Schöpfung, Vernunft und Gesetz in Luthers Theologie*, 296ff., 303ff.

7 See especially Ljunggren's ideas in *Synd och skuld i Luthers teologi*, 1ff., 123ff., 200ff., where he analyzes original sin and the connection between original and actual sin; Olsson, *Schöpfung, Vernunft und Gesetz in Luthers Theologie*, 320ff.; Harnack, *Luthers Theologie*, 1:193ff.; and Althaus, *Die Theologie Martin Luthers*, 144.

8 See especially Olsson, *Schöpfung, Vernunft und Gesetz in Luthers Theologie*, 323ff. See

Humanity—characterized as it is by unbelief, rebelliousness, self-righteousness, and self-centeredness—is the receptor of the church's mission and evangelization. The message is directed at a sinful humanity, a humanity in conflict with God and under God's wrath. In its relationship to God, humanity is totally depraved.

2. Furthermore, Luther asserts that the fall's depravity impinges significantly on psychological/physical life (*vita animalis*) and in natural humanity's dominion over creation, though in the psychological/physical life, humanity is not totally depraved. In the beginning, humanity possessed an unspoiled "practical" reason and knew instinctively how it ought to behave in relation to creation and its fellow human beings. Since the fall, this knowledge has been largely lost. Using its reason and will, humanity seeks only its own concerns. It does not possess any sure insight into how it ought to behave in creation and toward its fellow human beings. Therefore through the worldly regiment (*politia*), God, by means of vocations, laws, and ordinances, must bring about the works that serve life in creation and among people.

   Even humanity's will and emotions are now depraved. We no longer possess the total, spontaneous devotion to God's will and the freedom from fear that we enjoyed before the fall. Fallen humanity lives in fear of God and creation. The reason-bound treasures of human activity, namely, will and emotions, are now ruled by evil desire (*concupiscentia*) and no longer spontaneously exercise their duties toward creation and humanity. Civil law and the worldly regiment must force the rebellious and concupiscent human being to behave properly.[9] Indeed, according to Luther, fallen humanity possesses a weakened ability of physical sensation and a darkened knowledge of God.

In summary, the perfect pre-fall humanity has, through the fall, experienced a catastrophic negative transformation in its relation to God and in its relation to creation and its fellow human beings. Humanity is no longer in any respect God's image. In view of the seriousness of the fall and of sin, Luther can even say that natural humanity has been transformed from *imago Dei* to *imago diaboli* (the image of the devil). This dark picture of humanity is true for Adam and for all his children. Humanity is by nature placed under God's wrath, judgment, and death

---

also Ljunggren, *Synd och skuld i Luthers teologi*, 100ff.; and Harnack, *Luthers Theologie*, 1:193ff., 205ff. Concerning God's temporal and eternal punishments, see Harnack, *Luthers Theologie*, 1:252ff.; 2:47ff.

9 Olsson, *Schöpfung, Vernunft und Gesetz in Luthers Theologie*, 328ff.

(Genesis 2:17). It is this depraved humanity that the church and mission addresses with its message. According to the reformer, there is nothing positive in humanity to which that message can attach. Humanity is simply characterized by unbelief, self-centeredness, and self-righteousness, an active rebellion against God's will—both in respect to humanity's relation to God and in respect to its relation to creation and its fellow human beings.

Fallen, But Still God's Creation

The above sketch has shown that humanity has wholly and radically lost its spiritual life (*vita spiritualis*) through the fall. Faith, devotion, and spontaneous obedience to God are gone. Adam and all people are, at their core, enemies of God. For all this, Adam and all his children are placed under the curse of death, which is the wages of sin. However, all humans possess from birth a psychological/physical life (*vita animalis*) with these faculties: reason, will, senses, procreative abilities, etc. But these faculties are severely damaged. They are no longer saturated with spiritual life and do not exercise perfectly their dominion over creation as they did before the fall. However, even after the fall, humanity possesses a certain ability to rule creation. We will see how a remnant of the *imago Dei* and the faculties given in creation are important for Luther when he speaks about the efforts (forced and imperfect as they are) of human beings in home, society, and a productive life.[10]

According to Luther, natural humanity is at the same time fallen/depraved and God's beloved creation. Through conception, the first Adam transmits sin to all his offspring (Psalm 51:7; John 3:6; Romans 5:12f.; 1 Corinthians 15:21ff., 45ff.). Every human is born a sinner and is ruled by depravity and sin in every respect. According to Luther, the question why a good and righteous God should create individuals and a whole species within Adam's fallen nature ought not to be and cannot be fully understood. In a similar way, the fact that God neither changes the nature of Adam's descendants nor alters sin's continued existence is something incomprehensible for human beings.[11]

Nevertheless, fallen humanity remains the creation of the good and righteous God. Among other things, this means that God creates depraved humans with psychological and physical capacities such as reason, will, and the senses. It also means—and this is important to note—natural humanity possesses some knowledge of God and God's Law. Natural humanity witnesses in all its imperfection that God is the Creator of humanity and that humanity can never escape

10 Olsson, *Schöpfung, Vernunft und Gesetz in Luthers Theologie*, 334ff., 340ff.

11 See Ljunggren, *Synd och skuld i Luthers teologi*, 201ff., 220ff., 381ff.; and Olsson, *Schöpfung, Vernunft und Gesetz in Luthers Theologie*, 320f., 358ff.

the question of God's existence. That God creates every person with some inkling of the Creator and the Law demonstrates that God does not want to abandon humanity to complete depravity. Through the natural law and the preached Law, God wants to convict every person of sin (*officium theologicum legis*) and thereafter lead every person to Christ, the Gospel, and faith. Through the Law, God also wants to compel unwilling people to serve their neighbors in civil life (*officium politicum legis*).

According to Luther, even by his work through the Law, God shows that he does not want to abandon fallen humanity. Despite everything, God wants humanity to become the image of God (*imago Dei*) in its relationship to God, to neighbor, and to all creation. In other words, sin cannot change the fact that fallen humanity is God's creation, and God himself aims finally to save and to transform humanity into his likeness. Luther draws this conclusion from the fact that every person possesses psychological and physical capacities, some intimation of God's existence, and some recognition of God's Law. After all, humanity is God's creation and God is the Creator and Savior of humanity. In addition to all the earthly good that God grants to both good and evil people, as Creator and Savior he wants ultimately to make everyone into the *imago Dei*—through the Gospel of Christ, through faith, and through the final making of all things new. Indeed, according to Luther, God wants to make humanity into something higher and more glorious than it was originally.[12]

Luther's view of mission must be seen from this broader perspective. The outlook for fallen humanity has to be characterized as rather gloomy. But when seen from the perspective of God's hold on every human heart, his desire to save, and his plan for the recapitulation of humanity, the situation is not so dreary. For Luther, what God wants and does is always decisive. Thus God's plan for salvation and mission are nearly identical. The efforts of the church and mission are important, but more important still is that God will not abandon us, that he still seeks our rehabilitation and salvation.

The Continuing Work and Presence of the Creator

On the basis of Scripture, Luther asserts that God is the Creator of all, continuously creating and sustaining all. This is expressed particularly in Luther's *Magnificat* (1521) and *Bondage of the Will* (1525). God creates and sustains everything that exists. Everything has its origin, its life, and its existence in God alone. For Luther, creation theology is not only connected with *perfectum* (the past tense) but also with *praesens* (the present tense). God created in the beginning

---

12 Olsson, *Schöpfung, Vernunft und Gesetz in Luthers Theologie*, 357ff., 361ff. See also Wingren, *Luthers lära om kallelsen*, 69ff.

(*creatio prima*), continuously creates anew (*creatio continua*), and is living and active over all things, present with his creative authority and compelling power.

For a missiological investigation, it can be important to point out how the reformer asserts that the Creator continually works and is present in the whole world, in all that happens, among all people under the sun. When in mission we preach about the Creator, the Word gives us the necessary interpretation of God's works—that God is already there in his providence and in his creative-sustaining-caring work. All people encounter the Creator's active and sovereign power whether they realize it or not. Taking creation theology seriously, the mission message communicates that our relationship to God the Creator is given with life itself. Nothing exists in and of itself. All is and exists only through God the Creator. Ultimately, nothing and no one can escape God the Creator and Sustainer.[13]

Thus Luther asserts that God is present in and above all with his authority and life-giving power. However, God's omnipresence (ubiquity) must not be identified with creation itself or with the reality of the world. God remains transcendent to the world, nature, and all creation. With his omnipotence and creative power, he is beyond all things and not pantheistically identical with creation or nature.[14]

---

13 Among the secondary works on Luther's creation theology, see Harnack, *Luthers Theologie*, 1:86ff., 91ff.; Köstlin, *Luthers Theologie*, 2:95ff.; Elert, *Morphologie des Luthertums*, 1:386ff.; Pedersen, "Schöpfung und Geschichte bei Luther," 6ff.; Althaus, *Die Theologie Martin Luthers*, 99ff.; Olsson, *Schöpfung, Vernunft und Gesetz in Luthers Theologie*, 369ff., with bibliography; Pinomaa, *Sieg des Glaubens*, 26ff.; and Wingren, *Luther frigiven*, 9ff., 85ff., 97. Wingren truly captures what Luther, in his colorful language, has to say about the active Creator in present daily life. Concerning the importance of keeping creation theology alive in mission work, see, among others, the following works: Aagaard, "Kap. Missionstheologie," 225ff.; Öberg, "Mission und Heilsgeschichte," 25ff.; and Pörsti, "Luthers syn på evangelisation," 24f.

14 See Harnack, *Luthers Theologie*, 1:86ff.; Althaus, *Die Theologie Martin Luthers*, 100; and Olsson, *Schöpfung, Vernunft und Gesetz in Luthers Theologie*, 371ff. Luther describes God's omnipresent but never localized right hand in his treatise on the Lord's Supper, "That These Words of Christ, 'This Is My Body,' etc. (1527)": "... the right hand of God ... is the almighty power of God, which at one and the same time can be nowhere and yet must be everywhere. It cannot be at any one place, I say. For if it were at some specific place, it would have to be there in a circumscribed and determinate manner . . . . But the power of God cannot be so determined and measured, for it is uncircumscribed and immeasurable, beyond and above all that is or may be. On the other hand, it must be essentially present [*wesentlich und gegenwertig*] at all places, even in the tiniest tree leaf. The reason is this: It is God who creates, effects, and preserves all things through his almighty power and right hand, as our Creed confesses. . . . If he is to create or preserve it . . . he himself must be present in every single creature in its innermost and outermost being . . . so that nothing can be more truly present and within all creatures than God himself with his power" (LW 37:57–58 [WA 23:133.21ff.]).

This is significant for mission work in at least two ways. First, there is no reason to accept the accusation that for original Lutheranism the Christian God is a distant God. Second, Luther decidedly opposes any tendency to identify God with the created, a misunderstanding that occurs in many non-Christian cultures.

For Luther, God's omnipresent work in creation and in the life of humans must not be considered an impersonal natural power. In Luther, one deals with a personal God, the God of righteousness and love. The Creator can use things (fire and water), occurrences (pestilence, accidents, war, and death), and the ordained person's ministry as tools for his discipline and wrath. God's creative, sustaining, and caring work is, however, first an expression of God's unconditional goodness and giving love (*gebende Liebe*).[15]

THE CREATOR'S WORK AND THE INTERPRETING WORD

Earlier we noticed how forcefully Luther asserts God's providence, God's creative and sustaining activity of all that is, God's omnipresence, God's authority, and God's power. Similarly, Luther emphasizes that natural fallen human beings cannot fully understand the work of the Creator or see God immediately in what they meet in nature, creation, and the course of history and life. The work of the Creator, which expresses both his sustaining goodness and his discipline and wrath, is, therefore, constantly misunderstood. The natural human does not trust in God but in those gifts God gives to both the evil and the good. When the natural human meets the wrath of the Creator (God's reaction to sin and evil, God's merciful discipline, *ira misericordiae*, in external occurrences), he or she is filled with cowardice and despair.

In this way, the reformer asserts that the natural human cannot really understand God's works in creation (nor in salvation, for that matter) without the Word of law and the Word of promise. Therefore Luther links God's creative activity and his leading in history with the Word of God, which interprets and communicates the significance (*significatio*) of God's work. The natural human "objectively" meets God in life and creation but only understands what is happening through the Word as Law and Gospel. In time and creation the natural human never comprehends God in his naked majesty (*deus nudus*). Instead, he or she understands God as he is in his works as interpreted by the Word. The God of creation is hidden from the natural (unregenerate) person even in his works. Only through the Word as Law and Gospel can natural humanity learn to believe in the Creator and hold fast to him in both his severity and goodness. According

---

15 Althaus, *Die Theologie Martin Luthers*, 104ff., 107ff.; Olsson, *Schöpfung, Vernunft und Gesetz in Luthers Theologie*, 376ff.; and Pedersen, "Schöpfung und Geschichte bei Luther," 12.

to Luther, faith in God's work and God's Word together characterizes Christian creation theology.[16]

Such a view of natural theology has consequences for mission work and evangelism. The First Article about creation and God's sustaining work, the fundamental way of seeing the world, should not be ignored in preaching. All genuine evangelical-Lutheran preaching includes preaching about creation. Creation faith is not a theology of secularization but the first part of Christian faith. Second, one must remember how little natural humanity understands the work of the Creator and Sustainer, even if living by and in the same work as the Christian. The God whom the natural human experiences in creation and history is hidden. God must be explained, known, and believed through his Word as Law and Gospel. The complete meaning of creation can in no way be fully understood by the natural mind. Yet perhaps nothing in all theology is so universal and true as the doctrine of creation, the sustaining of all life, the Creator, God's activity in the occurrences of everyday life, and God's good foreknowledge. God is the Creator and Sustainer of everything and everyone, even of the heathen. But if that is true, everyone also must be provided with the opportunity to hear about God's creative activity and his other great work, namely, salvation in Jesus Christ. That is how, in Luther's theology, creation and the history of all people are intertwined with the history of faith and the church. The inner mystery of history is God's work in creation and salvation, which the Word alone can explain to the human mind.

That Luther has so clearly perceived this mystery is demonstrated by how often and how exhaustively he teaches and preaches Christian creation and faith. An extraordinary example of how he describes the Creator's *gebende Liebe* (giving love) is in these well-known sentences from the Large Catechism:

> What is meant by these words . . . "I believe in God, the Father almighty, creator," etc? Answer: I hold and believe that I am God's creature, that is, that he has given me and constantly sustains my body, soul, and life, my members great and small, all my senses, my reason and understanding, and the like; my food and drink, clothing, nourishment, spouse and children, servants, house and farm, etc. Besides, he makes all creation help provide the benefits and necessities of life—sun, moon, and stars in the heavens; day and night; air, fire, water, the earth and all that it yields and brings forth; birds, fish, animals, grain, and all sorts of produce. Moreover, he gives all physical and temporal blessings—good government, peace, security. Thus we learn from this article that none of us has life—or anything else . . . . All this is comprehended in the word "Creator."

---

16 Olsson, *Schöpfung, Vernunft und Gesetz in Luthers Theologie*, 436ff., 448ff.; Harnack, *Luthers Theologie*, 1:93ff., 98ff.; and Pedersen, "Schöpfung und Geschichte bei Luther," 10ff., 21ff.

Moreover, we also confess that God the Father has given us not only all that we have and what we see before our eyes, but also that he daily guards and defends us against every evil and misfortune, warding off all sorts of danger and disaster. All this he does out of pure love and goodness, without our merit, as a kind father who cares for us so that no evil may befall us.[17]

Human Beings
as God's Co-Creators (*Cooperatores Dei*)

Luther claims that God, in his creating providence, uses creation itself as the means of his creative activity. Everything created is God's tool and mask (*larvae Dei, Gottes Mummerei*). God alone is the *causa prima*; the tools are the *causae secundae* or *instrumentales*. God could have worked in creation directly without these instruments, but it has pleased him to work through and hide himself behind these masks. There is no place in all creation and the historic process where one may see God directly and immediately, but faith sees God working everywhere. Everything created, especially humankind, is assigned by God to be a tool of creation, a tool that accomplishes his work. God creates and cares for every individual. For example, he creates and cares through the sexual intercourse of parents and their care for the child. God gives seed in the field, but the farmer is assigned to work with that seed. All activities in the field, in the city, at home, in government, and in the military are masks of God's work among people. God's work through nature and people is primarily an expression of the Creator's care and love. But it also can represent God's wrath against evil and godless people.[18]

Luther's view of people as God's masks and tools automatically assigns a high value to all earthly activities. Luther research has clarified the reformer's comprehensive doctrine of vocation (*Beruf*), of different estates and services, of work and biological processes. According to Luther, the Creator takes people, even the godless, into his service to sustain life on earth and to serve—willingly or unwillingly—the best for neighbor and for creation. Of course, Luther recognizes that

---

17 LC II 13–17 (K-W, 432–33; *BSLK*, 648); cf. SC II 2 (K-W, 354–55; *BSLK*, 510f.). See also Öberg, "Mission und Heilsgeschichte," 26f.

18 Wingren, *Luthers lära om kallelsen*, 12ff., 18ff., 148ff, and elsewhere; Josefson, *Den naturliga teologins problem hos Luther*, 107ff.; and Olsson, *Schöpfung, Vernunft und Gesetz in Luthers Theologie*, 373ff. Cf. LC II 26: "Creatures are only the hands, channels, and means through which God bestows all blessings. For example, he gives to the mother breasts and milk for her infant or gives grain and all sorts of fruits from the earth for sustenance—things that no creature could produce by itself" (K-W, 389). On how God opposes Satan by way of work, school, city hall, church, etc., see "On the Councils and the Churches (1539)," LW 41:176ff. (WA 50:652.7ff.).

sinful types of work do exist—for example, prostitution, life in the cloister, and usury—work in which a Christian must not participate.

For Luther, the various ordinances, ranks, careers, and kinds of work are not merely sterile jobs. They are ordained and chosen by God and are ultimately parts of God's creative activity. They are an expression of God's love and care for creation and for life on earth. God takes people into his service by caring for and developing his world. Thus people become God's co-creators (*cooperatores Dei*) whether they know God or not. In all this co-creation and work, the need of the neighbor is the aim. Human beings, God's co-creators, become the means and the channels for the giving and sustaining love of the Creator.[19]

Christians will, of course, serve their neighbor in natural ways that are near to them. As Mary after the annunciation continued her work among the livestock and in the kitchen, so every Christian ought to flee from super-spiritual piety and serve fellow human beings in their given vocations. In this matter, Luther's struggle against monks and enthusiasts is significant. If the godless are legally forced to serve, those who believe and are driven by God's Spirit will serve willingly. But this service ought to occur in an everyday and natural manner. It is through such service, not through some kind of spiritual specialization, that Christians communicate God's love and true care for the neighbor.[20]

THE TWO REGIMENTS DOCTRINE AND THE CIVIL LIFE

For this investigation of Luther and mission, it is important to observe that the reformer often highly values the orders of creation and vocation (*Beruf*), even in non-Christian cultures. Luther can do this because of the concept of people as *larvae Dei* and as *cooperatores Dei*. Indeed, the whole cluster of ideas about God's creative and sustaining activity are central to Luther. Especially important is the reformer's understanding of the two regiments doctrine.[21] According to this

---

19 Törnvall, *Andligt och världsligt regemente hos Luther*; Wingren, *Luthers lära om kallelsen*, 12ff., 135ff., with references; and Wingren, *Luther frigiven*, 64ff. See also Kinder, *Geistliches und weltliches Regiment Gottes nach Luther*, 20ff.

20 See Wingren, *Luthers lära om kallelsen*, 140ff., 185ff. In his sermon on the Magnificat, Luther writes that the Virgin Mary did not begin to perform remarkable works of power; instead, after the annunciation, she served in the natural sphere: "Behold, how completely she traces all to God, lays claim to no works, no honor, no fame. . . . She seeks not any glory, but goes about her usual household duties, milking the cows, cooking the meals, washing pots and kettles, sweeping out the rooms, and performing the work of maidservant or housemother in lowly and despised tasks, as though she cared nothing for such great gifts and graces" (LW 7:329 [WA 7:575.13ff.]). Cf. especially the clarifying theses about faith and life in the given vocation in Luther's sermon on John 21:19–24 in *Church Postil* (1522), WA 10/1.1:306.15ff., 308.6ff., 310.14ff., 323.8ff.

21 See these basic works: Törnvall, *Andligt och världsligt regemente hos Luther*, 1ff., 30ff.;

doctrine, God is present and active in this world through the ordinances, both worldly and spiritual, which he created and established. It is essential to observe that both regiments or hands are established by God against Satan's reign. If this is not the case, one concludes with dualistic nineteenth-century liberal theology that God's work in creation is merely temporal, external, and relative, whereas Christ's reign is connected inextricably with salvation, directed toward ethics, and absolute. Luther speaks of the earthly regiment, or the regiment of the sword, as something that limits evil by force and laws, that orders society in peace, and that establishes justice at home and in governments. He speaks of the spiritual regiment, or the regiment of the Word, as something that offers justification with God. God establishes both regiments. Both are God's means to work against Satan's destruction, God's hands to govern the world and to save people. Through the earthly regiment—which consists of government leaders, magistrates, judges, parents, and the like—order and peace are ensured so work life and family life can function properly. Through the spiritual regiment—consisting of Christ, the Word, the sacraments, pastors, and the like—God provides forgiveness and eternal life. Consequently, the difference is clear between the task and the goal of each regiment. In this context, what interests us most is the earthly regiment.

For Luther, it is by no means self-evident that Christian princes, parliaments, and judges always rule and judge more effectively or more reasonably than those in non-Christian lands. God does not begin to be active in the earthly regiment only after a nation and its leaders have become Christian. Similarly, Luther evaluates positively all legitimate positions, biological ordinances, etc., wherever they exist. One need not depend on the Gospel or the church or God's so-called right hand for this world to function—an important presupposition for Luther's ecclesiology and missiology. The Creator has ordained the earthly regiment and established the orders of creation and earthly occupations. God's so-called left hand stretches forth to all and works among all people. God's left hand is intimately connected with natural law (*lex naturalis*), the law written in all human hearts and the regulating principle of the civil use of the law in all cultures. The civil life, the organs of society, rankings, and different types of work are things that God has appointed, not something base or evil. God directs people everywhere to build up a civil order in which people, willingly or unwillingly, serve one another and the neighbor's good. The righteousness, order, and peace that is created in this way,

---

Lau, *Luthers Lehre von den beiden Reichen*, 28ff., 34ff.; Wingren, *Luthers lära om kallelsen*, 33ff., 97ff.; and Wingren, *Luther frigiven*, 65ff. See also Lau "Aüsserliche Ordnung" und "weltlich Ding" in *Luthers Theologie*, 12ff.; Kinder, *Geistliches und weltliches Regiment Gottes nach Luther*, 7ff.; Iserloh and Müller, *Luther und die politische Welt*; and Manns, "Luthers Zwei-Reiche- und Drei-Stände-Lehre." Especially enlightening is *Temporal Authority*, LW 45 (WA 11:247ff.). Cf. WA 19:629.14ff. and 29:244f.

namely, *iustitia civilis,* is in no way a saving righteousness. But it is important for humanity's common life, and it is an assertion that the Creator is not distant from creation and humanity.

Luther claims that humanity possesses natural law, reason, and a sense of what is fair (*Billigkeit*) in amounts sufficient to manage civil life and to sustain order and peace in society. He also believes that leaders in civil service and authorities can, through Satan's destructive work, abuse the power they have been given by God, even in the earthly regiment.[22] Concrete laws and ordinances (positive rights), which grow out of society, do not have absolute autonomy. Their source and their correcting court of appeal are in natural law (*lex naturalis*).

The actual government is not only conditioned by sinful circumstances, it is itself sometimes evil and destructive and needs open criticism. Among other things, the Decalogue (revealed Law) has an important function as a clear expression of natural law. The independent civil life, which is directed by reason, cannot liberate itself from the will of the Creator or legitimate itself (*Eigengesetzlichkeit*). Luther, however, opposes revolution as a solution for problems such as oppressive government leaders or inhumane government. He does so primarily because experience has shown that the misery resulting from revolution is worse than the original evil. Also, the ruling authorities have been commissioned by God (Romans 13:1ff.). Luther often considers an inhumane regime to be God's punishment or discipline, an idea our time considers too passive and pacifying. Luther stressed that God as the Lord of history topples tyrants from their thrones. He often says God helps the oppressed by sending great and reasonable leaders (*viri heroici, Wunderleute*). With a clear perspective, they defeat oppression and establish a reasonable and humane order. Like others, Luther lived in a patriarchal society that could not at the time think of rectifying oppression through democratic processes. Luther believed people must be ruled consistently and with the force of law so they would not develop into a revolutionary mob. God will not release the reins that control earthly government so that it devolves into anarchy.

According to Luther, the church in its preaching of God's Law and command ought to teach about life in the various vocations and ought to punish gross abuses in earthly government. Luther did so in speaking and in writing by interpreting the second table of the Decalogue. For example, Luther reacted to the Roman Catholic hierarchy's greed for money and its abuse of power. In connection with the Peasants' War in the mid-1520s, Luther criticized both sides of the conflict. On the one hand, he criticized the lords who turned a blind eye to the

---

22 Törnvall, *Andligt och världsligt regemente hos Luther*, 113ff.; Wingren, *Luthers lära om kallelsen*, 9ff., 158ff.; Lau *"Aüsserliche Ordnung" und "weltlich Ding" in Luthers Theologie*, 37ff.; and Pedersen, "Schöpfung und Geschichte bei Luther," 14ff., 18ff.

peasants' social destitution and lack of rights. On the other hand, he criticized the peasants for revolting against the ruling authorities. Luther's social-ethical preaching often attacked usury and the lucrative interest rates that made those who took out loans destitute. Luther also wrote about education and the Christians' stance toward war.[23] Although the preaching ministry uses only the Word, not agitation and political demonstrations, Luther's involvement in contemporary political and social problems shows that he often wished to speak a critical word (law) about sociopolitical problems. As Franz Lau rightly cautions, however, Luther did not want to make the church into city hall and mix the two regiments. When Luther teaches from the second table of the Decalogue, he touches on a wide range of social and political questions. When confronted with extraordinary events or when requested, Luther felt preachers ought to give the worldly power a word of advice or warning while remaining basically loyal. Position and status are good, but the person in the position can be evil and abuse power.

---

23 See Ivarsson, *Predikans uppgift*, 146ff., 158ff.; Törnvall, *Andligt och världsligt regemente hos Luther*, 113ff.; and Wingren, *Luthers lära om kallelsen*, 113ff. About how Luther's theology actually contradicts the German *Schöpfungstheologie* of the 1930s with its *Eigengesetzlichkeit* and how, according to Luther, the world is independent in relation to the church but never in relation to the Creator and his Law or will, see Wingren, *Luther frigiven*, 76ff. Cf. Öberg, "Mission und Heilsgeschichte," 26f.

See especially Lau (*Luthers Lehre*, 8ff.), who shows Luther's *Die Berichtigung aller Stände durch das Predgtamt* against the complaints of Karl Barth and others in the 1900s. Nevertheless, Lau also shows this is a more general type of teaching/preaching without addressing the details of specific political questions. Lau considers the role preaching on the Decalogue has in correcting abuses of the civil life on pp. 74ff. and cites, among other things, WA 31/1:191ff.; 32:399ff., 344ff. This is especially clear in "A Sermon on Keeping Children in School": "Beyond that, however, [God] does great and mighty works for the world. He informs and instructs the various estates on how they are to conduct themselves outwardly in their several offices and estates, so that they may do what is right in the sight of God. . . . For a preacher confirms, strengthens, and helps to sustain authority of every kind, and temporal peace generally. He checks the rebellious; teaches obedience, morals, discipline, and honor; instructs fathers, mothers, children, and servants in their duties; in a word, he gives direction to all the temporal estates and offices. . . . Therefore, to tell the truth, peace, the greatest of earthly goods, in which all other temporal goods are comprised, is really a fruit of true preaching" (LW 46:226 [WA 30/2:357.4ff.]).

Cf. LW 13:195 (WA 51:240.7ff.): "Now, if a preacher in his official capacity says to kings and princes and to all the world, 'Thank and fear God, and keep His commandments,' he is not meddling in the affairs of secular government. On the contrary, he is thereby serving and being obedient to the highest government. Thus the entire spiritual government really does nothing else than serve the divine authority." Cf. also Olsson, *Grundproblemet i Luthers socialetik*, 1:92ff., about "natural and divine right"; and Lau, "Äusserliche Ordnung," 40ff, 85ff.

Generally, Luther wants to let the world be led by people who are enlightened by reason. Civil righteousness and political systems are not in themselves Christian, but they ought to be reasonable and they ought to protect the rights of citizens. In Luther's view, the relative order that emerges from reason and reasonable authorities is also important so that the Gospel can be preached freely.

Social and Political Issues, Creation, and the Law

Within church and mission, what role should the church or mission play in oppressive social-ethical and sociopolitical contexts? In general, Luther and the Lutheran Confessions maintain that one should never mix the earthly and spiritual regiments. God's regiments each have different goals, characters, means, and the like. The church and its ministers should not direct political life. The earthly power should not involve itself in the work of the church, in the Word and Sacraments. God has two regiments in this one world: God's right hand works through the Word/Gospel and God's left hand through civil government. These regiments cannot be mixed without damage to both.[24] In the earthly regiment, the Creator/Sustainer works through law, force, and the sword. The spiritual regiment is concerned with God as Savior in a heavenly, eternal regime in which God grants righteousness through the Gospel (preceded by the Law in its second use).

In different lands and in the concrete lives of individuals, relations and mutual service exist between the two regiments. The leaders in both ought to support and promote each other's work, though they have different goals in their particular sphere. On the one hand, the servant of the Word should mind his own business and not exercise political power. On the other hand, civic leaders should govern society and not get involved in the work of the church. But most Christians are at home in the spiritual realm of the church and up to their ears in natural, worldly pursuits, positions, and vocations. Luther clearly believed the faithful should exercise their faith, crucify the "old man," and serve their neighbors in the natural, civil ordinances, vocations, and ministries. In their earthly pursuits and vocations, they naturally influence and direct sociopolitical life as actively as non-Christians. In many passages, Luther has said Christians who live their lives responsibly toward God should be set aside especially for civil tasks.[25]

---

24 Törnvall, *Andligt och världsligt regemente hos Luther*, 70ff., 216ff. Cf. Wingren (*Luthers lära om kallelsen*, 120ff.) about how the pope and the enthusiasts, instead of fighting with the Word, take the sword in hand and how the princes and judges attempt to control the preaching office. In either direction, one fatefully mixes the two regiments. Cf. Pedersen, "Schöpfung und Geschichte bei Luther," 15ff.; and Kinder, *Geistliches und weltliches Regiment Gottes nach Luther*, 37ff.

25 See Kinder, *Geistliches und weltliches Regiment Gottes nach Luther*, 20ff., 41ff., 47ff.; Törnvall, *Andligt och världsligt regemente hos Luther*, 73, 190ff.; Wingren, *Luthers lära*

Finally, Luther considers political and social-ethical questions primarily in connection with the First Article, namely, from the perspective of creation faith and the Law. This is quite different from much of nineteenth- and twentieth-century theology. The twentieth century has often confused God's regiment of grace and salvation from sin with God's regiment of power that fosters a good and just social and political life. For nineteenth-century Protestantism, God's reign became mostly a this-worldly, ethical reign. During the past century, the so-called social gospel interpreted sin and salvation together. The focus was on the social conditions from which one needed to be saved. Peace with God and peace in sociopolitical questions were equated. This theological shift occurred because enormous world problems influenced the Ecumenical Movement and the international mission debate (Bangkok 1973 and Melbourne 1980). Karl Barth's ideas about *Königsherrschaft Christi*, in which God's reign is supposed to bring about new structures in the sociopolitical plane, have exercised a profound influence, especially on liberation theology.

Especially from the golden age of Pietism through the revival movements of the nineteenth century to contemporary theological existentialism, creation and social-ethical questions have had little place in the exercise of theology. In the past 150 years of mission, the mission task often has been defined narrowly with the well-known formula "to make Christ known." Many have not understood that it is impossible to sweep social-ethical questions under the rug, whether at home or in the mission field.

It can be helpful to compare Luther's thinking with theologians who equate peace with God and peace in sociopolitical questions and with pietists who ignore creation and related social-ethical questions. Luther would have criticized the first for mixing earthly freedom with the peace of the Gospel (compare his dispute with the political enthusiasts of the radical Reformation). Likewise, Luther would have cautioned against neglecting the creation dimension and the many shifting problems of life and world. We must deal with human rights, economic and political oppression, and the origin of famine in connection with the First Article, creation, and law. Otherwise these problems will fall under the Second and Third Articles and corrupt them—as happens in contemporary ecumenical debates and in much of contemporary mission theology. Instead of focusing on Christ and the forgiveness of sins and eternal life, many contemporary theologians discuss social distress and politics. By emphasizing laws and efforts to help the oppressed and distressed, the Gospel is apt to become Law.[26] Luther would have cut immediately

---

om kallelsen, 36ff., 127ff.; and Pedersen, "Schöpfung und Geschichte bei Luther," 18ff., about, among other things, Baptism, crucifixion, and vocation.

26 Cf. Vikström, "Mission und Reich Gottes," 60ff.; and Öberg, "Mission und Heils-

through the confusion of the contemporary debate with a clear distinction among the articles of the Creed and by upholding the doctrine of the two regiments. As will be examined later, Luther identified God's reign with salvation from Satan, sin, death, and the accusing Law through the Gospel of the forgiveness of sins. At the same time, Luther taught the First Article, God as Creator, and his created people as co-creators with social responsibility as stated in the second table of the Decalogue. For the sake of the Gospel, Luther strictly defined the sphere and specific task of each of the three articles of the Apostles' Creed.

Social-ethical questions must be handled primarily under the First Article (creation and Law). If not, Christ as Savior from sin and death, God's unconditional grace, and the forgiveness of sins will become strange birds in evangelical-Lutheran Christianity. These issues must be handled and acted upon; they must not be corrupted with alien content. But to ensure the quality of humanity's dominion in the world and its management of natural resources, Christ as Co-Creator and Co-Sustainer (cf. Colossians 1:16) also must be confessed.

THE CREATOR, THE LAW, AND HUMANITY

All creatures exist and subsist in the Creator. Nothing and no one can avoid this relation to the Creator. To this, Luther attaches a second important thesis: God has placed humanity and all creation under the Law. This implies that God has not abandoned the world and humanity, despite our sin and our fall from grace.

On the basis of Romans 2:15, Luther says God has written the Law on human hearts.[27] Whether we realize it or not, we are, therefore, connected with the Creator. The so-called *lex naturalis* can never be erased from human hearts and consciences, despite our fall and revolt against God, our unbelief and sin.[28] In Luther's

---

geschichte," 27, 38ff. See also Wingren, *Luthers lära om kallelsen*, 11ff., 20ff.; and Wingren, *Luther frigiven*, 73.

27 See the studies of Josefson, *Den naturliga teologins problem hos Luther*, 73ff., 84ff., 93ff.; and especially Olsson, *Grundproblemet i Luthers socialetik*, 1:19ff., 51ff.; and Olsson, *Schöpfung, Vernunft und Gesetz in Luthers Theologie*, 24ff., 160ff. Olsson criticizes Troeltsch's and Holl's interpretations of Luther.

28 Olsson, *Schöpfung, Vernunft und Gesetz in Luthers Theologie*, 17ff., 157ff. Olsson cites many examples in Luther's writings about the law written on human hearts, among them LW 27:355 (WA 2:580.19): ". . . written [law] in the hearts of all people"; WA 30/1:192.19: "Die zehen gepot sind auch sonst ynn aller menschen hertzen geschreiben"; LW 25:19–20 (WA 56:23.8f.): "By nature and indelibly the law of nature is imprinted on their minds, *while their conscience bears witness to them* [Romans 2:15], a good witness about the good works and an evil witness about the evil works" (*original emphasis*). See also Josefson, *Den naturliga teologins problem hos Luther*, 73ff., 84ff., 93ff.

understanding of mission, even the heathen are said to know the Law and to do some superficial works of the Law. Above all, natural law is a judging and affirming authority over concrete human works—natural law, not the Law revealed in God's Word.

The reformer emphasizes that this does not imply that the heathen concretely know and fulfill the Law's innermost demands for a love connected with faith and the Holy Spirit. Luther rejects the Scholastic theologians' notion that by nature we have a pure natural moral knowledge. Romans 2:14–15 ultimately shows sin is deeply ingrained and inextinguishable. We need grace and justification. Even the natural law through conscience ought to condemn us, reveal our sin, and drive us to grace and to Christ. Luther says human beings by nature have a deficient knowledge of the Law's external, surface work. But notwithstanding the impairment of our knowledge caused by sin, we can still recognize the natural law and the Golden Rule (Matthew 7:12).[29]

Humanity does not understand the full dimensions of *lex naturalis* and can, of course, abuse it, sin against it, and hate it, but humanity can never ultimately flee from the condemnation of the law in the conscience. Therefore everyone experiences guilt. Because knowledge of the Law has been obscured through the fall and unbelief—though not completely erased—the Law must be preached for humanity to see its situation under sin. This *officium spiritualis legis* ought to be used so there is a movement from the Law to the Gospel. For Luther, it is also important that natural law, written on human hearts, resonate with the preaching of the revealed Law. An ox or a donkey does not react to such preaching, but humanity does and either accepts or becomes annoyed by the demands of the Law.[30] In this way, natural law becomes a kind of point of contact for the Word/Gospel.

The eminent Luther scholar Herbert Olsson, writing against Karl Holl, emphasized that in Luther's thought the Law cannot be considered an eternal, objective order. It is an expression of the will of the living Creator. The command in paradise (Genesis 2:17) and the first command of the Decalogue actually

---

29 Olsson, *Grundproblemet i Luthers socialetik*, 1:51ff., 62ff., 65ff.; Olsson, *Schöpfung, Vernunft und Gesetz in Luthers Theologie*, 87, 110ff.; Josefson, *Den naturliga teologins problem hos Luther*, 79, 101ff.; and Althaus, *Die Theologie Martin Luthers*, 221, 227ff.

30 Josefson, *Den naturliga teologins problem hos Luther*, 87ff., 93ff.; Althaus, *Die Theologie Martin Luthers*, 128, 221ff., 227ff.; and Olsson, *Schöpfung, Vernunft und Gesetz in Luthers Theologie*, 19f., 87, 98, 110ff. Cf. also Wingren, *Luther frigiven*, 45ff. In *Himmelrikets nycklar och kyrklig bot i Luthers teologi*, 142ff., I have criticized Wingren, among others, because he does not sufficiently recognize that in Luther the natural knowledge of the Law is deficient and that it is, therefore, necessary to preach the Law/command. See also Öberg, ". . . i hans navn skal omvendelse og tilgivelse for syndene forkynnes for alle folkeslag," 118ff.

contain both threat and promise, Law and Gospel. This characterizes the content of all the laws and all the commands of the Bible. The person who trusts in God and who loves him is commanded to love the neighbor. Faith in God and love for neighbor is the basic context of the Law. The Law is more than some kind of objective command.[31]

Luther makes a distinction between what God commands in the Law (*officium legis*) and how the natural, fallen human being understands and uses this command (*usus legis*). Humanity before the fall understood the Law as something inexpressibly desirable, but after the fall, humanity experiences it as a threat and punishment. By nature, the fallen, depraved human knows something of the Law but distorts its meaning. By attempting to do good works, humanity seeks to silence the threat of the Law and to win God's favor.[32] Having lost our original state, our spontaneous love for God, by nature we now believe that fellowship with God depends on a righteous life. That affects our view of God and our exercise of religion. Natural man is curved in on himself (*incurvatus in se*), seeking his own welfare by avoiding punishment and attempting to earn a reward but actually hating the Law that commands the same good conduct. In fact, natural humanity does not have a correct understanding of the Law but perverts it. Only through the Gospel, faith, and the Holy Spirit can humanity understand that the Law speaks of faith toward God and love toward one another. For natural humanity, the way of the Law is simply a false way to salvation.

Although humanity abuses and breaks the Law, it cannot escape its demands. The Law can drive and tyrannize the conscience, but it cannot produce righteousness before God. Luther emphasizes that the unwillingness of the depraved human heart is aggravated by the Law (Romans 5:20). However, Luther does not conclude that the Law should not be preached. As an expression of God's will, the Law should be kept alive through preaching because the Law ultimately shows it is impossible to earn salvation (*impossibilitas legis*). At this point, the Law has completed its task: to reveal sin and to drive the human heart to contrition, *officium spiritualis*.[33] Then man is no longer closed to the Gospel and unconditional grace.

---

31 Olsson, *Schöpfung, Vernunft und Gesetz in Luthers Theologie*, 24ff., 119ff., 124ff., 214ff., 438ff. See also Josefson, *Den naturliga teologins problem hos Luther*, 73ff., especially: "Natural law is consequently not an objectively existing natural law, but instead the will of the Creator God, as he appears to sinful humanity" (109). Cf. Althaus, *Die Theologie Martin Luthers*, 191ff.

32 Olsson, *Schöpfung, Vernunft und Gesetz in Luthers Theologie*, 31ff., 105ff., 170ff.; Josefson, *Den naturliga teologins problem hos Luther*, 65ff., 79f.; Wingren, *Luthers lära om kallelsen*, 20ff., 105ff.; and many other passages.

33 Josefson, *Den naturliga teologins problem hos Luther*, 65ff., 75ff., 96ff.; Wingren, *Luthers lära om kallelsen*, 69ff.; Olsson, *Schöpfung, Vernunft und Gesetz in Luthers Theologie*, 70ff.; and Althaus, *Die Theologie Martin Luthers*, 221ff.

We previously touched on the civil function of the Law (*officium civilis legis*) in addition to its spiritual function. Through this function, the Creator brings about a civil order in which evil is suppressed. But Luther notes that even in civil life natural humans easily lose sight of the neighbor, seek their own honor, or try to gain merit before God. Human beings are curved in on themselves and guilty.[34] The civil law creates no righteousness before God that could count toward salvation.

The Universal Struggle between God and Satan

We have sketched Luther's view that humanity after the fall was completely depraved in its spiritual life in relation to God and also to a high degree in the psychophysical life in relation to creation and fellow human beings. We have also shown how despite the fall and sin the Creator energetically and constantly renews, takes care of, and sustains the world and humanity through his own power and love and through the Law. We also have surveyed briefly God's great soteriological plan for a new creation through Christ, which would restore humanity's full fellowship with God. In this context Luther also reckons with the devil, his power, and his constant efforts in history. The devil actively opposes God's positive work both in creation and in salvation.[35] The world is a battlefield between God and Satan. Luther often uses the traditional, contemporary conceptions of devils and demons, but behind all his ways of expression is the cosmic struggle between the rule of God and the rule of Satan. This dualism between God and Satan, couched in personal terms, is important for Luther's reflections on evangelism. Luther speaks not only of the negative conditions in every individual but also of that destructive spiritual power that seeks to thwart God's work. Luther depicts the work of the church and of mission as a cosmic struggle against Satan,

---

34 Ljunggren, *Synd och skuld i Luthers teologi*, 308ff.; Törnvall, *Andligt och världsligt regemente hos Luther*, 154ff., and other passages; Josefson, *Den naturliga teologins problem hos Luther*, 83, 106ff.; Wingren, *Luthers lära om kallelsen*, 23ff., 65ff.; Althaus, *Die Theologie Martin Luthers*, 220ff; and Olsson, *Schöpfung, Vernunft und Gesetz in Luthers Theologie*, 67ff.

35 See Harnack, *Luthers Theologie*, 1:254ff.; Köstlin, *Luthers Theologie*, 2:95ff.; Bring, *Dualismen hos Luther*, a thorough survey; Obendiek, *Der Teufel bei Martin Luther*; Althaus, *Die Theologie Martin Luthers*, 144ff.; Pedersen, "Schöpfung und Geschichte bei Luther," 25ff.; and Aagaard, "Kap. Missionstheologie," 229f.

In his monumental work *Schöpfung, Vernunft und Gesetz in Luthers Theologie*, Olsson seems to have lost sight of the dualism between God and Satan by concentrating on that which happens to humanity through the fall and on God's creating work through the Law. This criticism also is relevant to some degree of Törnvall's otherwise important work from 1940, *Andligt och världsligt regemente hos Luther*.

his servants, and his armory. One could say the mission field is a fortified and mined battlefield.

According to Luther, Satan or the devil is God's constant opponent and enemy, even in the dimensions of creation and nature. Satan is connected to and stands behind disease, accidents, and death. He is active in those persons who do everyday work in such a way that they lose sight of their neighbor. The devil contributes to government officials' misuse of their offices, to tyranny, anarchy, and confusion of the spiritual and worldly regiments. An *opus diaboli* lurks behind all the Creator's works and ordinances. For Luther, these were not medieval notions about the devil but actual reality as described in the Scriptures and by believers who were members of the early church. But Luther is not a Manichaean. He considers the conflict between God and Satan in personal terms, a kind of antagonism.

Above all, Satan aims his work at the Word and faith, exactly as he did in the Garden of Eden. The devil wants to break down the truth of salvation and faith in God's Son. He opposes Christ and the work of Christ's church in the world. Therefore Luther considers his reformation for the Gospel to be aimed at Satan, who is incarnated in the papacy, the enthusiasts, and elsewhere and who is working in all heresy to tempt and harden people and prevent them from understanding the Gospel. Above all, God's archenemy has attempted throughout history to extinguish faith in Christ and in the doctrine of justification through faith alone without works of the Law.

Luther often notes that only God is omnipotent but that Satan nevertheless accomplishes powerful destruction in people, in nature, and in that which concerns faith and the Gospel. Luther observed that humanity can never place itself in a neutral position but must follow either God or the devil.[36] The bitter struggle between God and the prince of this world, God and God's opposing god (that is, Satan), permeates all of natural and spiritual life. This unavoidable antagonism means that those who belong to God often long for the Last Day and the new creation. The reformer connects creation's and humanity's involvement in the struggle between God and Satan with his powerful eschatological perspective. The world in which we now live will never become a heavenly reign in this age. According to Luther, the devil tempts and destroys at every time and in every place in human life. However, these divine characteristics of Satan (if one may speak of them as "divine") do not mean that God's divinity and power are less than absolute. In his omnipotence and grace, God subverts even Satan to himself. God's enemy is allowed to serve as an instrument of God's wrath. Luther bases this idea on the story of Job, the physical and spiritual temptations of humankind, and

---

36 *Bondage of the Will* (1525), WA 18:635.7ff., 626.22ff. See also "Psalm 118 (1530)," WA 31/1:119.19ff. Cf. Bring, *Dualismen hos Luther*, 261ff.

humanity's physical death. Satan works in all of life's bitterness and misery, but God has power to use this evil for his positive, saving work. God alone is omnipotent. God maintains control over all that happens. In all its physical and spiritual difficulty, God creates in humanity a humility that seeks God's help and grace. The devil is completely destructive and seeks to tear humanity away from God. However, God will help and save. God can use testings and temptations to draw humanity into the embrace of the Creator and Savior.[37]

Luther ceaselessly returns to the fact that Satan and all his helpers seek to hinder and abolish the work of the Gospel and to create divisions and confusion among Christians. So Luther concludes that the cross and suffering will follow those who seek to spread the Gospel in the world.   .

The Problem of Natural Religion in Luther

That religion is a basic category in all human life was obvious to Luther. He experienced that all humans have wrestled and will wrestle with the question of God. They give their hearts to something they consider divine. Luther believed that general religiosity did not spring from some naturally given religious disposition, a view commonly held during the eighteenth and nineteenth centuries. The Scriptures show that natural religion is part and parcel of a certain notion or knowledge of God (Romans 1:19f.) and of the fall of humanity from God (Romans 1:21ff.). To understand Luther on evangelism, knowledge of his view of natural religion is obviously important. But it is also a major problem for systematic theology and for missiology: the meeting of Christianity with other religions. In our contemporary theological period after Karl Barth, Hendrik Krämer, the Tamburam Conference (1938), and Vatican II (1962–1965), the question of natural religion has become especially important for the mission of the church.

Luther scholars have wrestled with the reformer's understanding of natural theology and religion. Modern concerns with this topic were not central to Luther's theological reflection; therefore he did not deal with them comprehensively. Luther scholars have not reached a consensus on this because Luther is sometimes positive and at other times negative on the subject. Moreover, some scholars make Luther into their own image. Luther describes reason and the natural philosophical knowledge of God as imperfect but also as the Law's false way to salvation.[38] Some scholars find a distinction in Luther's theology, a distinction

---

37 Concerning Luther's rather complex reasoning about God's omnipotence and Satan as a tool for God's will and about how the devil's work is neither autonomous nor absolute, see Harnack, *Luthers Theologie*, 1:257ff.; Bring, *Dualismen hos Luther*, 258ff., 264ff.; and Althaus, *Die Theologie Martin Luthers*, 146ff.

38 Among the many contributions to the problem of natural theology and religion in

between the intuitive, abstract, and imperfect knowledge of God (*notitia*) and the existential use of this knowledge in the individual's faith/nonfaith and practical life (*usus*). The general knowledge of God is true in some respects, but as soon as the fallen natural human being attempts to describe more about God's nature and

---

Luther, the following can be cited: Karl Holl, "Was verstand Luther unter Religion?" in vol. 1 of *Gesammelte Aufsätze zur Kirchengeschichte*, 7th ed. (Tübingen: J. C. B. Mohr, 1948), 52ff. Holl investigates primarily Luther's coming to terms with Catholic faith and spirituality. Engeström, *Luthers trosbegrepp med särskild hänsyn till försanthållandets betydelse*. Vossberg, *Luthers Kritik aller Religion*. This is an important historical-systematic work. Vossberg asserts that, according to Luther, the cosmic (through creation) and ethical (through natural law) religion is something generally available and generally worthless. Vossberg surveys different forms of natural religion without and within the church and the criticism Luther aims against them. He emphasizes how Christianity, according to Luther, is a theocentric religion, simply the true and unique religion. Holsten, "Christentum und nicht-christliche Religion nach der Auffassung Luthers." Holsten emphasizes, against Vossberg, that Luther's understanding and critique of non-Christian religion and perverted Christianity is determined by the centrality of the Gospel and the doctrine of justification in his theology. Holsten analyzes the Luther texts that illustrate that non-Christian religion exists within the Roman Catholic Church. He also illustrates the reformer's religio-historical observations in his exegesis of the Old Testament; in his commentaries on the New Testament that deal with natural religion and revelation; and in his view of the relationship between the Christian faith and Judaism and heathenism. Luther has found in the rich and variegated world of religion a common denominator, that is, the way of the Law, works, and self-righteousness to God. Arnold, *Zur Frage des Naturrechts bei Martin Luther*. This Catholic scholar reviews especially Luther's positive stance toward general religiosity and interprets this in the direction of a Roman Catholic view of reason and revelation. But reason is incapable in the arena of faith and salvation, according to Arnold's interpretation of Luther.

Among the more recent research, the following works are important: Pedersen, "Luthers Laere om Gudserkendelsen," 67–97. Josefson, *Den naturliga teologins problem hos Luther*, in which he reviews Luther's statements and reservations about natural religion among all peoples. Josefson emphasizes especially how such natural religion is characterized by the false way to salvaton of the Law and works. The topic of natural law (*lex naturalis*) is comprehensively investigated. H. Bornkamm, *Luther und das Alte Testament*, 38ff. Bornkamm studies Luther's observations and judgments about heathen religion on the basis of the Old Testament stories. Pedersen, *Luther som skriftfortolker*, 71ff., 83ff., 107ff. Regin Prenter, *Skabelse og genløsning: Dogmatik* (Copenhagen: G. E. C. Gad, 1955), 150ff. Hägglund, *Theologie und Philosophie bei Luther*. Hägglund focuses on the opposition between theology and philosophy and the reformer's criticism of the medieval concept of faith. Lohse, *Ratio und Fides*, 59ff. Olsson, *Schöpfung, Vernunft und Gesetz in Luthers Theologie*, 149ff., 157ff., 174ff., 190ff. Olsson's investigations are well documented with many references to source material. Brosché, *Luther on Predestination*, 27–47. The weakness in this examination is that Brosché does not do justice to Luther's pointed attack against the preoccupation of natural religion and natural theology with what an individual ought to do to please God, that is, *opera legis*.

proceeds to worship God on that basis, he is soon on a false, even idolatrous, path. Most scholars feel Luther views natural religion negatively. For Luther, it is not simply that natural knowledge of God needs to be complemented by revelation.[39]

The Witness of Natural Religion in Luther Source Material

I will now examine some texts that represent Luther's understanding of the subject. In these texts, Luther uses the terminology of medieval scholasticism on the knowledge of God through reason and revelation. Nevertheless, Luther does not resolve the issue with the scholastic paradigm (reason-revelation, nature-supernature) that finds a kind of harmonic, complementary relationship between natural and revealed knowledge. Many scholars have noted that Luther is not especially interested in the absolute God of metaphysics and in epistemological speculations about natural knowledge and special revelation. Instead, Luther creates a theological-realistic-existential view.[40] For him, the true relationship to God and knowledge about God is borne by the revelation in Christ, by the Word, and by faith's trust in God's help and grace. Luther opposes any notion that Christian truth could be primarily of a theoretical nature (a higher knowing), as high scholasticism often reasoned. Luther speaks of a wisdom given through Christ, the Gospel, and faith and appropriated personally.[41]

---

39 Josefson, *Den naturliga teologins problem hos Luther*, 23ff., 36ff., 54ff., has interpreted Luther to mean that natural religion is true only insofar as it provides an abstract knowledge of God. This is something that God provides. But because Luther broke with the intellectual interpretation of revelation and focused on the natural human's concrete thoughts about God and, thereby, on the natural human's worship and cult, he classified natural religion as a way to fellowship with God through false reason and the Law. Cf. Pedersen, *Luther som skriftfortolker*, 71ff. Pedersen understands how Luther reckons with the truth in the knowledge of God. At the same time, humanity loses this truth as soon as the abstract divinity is filled with content and is united with an actual cult. Brosché, *Luther on Predestination*, 30ff., in a somewhat oversimplified manner, contrasts true *notitia* and false *usus* in natural religion.

40 *Publisher's note:* This does not suggest the existentialist theology of Rudolf Bultmann.

41 Josefson, *Den naturliga teologins problem hos Luther*, 8ff., 28, 32. Josefson emphasizes how Luther breaks with the Scholastic intellectual understanding of revelation. He argues persuasively against Arnold (*Zur Frage des Naturrechts bei Martin Luther*, v, 13, 17), who chose to frame the reformer's thinking about natural theology in the scholastic paradigm of reason-revelation. Thus, according to Arnold, the naturally given partial knowledge of God and some of God's attributes would only need to be complemented and rectified by the fuller knowledge that Christian revelation supplies. Even if Arnold rejects the idea that humanity in Luther's thought can naturally embrace all the main articles of Christian faith, he has not seen, as Josefson has, that Luther categorically rejects the complementarity paradigm and, as a principle, considers the way of reason to be the false way of the Law. The reformer does not construct a theoretical

Luther seeks to attain a logical, theoretical understanding of the natural knowledge of God by using a so-called practical syllogism constructed with a major premise (*propositio maior*) and a minor premise (*propositio minor*):

(a) There is a God who is omnipotent, good, and who helps in times of need, etc.

(b) This or that in the world, this or that created, is the divine.

Luther means: (a) The undefined and abstract knowledge of God (or the concept of God as far as it goes and whatever degree of truth it possesses) is written by God on human hearts (Romans 1:19ff.). (b) Humanity's concretization and application of this intuitive knowing of a particular god only increases sin. Such knowledge does not lead to true worship of God but to idolatry. When humanity moves from a general, conceptual level (*notitia*) to a deeper personal appropriation and to the worship of the heart (*usus*) or attempts to consider the general divinity as a

---

epistemology but a theological-religious way of knowing in which there is opposition between the knowledge of reason and the Word/faith.

See also the following: Skydsgaard, *Metafysik og tro*, 94ff., 211ff. Skydsgaard points out that Thomism sees reason and revelation as complementary. Thomism understands truth theoretically. Engeström, *Luthers trosbegrepp med särskild hänsyn till församthållandets betydelse*, 148ff. Hägglund, *Theologie und Philosophie bei Luther*, 8ff., 13ff., 20ff., 60ff., with the help of the doctrines of late scholasticism, shows how Luther opposes reason to revelation, the knowledge of reason to the trust of faith. Persson, *Sacra doctrina*; Brosché, *Luther on Predestination*, 27ff.; and Ebeling, *Luther*, 76–92 (English edition). This renowned Luther scholar says this about Luther: "Thus, for example, he asserts that *intellectus,* instead of being understood as in philosophy as a human faculty, is used in the Bible in a sense which is defined by its object, so that the formal concept is replaced by a concern for the particular thing towards which the mind is orientated. Accordingly, true *intellectus* is not the knowledge of an arbitrary object, but something specifically biblical, namely the wisdom of the cross of Christ, that is, faith. By contrast, the so-called human intellect is mere *sensualitas,* and this includes the human *ratio,* since it is likewise incapable of understanding spiritual things (*spiritualia*)" (87).

The following are some examples of how Luther flees from philosophical epistemological theories and metaphysics: WA 21:509.6ff., 510.39ff.; 18:663.19ff., 663.27ff.; and especially 49:164ff. In a 1544 sermon on 1 Corinthians 10:1–6, Luther writes: "Oportet nos habere Deum, qui se revelat. Quomodo? per verbum. Sic omnes patres ab Adam usque ad Christum crediderunt in Deum promissum loquentem cum eis, et dixit: 'Semen mulieris' [Genesis 3:15]. Is erat Christus promissus venturus. Et ad Abraham: 'In semine' [Genesis 22:18]. Das war Christum, promissorem Deum habere, non metaphysicum, absolutum. Si non se revelat, non sequitur fides, invocatio. Sic omnes crediderunt in Christum propter promissionem factam. Sicut nos in eum credimus et promissiones factas patribus promissas nobis factas per Christum venientem" (WA 49:536.17–537.3).

specific, particular divinity, humanity does not attain true knowledge of God but, because of its endless depravity, ends up in heresy and idolatry.[42]

In such logical, conceptual exploration, Luther believed that theology should always and only serve the exposition of Scripture. Only Scripture can decide a theological issue, even one as complex as the natural knowledge of God and its existential application. In Luther's Bible commentaries and sermons, Romans 1:19ff. is always in focus. Even texts such as Jonah 1:5ff., John 1:4–5, and Galatians 4:8 are important. But in arguing for a natural knowledge of God, Luther did not use Psalm 19:1ff. ("The heavens declare the glory of God"), John 1:9 ("The true light that gives light to every man"), or Paul's speech at the Areopagus (the worship of the Athenians in Acts 17:22ff.).[43]

Concerning Luther's concrete Bible exposition, Luther's 1515–1516 commentary on Romans contains clear Reformation-like passages, but the true Reformation breakthrough did not occur before 1517–1518, according to most contemporary scholars. Already in the introduction to the commentary, Luther says the goal of Romans is to destroy self-righteousness and self-wisdom to make room for Christ and his righteousness. God's righteousness (*iustitia Dei*), of which the Epistle speaks, cannot be separated from the knowledge of God (*sapientia Dei*). It is implied that knowledge of God is of a practical/existential nature and concerns justification with God.[44] The commentary discusses Romans 1:19ff. in connection with Gabriel Biel. Luther claims that all people from creation, through nature and reason, possess an abstract knowledge of the divine (*divinitas*), a knowledge of God's eternity, power, wisdom, righteousness, and goodness. There is no excuse for the fact that humans have applied this imperfect and abstract knowledge to created things and idols "fabricated" after the desires of their own hearts. However, in this early commentary, Luther says people could have been saved if they had remained in their naturally given knowledge of God and faith without reasoning, if they had worshiped *the* true God and not turned to idols.[45] This conclusion does not appear in Luther's later clear Reformation writings.

---

42 We can refer to the following: *Romans* (1515/1516), WA 56:177.11ff.; *Deuteronomy* (1529), WA 28:611.1ff.; *Lectures on Isaiah* (1527/1530), WA 31/2:235.15ff.; and *Galatians* (1531/1535), WA 40/1:411.1ff., 608.8ff., 608.25ff. See also Arnold, *Zur Frage des Naturrechts bei Martin Luther*, 25ff.; Josefson, *Den naturliga teologins problem hos Luther*, 27ff.; Olsson, *Schöpfung, Vernunft und Gesetz in Luthers Theologie*, 156f; and Brosché, *Luther on Predestination*, 30ff.

43 Examples are given in *Luther and World Mission*, 48ff., 52ff.

44 WA 56:2.6ff. Cf. WA 4:597.8–600.21 for Luther's early position. On the discussion about the chronology of Luther's breakthrough, see Öberg, *Himmelrikets nycklar och kyrkligt bot i Luthers teologi*, xviiif., with the adduced secondary works.

45 WA 56:176.14ff., especially 177.11ff. See Josefson, *Den naturliga teologins problem hos*

However, this does not prevent the mature reformer from claiming that a general knowledge of God and of some of God's characteristics are inextricably written into the reason of natural humanity and that each individual human is held responsible for the use of this naturally given knowledge. After the Reformation breakthrough and the break with Roman Catholic theology, Luther turns sharply against all notions about the possibility for salvation by the knowledge available through creation and reason. Luther disputes scholasticism's speculative knowledge of God, especially because it always couples rationalism with legalism/moralism. Luther accuses the Scholastic theologians of introducing Plato and Aristotle into theology. This objection to using philosophy when dealing with theology appears everywhere in Luther's writings. For an existential knowledge of God, one must have access to the special revelation from God, the wisdom in the cross of Christ, which is proclaimed through the Gospel and is appropriated through faith alone in God's Son.[46]

Already in the 1517–1518 lectures on Hebrews, Luther writes that the abstract concept of God that poets and philosophers know and that Paul discusses in Romans 1:19ff. is a human faith (*fides humana*). Like everything human, it is inconstant, even empty, dishonest, and dead. It cannot withstand doubt. This speculative *fides humana* lacks personal trust in God's help and grace. It believes that God helps others in general, but it does not know the language of true faith: that God helps me or is for me (*pro me*) in his grace. Luther says true faith is not given by way of nature but by grace (*non ex natura, sed ex gratia venit*). The human or naturally given "faith" does not understand God as a God of grace but as a tyrant and judge from whom one must flee. Already at this early stage, Luther says that the abstract and natural knowledge of God and "trust" is dominated by the threat of the Law. Human faith in God is as easily extinguished as a candle in the wind. But as the wind does not extinguish the sun and its rays, so God's grace and true faith remain.[47] There is no complementary relationship between nature and grace, no theoretical epistemology leading to a true knowledge of God.

Luther, 27ff., 36ff. I have reservations about to what degree Luther's Reformation doctrine of justification by faith appears in these lectures on Romans. See also Pedersen, *Luther som skriftfortolker*, 73; Olsson, *Schöpfung, Vernunft und Gesetz in Luthers Theologie*, 156f.; and Brosché, *Luther on Predestination*, 30f.

46 Concerning this, see the works adduced in *Luther and World Mission*, 38n38, 39–40n41, by Vossberg, Engeström, Josefson, Hägglund, Lohse, Olsson, and Ebeling.

47 LW 29:235 (WA 57:232.27ff.): " 'To believe that God exists' seems to many to be so easy that they have ascribed this belief both to poets and to philosophers, as the apostle also asserts in Rom. 1:20. In fact, there are those who think that this is self-evident. But such human faith is just like any other thought, art, wisdom, dream, etc., of man. For as soon as a trial assails, all those things immediately topple down. Then neither reason

At the disputation in Heidelberg in 1518, Luther contraposes *theologia gloriae*, characterized by speculation and works of the Law, and *theologia crucis*, borne by the revelation in Christ.[48] Luther says that the Law *per se* is holy and good. But the Law and works of the Law cannot lead to salvation. The Law increases sin in fallen humanity, which is occupied with works of the Law. Only the righteousness revealed in Christ leads to true knowledge of God and salvation.[49] A major thesis of the Heidelberg Disputation reads: "He is not righteous who does much, but he who, without work, believes much in Christ" (Thesis 25).[50] Luther supports this thesis with Paul's words about justification (Romans 1:17; 3:20, 28; 10:10).[51]

The knowledge of God that is communicated by reason and nature is connected to *theologia gloriae.* According to Luther, the rationalism and the legalism of the Roman Catholic Church fit together like hand and glove. Reason in its

---

nor counsel nor faith has the upper hand. Ps. 107:27 says: 'They reeled like a drunken man, and all their wisdom was swallowed up.' For this reason the apostle James calls this faith 'dead' (2:17), and others call it 'acquired' faith. But in man there is nothing that is not vanity and a lie. In the second place, such faith believes nothing about itself but believes only about others. For even if it believes that God exists and rewards those who see Him, yet it does not believe that God exists and rewards it itself. Therefore, as the saying goes, it is faith about God, not in God. For this reason another faith is needed, namely, the faith by which we believe that we are numbered among those for whom God exists and is a Rewarder. But this faith does not come from nature; it comes from grace. For nature is terrified and flees from the face of God, since it believes that He is not God but is a tyrant, a torturer, and a judge, as the well-known words in Deut. 28:65 state: 'The Lord will give you a trembling heart . . . and your life shall hang in doubt before you.' And let us give a simile applicable to the two kinds of faith. Just as a candle exposed to the wind loses not only its rays but all light, while the sun shining from above can be disturbed by no power of the winds either in its rays or in itself, so the first kind of faith is extinguished, the second kind never." This quotation is an excellent demonstration of how the incipient reformer uses the Scholastic conceptual pair *natura/gratia* but fills it with partially new content.

48 See Loewenich, *Luthers Theologia crucis*, 7ff., 21ff.; Pinomaa, *Sieg des Glaubens*, 22ff.; Josefson, *Den naturliga teologins problem hos Luther*, 24ff.; and Brosché, *Luther on Predestination*, 42ff., with references.

49 Heidelberg Disputation Thesis 1: "The law of God, the most salutary doctrine of life, cannot advance man on his way to righteousness, but rather hinders him" (LW 31:39 [WA 1:353.15ff.]). Cf. the explanation of this thesis (WA 1:355.30ff., 357.6ff.), which, on the basis of Romans 3:10ff.; 3:21; 5:20; 7:9; 8:2; and 2 Corinthians 3:6, argues that the Law cannot save but in one way increases sin and reveals and places all people under God's wrath and judgment. Paul teaches, therefore, that a righteousness apart from the Law has been revealed for the salvation of a powerless, condemned humanity.

50 LW 31:41.

51 WA 1:364.2ff.

pursuit of God is always tuned into the Law and works. Natural humanity is deeply self-righteous. According to Luther, creation communicates some knowledge of God and of some of the divine attributes;[52] nevertheless, Luther does not base true and saving knowledge of God on anything that is given through nature/reason. He expressly says that the naturally given, abstract knowledge of God and of God's attributes (*virtus, divinitas, sapientia, iustitia, bonitas*) can attain some truth. But in the same breath, he says that this knowledge does not make one worthy before God nor does it provide any wisdom about God. It is masterfully said in Theses 19–20:

> 19. That person does not deserve to be called a theologian who looks upon the invisible things of God [*invisibilia Dei*] as though they were clearly perceptible in those things which have actually happened [*ea, quae facta sunt*] [Rom 1:20].
>
> 20. He deserves to be called a theologian, however, who comprehends the visible and manifest things of God seen through suffering and the cross [*qui visibilia et posteriora Dei per passiones et crucem conspecta intelligit*].[53]

Humanity's knowledge of God is not able to search the hidden God (*Deus absconditus*) who first accuses the one whom he wants to justify. This means that the attempt of the Gentiles and the philosophers to know God in his absolute being has proven to be in vain. One gets to know God indirectly in Christ's weakness (and secondarily in one's own), suffering, and cross. Luther expressly says that *theologus gloriae* calls the evil good and the good evil, while *theologus crucis* sees and says what truth is. Ultimately, the blindness of the theologian of glory is that he does not see but ignores the God hidden behind Christ's cross and suffering, the same God whom true faith sees and whom it grasps. As concerns true wisdom about God, justification, and salvation, humanity must be enlightened by divine revelation, that is, by the Gospel of Christ and Christ's cross. The foolishness of this God or *theologia crucis* alone leads to true certainty and salvation. Speculative theology, grounded as it is in nature and reason, does not lead to salvation. Humanity's use/misuse of the imperfect, natural knowledge of God does not lead to true wisdom but to false foolishness. Luther writes similarly in other material from the beginning of the 1520s.[54]

---

52 WA 1:354.17f., 354.27, 361.35. Cf. WA 7:205.16ff.: "Dan das leret die natur, das eyn gott sey, der do alles gutis gebe und yn allen ubel helffe, wie das antzeygen die Abgotter bey den Heyden." See Loewenich, *Luthers Theologia crucis*, 13; Bandt, *Luthers Lehre vom verborgenen Gott*, 90f.; Althaus, *Die Theologie Martin Luthers*, 35; Pinomaa, *Sieg des Glaubens*, 23f.; and Brosché, *Luther on Predestination*, 42ff.

53 LW 31:40 (WA 1:354.19ff.). Cf. the explanations in WA 1:361.32–362.19.

54 Heidelberg Disputation Thesis 21: "*A theology of glory calls evil good and good evil. A theology of the cross calls the thing what it actually is.* This is clear: He who does not

In the middle of the 1520s, on the basis of Romans 1:19ff., Luther continues to claim that humanity through nature/reason possesses some knowledge of God's existence and knows that God gives everything good, helps in times of need, etc. Therefore humanity cannot avoid the question about God. This is further verified by Gentile religion, even if it is *per se* false and a false knowledge of God. Humanity always trusts in something, some kind of helper. Because it lacks God's Word, which provides an understanding of who God actually is, natural religion becomes unavoidably false.[55]

In *Bondage of the Will* in 1525, Luther argues that natural humanity lacks true knowledge of God and the power to do what God commands. Even if he can ascribe some freedom to human will within the sphere of civil righteousness (*iustitia civilis*), human will is so depraved in relation to God that it neither knows God nor is able to follow God's will. Luther writes:

> For here the text applies that Christ and the Evangelists so often quote from Isaiah: "You shall indeed hear but never understand, and you shall see but never perceive" [Isa. 6:9–10; Matt. 13:14; etc.]. What else does this mean but that free choice or the human heart is so held down by the power of Satan that unless it is miraculously raised up by the Spirit of God it cannot of itself either see or hear things that strike the eyes and ears themselves so plainly as to be palpable? Such is the misery and blindness of the human race! . . . [M]an left to himself sees but does not perceive and hears but does not understand.[56]

Luther claims that no one can obtain saving knowledge or faith and blessedness without the help of the Word and the Spirit (1 Corinthians 2:9ff.). The Acts

---

know Christ does not know God hidden in suffering. Therefore he prefers works to suffering, glory to the cross, strength to weakness, wisdom to folly, and, in general, good to evil. These are the people whom the apostle calls 'enemies of the cross of Christ' [Phil. 3:18], for they hate the cross and suffering and love works and the glory of works" (LW 31:53, *original emphasis* [WA 1:362.21ff.]). Cf. WA 1:355.2, 357.3ff. See also "Explanations to the 95 Theses," WA 1:614.17ff., about *theologus gloriae* and *theologus crucis*; and *Church Postil* (1522), WA 10/1.1:239.20ff., 240.22ff.

55 WA 12:291f.; 16:43.10ff.; 18:80.18ff.

56 LW 33:98 (WA 18:658.21ff.). *Bondage of the Will* points to humanity's double imprisonment, partly to speculation, partly to moralism and legalism. These imprisonments are inextricably connected. For humanity to perceive its fundamental depravity and its sin and thereby to flee to Christ, God has given his Law. The Law commands, but humanity is unable to fulfill its demands. Therefore the Scriptures are also full of Gospel, that is, the word about what God wants to grant to sinners. This is one of the decisive arguments in Luther's struggle with Erasmus. See WA 18:673ff., 683ff. For exegesis of *Bondage of the Will*, see Loewenich, *Luthers Theologia crucis*, 27ff.; and Josefson, *Den naturliga teologins problem hos Luther*, 38ff. See also Pinomaa, *Sieg des Glaubens*, 46ff.; and Vossberg, *Luthers Kritik aller Religion*, 33ff.

of the Apostles shows that the most educated heathen came to reject the church's faith in the resurrection and eternal life. Luther writes:

> Now, the things which lead to eternal salvation I take to be the words and works of God, which are presented to the human will so that it may apply itself to them or turn away from them. By the words of God, moreover, I mean both the law and the gospel, the law requiring works and the gospel faith. For there is nothing else that leads either to the grace of God or to eternal salvation except the word and work of God, since grace or the Spirit is life itself, to which we are led by God's word and work. The life or eternal salvation, however, is something that passes human comprehension [Isaiah 64:4 and 1 Corinthians 2:9 are adduced here] . . . . This means that unless the Spirit had revealed it, no man's heart would have any knowledge or notion of it, much less be able to apply itself to it or seek after it.[57]

Natural humanity without the light of the Word and Spirit can neither know who God is nor follow God's will and commands.[58] The blindness of reason and the powerlessness of the will are interwoven with natural humanity's imprisonment to Satan, sin, and death. Humanity is in such a miserable condition that it cannot even perceive its own blindness and imprisonment; therefore God must, by the Law, reveal and convict humanity so it will seek help through the Gospel of Christ.[59]

---

57 LW 33:105–6 (WA 18:663.12ff., 27ff.). Luther shows how the great Gentile thinkers were confounded by Christian faith in the resurrection. At the Areopagus, Paul was called a babbler and an advocate of foreign gods (Acts 17:18). Porcius Festus believed Paul was insane (Acts 26:24). Observe that Luther did not consider the speech at the Areopagus a support for natural theology.

58 See Luther's barrage of Scripture passages against Erasmus's faith in free will and the religion of natural humanity (WA 18:756ff.), especially the summary: "Agree now, then, when you hear that the most excellent thing in all men is not only ungodly, but ignorant of God, contemptuous of God, inclined to evil and worthless as regards the good. For what does it mean to be wicked but that the will—which is one of the most excellent things—is wicked? What does it mean to be without understanding of God and the good but that reason—which is another of the most excellent things—is ignorant of God and the good, or is blind to knowledge of godliness? . . . What does it mean not to fear God, but that in all their parts, and especially the higher ones, men are despisers of God? But to be despisers of God is to be at the same time despisers of all the things of God—his words, works, laws, precepts, and will, for example. What now can reason dictate that is right when it is itself blind and ignorant? What can the will choose that is good when it is itself evil and worthless? . . . With reason in error, then, and the will misdirected, what can man do or attempt that is good?" (LW 33:254–55 [WA 18:761.39ff.]).

59 WA 18:671ff., 683ff.

In *Bondage of the Will*, Luther gives the solution to natural, imprisoned humanity's hopeless situation: Scripture sheds clear light and gives certain guidance for the human situation.[60] To find the true and saving knowledge of God, one must leave behind the speculations of reason about God's eternal being and God's will toward humanity. One must differentiate between the preached God and the hidden God, between God's Word and God in his inscrutable majesty. Luther says:

> God must therefore be left to himself in his own majesty, for in this regard we have nothing to do with him, nor has he willed that we should have anything to do with him. But we have something to do with him insofar as he is clothed and set forth in his Word, through which he offers himself to us .... For it is this that God as he is preached is concerned with, namely, that sin and death should be taken away and we should be saved. For "he sent his word and healed them" [Ps. 107:20]. But God hidden in his majesty neither deplores nor takes away death, but works life, death, and all in all. For there he has not bound himself by his word, but has kept himself free over all things.[61]

Because God "lives in unapproachable light" (1 Timothy 6:16), a presumptuous humanity must be restrained from its attempt to seek God in his majesty. All are encouraged to quell their curiosity about God's secret will and to see God as he has been revealed in Jesus Christ. Faith ought to

> occupy itself instead with God incarnate, or as Paul puts it, with Jesus crucified, in whom are all the treasures of wisdom and knowledge, though in a hidden manner [Col. 2:3]; for through him it is furnished abundantly with what it ought to know and ought not to know. It is God incarnate, moreover, who is speaking here: "I would . . . you would not"—God incarnate, I say, who has been sent into the world for the very purpose of willing, speaking, doing, suffering, and offering to all men everything necessary for salvation.[62]

---

60 WA 18:654ff., 606ff., contains some of the most exhaustive accounts of Luther's view of Scripture's authority, its clarity, and its center in Christ and in faith in him. Concerning knowledge of God and the word of Scripture, see Pedersen, "Luthers Laere om Gudserkendelsen," 73ff.

61 LW 33:139–40 (WA 18:685.14ff.). Cf. LW 33:140 (WA 18:685.25ff.): "Diatribe, however, deceives himself in her ignorance by not making any distinction between God preached and God hidden, that is, between the Word of God and God himself. . . . Thus [God] does not will the death of a sinner, according to his word; but he wills it according to that inscrutable will of his. It is our business, however, to pay attention to the word and leave that inscrutable will alone, for we must be guided by the word and not by that inscrutable will. After all, who can direct himself by a will completely inscrutable and unknowable?" Luther bases his distinction between the revealed/preached God and the hidden God on 2 Thessalonians 2:4. See Loewenich, *Luthers Theologia crucis*, 28ff.

62 LW 33:145–46 (WA 18:689.22ff.).

As is apparent in *Bondage of the Will*, Luther does not allow any room for natural theology. Because the knowledge of faith is the only true knowledge of God, reason and revelation (primarily the word about Christ) actually stand in diametrical opposition to each other. Luther's commentary on Jonah (1526) supplies important information about his view of natural religion. Jonah 1:5 includes the sailors' cries, each to his own god, when God sent the storm because of Jonah's flight to Tarsus. Luther comments on "All the sailors were afraid and each cried out to his own god." This provides an opportunity for Luther to develop his ideas about the natural knowledge of God, its limitations, and its ineluctable decline into unbelief and idolatry. Luther says there has never been a true atheist. He claims that the cry of the Gentiles, each to his own god, supports the idea that all humans—even if they do not truly believe—possess an intuitive knowledge of God's being.

> Here you find St. Paul's statement in Rom. 1:19 concerning the universal knowledge of God among all the heathen, that is, that the whole world talks about the Godhead and natural reason is aware that this Godhead is something superior to all other things. This is here shown by the fact that the people in our text called upon a god, heathen though they were. For if they had been ignorant of the existence of God or of a godhead, how could they have called upon him and cried to him? Although they do not have true faith in God, they at least hold that God is a being able to help on the sea and in every need. Such a light and such a perception is innate in the hearts of all men; and this light cannot be subdued or extinguished. There are, to be sure, some people, for instance, the Epicureans, Pliny, and the like, who deny this with their lips. But they do it by force and want to quench this light in their hearts. They are like people who purposely stop their ears or pinch their eyes shut to close out sound and sight. However, they do not succeed in this; their conscience tells them otherwise. For Paul is not lying when he asserts that they know something about God, "because God has shown it to them" (Rom 1:19).[63]

It can hardly be expressed more clearly: Natural humanity in all lands and in all places possesses some intimation and insight about the divine being and that this God helps in time of need. It can be denied with the lips, but it is nevertheless written on the heart and conscience and can, therefore, never be completely obliterated. Luther says: "It follows from this that natural reason must concede that all

---

63 LW 19:53–54 (WA 19:205.27ff.). About Luther's commentary on Jonah, see Josefson, *Den naturliga teologins problem hos Luther*, 61f.; H. Bornkamm, *Luther und das Alte Testament*, 27f.; Pedersen, *Luther som skriftfortolker*, 73; Lohse, *Ratio und Fides*, 59ff.; Olsson, *Schöpfung, Vernunft und Gesetz in Luthers Theologie*, 150f.; and Brosché, *Luther on Predestination*, 35f. Bornkamm points out how Jonah is, for Luther, an excellent example of the saints, their doubts, and their prayers.

that is good comes from God; for He who can save from every need and misfortune is also able to grant all that is good and that makes for happiness. That is as far as the natural light of reason sheds its rays—it regards God as kind, gracious, merciful, and benevolent. And that is indeed a bright light."[64]

Luther's commentary on Jonah contains perhaps his most positive passages about natural knowledge of God. It is "a bright light," in no way only darkness—as far as it goes. The above statement can with the words *gracious* and *merciful* seem to make problematic much of what has already been said about how seriously Luther limits the ability of the light of reason, indeed, how he contraposes the naturally given knowledge of God and the knowledge of God's salvation that is revealed in the Word. One needs to be careful not to draw the conclusion that Luther advocates a doctrine of salvation by way of the light of natural reason. [For example, in the Small Catechism's explanation of the First Article, Luther can speak of fatherly grace and goodness, even in creation and the natural life.] Also, every Luther expert knows that Luther does not spare words when arguing a point. Such overstatement can sometimes sound like contradiction. This can partially account for the different interpretations of Luther on this question. Luther is certainly not always conceptually clear and precise in his writings.

In the exposition of Jonah 1:5, Luther clearly rejects the notion that humanity could attain a true and saving knowledge of God through the light of nature and reason. Humanity possesses a light that is communicated by God himself, but in many ways it is imperfect and does not lead to true worship of and faith in God. Luther writes:

> However, it manifests two big defects: first, reason does admittedly believe that God is able and competent to help and to bestow; but reason does not know whether He is willing to do this also for us. That renders the position of reason unstable. Reason believes in God's might and is aware of it, but it is uncertain whether God is willing to employ this in our behalf, because in adversity it so often experiences the opposite to be true. . . . [The mariners] believe that He may help others. But that is as far as they can go; they cannot transcend that. They exhaust every means at their command; they try their utmost. Free will cannot go beyond that. But they do not believe that God is disposed to help them.[65]

Thus Luther points out the difference between possessing theoretical knowledge about God, his power, his ability to help people, etc., and possessing a sure faith that God will stand by one's own side and help in one's own personal need. The natural knowledge of God lacks the *pro me* that is so important for existential

---

64 LW 19:54 (WA 19:206.9ff.).

65 LW 19:54 (WA 19:206.13ff.).

faith. Natural humanity does not believe that God unconditionally wants to help just me. Therefore it seeks to ensure its own safety with its own actions. The reformer expressly says that existential trust in God's help and grace is a gift of the Holy Spirit: "But this situation calls for a faith that does not doubt but is convinced that God wants to be gracious not only to others but also to me. That is a genuine and a live faith; it is a great and rich and rare gift of the Holy Spirit, and so we shall see it in Jonah."[66]

But reason's knowledge of God has another serious problem. Reason knows that God exists but does not know God's true nature, least of all God's will to love. Luther says:

> The second defect is this: Reason is unable to identify God properly; it cannot ascribe the Godhead to the One who is entitled to it exclusively. It knows that there is a God, but it does not know who or which is the true God. It shares the experience of the Jews during Christ's sojourn on earth. . . . It was incredible to them that Jesus of Nazareth was the Christ. Thus reason also plays blindman's bluff with God; it consistently gropes in the dark and misses the mark. It calls that God which is not God and fails to call Him God who really is God. Reason would do neither the one nor the other if it were not conscious of the existence of God or if it really knew who and what God is. Therefore it rushes in clumsily and assigns the name God and ascribes divine honor to its own idea of God. Thus reason never finds the true God, but it finds the devil or its own concept of God, ruled by the devil. So there is a vast difference between knowing that there is a God and knowing who or what God is. Nature knows the former—it is inscribed in everybody's heart; the latter is taught only by the Holy Spirit.[67]

---

66 LW 19:54 (WA 19:206.27ff.).

67 LW 19:54–55 (WA 19:206.31ff.). Cf. the Latin lectures on Jonah (WA 13:228f., especially 229.8ff.). See also the *postil* on Romans 11:33ff.: "The reason and wisdom of man may go so far as to reach the conclusion, although feebly, that there must be one eternal divine being, who has created and preserves and governs all things. Man sees such a beautiful and wonderful creation in the heavens and on the earth, one so wonderfully, regularly and securely preserved and ordered . . . Rom 1,20. This is (a posteriori) the knowledge that we have when we contemplate God from without, in his works and government; as one, looking upon a castle or house from without, would draw conclusions as to its lord and keeper. But from within (a priori) no human wisdom has been able to conceive what God is in himself, or in his internal essence. Neither can anyone know or give information of it except it be revealed to him by the Holy Spirit" (Lenker 8:8 [WA 21:509.6ff., 18ff.]). For how the Spirit alone, through the word of Scripture and preaching, explains the doctrine of the Trinity and God's salvation through Christ's death and resurrection, see WA 21:510ff., 517ff. But all people without the grace of special revelation oppose, indeed, struggle against, these fundamental

In brief, one can say that natural humanity intuitively knows a God who is powerful and can help. But it does not understand and does not believe that God can and will help "just me." Therefore it does everything to ensure its safety. But it does not know God's faithful will to love, that is, it does not know who God is in truth.

Luther shows with many examples from the history of Israel and the church how those who have left the guidance of God's Word end up in grave idolatry or, in Christian circles, in a refined self-righteous worship of God that is authored by the devil. Humanity has consistently created a god after its own ideas and fantasies, serving false gods, indeed, serving Satan himself. According to Luther, this mistaken and false faith in God is characterized by the Law, works of the Law, and self-righteousness. Natural humanity seeks to please God and win his goodwill through sacrifices, works, and false spirituality—the nucleus of all natural religion. It is not a religion of grace but a religion of the Law.[68]

The fact that the sailors of Jonah 1:5ff., despite their earnest intercession to all sorts of gods, nevertheless panic and throw all the cargo off the ship and run to Jonah to obtain help from his God shows that natural, false, law religion cannot stand up in emergencies and in doubts. It soon finds itself in despair. Therefore to know and to worship the true God means that one does not serve God through works of the Law but through faith in God's unconditional grace. Luther says: "There you can see that a false faith will not stand the test of adversity, but that both god and faith, idol and superstition, become engulfed and vanish, and that nothing but despair remains. Therefore only the one living God is entitled to the name and reputation of being a helper in every trouble, Ps. 9:10; Ps. 46:1; for He can rescue from death, Ps. 68:20."[69] Concerning the true faith's relation with God, Luther writes: "For the real and the true God is He who is properly served not with works but with the true faith and with sincerity of heart, who gives and bestows mercy and benefactions entirely gratis and without our works and merits. That they do not believe, and therefore they do not know God but are bound to blunder and to miss the mark."[70] True knowledge of God or wisdom comes only by grace through faith.

We next look at Luther texts from 1529 and later. In his 1529 commentaries on Deuteronomy, Luther exposits Deuteronomy 4:6 with the help of Romans 1:19ff. By the testimony of creation, all people possess an intuitive and abstract knowl-

---

doctrines of the Christian faith as if they were heresy (WA 21:510.11ff., 512.13ff.). This is because they lack God's Word and faith (WA 21:513.9ff., 514.9ff., 515.19ff., 519.16ff.).

68 WA 19:207.11ff. Cf. WA 21:512.13ff., 513.28ff., 518.18ff.

69 LW 19:57 (WA 19:208.31ff.).

70 LW 19:55–56 (WA 19:207.26ff.).

edge of a divine being or creator. This speculative insight derived from nature understands that God exists and that God helps and gives all good to humanity and that humanity does, to some extent, trust in God in times of need and doubt.[71]

For Luther, this natural and rational knowledge of God is not negative as long as humanity does not attempt to define further the content of the knowledge. Natural knowledge of God has never led to a true and personally appropriated knowledge of God. Abstract knowledge of God led the ancient Romans to worship Jupiter, Mars, and Venus and to seek the help of specialized gods in the various distresses of life. Some in the Roman Catholic Church, in a paganized folk religion, have sought the help of specific saints in different types of trouble. Indeed, even the Jews, who had access to Deuteronomy 4:6, set up altars to idols. The greedy have always and above all trusted in mammon, that is, in money and possessions. Briefly said: Through reason, humanity knows God only abstractly or partially and uses this knowledge of God, written on their hearts, only for idolatry.[72] Because natural knowledge of God is so imperfect, full of uncertainty and without true personal appropriation, when humanity cannot in fact find the true God through nature/reason, God was constrained to help humanity by sending his Word and giving his Son. Humanity can truly hear, see, touch, and understand who God is—that God does what is good and saves in all types of need—only by way of God's revelation. Through the Word from God, humanity learns to know God's true heart and nature, that is, that God does what is good and saves in all types of need.[73]

---

71 WA 28:609.28ff.: "als Paulus zum Röm. 1. anzeigt. Alle welt heisst das einen Gott, darauff der mensch trawet in not und anfechtung, darauff er sich tröstet und verlesst, da man alles guts wil von haben und der helffen könne." WA 28:610.16ff.: "So beschreibet die vernunfft Gott, das er sey, was einem menschen hülffe thue, jm nütze und zu gut gereiche. Daraus spürt man, das vernunfft nur so viel weis von Gott, als Paulus zur Röm. am 1. Cap. saget: 'das man weis, das Gott ist, das ist jnen kund gethan damit, das Gottes unsichtbares wesen ist zu mercken an den wercken, die er thut an der welt, die er geschaffen hat.' 'Das Gott sey,' das ist: das Gott nütze sey und helffe in nöten."

72 WA 28:609.32ff., 610.22ff., 611.15ff., 611.29ff.

73 Luther's writings here are clear, see WA 28:611.26ff., 612.12ff.: "Darumb sag ich noch einmal, die vernunfft wisse etlichermasse, das Gott könne und solle helfen, aber den rechten Gott kan sie nicht treffen, sie mag wol von jm reden, aber wer er sey und wie er helffe, das weis sie nicht . . . Nicht anders thut die vernunfft, wenn sie Gottes Wort nicht hat: sie weis wol von jm zu sagen und zeugt, das ein Gott sey, aber sie kans nicht recht treffen, denn sie weis nicht, wer er ist. Dieser ungewisheit halben mus Gottes Wort uns zu hülffe komen und mus Gott sich heraus an tag geben und sich selber abecirckeln in ein eusserlichen wort und zeichen, das man jn hören, sehen, greiffen, fassen un erkennen möge, sonst ist uns ungeraten. Das sihest du auch in diesem Text 'Ich bin der Herr dein Gott, der ich dich aus Egypten gefüret habe.' Da erzelt er, was

In the Large Catechism (1529), Luther says that a right concept of God is conditional on a right faith, but idolatry has its source in a false or incorrect faith. In connection with the First Commandment, Luther writes:

> A "god" is the term for that to which we are to look for all good and in which we are to find refuge in all need. . . . As I have often said, it is the trust and faith of the heart alone that make both God and an idol. If your faith and trust are right, then your God is the true one. Conversely, where your trust is false and wrong, there you do not have the true God. For these two belong together, faith and God. Anything on which your heart relies and depends, I say, that is really your God.[74]

Using this standard, Luther measures the practice of religion in our world. As concerns the "Christian" West, he finds that people in general often trust in possessions and money, in power, expertise, and prestige. These are their "gods." Likewise, it is idolatry when one cries out to a saint in the time of need or when one practices black magic. Within Christendom, from the time that faith was replaced with spiritual blindness, a different kind of idolatry, "faith in something other than the true God," has appeared. Monks and nuns, amid the religious life and church worship, set up an idolatry of works and self-righteousness. Luther says: "[This false worship] involves only that conscience that seeks help, comfort, and salvation in its own works and presumes to wrest heaven from God. . . . What is this but to have made God into an idol—indeed, an 'apple-god'—and to have set ourselves up as God?"[75] In the heathen world, people have throughout history created a god for every different area of life and need. This is the root of idolatry: false faith coupled with the pursuit of good fortune. Luther concludes: "Accordingly the pagans actually fashion their own fancies and dreams about God into an idol and rely on an empty nothing."[76] Luther remarks that even in worship humanity is occupied with itself, that is, curved in on itself. Works of the Law (*opera legis*) have left their imprint on worship of God, transforming it into idolatry. In these wretched conditions, Luther saw motivation both for mission among the heathen and for his own reformation work. Heathenism existed not only in faraway lands. Because the work of God's reign is the corrolate of heathenism, Luther could never draw a definitive border between the reformation of the church/inner mission and the exterior mission among non-Christian peoples.

Gott sey, was seine Natur und Eigenschaft sey, nemlich, das er wolthue, erlöse aus gefehrlichkeiten und helffe aus nöten und allerley widerwertigkeiten."

74 LC I 2–3 (K-W, 386). Concerning natural and revealed knowledge of God in the Large Catechism, see Josefson, *Den naturliga teologins problem hos Luther*, 48ff.

75 LC I 22–23 (K-W, 388–89).

76 LC I 20 (K-W, 388).

The Gospel and faith must struggle against humanity's religion of law, against its idolatry.

In the Large Catechism, the reformer explains the three articles of faith so people, through God's Word, might get to know the true God and what one might expect of and receive from him. He concludes his rich explanation of the Creed with some interesting ideas about how only God's revelation in the Word can give help and certainty to humanity's struggle with the question about God and its pursuit of salvation. Luther says:

> Here in the Creed you have the entire essence, will, and work of God exquisitely depicted in very brief but rich words. In them are comprehended all our wisdom, which surpasses all human wisdom, understanding, and reason. Although the whole world has sought painstakingly to learn what God might be and what he might think and do, yet it has never succeeded in the least. But here you have everything in richest measure. For all three articles God himself has revealed and opened to us the most profound depths of his fatherly heart and his pure, unutterable love. For this very purpose he created us, so that he might redeem us and make us holy, and, moreover, having granted and bestowed upon us everything in heaven and on earth, he has also given us his Son and his Holy Spirit, through whom he brings us to himself. For, as explained above, we could never come to recognize the Father's favor and grace were it not for the LORD Christ, who is a mirror of the Father's heart. Apart from him we see nothing but an angry and terrible judge. But neither could we know anything of Christ, had it not been revealed by the Holy Spirit.
>
> These three articles of the Creed, therefore, separate and distinguish us Christians from all other people on earth. All who are outside this Christian people, whether heathen, Turks, Jews, or false Christians and hypocrites—even though they believe in and worship only the one, true God—nevertheless do not know what his attitude is toward them. They cannot be confident of his love and blessing, and therefore they remain in eternal wrath and condemnation. For they do not have the LORD Christ, and, besides, they are not illuminated and blessed by the gifts of the Holy Spirit.[77]

This is a deathblow to all natural theology and religion. Luther assumes that an abstract knowledge of the divine being lies behind all searching for God. But in practice, the human heart is depraved and curved into its own wishes and false faith so only through God's Word can we get to know God's heart, God's

---

77 LC II 63–66 (K-W, 439–40). Cf. the *Magnificat* (1521) and the lectures on Isaiah (1527–1529) where it is expressly said that God's work of creation from nothing is to make sinners righteous and to give life to the dead and that Christ's work of reconciliation is the difference between Christianity and other religions (WA 7:546.32ff, 559.19ff; 31/2:332.9ff; 40/3:154.11ff.). See also Althaus, "Gottes Gottheit als Sinn der Rechtfertigungslehre Luthers," 15ff.; and Pedersen, *Luther som skriftfortolker*, 75.

inscrutable love toward us. Above all, the Word/revelation discloses the mystery of Christ without which no one can know God's heart. Those who know the Law to some degree must be given an opportunity to hear the Gospel. Because Luther's Europe had become paganized, there was no need for him to apologize for not traveling abroad with the Gospel. Europe was mission field enough!

In the later commentaries on Galatians (1531/1535) and Genesis (1535–1545), Luther's theological evaluation of natural religion and theological knowledge are central. Here again, Luther notes that all people—in Christian and heathen cultures—have a natural knowledge of a divine being. They know this divine helper ought to be served and worshiped even as they know the Golden Rule that one ought to treat one's neighbor as one wants to be treated. Luther based his comments on Romans 1:19ff. and on the philosophers' concepts of God, however distorted and false they are.[78]

In the *Larger Commentary on Galatians*, Luther asks how Paul can claim both that the heathen know God and that they do not know God. Romans 1:19ff. says that natural humanity possesses some naturally given, intuitive knowledge of God. But Galatians 4:8–9 says: "Formerly, when you did not know God, you were slaves to those who by nature are not gods. But now that you know God—or rather are known by God—how is it that you are turning back to those weak and miserable principles? Do you wish to be enslaved by them all over again?" Luther resolves the problem first by recognizing that there are clear limitations to natural knowledge of God and second by making a clear distinction between the general, natural knowledge of God and the special or true knowledge of God. Luther says:

> "If all men know God, why does Paul say that before the proclamation of the Gospel the Galatians did not know God?" I reply: There is a twofold knowledge of God: the general and the particular. All men have the general knowledge, namely, that God is, that He has created heaven and earth, that He is just, that He punishes the wicked, etc. But what God thinks of us, what He wants to give and to do to deliver us from sin and death and to save us—which is the particular and the true knowledge of God—this men do not know. Thus it can happen that someone's face may be familiar to me but I do not really know him, because I do not know what he has in his mind. So it is that men know naturally that there is a God, but they do not know what He wants and what He does not want. [Romans 3:11; John 1:19; and the false worship of the Jews and Muslims are adduced here.] . . . But all of them are deceived and, as Paul says in Rom. 1:21, "become futile in their thinking"; not knowing what is pleasing to God and what is displeasing to Him, they adore

---

78 *Galatians*, WA 40/1:607ff.; 40/2:66.34ff.; and *Genesis*, WA 42:631.36ff.; 44:84.15ff. See Josefson, *Den naturliga teologins problem hos Luther*, 41ff., 60f., 102; Pedersen, *Luther som skriftfortolker*, 74f.; and Brosché, *Luther on Predestination*, 38.

the imaginations of their own heart as though these were true God by nature, when by nature these are nothing at all.[79]

In the commentary on Genesis, Luther remarks that the naturally given *notitia Dei,* which one finds among the heathen and in all speculative thought about God, consists of abstract and purely objective notions about the Creator. Natural knowledge of God cannot attain *Deus cultus et adoratus,* the existential knowledge and experience of God in true worship and faith. Luther acidly suggests that the God of the pope, the Turks, and the Jews is the same as the speculative God of philosophy and metaphysics. One may speak of God's absolute being and majesty, but, says Luther, even the devil knows that God exists.[80]

Luther uses a syllogism to illustrate the relation between natural knowledge of God and humanity's perverted use of that knowledge:

> From the acceptance of the major premise, "There is a God," there came all idolatry of men, which would have been unknown in the world without the knowledge of the Deity. But because men had this natural knowledge about God, they conceived vain and wicked thoughts about God apart from and contrary to the Word; they embraced these as the very truth, and on the basis of these they imagined God otherwise than He is by nature.[81]

Luther observes in the *Larger Commentary on Galatians* that idolatry derives from the concept of God that is written on the human heart. Depraved reason and the human heart abuse the knowledge of God that nature provides. Natural and fallen humanity cannot correctly use this knowledge but necessarily misuses it when it lacks or sets aside what God's Word communicates about God and true worship. Some years later Luther emphasizes a similar point in his commentary on Genesis: the worship of Abraham, Isaac, Jacob, and Joseph is not abstract and objective but a personal trust in the God of the Word and grace. This personal trust takes expression in the worship of the heart, having its source in the promises of the Word about Christ and eternal life. These promises have been given not only to Abraham but also to all peoples.[82]

---

79 LW 26:399–400 (WA 40/1:607.26ff.). See Josefson, *Den naturliga teologins problem hos Luther,* 41f.; and Watson, *Let God Be God!* 73ff.

80 WA 43:240.22ff.; 44:591.34ff.

81 LW 26:400 (WA 40/1:608.25ff.). Cf. WA 40/1:110ff., on how all worship without God's Word and command and without Christ is idolatry.

82 WA 42:631f. on Genesis 17:7, especially: "For 'to be God' not only means to be the creator of something but includes the worship of God. God is also the God of the heathen, for He created them; but He is neither acknowledged nor worshiped by the heathen. When God says: 'I shall be your God,' He points out that Abraham will always have the Word of God in his family and house, in order that his descendants may learn

True, the reformer in this later material does not touch on the question of the tension between the naked, hidden God and the God revealed in Christ and the Word. But some passages in the 1535–1545 Genesis commentaries highlight the tension between *Deus absconditus* and *Deus revelatus*. Hiddenness and opposition also characterize God's saving work in the crucified Christ and in faith's meeting with the God who kills and makes alive. Therefore a Christian who is firmly anchored in the promises and the Gospel believes and hopes against all that he sees. That is the difficult art of true faith, which the heathen and false Christians in their wisdom and "certain faith" do not know.[83] God is hidden and revealed even for the Christian. God is unapproachable through reason and flesh. But God has been clearly revealed and can be grasped by faith in the Word and Sacraments.[84]

This is the overarching theme: To know God's salvation, one must completely refrain from speculating about God. Speculation drives everyone, unbelievers and Christians, toward heresy and away from the true knowledge of God. Therefore one ought to flee all speculations and get to know God in Jesus Christ.

---

from it to know God and to worship Him aright. Thus the First Commandment says: 'I am the Lord your God' [Ex. 20:2], that is, 'I reveal Myself through the Word, and you shall worship Me and acknowledge Me.' The name God must be understood in a relative sense, to mean the God who is worshiped and adored, not in an absolute sense, to mean God according to His essence and majesty. . . . To adore God is to go to Him for help when you turn your face toward Him and call upon Him in trouble, when you give thanks for deliverance, when you recall and proclaim His acts of kindness by declaring that He is the Creator, the Benefactor, the Promiser, and the Savior" (LW 3:116–17 [WA 42:631.18ff.]).

83 Loewenich, *Luthers Theologia crucis*, 38ff., with references. See also Harnack, *Luthers Theologie*, 1:84; and Pedersen, "Luthers Laere om Gudserkendelsen," 94ff., on the knowledge of God, the hidden God, and faith. About God's hiddenness under God's works and words, see LW 4:7 (WA 43:140.28ff.): "Therefore the prophet (Is. 45:15) calls Him 'a God who hides Himself' [*Deum absconditum*]. For under the curse a blessing lies hidden; under the consciousness of sin, righteousness; under death, life; and under affliction, comfort." But faith can grasp the true God despite all the contradictions: "For this reason nothing in the world seems more uncertain than the Word of God and faith, nothing more delusive than hope in the promise. In short, nothing seems to be more nothing than God Himself. Consequently, this is the knowledge of the saints and a mystery hidden from the wise and revealed to babes (Matt. 11:25)" (LW 4:355–56 [WA 43:392.16ff.]). Cf. LW 4:357 (WA 43:393.16ff.): "For it is the wisdom of the saints to believe in the truth in opposition to the lie, in the hidden truth in opposition to the manifest truth, and in hope in opposition to hope."

84 LW 6:148 (WA 44:110.23ff.): "God is the One who is hidden. This is His peculiar property. He is really hidden, and yet He is not hidden, for the flesh prevents us from being able to look at him. . . . But in faith, in the Word, and in the sacraments He is revealed and seen." LW 5:46 (WA 43:460.26ff.): "If you believe in the revealed God and accept His word, He will gradually also reveal the hidden God." Cf. WA 41/2:77.21ff.

According to Luther, there is no other God than the one whom one meets in Jesus Christ, the incarnated mediator who shows us the God of love.

> You have often heard from us that it is a rule and principle in the Scriptures, and one that must be scrupulously observed, to refrain from speculation about the majesty of God, which is too much for the human body, and especially for the human mind, to bear. "Man shall not see Me and live," says Scripture (Ex. 33:20). The pope, the Turks, the Jews, and all the sectarians pay no attention to this rule. They put Christ the Mediator out of their sight, speak only of God, pray only to Him, and act only in relation to Him . . . . In short, whoever does not know the doctrine of justification takes away Christ the Propitiator.[85]

Luther also emphasizes the connection between speculation and works of the Law in which one seeks reconciliation with the Mediator, Christ. He claims that God is unapproachable via speculation and therefore encourages people to flee from it. First Corinthians 1:21 says that the world in its wisdom has not learned to know God but that the foolish preaching of the crucified Christ provides salvation to those who believe. Therefore Luther exhorts his readers in this way:

> Therefore begin where Christ began—in the Virgin's womb, in the manger, and at His mother's breasts. For this purpose He came down, was born, lived among men, suffered, was crucified, and died, so that in every possible way He might present Himself to our sight. He wanted us to fix the gaze or our hearts upon Himself and thus to prevent us from clambering into heaven and speculating about the Divine Majesty. Therefore whenever you consider the doctrine of justification and wonder how or where or in what condition to find a God who justifies or accepts sinners, then you must know that there is no other God than this Man Jesus Christ.[86]

In the commentaries on Genesis, Luther warned his students against pondering over the *Deus absconditus*, about whom he had written so energetically in 1525 in *Bondage of the Will*. Such speculation about the naked God (*Deus nudus*) accomplishes nothing. One must strictly hold to the God revealed in Jesus Christ. There is no other God who saves. One meets this true God concretely in the message of the church and only in the church.[87] Such a fundamental perspective

---

85 LW 26:28 (WA 40/1:75.29ff.).

86 LW 26:29 (WA 40/1:77.28ff.). Cf. LW 26:30 (WA 40/1:78.31ff.): ". . . or when it comes to satisfaction for sin, the forgiveness of sins, reconciliation, and eternal salvation, then you must disabuse your mind completely of all speculation and investigation into the majesty of God, and you must pay attention only to this Man, who presents Himself to us as the Mediator and says: 'Come to Me, all who labor, etc.' (Matt. 11:28). When you do this, you will see the love, the goodness, and the sweetness of God. You will see His wisdom, His power, and His majesty sweetened and mitigated to your ability to stand it."

assigns a central place in God's plan of salvation to the Gospel, through which one really gets to know God.

I have previously pointed out how works-righteousness characterizes natural religion according to Luther. It is not borne by God's love, grace, and faith; instead, it knows ultimately only the God of creation, of power, of righteousness, of the Law, and of judgment. God's help and blessing are conditional in natural religion. Therefore one seeks through sacrifices and works to ensure earthly blessing and God's forgiveness. In the Heidelberg Disputation of 1518 and later, Luther often explained that the works of the Law (*opera legis*) are the center of the natural, reason-inspired exercise of religion.[88] This theme appears with special clarity in the *Larger Commentary on Galatians* (1531/1535) in which Luther chisels out his doctrine of justification through faith without works of the Law: "All men have the general knowledge, namely, that God is, that He has created heaven and earth, that He is just, that He punishes the wicked, etc."[89] Natural humanity, moving about in the spheres of creation, the Law, and justice, enjoys a relationship to God (as Creator and under the Law).[90]

In the commentary on Galatians, Luther draws a sharp distinction between the passive righteousness of faith and all active, human righteousness that is characterized by the Law and works.[91] Luther postulates: "Thus human reason cannot refrain from looking at active righteousness, that is, its own righteousness; nor can it shift its gaze to passive, that is, Christian righteousness, but it simply rests in the active righteousness."[92] Natural humanity—including Jews and false Christians—

---

87 LW 5:50 (WA 43:462.29ff.): ". . . because after my death many will publish my books and will prove from them errors of every kind and their own delusions. Among other things, however, I have written that everything is absolute and unavoidable; but at the same time I have added that one must look at the revealed God, as we sing in the hymn: *Er heist Jesu Christ, der HERR Zebaoth, und ist kein ander Gott,* 'Jesus Christ is the Lord of hosts, and there is no other God'—and also in very many other places. But they will pass over all these places and take only those that deal with the hidden God. Accordingly, you who are listening to me now should remember that I have taught that one should not inquire into the predestination of the hidden God but should be satisfied with what is revealed through the calling and through the ministry of the Word." Loewenich (in *Luthers Theologia crucis*) should have paid more attention to this warning because he is preoccupied with what Luther wrote about the *Deus absconditus.*

88 See Harnack, *Luthers Theologie,* 1:69ff., 135ff.; and Josefson, *Den naturliga teologins problem hos Luther,* 46f., 60f., 64ff.

89 LW 26:399.

90 See *Luther and World Mission,* 15–25, 32–35.

91 WA 40/1:40ff.

92 LW 26:5 (WA 40/1:42.12ff.).

always seeks God's favor and goodwill through works of the Law.[93] This is the stance of all fallen, natural humans, a position that had been strengthened further by the teachers of the Law among the Galatians (1:7–9). The Law and works-righteousness unsettle the conscience, distort the Gospel, and lead to a false faith. The curse rests on those who through this doctrine extinguish the Gospel and kill faith.[94] Luther comments on Galatians 4:7:

> Whoever falls from the doctrine of justification is ignorant of God and is an idolater. Therefore it is all the same whether he then returns to the Law or to the worship of idols; it is all the same whether he is called a monk or a Turk or a Jew or an Anabaptist. For once this doctrine is undermined, nothing more remains but sheer error, hypocrisy, wickedness, and idolatry, regardless of how great the sanctity that appears on the outside. The reason is this: God does not want to be known except through Christ; nor, according to John 1:18, can he be known any other way. Christ is the Offspring promised to Abraham; on Him God founded all His promises. Therefore Christ alone is the means, the life, and the mirror through which we see God and know His will.[95]

In connection with Galatians 3:28—"There is neither Jew nor Greek"—Luther says that neither those who are circumcised and seek to follow the Law of Moses nor the many shining examples of morality among the heathen can attain a true fellowship with God or salvation. The Law and works are irrelevant for salvation. All that matters is Christ alone, in whom one is clothed in Baptism.[96] Concerning Galatians 4:8, Luther writes: "Therefore it does not make much difference whether you call the 'elements' here the Law of Moses or some of the traditions of the Gentiles. For someone who falls away from grace into the Law is no better off in his fall than someone apart from grace who falls into idolatry. Apart from Christ there is nothing but sheer idolatry, an idol and a false fiction about God, whether it is called the Law of Moses or the law of the pope or the Koran of the Turk."[97]

As previously noted, Luther integrates the work of mission and church. The line between the evangelization of the church and foreign mission fluctuates. Walter Holsten and E. Danbolt have stated rightly that this hangs together with Luther's notion that both unbelief and the saving Gospel are universal.[98] We have

---

93 WA 40/1:86.18ff., 152.14ff., 611ff.

94 WA 40/1:110ff.

95 LW 26:395–96 (WA 40/1:602.12ff.). Cf. the clarifying explanation of this thesis about *opera legis* and heathenism in WA 40/1:603ff. See also WA 40/2:110ff. Cf. Vossberg, *Luthers Kritik aller Religion*, 62ff., 88ff., 103ff.; and especially Holsten, "Christentum und nicht-christliche Religion nach der Auffassung Luthers," 16ff., 67ff., 145ff.

96 WA 40/1:542f.

97 LW 26:400–401 (WA 40/1:609.15ff.).

repeatedly seen that Luther finds natural religion, characterized as it is by the Law and self-righteousness, among all the heathen, circumcised Jews, among the nominal Christians of the Catholic Church, and among enthusiasts and false Christians in the evangelical camp. Wherever this false worship of God appears, the false worship in which one believes that relationship to God is decided by the Law and works, there is idolatry or heathenism. Wherever the Gospel of unconditional grace and faith in Christ is not preached and believed, there is darkness and heathenism. The Great Commission is relevant not only in non-Christian lands but also in those lands regarded as Christian. Luther understands that cross-cultural mission is a special kind of ministry, but nevertheless he believes that Jesus' commission to preach the Gospel is applicable even to the new heathenism and the nominal Christianity of old Christian lands. One cannot draw a fundamental line of demarcation between the church's domestic work and her foreign mission. Both fields of the church's activity share injury and require healing.

Finally, there is a special problem in connection with the *locus classicus* of natural knowledge of God in Romans 1:19–23. In Romans 1:20, Paul says God's power and glory have been visible from the beginning of creation and humankind is, therefore, without excuse when it comes to worship of the created. In his comments on this problem in 1545, Luther emphasizes (along with a respondent whom Luther does not correct) that only through God's Word may humanity receive the knowledge of God and of God's will that leads to justification and salvation. Nevertheless, all humanity receives a general, philosophical knowledge of God, even if they do not, for example, understand and believe that God has created the world from nothing (*creatio ex nihilo*). But if humanity from creation enjoys a merely imperfect and abstract knowledge of God, how can Paul reject all excuses? Already in the 1515–1516 commentary on Romans, Luther joins Paul in rejecting all such excuses. The aging reformer, on the last occasion when he is present at a disputation, says that the apostle in Romans 1:19–23 actually answers this question about responsibility. The heathen (*gentes*) knew that a God exists. They did not honor the true God, however, but worshiped idols they knew were wood and stone. Therefore they were without excuse and were placed under guilt and punishment.[99] Even the general, abstract, or philosophical knowledge about the divine being, that being's power, righteousness, etc., makes humanity responsible according to Luther. Even if the depraved human heart turns itself toward and

---

98 Holsten, "Christentum und nicht-christliche Religion nach der Auffassung Luthers," 30ff., 45ff., 55ff., 67ff.; and Danbolt, "Misjon—evangeliets frie løp," 246f., 250f.

99 "Die Promotionsdisputation von Petrus Hegemon (1545)," WA 39/2:344.22ff., 345.24ff. Cf. WA 14:588.8ff., 26f. Concerning the naturally given knowledge of God and the question of responsibility, see also WA 39/2:346.26ff., especially 347.10ff.

worships the created and idols, humanity does not receive any direction toward such behavior from the general, natural intimation/knowledge of God. The driving force toward idolatry lay in humanity's depraved heart. Therefore humanity must answer for its own false worship of God.

SUMMARY

The following are Luther's main points concerning natural theology.

1. Through the testimony of creation, all people have in their reason and their hearts a God-given notion of God and of some of God's characteristics. Luther bases this position on Romans 1:19ff. and on the fact that all cultures practice religion. The natural man always reckons with something or someone divine, who is all-powerful and righteous, helps those in need, demands works, punishes, and rewards. Human beings can never avoid the question about God and salvation. This kind of questioning is an important point of contact for mission and evangelization, even if it is the Gospel of Christ alone that can supply an answer.

2. As soon as individuals, by their natural knowledge alone, seek to be more precise and express who God is, they invariably create a god from their own thoughts and fantasies. Because of the absolute depravity of human beings, they cannot avoid this. So they end up praying to and worshiping that which is not God. Without revelation and the Scriptures, humans always and unavoidably become idolaters. This kind of natural religion is widespread among unbelievers, Jews, and even within the Christian West. Because everyone has some knowledge of God, atheism is really a confession of the mouth, not of the heart. Luther concedes that there is a natural knowledge of God, but this is not a true knowledge, faith, or worship of God. Such an understanding opens a wide field for foreign mission and re-Christianization on all continents.

3. Although natural knowledge of God is true in some respects, one cannot, on the basis of reason alone, comprehend the inner working of creation, to say nothing of understanding God's heart and God's saving work—that God created from nothing; that Christ's incarnation, death, and resurrection are the way to eternal life; and that we are justified only through faith in Christ without works of the Law. Therefore a developed natural theology and a practiced natural religion cannot be true.

4. Because a truly accurate knowledge of God is acquired only through Jesus Christ, the Word, and the Gospel, one should flee all philosophical speculation about God's majesty, holding only to that which God reveals through his Word, above all the word about Jesus Christ. Through the

Word, we receive the Spirit and true saving wisdom and faith, which is not primarily an objective, theoretical knowledge.

5. The difference between natural theology/religion and the revealed knowledge of God/faith is that natural knowledge lacks personal trust and dedication to God's goodness. One may understand something about God without having faith in or fearing God. Natural theology speculates about the divine majesty (*theologia gloriae*). Both within Christendom and in the heathen world, natural theology is characterized by rationalism, legalism, and moralism, by the Law and self-righteousness. True and saving knowledge of God looks only to God in Christ (*theologia crucis*). Only the theology of the cross leads to true knowledge of God, his heart, his will to save, and to justification and salvation.

The natural man is not oppressed with temptations and vexations because, according to natural religion, God's help and grace are always conditional on human works. But the person who has true knowledge of God is always oppressed with setbacks and spiritual battles because it has its stronghold in Christ and unconditional grace, which is revealed through the Holy Spirit through the Word/Gospel. In short, natural theology/religion is characterized by the Law and what humans do. The wisdom of faith is always carried by what God's Word and the articles of faith say that the Father, the Son, and the Spirit do and give. There is an unbridgeable gap between the anthropocentric and theocentric knowledge and worship of God. Special or true knowledge of and faith in God has its source in the Gospel and is characterized completely by trust in God's undeserved grace. Ultimately, this is a question of the difference between the way of the Law and the way of the Gospel to fellowship with God, between the active and the passive ways to righteousness. Works of the Law and self-righteousness are in this way the marks of natural religion both in Christian and non-Christian lands. Christ, grace, and faith in the forgiveness of sins are always signs of true wisdom, that which revelation, the Word, and the Spirit give. All natural theology and religion is an expression of the human way to God through speculation and works of merit, a false and inescapable way. Whatever notion of God one might have, true wisdom and faith in God come through the illuminating Gospel of Christ. Herein lies the basic motivation for all mission, evangelization, and reformation.

The Source and Content
of True Knowledge of God according to Luther's
Commentaries on John's Prologue

Our study of a true, saving knowledge of God continues by highlighting one pericope, John 1:1–18, in Luther's exposition of Scripture. Luther's commentary on John's prologue and the incarnation includes ideas fundamental to his "missiology." Luther emphasizes that God seeks fellowship and comes near to humanity in the Son of Man and that Christ through history meets people "in the flesh" in the Word and Sacraments.[100]

Naturally, Luther's commentaries on John's prologue stress Christ's incarnation. But for Luther, one rule is always important: The person is as his or her works. Therefore I refer the reader to the study of Luther on the important theme: Jesus Christ's works, especially in the crucifixion and the resurrection. The notes give information about the relevant literature.

Luther is not especially interested in theoretical and speculative epistemology. He does not consider the wisdom that is given to us through Christ, the Word, the Spirit, and faith to be a philosophical knowing. Faith's existential appropriation of the mystery of salvation in Christ is not a species of philosophical conceptuality. Although Luther has some references to theoretical epistemology, generally he avoids philosophical concepts and philosophical arguments. He uses the language of the Scriptures and faith when he wants to discuss the source and content of true wisdom.[101] In the commentaries on John 1:1–18 previous to the Reformation breakthrough, Luther is influenced by scholastic distinctions and concepts. He recognizes no conflict between the use of reason and revelation,[102] but he articulates it later in his exposition of John's prologue.[103]

---

100 See Loewenich, *Luther und das Johanneische Christentum*, 23ff., 35ff.; Öberg, "Mission und Heilsgeschichte," 3; and Pörsti, "Luthers syn på evangelisation," 25.

101 See the clear-sighted observations of Althaus, *Die Theologie Martin Luthers*, 17f., with references. Cf. Loewenich, *Luthers Theologia crucis*, 107ff., on how faith's *intelligere* has as its object God's work in Christ's cross and the promises of the Word. The knowledge and confidence of faith are not based on some empirical-psychological foundation. See also the viewpoints of the scholars listed in *Luther and World Mission*, 39–40n41, especially the quotation from Ebeling, *Luther* (p. 40n41). An enlightening text on this subject is WA 49:536.17ff.

102 WA 1:23–29 (probably from December 1514) shows that Luther is ensnared in a mass of philosophical and psychological speculations that he connects to Aristotle, Augustine, and the Scholastic theologians. Concerning the Christology of the young Luther, see Seeberg, *Luthers Theologie*, 2:4ff., 22ff.

103 *Church Postil* (1522), WA 10/1.1:180–247, especially WA 10/1.1:202ff., 209ff., 220ff. See

On the basis of John 1:1–3, Luther claims:

1. God's eternal Son, the Word or Logos, Christ, is true God.

2. He is eternally begotten of the Father, before the creation of the world and before his own birth as a human being.

3. God the Father has created everything and sustains everything that exists through the Word, the only begotten Son. Cf. John 1:14.

John's prologue includes scriptural support both for classic Christological dogma and for the church's belief that Christ is Co-Creator and Co-Sustainer with the Father. However, natural humanity knows nothing of this.[104] We will return to Christology in connection with John 1:14.

Luther translates John 1:5b: ". . . and the darkness has not *understood* it" (*emphasis added*). The translation of the final clause is similar to the latest Norwegian translation, while the latest official Swedish translation (cf. with the 1917 translation) has the words "and the darkness has not overcome it" (κατέλαβεν; RSV: *overcome*). Any of these translations are probably valid. Luther's translation suggests a limitation of natural humanity's ability to receive the true light from the so-called cosmic Christ. Luther is well acquainted with the philosophical interpretations of Augustine and the medieval Scholastics and confesses that he was tied to their interpretations for some time. They had said that the cosmic Christ with his divine light enlightens the reason of all, even of the heathen. For the Scholastics, the cosmic, preincarnation Christ gave life and light for salvation without the media of Scripture and Gospel. Luther rejects this view. He repeats *solus Christus,* emphasizing the Christ incarnated on earth. Augustine and the medieval Scholastics led people away from the life and the light of the revealed Jesus Christ toward the light of human reason and speculation. But Luther says that John in his prologue tried to stress the exact opposite. John is an evangelist, not a Platonist. To acquire knowledge about God, therefore, one ought not turn to something created or to the light of one's own reason. Human speculation leads nowhere. One can learn to know God if and only if one contemplates the human Jesus, the Jesus of flesh and blood, and learns to know this person more closely

---

also WA 11:226f.; 15:802f.; *Festival Postil* (1527), 17/2:320–26; 27:529ff.; 29:9ff., 37.3ff.; "Sermons on John 1 and 2 (1537/1538)," especially 46:563ff., 593ff., 614ff.; and "The Disputation concerning the Passage: 'The Word Was Made Flesh' (1539)," 39/2:3ff. Among the secondary literature about Luther and the Gospel of John, see Loewenich, *Luther und das Johanneische Christentum,* 20ff., 35ff.; Ebeling, *Evangelische Evangelienauslegung*; and Wolf, "Die Christusverkündigung bei Luther."

104 On John 1:1–4, see WA 10/1.1:194ff.; 11:226f.; 15:801f.; 17/2:318.28ff.; 27:529.2ff.; 37:1.16ff., 3.16ff; 46:547–63. Cf. *Luther and World Mission,* 67n110, and the literature referred to in *Luther and World Mission,* 71–72n118.

through the Word of Scripture and the preaching of the church. Luther acknowledges that he has abandoned his doctrinal father Augustine's interpretations and especially the Scholastic extension of them toward a natural theology.[105] Luther does not deny that reason in earthly life is enlightened by a light that the cosmic Christ has communicated. He decidedly denies that the light of nature and reason can teach humanity the heart of God and of Christ. Reason opposes the light of Christ, which is a light of grace. Therefore God must send preachers who preach about this light in words and deeds.[106]

---

105 LW 52:57 (WA 10/1.1:202.7ff.): "He does not want to disperse us into the creatures which are created through him, so that we should run after him and seek him there and speculate as do the followers of Plato. On the contrary, he wants to gather us together out of these farfetched high flown thoughts into Christ." Concerning the incarnated Christ as the revelation of God, see WA 10/1.1:200.17f., 207.23ff. See especially Luther's own testimony about John 1:5: "Oh, that this interpretation might be eradicated from my heart where it is so deeply rooted! It is not that this interpretation is wrong or incorrect in itself, but that at this point in the Gospel it does not fit and is out of place. . . . Why do they not also say this of natural life? For natural life is quickened by the divine life in exactly the same manner as the light of reason is illuminated by the divine light. Hence, in all fairness, they should also say that life quickens the dead, and the dead do not comprehend it, as they say that the light illumines dark reason and reason does not comprehend it. . . . Platonic philosophers first led St. Augustine to this interpretation of this text with their unprofitable and silly babbling. . . . Augustine in turn pulled all of us after him" (LW 52:62–63 [WA 10/1:209.23ff.]). Cf. WA 11:227.26ff.; 27:529.9ff.; 29:11.9ff.; 46:562ff. See Augustinus, *In Ioh.ev.tract* 1.16.17, MPL 35:1387. See especially Ebeling's helpful study, *Evangelische Evangelienauslegung*, 251ff.; and Prenter, *Spiritus creator*, 12f.

106 WA 10/1.1:203.3ff. See how the light of grace is something that people cannot understand naturally according to John 1:5 (supported by Acts 17:27) in WA 10/1:210.18ff. Especially enlightening are Luther's words: "Therefore let us cling to the simple interpretation which the text furnishes freely and easily. All who are illumined by natural reason comprehend the light and are illumined, each one according to his measure. But this light of grace which is given to men in addition to the natural light shines in the darkness, i.e., among the blind people of this world who are without grace, but they do not accept it. On the contrary, they persecute it; this is the meaning of his words in John 3[:19]: 'This condemns the world, that the light has come into the world, and men loved darkness more than the light.' . . . . [A]s St. Paul says in I Corinthians 2[:8]: 'Had they recognized the wisdom of God, they would not have crucified the King of Glory.' In such a manner, too, Christ, even before his birth, from the beginning and until the end, has always been life and light, and he shines at all times in all creatures in the Holy Scriptures through his holy people, prophets and preachers, with works and words, and he has never ceased to shine. But there is darkness whenever he sheds his light, and the darkness does not comprehend him" (LW 52:64 [WA 10/1.1:212.6ff.]). Cf. WA 11:227.31ff.; 15:802.16ff.; 17/2:320.18ff.; 27:530.1ff., 531.6ff.; 37:4.17ff.; 46:564ff.

According to Luther's 1522 *Church Postil*, this is connected with the fact that humanity's nature and reason are depraved after the fall. All Adam's children are created by God, but after the fall, they possess nothing divine, only evil.[107] Pride and love of self characterize natural humanity. It knows that it ought to serve God, but in its blindness, it does not know how one becomes pious and righteous in relation to God. Luther says reason is always tuned into works as the means to win God's favor and grace. And the ingrained self-righteousness of natural humanity is the root of all the delusions and all the idolatry of religious practice. But the light of grace in Christ teaches something incomprehensible for natural humanity, namely, that one becomes pious and righteous in relation to God through faith without works of the Law. Natural reason always despises the light of grace and the righteousness of faith and instead constantly demands works to please God.[108] The Gospel creates a crisis for all natural religion. The previous quotations from the commentaries on John's prologue mesh well with what we have discovered about Luther's view of the consequences of the fall and natural humanity's ingrained tendency to seek God's favor through works of the Law.[109] Luther says:

> Behold, there you have in brief the cause and origin of all idolatry, of all heresy, of all hypocrisy, of all error; this is what all the prophets deplored and why they were killed, and against this all Scripture takes a stand. All of this comes from the stiff-necked, self-willed pride and delusion of natural reason which is puffed up because it knows that we must be godly and serve God; moreover, it does not want to listen to or tolerate any teacher.[110]

Luther makes a clear distinction between the natural light, given to both evil people and good, and the special light of Christ that is given through faith and the Holy Spirit.[111] John the evangelist speaks primarily about this light of grace and faith. Luther says:

---

107 WA 10/1.1:203.5ff., 203.15ff., 204.9ff. Cf. WA 11:227.29ff., 802.18ff.; 17/2:320.22ff., 320.36ff.; 46:563ff. Loewenich writes: "Luther fasst das 'Licht' bei Johannes durchweg als Bild für die Offenbarung und damit zugleich antithetisch zum 'naturlichen Licht'" (*Luther und das Johanneische Christentum*, 53f.).

108 WA 10/1.1:205.4, 206.6. Cf. the passages in WA 27:530.5ff.; 46:567.1ff. See Wolf, "Martin Luther," 14ff., 22ff.

109 See *Luther and World Mission*, 17–19, 34–35, 43ff., 50–51, 58, 59ff.

110 LW 52:59–60 (WA 10/1:206.16ff.). Cf. WA 10/1:239.17ff., 240.22f.; 27:531ff.; 46:563ff., 577.17ff.

111 See, among others, WA 10/1.1:203.5ff., 203.15ff., 206.17ff. See especially LW 22:30 (WA 46:562.23ff.): ". . . but with this light He illumines men, so that all reason, wisdom, and dexterity that are not false or devilish emanate from this Light, who is the Wisdom of the eternal Father. But in addition to this light, which all men, both the good and the bad, enjoy in common, there is a particular light which God grants only to His

This is also the import of the words themselves when he says: "the life was a light of men" [John 1:4]. If it is a light of men, then it must be a light different from that which is in man. . . . Therefore, this light must be understood as the one which is revealed to the world in Christ on earth. . . . He does not say that the light was the life of men, but "the life was the light of men," for the reason that in Christ are reality and truth, and not just the appearance of these things, as in man.[112]

In this passage, Luther overinterprets the Scholastics' use of John 1:4. Although they spoke of a light of reason and nature, they meant that this light had been given through Christ and ultimately was not a light *from* humanity but a light from Christ *in* humanity. The Scholastics did, however, emphasize the light of reason so much that they often spoke of its distance from the incarnated Christ and from the Gospel.

John 1:7 says this about John the Baptist: "He came as a witness to testify concerning that light, so that through him all men might believe." Based on this verse, the reformer emphasizes that human instruments of the Gospel are simply witnesses. Just as certain as the flesh and blood of Christ are the only light that leads to true knowledge of God and to a saving faith, so it is certain that Christ must be testified and preached for the same goal to be reached. This connection between *Christus revelatus* (the Christ who is revealed) and *Christus praedicatus* (the Christ who is preached) is decisive for Luther. He rejects any notion of a saving natural revelation, any human attempt to reach heaven, and all spiritualistic attempts to produce a true faith without the medium of the Word. Instead, the Word/Gospel and faith appear as the true pillars of Luther's missiology and ecclesiology. The light of Christ is offered as a light of grace for all, Jews and Gentiles, even if not all want to receive the Gospel. Luther has a kind of chain of revelation: God—Christ—the Scriptures—the Gospel of the church—grace/faith.[113] Thereby

---

own. To this applies everything that John later writes about the Word, namely, that He reveals Himself to His elect through the Holy Spirit and the oral Word, and that He wants to be the Light of His people."

112 LW 52:60 (WA 10/1.1:206.20ff., 207.10ff., 207.14f.).

113 See especially LW 52:66–67 (WA 10/1.1:215.23ff.): ". . . just as [John] was the forerunner of Christ and directed the people to him, so the spoken word of the gospel should preach only Christ and point only to him. For only to that end was it ordained by God, just as John was sent by God . . . . Just as the darkness was unable, on its own, to comprehend this light, even though it was present, John had to reveal and to bear witness of it. To this day natural reason on its own is unable to comprehend it, even though it is present in all the world. The spoken word of the gospel must reveal and proclaim it. Now we see that through the gospel this same light is brought to us, not from afar, nor is it necessary to run after it a great distance; it is very near to us and also shines in our heart. Nothing more is necessary but that it be pointed out and preached. And who-

the Gospel message of church and mission is given a powerful principal foundation and motivation. There is a motivation for the work of church and mission in the way that Christ, grace, and faith are given to humanity through the Word and Sacraments. God's salvation is communicated to and entrusted to the apostolic church.

Especially interesting are the commentaries on John 1:9: "The true light that gives light to every man was coming into the world." Is it possible that Luther agrees with both older and newer teachings about the cosmic Christ who can save even outside the sphere of influence of the Gospel and church? Luther says in connection with John 1:9 (compare with Luther's comments on John 1:4 above) that Christ communicates a natural light for the life of humanity, its thoughts, and its pursuits here on earth. But that natural light, given through reason, is not the same as the light of revelation, grace, and faith that comes from the same Christ. John 1:5 and John 1:10ff. say that humanity in its darkness neither understands nor receives Jesus Christ. That Christ "gives light to every man" means that he alone gives the true light (through the Word) and is revealed or illuminates all humanity, Jews and Gentiles. Many do not understand or may indeed directly reject the revealed light of Christ (John 1:10–11). Luther believes that Christ is known only through the incarnation and received in faith. This thesis is expertly honed by Luther in many passages on John 1:9ff.[114]

---

ever hears it preached, and believes, finds it in his heart; for faith can only be in the heart, and so this light cannot be anywhere except in faith." See also WA 29:9.6ff., 15ff.: "Haec erat conclusio, quod Euangelista scribit Iohannem non fuisse lucem, sed debebat testimonium dare de luce ut omnes homines per illum. . . . Notanda haec verba his praedicari, quia es sol bleiben so: Iohannes sols liecht nicht sein . . . . Das wort ist nicht zu bezalen. Summa summaraum: es sol kein ler, gesetz, mediator, doctor nicht gelten nisi de quo Iohannes testatur. Contra hunc textum peccant Papistae, Rottae, quia omnes voluerunt esse lux, non contenti ut testarentur. . . . Ergo quisque audiat hunc unicum magistrum . . . . Qui Christum non monstrat, den las faren." See the extensive argument for Christ's kingdom as a kingdom of preaching in WA 10/1.1:214–20 (with many Scripture citations); 15:802.28ff.; 17/2:322.16ff.; 27:531.11ff., 535.1ff. (a strongly antispiritualistic text); 46:569ff., 578ff. (with a barrage of Scripture passages that speak of Christ, preaching, and faith). Concerning *viva vox*, see especially WA 46:582ff. In the secondary literature, see Bizer, *Fides ex auditu*; Öberg, *Himmelrikets nycklar och kyrklig bot i Luthers teologi*, 147, with the adduced studies; and Prenter, *Spiritus creator*, 114ff., 130ff.

114 WA 10/1.1:220.18–227.12, especially: "If this is said of the natural light, his words are contradicted that it is the true light; for he said above: 'the darkness does not comprehend it' [John 1:5], and all his words are aimed at the light of grace. Then follow the words: 'He came into the world and the world did not recognize him and his own did not accept him' [John 1:10]" (LW 52:70 [WA 10/1.1:221.1ff.]). WA 29:11.13ff.: " 'Erat lux vera.' Da stehts ja dur ausgetruckt. Multi quesierunt, an omnes

Concerning John 1:12–13—"Yet to all who received him, to those who believed in his name, he gave the right to become children of God—children born not of natural descent, nor of human decision or a husband's will, but born of God"—Luther says that natural reason leads no human to become God's child nor does it receive the light in Christ; instead, natural reason despises it. Only faith in Christ provides knowledge of God, makes a person a child of God, and brings liberation from Satan, sin, death, and God's wrath. This occurs without works of the law or human achievements, only through faith in the Gospel about God's Son. Those who have become God's children already possess perfect righteousness and freely and spontaneously bear the fruit of good works.[115]

Luther notes that faith which is enlightening and saving does not operate through something that is in humanity (John 1:13). One cannot trust in a blood connection to Abraham, as the Jews do. Divine birth is not won through flesh and blood but only through the Gospel received in faith. True knowledge of God's will to save is always a gift from God. And only those who are so begotten of God can be called God's children. Luther is radically theocentric in describing how true wisdom of God and salvation come through faith alone.[116] Only those who trust

---

. . . Augustinum quoque? Das las wir faren. . . . Non loquitur de iis qui audire sollen, wie viel er sein, sed de iis qui docturi, i.e., nemo sol sich unterwinden zu leren nisi unica lux illa. Omnes homines quicunque nascuntur, sollen sie geleret werden, mussen den lerer haben." Cf. WA 17/2:323.15ff.; 37:7.30ff.; 46:593ff. Concerning the connection between the light of Christ, the promises of Scripture, and the true preaching of Christ, see especially WA 46:595.6ff., 596.3ff., 597.5ff. Cf. Loewenich, *Luther und das Johanneische Christentum*, 53.

115 WA 10/1.1:227.16ff.; 15:803.5ff., 803.19ff.; 29:16.8ff.; 37:8.34ff.; 46:610ff., with extensive Bible argumentation. See the matter briefly and clearly put in *Festival Postil* (1527), WA 17/2:324.6ff.: " 'Wieviel yhn aber auffnamen, denen gab er macht, Gottes kinder zu werden, die da an seinen namen gleuben.' Da stehet beyde, unser shande und ehre, damit er uns begabt hat, Die schande ist gros, das wir bisher sind des Teuffels kinder gewesen, Die ehre aber viel grösser, das wir nu Gottes kinder sind. Denn wie kündten wir grössern rhum und trotz haben ynn hymel und erden, denn das wir der höhisten Maiestet kinder heissen und alles haben, was er ist und hat? . . . Wie komen wir aber dazu? Durch den glauben (sagt er) an seinen namen, Da sind alle unsere weise und wege auffgehaben, alle werck und verdienst ausgeschlossen . . . . Also ist es alles yn den glauben gefasset, was wir haben an geistlichen gütern, das uns Gott der sunde und Teuffel aus dem rachen reisset und aus kindern des zorns seine liebe kinder machet."

116 WA 10/1.1:228.20ff., 229.19ff., 231.16ff., 234.12ff.; 15:803.12ff.; 17/2:325.3ff.; 46:614ff., 621ff. See especially the following passages from the 1537–1538 commentaries: "Thus both John the Baptist and the evangelist John reject the physical birth of all men, even the Jews' especially chosen and select descent from Abraham, as a basis for becoming children of God. . . . Yet all this is of no help or service toward the attainment of the spiritual birth. This is God's work alone and it preserves us eternally" (LW

God's will to save and are firmly anchored in faith in Christ can survive severe doubts and spiritual struggles.[117]

The above passages on John's prologue show that Luther has abandoned theoretical epistemology. He speaks with the religious-existential language of the Bible about how one gets to know God, to be begotten of God, to believe the Gospel, to become God's child, etc.

Jesus Christ's incarnation, atoning death and resurrection are the essential elements of Luther's doctrine and preaching about God's salvation. So Christ's person and work are held together. The reformer ceaselessly repeats the thesis: As the person is, so are the works. Among the works of God's Son, the substitutionary death on the cross and his resurrection are central. There is a great breadth to Luther's writing on this. It is not possible here to review the secondary literature on this theme. However, I must say against Gustaf Aulén that Luther in no way hides or deemphasizes Jesus' death as an atonement for sins. As Harm Alpers and others have shown, Luther unites the satisfaction and victory motifs, a double perspective that ought to be important for all mission preaching. Because non-Christians are often more open to the struggle and victory motifs than the atonement motif, genuine Lutheranism must preach both. Luther believed that he followed the Scriptures, especially Paul's preaching on Christ's cross and resurrection, on this point.

Not only because of church tradition but also primarily on the basis of the Scriptures, Luther confesses the church's ancient Christology, namely, the doctrine of the two natures. He particularly emphasizes Christ's true humanity, the fact he took on our weak flesh.[118] At the same time it is clear that the question of salvation

---

22:93 [WA 46:616.15ff.]). LW 22:99 (WA 46:621.37ff.): "St. John casts aside as a rotten apple everything of which man might be tempted to boast self-reliantly; he eliminates everything but the birth from God and recognizes as children of God only those who accept Christ. These alone shall be enabled and entitled to glory in the fact that God is their Father and that they are His children." LW 22:101 (WA 46:623.25ff.): "Therefore they and only they are children of God who are born of God, that is, who believe in Jesus Christ, the Son of God and of Mary. And these believers are not 'born of blood nor of the will of the flesh nor of the will of man, but of God.' " See also Loewenich, *Luther und das Johanneische Christentum*, 55f., about Christians as children begotten of God.

117 WA 10/1.1:232.16ff.; 31/1:127.7ff., 146.31ff. See Althaus, *Die Theologie Martin Luthers*, 147; and Lennart Pinomaa, *Die Anfechtung als Hintergrund des Evangeliums in der Theologie Luthers* (1943). See also Öberg, *Himmelrikets nycklar och kyrklig bot i Luthers teologi*, 220ff., with the references on doubt and its solution.

118 See Harnack, *Luthers Theologie*, 2:87–310. Especially about the incarnation and the Christ dogma, see Wolf, "Christusverkündigung bei Luther," 49ff., 53ff. For a thorough investigation, see Seeberg, *Luthers Theologie*, vol. 2, especially 233ff. See also Watson,

and the fact that one comes to know God's heart through the incarnation are overwhelmingly the most significant aspects of his Christology.

Luther comments extensively on John 1:14: "The Word became flesh and made his dwelling among us. We have seen his glory, the glory of the One and Only Son, who came from the Father, full of grace and truth." This text is a central and decisive text for Luther's Christology. The fact that Luther had already disputed with the old heresies that had their origin in natural reason and with more contemporary watered-down formulations of Christology make it easy to understand that the doctrine of the incarnation of God's eternal Son is important for the reformer. Luther presents a veritable arsenal of proof from the Old and New Testaments to show that faith in the incarnate Christ confesses and praises the mystery of salvation itself, which humanity could never understand through its own wisdom. It is the incarnate Jesus Christ and his work of salvation through which one learns to know God, God's heart, grace, and truth. Those who do not know God in Jesus as true God and true man do not know God, however they would like to speak about him.[119]

The words of the ancient dogma about Christ, "true God and true man," that is, the mystery of the incarnation, is, for Luther, the richest source and the true foundation of all faith and joy. Few theologians have done as much as Luther with the words "The Word became flesh and made his dwelling among us." Luther

---

Let God Be God! 102ff., 116ff.; Althaus, *Die Theologie Martin Luthers*, 159ff., 171ff.; and Frostin, *Politik och hermeneutik*, 75ff., who, against Bultmann, Loewenich, and Ebeling, emphasizes that Luther always attaches great significance to the natural or historical side of Christ's incarnation and works. Cf. Vogelsang, *Der angefochtene Christus bei Luther*, 100ff. See especially the comprehensive investigation of Luther's Christology during the various phases of his career and the constant elements of his Christology in Lienhard, *Martin Luthers christologisches Zeugnis*, especially 274ff. Aulén, *Den kristna försoningstanken*, 174ff., 199ff., believes that Luther breaks with the so-called Latin theory of reconciliation, that is, *satisfactio vicaria*. It is supposed that Luther sees Christ's suffering on the cross and his resurrection as only God's work of struggle and victory. See Althaus, *Die Theologie Martin Luthers*, 191ff. (English: 218ff.), for a severe critique of Aulén. Cf. especially Alpers, *Die Versöhnung durch Christus*, 184ff. He shows that Luther unites the Latin (satisfaction motif) and the classic (struggle motif) doctrines of reconciliation. The investigation of Alpers should once and for all put to rest the notion that Luther hesitated to speak of God's wrath, the debt of sin, or Christ's *satisfactio vicaria*.

119 WA 10/1.1:236.15ff., 237.4ff., 239.15ff.; 46:631.35ff., 633.21ff. Luther aims his sting against the Arian denial of Christ's divinity, against the Apollinarian denial of Christ as truly human, and against the Jews who deny that Jesus was God's Son, even if they confess God as creator of heaven and earth. Concerning the theme of the Word become flesh, see especially Wolf, "Die Christusverkündigung bei Luther," 49ff., 53f.; and Ebeling, *Evangelische Evangelienauslegung*, 241ff., 360ff.

emphasizes Jesus' true humanity, that he was not a ghost but shared all the characteristics of humanity. In his earthly life, in his gestures and his needs, Jesus was like any other citizen of Nazareth or Capernaum. Christ's destitution (from the Greek *kenosis*, which means "emptying") occurred so humanity might find God and receive the right to become children of God. Luther writes: "Here [Christ] decides now that which must be done for our sake. In order that we might become God's children through faith in the Word, the Word must reveal itself to us and become flesh, i.e., a natural human being. And he has lived among us, i.e., had relationship with us, tasted all human distress and fragility, indeed made the divine majesty nothing as Paul says (Phil. 2:7)."[120] The incarnation is an incomparable source of comfort. With the ring of ancient Christology, Luther writes in the 1537–1538 commentaries on John:

> Thus the most precious treasure and the strongest consolation we Christians have is this: that the Word, the true and natural Son of God, became man, with flesh and blood like that of any other human; that He became incarnate for our sakes in order that we might enter into great glory, that our flesh and blood, skin and hair, hands and feet, stomach and back might reside in heaven as God does, and in order that we might boldly defy the devil and whatever else assails us.[121]

There is a connection among the miracle of the incarnation, God's will to save, and the existential comfort these give to faith. Like the ancient church and the Eastern churches throughout the centuries, Luther has the ability to hear Gospel in the incarnation, God's pursuit of nearness to humanity, and his incorporation into the life of humanity characterized as it is by sin and death. Nevertheless, Jesus' special work for our salvation—the cross, reconciliation, and his resurrection—in connection with the incarnation is never far from Luther's thought.[122] He

---

120 WA 17/2:326.11ff. Cf. WA 10/1.1:236.11ff., 243.7ff.; 46:631.17ff.; and especially LW 22:112 (WA 46:633.2ff.): "The same Word, which became man, Mary suckled and carried in her arms as any other mother does her child. He came to men, lived and dwelt among them. Thus it was no ghost but a true man, 'taking the form of a servant,' as St. Paul says (Phil. 2:7), 'being born in the likeness of man' with regard to seeing, hearing, speaking, eating, drinking, sleeping, and waking, so that all who saw and heard Him were constrained to confess and say that He was a true and natural man." Concerning the significance of Christ's true humanity for the knowledge of God, see Wolf, "Die Christusverkündigung bei Luther," 68f.; and Loewenwich, *Luther und das Johanneische Christentum*, 35ff., especially 38.

121 LW 22:110 (WA 46:631.27ff.). Cf. WA 46:624.24ff.

122 For example, WA 46:624ff., 632.21ff., 669.1ff. The works to which *Luther and World Mission*, 74n125, refer show to what breadth Luther speaks of Christ's atoning death and the victory of the resurrection over the forces of depravity.

often includes both becoming man and the death on the cross under the concept "incarnation."

In this context, Luther also refers to the divine glory of Jesus Christ, that he is the only begotten Son or true God, that he has all authority to help and to save. Luther's translation of and the commentary on John 1:14b show that the reformer jealously guards Christ's true divinity: "Und wir sahen seine Herrligkeit . . . als des eingeboren Sons vom Vater."[123] He also supports this doctrine with a long list of texts from both the Old and New Testaments. The *Logos* (Christ) shares in or is the mediator in creation (see Luther's commentary on John 1:1–3). Through the words spoken from heaven, Jesus is certified to be God's beloved Son (Mark 1:11 and parallels). Jesus' divine power has been displayed by signs and wonders. In the crucifixion and resurrection, Christ has defeated Satan, sin, and death. Luther emphasizes that Jesus Christ is called God's only begotten Son and is given divine glory and power in a clear word of Scripture (John 1:14 and supporting texts). We can become the children of God only through the only begotten Son.[124] In the 1537–1538 commentaries on John (and in other passages), one sees, however, how Luther holds together Christ's humanity and divinity:

> Thus the Word, through which all things are made and preserved, was made flesh, that is, man, was born according to the flesh from the seed of Abraham and David, dwelt among us, and redeemed us from the curse and the power of the devil. By virtue of His incarnation and His eternal and glorious divinity we poor mortals who believe in His name became children of God, and God becomes our Father . . . (Rom. 1:4) . . . . We must treasure this text and take comfort from it in hours of sadness and temptation. Whoever lays hold of it in faith is lifted out of his distress, for he is a child of eternal bliss. And to this honor he falls heir through the only-begotten Son, who is God from eternity. . . . That Jesus Christ is very God and very man, the only-begotten Son of the Father, begotten of Him in eternity, and born of the Virgin Mary in time, and that believers in Him are redeemed from sin and all evil—this is our Christian faith. This alone makes us Christians. It makes us adopted sons of God, but not His natural children; for Christ, our Head, alone is the natural, true, and only-begotten Son of God the Father.[125]

---

123 WADB 6:327.

124 See WA 10/1.1:244.6ff.; 17/2:326.16ff.; especially 46:634.37ff., 635. 21ff., 637f. Concerning Christ as true God, see Wolf, "Die Christusverkündigung bei Luther," 56ff.; and Ebeling, *Evangelische Evangelienauslegung*, 241ff.

125 LW 22:115–16 (WA 46:635.40ff., 636.8ff., 636.21ff.). That Jesus is God's Son in a way other than the saints are children of God and that he is the origin of the divine childhood of all believers, see WA 46:637.30ff., 638.10ff., 638.17ff.; 10/1.1:245.6ff.

The texts show how Luther defends the truths about Christ and at the same time attempts to explain how these truths can be used by existential faith. We have excellent examples of this in Luther's frequently occurring paradigm: *historia et fructus (usus) historiae*.[126]

For Luther, this rule always applies: The person is such as his works are. Luther is interested in explaining the natures and the power of Jesus Christ, to speak of what he does and gives. Discussion of his saving works (*factum*) and their existential use (*usus facti*) through faith are connected with what Luther writes about the central words of John's prologue: "full of grace and truth" (John 1:14). In his writings from the 1520s, Luther finds in these words a summary of the Gospel and a stronghold for faith.[127] In the thorough exposition of John (1537–1538), Luther spares no words to describe the situation of all Adam's children under sin, God's wrath, and judgment. Even those who believe in Christ sin. Into this situation, the prologue inserts a powerful promise that summarizes the entire Gospel of the power, the glory, and the unconditional and overflowing grace of Jesus Christ. He is the only one without sin. Therefore he can make the children of Adam who live under sin into children of God. As the Son enjoys the grace and goodwill of the Father, so all who receive the Son and believe in him are clothed in the fullness of grace and truth without works of the Law and without deserving such grace.[128]

Luther makes similar comments on the words "From the fullness of his grace we have all received one blessing after another" (John 1:16). Natural humanity is not only deficient in its knowledge of God, it also lies under God's wrath and judgment because of its sin. In Christ the fullness of grace and truth exists without human works and synergism, but only through faith.[129]

Luther contrasts the way of the Law and the way of grace to salvation when he comments on John 1:17: "For the law was given through Moses; grace and truth

---

126 See Öberg, "Mission und Heilsgeschichte," 30f., with citations from Luther's Christmas, Good Friday, and Easter sermons.

127 LW 52:88 (WA 10/1.1:246.1ff., 246.20ff.): " 'Full of grace and truth.' These two words Scripture normally places next to each other. 'Grace' means that everything he is and does is pleasing in the sight of God. 'Truth' means that everything he is and does is good from the start and right in him; there is nothing in him that is not pleasing and upright. The opposite is the case with men: there is nothing but lack of grace and falseness so that everything they do is displeasing to God. . . . There is no need to look for the most solid portion of this Gospel. It is all solid and important, laying a foundation for the article of faith that Christ is true God and man and that, without grace, nature, free will, and works are nothing but lies, sin, error, and heresy—contrary to the views of the papists and the Pelagians." Cf. WA 15:803.38ff.; 17/2:326.26ff.

128 WA 46:636.40ff., 637.17ff.

129 WA 46:649–57.

came through Jesus Christ." God's Law is good, holy, and life-giving (Romans 7:10, 12; Acts 7:53). Because of sin, human beings are unable to keep the Law, so they are placed under judgment and death. The Law continues to be a great blessing for civil vocations and secular work in society, but the Law never leads to salvation, to grace, and to truth. Concerning salvation, there is a definite difference between Law and Gospel, between those who, with works of the Law, approach God and are laid low and those who, through faith in the Gospel, have fellowship with God. The Law and the Gospel do their own work and have two types of disciples. The Law shows what should be done. Its task is to show that we have not kept God's command and are sinful (*officium spiritualis legis*). Therefore the Law and the Gospel ought not be confused. Whoever believes in God's Son shares in grace and truth, but whoever trusts the Law for salvation is a slave to the Law and is completely beyond salvation. The knowledge of grace and truth or the knowledge of God is won only through the Gospel, the Spirit, and faith.[130] Faith is distinct from all legalistic, moralistic, and intellectual models of salvation.[131]

In his exposition of John's prologue (1537–1538), Luther hones and summarizes his understanding of natural and revealed knowledge of God. He emphasizes the concluding verse of the prologue: "No one has ever seen God, but God the One and Only, who is at the Father's side, has made him known" (John 1:18). Luther discusses his own questions and those of the Scholastic theologians in the *Larger Commentary on Galatians*. How can Romans 1:19ff. and 2:14f. be harmonized with John 1:17f.?[132]

---

130 WA 46:657–65, especially LW 22:144 (WA 46:662.1ff.): "The Law, given through Moses, is indeed a Law of life, righteousness, and everything good. But far more was accomplished through Christ. He comes and fills the empty hand and purse; He brings with Him the fulfillment of the Law's precepts and demands. He supplies grace and truth, and the means that enable me to keep the First, the Second, and the Third Commandment. Thus I acquire a trust and a faith in God as my Father, and I begin to praise His name with a cheerful heart and to hallow His name. But from what source does this come to me? It is not attributable to my own ability, nor is all this attainable by my merits and by my performance of the works of the Law. No, we owe it all to our illumination by the Holy Spirit, our regeneration by the Word of God, and our faith in Christ." See also Loewenich, *Luther und das Johanneische Christentum*, 32ff.

131 See Josefson, *Den naturliga teologins problem hos Luther*, 37f., 60ff., 79ff., 104ff.; and Olsson, *Schöpfung, Vernunft und Gesetz in Luthers Theologie*, 39ff., 55ff., 66ff. See also Öberg, *Himmelrikets nycklar och kyrklig bot i Luthers teologi*, 138ff., which includes a thorough discussion concerning the treatment of the Law/Gospel theme by Luther scholars.

132 WA 46:666.11–667.6. Concerning Luther's later opinions on John 1:18, see Harnack, *Luthers Theologie*, 1:70ff.; and Josefson, *Den naturliga teologins problem hos Luther*, 69ff.

Luther holds fast to Paul's words about the knowledge of God written on the heart and knowledge of the Law, making all people responsible and without excuse.[133] Luther criticizes the Scholastics' unfortunate interest in and too eager pursuit of a theoretical epistemological solution to the issue of natural and revealed knowledge of God. For Luther, the only solution is to distinguish the knowledge that the Law gives from a true knowledge of God given through the Gospel and faith in God's Son. God has provided both the Law and the Gospel so humanity might learn to know him, what he commands, demands, and gives. The issue is about two types of knowledge of God: *cognitio legalis* and *cognitio euangelica*. In his commentary on the final verse of John's prologue, Luther identifies the natural knowledge of God with a knowledge of God's Law, equating *cognitio naturalis* with *cognitio legalis*. Distinguishing the legal from an evangelical knowledge of the Law solves the superficial contradiction between Romans 1:19ff. and John 1:17f.[134]

The Law and a knowledge of God and his will is written on our hearts (Romans 2:15). The Law given through Moses may appear to be more clear, but natural knowledge is, to a large degree, identical with the external commands of the Decalogue's second table. All reasonable people know that it is wrong to disobey father, mother, and ruling authority; to commit adultery; to steal; or to curse. Even in non-Christian lands, laws condemn such behavior. However, we do see people abuse their natural knowledge of the Law, especially the unrighteous who have great success and act freely. But everyone who breaks the commandments (if they are reasonable people and not Epicureans) experiences in their consciences the judgment of God's Law. The Law written on the heart accuses when the letter of the Law is broken. Luther does not speak of reason's "inherent principles" nor does he claim that reason produces ethical norms. He does, however, claim that by nature we already know the major points of the Law and the fact that God wants to give all good things and to help humanity in its earthly problems.[135] When

---

133 WA 46:666.20ff., 668.6ff.

134 LW 22:150 (WA 46:667.7ff.): "Someday this question is going to cause trouble. But you must learn to answer it in the following way: There are two kinds of knowledge of God: the one is the knowledge of the Law; the other is the knowledge of the Gospel. For God issued the Law and the Gospel that He might be known through them." Cf. LW 22:151 (WA 46:668.9ff.): "Reason can arrive at a 'legal knowledge' of God. It is conversant with God's Commandments and can distinguish between right and wrong. The philosophers, too, had this knowledge of God. But the knowledge of God derived from the Law is not the true knowledge of Him, whether it be the Law of Moses or the Law instilled into our hearts." See Josefson, *Den naturliga teologins problem hos Luther*, 70ff. Cf. the literature referred to in 78n138 and to Wolf, "Martin Luther," 13f.; and Ebeling, *Evangelische Evangelienauslegung*, 254.

135 WA 46:667.10ff., 667.34ff., 668.13ff., 668.22ff. Cf. *Luther and World Mission*, 32ff., 40ff.

harshly indicting the false and asocial worship of God by monks, Luther notes that unbelievers and philosophers actually know God better and do what is required better than the monks. But the knowledge of unbelievers and philosophers is nevertheless *cognitio legalis*, not a true, saving knowledge of God.[136]

The only true knowledge of God is that received through faith in the Gospel of Christ's incarnation, atoning death, and resurrection from the dead. This true knowledge is not the Law's ambiguous, theoretical, and one-sided knowledge of God and God's will. The only true knowledge of God is the evangelical knowledge of grace, mercy, and truth in Jesus Christ. "It doesn't grow up in our garden," says Luther.[137] What we need is a superrational, heaven-revealed knowledge of God's will to save and of his mercy toward sinners who live under the Law. Few theologians have been able to express the radicality of the Gospel and grace as Luther does. No one understands this true knowledge through creation, through the law written on the human heart, nor even through Moses' Law. Through the Law, one gets to know only God's left, condemning, and killing hand. For a true knowledge of God one must pass through *cognitio legalis* and insight into one's own guilt and condemnation and come to the knowledge of God and Christ, a knowledge borne by the Gospel and grace. That is what John 1:18 tells us: "No one has ever seen God, but God the One and Only, who is at the Father's side, has made him known." The faith of the heathen and often even the faith of the papists is not only imperfect but also perverted and characterized by works of the Law. There is an unbridgeable chasm between knowing God through Moses and the Law and knowing God through Christ and the Gospel.[138]

---

136 WA 46:668.28ff.

137 See LW 22:152–53.

138 LW 22:152–53 (WA 46:669.1ff.): "The other sort of knowledge of God emerges from the Gospel. There we learn that all the world is by nature an abomination before God, subject to God's wrath and the devil's power, and is eternally damned. From this the world could not extricate itself except through God's Son, who lies in the bosom of the Father. He became man, died, and rose again from the dead, extinguishing sin, death, and devil. This is the true and thorough knowledge and way of thinking about God; it is called the knowledge of grace and truth, the 'evangelical knowledge' of God. But this knowledge does not grow up in our garden, and nature knows nothing at all about it. Reason has only a left-handed and a partial knowledge of God, based on the law of nature and of Moses; for the Law is inscribed in our hearts. But the depth of divine wisdom and of the divine purpose, the profundity of God's grace and mercy, and what eternal life is like—of these matters reason is totally ignorant. This is hidden from reason's view. It speaks of these with the same authority with which a blind man discusses color" (Luther cites John 1:18). Cf. LW 22:153 (WA 46:669.22ff.): "Reason is confined to the first type of knowledge of God, which proceeds from the Law; and it speaks a vague language. All Turks, Jews, papists, Tartars, and heathen concede the

Therefore theologians should refrain from discussing salvation on the basis of the Law and natural knowledge of it. Instead, they should focus on knowing the God who is revealed through Jesus Christ and faith. This is the true art and the true wisdom that all the saints from the beginning of time (Genesis 3:15) have exercised. In the natural law and in Moses' Law, God remains unknown and hidden. Only through the grace and truth that is revealed to humanity through Jesus Christ and the Gospel does humanity get to know God and God's heart. No law of any kind can lead to wisdom and salvation.

Even if Luther in many ways assigns positive tasks to the Law and its work, he reacts here precisely as violently as he does in the *Larger Commentary on Galatians* against the practice of associating the Law with salvation or the true knowledge of God. The true knowledge of God is not a fleshly or earthly striving but is attained only through revelation from God alone, through the preaching of the Gospel.[139]

Summary

Luther in his commentaries on John's prologue is critical of the Scholastic theologians and their teaching of a legalistic way to salvation. (1) Luther considers fallen humanity to be so depraved that it always perverts natural law and Moses' Law. (2) Therefore fallen humanity pursues God's goodwill through personal performance (*opera legis*). (3) By nature, fallen humanity does not know and perceive God's will to save or his mercy toward sinners. That is not the way of divine mercy revealed to humanity in Christ. For Luther, it is more important to emphasize God in Jesus Christ and the Gospel rather than God's transcendence. The Scriptures show that from the beginning (Genesis 3:15) Christ illuminated the path of the saints and revealed God's grace and truth.[140] Luther says the Gospel's

---

existence of a God, the Creator of heaven and earth, who, as they say, makes life contingent on our observation of His commandments and prohibitions. The pope goes a step beyond this and also speaks about Christ, but what he says is merely historical. But the fact and the knowledge that all men are born in sin and are damned, that Christ, the Son of God, is the only source of grace, and that man is saved solely through Jesus Christ, who is the grace and truth—this is not Mosaic or legal knowledge but evangelical and Christian knowledge." Cf. WA 46:672.21ff., 673.1ff., on Genesis 33:20. See also Loewenich, *Luther und das Johanneische Christentum*, 38f.

139 WA 46:670.2ff., especially: "That is the spiritual and Christian knowledge of God. The other is carnal and earthly and issues from reason, for it is written in our hearts. But this knowledge must be proclaimed from above and take form in the heart; that is, one must learn that God confers grace through His beloved Son. Therefore behold how blind the world is in its way of knowing God. Thus we must take note of this plain and clear text, which informs us that no one has ever seen God; for it is true that no one, of himself, can know God in the evangelical sense. The barefooted friars were much blinder than the heathen" (LW 22:154 [WA 670.19ff.]).

140 LW 22:155–56 (WA 46:671.22ff.): "To summarize, we have been so abominably cor-

way to salvation is something completely new and distinct from the way of the Law and works. Divine revelation in the Word places all people under sin and judgment. At the same time, the only possibility for salvation is offered in Christ. That possibility surpasses the knowledge of reason and nature and is indeed incomprehensible. Through the Law and reason, jurists, philosophers, and the heathen have seen only God's back. Through Christ alone can one see God's face, that is, his will to save.[141]

God's history of promise and salvation indicates that the grace revealed in Christ must be preached among all people; otherwise it does not become known. Luther couples these two categorical theses: (1) Christ is the only revealer of God, God's heart, and God's will to save; and (2) Christ must be preached for the Gospel to create faith and be received in faith.[142] This second thesis is a powerful

---

rupted by sin that we not only know nothing about our first and natural knowledge of God any longer, but we have also defected from the righteousness of the Law and fallen into lies. With our own fabricated works we presumed to reconcile God. Thus reason recognizes God from the Law of Moses, as we find stated in Rom. 1:19, 32. But in the sense of the Gospel reason knows nothing of God. For this is a new revelation from heaven, which not only acquaints us with, and instructs us in, the Ten Commandments but also informs us that we mortals are all conceived in sin and are lost, and that no one keeps the Law, but that those who want to be saved will be saved solely through the grace and truth of Jesus Christ. Here is the depth of His nature; here is the will of God. [*Das ist der abgrund seiner natur und Göttlicher wille.*] . . . [T]here is no salvation or knowledge of God outside Christ. No one is approved by God unless he is marked with the grace and truth of the Son. This knowledge is concealed from reason. Even today the papists and all the others are ignorant of it. . . . Thus after the Fall Adam knew God through the Son, as did all the patriarchs and prophets. They hoped for the advent of the promised Messiah. Through Him they received grace from God. They did not linger with the Law . . . . [I]t is impossible to see God by means of the Law or by reason. No one can fathom Him, or climb to His heights. He is too lofty. He is seen only by those born of God, not by those born of the blood [John 1:13]."

141 LW 22:156–57 (WA 46:672.14ff.): "Whence comes the knowledge of the God of grace and truth? It is given by the only-begotten Son of God. The Son of God, who is in God and who Himself is God, is indispensable for this. For He comes from the Father, and He knows the truth. There is no other doctor, teacher, or preacher who resides in the Godhead and is in the bosom of the Father but the one Doctor, Christ. . . . Who else could have revealed God to us? Consult all the law books of the jurists, all the books of the philosophers and of all heathen. You will find that they do not exceed the knowledge of God contained in the Law of Moses, enjoining us not to steal, not to commit perjury, and to love government and parents. To know God from the Law with His back turned to us is a left-handed knowledge of Him. Therefore walk around God and behold His true countenance and His real plan. God is seen properly only in Christ. . . . [T]his is the true mind of God. We must depend on Christ; this is the true knowledge of God."

142 WA 46:670.21ff., 672.33ff., 673.8ff., 673.31ff. See especially LW 22:59–60 (WA

motivation for the church to spread the Gospel. Grace and truth in Christ must not be allowed to become simply one idea among others. So people might learn to know God, the Gospel must be preached to human hearts under the Law, sin, and death.

The Church, the Priesthood of All Believers, and the Ministry of Preaching

We have seen that Luther stressed that a saving knowledge of God comes only through revelation. This revelation, this wisdom and faith, has its center in Jesus Christ and must be communicated to people through the Word and Sacraments. And in this respect, Luther never differentiates between what is relevant for the domestic work of the church and for mission abroad. Luther considers writings from the first great mission epoch of the church to be guidance for his own church reformation—except in some external matters concerning order. Luther integrates church and mission. Luther knew that foreign mission has its own special contexts and must employ methods particular to those contexts, but, as a matter of principle, he never differentiated between church and mission. For Luther, the church of Christ always preaches the Gospel to all countries, however great the concentration of Christians may be. With this, we now have to consider the human factor in the work of God's reign. For this activity, organization, workers, and representatives are needed—laypeople and the ordained ministry of preaching as communicators of the Gospel. Luther's perspective on these issues is basic for his missiology.

The Word, the Gospel, and the Church

Luther's ecclesiology is theocentric. God—Father, Son, and Spirit—is ultimately the working subject, the driving force, and the guarantee of the church's growth and existence. The church is created and sustained by God through those works he already has accomplished and those he continues to do until the coming of his reign of glory. Luther emphasizes that God builds and gathers his church through the Word/Gospel. The Gospel message must be pure and clear and must place Christ in the center. When the church seeks to fulfill the Great Commission, one should always remember that, ultimately, the Father, the Son, and the Holy Spirit, through the Word and Sacraments and through human means, builds,

---

46:587.8ff.): "Thus throughout the dispersion of the Christian Church among all the peoples of the world, from the east to the west and from the north to the south, she must be firmly united in this, that she acknowledges Christ as her sole Light and that she knows and preaches none other than Christ. Thank God, we are doing this, making all our instruction, writings, and sermons conform to it."

expands, and sustains the church or God's reign in time. For Luther, church and mission is ultimately the work of God (*missio Dei*).[143]

In his ecclesiology and missiology, Luther stresses Christ's lordship through the Gospel in the Word and Sacraments. He rejects the Roman Catholic Church's exaggerated view of Christ's work through vicars or Christ's representatives. The reformer also criticizes the enthusiasts' accent on the baptism of the Spirit and discipleship. The ascended Lord Jesus Christ in his kingship and Melchizedek-like priesthood builds his church and congregation through the manifold forms of the Gospel. Emphasizing this ensures the church's Gospel-centered character. The church is threatened as soon as ministry's desire to dominate is allowed to develop and as soon as the Gospel begins to be interpreted as a new law (*nova lex*) in either a Roman Catholic or enthusiastic manner.[144] We will see in chapter 3 how impor-

---

143 See Aulén, *Till belysning af den lutherska kyrkoidén*, 7–79. Kinder, *Der evangelische Glaube und die Kirche*, 81ff., 85ff., 103ff., has many valuable and helpful insights. See also Öberg, *Himmelrikets nycklar och kyrklig bot i Luthers teologi*, 459ff., with references; as well as Aagaard, "Lutheran Tradition and Mission Theology," 6; and Becker, ". . . like a traveling rain shower . . ." 27f., about how the Gospel is introduced into the world by God. A helpful Luther text is "That a Christian Assembly (1523)," LW 39:305 (WA 11:408.8ff., 408.16ff.): "The sure mark by which the Christian congregation can be recognized is that the pure gospel is preached there. For just as the banner of an army is the sure sign by which one can know what kind of lord and army have taken to the field, so, too, the gospel is the sure sign by which one knows where Christ and his army are encamped. . . . Thus we are certain that there must be Christians wherever the gospel is, no matter how few and how sinful and weak they may be. Likewise, where the gospel is absent and human teachings rule, there no Christians live but only pagans, no matter how numerous they are and how holy and upright their life may be." Cf. a 1525 sermon on the Great Commission: "Dic mihi, an verbum sit uber Christenheit an econtra? muss verbum an die Christenheit glauben vel econtra? Verbum potest esse sine ecclesia, non econtra. Per verbum generatur, ergo dicere cogeris, quod ecclesia geringer quam verbum, quare dicis Ecclesiam uber das Wort?" (WA 17/1:99.7ff.). Cf. among the numerous texts WA 7:721.9ff.; 12:191.16; 29:510.18ff.; 38:252.24ff.; 42:334.12ff., 423.37ff.

144 Concerning Christ's lordship through the Gospel, see Vajta, *Die Theologie des Gottesdienstes bei Luther*, 119f.; Kinder, *Der evangelische Glaube und die Kirche*, 65ff., with the references on 57f.; Forck, *Die Königsherrschaft Jesu Christi bei Luther*, especially 85ff.; Persson, *Kyrkans ämbete som Kristus-representation*, 283ff.; and Öberg, *Himmelrikets nycklar och kyrklig bot i Luthers teologi*, 105ff. In connection with Psalm 110, Luther says that the Aaronic priesthood is characterized by God's wrath while Christ's kingship/priesthood is characterized through the Gospel by righteousness, grace, comfort, peace, and blessedness. See WA 41:183.15ff. Cf. WA 1:703.30ff. and 31/1:533.27ff. The distinguishing mark of the church is the Gospel. Cf. WA 10/1.1:711.11ff.; 14:579.20ff.; 25:248.16ff.; 31/2:264.21ff.; 40/1:562.12ff.; etc.

tant Christ's lordship through the Gospel is in Luther's understanding of world mission.

As we have seen in the section on humans as *cooperatores Dei* (p. 25ff.), Luther distinguished between the earthly regiment as a power given to humanity and the spiritual regiment as the power that God has retained.[145] This means that the Trinity is the acting subject in the work of the church through the Word and Sacraments. That gives a marked realism to Luther's view of the Word and Sacraments in the life of the church. The Father, the Son, and the Spirit are actually present with the fullness of grace to awaken and strengthen the faith of the people.

However, this theocentric view does not exclude the fact that God uses people to accomplish his will in both earthly and spiritual matters. In *Bondage of the Will*, Luther writes:

> ...but [God] does not work in us without us, because it is for this he has created and preserved us, that he might work in us and we might cooperate with him, whether outside his Kingdom through his general omnipotence, or inside his Kingdom by the special virtue of his Spirit.... But he does not work without us, because it is for this very thing he has recreated and preserved us, that he might work in us and we might cooperate with him. Thus it is through us he preaches, shows mercy to the poor, comforts the afflicted.[146]

However much Luther sets the work of the Father, the Son, and the Spirit in the center, here and elsewhere Luther shows the importance of the testimony of laypeople and of the ordained ministry of the Word and Sacraments.

From 1519 until his death, Luther emphasized the following scheme of soteriological economy: the Father, the Son, and the Spirit; the Word and Sacraments; the testimony of laypeople and the ordained ministry of the Word and Sacraments; and a created and sustained faith. Throughout his life, but especially after the dispute with the spiritualism of the enthusiasts, Luther emphasized the necessary connection between the means of grace and faith. No one can receive saving faith without the Word and Sacraments. Wherever the true Gospel is in motion, faith and the community of saints are created. The church as the institution of the means of grace and the spiritual importance of faith are connected to each other. Luther often points out that one does not receive grace and the forgiveness of sins through some kind of inwardness or by "staring at the sky." The Gospel of the church and mission is the instrument of God's salvation, something unavoidably necessary. Forgiveness of sins and eternal life are received only where the Father, the Son, and the Spirit communicate these blessings in the means of

---

145 Törnvall, *Andligt och världsligt regemente hos Luther*, 89f.; and Vajta, *Die Theologie des Gottesdienstes bei Luther*, 203f.

146 LW 33:243 (WA 18:754.5ff.).

grace.[147] These general rules of the economy of grace do not limit God's power. But it has pleased God to accomplish his work through the church. The task of the church to spread the Gospel is an important part of the history of salvation. The task of the church and mission is immeasurably important.

Even the concept *notae ecclesiae* is, in Luther, determined primarily with a view toward God's salvation and the expansion of the church in the world. In Luther's view, neither the right kind of hierarchy (a Roman Catholic criterion) nor the holy lives of the church members (an enthusiast criterion) are the criteria for being a true church. Instead, the signs of the church are primarily the church-creating means of salvation that rest on divine mandate and promise. Luther spoke of the Word or the Gospel as *symbolum unicum* or *unica nota*. But he often names also the Word, Baptism, Communion, the power of the keys, and the ministry of the church as the signs of the church (*notae ecclesiae*). Through them God creates and sustains faith and the church. Through them the church emerges from hiddenness so the individual can orient himself or herself.[148]

The Church as the Communion of Saints

We have emphasized what, according to Luther, creates and sustains the church. But his ecclesiology is by no means adequately described by speaking only about the church-creating and incorporating work of the Father, the Son, and the Holy Spirit through the Gospel. As early as the pre-Reformation lectures on the Psalms (1513–1515), Luther speaks about the church as *Gemeinde, Volk der*

---

147 Cf. Öberg, *Himmelrikets nycklar och kyrklig bot i Luthers teologi*, 108ff., 298ff., with the references to Luther's writings and secondary literature. See also Vajta, *Die Theologie des Gottesdienstes bei Luther*, 118; and Ivarsson, *Predikans uppgift*, 21f., on how Christ comes to us through the Gospel. Some passages on the subject include WA 6:560.33ff.; 7:50.33ff.; 10/1.1:14.1, 249.31ff.; 28:314.1ff.; 30/2:487.12ff.; 40/2:518.30ff.; 41:454.18ff. See especially LC II 38–39: "Neither you nor I could ever know anything about Christ, or believe in him and receive him as Lord, unless these were offered to us and bestowed on our hearts through the preaching of the gospel by the Holy Spirit. . . . In order that this treasure might not remain buried but be put to use and enjoyed, God has caused the Word to be published and proclaimed, in which he has given the Holy Spirit to offer and apply to us this treasure, this redemption" (K-W, 436; *BSLK*, 654). Cf. SA (*BSLK*, 453f.).

148 See Kinder, *Der evangelische Glaube und die Kirche*, 103ff.; and Öberg, *Himmelrikets nycklar och kyrklig bot i Luthers teologi*, 94ff., with references to Luther texts and to secondary literature. From the Luther material, one might mention WA 11:408.8ff.; 25:97.27ff. on the Word/Gospel as *unica nota*; WA 7:720.32ff. on the Word and the Sacraments; and WA 38:252.27ff.; 50:628ff.; 51:478ff. on definitions with further signs of the church, among them prayer, the keys and the ministry, the cross, and the suffering of the church.

Glaubenden, populus Christi, congregatio sanctorum, and *populus fidelium*. Later, in his struggle to oppose the hierarchical layering and the exaggeration of the church as a sacred institution, Luther clearly pronounces that the church is and consists of the people of God gathered through the Gospel and in faith, the communion of the saints (*congregatio* or *communio sanctorum*), and the body of Christ. Through the same Savior and the same Gospel, sacraments, and justification through faith in Christ, the church constitutes—despite different gifts of grace, duties, and vocations—a holy fellowship in which all are equal through the same grace and the same faith. The church is not only the reign of the Gospel but also a fellowship of people, characterized by faith in Christ and love, a spiritual body united with its head, Christ, through faith in him.[149]

The *communio sanctorum* is constituted, however, not as a voluntary association of repentant believers and saints. Luther is just as emphatic in his rejection of the Anabaptist faith-fellowships, such as those established by Andreas Bodenstein von Karlstadt and Thomas Münzer, as he is in his rejection of the hierarchical, canonical Roman Church. In the congregationalism of the Anabaptists, the voluntary decision, the degree of faith, and the holiness of the individual members becomes too central. Luther does not speak about how one associates with sanctified faith-fellowships, but how one is won by the Gospel, is given faith, and is, thereby, incorporated into the church/congregation. Luther's ecclesiology is expansive—incorporating and not exclusive, demarcating and sectarian.[150] The church—built by Father, Son, and Spirit through the Gospel, by unconditional

---

149 See Althaus, *Communio sanctorum*, 37ff., 54ff.; Althaus, *Die Theologie Martin Luthers*, 249ff., 254ff.; Kinder, *Der evangelische Glaube und die Kirche*, 78ff.; and Öberg, *Himmelrikets nycklar och kyrklig bot i Luthers teologi*, 461ff. These refer to the relevant secondary literature and to a number of Luther texts. Among the Luther texts, these can be mentioned: WA 6:292ff. (*communio* motif) and 6:310.30ff. (*corpus Christi* motif). Futhermore, *communio sanctorum* is a defining element of the Creed's "holy catholic church." Cf. WA 2:190.18ff., 415.28ff.; 6:606.33ff.; 50:624.14ff.; and LC II 51–52: "I believe that there is on earth a holy little flock and community of pure saints under one head, Christ. It is called together by the Holy Spirit in one faith, mind, and understanding. It possesses a variety of gifts, and yet is united in love without sect or schism. Of this community I also am a part and member, a participant and co-partner in all the blessings it possesses. I was brought into it by the Holy Spirit and incorporated into it through the fact that I have heard and still hear God's Word, which is the beginning point for entering it" (K-W, 437–38; *BSLK*, 657; see the entire section beginning with paragraph 43). About the church as *corpus Christi* united through a common and right faith in the Father and the Son through the Word and Baptism, see the sermon on Ephesians 4:4 in WA 22:299.18ff., 299.27ff. Cf. WA 31/1:15ff.; 40/1:662.2ff.; 50:624ff.

150 Cf. Kinder, *Der evangelische Glaube und die Kirche*, 81ff., and the quotation from the Large Catechism in the previous footnote.

grace and justification through faith alone—does not know any hopeless cases. The church does not seek the righteous, but through the Gospel, it grants forgiveness and life to sinners. The ship of the church carries many who appear to have failed in faith and life. Luther sometimes likens the church to a people under medical care, regaining health in a hospital.[151] One never ceases to be amazed at how Luther can maintain his optimism in his struggle with the Romanists and the enthusiasts and amid the discouraging incidents in the evangelical church and in individual lives. Through all, he trusted in God's power through the Word/Gospel.

What is meant, then, by the church's "holiness" in the communion of the holy, *communio sanctorum*? Luther argued that the holiness of the church is primarily the justification granted through faith in Christ. The church's uneven performances in this world speak against the idea that it is a fellowship of the holy people of God and Christ. True, faith and the Holy Spirit produce good fruit among people of faith, but human weakness, sin, factions, and errors always follow the church. The holiness and righteousness of the individual and of the church are, therefore, hidden under their opposites, just as Christ's holiness is hidden by the shame of the cross. Therefore those made holy by faith in Christ are condemned by the world, by reason, and by the legalists. One does not see the holiness of the church, yet one must believe in a holy church, says Luther. Luther allows talk about the church's sin, but he emphasizes that individual Christians and the church through faith in Christ are perfectly holy and righteous. Faith believes in something it cannot see: *Credo ecclesiam sanctam*. Faith confesses this despite the fact that apostles and thieves, the Virgin Mary, and the adulteress belong to the church. The well-known words from the *Larger Commentary on Galatians* are relevant: "The church is indeed holy, but it is a sinner at the same time."[152] Only the one whose ecclesiology is determined by the Gospel, faith, and justification through faith in God's Son can speak in this manner. This does not prevent the reformer from encouraging the justified in faith to live according to God's will, as he does, for example, in the commentaries on the New Testament's ethical teaching and *parenesis*. This fruit of faith, grace, and the Spirit is, however, always fallible and ought never to constitute a criterion for judging anyone's status before God. Faith and unbelief divide the world that exists in the church and nonchurch, and no person can draw a definitive line of demarcation between them.[153]

---

151 Cf. Öberg, *Himmelrikets nycklar och kyrklig bot i Luthers teologi*, 462f., 464ff. See also WA 15:726.7ff.; 20:369f.

152 LW 26:109 (WA 40/1:197.23f.).

153 See Althaus, *Communio sanctorum*, 42f.; Althaus, *Die Theologie Martin Luthers*, 252ff.; Kinder, *Der evangelische Glaube und die Kirche*, 97; and Olsson, "Kyrkans synlighet och

The realm of the means of grace (that is, of the empirical church) and the realm of true faith in Christ can never be split because faith is created and sustained by the Gospel. Nevertheless, these realms are not to be equated because not everyone who "belongs" to the church possesses the true life in Christ and faith. Here, Luther believes, one should carefully guard against the desire to judge and against naïveté. We should invest all our power in edifying, helping, and bearing those who are outside the fellowship so they are reinstated in a true faith and Christian lifestyle. This happens primarily through the preaching of the Word and the loving care of believers. On the other hand, church discipline must have its place in a church that is conscious of its responsibility.[154]

As previously stated, Luther believed individual Christians and the church always struggle with God's opponent, Satan. Satan tempts, distorts God's Word, and perverts faith in God's Son. He splits the church. Luther's primary weapon is always the positive preaching of God's Word. Although he never believed that one could create a true church through discipline, at times Luther used church discipline, especially in doctrinal matters, because false doctrine compromised the Gospel. Even then, church discipline was primarily pastoral, a means to be helpful. Such discipline relied on the power and authority of the Word. Still, Luther believed no church or congregation in this age could become perfect and completely pure. The enthusiasts who sought to realize such an ideal had forgotten

---

fördoldhet enligt Luther," 348ff. Cf. Öberg, *Himmelrikets nycklar och kyrklig bot i Luthers teologi*, 463ff., with numerous examples from Luther's writings. Some good examples include WABr 6:227.12ff.: "Christus hie auff erden ynn den seinen schwach, gebrechlich und ergerlich sein mus, wie er selbs spricht: Selig ist, der sich nicht ergert an mir [Matthew 11:6], Und seine Christenheit also lesst verbergen mit trubsal, rotten, gebrechen und schwacheit, das man sie mit der vernnufft nicht finden kan, sondern allein mit dem glauben ersehen und bey dem Euangelio erkennen muss, wie wir ym Credo sagen: Ich gleube eine heilige Christliche kirche. Ob nu wol die Christen viel fruchte des geists bringen und heiliglich leben, So bleiben doch da neben viel sunde und gebrechen." Cf. LW 33:89 (WA 18:652.23f.): "What, then, are we to do? The Church is hidden, the saints are unknown." Cf. WA 34/2:518.1ff., 518.17ff., and especially the words from the *Larger Commentary on Galatians*: "Therefore we correctly confess in the Creed that we *believe* a holy church. For it is invisible, dwelling in the Spirit, in an 'unapproachable' place (1 Tim. 6:16); therefore its holiness cannot be seen. God conceals and covers it with weaknesses, sins, errors, and various offenses and forms of the cross in such a way that it is not evident to the senses anywhere. Those who are ignorant of this are immediately offended when they see the weaknesses and sins of those who have been baptized, have the Word, and believe; and they conclude that such people do not belong to the church. . . . Anyone who thinks this way turns the article of the Creed, 'I believe a holy church,' upside down; he replaces 'I believe' with 'I see'" (LW 27:84–85 [WA 40/2:106.19ff.]).

154 Öberg, *Himmelrikets nycklar och kyrklig bot i Luthers teologi*, 466ff., with cited texts.

Jesus' parable of the weeds and the wheat (Matthew 13:24–30, 36–42) and Paul's words that heresies and the church would always coexist (1 Corinthians 11:19). But Luther never condoned irresponsible passivity toward Satan's work in the church or among Christians.[155]

The Priesthood of All Believers and the Ordained Ministry of the Church

We cannot forget that Luther considered the church to be a tool for the expansion of the Gospel. The people of faith are created through the Word/Gospel; they also are involved in evangelization and mission, the business of all Christians. According to the Roman Catholic ecclesiology of Luther's time, official ecclesiastical power (*potestas ecclesiastica*) belonged only to the priests and the hierarchy. The church as a whole had received a priestly character, but the sacrament of ordination created a special priesthood that possessed the privilege of blessing, consecrating, and administering the sacraments. Through sacred ordination, the priest was given a unique, indelible sacramental character (*character indelebilis*), which through a chain of many ordinations went back to Christ. This view divided the church between priests and laypeople, making priests and the hierarchy mediators between God and people. The clergy were to communicate the blessings of salvation to laypeople.

Luther, however, asserted that the blessings of salvation were communicated to people through the Word and Sacraments, and these were the instruments of the Spirit and of grace. The ministries of the church served these means of grace. Furthermore, Luther stressed the important biblical concept of the priesthood of all Christian believers (*sacerdotium omnium*). On the basis of Deuteronomy 7:6; John 6:45; 1 Corinthians 14:30 (in his earlier writings); 1 Peter 2:5, 9; and Revelation 1:6; 5:10; 20:6, the reformer asserted the nearly subversive thesis that all Christians are priests. He wanted to emphasize the fundamental unity and equality of the laypeople and the ordained in *communio sanctorum*. Because all Christians constitute the body of Christ and possess the same Baptism, Gospel, and faith, they also are one single spiritual and priestly people. That means all Christians can approach God in faith and prayer without a mediator and offer their lives as a thankoffering to God and neighbor. Furthermore, all Christians have the responsibility to see that the Gospel is preached. They themselves witness to and proclaim God's salvation wherever in the world they may live. In emergencies they may baptize and preach publicly. The priesthood of all believers means that all believers in Christ are equal and have authority in him. Therefore only unbelief

---

155 Öberg, *Himmelrikets nycklar och kyrklig bot i Luthers teologi*, 470ff., 490ff., 494ff., 500ff.

disqualifies one from the priesthood of all believers. However, for Luther, the priesthood of all believers does not in itself grant one the right to preach in a congregation or to administer the sacraments because this is public ministry and ought to be performed by the publicly ordained ministers of the church.[156]

The priesthood of all believers, the *communio sanctorum*, has the responsibility for all the church's means of grace, services, and ministries. All Christians are commanded and responsible for preaching the Gospel. Where a true spiritual life exists through the Gospel, laypeople should not be deprived of their right and responsibility. According to Luther, though the Word and Sacraments in the church ought to be preached and administered publicly by a publicly called minister, the blessings of the Word, Baptism, Communion, and the power of the keys have, in principle, been entrusted by God/Christ to the entire church/congregation. In Luther's view, the clergy administer the means of grace as a mandate from both Christ and the congregation. Therefore the congregation must never be passed over when congregational priests are called and ordained. On the basis of the doctrines of *sacerdotium omnium* and *communio sanctorum,* Luther concludes that the church as a whole, the congregations, and all individual Christians have responsibility for the work of God's reign. This is not merely a matter of the preaching ministry. The broader responsibility and testimony of the congregation is also important in Luther's ecclesiology and missiology. Later Lutheranism often lost sight of the concrete *communio sanctorum* as the church became a place, an institution, and the priesthood.[157]

What place does the ministry of preaching have in Luther's theology? There is a connection between ecclesial ministry and the priesthood of all believers in the *communio sanctorum* in which the latter is the true subject for all the means of grace, the services, and the ministries. At the same time, a distinction is made between becoming a priest through Baptism, the Gospel, and faith and the ministry of preaching. Therefore the priesthood of all believers does not imply a general, public ministry of the Word and Sacraments that applies to all Christians.

---

156 See the following: Hök, "Luthers lära om kyrkans ämbete," 148; Brunotte, *Das geistliche Amt bei Luther*, 133ff.; Prenter, *Embedets guddommelige indstiftelse og det almindelige praestedømme hos Luther*; Lieberg, *Amt und Ordination*, 26, 45, 227ff.; Öberg, *Himmelrikets nycklar och kyrklig bot i Luthers teologi*, 60ff.; and Öberg, "Den lutherska reformationen och ordinationen," 60ff. Among the representative Luther texts, see WA 6:407.8ff., 408ff., 563ff.; 12:169ff.; 38:229.19ff.; 41:153.9ff.

157 Öberg, *Himmelrikets nycklar och kyrklig bot i Luthers teologi*, 67ff., with citations from Luther and a review of the secondary literature. Cf. also Aagaard, "Lutheran Tradition and Mission Theology," 6f.; and Aargaard, "Luther og laegfolket," 118f.

Luther holds together but differentiates the priesthood of all believers and the public ministry of preaching.[158]

For a century, Luther scholars have discussed how much Luther bases the ordained ministry on the priesthood of all believers and how much on divine institution. Some hold that the ministry of the church possessed only an authority delegated by the priesthood of all believers. But many have overinterpreted Luther's statements, claiming that Luther believed in some kind of natural right as the basis for the public call. They did not see that the *corpus Christi* motif cut through any theory of natural right and that Luther believed that the church's ministry also was given and established by God. According to Luther, God himself calls through the congregation's call to ministry. Thus the public ministry is not merely a question of human delegation of authority, but public ministry is the ministry of Word and Sacraments and rests on divine mandate.[159]

This relationship between the church/congregation and the divine institution of the ministry of preaching is made clear in "On the Councils and the Church (1539)." Here the ministry of preaching is listed as one of the signs of Christ's church (*notae ecclesiae*). Luther writes:

> [T]he church is recognized externally by the fact that it consecrates or calls ministers, or has offices that it is to administer. There must be bishops, pastors, or preachers, who publicly and privately give, administer, and use the aforementioned four things or holy possessions [namely, God's Word, Baptism, Holy Communion, and the power of the keys] in behalf of and in the name of the church, or rather by reason of their institution by Christ, as St. Paul states in Ephesians 4 [:8], "He received gifts among men . . ."—his gifts were that some should be apostles, some prophets, some evangelists, some teachers and governors, etc. . . . It must be entrusted to one person, and he alone should be allowed to preach, to baptize, to absolve, and to administer the sacraments. The others should be content with this arrangement and agree to it. Wherever you see this done, be assured that God's people, the holy Christian people, are present.[160]

Luther reckons that ordained ministry is not only something that the congregation grants but also a divine ordinance and institution. He uses elevated lan-

---

158 Brunotte, *Das geistliche Amt bei Luther*, 34–116, 154ff.; and Öberg, "Den lutherska reformationen och ordinationen," 61f.

159 See the studies about ministry as an authority delegated by the congregation or given by God in Brunotte, *Das geistliche Amt bei Luther*, 8ff., 118ff.; and Lieberg, *Amt und Ordination*, 113ff.

160 LW 41:154 (WA 50:632.36ff.).

guage to describe the loftiness and the necessity of the ecclesial ministry.[161] He speaks of the servants in the ministry of the church as the servants and legates of God and of Christ.[162] The ecclesial ministry is established to serve the congregation with the preaching of the Word, Baptism, Communion, and pastoral care. Consequently, it is a servant ministry, a *ministerium*, of the means of grace. This dynamic relationship between ministry and the means of grace is important. By it the ordained are prevented from bullying and tyranny. They are constantly held to the work that builds the body of Christ. Only the one who preaches the Gospel and administers the Sacraments rightly exercises his ordination.[163]

Because it is a public ministry (*ministerium publicum*), Luther always insists on a public call in connection with the congregation—especially after the beginning of the dispute with the enthusiasts.[164] Public ministers must be called publicly. The call of the congregation puts one into a ministry of preaching, not the wishes of the individual or his inner urge. Timothy and Titus assigned the ministry of preaching to trusted men after the congregation had been consulted. The inner call (*vocatio interna*) in and of itself is not sufficient ground. It is not always clearly experienced, and even the enthusiasts build their calls on it. The outer call (*vocatio externa*) is not based only on an inner call or on a subjective experi-

---

161 This idea exists already in an essay that is important for the priesthood of all believers—"To the Christian Nobility (1520)," LW 44:176 (WA 6:441.22ff.): "I am not referring here to popes, bishops, canons, and monks. God has not instituted these offices. . . . I want to speak only of the ministry which God has instituted, the responsibility of which is to minister word and sacrament to a congregation, among whom they reside." Cf. WA 6:440.20ff.; 8:550.16ff., 501.3ff., 501:18ff. Beginning about 1530, the ministry's divine institution is mentioned more often in Luther's writings. Cf. WA 28:470.39ff.; 30/2:554.9ff.; 38:240.24ff., 243.29f.; 41:241.39f.; WABr 10:255.18ff.; and many other passages. See also how Luther describes the ministry as "most important and necessary for all churches" (LW 53:124n1) and as *sanctum divinum ministerium* and *heiliges, liebe Pfarramt* in WA 38:423.21f., 425.1f., 243.29; 30/2:527.1ff., 554.2ff.

162 See Brunotte, *Das geistliche Amt bei Luther*, 118ff.; and Lieberg, *Amt und Ordination*, 108ff., 121ff., with many citations from Luther. Cf. also Öberg, *Himmelrikets nycklar och kyrklig bot i Luthers teologi*, 73, with the citations in the notes.

163 Hök, "Luthers lära om kyrkans ämbete," 142f.; Vajta, *Die Theologie des Gottesdienstes bei Luther*, 196ff.; Persson, *Kyrkans ämbete som Kristus-representation*, 285ff.; and Lieberg, *Amt und Ordination*, 19ff., 94ff. See also Öberg, *Himmelrikets nycklar och kyrklig bot i Luthers teologi*, 73f.

164 Concerning the public call, see Elert, *Morphologie des Luthertums*, 1:303ff.; Brunotte, *Das geistliche Amt bei Luther*, 174ff.; Lieberg, *Amt und Ordination*, 132ff.; Vajta, *Die Theologie des Gottesdienstes bei Luther*, 200, 216; Althaus, *Die Theologie Martin Luthers*, 284ff.; and Öberg, "Den lutherska reformationen och ordinationen," 64ff., 68ff.

ence, but one must be approved and called by others, taken into service, and bound to God's Word before God and people.[165]

The fact that the priesthood of all believers is responsible for ministry and witness is important, but this fact does not grant the public ministry of the Word and Sacraments to all Christians. In his 1530 exposition of Psalm 82, Luther speaks of the necessary, public call to the ministry of the Word.[166] Responding to a common misunderstanding of the priesthood of all believers, he writes: "It does not help their case to say that all Christians are priests. It is true that all Christians are priests, but not all are pastors. For to be a pastor one must be not only a Christian and a priest but must have an office and a field of work committed to him. This call and command make pastors and preachers."[167] In the *Larger Commentary on Galatians*, Luther explains how this should work out in practice:

> God calls in two ways, either by means or without means. Today He calls all of us into the ministry of the Word by a mediated call, that is, one that comes through means, namely, through man. But the apostles were called immediately by Christ Himself, as the prophets in the Old Testament had been called by God Himself. Afterwards the apostles called their disciples, as Paul called Timothy, Titus, etc. These men are called bishops, as in Titus 1:5ff.; and the bishops called their successors down to our own time, and so on to the end of the world. This is a mediated calling, since it is done by man. Nevertheless, it is divine. Thus when someone is called by a prince or a magistrate or me, he has his calling through man. Since the time of the apostles this has been the usual method of calling in the world. It should not be changed; it should be exalted, on account of the sectarians, who despise it and lay claim to another calling, by which they say that the Spirit drives them to teach. But they are liars and impostors, for they are being driven by a spirit who is not good but evil. . . . Therefore when I preach, baptize, or administer the sacraments, I do so as one who has a command and a call. For the voice of the Lord has come to me, not in some corner, as the sectarians boast, but through the mouth of a man who is carrying out his lawful right. But if one or two citizens were to ask me to preach, I should not follow such a private call; for this would open the window to the ministers of Satan.[168]

These quotations show how Luther bases the public call to the ministry of the church partly on the praxis of the early church and partly in view of the danger for factions if one is to build a public ministry only on the inner call. But what becomes of the congregation's fundamental right to call when Luther, in his state-

---

165 Öberg, "Den lutherska reformationen och ordinationen," 64f.

166 WA 31/1:210ff.

167 LW 13:65 (WA 31/1:211.16ff.).

168 LW 26:17–19 (WA 40/1:59.2ff.).

church context, speaks of a call through the princes and electors? First, in principle the local congregation has the right to call. And the call of the congregation is at the same time God's call. The local congregation as part of the *ecclesia universalis* has the authority to test the doctrine of the preacher (*ius iudicandi*). God gives the congregation the responsibility to see that the Word is preached and the Sacraments are administered. The reformer assigns the responsibility and right to call ministers of the Word and Sacraments primarily to the local congregation. All calls ought to be extended in the name of the congregation. No one ought to assign or reassign a congregational pastor against the expressed will of the congregation.[169] This right, which belongs to the congregation, can nevertheless in practice be exercised by princes, diets, patrons, and bishops. But they must call in consultation with the congregation or a representative of the congregation—for example, concerning the pastoral candidate's doctrinal orthodoxy.[170]

The local congregation is central to Luther's view of church and ministry. In "That a Christian Assembly (1523)," Luther claims that in normal circumstances the congregation's right to call may in no way be questioned by either defiant pastoral candidates or self-indulgent bishops. Luther writes: "[I]f he is at a place where there are Christians who have the same power and right as he, he should not draw attention to himself. Instead, he should let himself be called and chosen to preach and to teach in the place of and by the command of the others."[171] A little later, the reformer writes:

> Otherwise, if there is no such need and if there are those who have the right, power, and grace to teach, no bishop should institute anyone without the election, will, and call of the congregation. Rather, he should confirm the one whom the congregation chose and called; if he does not do it, he [the elected man] is confirmed anyway by virtue of the congregation's call. Neither Titus nor Timothy nor Paul ever instituted a priest without the congregation's election and call. [Luther refers to Titus 1:7 and 1 Timothy 3:10.][172]

In normal circumstances, a proper ecclesial ministry is bound by the will, choice, and call of the local congregation. The following characterize the pastoral ordination introduced by Luther in 1535 for Wittenberg.

---

169 The local congregation's right to call is emphasized in, among other writings, "To the Christian Nobility (1520)," LW 44:123ff. (WA 6:407f.); and "That a Christian Assembly (1523)," LW 39:305ff. (WA 11:408–16).

170 See Rietschel and Graff, *Lehrbuch der Liturgik*, 2:844ff.; Brunotte, *Das geistliche Amt bei Luther*, 174ff.; and Lieberg, *Amt und Ordination*, 145ff.

171 LW 39:310 (WA 11:412.30ff.).

172 LW 39:312 (WA 11:414.11ff.).

1. The public sanction and establishment of the congregation's choice/call (*confirmatio*).

2. The congregation's official right to the means of grace and to putting someone into the servant ministry (*missio*).

3. The strengthening through God's Word and prayer for the power and guidance of the Spirit in service to the reign of God (*benedictio*).[173]

Of course, Luther does occasionally describe emergency situations in which one cannot follow this order. One ought to observe, however, that when Luther speaks of *Not* or *Notstand* (an emergency or emergency situation), measures are taken that are never meant to establish a new rule. In "That a Christian Assembly . . ." Luther touches on such emergency situations. He gives the right and responsibility to arrange things so that the Gospel is preached to the priesthood of all believers. As for the emergency right of individual Christians to preach where there are no other Christians or in pagan settings, Luther writes:

> [I]f he is in a place where there are no Christians he needs no other call than to be a Christian, called and anointed by God from within. Here it is his duty to preach and to teach the gospel to erring heathen or non-Christians, because of the duty of brotherly love, even though no man calls him to do so. [Here Luther cites the examples of Stephen in Acts 6–7, Philip in Acts 8:5, and Apollos in Acts 18:24ff.] In such a case a Christian looks with brotherly love at the need of the poor and perishing souls and does not wait until he is given a command or letter from a prince or bishop. For need breaks all laws and has none.[174]

Luther believes that 1 Corinthians 14:34ff. constitutes a prohibition for the access of women to the ministry of the Word. However, in a cloister of nuns, it can sometimes occur that there is no man to preach the Gospel. In such a situation, one of the women can be allowed to preach.[175] In "To the Christian Nobility (1520)" and in "Concerning the Ministry (1523)," Luther gives isolated Christians and repressed congregations without pastors the right to call their own pastors. These can rightly be installed into the ministry of the church.[176] He always legitimates these emergency measures on the basis of the priesthood of all believers.

---

173 Öberg, "Den lutherska reformationen och ordinationen," 75ff., especially 84f.

174 LW 39:310 (WA 11:412.16ff.).

175 WA 12:309.16ff., 309.22f.

176 "To the Christian Nobility (1520)," WA 6:407.34ff. Cf. the advice Luther gives to the Utraquists in Prague that they might, after humble prayer, call and employ pastors in their difficult and special situation. The Bohemians were forced to let their pastors be ordained by a Roman bishop in Italy, but when the newly ordained pastors returned to Prague, they were forced to recant their promises about communion *sub una specie*.

Luther's opinion about emergency situations should continually be considered and applied in the frequently extraordinary contexts of the mission field. But I have found nowhere in Luther's writings where he draws up a new set of regulations for establishing new congregations in foreign mission fields. For Luther, both the priesthood of all believers and the ministry of the church are instituted by God and are important in reformation, evangelization, and mission. In prayer and testimony and by taking responsibility for the church's means of grace and for ministry, the priesthood of all believers ought to work together with those who, out of and by the priesthood of all believers, have been called to the public administration of the Word and Sacraments. Both the priesthood of all believers and the church's ordained ministry constitute the superstructure of Luther's ecclesiology and missiology. They are tightly intertwined but are not to be confused. We will return to this question when I survey Luther's exposition of the New Testament Epistles.

Summary

According to Luther's ecclesiology and view of ministry, the church is a creation of the Gospel (the Word and Sacraments). The church grows and is sustained by the work of the Father, the Son, and the Spirit. The church is a fellowship of faith and of people, all possessing the same grace and righteousness through the same Gospel and faith in Christ. The priesthood of all believers is united, possesses the gifts of grace, and is responsible for the work of God's reign. Likewise, the church's public ministry of Word and Sacraments is important. All Christians have the responsibility to see that the Gospel is preached. At the same time, the ordained ministry of the Word is important. While evangelical mission movements of the last two centuries have primarily emphasized the personal inner call to service in God's reign, Luther ascribes more importance to the outer call of the congregation to the ministry of Word and Sacraments. Later, in connection with the apostolic letters, Luther describes a plurality of ministries in the work of God's reign, but he does not describe a special mission ministry.

See "Concerning the Ministry (1523)," WA 12:190ff., especially 193.22ff. See also Öberg, "Den lutherska reformationen och ordinationen," 71f.

CHAPTER THREE

THE MISSION PERSPECTIVE IN LUTHER'S COMMENTARIES, LECTURES, AND SERMONS ON THE BIBLE

IN THIS CHAPTER, I WILL SHOW HOW LUTHER develops his mission thinking in his comprehensive exegesis of and commentaries on the Old and New Testaments. It is above all in Luther's commentaries and sermons that one can get a clear picture of his mission thinking. We begin with Luther's commentary on Genesis and end with his comments on the letters of the New Testament. In this way, we can trace Luther's thinking on mission as we follow the salvation history of the Bible. Chapter 3, which is the anchor for this book, does the following: The first major division examines Luther's comments on the expansion of the reign of God and Christ based on the Old Testament. The second major division surveys and analyzes Luther's commentaries on the Gospels, focusing on the new covenant and the message of the Gospel for all people. The third major division examines what Luther says about mission among Jews and Gentiles based on the Acts of the Apostles. It also surveys how Luther describes the content of the Gospel and the methods for its expansion on the basis of the reformer's work with the New Testament Epistles.

THE MISSION MOTIF IN THE OLD TESTAMENT COMMENTARIES

As an exegete, lecturer, and preacher, Luther often worked with the Old Testament, especially Genesis, the Psalms, and the Major Prophets.[1] Clearly, the

---

1 For Luther's general view and prophetic-Christological interpretation of the Old Tes-

reformer sees a difference or even an antithesis between the Old and the New Testaments. The Old Testament and the old covenant is often linked to the Law and to the tyranny of the Law from which the new covenant is clearly separated. Luther also sees the Old and the New Testaments in the light of revelation and salvation history under the scheme promise-fulfillment. Luther emphasizes a positive connection between the Old and the New Testaments, though the antithetical undertone is not completely absent.

As noted previously, even the Law (*usus spiritualis legis*) serves the Gospel. But God's revealed Word about salvation by grace through faith in the (coming) Christ is, for Luther, already a reality in the Old Testament. The Old and New Testaments are a unity in the sense that they both point to Christ and that they are both revealed by God. Luther uses a prophetic-Christological method of interpretation in which the Old Testament is seen in the light of the New and all Scripture becomes a unity. Unity pervades both Testaments. The themes curse-promise and Law-Gospel permeate both Testaments, though the Old Testament has primarily Law and the New Testament primarily Gospel.

Luther places world and salvation history into three periods: (1) from the beginning to the flood, (2) from the flood through the prophets to Christ, and (3) from Christ to the end of the ages. Through these three epochs, two themes are the same: (a) the curse through the fall and the sin of Cain with all the consequent unfaithfulness and sin of a fallen humanity, and (b) the blessing through the promised seed of Eve and the incarnated and revealed Jesus Christ. This important tension between curse and blessing, fall and faith, Law and Gospel must always be kept in mind when studying Luther.

The fact that Luther sees the promises about the Messiah and the faith of the saints as realties in the Old Testament cannot be overemphasized. These realities hold everything together in the Old Testament. For Luther, the list of the Old Testament faithful found in Hebrews 11 is not simply a nice piece of prose. Abraham, the father of faith and the greatest saint of the Bible, as well as the other principle figures of the Old Testament, had a real faith in Jesus Christ. To a certain degree, the Gospel was concealed from them and their faith was focused forward on a promised Savior, but they still possessed an actual faith and belonged to the true people of God through that faith. Luther firmly believed that the promises of the church, faith, and the fight of faith already existed during the time of the Old

---

tament, see the following: H. Bornkamm, *Luther und das Alte Testament*, 69ff., 209ff., with impressive insights; Althaus, *Die Theologie Martin Luthers*, 73, 77ff., 88ff.; and Juhani Forsberg, *Das Abrahamsbild in der Theologie Luthers* (1984), 18ff., 24ff., 42ff., 60ff., et al. See also Pedersen, *Luther som skriftfortolker*, which in different contexts considers Luther's interpretation of the Old Testament. The literature cited above refers to other relevant works.

Testament patriarchs. Where Christ and faith are, there is God's church, according to Luther.

For Luther, the Old Testament is primarily a history of Christ and of faith (*sensus literalis propheticus*). Those who do not understand the presence of Christ and faith in the Old Testament have not really understood the Old Testament. Heinrich Bornkamm and Ebbe Thestrup Pedersen have shown how Luther disposed of nearly all the church's allegorical interpretations of the Old Testament. These interpretations are phantoms that lose the Old Testament as the history of Christ and faith. Likewise, Luther rejected the Anthiochene typological interpretations that emptied the events of the Old Testament of any historical value and made them into mere shadow plays of that which was to come in the New Testament. For Luther, the Old Testament is not mere shadow play but actually has to do with God and Christ. Therefore Luther gives most of his attention (outside of his creation theology) to those Old Testament passages in which he finds Christ and the people who receive the promises. He believes that those Old Testament figures who receive the promises are Christians and the true church. And for Luther, mission is everywhere in the Old Testament.

It is important to keep a few principles in mind as we examine Luther's work with the Old Testament. First, Luther combines systematic exegesis and preaching in his biblical interpretation precisely as Augustine did. Second, Luther focuses on the simple, literal sense of the text. Third, he constantly searches for the Gospel in the text. While Luther stigmatizes and jokes about the ancient and medieval church's Old Testament allegorizing, he himself occasionally allegorizes. Despite his warning (*caveate ab allegoriis*), he exploits a limited allegorical interpretation but says it must be exercised strictly according to *analogia fidei*. So if Luther uses allegorical interpretation, it is to place Christ, Christ's kingdom, and faith in the center of the interpretation. Luther's interpretation can be referred to as a Christological-prophetic method. But this does not prevent him from recognizing that the Scriptures often describe an actual historical problem (*sensus literalis historicus*).

THE MISSION MOTIF IN THE GENESIS COMMENTARIES

While an exhaustive survey is not possible, we will first look at some passages in Luther's commentaries on Genesis. In his German translation of the Bible, Luther wrote: "Indeed Moses is a source of all wisdom and understanding from which has streamed all that the prophets have known and said. The New Testament also flows from Moses and is grounded therein."[2] According to Luther's high estimation of Genesis, this book contains everything there is to know about the Gospel and faith.

---

2 WADB 8:29.27ff.

This is obvious in Luther's commentaries on the so-called *protoevangelium* about the woman's seed in Genesis 3:15. In the mid-1520s, Luther said this about the seed or Christ:

> This seed will crush the serpent's head, i.e. the seed will subvert, trample under his feet and crush the damage which the serpent has caused. When Adam heard this, he reemerged from hell and was again comforted. This is the faith that the Seed will take all the power of the devil and crush it so that it is destroyed. . . . After they lived and died, their descendants waited and believed on this promise and always preached that a fruit would come and crush the serpent's head. All the content of gospel and faith are contained in these few words. . . . It states there that Adam has been a Christian already long before the birth of Christ because he had the same faith in Christ that we have. Time makes no difference as it concerns faith. Faith is one and the same from the beginning of the world to its end.[3]

This quotation states that the same Adam who through the fall, unbelief, and sin has been condemned to death also and actually shares in the Gospel about Christ and in faith. Luther's statement here is not allegorical or typological. He believes that Adam actually has faith. Adam hears the message of Christ's victory over the forces of destruction and he hears about redemption. Adam and his descendants also have preached about the salvation that comes through the seed, Christ. Adam shares in the totality of the Gospel and believes that he so shares. This Gospel lives on with his descendants and is the basis for their faith as well. Adam believes the Gospel, thus he is called a Christian. Faith is not bound by time and is the same under both the old and the new covenants.

God later renewed and clarified the promises of salvation in Christ. Luther focuses here on the promises to Abraham and his seed, on Abraham as the premier example of faith in Christ, and on Abraham's struggling and expanding church. In Genesis 12:3—"and all peoples on earth will be blessed through you"—Luther sees an unambiguous promise of universal salvation in Jesus Christ. That is why Luther considered this to be the noblest chapter in the entire book of Genesis. The true promise in Genesis 12:3 says not only that Christ will crush all the forces of destruction but also that his work will provide a spiritual blessing to the entire world. This promise ought to be written with golden letters, to be honored and praised in all the languages of the world. Through Christ, the seed, the promise is given to all the nations of the world, even before the Law, circumcision, and the Jewish people appeared. Luther notes that Genesis 12:3 clearly rejects any notion that only the Jews will share in God's salutary blessing.[4]

---

3 WA 24:98.28ff. Cf. WA 14:139ff.; 40/1:513f.; 42:142ff.

4 WA 14:223.17ff.; 24:243ff.; 42:447ff. Concerning Luther's work with these texts that he

According to Luther, the content of the *protoevangelium* in Genesis 3:15 is defined in Genesis 12:2–3. The woman's seed is identified with Abraham's seed, Jesus Christ. But the message of this promised seed must be preached in the world. Thus Abraham preached the Gospel about the blessed seed, Christ, and taught his servants and his neighbors among the Canaanites. Because Abraham always wanted to lead people to the true faith in and worship of God, he did not fear the opposition of the Gentiles. In this way he established a church, preaching the Word and establishing a cult in a way similar to the church of the new covenant.[5]

Luther identifies the blessing of Abraham with the woman's seed or Christ (Galatians 3:16). He finds in Genesis 17:4ff. another expression of the universality of God's salvation through the woman's seed and the covenant with Abraham. He often notes how Paul refers directly in Romans 4:16 to Genesis 17:4–5: "As for me, this is my covenant with you: You will be the father of many nations. No longer will you be called Abram ["God hears"]; your name will be Abraham ["father of many"], for I have made you a father of many nations." Luther describes the covenant with Abraham as a covenant "for the generations to come," an eternal covenant (Genesis 17:7). Here is a clear indication that the pact with Abraham will finally include even Gentiles. Already in Genesis the limiting of God's salvation to the Jews is *de facto* repudiated. The comprehensiveness of the pact and its universal direction is important for Luther, but Paul's interpretation of the qualitative or material side of the pact with Abraham is even more important. According to Romans 4:16f. and Galatians 4:21ff., the covenant with Abraham is characterized by God's promises of grace, faith, and freedom, not by the Law or slavery under works of the Law.[6] Here is an example of how Luther interprets the Old Testament in light of the new covenant. He believes this is the correct method and that Christ and the apostles also used this method.

---

believes concern Christ, see H. Bornkamm, *Luther und das Alte Testament*, 86ff.

5 Cf. "Sermon on Genesis 12 (1523)," WA 14:223.18ff., 224.15ff., 225.1ff.; 42:500.14ff. See the exhaustive investigation by Juhani Forsberg, "Abraham als Paradigma des Glaubens, der Hoffnung und der Liebe" (1983): 106ff., especially the passage "Universalität und 'Mission' der Kirche Abrahams," 118ff., 123ff., 136ff. Pedersen, *Luther som skriftfortolker*, 223ff., helpfully shows how Luther differentiates between priestly rites in the Old Testament (= types) and the New Testament's sacraments. However, the signs that accompanied the promises to the patriarchs are full of realism. The New and Old Testament have the Christ, the Spirit, a faith, and a people of God. Cf. also Bunkowske, "Was Luther a Missionary?" 164.

6 WA 56:45.10ff.; 57:46.6ff. See especially WA 14:256f.; 24:318ff., 321ff. Cf. the passage in Forsberg, "Abraham als Paradigma des Glaubens," 47ff., 60ff., with references. See also Pedersen, *Luther som skriftfortolker*, 219f.

Genesis 22:18 says: "[A]nd through your offspring all nations on earth will be blessed, because you have obeyed me." Luther's understanding is that these words, spoken after Abraham's distress at the sacrifice of Isaac, more than all other Old Testament texts, mean that God's salvation is for all peoples and lands. In a 1525 commentary, Luther writes:

> But the blessed Seed which was promised to Abraham . . . he is a different kind of person than Moses. About him it has been said: And a Seed will come through whom not only your people, your flesh and blood, but also everything on earth will be blessed. It is as if he were to say: I want to govern and maintain your flesh and blood and this seed for my people, but when the people who belong to the true Seed come then a preaching will go out so that all Gentiles under heaven will be blessed and so that God will be a Father for all believing Gentiles under the sun.[7]

Luther recognizes the difference between the covenant at Sinai and the covenant established through Jesus Christ. The former covenant is limited to the Jews, but the covenant promised to Abraham and established in Jesus Christ has a universal horizon. And the blessed seed (Christ) has a different message than Moses. Long before the appearance of the Law and the Jews, the Abrahamic promises speak of the Gospel and salvation by grace. A message will go out to both Jews and Gentiles that all under the curse and judgment will be given grace in Jesus Christ. With a profound seriousness and consistency, Luther argues on the basis of Genesis 22:18 that Abraham's blessing has a universal horizon and a universal quality.[8]

---

7 WA 16:162.13ff.

8 In a 1523 commentary, Luther writes: "Dictum est regnum Christi et Euangelium in his brevibus verbis, et quis potest satis explicare? Abraham intellexit et prophetae, paucissimi Iudeorum intellexerunt. Etiamsi non aliud verbum haberemus quam hunc unicum locum, sat esset. Et credo patriarchas non plus habuisse scripturarum, qui locus comprehendit totam scripturam. Non exponendus iste locus de benedictione carnali simpliciter. 'Ego mittam', inquit, 'benedictionem per universum mundum' in hoc 'per semen tuum'. Per Adae lapsum et nos immersi sumus peccatis et maledicti, et quicquod nascitur e femina, puer maledictionis . . . . Illa benedictio sol ghen uber alle heiden, doch in semine Abrahae. Hoc est Euangelium . . . super omnes benedictio venit, qui sunt sub sole sive sint Iudei sive gentes. Benedictio adest omnibus, sed non omnes arripiunt . . . . Verum est: omnes gentes benedicentur, hoc est: praedicatur omnibus verbum . . . Iudeis scopus positus est, quod gloriari non possunt se meritos esse hanc benedictionem, Inquit Paulus [Galatians 3:17]. Eo tempore quo promissio ista facta est Abrahae, non fuit lex neque Moses neque Iudei etc. Ergo ex mera misericordia provenit istud beneficium nostrum" (WA 14:302.18ff., 303.12ff., 303.23ff.). Cf. WA 16:161–64; 20:550.11ff.; 24:392ff.; 40/1:278ff., 373ff., 453ff., 472ff., 546f.; 43:245ff.; 45:245ff., 260ff.; 54:70ff., 54.75f. It is worth noting how the reformer, when considering the promises to Abraham, draws in many texts from the New Testament and forcefully emphasizes that the universalism of the Gospel of salvation was established before

In a 1527 commentary on Genesis, Luther notes parenthetically that all people in Adam lay under sin and judgment. But in Abraham's blessed seed (Christ), God will also have mercy on all people, according to Galatians 3:22 and Romans 11:22. Luther says:

> The blessing should now have reached all Gentiles. However it would have reached them in Abraham's name. This message is the Gospel. . . . The Gospel is the kind of message which offers us God's grace and mercy, the grace which has been won by Jesus Christ and given to us in his blood. . . . The blessing has gone out to the whole world. It has reached Gentiles and Jews and continues ceaselessly to progress. . . . See, this promise (Genesis 22:18) proceeds in such a manner that God wants the Gospel to be announced in all the world. This is what is meant by "blessed." The blessing is there, the invitation is to everyone, but not everyone receives it.[9]

This passage shows how Luther weaves together texts from the Old and New Testaments and how he, in a Christological-prophetic interpretation of the Old Testament, finds the sum of the Gospel in Christ's work of redemption. The Gospel of salvation has gone out to all peoples. It also is important to note in the quotation that the Gospel progresses ceaselessly in the world, received or rejected, even in Luther's time. Luther's words "it has gone out to the whole world" and similar statements have unfortunately led certain scholars to believe that Luther thought the mission task had been fulfilled in the time of the apostles. Whoever carefully reads the passage, however, understands that Luther clearly speaks of the Gospel's continuing expansion.

The comprehensive 1535–1545 Genesis commentary discusses the above themes in connection with Genesis 22:18. Luther forcefully emphasizes that Abraham's seed is Christ. The salvation promised through Christ is consequently not addressed only to the Jews but also to all the peoples of the world. It is surprising how full of references to the New Testament these commentaries are.[10] Even in the *Larger Commentary on Galatians* (1531/1535), one notices how, among other things, Galatians 3:17ff. (Abraham's children = the people of faith) is important for Luther's understanding of Genesis 3:15 and 22:18. Luther not only emphasizes here the Gospel and faith against works of the Law but also emphasizes powerfully

---

Moses and the Law and the chosen people. That the promise is universal does not, however, mean that all receive the blessing. Concerning the promise to Abraham and the mission motif, see the excellent essay by Forsberg, "Abraham als Paradigma der Mission in der Theologie Luthers," 114ff., and especially Forsberg's dissertation, "Abraham als Paradigma des Glaubens," 118ff. See also Pedersen, *Luther som skriftfortolker*, 220ff.

9 WA 24:392.19ff.

10 WA 43:245–64, especially the conclusion, 263.42ff. Cf. WA 44:753ff.; 54:75.12ff.

that God's salvation in the blessed Seed/Christ belongs to all peoples, even Gentiles.[11] In his Genesis commentaries, Luther speaks energetically about mission, as if he had the mission commissions of the New Testament before him.[12]

The promises to Abraham in Luther's interpretation are more germane for mission than the *protoevangelium* in Genesis 3:15. It is because of these promises and because of faith that the time of Abraham is something of a golden age in which the Gospel, faith, and the church owned a clarity and power that they did not have again until Christ's incarnation. The Gospel, faith, and the universality of salvation make this epoch extraordinary. It ought to be emphasized that the reformer means that the church has existed from the beginning of the world and that it continues its existence through the Word and faith until the end of the age. The church of the Old Testament lives under the horizon of the promises, while the church of the New Testament is established after the promises receive their *yes* and *amen* in Jesus' incarnation, death, and resurrection. But for Luther, as Juhani Forsberg rightly expresses, Genesis is the real history of the one true church. The church can be defined as the reign borne by the Word of the Seed/Christ and faith. Where the Gospel and faith have a place among people, there is God's church.

One ought to be aware, however, that this church always has an antichurch that opposes it, that is, Satan and his followers. From the time of Cain, the church has been forced to fight against false doctrine, idolatry, and other types of enemies. The patriarchal "mission" is also characterized by this dualism between the true church and the false church (also the world). It is possible that Luther is influenced by Augustine's ideas about *civitas Dei* and *civitas terrena* (*diaboli*) in which the power of God's reign is thought to be realized in a gripping way within the frame of human history.[13] However, it is likely that

---

11 WA 40/1:3734ff., 380ff., 453ff., 472f., 491f., 513ff., 546ff.

12 LW 2:260 (WA 42:447.30ff.): "No doubt Christ referred to these thoughts of the holy patriarch when He said (John 8:56): 'Your father Abraham rejoiced that he was to see My day; he saw it and was glad.' The statement of the text, 'all the families of the earth,' is not to be understood of extent only, of the families of one time, but of duration, as long as the world will stand. It is altogether in accord with the statement of Christ (Mark 16:15–16): 'Go, preach the Gospel to the whole creation . . .' This blessing has now endured for one thousand five hundred years, and it will endure until the end of the world, since the gates of hell (Matt. 16:18), tyrants, and ungodly men will oppose it and rage against it in vain. But above all it must be noted that the text does not say that all the nations will flow together to the Jews and will become Jews; but it declares that the blessing this people is to possess will be transferred from this people to the heathen, that is, to those who are not circumcised and who know nothing of Moses and his statutes." Cf. also WA 42:521.18ff., 521.32ff.

13 Cf. Forsberg, "Abraham als Paradigma der Mission in der Theologie Luthers," 115, and "Abraham als Paradigma des Glaubens," 107–18. Cf. Hallencreutz, "Luther och Olaus

Galatians 3 and Hebrews 11 exercise the more significant influence on Luther's idea of the Old Testament church.

It is worth noting how Luther finds in the wandering church of the patriarchs the anticipatory presence of the public ministries and of the public, ordered worship with preaching, prayer, and offering. One often notices in this regard those writings of Luther with an anti-enthusiast emphasis. The reformer meant that the church with its means of grace can never become some kind of *civitas platonica*. The patriarchal *ecclesia peregrinans* is ultimately a preaching and missionary church. Faith always gives birth to confession and testimony/preaching about Christ and blessing through him. Patriarchal history is woven with the history of the Egyptians and the Canaanites. Therefore the history of the patriarchs is also a chapter in mission history. That the Gentiles who lived in the same areas as the patriarchs are said to be incorporated in their worship is probably the most common feature that Luther notices about the patriarchal mission. However, one does not find only this centripetal movement but also an extrovertive, centrifugal movement.[14]

Even during the time of the patriarchs, people of faith sought to spread knowledge of God's promises and faith among their friends and among the Gentiles whom they met during their wanderings. The promises of the Old Testament are given to all the world; therefore there is a centrifugal mission in the world. To distribute his message, God can exploit persecutions, hunger, and distress. On the

---

Petri om 'missionsbefallningen,' " 13f. See WA 42:79ff., 425.1ff. One ought, however, to be careful about framing Luther too categorically in Augustine's scheme of *civitas Dei/civitas terrena*. In the source material, one does not often find where Luther explicitly refers to the concept. It is the biblical concepts of light and darkness, truth and lie, true doctrine and false doctrine, and God and Satan in an unavoidable struggle that characterize Luther's thought. This Luther was considered to be too difficult and gloomy by the humanists as they attempted cultural synthesis. Cf. *Luther and World Mission*, 35–37.

14 Cf. the typical commentary on Genesis 12:3 from 1523 in WA 14:223.18ff., 224.17f.: " 'In te benedicentur' [12:3]. Benedictio enim hec est Euangelium. Hoc ipse praedicavit, per hoc declaratum est amplius quod Adam promissum erat, 'Ipsum conteret serpentis caput' [Genesis 3:15] . . . Ubi fides, tum sequitur confessio et praedicatio gratiae dei . . . 2. peregrinatio, qua ivit 'Bethel versus orientem', 'erexit altare'. Quid hoc? estne sacerdos? Nihil aliud ista re fecit, Nisi ut suos doceret, ut precarentur et offerrent. Ab initio fuit externum signum cultus divini mactatio pecorum et oblacio, Sicut nos habemus missam et participationem panis . . . oportet ut locus sit, in quo praedicetur, Sicut ipse mihi soli non praedico, quare praecipue propter praedicationem. Quid praedicavit? hoc 'promisit mihi In me benedicendas etc. et terram semini futuram' etc. Summus sacerdos fuit. Oravit certe, ut hoc impleretur, quod sibi promissum fuit. Hic Abraham est paterfamilias, et episcopus fuit." Cf. WA 24:253.10ff., 255.3ff., 257.1ff; 42:499.21ff.; 43:104.7ff.; 44:168.18ff.

basis of Genesis, Luther holds together *missio Dei* and a universal *missio ecclesiae*. For example, in the mid-1520s Luther comments on Genesis 12:14–16:

> In this manner God plagues his own people so that he does not allow them to settle in one place. He chases them here and there, not only for their own sake so that their faith might be strengthened, but also for the sake of other people. For Abraham was not able to be silent, and it would not have been appropriate for him to refrain from preaching to his neighbors about God's grace. Therefore through hunger God has driven him into Egypt in order that even there he might do something useful and give some revealed and right knowledge of God which he also doubtless did. For it cannot be tolerated that one mixes with people and does not reveal to them that which provides the blessedness of their souls. . . . So God acts in a wonderful way here on earth. He sends apostles and preachers to people before they ask or even think about it even though those who are sent do not know how they have found themselves on the way.[15]

In the 1535–1545 Genesis lectures, Luther writes this on Genesis 35:2:

> Moses, moreover, says that Jacob spoke to his household and all who were with him. . . . For I have often stated that it is quite credible that when the patriarchs were teaching, many of the heathen flocked to them, for they saw that the patriarchs were godly and holy men and that God was with them, and therefore they heard and embraced their doctrine. . . . Later on, Joseph in Egypt, Daniel in Babylon, and Jonah in Nineveh taught the doctrine of God. Therefore God gathered a church in the world not only from the one family of the patriarchs but from all nations to which the Word made its way.[16]

In a paraphrase of Joseph's conversation with his brothers and of his commandment to hasten with the message to their father (Genesis 45:9–11), Luther makes a connection to Christian mission (Matthew 10:27; Mark 16:15). The reformer wants his readers to learn for themselves to draw the consequences of their own reception of the Gospel. As soon as they have received God in his Son and the Spirit, the immediate consequences ought to be: "Go, and do not keep silence, in order that the rest of the multitude may be saved too, not you alone."[17]

It ought to be clear from the examination of these texts in Luther's commentaries on Genesis that the promise of the woman's seed and above all the promise of blessing to Abraham and all peoples contain promises that apply to all peoples and lands, Jews and Gentiles. Where the promises of God's grace and salvation in Jesus Christ are received in faith, there God's reign and the church already exist in

---

15 WA 24:261.26ff.

16 LW 6:227 (WA 44:168.13ff.).

17 LW 8:46 (WA 44:612.26f.).

the Old Testament. The reformer notices that this people is a people who trusts in God's promises. This people of faith worships in a specific way with the preaching of the Word. This people, especially their *summus pontifex* and *episcopus* Abraham, missionize and seek to lead Gentiles to God's salvation in faith. In this way, the conversion of the Gentiles and faith are important from the beginning of the Bible, according to Luther. We have even seen how Luther seeks in Paul, above all, a basis for the universality of the Gospel and God's reign.

It would not be difficult to find in Luther's commentaries on Genesis and the Pentateuch other examples that explicitly emphasize the task of the Gospel and that reject all limitation of God's salvation. But the passages to which I already have referred are enough. However, I will point out that the reformer, in his efforts to emphasize the universality of God's salvation, often says that Paul in Romans 10:19 uses the words from Moses' farewell: "I will make them envious by those who are not a people; I will make them angry by a nation that has no understanding" (Deuteronomy 32:21). Luther means that this provocation first began to be realized when the apostolic preaching and the Gospel went out to the peoples. The provocation functions even in the 1500s when one says that everyone who has rejected Christ (among the Jews and Gentiles) does not belong to God's people and at the same time that all (Jews and Gentiles) who believe in Christ are *populus Dei*.[18] For Luther, Moses in his farewell sings about how the limitations of the covenant at Sinai are superceded by a message of salvation in Christ for all peoples.

The Mission Perspective in the Commentaries on the Psalms

According to Luther, most of the psalms are prophetic and speak of Christ. As it concerns the mission motif in Luther's commentaries on the Psalms, it ought to be said immediately that the usual centripetal theme of the Psalms—that the Gentiles will make pilgrimage to and worship in Jerusalem—is consistently suppressed. For Luther, this part of salvation history is replaced and succeeded by Jesus Christ, his salutary work, and the outpouring of the Spirit. Centrifugal universalism, that is, that God's salvation will be carried out to all peoples under the sun, is the more dominant theme in the reformer's commentaries on the Psalms. The Psalms constantly provide Luther with the opportunity to emphasize the universal expansion of Christ's lordship through the preaching of the Gospel.

In Psalm 2:8, Luther considers the words "Ask of me, and I will make the nations your inheritance, the ends of the earth your possession." Luther under-

---

18 See *Deuteronomium Mosi cum annotationibus* (1525), WA 14:736ff. Cf. also WA 56:104.8ff. and 57:93.1ff. Luther cites Deuteronomy 32:21 often when he argues against Jewish or papistic narrowing of God's salvation. Cf. WA 41:499f.

stands that the deeper significance of this text is not a promise for Israel's nation-alistic dreams (cf. Psalm 2:9). Instead, the text speaks of a spiritual reign. This reign is grounded in God's own command and gathers its subjects from among both Jews and Gentiles. The psalm speaks of Christ's universal lordship, which originates in Zion/Jerusalem but will expand to all peoples. The sending of God's Spirit is an important prerequisite for this to happen. Similarly, the apostles and subsequent preachers call the peoples through the Gospel to faith in Christ.[19] Christ has been given to the Jews according to the promise to the patriarchs, but on the basis of God's undivided mercy, he also has been given to the Gentiles (Isa-iah 66:19f.; Romans 15:8). Therefore Luther writes concerning Psalm 2:8: "We can all see [that this verse is] fulfilled in the Acts of the Apostles when the disciples preached only for the Jews until Paul, who was called from heaven, was sent as the apostle to the Gentiles."[20]

Psalm 18:50–19:7 is interpreted similarly according to the new covenant's *reg-num Christi* in which the promises of salvation and mercy are fulfilled. Luther connects these verses directly to the preaching of Christ for all peoples from the days of the apostles until the return of Christ.[21] It is clear that Psalm 19:4 ("Their voice goes out into all the earth, their words to the ends of the world.") determines Luther's interpretation of the entire pericope. In *Operationes in Psalmos* (1519–1521), Luther claims in his Christological interpretation that Christ's lord-ship through the Gospel will be carried to all peoples and in all languages. Fur-thermore, he claims that this universal preaching has its true origin in the preach-ing of the apostles and continues in Luther's time and until the end of the world and of time. He says:

> The voice of the heavens, the days and the nights which preach God's glory and the work of his hands. But where do we hear these heavens? And among which peoples? Or with which languages do they speak? He answers: they speak in the languages of all peoples and throughout the whole earth as the following verse says. This was fulfilled when the apostles preached God's mighty works in different languages and it is still being fulfilled in the whole earth as long as the Gospel which was spread in different languages through

---

19 WA 5:61.24ff.; 31/1:268.5ff., 530.34ff.; 40/2:260.16ff. Peters, "Luthers weltweiter Mis-sionssinn," 165, sheds light on Luther's concern for mission through the exegesis of Psalm 8. Concerning the psalms that Luther connects with Christ's person and salutary work, his kingdom, or the church, see H. Bornkamm, *Luther und das Alte Testament*, 90ff. Cf. concerning Luther's early work on the Psalms, Ebeling, "Die Anfänge von Luthers Hermeneutik," 219ff.

20 *Operationes in Psalmos* (1519–1521), WA 6:62.19ff.

21 WA 5:541ff.; 40/1:386.10ff.; 40/2:263.31ff. See especially WA 5:546.6ff.

the apostles continues to sound in the same languages until the end of the world and time.[22]

The text clearly shows how Luther can say both that the apostles fulfilled the task of mission and that its fulfillment continues until Christ's return. Detractors (for example, L. Bergman) have interpreted this way of speaking, common in the Luther material, to mean that Luther did not believe a mission was needed after the time of the apostles. In his 1531 commentary on Psalm 19, Luther says:

> This is a prophetic and didactic psalm. It prophesies that the Gospel will be preached in the whole world. . . . [on 19:1] *The heavens are telling the glory of God; and the firmament proclaims His handiwork.* This is to say: "The glory of God is preached everywhere in all the lands under all of heaven." . . . The "handiwork" of God is all the works wrought by the Gospel, like justification, salvation, and redemption from sin, from death, and from the kingdom of the devil. . . . [on 19:2–3] This is to say that the Gospel will always be preached and that the Christian Church will stand and remain eternally. . . . "The Gospel will be preached in all lands, nations, and languages, not only among the Jews, not only in Jerusalem, but in all tongues." . . . [on 19:4] Here he teaches explicitly that in the future God's grace will be preached everywhere.[23]

In Luther's commentaries on the Psalms written at Coburg in 1530, he can even say concerning Psalm 19:6: "Christ began namely to rise up through the Gospel during the time of the apostles and continues to do so until the end of the world, as he says himself: 'I am with you always, to the very end of the age' [Matthew 28:20] . . . Christ is therefore the bridegroom which illuminates the ends of the earth from the beginning to the end of the world."[24] As the sun successively illuminates the heavens, so the Gospel of Christ will illuminate the world of people until the end of the age. The mission task has not been completed in Luther's time.

Luther does not, as many others have and still do, use Psalm 19:2 to argue for a knowledge of the Creator attested to in the witness of creation. The preaching of the heavens and the firmament is said to be the central message of the Gospel about redemption, justification, and the forgiveness of sins. This message will be preached among Jews and Gentiles in all lands and in all languages. Of course, one may legitimately question whether Luther's allegorical interpretation of Psalm 19:2 in fact corresponds to the original message of the text. Luther follows Paul's figurative exegesis of Psalm 19:4 in Romans 10:18. At any rate, Luther's exposition would seem to witness to two things. First, the theme about natural knowledge of

---

22 WA 5:546.8ff.

23 LW 12:139–41 (WA 31/1:580.1ff.) (*original emphasis*).

24 WA 31/1:341.14ff., 341.20ff.

God should not be overemphasized. Second, the gift of the Gospel and its scope until the end of the world and of time is of primary importance to the reformer.

The mission motif receives a powerful expression in a 1534 commentary on Psalm 110:1ff.: "The LORD says to my Lord: 'Sit at my right hand until I make your enemies a footstool for your feet.'" In his interpretation of this text, Luther follows Jesus' own and primarily the apostolic interpretation (Matthew 22:44; Acts 2:34ff.; Romans 8:34; 1 Corinthians 15:25ff.; Ephesians 1:20ff.; Hebrews 1:3, 13; 10:12; 1 Peter 3:22). After Luther has said that the psalm really witnesses to Christ as the glorified (that is, resurrected and ascended) king, he gives his own Christological-prophetic interpretation:

> Your reign's scepter, Lord. This is a different kind of reign than the earthly kingdom. He has a scepter, a scepter which goes out from Zion. The city of Jerusalem will become the city where his reign originates. The text clearly shows that Christ's reign [*Christi regnum*] will not be in heaven over the angels, but instead here on earth. Nevertheless, it will not be earthly. It is on the earth, but it is not earthly. It is among humans, but it is not human. We live in heaven and at the same time in our earthly bodies. Therefore this is a strange kingdom. In Jerusalem Christ begins to be the king. And from this place his reign will go forth in a way that the world will hear it, as Zechariah 2:2 says, a city so large that the wall reaches to the ends of the earth. This must be a big city . . . it cannot be understood corporally but it begins in Christ's own body. It is this that Christ said to the disciples (Luke 24:46): the Christ must suffer and rise and in his name the Gospel will be preached in the whole world starting in Jerusalem. . . . It originates in Jerusalem and has come to us and it progresses until the whole world has been brought in, until the walls of Jerusalem reach the ends of the earth.[25]

This text shows clearly that the reformer sees the expansion of Christ's reign from Jerusalem to the ends of the world as something that always continues. That the expanding Christ-led reign must reach all people is, for Luther, a major biblical theme. It should also be emphasized that Christ's royal priestly lordship belongs to the Gospel's spiritual reign on earth, according to Luther. Here the distance from contemporary Barthian *Königsherrschaft Christi* and its occasional coupling with the sociopolitical arena is completely apparent.

Luther interprets Psalm 110 as the authors of the New Testament do, that is, as a commentary on Christ's priesthood and lordship, his reign and his battle against all evil spiritual and worldly powers that oppose his reign, a reign that promises blessing for all lands. Here the Spirit predicts everything about Christ's person (true God and true human) and about Christ's work as the universal priest and king over a spiritual kingdom. Furthermore, Psalm 110 prophesies that Christ's

---

25 WA 37:389.5ff.

reign shall be borne by God's authority and power and be ruled by Christ's scepter, which is the public preaching of the Gospel in the world.[26] Luther says in a comprehensive commentary: "Hence this scepter is nothing else than the office of the public ministry, which the Lord Christ began Himself and later on commanded to be extended by His messengers, the apostles and their successors, and to be continued until the Last Day."[27] He adds:

> A building like that, therefore, proceeds successfully and keeps on growing larger and larger, as the psalmist also says here regarding the scepter, which, being sent out, "proceeds." There is power behind its activity, and it accomplishes what it should. It converts and changes hearts, so that they cling to this King Christ, willingly subject themselves to Him to be commanded as He wills. . . . Hence the Jews are unable to understand what was said here and everywhere in the prophets about the heathen joining this people in droves, or about the city of Jerusalem becoming so great that its walls stand at the ends of the earth . . . . But, as a matter of fact and experience, this kingdom of Christ, begun at Zion or Jerusalem, has been spread abroad in the world; and this King, born of the Jewish nation, is being accepted everywhere merely through the Word of the Gospel, which the apostles preached. It has run abroad in the whole world and still runs, as Psalm 19:4 reads: "Their line goes out through all the lands, and their speech to the end of the world."[28]

These passages clearly show that Luther knows that the Gospel must have messengers. The Gospel goes forth through the world, but it does so through the apostles of the word of Christ and their followers. Luther's commentaries on Psalm 51:15ff. and 68:11 show, among other things, that the confession and testimony of all believers is important for the expansion of God's reign. Despite their predilection to silence, Luther challenges believers in Christ to open their mouths and to witness to what they have experienced of God's salvation. Especially important for Luther is the preaching ministry's public work of Word and Sacraments in which God's salvation is carried forward to all people in the world. Of course, the remnant of those who believe can often be small, but Christ wants to establish over the whole world the pulpit, the baptismal font, and the altar with the Lord's Supper on it. In this way, Christ and his name are spread everywhere and remain in the lands of Gentiles and in Europe's cities and villages.[29] This

---

26 WA 31/1:531.16ff.; 41:79ff., 122ff. See H. Bornkamm, *Luther und das Alte Testament*, 91f., with many references to Luther passages.

27 LW 13:265 (WA 41:123.34ff.).

28 LW 13:269–70 (WA 41:127.29ff.).

29 See Peters, "Luthers weltweiter Missionssinn," 166f.; and Bunkowske, "Was Luther a

emphasis that the Word and Sacraments must have their place and always be practiced is typical of Luther's ecclesiology and missiology.

One notices in the above quotation how well Luther understands the centripetal motif in the Old Testament. But Christ's reign or the reign of the saving Gospel, about which Psalm 110 really speaks, does not have such limitations. Luther means that God's salvation will be brought to all peoples. One starts in Jerusalem, but the ultimate goal is not pilgrimage to and worship in Jerusalem. The ultimate goal is praise to and faith in Christ out among the peoples. The centrifugal aspect is powerful and destroys all particularism in the Sinai covenant. It also emphasizes that God/Christ through the Word is the power in the church's struggle to expand and sustain the reign of God.

The church year with its Sunday and festival pericopes reflects primarily the salvation history of the new covenant. It is interesting to see that Luther preaches long sermons on Psalm 110 between Ascension and Pentecost in 1535. The powerful emphasis on Christ's lordship and the universal preaching of the Gospel that Luther finds in this psalm makes it appropriate for this season of the church year when people gather to celebrate Christ's ascension to the Father's right hand and the sending of the Spirit. According to Luther, it is precisely Christ's Ascension and Pentecost that are the decisive prerequisites for the start of world mission. With these events, the ascended Lord takes the lead in the expansion of the Gospel from Jerusalem to the ends of the earth. The many workers in the reign of God—from the apostles onward—are activated to preach the Gospel and to build the reign of faith in Christ.

The mission motif is especially prominent in the reformer's commentary on Psalm 117:1: "Praise the LORD, all you nations; extol him, all you peoples." In 1530, Luther emphasizes how this psalm opposes every attempt to limit God's salvation to the Jewish people or, more relevant for Luther, to the pope's church. The universality of salvation does not tolerate binding either to Jerusalem or to Rome. It is a question about one Lord and one Gospel for all peoples, even if not everyone who is offered the Gospel accepts it. Even in the sixteenth century, world mission took the Gospel to people. Luther says:

> Now how can it be true that all the heathen will become subject to one Christ and praise God, when all heathen persecute Christ, as He Himself says in Matt. 5:11: "Men shall revile you for my sake"? The answer: The psalm does not say that all men, or even all those among the heathen, will praise Him, but "all you heathen." That is to say: Wherever there are heathen—or a country or a city—there the Gospel will penetrate and will convert some to the kingdom

---

Missionary?" 163, with cited texts. Cf. the quotations on Psalm 117 on pp. 112–13 (nn30–31), which follow.

of Christ. Regardless of whether all people believe it, still Christ rules wherever there are people: He preserves His Word, His Baptism and Sacrament, despite all devils and men. For the Gospel and Baptism must come to the whole world, as they have indeed come and every day come again. Thus He has said (Mark 16:15): "Go into all the world, and preach the Gospel to the whole creation"; and (Ps. 19:1): "The heavens are telling the glory of God, and the firmament proclaims His handiwork." That is, Christ is preached as far as the heavens and the firmament extend.[30]

Luther emphasizes that Psalm 117:1 clearly teaches "that God is not only the God of the Jews but the God of the heathen also, and not only of a small part of heathendom but of all heathen throughout the world."[31]

The Gospel's invitation is closely connected with repentance from idolatry and with faith in the Gospel. But repentance and faith are not something that the human subject does and creates by his or her own power. They are a work of God's Word as Law and Gospel. As previously emphasized, Luther generally demands a preaching of Law and Gospel, repentance and forgiveness of sins. This rule, so important for the reformer, is relevant for mission among unbelievers. Repentance and faith are created when the human turns toward and listens to the Word, which reveals sin and speaks God's grace and forgiveness of sins. But the Word/Gospel has no voice of its own. Someone must preach the Word with a view toward conversion and faith. Therefore mission workers and the sending with the Gospel stand in focus.

> If He is to be their God, then they must know Him, believe in Him, and give up all idolatry. One cannot praise God with an idolatrous mouth or an unbelieving heart. And if they are to believe, they must first hear His Word and thereby receive the Holy Spirit, who through faith purifies and enlightens their hearts. One cannot come to faith or lay hold on the Holy Spirit without hearing the Word first, as St. Paul has said (Rom. 10:14): "How are they to believe in Him of whom they have never heard?" and (Gal. 3:2): "You have received the Spirit through the proclamation of faith." If they are to hear His Word, then preachers must be sent to proclaim God's Word to them; for not all the heathen can come to Jerusalem or make a living among the small company of the Jews. He lets them stay where they are and calls upon them, wherever they may be, to praise God.[32]

---

30 LW 14:12–13 (WA 31/1:232.20ff.).

31 LW 14:8–9 (WA 31/1:228.20ff.).

32 LW 14:9 (WA 31/1:228.34ff.). Concerning Psalm 117 and the necessity of preaching among nonbelievers, see Elert, *Morphologie des Luthertums*, 1:340. See also Stolle, *Kirche aus allen Völkern*, 87ff. How Bergman, *Den lutherske Reformation og Missionen*, 57f., can summarize Luther's many commentaries on Psalm 117:1 by saying "de

Luther's commentaries on the Psalms touch even on the subject of mission work and contextualization, specifically the part of contextualization that concerns the laws, customs, and cultures of mission lands. Luther is quite open here. It is important to observe that mission, for Luther, does not mean that native laws and customs should be abolished. He writes:

> . . . the kingdom of Christ is not a temporal, transitory, earthly kingdom, ruled with laws and regulations, but a spiritual, heavenly, and eternal kingdom that must be ruled without and above all laws, regulations, and outward means. He tells the heathen to remain heathen; He does not ask them (as I pointed out before) to run away from their countries or cities to go to Jerusalem. He does not demand that they give up or abandon their secular laws, customs, and habits to become Jews, just as He does not demand of the Jews that they abandon their laws. What He demands is something different from, and higher than, external, worldly laws or ceremonies. Every country and city can observe or change its laws. He does not concern Himself about this. Where laws are retained, they do not hinder His kingdom; for He says: "Praise the Lord, all you heathen!" [Ps. 117:1].[33]

If later Lutheran mission was sometimes tempted toward cultural imperialism, Luther has excluded such an attitude. Of course, obvious idolatry must be abandoned when one believes in Christ, but native laws, customs, and cultures do not necessarily conflict with Christ's reign of salvation. For Luther, mission does not mean to change the laws and cultures of mission lands. This is consonant with what has been discussed in the second section of chapter 2 concerning Luther's important doctrines about the earthly regiment in which the Creator, through the Law, works so all peoples in a reasonable way develop and form civil law, cultural life, domestic life, etc. Mission need not and should not direct itself primarily to changing ordinances, customs, and uses in mission lands. Church and mission will focus on the Gospel and on faith, not on customs, laws, and the organization and formation of earthly life among the Gospel's hearers.

What has to this point been reviewed of Luther's reflections about mission on the basis of Old Testament texts probably cannot be considered a full-blown missiology. But there is surely a solid foundation for the universality of Christ's Gospel and for mission among Jews and Gentiles. The cornerstones are the promises of God's salvation in Christ and the promises that the Gentiles also share in those

---

bibelske Forjættelser om Hedningernes Delaktiggørelse i Frelsen, betrakter han . . . some allerede opfyldt" ("He considers that the biblical promises about the Gentiles' participation in God's salvation have already been fulfilled") is, for me, a riddle. He doesn't see with seeing eyes because his thesis that Luther lacked a vision for mission has blinded him.

33 LW 14:14 (WA 31/1:233.19ff.).

blessings through the preaching of the Gospel. Furthermore, Luther notes how all believers will witness about Christ and how the ministry of preaching will work in the Word and Sacraments. The unbelief of the peoples must be replaced by belief, but the focus of the preaching of the Gospel is not cultural transformation.

CHRIST AND THE PEOPLES ACCORDING TO THE COMMENTARIES ON ISAIAH AND ZECHARIAH

Luther is often engaged in the exposition of the prophets in the Old Testament. Here we will address the mission theme in Luther's commentaries on Isaiah. Luther often points out that the texts speak both to the time of the prophets and to the time of the church in the new covenant under the lordship of Christ. The prophetic texts also speak to the work of the church for the conversion and faith of the heathen.[34] In my examination here, I will concentrate on Luther's concern with how the prophetic texts speak to the work of the church.

According to the reformer, Isaiah 2:2ff. prophesies a future universal reign. Luther consciously abandons any interpretation that might focus on the earthly Jerusalem, an interpretation that the text could in fact sustain. Instead, on the basis of this passage, Luther envisions a spiritual reign or Christ's church in which the heathen are called through the Gospel to serve the living God willingly on the basis of God's mercy. Christ's reign originates in Jerusalem/Zion, but it will stretch forth with God's salvation to all peoples.[35]

Luther's commentaries on Isaiah 9:2ff., which is the second lesson for Christmas Day, are also characterized by the mission motif. A powerful light will shine on all peoples through the incarnation, death, and resurrection of Jesus Christ. This light will shine on all and call both Jews and heathen, all of whom live in the darkness of sin, death, and the accusing Law.[36] Here is prophesied a time of great joy because "as in the day of Midian's defeat, [the Lord has] shattered the yoke that burdens them, the bar across their shoulders, the rod of their oppressor" (Isaiah 9:4). As Gideon slew the Midianites with only 300 men (Judges 7:2ff.), so against all human reasoning the new spiritual reign will defeat sin, death, the accusing Law, hell, and all the other forces of evil in the birth of a little child and in the weakness of God in the cross of Christ. Luther forcefully emphasizes that Christ's

---

34 WA 19:166.21ff., 361.33ff.; 25:124.27f.; 31/2:72.13ff., 393.4ff., 500.3ff. Luther's comprehensive commentaries on Isaiah can be found in WA 25:89ff. and WA 32/2, which also includes sermons on Isaiah texts.

35 WA 25:97f.; 31/2:19–22. See also the comments on Isaiah 4:3, WA 25:104f.

36 WA 19:134.35ff., 135.15ff.; 25:121.5ff.; 52:579.4ff. For Luther, the hardening of the chosen people against God's Messiah appears as an unbelievably sad reality in the midst of his brimming eloquence on the limitlessness of God's salvation.

universal reign of joy is not built on human power and ability but on God's wisdom and authority.[37] *Missio Dei* and *missio Christi* announce the good news of salvation for all peoples.

Isaiah 9:6 describes the distinguishing mark of Christ's reign: "And he will be called Wonderful Counselor, Mighty God, Everlasting Father, Prince of Peace." Christ's reign is inexpressibly wonderful. In it, Christ through the Word opposes all spiritual enemies while at the same time feeding, propagating, and ruling his reign and his people. Ultimately, everything rests on Christ, the Gospel, and the forgiveness of sins.[38] God in Jesus Christ will build his reign and it will be great and glorious forever.[39]

In Luther's 1526 commentary on Isaiah 9:7f., he writes:

Why would he be given such a name? He answers and says: Because "there will be no end to his government." He doesn't say: Because he will sit high for his own sake. . . . Instead, it is because he must gather us through the Word and lead us into his reign. Therefore he must give us such names and accomplish such works in us and with us. His reign becomes great, however, because the number of Christians daily increases and becomes more from the beginning of the Gospel until the end of the world. Because the nature of this reign is also that it constantly increases and is formed, the Gospel is never unoccupied or rests but instead runs its course and expands in the whole world until the last day comes.[40]

These are clear words about Christ's government and the way of the Word and faith out to all peoples until the end of the world. For Luther, it is still the time of mission in the world.

Luther knows that while being opposed by the Jews and later being persecuted by the Roman Empire, a few Christians were engaged in mission and spread the Gospel among the heathen. The cross and persecution always follow the expansion of the Gospel. Therefore the work of world mission can never be accomplished with human power. In the work of the church and mission, it is God/Christ who is the functioning and sustaining subject.[41] Luther rejects any notion that salvation was intended only for God's chosen people, that is, Israel. He asks:

---

37 WA 19:145.17ff.; 25:122.28ff., 122.44ff.; 52:579. Cf. WA 5:635.26ff. in which Luther, without hesitation, interprets Psalm 22 as Christ's suffering.

38 WA 19:153–63; 25:123.22ff.; 31/2:71.3ff.; 52:583ff. See also H. Bornkamm, *Luther und das Alte Testament*, 94.

39 WA 19:165f.; 52:586.13f.

40 WA 19:164.2ff.

41 WA 19:164.18ff.

But what will happen with the heathen who have not heard about the kingdom of David? Won't we also enter Christ's reign or is it only the Jews who will become blessed? Answer: With this prediction, Isaiah follows the manner of Scripture and gives the promises about Christ and his reign to the Jews alone because Christ as Abraham's seed was promised to the Jews alone. But Christ has not continued to be the Savior of the Jews alone, as Paul says in Romans 15:8f: "For I tell you that Christ has become a servant of the Jews on behalf of God's truth, to confirm the promises made to the patriarchs so that the Gentiles may glorify God for his mercy . . ." So according to the promise Christ is only for the Jews, but according to actual fact he belongs to the whole world. He must, of course, be promised to a certain people among all the peoples since he could not be born from all peoples and all seed. But he would not bring blessing only for this people, but instead for the whole world.[42]

In this passage, Luther acknowledges the special promises to the Jews but also recognizes the universality of the Gospel. Christ will build his reign over the whole world. The gift of the Gospel to the peoples rests only on God's mercy.

Luther also points out that Isaiah 11:10–11 looks forward to the sprouting of Jesse's root, which in the Gospel without works of the Law stands up as a banner for the Gentiles: "In that day the Root of Jesse will stand as a banner for the peoples; the nations will rally to him, and his place of rest will be glorious. In that day the Lord will reach out his hand a second time to reclaim the remnant that is left of his people." When Christ has been raised up (John 12:32), then he will through the Word call all peoples, both heathens and Jews. Luther emphasizes that the peoples, or the heathen, will be visited during this era.[43] The servant of the Lord, or Christ, will, according to Isaiah 42:1, 6, preach a sweet Gospel. Hereby Christ will become the light of the peoples (*lumen gentium*).[44] Luther's mission universalism is also apparent in connection with Isaiah 49:1, 6. Not only Israel but also the heathen, or the lands by the sea, will be called, and in this way God's salvation will gather one single church from the entire world.[45]

Luther writes in a commentary on Isaiah from 1527–1530:

"It is too small a thing for you to be a servant" etc. Also the peoples will be saved through the Gospel. This is a crystal clear passage which shows that we heathen will be incorporated into Christ's body and reign so that we share in the covenant, the promises and God's grace. Christ must be the light of the peoples, the master and teacher of the peoples, so that the heathen will be saved through him. Therefore all we among the peoples who receive Christ are

---

42 WA 19:166.19ff.

43 WA 25:134.29ff., 135.37ff.; 31/2:88.12ff.

44 WA 25:268.26ff., 271.13ff.; 31/2:309.17ff., 314.22ff.

45 WA 25:303.16ff., 305.13ff.; 31/2:393.31ff.

truly Abraham's seed (descendants). . . . This passage contains the most effective solution to the arguments by which the Jews push themselves against us heathen (*gentes*).[46]

As in previously discussed texts, it is surprising how forcefully Luther opposes any narrowing of the field when it comes to defining those who have the right to hear the Gospel. The covenant with the chosen people has been expanded or passed over into a covenant with limitless dimensions. One also notices that Luther often says that both Jews and Gentiles—however, only those who in faith and sincerity receive the message of salvation—belong to Christ's reign. Luther reckons the Germans among the heathen who ought to be incorporated into Christ's reign.[47]

Luther forcefully discusses mission in his commentary on Isaiah 60:1ff. He interprets this text in 1522–1545 as the clearest prophecy about how God's salutary glory, light, and grace—and not the righteousness of the Law—would be proclaimed for the whole world because Christ, or Abraham's blessed seed, had come. Luther says that Isaiah and the other prophets draw on the promises to Abraham (Genesis 12:3; 18:18). "It follows clearly from these words that Christ, Abraham's seed, will become known in the whole world. This could not occur through his own person. It has therefore occurred through preaching . . . a preaching about blessing and grace . . . John 8:56: Abraham laughed (Genesis 17:17) that he should get to see my day. He has seen it and become glad."[48] Isaiah 60:1ff. prophesies about Christ's reign or the church. The dawn of the light and glory indicate not only Christ's birth but also primarily "the dawn of the Gospel after Christ's ascension, whereby Christ has spiritually and blessedly gone up and been glorified in the hearts of all believers in the world."[49]

As much as Luther can say about the natural knowledge of God in creation and the Law, the words in Isaiah 60:2 ("See, darkness covers the earth and thick darkness is over the peoples") indicate that this natural knowledge of God is ultimately nothing and darkness. It leads to idolatry, self-righteousness, and above all, this natural knowledge resists and does not recognize the Gospel or God's salvation.[50] Therefore God's glory in Christ must rise, and it continues to be revealed

---

46 WA 25:305.13ff. (cf. LW 17:175).

47 Cf. also the mission universalism in the commentaries on the originally centripetal text in Isaiah 49:3 (WA 25:304.13ff.). Luther also marks the movement of the Gospel out to the heathen in connection with Isaiah 51:4f. about the biding of the islands (WA 25:316.44ff.; 31/2:415.34ff.).

48 WA 10/1.1:524.2ff. Cf. WA 25:361.37ff.; 31/2:560.6ff.; 49:669.37ff.

49 WA 10/1.1:526.18ff.

50 WA 10/1.1:528ff.; 25:362.29ff.; 31/2:501.20ff.; 49:504.22ff. Cf. the investigation concerning natural religion, *Luther and World Mission*, 37–81.

through the Gospel, even in Luther's time. The heathen—even their princes—will become Christians and wander in the light of Christ. But the Jews, the pope, and the Turks gather the peoples against Christ.[51] Luther speaks of this coalition against faith in Christ throughout his active life as a reformer, not only during the so-called apocalyptic final phase of his life.[52]

Something of a missiological *locus classicus* exists in Isaiah 60:4–6, according to Luther's exposition. The words in Isaiah 60:4 ("All assemble and come to you") are not allowed to and cannot indicate a geographic assembly in Jerusalem. Instead, it is proclaimed here that God's salvation seeks to reach all peoples. Luther claims in 1522:

> Isaiah's meaning seems to be: "Look round about thee, unto the four quarters of the world. I will expand thee into all the earth, and thy children shall dwell everywhere." The words of the text were designed to comfort the first Christians at Jerusalem in view of the fact that they were few in number [and] despised. . . . [The] violence [of the persecuting Jews] only helped to fulfill this God-directed prophecy of Isaiah against themselves. Their persecution drove Christians into all the world and extended the Gospel until everywhere the sons and daughters of Jerusalem [i.e. of the church] were gathered to the light.[53]

This citation is an excellent example of how Luther unites mission and persecution. Evil designs against Christians can be transformed in the hands of God so Christians and the Gospel will truly go out to their intended goal, that is, to the whole world.

Luther understands Isaiah 60:5 as a description of how the Mediterranean region was Christianized because the Scriptures speak of the Mediterranean Sea as "the Sea." Jerusalem will swell with joy when the West (the Mediterranean area) receives Christ, primarily through Paul's preaching of the Gospel. Then "the wealth of the seas [peoples] and the riches of the nations [a great mass of Gentiles]" will turn toward Christ. "This prophecy of Isaiah was largely fulfilled through the instrumentality of Paul our apostle. Through his preaching 'the abundance of the seas' [*die menge des mehres*] was converted and 'the wealth of the nations' [*macht der heyden*] came into the faith. The latter part of this verse is designed to explain who are the sons and daughters that come from afar, namely, the abundance of the Gentiles on the great Mediterranean, whom Paul converted."[54] In Luther's interpretation, the words about joy and trembling belong

---

51 WA 10/1.1:539.13ff. and 49:504.22ff., 505.18ff., 669.37ff.

52 Cf. *Luther and World Mission*, 47–90.

53 Lenker 6:328–29 (WA 10/1.1:542.17ff.).

54 WA 10/1.1:544.11ff., 546.6ff. Cf. WA 31/2:502.27ff.

together with the Spirit of the new covenant according to Acts 10:45, for example.[55] Luther believes that Isaiah 60:6 describes the reception of the Gospel in the lands to the east of Jerusalem. The reformer mentions a list of peoples and lands in this context and proves himself to be an astute geographer.[56] Isaiah 60:4–6 speaks about how the Gospel has been offered to the most significant regions of the world and how they have received it. Both the Mediterranean regions and Arabia in the east have received the promises and the Gospel. The prophet foresees the time of the Spirit and the church, the time of the universal Gospel of salvation, the time of world mission.[57]

Luther has also focused on global mission in his exposition of Isaiah 66:19: "I will set a sign among them, and I will send some of those who survive to the nations . . ." The sign is Christ and the Gospel of Christ, and Luther makes a great deal of effort to understand who these peoples are who receive the Gospel. One also observes how a text with a centripetal mission motif can be transformed into a centrifugal text through a Christological-prophetic exposition by Luther.[58] For Luther, the mission epoch that was restricted only to God's chosen people has definitely passed away after Christ's ascension and the sending of the Spirit.

Finally, we will consider a few passages in Luther's commentaries on Zechariah. The reformer often interprets these texts in a spiritual or metaphorical way. In Zechariah 2:1–2, we read about the man with the measuring line. He is going to measure the breadth and length of Jerusalem. In his work on Zechariah in 1527, Luther interprets this metaphorically as the spiritual Jerusalem or the church. In this way, Zechariah 2 does not speak of the earthly Jerusalem as does Zechariah 1; "instead, it will become such a large Jerusalem that one cannot measure it, but it will be without walls and as wide as the world, so that God himself will be a burning wall around it."[59] In this allegorical exposition, Luther says the angel with the measuring line is Christ, and he measures his reign as long and as

---

55 WA 10/1.1:548.18ff.; 49:672.37ff.

56 WA 10/1.1:550.1ff.; 25:363.12ff.; 31/2:502.32ff.

57 WA 10/1.1:554.14ff. Cf. Isaiah 60:9 about the islands longing for Christ, WA 25:364.15ff.; 31/2:504.30ff.

58 WA 25:400.3ff.; 31/2:583.5ff. It should be pointed out that Luther, in the continuous commentary on Joel in *Lectures on the Minor Prophets* (1524), develops even further the mission motif on the basis of Joel 2:28f. Luther briefly emphasizes that with the sending of the Spirit, a universally directed and sweet message is given and that all who are touched by the Spirit witness about Christ. However, we will see how important the words in Joel 2:28f. are when Luther develops the thesis about God's salvation for all peoples.

59 WA 23:522.29ff. Concerning the cessation of the old priesthood and Christ's coming priesthood, cf. WA 23:501.17ff., 502.15ff. H. Bornkamm, *Luther und das Alte Testa-*

broad as God's Spirit reaches. God's Spirit and Christ as the foreman are central to Luther's interpretation.

> Therefore the measuring line has to do with a different kind of measuring, namely, that of the spiritual Jerusalem. The man with the measuring line, however, is Christ, our Lord, the one Master Builder of the New Jerusalem. The fact that He has the measuring line in His hand means, however, that He distributes the Holy Spirit with His gifts. . . . (Rom. 12:3ff.; Eph. 4:7ff.; 1 Cor. 12:4ff.). For Christianity goes no farther nor is it more confined than the Spirit of Christ goes and is offered, and that is this spiritual measuring. The Spirit, however, goes as far as the world goes, as He says through the prophet Joel (Joel 2:28), "I will pour out My Spirit on all flesh," that is, upon all the people in all the world. Not that all men receive the Holy Spirit, for the greater part persecute Him. . . . [T]he Holy Spirit is sent out upon all men in all the world through the Word of the Gospel and is offered to all of them. Poured out in this way, it hovers over all men in the world wherever the Gospel is preached.[60]

Luther speaks of the spiritual Jerusalem with a universal preaching of the Gospel of Christ and about how Christ's Spirit breaks down all limitations to Israel and Jerusalem. The reformer does not deny that the old Israel was chosen by God and has an important role in history and in salvation history. However, he believes that the physical Israel/Jerusalem has been succeeded by the spiritual and eternal Israel/Jerusalem. The reformer claims that, according to the prophets, Christ would come while the physical Jerusalem and the Jewish government were still intact. He would live in this Jerusalem but create a new, spiritual/eternal reign. This has occurred in Jesus' birth, life, and crucifixion. Luther believes the fact that the historical Jerusalem was destroyed and the Jewish government lost its power is one proof among others that this spiritual reign of Christ has come.[61] This does not mean that God as the Lord of history and of the Gospel has abandoned his chosen people. He continues to offer the Gospel to both Jews and Gentiles, and thereby he holds out the opportunity to be incorporated into the

---

ment, 28, points out that Luther's Zechariah commentaries are characterized by a thoroughgoing allegorization. Furthermore, it is emphasized that the prophet through the Word disciplines and points to Christ.

60 LW 20:182 (WA 23:522.32ff.).

61 WA 23:523, 532.4ff. Cf. WA 23:501.17ff. and 19:350ff. Concerning Luther's view of Israel's religio-political task in the old covenant, the careless self-idolatry and hardening of the people, and how the people ceased to be a gathered people after the crucifixion of Jesus and their dispersion, see Pauls, *Luther und die Juden*, 1:23ff.; and H. Bornkamm, *Luther und das Alte Testament*, 63ff., 92ff. *Luther and World Mission*, 326ff., investigates this problem and reviews the existing literature.

spiritual Israel. In the first major division of chapter 4, I will consider how Luther reflects on Romans 11:25 about the salvation of all Israel.

On Zechariah 2:8, Luther says that God himself, through the Son of Man and the preaching of his disciples, will make known his decision for salvation among all the Gentiles of the world. This *missio Dei* through the words of Christ and the preaching of the apostles and their followers always includes a struggle with heresy. Luther emphasizes in a surprisingly forceful manner the signficance of the apostles and the ministry of preaching for the expansion of God's reign. The expanding power and ambassadorial character of Christ's reign are prominent in Luther's expositions. Zechariah 2:11 and 9:16 provide Luther with an opportunity to emphasize that the Jews, dispersed as they are into numerous religious directions, and the Gentiles, who are even more split into different types of idolatry, can be united into one people and reign through the apostolic word. God's Gospel unites Jews and Gentiles in all parts of the world.[62]

In connection with Zechariah 9:17, Luther emphasizes that those who have recently come to faith carry their testimony further and lead new people to faith in Christ. Zeal for winning souls for Christ ought not be the task only of the ministry of preaching, but of all Christians.[63] This harmonizes well with what we have seen in chapter 2 about Luther's belief that all Christians are responsible for the expansion of God's reign and have the duty to witness about what they have experienced through their faith in Christ.[64]

In his commentaries on Zechariah, the reformer shows in many ways how he thinks about the centrifugal nature of the expansion of God's reign in the world. Christians are sown like seeds among the peoples, and both official preachers and laypeople preach and witness. As a fire, the Gospel goes forth in the power of

---

62 WA 23:534.24ff., 539.31ff., 622.1ff. Cf. WA 23:533.10f. concerning how "Christ through the Gospel has come to all places." This short sentence is opposed to Luther's usual thesis that the Gospel has not yet reached everywhere.

63 LW 20:297–98 (WA 23:622.32ff.): "But in this kingdom things happen in a wondrous way. There one finds the very finest and most pleasing bearing and increasing of people. For there no children are begotten that will lie in cradles. What else, then? Only fine, strong young men and full-grown, beautiful maidens are begotten there. . . . For when a man becomes a Christian, he can immediately teach and act and at once beget other Christians, just as if a mother bore a boy who at once could take a wife and beget children. That would be an unusual child. But so are all the Christians: they are full-grown young men who through the Word can beget other Christians, and full-grown maidens who can carry and bear other Christians. This bearing and increasing is brought about through grain and new wine, that is, through the Gospel. [Here Luther cites 1 Corinthians 4:15; Galatians 4:19; Isaiah 66:7.]"

64 See *Luther and World Mission*, 89–95.

the Spirit and wins people to Christ's reign. As Luther says in his metaphorical commentary on Zechariah 10:9:

"Though I scattered them among the nations, yet in far countries they shall remember Me." The increase is to take place in this way: They will be scattered among the nations, like a seed which is increased in a field. This must of course be a spiritual increase, because they are not to return home from the nations but are to be sown there among the people and then increased. All of this takes place in this manner, that they will be sent by God among the nations as preachers and thus draw many people to themselves and through themselves to Christ. "For," He says, "they shall remember Me in far countries, that is, they shall preach and teach of Me, and thus they shall be increased and shall convert many others to Me."[65]

In a metaphorical interpretation of Zechariah 12:6, Luther says:

Not only shall the persecutors rage in vain, but the Christians shall also, through the Word, harvest much fruit among all the Gentiles and shall convert and save many, and thus they shall devour round about them like a fire that is burning in the midst of dry wood or straw. The fire of the Holy Spirit, then, shall devour the Gentiles according to the flesh and prepare a place everywhere for the Gospel and the kingdom of Christ.[66]

It ought also to be observed that the reformer uses the word *Gentile* to refer to non-Christians, not non-Jews.

One finds many such mission passages in Luther's commentaries on Zechariah. In the two final citations, the Gospel and the way God's salvation goes out to the peoples are given a practical application. Both lay believers and public preachers carry the Gospel to all peoples who will be won by the Word and the Spirit, converted, and believe the Gospel. The reformer also has, through a metaphorical interpretation of such difficult things in Zechariah as chariots, horses, angels, construction workers, winds, etc., expressed his beliefs about the church's first mission era under the direction of the apostles and their followers. Those first preachers continued and courageously endured great difficulties and persecution. By means of the Gospel, they provided the peoples with faith and the Holy Spirit while struggling against heresies. Luther proves that he possesses good historical insight into the church's first mission period.[67]

---

65 LW 20:305–6 (WA 23:629.15ff.).

66 LW 20:326 (WA 23:645.30ff.). Cf. Danbolt, "Misjon—evangeliets frie løp," 254.

67 WA 23:524ff., 581ff. Concerning Luther and church history, see Schäfer, *Luther als Kirchenhistoriker*, and Headley, *Luther's View of Church History*.

SUMMARY

I have now finished the exploration and analysis of the mission motif in Luther's exposition of the Old Testament. A summary of the foregoing analysis could include the following major points.

1. Luther means that the whole Bible is fundamentally a message about universal salvation for all peoples in Jesus Christ. Already the Old Testament saints includes Jesus and the true faith. The reformer exposits the Old Testament with a Christological-prophetic method, and the relation between the Old and New Testaments is that of promise and fulfillment. But faith in Jesus and even the church itself are already realities in the Old Testament.

2. Already the *protoevangel* in Genesis 3:5 concerning the Seed/Christ points to world mission. This becomes more evident later in texts concerning God's covenant with Abraham and the promises about universal blessings through his seed, that is, through Christ (Genesis 12:2–3; 17:4–8; 22:18). Long before the covenant at Sinai and the giving of the Law, God's covenant with Abraham promised salvation by grace for all people who live under judgment and death because of their sins.

3. During the time of the patriarchs, the "wandering church" sought to spread the Gospel about Christ and his righteousness. This occurred partly when the heathen came to the settlements of the patriarchs (a centripetal motif) and partly when the patriarchs reached out to those whom they met during their wanderings or during their settlements in foreign lands (often a centrifugal motif).

4. The texts in the Psalms and the Prophets concerning the pilgrimage of the heathens and about their worship of YHWH in Jerusalem are constantly read backward and exposited in a New Testament centrifugal direction. Luther means that the covenant at Sinai, along with the heathens' pilgrimage to worship YHWH in Jerusalem, is replaced with Christ's work and the Spirit's sending in the new covenant. Therefore the Old Testament must be read in the light of the New Testament. Luther focuses especially on those texts in the Psalms and the Prophets that speak of a great era of salvation for all peoples. With power and consistency, Luther asserts on the basis of the Old Testament that God's salvation belongs to and should be announced to all people. He substantiates this universal aspect of mission with many additional texts from the New Testament.

5. Christ, the Word, and the Spirit gather one single people of God from both Jews and Gentiles. The chosen people's hardness of heart does not exclude

them from sharing in the blessings of the Gospel, as long as they repent and believe in God's Messiah. Therefore there is only one church of both Jews and Gentiles who are saved through faith apart from works of Law.

6. The reformer never ceases to emphasize that the message of universal salvation in its very nature is a good and wonderful message about undeserved grace and forgiveness through faith in the Seed/Christ. At the same time, this message belongs together with the Law/Gospel dialectic, with the heart's repentance, and with the abandonment of every form of idolatry.

7. It is emphasized that the reign of Christ is a spiritual reign in the middle of an existential-earthly reality. The reign of Christ will always be spread through the Gospel, not with earthly power and coercion. As the Gospel reaches different people groups, their habits, laws, orders, and culture are not cast aside. Luther in no way represents a kind of missionary cultural imperialism.

8. The commentaries on the Old Testament show that Luther defines mission—without, however, using the term—as God's people or church in movement with the Gospel to all those who have not heard or believed it. The true faith takes unavoidable expression in confessing and witnessing to others about God's salvation. The patriarchs were the first messengers as they declared the Gospel among relatives, among visitors to their camps, and among those whom they met during their journeys. On the basis of the Old Testament, Luther emphasizes that both the testimony of laypeople and the Word's public ministry are important for the expansion of God's reign. The importance the reformer assigns from an Old Testament perspective to public ministry (that is, ordained ministry), public preaching, the means of grace, and worship services indicates that he apparently sees these as important for all mission work.

9. Luther shows in many ways that it is at the same time the Father, the Son, and the Spirit who drive God's people forward in the spreading of the Gospel and the faith. It is the Trinity who works through the Gospel messenger. In his commentary on Psalm 110:1f., Luther especially emphasizes that it is the glorified Christ who becomes the one who drives the work of God's reign forward through the preaching of the Gospel. Therefore the Word/Gospel must have message carriers. The way the Gospel and the preachers reach the people is not a finished work by Luther's time but a continuing one.

10. The mission of God's people always encounters Satan's antimission, Satan's antichurch, heresies, and all types of evil. Therefore the spreading of the Gospel is always accompanied by opposition, crosses, and persecu-

tions. However, God can use these evils in such a way that they serve the Gospel. Through persecution, Christians are forced to move from place to place, and with them the Gospel is continuously taken to new fields.

11. On the basis of the Old Testament, Luther often speaks of how the mission of God and the church will enter a great era through the glorification of Christ and the Spirit's sending. This is a good segue to Luther's exegesis of the New Testament.

THE MISSION MOTIF
IN LUTHER'S INTERPRETATION OF THE GOSPELS

Despite everything that divides them, the Old and New Testaments are a unity because both contain the message about Jesus Christ. In the first major division of chapter 3, we have seen that Luther, in his prophetic-Christological interpretation of the Old Testament, spoke of Christ, of his work of salvation, of faith, of the church, etc. This does not prevent Luther, however, from developing aspects of salvation history on the basis of both Testaments. The Old Testament contains promises about the coming Messiah, and the New Testament speaks about how those promises are fulfilled through the incarnation of God's Son, his reconciling death, and his resurrection. The Christ-event is the center of the Scriptures, an event by which the Old Testament and the way of the church under the new covenant until the final judgment is illuminated.[68]

Luther's forewords to the New Testament (1522/1546) show that he recognizes the significance and the uniqueness of the New Testament and the new covenant. It is surprising how clearly the mission motif shines through in this text: "Thus this gospel of God or New Testament is a good story and report, sounded forth into all the world by the apostles, telling of a true David who strove with sin, death, and the devil, and overcame them, and thereby rescued all those who were

---

68 Luther's way of understanding salvation history is emphasized by Pedersen, *Luther som skriftfortolker*, 224ff. Although I have much esteem for how H. Bornkamm emphasizes that the Old Testament's words about Christ, faith, and the church ought not be considered as more or less empty anticipations of that which is to come in the new covenant (*Luther und das Alte Testament*, 209ff.), I cannot approve of the following statement: "Damit stürzt Luther das ganze heilsgeschichtliche Schema der altkirchlichen Exegese" (216). Periodically, Luther does note that the Old Testament stands under the horizon of the promises and the New Testament under the heaven of the fulfilled promises. That Luther can combine realism concerning faith in Christ in the Old Testament and a salvation history perspective is shown clearly in his forewords to the translations of the Old and New Testaments. See WADB 8:11–31; 6:3–11.

captive in sin, afflicted with death, and overpowered by the devil."[69] The Gospel is actually a public declaration about what people may receive in the saving work of Christ. In his testament, Christ has expressly said that that which he has won must be preached and distributed in the entire world. All who receive the message in faith share in that which Christ has won. "This report and encouraging tidings, or evangelical and divine news, is also called a New Testament. For it is a testament when a dying man bequeaths his property, after his death, to his legally defined heirs. And Christ, before his death, commanded and ordained that his gospel be preached after his death in all the world [Luke 24:44–47]. Thereby he gave to all who believe, as their possession, everything he had."[70]

The following section carefully investigates how the mission motif comes to expression in the reformer's exegesis and interpretation of the four Gospels of the New Testament.[71] In his interpretations of the Gospels, Luther takes up both the specific problems of the Reformation and those problems that concern church and mission in all times. In his interpretation of Scripture, Luther does not draw strict lines of demarcation between scholarly exegesis and preaching, between scholarship and edification.

THE MISSION MOTIF IN THE COMMENTARIES ON THE SYNOPTIC GOSPELS

The salvation history perspective becomes necessary for Luther when he sees that the work of Jesus and the disciples during the master's earthly life was limited to the Jewish people, the circumcised. Luther has to explain the pericope about the Canaanite woman in Matthew 15:21ff. (with parallels), among others. The words in Matthew 15:24, 26 are unambiguous: "I was sent only to the lost sheep of Israel. . . . It is not right to take the children's bread and toss it to their dogs." The reformer well understands that Jesus, as a rule, preached about the reign of heaven within the historical territory of Israel. At the same time, he understands from the Gospels as a whole that Christ's saving work and the Gospel of the New Testament has a universal vector. Because the history of salvation continued, one can, after Jesus' earthly life, no longer speak of a restricted or a closed offer of salvation. Therefore it is easy to understand that Luther would use Matthew 15:21ff. as a way to speak to his contemporaries about how faith defeats doubt through a perse-

---

69 LW 35:358 (WADB 6:5.4ff.).

70 LW 35:358–59 (WADB 6:5.12ff.).

71 Among the literature about Luther's interpretation of the Gospels, the following studies ought to be named especially: Bauer, *Die Wittenberger Universitätstheologie*; Ebeling, *Evangelische Evangelienauslegung*; Loewenich, *Luther als Ausleger der Synoptiker*; Pedersen, *Luther som skriftfortolker*; and Ingebrand, *Bibeltolkningens problematik*.

vering trust in the Word of Christ.[72] The reformer also has considered Jesus' commissioning speech in Matthew 10, which contains the well-known words in vv. 5–6, "Do not go among the Gentiles or enter any town of the Samaritans. Go rather to the lost sheep of Israel." Luther was well aware of the "conflict" between this limited sending (cf. Romans 15:8; Acts 13:46) and the universal sending that was to come and is expressed in Mark 16:15 and Luke 14:21. That the twelve apostles should wait for a time before evangelizing the heathen and the Samaritans depends on the fact that Christ was the servant of the circumcised (Romans 15:8) until the Law was fulfilled in his death. Afterward, the apostles were newly commissioned to go into all the world. Luther uses Matthew 10 to review the church's transformation from the closed synagogue to a church for all peoples with the Word and Christ in the center. Furthermore, the reformer writes about the church's predicament in the world and the antagonism between the missionizing church and the rulers of this age.[73]

When reflecting on the above texts, Luther argues against restricting true worship of God to Jerusalem or, in Luther's time, to Rome. He adduces Jesus' response to the Samaritan woman in John 4:21–23: "Believe me, woman, a time is coming when you will worship the Father neither on this mountain nor in Jerusalem. You Samaritans worship what you do not know; we worship what we do know, for salvation is from the Jews. Yet a time is coming and has now come when the true worshipers will worship the Father in spirit and truth." Luther means that the church with the Spirit after Pentecost is liberated from all geographic restriction. Of course, salvation comes from the Jews (John 4:22), but it is not limited to this closed group. Instead, it is offered to all and is received in worship in all the earth.[74] Thus on the basis of some New Testament passages, Luther understood that there was a limitation to Jesus' mission field during his earthly life. Later, this particularism is removed, according to the Scriptures. Church and mission are to spread the faith of Christ to all peoples. This is a special characteristic of the new covenant as it regards the expansion of God's reign, that is, mission. The Old Testament prophets had foreseen this great epoch. With the Spirit of Pentecost, it has arrived. We will first see how Luther develops this thesis on the basis of texts from the Synoptic Gospels.

---

72 WA 11:43f.; 15:455.19ff.; 37:314.21ff.; 38:594.18ff., 595.3ff., 595.14ff. Cf. Ebeling, *Evangelische Evangelienauslegung*, 81, 189, 193; and Loewenich, *Luther als Ausleger der Synoptiker*, 97ff., 159ff.

73 WA 12:600.13ff.; 38:494.17ff., 495.14ff., 497.29ff.

74 WA 47:224.29ff., 226.7ff. Cf. Ebeling, *Evangelische Evangelienauslegung*, 193, on how, in light of salvation history, Luther interprets a number of passages in the New Testament about Israel and about the church that consists of both Jews and Gentiles.

Luther's commentaries on the story about the Wise Men in Matthew 2:1–12 show that the mission motif is almost completely missing in the beginning of 1517. Later, and especially in the *House Postil* (1544), it occupies a relatively large place in the reformer's commentaries. The fact that the Magi first arrive in the glorious city of Jerusalem and later, led by the Scriptures, find Jesus in the humble village of Bethlehem shows that natural reason is blind concerning God's salvation, that the Word alone must be received in humility, and that faith alone leads to the Savior. The one who wants to find God's salvation ought not speculate. Instead, with the Wise Men, one ought to seek the poor incarnated God in Bethlehem's manger. This theme appears in all Luther's commentaries on this passage after the Reformation breakthrough. At the same time, Luther increasingly emphasizes that the story of the Wise Men is a clear testimony to the fact that God wanted to call even the Gentiles to Christ's reign. The Magi were called along with the Jews into the new covenant not through the Law and circumcision but on the basis of grace and mercy.[75]

Because Luther integrates God's reign/the church and their expansion (that is, mission), the commentaries on the parables of the kingdom of heaven in Matthew 13 (and parallels) indicate a great deal about the reformer's view of mission work. From Luther's comments, it is easy to see how completely decisive the seed

---

75 A sermon from January 6, 1517, lacks the mission motif completely. In connection with the traditional allegorical interpretation, Luther is occupied with the personal sacrifice of faith, hope, and love (gold, frankincense, and myrrh). The mission motif comes in later; see WA 10/1.1:557ff.; 27:13ff., 36.61ff. This is especially clear in *House Postil* (1544), WA 52:91.16ff.: "Das ist die Historia, in welcher wir erstlich sehen, wie das Gott auch die Heyden zum reich Christi foddert und zum volck annimbt, ob sie wol nit beschnitten noch wie die Jüden dem gesetz unterworffen waren. Solchs ist ein grosser trost, da wir Gott billich für loben und dancken sollen. Denn hie haben wir Heiden ein gewisse zeugnuss, das wir nicht verzweyfflen sollen, als gehörten wir nicht zu Christo, Sonder das wir uns sein sollen annemen als wol als die Jüden . . . . Denn dise Weysen sind ye Heyden gewest, die keinen Priester, keinen Gottes dienst, kein Gottes wort hetten und waren unbeschnitten, Und dennoch unangesehen solches alles, kommen sie als frembde und gar unverdiente leut zu dem liecht, dem Herren Christo, unnd nemen jhn an, Er nimbt sie auch an und lest jhm jhr anbetten und geschenck gefallen." Cf. WA 52:88.19ff. See Ebeling, *Evangelische Evangelienauslegung*, 475–95, with its detailed investigation; and Loewenich, *Luther als Ausleger der Synoptiker*, 81, 108, 153f. Bergman, *Den lutherske Reformation og Missionen*, 58ff., means that Luther with the frequently occurring "Wir Heiden" does not indicate the pagan world but the Christians of the West/Germany who were the descendants of the pagans. It is noteworthy that Bergman does not see that Luther follows Paul and divides the world into Jews/Gentiles, circumcised/uncircumcised. That Luther uses this vocabulary to speak about the Germans as pagans simply means that the Germans—however Christian they might be—do not exist under the old covenant, the Law, and circumcision.

(Matthew 13:3ff., 19ff.), or the preaching of God's Word in the whole world, is. Especially the Gospel about God's grace in Christ is to be preached. Luther emphasizes that God himself, through the Word, is the power of the expansion of his reign. Therefore those who trust in Christ need not become discouraged when many hearers of God's Word do not bear fruit nor when Satan sows his evil seed among the good seed (Matthew 13:24ff.). Luther emphasizes that weakness and hiddenness characterize God's reign in the world and that the church always struggles against heresies and sin. He energetically opposes the notion that people ought to try personally to build a reign of perfection. It is only the final judgment that will divide the good from the evil. In the present era, the church ought to preach and build the reign of God primarily through the Word and Sacraments. Even if one encourages and exercises church discipline, one will never be able to attain a completely pure church.[76]

Luther also considers the foundation of the building of God's reign. In connection with Matthew 16:18, Luther defends himself against the idea that Peter should be the rock of the church and its foundation. He also defends himself against the concept of the primacy of Rome that resulted from that interpretation. The reformer states that Christ has chosen to build a reign in the world that can-

---

76 A representative passage can be found in *Annotationes in aliquot capita Matthaei* (1538), WA 38:553–72, see especially 554.8ff., 558.5ff., 560.31ff., 561.1ff., 564.6ff., 567.24ff., 569.14ff. Surprisingly rich and fine are these words about the Gospel of Christ as the yeast: "Vult autem Christus hac parabola consolari nos et significare, quod Euangelium, novum fermentum, semel mixtum in genus hominum (id est pastam), non deficiet usque in finem mundi, sed penetrabit totam massam salvandorum . . . . Et sicut impossibile est fermentum semel pastae mixtum a pasta separari, qua immutavit paste naturam, Ita impossibile est rapi Christianos a Christo, Quia est in eis Christus fermentum ita incorporatus, ut unum sit corpus, una massa, ein kuche, ein brod etc." (WA 38:564.16ff.). About the church's humility and hiddenness, see WA 38:568.1ff.: "Ecclesiae thesaurum, scilicet Christum. Pii vero cognoscunt, et tamen non videntur esse Ecclesia, sed manent absconditi coram mundo. Ita stat illud argumentum a principio mundi: Ecclesia non est Ecclesia, et non Ecclesia est Ecclesia. . . . Quia et sine meritis, velut casu oblatus, accipitur, et tamen impiis manet absconditus, etiamsi verbis et factis et cruce et miraculis clarificetur." About the sorting of the wheat and the weeds (Matthew 13:24–30), see WA 38:561.32ff.: "Et sic sententia huius loci est de pacientia Sanctorum, qui coguntur ferre scandala et malos in Ecclesia, sicut dicit: De nobis exierunt, de nobis non fuerunt [1 John 2:19]. Ideo evellere malos ex Ecclesia nihil aliud est, quam Ecclesiam sine malis habere velle, quod est impossibile. Simul tamen stat, quod eos non toleramus, non probamus, non sinimus cum pace esse zizania, Sed increpamus, excommunicamus, facimus quae possumus." Cf. the many sermons on the parable of the sower (Luke 8:4ff.): WA 15:426ff.; 17/1:46ff.; 20:259ff.; 27:45ff.; 37:293f.; 52:142ff. See also Loewenich, *Luther als Ausleger der Synoptiker*, 31ff.; and Ebeling, *Evangelische Evangelienauslegung*, 52, 81, 105ff., 183f., 320, 448.

not be destroyed by any other power. The church is built on faith in Christ, on the confession of Christ, or simply on Christ. Luther has many arguments for his thesis, among them 1 Corinthians 3:11: "For no one can lay any foundation other than the one already laid, which is Jesus Christ." It is this Jesus Christ who enables the church to grow and who sustains it. Human authority and power can do nothing.[77]

Luther's commentaries on the second petition of the Lord's Prayer—"Thy kingdom come" (Matthew 6:10)—reveal an interesting development. In *An Exposition of the Lord's Prayer for Simple Laymen* (1519), one sees that Luther has barely begun to draw the missiological consequences of his new view of justification. In 1519, he is still completely preoccupied with the concepts of the coming of God's reign into the personal life of the individual who prays, that the power of God's grace might repress sin, and that the Christian both inwardly and outwardly might be clothed in the righteousness, discipline, humility, and goodness of the God-man. Mission among the heathen does not appear at all during this first period of Luther's work.[78] Already in "Eine kurze Form, etc. (1520)," Luther has something of an accent on prayer for the coming of the Gospel and on prayer for the propagation of faith and sanctification. In this work, Luther also distinguishes between the reign's partial coming in time and its fullness at Christ's parousia.[79] The more evangelistic and focused on the concrete work of church planting Luther became, the more "missionary" he became. In his *Sermons on the Catechism* (1528), Luther notes that God's/Christ's reign is not this-worldly but has to do with righteousness, salvation, and eternal life. Furthermore, God's reign grows in the present age and is perfected in the age to come. Luther prays for the success of the Gospel, the propagation of the faith, and growth in good works. The conditions under which God's reign exists are decided partly by the struggle between God and Satan and partly by the power and authority of the Gospel. Especially in the last of the sermons, the connection between the coming of Christ's reign and the preaching of God's true Word is emphasized.[80]

Not only the question about how one finds a graceful God but also the question about the practical work of Christ's reign must be considered. This is easy to

---

77 Öberg, *Himmelrikets nycklar och kyrklig bot i Luthers teologi*, 41ff., with the references.

78 WA 2:95ff. It is surprising that Luther connects the second petition in the Lord's Prayer only with the personal, even in *Personal Prayer Book* (1522). His interpretation is completely devoid of ecclesiological and missiological interests. See WA 10/2:398.10ff.

79 WA 7:22f.

80 WA 30/1:13.1ff.; 47:26ff., 100.4ff.

observe in the above texts, but it is even more clear in the explanation to the second petition of the Lord's Prayer in the Large Catechism (1529).

> What is the kingdom of God? Answer: Simply what we learned in the Creed, namely, that God sent his Son, Christ our Lord, into the world to redeem and deliver us from the power of the devil and to bring us to himself and rule us as a king of righteousness, life, and salvation against sin, death, and an evil conscience. To this end he also gave his Holy Spirit to teach us this through his holy Word and to enlighten and strengthen us in faith by his power.

> We pray here at the outset *that all this may be realized in us* and that God's name may be praised through his holy Word and our Christian lives. This we ask, both in order that we who have accepted it may remain faithful and grow daily in it *and in order that it may gain recognition and followers among other people and advance with power throughout the world.* So we pray that, led by the Holy Spirit, many may come into the kingdom of grace and become partakers of salvation, so that we may all remain together eternally in this kingdom which has now made its appearance among us.

> God's kingdom comes to us in two ways: first, it comes here, in time, through the Word and faith, and secondly, in eternity, it comes through the final revelation. Now, we pray for both of these, *that it may come to those who are not yet in it, and that it may come by daily growth here and in eternal life hereafter to us who have attained it.* All this is simply to say: "Dear father, we pray Thee, *give us thy Word, that the Gospel may be sincerely preached throughout the world* and that it may be received by faith and may work and live in us. So we pray that thy kingdom may prevail among us through the Word and the power of the Holy Spirit, that the devil's kingdom may be overthrown and he may have no right or power over us, until finally the devil's kingdom shall be utterly destroyed and sin, death, and hell exterminated, and that we may live forever in perfect righteousness and blessedness.[81]

On the basis of this long citation, one ought carefully to observe that the reign of God/Christ has to do with God's Word, faith, and sanctification. One notes even that the advent of God's reign is expressed as a divine work through the Word/Gospel. The vertical factor dominates the horizontal or human factor. The workers in the reign of God completely disappear before the divine active subject. Luther never spoke, for example, of a planned and programmed church growth "to evangelize the world in this generation." Church/mission stood on the front lines against Satan's reign. On that front line only God's power could decide the

---

81 LC II 51–54 (Tappert, 426–27; *Öberg's emphasis*). Cf. Scherer, *That the Gospel May Be Sincerely Preached*, 7ff. On how Luther uses the phrases "God's reign" and "Christ's reign" without differentiating between them, see Loewenich, *Luther als Ausleger der Synoptiker*, 208ff.

future of the church. It was God who led the growth of his own reign, and this reign would never be accepted by all people. The nerve in the church-building Gospel is Christ's redemption through which we are reconciled to God and liberated from Satan, sin, and death. The advent of God's reign occurs only partially in time and thereafter perfectly in eternity. In this way, Luther unites the present and the eschatological in his view of God's reign and mission. Prayer for the coming of God's reign is the same as prayer that God's Word might come more powerfully over the whole earth and that thereby God's Spirit might have the opportunity to create faith and Christian lifestyle. God's/Christ's reign becomes stronger where it has already broken in through the Gospel, the Spirit, and faith. But this reign also will be driven out into places in the world where it has not yet reached. Although Luther is occupied with the German Reformation, he has in no way neglected the universal perspective. Luther's words in the Large Catechism clarify how church and mission are integrated. Home in Germany and out on the front line of pure heathenism, it is a question of the coming of God's reign here on earth. And the same offer is given to everyone, wherever God's reign breaks in.

At least twelve examples of Luther's exposition of the parable of the wedding feast in Matthew 22:1–14 have been preserved. In different degrees in different years, it is emphasized how great and full of wedding joy God's reign is. It is emphasized that the Jews immediately—and in succession to them the Greeks, Romans, and Germans—have heaped more sins on their sins. They have despised the Gospel of Christ and received God's punishment: the destruction of Jerusalem and the disciplinary rod in Christian lands, that is, the Muslim invasion, the papacy, and the enthusiasts.[82]

It is especially important to note that in nearly every comment he makes on Matthew 22:1–14 Luther emphasizes the ongoing mission among the heathen who live without the promises of the covenant and the Law. He considers the words in Matthew 22:9–10: "Go to the street corners and invite to the banquet anyone you find. So the servants went out into the streets and gathered all the people they could find, both good and bad, and the wedding hall was filled with guests." The radical Gospel for everyone on earth without exception is described in a sermon from 1524:

> Afterward, the Gospel gets its start through the apostles. Now he says, "Go out!" Here no one is excluded. Christ concludes that all are children of the

---

82 See especially WA 12:668ff.; 20:523ff.; 36:342ff.; 45:175ff., 456f.; 52:504ff. Matthew 22:1–14 provides Luther occasions to emphasize how the church will never become free of sin and pure in time. He says something that is perennially relevant: "das man finde meuse treck unter dem pfeffer" (WA 37:181.23ff.; 52:512.3ff.). One can find a detailed analysis of Luther's exposition of Matthew 22:1–14 in Ebeling, *Evangelische Evangelienauslegung*, 61f., 174, 176, 192ff.

devil, so he sends out his own; otherwise it would have served no purpose. "Whoever you meet, bring here!" "Go out!" The apostles did this until the table was full. And this continues still every day, and the servants will continue to do so until the end of the world.[83]

After the Jewish people were invited to God's reign in Old Testament times and during Jesus' earthly life, a universal invitation to God's reign begins with the Great Commission to the apostles. This call still continues and will continue until the end of time. For Luther, now is the time of mission in the world, and the call to God's reign will, at Christ's own commission, continue as long as the world does. The Great Commission is not only an ethereal idea about universal salvation, but it also is realized through the consistent work of human beings. Furthermore, it is emphasized that everyone without exception shall be called. A passage in Luther's writings from 1525 in connection with Matthew 22:9 notes that it is still the time of mission:

> This is not yet completed. This era continues so that the servants go out onto the highways. The apostles began this work and we continue inviting all. The table will be full at the advent of the last day and when the Gospel has been made known in the whole world. . . . "But when the king came in to see the guests. . . ." This will happen on the last day. Then the table will be restricted, but not yet. Today, we have apostles and preachers.[84]

It is interesting to see how, in his expositions of the wedding feast in Matthew 22:1–14, Luther completely integrates the work of the domestic churches and of foreign mission.

The parable of the great banquet, the invitation, the many excuses, and the master's reaction (calling out on all streets and alleys) in Luke 14:16–24 provide Luther with the opportunity to speak about world mission.[85] The parable is not concerned with the Sacrament but with God's reign (the church) and the preaching of the Gospel about Christ and faith, says Luther in his allegorical and Chris-

---

83 WA 15:714.35ff.

84 WA 17/1:442.46ff. Cf. WA 52:511.26ff and especially 37:181.15ff.: " 'Ladet, wen ir findet.' Macht kein unterscheid. Er heisst Man, weib, Jung, Alt, als laden, Sic omnes sumus vocati, Id est: vocate omnes on all unterscheid, wen ir nur findet etc. Hoc est: venite, credite in Christum, lasst euch tauffen, horets Euangelium, diligite vos mutuo, das ist die ladung, Da solt ir zu essen finden, Id est: remissionem peccatorum, Vitam aeternam, victoriam mortis, inferni etc. Sic omnes invitamur, darff keiner sagen, quod non sit vocatus. Servi ghen hin aus und laden aus allen landen und leuten." Cf. Loewenich, *Luther als Ausleger der Synoptiker*, 42f.

85 WA 11:131ff.; 12:598ff.; 20:437ff.; 27:196ff.; 29:390ff.; 34/1:514ff.; 36:187ff.; 46:440ff.; 49:221ff.; 52:357ff. See Loewenich, Luther als Ausleger der Synoptiker, 47f.; and the detailed analysis in Ebeling, Evangelische Evangelienauslegung, 75f., 193f., 210.

tological interpretation. It is emphasized how great the invitation to God's reign is. The banquet, that is, God's reign, was prepared through Christ's life, death, and resurrection. Furthermore, it is noted that the apathy of the Jews and of others to the invitation is a great sin. Therefore already during Jesus' life, the message went out to the poor and the insignificant in Israel. It came out "into the streets and alleys" in Jerusalem (Luke 14:21).

Mission among the heathen enters the picture first in connection with Luke 14:23: "Then the master told his servant, 'Go out to the roads and country lanes and make them come in, so that my house will be full.'" Luther understands this verse to indicate the peoples or the heathen outside the Jewish urban context. Because the majority of the Jews were hardened, the invitation to the banquet of God's reign was offered to the heathen. The heathen lack the covenant promises and the Law of Moses and are idolaters. Nevertheless, they are invited—completely, unconditionally. The reformer also presses the point that one ought never to force another into God's reign. One strains and works persistently so people will receive the Gospel and come spontaneously to Christ in faith. Even in Christian lands later in history, Satan follows and people make excuses to decline the invitation of God's reign. In a number of sermons, Luther points out that compulsion to God's reign occurs through preaching of the Law and Gospel, that is, a preaching that rouses consciousness of sin and knowledge of God's grace.[86]

There is no doubt that the reformer uses the perspective of salvation history, that is, he differentiates between a particular call to the Jews for a time and a universal call after Christ's death, resurrection, and glorification. *House Postil* (1544) collects Luther's many commentaries on the call within the Jewish people and the universal call to all peoples.

> "*Go out quickly into the streets and lanes of the city . . .*" . . . This was also done among the Jews. For as the great lords, princes and priests, and those who were best among the people would not accept the Gospel . . . our God and Lord accepted the humble fishermen, the poor, miserable and despised little flock, as St. Paul also says, 1 Cor. 1:26–28. . . . "*Go out into the highways and hedges, and constrain them to come in that my house may be filled.*" This refers to us, the heathen, who have dwelt in no city, who were without any worship of the true God, but were idolatrous, and did not know what we or God were. Therefore our condition is properly called a free, open place on the highways, in the field, where the devil walks over us and has his quarters. Go thither, he says, and constrain them to come in. . . . Now, because his servants bring the precious Gospel to us, is an indication that we who are baptized and believe, also belong to this supper, for we are the great lords of the hedges, who are blind, poor and lost heathen. . . . [Mark 16:16]. . . . Therefore he must himself com-

---

86 WA 12:600.22ff.; 20:440.34ff.; 29:393.5ff.; 52:365.12ff.

mand and work that men continue and persevere evermore to constrain and urge as much as possible, both by holding forth wrath for the wicked and grace for the faithful. Wrath and repentance urge man to run and cry for grace. This is then the right way a person goes to this supper, and thus from Jews and Gentiles there will be one Christian church, and all will be called alike poor, miserable people, lame and crippled, for they accept the Gospel heartily and with joy.[87]

In this late commentary on Luke 14:21–23 Luther says that both Jews and Gentiles are invited to Christ's reign in the new covenant. The call to the heathen occurs on the basis of a perfectly unconditional grace. God's call always involves the Law/Gospel scheme. Finally, one ought not to lose sight of how markedly universal the invitation of the new covenant is. Until the end of the age, one ought to take the Gospel of Christ to all people who walk the earth. Luther writes:

> In the first place, he calls this doctrine a feast (i.e., the Gospel) because it is the last feast which will be given here on earth. . . . Secondly, he calls it a great feast, indeed truly great in all dimensions of greatness. For greatness is expressed in length, breadth, and depth according to the mathematicians. . . . Length [*longitudo*] expresses that this feast continues uninterrupted until the end of the world because the Gospel always remains and is carried forward. Breadth [*latitudo*] expresses that the Gospel spreads out over the entire world. "Their voice goes out into all the earth" (Psalm 19:4). Likewise "Go . . . [to] all nations" (Matt. 28:19). Depth [*profunditas*] expresses the power and firmness of this feast, i.e. the power of the Gospel which is Christ himself, the sustenance of a limitless power.[88]

This and the previous citation prove false all those who have believed that Luther lacked a sense for mission and believed that the Great Commission had been fulfilled in the apostolic age. For Luther, the Gospel must be preached until the end of this world and of time.

Already we have seen the eschatological perspective and the thesis about universal mission until the end of the age many times. Luther also comments on Matthew 24:14: "And this gospel of the kingdom will be preached in the whole world as a testimony to all nations, and then the end will come." In a series of sermons from 1537–1540, Luther writes on this verse:

> Before the last day comes, the church's regiment and Christian faith must spread out over the entire world as Christ in one of the previous chapters has already said; not one town will remain where the Gospel has not been

---

87 Lenker 4:48–49, 51, 54 (*original emphasis*) (WA 52:363.21ff., 364.32ff., 366.6ff.).

88 "Conciunculae quaedam, etc. (1537)," WA 45:448.10f., 448.17ff.

preached. And the Gospel will run through the entire world so that all have a testimony to their consciences whether they believe or not. The Gospel has been in Egypt. There it is gone. Likewise, it has been in Greece, in Italy, in Spain, in France and in other countries. Now it is in Germany. Who knows for how long? The Gospel is now with us, but our ingratitude and disdain for God's Word, our greed and pomp, mean that it will not stay for long. And because of this the enthusiasts will enter the picture and thereafter great wars. . . . Then the last day will come. St. Paul says this to the Romans in the eleventh chapter [Romans 11:25], the Gospel must be preached until the Gentiles in full number have come to heaven.[89]

This passage shows that Luther believes the end of world mission will come first when the end of the world comes, that is, at Christ's parousia. The Gospel has gone out and continues to go out into the world. When it has been despised, the lampstand has been moved. Even if Luther believes that the last day is not far off, in 1540 he believes it is still the time of mission in the world.

THE MISSION COMMISSIONS IN THE SYNOPTIC GOSPELS

The New Testament has many commands about mission. It has been rightly observed that Luther connects Matthew 28:18–20 primarily to his trinitarian theology and his teaching about the Baptism of the church. Therefore Matthew's Great Commission is not central to Luther's missiology. However, one often has left the question too easily at that without examining what role Jesus' mission commissions have played for Luther's missiology in general.[90] The following will examine what Luther has to say about various mission commands/instructions from the Scriptures with special attention to his comments on the following passages: Matthew 28:18–20; Mark 16:15–16; Luke 24:45–49; and John 20:19–23. First, it is interesting to note that Matthew 28:18–20 is almost never the subject of an exhaustive commentary by Luther. Indeed, in Luther's early writings, it is less important as a proof text for Baptism than Mark 16:15–16.[91]

---

89 WA 47:565.11ff.

90 Hallencreutz, "Luther och Olaus Petri om 'missionsbefallningen,'" 12, 22. In his examination of Luther and the Great Commission (Matthew 28:18–20), Hallencreutz apparently has not considered the other mission commands in the New Testament and their importance for Luther. Cf. concerning sermon and text choice in Luther, Ebeling, *Evangelische Evangelienauslegung*, 21ff.

91 Cf. "Babylonian Captivity of the Church," which uses Mark 16:16 but not Matthew 28:18–20 (WA 6:527.33ff.). In fact, Luther's 1523 and 1526 Orders of Baptism lack both texts. The Small and Large Catechisms have both texts as witnesses or proof texts for Baptism (K-W, 359, 457; *BSLK*, 517, 691). That is also true of the comprehensive Baptism sermons; see WA 37:627ff. Cf. WA 20:386.36ff. and 27:135.16f.

When considering the relative insignificance of Matthew's Great Commission in Luther's writings, it is important to remember that it is the commission from Mark that functioned as a lectionary text in Luther's context. Therefore Luther comments on Mark's text in his sermons nearly every year. The three-year lectionary did not exist in the 1500s. Also Luther did not have the text-critical problems with Mark 16:19–20 that his contemporary Roman Catholic scholars had, which are indicated in modern translations by setting that passage in parentheses. One might even venture to suggest that Luther found in the words of Mark's text about the preaching of the Gospel, Baptism, and faith an especially enlightening text for mission and Baptism. One ought to keep all this in mind when considering the weak place Matthew's commission has in the Luther material.

Nevertheless, Luther comments on Matthew 28:18–20 once in a sermon from 1525 (which was recorded by Rörer and Roth). In this sermon, Luther focuses on Baptism and teaching (especially ethics) in the name of the Trinity. Furthermore, Luther notes that mission has its basis in Christ's authority and command to make disciples of all peoples. It is emphasized that the work of the church is not a human business but a divine work done in God's name. In a surprisingly weak and inarticulate manner, Luther also mentions that the work of God's reign in the Word, Baptism, and teaching that began with the apostles would continue with their followers.[92] As previously mentioned, Luther sometimes uses the Matthew pericope as a proof text to develop a clearly centrifugal missiology.[93] As a whole, Luther's commentaries on Matthew 28:18–20 indicate little about his missiology. But the Gospels have other mission commands that Luther has used in a completely different manner.

Luther's commentaries on Mark 16:15–16 (within the whole context of vv. 14–20) are many and are filled with ideas about world mission. More than one hundred pages in the Weimar Edition[94] are filled with comments on this passage in the context of sermons on Christ's ascension. The passage itself reads as follows: "Go into all the world and preach the good news to all creation. Whoever believes and is baptized will be saved, but whoever does not believe will be condemned." It is important to observe how mission and Christ's authority are connected. Luther grounds such a sending of the disciples in Jesus Christ's universal authority and lordship, which has been revealed through his ascension to the Father's right hand (Mark 16:19; Luke 24:50f.; Acts 1:9–11). A passage from a 1523 sermon is significant.

---

92 WA 17/1:97.8ff., 99.14ff., 100.17ff.

93 WA 10/1.2:267.12ff.; 20:382.12; 38:448.17ff.; 46:393.19.

94 WA 10/1.2:266ff.; 10/3:139ff.; 12:555ff.; 15:550ff.; 17/1:256ff.; 20:382ff.; 27:131ff.; 34/1:412ff.; 37:77ff.; 41:73ff., 591ff.; 45:377ff., 442ff.; 46:389ff.

We must, therefore, conceive of his ascension and Lordship as something active, energetic and continuous, and must not imagine that he sits above while we hold the reins of government down here. Nay, he ascended up thither for the reason that there he can best do his work and exercise dominion. Had he remained upon earth in visible form, before the people, he could not have wrought so effectually, for all the people could not have been with him and heard him. Therefore, he inaugurated an expedient which made it possible for him to be in touch with all and reign in all, to preach to all and be heard by all, and to be with all. . . . [N]ot only does he sit up there but he is also down here. And for this purpose did he ascend up thither, that he might be down here, that he might fill all things and be everywhere present; which thing he could not do had he remained on earth, for here in the body he could not have been present with all. He ascended to heaven, where all hearts can see him.[95]

Luther always emphasizes that Christ's ascension does not mean that he has abandoned his church through the ages. On the contrary, the ascension means that with revealed authority in heaven and on earth Christ does everything to build his church throughout the world by his Spirit and through the Word and Sacraments. Few theologians have made the ascension into something actually important for Christian faith as Luther has. The reformer often says that the many Old and New Testament passages about the Messiah's universal lordship have been fulfilled after Easter through Jesus' ascension, the sending of the Spirit, and the proclamation of salvation through the Gospel in Word and Sacrament. Among the substantiating texts for Christ's lordship and universal mission, one might name—in addition to the texts already listed—Psalm 2:7; 68:19; and 110:1, 5–6. Luther even uses Matthew 28:18–20 for this purpose. Ephesians 4:8–9 also is important for the interpretation of Christ's ascension. Christ ascended to imprison the forces of darkness and to fulfill everything by means of the Gospel. Luther also connects John 20:23 and 21:15ff. with Christ's lordship through the Gospel. In this way, Jesus' ascension and session at God's right hand also are connected to the highest degree with world mission as *missio Christi* and *missio ecclesiae*.[96]

---

95 Lenker 3:190–91, 193 (WA 12:562.15ff., 564.17ff.). See these similar passages: WA 10/1.2:267.7ff.; 12:565.9ff.; 15:553.27ff.; 20:382.1ff., 383.10ff.; 27:138.26ff.; 41:592.21ff.; 45:443.9ff.; 46:392.7ff., 392.19f., 393.15ff. Cf. also LC II 31: ". . . and finally ascended into heaven and assumed dominion at the right hand of the Father. The devil and all his powers must be subject to him and lie beneath his feet until finally, at the Last Day, he will completely divide and separate us from the wicked world, the devil, death, sin, etc." (K-W, 435).

96 WA 12:563ff.; 15:553.27ff.; 20:382.7ff., 383.10ff.; 27:138.26ff.; 41:592.21ff.; 45:443.19ff.; 46:392.7ff., 393.15ff. Cf. Öberg, *Himmelrikets nycklar och kyrklig bot i Luthers teologi*, 105ff., about the church as Christ's lordship through the Gospel. Cf. *Luther and World Mission*, 81–84, with references in 82n144.

What does Luther say, then, about the command for universal preaching of God's salvation in Mark 16:15–16? The pericope begins with these words: "Go into all the world and preach the good news to all creation" (Mark 16:15). In his commentaries on this verse, Luther lets fly all his eloquence and his earthy language to underline how perfectly unconditional and comprehensive Christ's Gospel of salvation is. The universalism of the radical Gospel actually implies that all people lie under sin and death without being able to help themselves. Into this situation, God in Christ acts in a way beneficial to all and for the entire world. The old covenant's restriction of salvation to the chosen people is replaced with a call directed to all people on earth through the Gospel when Jesus ascends to the Father's right hand. This call includes Jews and heathen, high and low, rich and poor—briefly said, all people on earth. It shall be preached publicly everywhere, in all corners and alleys. Indeed, the phrase "to all creation" expresses, according to the reformer, that stones and trees, sun and moon—if they had ears to listen— should be able to certify that the Gospel has been announced everywhere in the world.[97]

In a sermon from 1536/1544, Luther speaks about how Christ has commanded that the Gospel of unconditional grace will be preached in all the earth to both pure heathens and the new heathens, that is, the self-righteous. Luther says on Mark 16:15:

> These are words of a sovereign Ruler, words that are becoming his majesty—
> commissioning these poor beggars to go forth and proclaim this new message,
> not in one city or country only, but in all the world, in principalities and
> kingdoms—and to proclaim it publicly and cheerfully; to speak before all
> creatures, so that all humanity might hear the message. That certainly means,
> to stretch forth the arms and gather unto Christ a great multitude. Indeed, it is
> such a mighty commission, that the like of it was never issued in the world.[98]

Later in the same sermon, Luther emphasizes that the means and the power for the expansion of Christ's reign do not come from within or from some earthly prince but from Christ and his command (Matthew 28:18; Psalm 2:8).

In the above texts, there is nothing to indicate that Luther should have differentiated between the Gospel for the purely heathen world and for those who have had the Gospel for a longer or shorter period of time. He says:

> This is also a consoling message to us, because we, too, are included in these
> words of Christ when he says: Go into all the world, and preach the Gospel to

---

97 WA 10/1.2:267.23ff.; 10/3:138.29ff., 143.16ff.; 12:556.1ff.; 15:550.14ff.; 17/1:257.19ff.;
   20:384.9ff.; 21:386ff.; 27:132.3ff., 140.16ff.; 34/1:412.6ff., 417.17ff.; 37:77.16ff.; 41:74.2ff.,
   592.16ff.

98 Lenker 3:214 (WA 21:387.1ff.).

the whole creation. Herein are inclosed all who hear this message, wherever they may live, be they few or many. "All the world" does not mean one or two parts of it, but everywhere within it wherever people may dwell. Therefore, the Gospel had to be proclaimed according to the command, as it is yet being proclaimed today. Although it is not steadily triumphant in every place, yet it is destined to reach to the ends of the earth and to resound in all places and corners of the world.[99]

For Luther, Jesus' mission command includes an order to preach the Gospel in all lands, even in those lands that have had the Gospel and faith for some time. On the basis of Jesus' command, the Gospel has gone out into the world—and it continues constantly to go out to those who lack it wherever they live. Luther's idea of mission is comprehensive, as is the Gospel about Christ.

Furthermore, it ought to be noted here how Luther—without forgetting the Law/Gospel motif in the preaching of repentance—emphasizes that it is not the Law and asceticism and human striving that will be preached as a way to salvation. It is the Gospel or the good news about God's mercy and the forgiveness of sins that will resound throughout the whole earth to the most distant corner. God's salvation is something sweet, something wonderful, something only the Gospel can give. Here exists no force and no works of the Law.[100]

Because all humans have the ability through their own reason to organize civil life, mission preaching does not need to deal with external matters and ordinances. It ought, instead, to focus only on the Gospel of Christ. Luther writes:

> On the other hand, Christ's kingdom has nothing to do with the kingdoms of men. He permits them to continue in their own observances. Christ commands that the disciples should preach the Gospel to all creatures. The creatures existed before the Gospel came to them. Governments are instituted, and laws formed, by men, through God-given reason and wisdom. . . . I Pet 2, 13. . . . Rom 13, 2. In such things, Christ would establish no change; he permits them to remain as they are, in fact and in name.[101]

---

99 Lenker 3:221 (WA 21:392.32ff.).

100 WA 10/3:139.5ff., 143.16ff.; 12:556.9ff.; 15:551.4ff.; 17/1:258.17ff.; 27:132.3ff.; 34/1:412.6ff., 420.1ff.; 37:78.1ff., 81.1ff.; 41:74.25ff., 75.12ff. Cf. this representative text: "The meaning of this message Christ plainly shows. In the first place, he gives it a worthy name, calling it Gospel-preaching. . . . For the word 'Gospel' means a new message—a good message bearing joyful tidings, proclaiming something, that one gladly and eagerly hears. Not a law or a commandment, forcing or demanding from us and threatening punishment and condemnation if we do not obey it" (Lenker 3:218 [WA 21:390.7ff., 390.14ff.]).

101 Lenker 3:223 (WA 21:394.24ff.).

This is an enlightening passage about the task that is specific to the spiritual regiment, that is, the Gospel. It also touches on mission and contextualization. It is not the task of mission to destroy the social ordinances, customs, and practices that one meets in the mission fields. The Creator is already active in the ordinances of the natural life long before the Gospel arrives.[102]

Luther says in many of his comments on Mark 16:15 that though all preaching must be faithful to the written Word, nevertheless the message from the apostolic age and through all the ages should be a public and oral preaching (*viva vox*).[103] God has a purpose with this, namely, that everyone should be reached with the Gospel and that even the illiterate should be able to share in the Gospel of salvation. We have a clear and representative text about this universal, oral mission preaching of the Gospel in the above-cited sermon from 1523:

> We have often said heretofore that the Gospel, properly speaking, is not something written in books, but an oral proclamation, which shall be heard in all the world and shall be cried out freely before all creatures, so that all would have to hear it if they had ears; that is to say, it shall be preached so publicly that to preach it more publicly would be impossible. For the Law, which was of old, and what the prophets preached, was not cried out in all the world before all creatures, but it was preached by the Jews in their synagogues. But the Gospel shall not be thus confined; it shall be preached freely unto all the world. . . . [I]t shall be cried out before the whole creation, so that earth shall not have a nook or corner into which it shall not penetrate before the last day. Such is the counsel of God, wherein he has decreed that even they who cannot read and have not heard Moses and the prophets shall, nevertheless, hear the Gospel.[104]

After reviewing all this material on Mark 16:15, it is apparent that this message will be preached and heralded. A mission and preaching task is part and parcel of the universality of the Gospel, a task that is based on Christ's own command and sending. The mission idea about the Gospel's way to all peoples implies that one must deal with the expansion of the Gospel practically as well.

This understanding can be found in the mission command from Mark 16:16: "Whoever believes and is baptized will be saved, but whoever does not believe will be condemned." According to Luther, the mission command in Mark speaks not only about a universal preaching of the Gospel but also about the Gospel and faith, Baptism and faith. In this material, Luther emphasizes against all attempts to

---

102 Cf. *Luther and World Mission*, 25–32, 253–66.

103 See Prenter, *Spiritus creator*, 127ff.; and Vatja, *Die Theologie des Gottesdienstes bei Luther*, 139ff. See also Ivarsson, *Predikans uppgift*, 20ff.; and Öberg, *Himmelrikets nycklar och kyrklig bot i Luthers teologi*, 147ff. Cf. *Luther and World Mission*, 205–10.

104 Lenker 3:183–84 (WA 12:556.9ff.).

connect good works with salvation that salvation/blessedness is received only through faith in Christ, which humanity shares through preaching and Baptism. It ought, however, also to be noted that faith for Luther is not a quality or something inherent in humanity that motivates God's grace and salvation. Faith is something that God gives humanity through the Word, Baptism, etc. Faith is a work of God and a gift of God, not a specific, evangelical qualification for God's grace.

There are many scholarly investigations that show that Baptism is, for the reformer, the source of salvation, grace, and forgiveness. To share in Christ, the forgiveness of sins, the new birth, the Holy Spirit, to be and to remain a Christian, to win eternal life, etc., is decidedly connected to Baptism as God's election and activity of grace within the individual. This is no less clear in Luther's commentaries on Mark 16:15–16. Just as Luther connects the Word with faith, so Baptism and faith are bound together. Only the one who trusts in the Christ of Baptism shares in the blessings of Baptism. Luther emphasizes that, like the Word, Baptism creates and sustains faith. In both cases, the glorified Lord Jesus is active as the Savior from Satan, sin, death, and the accusing conscience. Faith is followed by a life of killing the sinful nature and of good works.[105]

There are some helpful passages about Gospel preaching, Baptism, and faith in the previously cited sermon from 1536/1544. On the basis of Matthew 28:19 and Mark 16:16, Luther says:

> Now, we find in this text, Mt 28, 19–20, that Christ first commands the eleven to go and make disciples of all nations, and to baptize them into the name of the Father, Son and Holy Spirit. That is, they are to preach to them the teaching of the Gospel, how they must be saved—which, as yet, neither the Jews nor the heathen knew—and in this knowledge to baptize them, making the people disciples or Christians. These are the first essentials and thereto the words agree: "He that believeth and is baptized" etc.[106]

For Luther, however, both Baptism and faith are a work of God in humanity: "Christ intentionally made the statement thus plain: 'He that believeth, and is baptized' etc., in order to set right the delusions and pretensions of the Jews and of all the world regarding salvation by man's own works. On faith and baptism, not

---

105 WA 10/3:140.17ff., 141.28ff.; 12:556.25ff., 560.20ff.; 15:551.26ff., 552.16ff.; 17/1:258.18ff.; 21:390–408; 27:133.7ff., 136.16ff.; 34/1:418.1ff., 420.4ff.; 37:78.25ff., 81.13ff.; 41:75.10ff., 77.30ff., 593.11ff., 593.33ff., 594.11ff.; 46:393.18ff., 394.9ff. The Large Catechism also formulates the meaning and content of Baptism (K-W, 456ff.). Concerning Luther's theology of Baptism, see Öberg, *Himmelrikets nycklar och kyrklig bot i Luthers teologi*, 191ff., with the adduced literature of, among others, Julius Köstlin, Ruben Josefson, and Lorenz Grönvik.

106 Lenker 3:226 (WA 21:397.16ff.).

on our own but on his works, he bases all."[107] About the gifts and blessings of Baptism, that is, to be received as God's child and admitted to Christ's reign, Luther writes: "Thus, baptism is a sign and seal, in addition to the Word or promise, that we have been called and brought into the kingdom of Christ, have become God's children and heirs of eternal life, if, by faith we cling to Christ."[108]

Baptism also provides a public sign of the doctrine of the Gospel and the place where Christ has his reign. Baptism shows not only where the Gospel is preached but also where it is received, believed, and confessed. The tangible gathering and identity of Christ's reign through Baptism and faith is an important part of the expansion of the Gospel, that is, mission. Luther says:

> . . . in order that it may become evident, not only where this Gospel is preached, but also where it is accepted and believed, that is, where the church and kingdom of Christ may be in this world, Christ wants to unite and hold us together by virtue of this divine sign, baptism. If Christians were without such an ordinance, if they had no common bond in the way of seal or sign, the organization would neither be expanded nor preserved. Christ wishes to bind us together by a divine communion, to further the spread of the Gospel; that others through our confession, may be brought into the fold. Therefore, baptism is a public testimony to the Gospel teaching, and to our faith, by which the world may know where and within whom the Lord rules.[109]

In connection with Mark 16:15–16, Luther clearly expresses the centrifugal aspect of mission. God's salvation will be preached in the entire world, for all peoples, for all creation, until Christ's parousia. It will be preached and people baptized for salvation through faith in God's Son.

The texts reviewed already have answered the important question about whether Luther understood that this preaching of God's salvation among the heathen would continue even in his own generation and later or whether he believed, as some medieval and later Lutheran orthodox theologians did, that the Gospel already had reached all peoples and lands during the apostolic age.[110] As

---

107 Lenker 3:224 (WA 21:395.10ff.).

108 Lenker 3:234 (WA 21:404.2ff.).

109 Lenker 3:234 (WA 21:403.22ff.).

110 Holl, "Luther und die Mission," points out that even before Lutheran orthodox theologians took the position, some medieval Scholastics believed that Psalm 19:5 and Romans 10:18 indicate that the apostles already had succeeded in spreading the Gospel throughout all the world. Even in the 1519 commentary on Galatians, Luther had repudiated the legend from the early papacy that the apostles had divided the world into twelve regions for their mission fields (WA 2:476.33ff.). Concerning how orthodoxy's Johann Gerhard defends himself against the tough criticism from the Roman Catholics (among whom was the Jesuit Bellarmine) that the Lutheran churches did not

Luther understands it, as long as he does not see Christ coming on the clouds of heaven, his marching orders about universal mission remain. Many have wanted to find a correlation between Luther's progressively stronger emphasis on eschatology and apocalyptic and his alleged weak interest in mission.[111] I believe that the scholars behind these ideas have not considered what terrible injustice one does to the reformer in drawing such conclusions. Luther would probably turn over in his grave if he, after his lifelong struggle with the enthusiasts, should nevertheless be connected with their apocalyptic brand of Christianity. This is he who said that he would plant an apple tree if he heard about the immediate arrival of the Last Day. Despite the many signs of the times that prove the *mundus advesperans* (for example, the Antichrist in the pope and the problems with Muslims, the enthusiasts, and the increasing backsliding among the evangelical Germans), Luther did not proclaim that the time of mission had passed. According to the reformer, there are still people both at home in Germany and out in the world who have not heard the Gospel. The Gospel must be preached until Christ's parousia, which has still not occurred.

To make this even clearer, one can evaluate this extensive quote from Luther's 1522 Ascension Day sermon in which he explains Mark 16:15:

> A question arises about this passage, "Go ye into all the world," as to how it is to be understood, since the apostles certainly did not visit all the world. No apostle came hither to us; and many a heathen island has since been discovered, where the Gospel has never been preached. Yet the Scriptures say: "Their sound went out into all the earth." Rom 10, 18. Answer: Their preaching went out into all the world, although it has not yet come into all the world. This going out has been begun and continues, although it is not yet completed; the Gospel, however, will be preached even farther and wider, until the judgment day. When this preaching shall have reached all parts of the world, and shall

---

have any foreign mission, see Scherer, *Mission and Unity in Lutheranism*, 13f. Gerhard reckons apparently with a call to established domestic congregations. The mission command is not in and of itself any basis for a mission activity in heathen lands because the command was fulfilled by the apostles. This conclusion was fateful for Lutheran mission.

111 Here are some recent examples, Hallencreutz, "Luther och Olaus Petri om 'missionsbefallningen,'" 16ff.; Oberman, "Luthers Beziehungen zu den Juden," 1:525ff. It may well be that the older Luther emphasizes eschatology and apocalyptic more powerfully, but these biblical themes were important even for the younger Luther. There are innumerable proofs of this. One can, for example, compare the reformer's foreword to Revelation written in 1530 and the one written in 1546 (WADB 6:409–18). The concretion of Satan's struggle against Christ's reign concludes in both cases with "[a]fter the Turks, the Last Judgment follows quickly . . ." (LW 35:409 [WADB 6:416.36f., 417.36f.]).

have been everywhere heard, then will the message be complete and its mission accomplished; then will the last day also be at hand. The preaching of this message may be likened to a stone thrown into the water, producing ripples which circle outward from it, the waves rolling always on and on, one driving the other, till they come to the shore. Although the center becomes quiet, the waves do not rest, but move forward. So it is with the preaching of the Word. It was begun by the apostles, and it constantly goes forward, is pushed on farther and farther by the preachers, driven hither and thither into the world, yet always being made known to those who never heard it before, although it be arrested in the midst of its course and is condemned as heresy. As we say, when one sends a message, the message has gone forth, although it has not yet arrived at its destination, but is still on its way; or as we say that the emperor's message is sent to Nurenburg, or to the Turk, although it has not yet arrived: so we are to understand the preaching of the apostles.[112]

If it were only for these lovely words, one could easily conclude that the reformer possessed a mission perspective. Only ignorance or unwillingness to see could lead to the conclusion that Luther lacked a sense for and an interest in world mission. As Karl Holl states, Luther is cognizant of the mission task, the task that even the Christians of his own time had the responsibility to accomplish. One must notice how forcefully Luther, in connection with Mark 16:15, emphasizes that the Gospel has not reached all places and people and that mission preaching, therefore, should continue to the Last Day.[113]

---

112 Lenker 3:201–2 (WA 10/3:139.17ff.).

113 Cf. the continuity with other comments on Mark 16:15–16 through the years: WA 15:552.26ff.; 17/1:257.19ff.; 20:384.9ff. The following passage is especially clear: " 'Ite in' [Mark 16:15]. Ire debent in totum orbem et 'omni creaturae'. Tamen in Germania non fuit Apostolus et alibi? Magnus Jacobus primo anno occisus, quo ivit? Minor quoque mansit Hierosolymis, quomodo ergo verum? Hoc intelligendum de cursu Euangelii, non fine. 'Ite' i.e. praedicatio, quam incipio, est naturae, ut reiche de uno termino ad alium, ut erschal unter allen orten, das, wenn alle creatur ohren hetten, musten zeugniss geben, das gepredigt wer worden, quare dedit tam varios viros. Cum ergo ipsi 1. sint et in hoc cursu, qui debebat ire per totum orbem, impletum est, eciam si non egressi Hierosolymis. Sic dico: nuntius ivit Lipsiam, cum vix abiisset, quia in cursu est offitii, quod facere debet. Non consummabitis, ir sol khaum alle orter bepredigt haben, ich etc. Euangelium est enim nuntius ante extremum diem" (WA 17/1:257.19ff.). On how Luther's interpretation of Mark 16:15 reveals that the Gospel has not reached the entire world, see Holl, "Luther und die Mission," 235f.; and Loewenich, *Luther als Ausleger der Synoptiker*, 69f. See also Bergman, *Den lutherske Reformation og Missionen*, 61f., who has difficulties with these many clear passages in Luther because he believes Luther lacks a mission perspective in the sense of organizing a foreign mission. On p. 56, Bergman is occupied with only a few passages of Luther's interpretation of Mark 16:14–18 (WA 21:410.8f.; 10/3:145.26ff.) and does not seem to give as much weight to the more comprehensive arguments cited above.

We ought briefly to consider a special matter at this point. Immediately after the mission command, Jesus speaks in Mark 16:17–18 of wonders and signs that would follow the Gospel and faith. The enthusiasts asked why these signs do not accompany the Gospel of the Reformation. Luther responds that signs were given to the early church to confirm the Gospel, but after the expansion of the Gospel into the world, such signs are no longer common. Nevertheless, these signs— exorcism of demons, healing of physical and psychological ailments, and speaking in tongues (for Luther, preaching in new languages)—continue to occur where Christianity is suppressed or oppressed. But for the reformer, the wonder above all wonders is that God sustains the Word, the Sacraments, faith, the confession of Christ, and the church against Satan, all tyrants, and heretics.[114]

We already have seen how the preaching of God's Word stands in the center of Luther's missiology. Especially in connection with Psalm 117:1; Acts 10:44; Romans 10:14; and Galatians 3:2, the reformer argues that the preaching of the Word/Gospel is necessary so people might come to faith. For Luther, the preaching of the Gospel often distinguishes itself as God's foremost work on earth. This preaching of the Word/Gospel is filled with God's own authority and power. In connection with Mark 16:15, the reformer can say: "From this we see that the

---

114 Cf. WA 10/3:145.26ff. and comprehensively in a commentary from 1536/1544: " '*And these signs shall accompany them that believe.*' Here the sectarians have brooded over the question of signs, vainly asking why they do not accompany our preaching and whether they can no longer be expected. It is enough to know, that these signs followed as a testimony to, and public confirmation of, this Gospel message. . . . But with the preaching of the Word in all lands and tongues accomplished, their prevalence became less frequent, and their testimony less necessary" (Lenker 3:240 [*original emphasis*] [WA 21:408.17ff.]). Lenker 3:240–41 (WA 21:408.27ff.): "Yet it is true that the same power and efficacy of Christ remains in Christendom. If it were necessary, such signs could even now be performed. It often took place, and still does, that devils were cast out in Christ's name; likewise the sick are healed by prayer in his name, and many receive help in great distress of both body and soul. The Gospel is now being preached in new tongues, where it was unknown before. Signs are given to all Christendom, as Christ says—to those who believe. True, we do not always observe this gift in every Christian believer, and even the apostles did not do these wonders with equal power." Luther reminds his audience that the sustenance of the Word, faith, and Christians against the devil and all the enthusiasts is a greater miracle than exorcism and speaking in tongues (WA 21:408.38ff.). See Lenker 3:242 (WA 21:409.23ff.): "Thus, even in our day, are great signs and wonders upon wonders. Here is an example: In a great city a little flock of Christians is kept in the knowledge of God and in true faith, notwithstanding that more than a hundred thousand devils are turned loose upon them and the world is filled with sects, with scoundrels and tyrants. In spite of the opposition of all these, the Gospel, baptism, Lord's Supper and confession of Christ are still preserved."

Word of God must be an almighty power of God (Rom. 1:16) ... This is the greatest work God has done on earth. . . . The Word has done many wonders in the world, and it is not finished yet."[115]

This passage can serve as a transition to the important mission instructions in Luke 24:45–49, especially vv. 46–47, which read: "He told them, 'This is what is written: The Christ will suffer and rise from the dead on the third day, and repentance and forgiveness of sins will be preached in his name to all nations, beginning at Jerusalem.'" This text gives Luther reason to consider what should be preached in the work of God's reign and toward whom the message should be aimed. In my 1970 dissertation and, among other places, in the jubilee collection of essays for the 1984 *Menighetsfakultet* in Oslo, I have reviewed the connection between Luke 24:45–49 and Luther's ideas about proper preaching.[116] In addition to Baptism, the faith of the Christians, daily repentance, and the conversion of all people is related to the public preaching of Law and Gospel, to conversion, and to the forgiveness of sins. In penance, men and women listen to the Word as Law and Gospel. In this way, penance is not a human work but a work of God in the human heart through the Word as Law and Gospel. In true evangelical penance, humanity turns toward the Word as Law and Gospel. At the same time, this so-called passive penance engages the person justified through faith in service to the neighbor and in good works.

What does the reformer say about the Bible passage that indicates on the basis of Jesus' death and resurrection that a preaching of repentance and forgiveness would follow in his name "to all nations, beginning at Jerusalem"? In a number of sermons from the week after Easter, Luther has commented on these instructions from the risen Lord, instructions the reformer believes are connected with the scene presented in John 20:19–31. According to Luther, the universal preaching of God's salvation would begin in Jerusalem and begin with the pouring out of the Spirit. This is a question of a preaching on the basis of Jesus' death and resurrection that applies to all people and the entire world. The reformer forcefully emphasizes that this description of mission from Jesus' own mouth first places all humanity under sin and judgment and second promises a perfectly unconditional forgiveness to all who, on the basis of the knowledge of their own sin, flee to Christ, that is, receive the Gospel and the forgiveness of sins in Jesus' name. The age of mission will begin in Jerusalem among the chosen people and the spiritual elite. Then the Gospel will go out into the entire world. But for Jews and later for the heathen, it is always true that they attain salvation and eternal life only by lis-

---

115 LW 14:10–11 (WA 31/1:230.17ff.).

116 See Öberg, *Himmelrikets nycklar och kyrklig bot i Luthers teologi*, and the jubilee collection of essays for the 1984 *Menighetsfakultet* in Oslo.

tening to the preaching of repentance and forgiveness of sins, that is, by leaving all else in which they might trust and believing in God's crucified and risen Son. Luther's commentaries are highly critical of the Roman Catholic doctrine of penance. He opposed all superficial penance and all performance thinking in soteriological matters. It is another matter that a new heart and a new lifestyle follow from a right repentance as the fruit of faith. Luther emphasizes that this penance related to the Law and Gospel is a penance in Jesus' name that rests completely on Jesus' work of salvation for us and for the forgiveness of sins.[117]

Instructive for Luther's view of the mission preaching of repentance and forgiveness among all peoples and tribes is the commentary on Luke 22:46–47 in *House Postil* (1544):

> He says, this preaching will start in Jerusalem and thereafter resound in the whole world, i.e., the preaching that Christ had to die and rise from the dead. In whose name? In his name and no other shall repentance and the forgiveness of sins be preached. Consequently, repentance and the forgiveness of sins are not valid in St. Peter's or St. Paul's name. Even less valid are they in my own name so that I should become a monk, do this or some other work in order

---

117 See these sermons from the 1520s: WA 11:90ff.; 12:514ff.; 15:530ff.; 20:348.350f. Especially enlightening is the text recorded by Rörer in WA 15:530.15ff.: "docet praedicari debere poenitentiam, quae est ein veranderung und verwerfung des ienigen, quod sumus, quod non peccata illa externa puss, sed iusticiam et sapientiam mundi, ita ut sonet verbum super omnia extra Christum, quia Christus dicit 'in omnes gentes', neminem eximit et dicit totum mundum esse in eo statu, quo sit zu besseren, sequitur omnia esse damnata. Igitur extollit suum Euangelium super omnia quae in mundo sunt, immo damnat." Cf. WA 15:530.31ff. The Gospel of forgiveness can be articulated in the following manner: "Haec est 2. pars praedicationis. Prima te deiicit, cum dicit pus deiicit, cum remissionem dicit, erigit. Hoc in inferos detrudit, hoc erigit. Remissio, hoc verbum sonare in corde debet . . . . Deus de celo mittit. Primo dicit: poenitentiam fac i.e. tua nihil sunt, tum sequitur: remitto tibi peccata. Si hoc credo, so sein sie hin. . . . Aliud est: remissa peccata und ausgefeget. Quando remissa sunt, incipit regnum Christi" (WA 15:531.8ff., 531.23ff.). Repentance "in Jesus' name" rests always in forgiveness: "Haec remissio durat, quamdiu vivis, quando primum audis Euangelium. Sicut sol, quando incipit, non cessat, sed per diem totum lucet, ut omnes possint capaces lucis. . . . Iterum remissio semper durat . . . . Remissio ist der glantz. Ideo tota vita Christiani non est ordinata, ut satisfaciat pro peccatis, quia hic habes verbum. Sol lucet, splendet, ist auffghangen, es ist unverdint, es ist dir geben. Ista remissio fit, dicit, in meo nomine, et hoc magnum est: deus donat tibi remissionem, quo incipias novam vitam" (WA 15:531.37ff.). About the special themes of Law/Gospel and repentance/forgiveness of sins, see Öberg, *Himmelrikets nycklar och kyrklig bot i Luthers teologi*, 138ff., especially 149–99, in which a number of texts are reviewed and the relevant literature is discussed. See also Öberg, ". . . i hans navn skal omvendelse og tilgivelse for syndene forkynnes for alle folkeslag," 109–26. Cf. Ivarsson, *Predikans uppgift*, 69–112. Cf. *Luther and World Mission*, 211–18.

that I might thereby earn the forgiveness of sins. In his name one shall preach forgiveness, that he has acquired this by his suffering and his resurrection, that whoever wants the forgiveness of sins shall believe that Christ has suffered for him and rose again from the dead. This shall be the right preaching. . . . But the Lord wants to say this: My dear Levites and Jews, you will be the first and with you one will begin to preach repentance, that you ought to repent or so you will never attain the forgiveness of sins. . . . The Lord wants such a preaching of repentance to go out into the whole world. So one can make no excuses; we must all accuse ourselves of sin and confess it. . . . Indeed, he wants such a preaching to begin in Jerusalem among God's people and in the most holy city. . . . To summarize: In this commission, Christ judges the whole world, barks at them as sinners in order that we will want to become holy and that all will kneel, lift up their hands and say: Lord, I am a sinner. It is necessary that I repent, but I am not able. Therefore, Lord, have mercy on me and help me. . . . To the one who does so and gives up all hope in life and works, the second part which is called the forgiveness of sins is added. . . . For there is the promise that all who receive the Gospel, their sins will be remitted and forgiven. For one shall in Christ's name preach the forgiveness of sins. . . . Consequently, a Christian is at the same time a sinner and holy. A Christian is at the same time evil and pious. For according to who we are in ourselves, we are sinners, and in our own name, we are sinners. But Christ gives us another name, which is called the forgiveness of sins, that for his sake sins are remitted and forgiven.[118]

In connection with the commentaries on Luke 24:45–56, it ought to be emphasized that Luther in no way distinguishes between that which ought to be preached in mission to the heathen and that which ought to be heard in Rome or Wittenberg. In all the earth, there is actually only one front, the front between unbelief and faith, between works-righteousness and faith in Christ. Therefore the same double-edged Word will resound to all of Adam's children in all parts of the world who are under guilt and judgment. This preaching is to put Christ's death and resurrection to practical use and to let it be a blessing to all those for whom God's Son suffered death and rose again to life. According to Luther, not only is it a struggle to spread faith in Christ on the heathen front in the beginning, but it is always a struggle, even to preserve faith in Christ in Christian contexts. Luther saw that Christ's reign was attacked in the West by the papacy, the enthusiasts, and the advance of the Muslims (and to a lesser degree by the Jews). One ought not to judge Luther's ideas about this spiritual struggle as merely a case of apocalyptic exaggeration. Only the type of Lutheranism that lives in theological obscurity

---

118 WA 52:261.34ff., 262.18ff., 263.19ff., 264.32ff.

can deny that Luther in this text understands and clearly expresses the chief problems of both domestic and foreign mission.

The Mission Motif in the Commentaries on John

I continue now by reviewing the mission motif in Luther's exposition of the Gospel according to John. Both Luther and later biblical scholars have heard echoes of the early church in John's Gospel. Therefore one ought to expect that this Gospel should provide Luther with numerous opportunities to comment on the church's growth in the world, that is, mission. This relatively comprehensive review addresses Luther's commentaries on the texts that in his understanding are connected with the expansion of the Gospel and the church in the world. In his commentaries on John, Luther wants, among other things, to develop his thesis about the fundamental significance of Christ's ascension and the Holy Spirit for the church's universal sending with the Gospel. He also provides clear instructions about what church and mission ought to communicate to people and what means Christ and the Spirit use in mission. In a surprisingly energetic manner, Luther also emphasizes that church and mission in all their work must follow Christ's Word and hold him always in the center. In other words, the formal and material principles of Scripture are in this manner important for the reformer.

Luther remarks in his commentaries on John's prologue (1:1–18) that all people on earth—whatever they might know naturally about God by way of creation and the Law—without exception must be enlightened and born again spiritually by Logos/Christ, or the true light, if they should win salvation. The reformer believes that the Christ-light has shone in the world from the time of the promise in Genesis 3:15 through all the prophets to John the Baptist and Christ's own appearance. In this final age, it has with powerful force illuminated the entire world from the first Christian Pentecost to today. The light is God's Word of promise, the Gospel about Christ, which has been preached and must be spread constantly in the entire world through preachers sent by God.[119]

---

119 See especially "Sermons on John (1537)," WA 46:541ff., 564ff., 593ff., 614ff. See also WA 29:8–36. Cf. also the investigation in *Luther and World Mission*, 64–84. In Luther's 1537–1538 commentaries on John 1:4–5, one passage can be interpreted to indicate that the Gospel already should have reached the entire world: "And this actually did come to pass when the Gospel was preached and when, by means of its preaching, the kingdom of Christ was established everywhere under the dome of heaven. Now it extends to the ends of the earth" (LW 22:41 [WA 46:571.18ff.]). Bergman, *Den lutherske Reformation og Missionen*, 56, cites this passage that is, of course, an exception to the rule that Luther assumes the Gospel will continue to spread throughout the world until the end of time.

The reformer has not passed over the universal aspect of Christ's reign that is implied in John 3:16–17: "For God so loved the world that he gave his one and only Son, that whoever believes in him shall not perish but have eternal life. For God did not send his Son into the world to condemn the world, but to save the world through him." Luther's commentaries on this verse contain many beautiful praises to God's unconditional mercy and love for a stubborn humanity and about how God in his Son has prepared salvation for all on earth.[120] It is clear that, in these words about God's love for the whole world in his Son, Luther has seen an indication of the Gospel's universality, that it concerns everyone without exception. Sometimes this is expressed explicitly. Because Luther does not allow that one may seek to reach God by works-righteousness or sublime enthusiast spirituality, world mission becomes necessary according to his commentaries on John's prologue and John 3:16–17. The Gospel through the Word, Sacraments, and soul care must be taken out to as many places as God's love in Christ reaches.[121]

On the Second Sunday after Pentecost, Luther preaches often on John 10:12ff. about the Good Shepherd. The reformer emphasizes that Christ has risen and taken his place by the Father's right hand, not to be passive and to do nothing but through his Word to get people to listen to his (that is, to the Shepherd's) voice and to lead them in the difficult struggle that follows the people of faith.[122]

The mission motif is further articulated in Luther's comments on John 10:16: "I have other sheep that are not of this sheep pen. I must bring them also. They too will listen to my voice, and there shall be one flock and one shepherd." When Luther preaches on this pericope, he nearly always discusses the question of who the other sheep are and identifies them with the heathen. Luther says expressly that since Jesus was glorified through his ascension, he has begun to establish his reign through the preaching of the apostles and their followers.[123] In Christ's reign, both Jews and heathen have access to the same salvation and grace by listening to the same Shepherd. The expansion of Christ's reign, that is, mission, continues constantly until Christ's return. Luther has many comments on this passage.[124] The following passage from 1523 is indicative:

---

120 Cf. WA 10/1.2:284ff.; 10/3:160ff.; 11:114ff.; 17/1:271ff.; 20:401ff.; 27:167ff., 181ff.; 36:180ff.; 41:753ff.; 45:84ff.; 47:78ff., 86ff. Cf. about true worshipers, *Luther and World Mission*, 127–37.

121 Especially WA 17/1:272.5ff.; 20:402.22ff., 404.22ff.; 27:167.11ff.; 41:754.1ff., 756.40ff.; 45:84.22ff. There is a reason why the church preaches on John 3:16f. during Pentecost, the birth of mission. This ecclesiastical choice of pericopes implies a salvation history concept.

122 WA 10/1.2:241ff.; 52:275ff.

123 WA 11:98.17ff.; 12:530.11ff., with many other passages.

124 WA 10/1.2:284.34ff.; 10/3:124.5ff.; 11:101.23ff.; 15:537.3ff.; 36:164.9ff. See especially

. . . for this passage was verified and fulfilled shortly after Christ ascended into heaven, and is still in process of fulfillment. When the Gospel was first proclaimed, it was preached to the Jews; that nation was the sheepfold. And now he says here: "And other sheep I have, which are not of this fold: them also must I bring." Here he declares that the Gospel is to be preached to the gentiles also, so that they also might believe in Christ, that there might be one Christian communion, composed of Jews and gentiles. This was afterwards brought about through the apostles, who preached to the gentiles and converted them to the faith. Accordingly there is now but one church or communion, one faith, one hope, one love, one baptism, etc. And this continues to the present day, and will continue until the day of judgment. Hence, you must not understand this to mean that the whole world, and all men, will believe in Christ; for this holy cross will always be with us. They are in the majority who persecute Christ, and therefore the Gospel must ever be preached, that some may be won for Christ. The kingdom of Christ is in process of growing and is not something that is completed [*das reych Christi stehet ym werden, nicht ynn geschehen*].[125]

Mission among the peoples is central when Luther reflects on salvation history after Christ's ascension. Nevertheless, it ought to be observed that for Luther mission and the church are integrated in the new covenant and that the Gospel creates one single people of God from Jews and heathen. The true time of mission has begun with the preaching of the apostles, but the time of world mission continues until the last day.

Early on, Luther did not connect the words in John 12:32 ("But I, when I am lifted up from the earth, will draw all men to myself") with world mission.[126] But in his later writings, Luther believes that these words of Jesus indicate the ascended Christ's active struggle through the preaching of the apostles and their followers to spread God's salvation in the entire world.[127]

---

the 1544 *House Postil*: "Das aber der Herr von andern Schaffen sagt, die er auch füren soll, auff das ein Hirt und eine Herd werd, Solchs hat sich als bald nach Pfingsten angefangen, da das Euangelion in aller welt durch die Apostel ist gepredigt worden, unnd gehet noch biss zu ende der welt. Nit der massen, als solten alle menschen sich bekeren und das Euangelion annemen. Denn da wird nicht auss, der Teuffel lests da zu nicht kommen, So ist die welt on das dem wort feind unnd wil ungestraffet sein. Derhalb werden für unnd für mancherley glauben unnd Religion in der welt bleyben. Das aber heyst ein Hirt unnd ein Schaffstal, das Gott alle, so das Euangelion annemen, Umb Christus willen zu Kindern auffnemen will, es seyen gleich Jüden oder Heyden. Denn das ist die rechte, einige Religion, disem Hirten unnd seiner stym volgen" (WA 52:282.24ff.)

125 Lenker 3:31 (WA 12:539.33ff.).

126 Cf. WA 10/1.2:367; 10/2:332ff.; 17/2:483ff.

127 For example, WA 45:538.31ff.

In a fumbling manner at first[128] and later clearly, Luther connects John 14:12 ("I tell you the truth, anyone who has faith in me will do what I have been doing. He will do even greater things than these, because I am going to the Father.") with the church's mission led by the glorified Christ. The reformer says that God's people of faith will do greater works than Christ did because the apostles, their followers, and the Christians will spread the Gospel farther out into the world than he himself did. But in a manner that we already have seen, Luther says also that Jesus Christ is the power and mechanism of these "greater works." The work of mission will continue until the Last Day. In the comprehensive commentaries on John from 1538, Luther says:

> Here I accept the general sense of the verse. It can have no other meaning than this, that the works of Christians are called greater because the apostles and the Christians had a wider field for their works than He did, that they brought more people to Christ than He Himself did during His earthly sojourn. Christ preached and worked miracles only in a small nook, and for just a short time. The apostles and their successors, however, have come to all the world, and their activity has extended . . . farther and farther through the apostles and the preachers who came after them; it must go on until the Day of Judgment. Thus it is true that the Christians do greater works, that is, more works and more extensive works, than Christ Himself did. Yet the works are identical; they are the same as His. For when Christ declares that he who believes in Him will do greater works, He does not deny that such works must be done through His power and must issue from Him as the Fountainhead.[129]

After Luther, in connection with John 14:12, has praised the Gospel, Baptism, the Lord's Supper, and Christian prayer as the greatest of works compared with

---

128 As is well known, Luther connects miracles mostly with the first breakthroughs of the Gospel in its meeting with an obdurate heathenism. In one sermon (WA 20:385.21ff.), Luther discusses the connection only between the Word, a strong faith, and miracles. In the *Festival Postil* (1527), Luther writes: "dann wa ir an mich glaubet, werdet ir nicht allain solche werk und wunderzaichen thun, die ich thu, sonder auch grössere, Welchs dann geschehen ist nach der himelfart Christi, da die Apostlen vil grössere zaychen, bayde under den Juden und Hayden gethon haben, dann Christus selbs. Was ist aber der ursache? Der HERR saget hie selbs und spricht: 'Dann ich gee zum vatter.' Das ist: Ich vil das raych anfahen, da ich alle ding erfülle, dann ich bin im vatter, Darumb seind auch Christo alle ding underworffen, das er der son ist . . . 'Ich gee zum Vater'? Antwort: Darumb, das Christus im Vater ist, so thut er die werck des vaters, aber nicht darumb thun wir auch dieselbigen werck, Sondern das Christus, der im vatter ist, nun in uns ist. Dann zum vater geen ist alle ding erfüllen . . . [Ephesians 4:8 and Psalm 68:19 are here adduced.] . . . Dann das ist das reich Christi, dadurch er auff erden regirt in den hertzen der glaubigen, und sitzet auff dem stul David seines vatters" (WA 17/2:420.7ff., 420.25ff.). Cf. *Luther and World Mission*, 157ff.

129 LW 24:78 (WA 45:531.23ff.).

dramatic miracles—among other things, he says the prayers of Christians sustain the ever-changing course of the planet—he comments on the concluding words: ". . . because I am going to the Father." Jesus Christ's enthronement on the right hand of the Father is, says Luther, a prerequisite to his building of his church in the world in his omnipotence.

> By "going to the Father" Christ means that He is to be made Lord and placed on the royal chair at the right hand of the Father, that all power and might in heaven and on earth are given to Him, as He says in Matt. 28:18. "You will get the power to perform such works because you are My members and believe in Me." . . . "But afterwards—after My crucifixion, death, and burial—I shall first leap from death into life, from the cross and the grave into everlasting glory, divine majesty, and might. Then—as Christ states elsewhere (John 12:32)—I will draw all men to Myself, and all creatures will have to be subject to Me. Then I shall be able to say to you apostles and Christians: 'You, Peter or Paul, you must go forth and overthrow the Roman Empire if it refuses to obey My Word.' "[130]

Can the fact that God's salvation will be offered to all people be more clearly expressed? Can the fact that the glorified Christ is the driving motor or the active subject in the workers of God's reign be more clearly expressed? Hardly. It is Christ, with all power in heaven and on earth, who accomplishes mission work among the peoples. The conclusion of the citation does not mean that Luther links mission with political revolution. That interpretation is excluded by countless passages in the source material. A Luther scholar must become used to the fact that the reformer often uses drastic metaphorical language.

A pair of passages in Jesus' farewell speech in John 13–17 concern especially the time of the Spirit and the church during which the Word/Gospel will be preached for all people. John 14:23–31, the Gospel for Pentecost, shows that, according to Luther's commentaries, Christ will leave the world and as the glorified Lord work for the establishment of his reign as never before. This he does through the Holy Spirit who will comfort, give joy, and teach in all truth. But the Spirit has his own determined ways, according to Luther's common words. The Spirit works through the Word and the means of grace as a unified entity. Luther says quite powerfully that the ascended Lord in no way gives dispensation from obedience to the words that he himself has spoken. Quite the opposite, Jesus says that the Helper "will teach you all things and will remind you of everything I have said to you" (John 14:26). Just so, the content of love to Christ—which during the time of farewell and all the time of the church is important—is described in such a way that one keeps Jesus' words (John 14:23f.). This means, above all, that no

---

130 LW 24:85–86 (WA 45:538.14ff., 538.31ff.).

instance or power ought to be allowed to do violence to or to extinguish the Gospel, says Luther.[131] It ought to be observed that this pericope is used by Luther during the season of Pentecost when sermons on the ascension and the outpouring of the Spirit occur close to each other. For Luther, Christ's ascension and the outpouring of the Spirit constitute a general start for the work of building Christ's reign through the Gospel in the mouths of fragile humans.

John 16:5ff., Jesus' farewell discourse, provides the reformer with an occasion to speak about the growth of Christ's reign or mission.[132] Jesus' speech about the reality of persecution for disciples (John 15:19–16:4) had, according to Luther, confused the disciples, so they simply could not understand that to fulfill God's plan of salvation he must suffer death on the cross, rise from the dead, and through the ascension bodily leave earth and the disciples. In the reformer's understanding, Jesus wants, therefore, to say that both from the perspective of God's plan of salvation and from that of one's own salvation it is most useful and best (John 16:7–8) that Jesus should go to the Father through suffering, death, resurrection, and ascension. Hereby the whole foundation of salvation is laid and the possibility for the sending of the Spirit-Helper and for the expansion of Christ's reign through the Gospel is established.

In a 1538 commentary on John, Luther writes:

> "For if I do not go away, the Comforter will not come to you; but if I go, I will send Him to you." Christ wants to say that it has been proclaimed in Scripture and foretold by all the prophets that Christ will suffer, die, be buried, and rise again, and thus establish a new, eternal kingdom in which mankind has everlasting life and is redeemed from sin, death, and hell. This must be fulfilled; and the hour of its fulfillment has now come. "For the predictions of all the prophets point to this time, and I am the Person who is to carry them out. Therefore your joy and salvation are now beginning; but you must learn to forget about My physical presence for a little while and to look for the Comforter. For My kingdom cannot be ushered in, nor can the Holy Spirit be given, until I have died and departed this life. My death and resurrection will renew everything in heaven and on earth, and will establish a rule in which the Holy Spirit will reign everywhere through the Gospel and your ministry." . . . But if I go, die, and accomplish what God in His counsel has decreed to accomplish through Me, then the Holy Spirit will come to you, work in you,

---

131 See, for example, WA 12:568ff.; 20:398ff.; 29:351ff.; 41:248ff.; 47:772ff. Cf. Ebeling, *Evangelische Evangelienauslegung*, 459, 470f.

132 The important passages are WA 10/1.2:259f.; 10/3:124ff.; 11:104ff.; 12:542ff.; 15:542ff.; 17/1:243ff.; 28:45ff., 50ff.; 34/1:361ff., 369ff.; 37:74ff.; 41:63ff.; 46:363ff. All is gathered and developed in the monumental "Sermons on John 16 (1538)," WA 46:30ff. Cf. Loewenich, *Luther und das Johanneische Christentum*, 25.

and instil such courage in you that you will be My officials and corulers, will turn the whole world topsy-turvy, will abolish the Law or Judaism, will destroy pagan idolatry, and (as we shall hear) will rebuke all the world and change it. And your doctrine will endure and prevail forever. . . . I will receive power from My Father, will be Lord over everything, and will give you the Holy Spirit, who will glorify Me in the world. Thus I will initiate and promote My everlasting kingdom through you.[133]

Luther energetically anchors world mission in Christ's death and resurrection and understands Christ's enthronement at the right hand of the Father and the sending of the Spirit as decisive presuppositions for centrifugal, universal mission. At the same time, the expansion of God's reign is concretely anchored in the work of Christ's church, that is, the Word and the Sacraments, in the work of many servants, etc. But it is always the glorified Christ and the Holy Spirit who are the ultimate, active subjects. With their authority and power, Christ and his Spirit work in the ministry of the church.

Above, I have often shown how Luther is occupied with the message of the work of the church/mission. Luther sees in John 16:8–11 a basic teaching about the content of the preaching of God's reign in church and mission. Those who are familiar with Luther know that he often uses just these words to support the thesis (which is also based on Luke 24:47 and some passages in Paul) that repentance and the forgiveness of sins, Law and Gospel, shall be preached wherever the church works. First, in connection with John 16:8–11, the reformer emphasizes that the Spirit through the apostles and the church in all times will accuse the world of sin, that is, reveal its defection, its unbelief, and its actual sins. The church especially emphasizes that sin is not only superficial; sin goes through all layers of the human subject. So the Spirit through the preached Word will reveal unbelief and the defection of the heart as the archsin. Sin in this understanding is incomprehensible for works-righteousness: "because men do not believe in me" (that is, Christ). This is the source of sins against the Law.[134] This agrees with the discussion about the original fall and Luther's hamartology in chapter 2 (pp. 16–20).

Concerning John 16:10 (". . . in regard to righteousness, because I am going to the Father, where you can see me no longer"), the reformer says that the world will come to know that saving righteousness does not consist in works of righteousness, civil decency, or something else that the human performs. Righteousness vis-à-vis God is simply this: to receive in faith Christ as dead, risen, and enthroned at

---

133 LW 24:334–35 (WA 46:32.33ff., 33.23ff.).

134 WA 10/3:125.2ff.; 12:542ff.; 15:543.28ff.; 17/1:244.28ff.; 34/1:362.6ff.; 37:75.33ff.; 41:64.29ff.; and especially 46:37–43.

God's right hand.[135] That which is always conspicuous in Luther's exegesis and preaching on the ascension and the sending of the Spirit is that Christ's enthronement at the Father's right hand is a living reality for the reformer. The foundation of the Good News is laid deep in the cross and the resurrection. Then the glorified Christ, who possesses all authority in heaven and earth, works through the Holy Spirit and through preaching, Baptism, the Lord's Supper, and the keys to grant saving righteousness and to build his reign. At a certain level, the real drama begins with the ascension and the outpouring of the Spirit. This is world mission as a "sharing out" to people of the righteousness Christ accomplished in his death and resurrection. This powerful vision is reliably and firmly anchored in the doctrine of sin and grace, Law and Gospel. Luther does not for a moment deny the need for workers in the expansion of God's reign. But it is always ultimately the glorified Christ and the Spirit who drive the work forward. In a 1523 sermon, Luther says:

> For this reason he is risen from the dead and ascended to heaven, that he might begin a spiritual kingdom, in which he reigns in us through righteousness and truth. Therefore, he sits above; he does not rest and sleep, does not play with himself, but, as Paul says, Eph 1, 22, has his work here upon the earth, governing the consciences and the souls of men with the Gospel. Wherever Christ is now preached and acknowledged, there he reigns in us, from the right hand of his Father, and is himself here below in the hearts of men . . . and guards you from sin, death, devil and hell.[136]

If unbelief is the sum of all sins, so Christian righteousness consists in the phenomenon that the human through the Gospel receives grace and help to believe in Christ's saving work. This radical view of Law and Gospel, works and faith, sin and grace has consequences for Luther's understanding of the words in John 16:11: ". . . and in regard to judgment, because the prince of this world now stands condemned." Even if reason is enough to organize a civil order and righteousness, this world and its prince know nothing of the meaning of righteousness before God. The world does not understand that the one who is without Christ is helplessly and hopelessly lost under sin and death. This is judgment.[137]

Luther also emphasizes that the Holy Spirit's treble truth about sin, righteousness, and judgment on the world in all times unavoidably leads to the confrontation between God's/Christ's reign and the devil's reign. The commentaries in ques-

---

135 WA 10/3:127.26ff.; 15:544.16ff.; 17/1:245.15ff.; 34/1:365.1ff.; 37:76.33ff.; 41:66.20ff. See especially WA 46:43–46.

136 Lenker 3:117 (WA 12:546.35ff.).

137 WA 10/3:131.23ff.; 12:548.1ff.; 15:544.28ff.; 17/1:246.26ff.; 34/1:368.1ff.; 37:76.19ff.; 41:67.31ff.; and especially 46:46.27ff.

tion were written throughout Luther's life as an active reformer and are occupied with how the fact that Christ forms the church for work and through the Spirit drives the Gospel throughout the world is, for Christians, unavoidably connected with the cross and suffering. Luther does not at all reckon with some kind of synthesis or civil peace between this age and Christ's coming reign. He comforts Christians, however, by reminding them of the fact that Satan is a condemned loser.[138]

Luther has reflected occasionally on the consequences of John 16:12–14 for church and mission. Here the usual debate with the Roman Catholic theologians looms large: whether the church stands over Scripture or the Scriptures over the church. From the words "I have much more to say to you . . . . [T]he Spirit of truth . . . will guide you into all truth" (John 16:12–13), one had given the hierarchy and the councils—if not principally, at least practically—authority over the apostolic word in the Scriptures. As a reformer and a man of the church, Luther orients his people in another direction. If the Holy Spirit would reveal other secrets that Jesus had not revealed to those who could not yet bear all, that additional revelation had nevertheless been given completely while the apostles still lived. It was, after all, the apostles who received the promise about the leading of the Spirit "into all truth." Above all, Luther wants to emphasize the congruence between what Christ taught and what the Spirit teaches. In a manner of speaking, the Spirit of truth does not add anything to but instead develops Christ's words, says Luther.[139] In this respect, he points to the abrupt words in John 16:13–14: "He will not speak on his own; he will speak only what he hears . . . . He will bring glory to me by taking from what is mine and making it known to you." On the basis of these words, Luther has developed an entire fundamental doctrine about how the church and mission as the tool of Christ and the Spirit in proclamation and in defense of Christ's teaching must carefully follow Christ's teaching as it exists in the Scriptures. The church and mission must follow not only Jesus' words but also the whole of Scripture, naturally as read with insight into the difference between the old and new covenants, etc. The filtering of the Scriptures that one often labels "Lutheran" in our time is not at all in agreement with Luther's commentaries on these texts. Luther says energetically that the Spirit, the church, and mission build Christ's reign on the foundation of the Word. He also emphasizes powerfully that God's Spirit works realistically through the Word and Sacraments

---

138 WA 10/3:132.2ff.; 12:549.23ff.; 37:76.22ff.; 41:68.1ff.; and above all 46:47.11ff.

139 WA 12:550.7ff., 550.29ff. Those who oppose the words of Christ in the Scriptures cannot be part of Christ's church. Luther can, however, while guarding the continuity between the words of Christ, the apostles, and the church, sometimes say that the Spirit would further develop that which Christ had said only briefly. Cf. WA 34/1:371.23ff., 372.10ff., 373.11ff. Concerning the Spirit of truth, see Loewenich, *Luther und das Johanneische Christentum*, 54f.

as the instruments of grace. Church and mission must hold dear the Scriptures, preaching, Baptism, the Lord's Supper, and the power of the keys. Through these, one learns above all to know grace in Christ. In this way, the Spirit builds the reign where Christ is believed and glorified. Luther says in an exposition from 1538:

> "For He will not speak on His own authority, but whatever He hears He will speak." Here Christ makes the Holy Spirit a Preacher. He does so to prevent one from gaping toward heaven in search of Him, as the fluttering spirits and enthusiasts do, and from divorcing Him from the oral Word or the ministry. One should know and learn that He will be in and with the Word, that it will guide us into all truth. . . . ". . . His message will have substance; it will be the certain and absolute truth, for He will preach what He receives from the Father and from Me. . . . Thus He will speak exclusively of Me and will glorify Me, so that the people will believe in Me."[140]

Even the Gospel of John has its own mission command: John 20:19–23, which Luther often exposits and on which he preaches the First Sunday after Easter (*Quasi modo geniti*). This text is, for the reformer, a primary witness for the use of the power of the keys in public church confession (*Bann*) and in private confession (*Beicht*). The pericope is also used—though not often—to describe the general use of the power of the keys in the preaching of Law and Gospel. Luther also extracts from this text an anti-theology against Roman Catholic theories about the authority of the papacy. In this anti-theology (which he supports with Matthew 18:15ff.), Luther says that the church is the true subject of the power of the keys and that all of the church's ordained ministers have the same authority and task of service.[141]

For Luther, John 20:19–23 concerns the general sending of the disciples/apostles into the world with God's salvation message. The risen Christ's greeting of peace to the disciples after Good Friday's wonderful duel (*mirabile duellum*) with Satan, sin, and death is an important starting point for this sending or *missio*. The Savior's *pax* gives birth to a faith, joy, and peace in those first disciples. In this way, the Gospel about Christ's death and resurrection gives anxious and trembling disciples throughout all times faith, joy, and a hope for the future. This ought to be the main task of all who are sent out with the Gospel.[142]

---

140 LW 24:362–63 (WA 46:57.19ff.). Cf. WA 12:550.7ff.; 15:545.4ff.; 34/1:369–76; and the exhaustive passage in 46:49–68.

141 Öberg, *Himmelrikets nycklar och kyrklig bot i Luthers teologi*, 41ff., 116ff., 200ff., 446ff. My dissertation reviews an abundance of source material on the power of the keys and churchly confession, as well as the relevant literature.

142 WA 10/1.2:235ff.; 12:517ff.; 20:363ff.; 37:380.27ff.; 49:135ff., 143ff.

Furthermore, Luther often points to Jesus' express sending of the apostles in John 20:21–23: "Peace be with you! As the Father has sent me, I am sending you. . . . Receive the Holy Spirit. If you forgive anyone his sins, they are forgiven; if you do not forgive them, they are not forgiven." According to Luther, these sending words mean first that just as Jesus was sent by the Father to accomplish and announce salvation for poor sinners, so Christ sends his disciples—here the ministry of preaching is central but not solitary—to announce or distribute God's salvation to people. *Missio ecclesiae* has its starting point and foundation in *missio Christi*. Thus Jesus entrusts his church with this dizzying task: the proclamation of the Gospel of salvation in the entire world. This general and universal sending is used by Luther in some early texts in an ethical direction. As Christ served his disciples in life and death, so Christians will serve their fellow humans in self-sacrificing love and good works.[143] Later, Luther connects Jesus' sending words in John 20:21 almost exclusively with the message that the church, the apostles, preachers, etc., ought to preach for people in our world.

On the basis of John 20:21–23, the reformer develops further not only the church's universal sending by Christ with the Gospel but also and above all the task/authority given by Christ to forgive and bind sins. One sees in the source material how Luther both differentiates and integrates two tasks. He emphasizes that one ought to connect neither the general sending nor the special use of the power of the keys to civil exercise of power. Private confession ought not be allowed through exaggeration of regret, feelings, and confession of sins to be made into a trap for the soul. Both in the general (the preaching of the Word) and in the special (pastoral care and church discipline) application of the power of the keys that Christ has given, the purpose is always the salvation of the sinner and spiritual help to people. For these tasks, the ministry of the church will administer public preaching, the sacraments, and institutional confession. Laypeople are not only allowed but ought to witness to and exhort the forgiveness of sins in private conversations with distressed people.[144] As we have seen in chapter 2 (pp. 25–35), Luther says that faith will serve its neighbor in practical care for the neighbor and in natural ways, in ways that are near at hand. Nevertheless, he can say that this Gospel invitation to the neighbor is the most important of all services to the neighbor. This task ought to be practiced by all the faithful in their contact with other people. The ministry of the church as *ministerium publicum* will again,

---

143 WA 10/3:94ff.; 10/1.2:230ff. See also WA 12:522.1ff.

144 See Öberg, *Himmelrikets nycklar och kyrklig bot i Luthers teologi*, 338ff., 356ff. See also WA 2:716.27ff.; 6:547.1ff.; 8:183.7ff.; 10/1.2:239.11ff.; 10/3:96.9ff.; 15:96.15ff., 486.25ff.; 32:426.19ff.; 47:287.12ff., etc. In Luther, Matthew 18:15f. constitutes the basis of the right of laypeople to forgive sins.

through the Word, the Sacraments, pastoral counseling, etc., publicly distribute the blessings of Christ's death and resurrection.[145]

When commenting on John 20:19–23, Luther often connects the general sending with a powerful emphasis on and extensive discussion about confession and absolution. Year after year, he preaches extensively to the congregation about the importance of anxious and regretful people being able to confess in private and receive forgiveness for that which troubles the conscience.[146] Private confession and absolution were of great value to Luther. He personally confessed to Pastor Bugenhagen. He wanted each evangelical Christian to have his or her own confessor. Luther often thanked God because he had placed his forgiveness and grace so low and so near that pastors and siblings in the faith could proclaim God's own forgiveness. The unbelievable can occur because Christ in John 20:23 had given the command to absolve people from their sins.[147]

---

145 WA 8:156ff., 173ff.; 10/1.2:239.8ff.; 10/3:96.11ff.; 12:521.15ff., 522.5ff.; 20:366.16ff.; 34/1:319.1ff.; 37:381.3ff.; 41:541ff.; 49:139ff.

146 Cf. the sermon on John 20:19ff. from 1522: ". . . for it follows thus in the text: 'As the Father hath sent me, even so send I you.' The first and highest work of love a Christian ought to do when he has become a believer, is to bring others also to believe in the way he himself came to believe. . . . My Father sent me into the world only for your sake, that I might serve you. . . . [R]emember and do ye also likewise, that henceforth ye may only serve and help everybody, otherwise ye would have nothing to do on earth. For by faith ye have enough of everything. Hence I send you into the world as my Father hath sent me; namely, that every Christian should instruct and teach his neighbor, that he may also come to Christ" (Lenker 2:358–59 [original emphasis] [WA 12:521.18ff.]). "Furthermore Christ now gives a command, he breathes upon the disciples and says: 'Receive ye the Holy Spirit: whosoever sins ye forgive, they are forgiven unto them; whosoever sins ye retain, they are retained.' This is a great and mighty power which no one can sufficiently extol, given to mortal men of flesh and blood over sin, death and hell, and over all things" (Lenker 2:359–60 [original emphasis] [WA 12:522.5ff.]). Christ does not want the power of the keys to be connected with the exercise of worldly power. ". . . [Christ] gives spiritual power and rule, and wishes to say this much: When ye speak a word concerning a sinner, it shall be spoken in heaven, and shall avail so much as if God himself spake it in heaven. . . . Again, if he says: Thy sins shall not be forgiven thee; then they shall remain unforgiven" (Lenker 2:360 [WA 12:522.12ff.]). "Hence we have no authority to rule as lords; but to be servants and ministers who shall preach the Word, by means of which we incite people to believe" (Lenker 2:362 [WA 12:523.37ff.]). The same motif is apparent in the corresponding sermon from 1526 (WA 20:366.16ff.). The general sending and corporate/private confession are integrated.

147 In the Large Catechism, Luther writes this about private confession: "Thus by divine ordinance Christ himself has entrusted absolution to his Christian church and commanded us to absolve one another from sins" (LC VI 14; Tappert, 458). Cf. "Conciunculae quaedam etc. (1537)," Luther writes this about John 20:19: "IN ISTIS VERBIS

Luther indicates that the church ought not in any way abandon some part of the means of grace that Christ established. According to Luther, Christ has, through absolution, *de facto* established a source of salvation in his church. If someone despises that, then he or she opposes Christ.[148] Luther never believed that preaching and the administration of the sacraments alone could suffice in the work of the congregation. Luther would add the private care of souls to contemporary Lutheranism's concentration on Word and Sacrament ministry. For the reformer, absolution was an indispensable part of the gifts of the Gospel. Even church discipline with the binding of sin so the sinner might later repent and be absolved of the same was cherished by the reformer on the basis of Matthew 18:15ff. and, among other texts, John 20:23. On the other hand, one could never produce a perfect and believing congregation by church discipline. Faith is created only by the Gospel publicly or privately communicated.

The sermon for the First Sunday after Easter 1544, which is recorded in *House Postil* (itself a revision of a sermon from 1531), summarizes well Luther's emphasis on both the general sending with the Gospel and this sending's special application above all in private pastoral care. In the commentaries on John 20:21, 23, Luther writes:

> "As the Father sent me, so I am sending you." These are remarkable words by which he *delivers the ministry of preaching to them and brings Christ's suffering and resurrection into their right use and exercise. . . .* The holy Isaiah in his 61st chapter (v. 1f) teaches us how the Father sent Christ. "The Spirit of the Sovereign LORD is on me, because the LORD has anointed me to preach good news to the poor. He has sent me to bind up the brokenhearted, to proclaim freedom for the captives and release from darkness for the prisoners, to proclaim the year of the LORD's favor etc." This is the command with which Christ was sent. *And he says here that he sends the disciples in the same way that he himself*

TRIA sunt observanda. Primum est institutio divina, scilicet, quod ipse Deus sese dimittit et ordinat auctoritate divina, quod absolutio hominis debeat esse absolutio ipsius Dei. Ita ut qui audit hominem absolventem, certus esse debeat sese ab ipso Deo in coelis esse absolutum. Et haec institutio est vis et robur clavium. Nam quid esset absolvere humanum aut retinere, Si hoc fieret temere et arbitrio humano sine Dei mandato seu instituto? Nunc cum Deus ita statuat et mandet absolvi seu remittere et ligare seu retinere, Valet remissio et retentio non virtute operis seu facti, sed virtute ordinantis et statuentis Dei" (WA 45:460.5ff.) See n146 and n151., WA 37:381.3ff.; 45:460ff. Cf. also Öberg, *Himmelrikets nycklar och kyrklig bot i Luthers teologi*, 280ff., "Avlösningen meddelas på Kristi befallning," and pp. 285ff., "Förhållandet mellan Guds och kyrkans förlåtelse."

148 See Öberg, *Himmelrikets nycklar och kyrklig bot i Luthers teologi*, 226ff., about how Christ's institution of the authority to absolve sins gives absolution a regular place in the church that aspires to completeness.

was sent. And he commands them to continue the same ministry which he him-
self had exercised so that they shall preach as he preached and so that this com-
mand and sending here is directed toward teaching alone.[149]

Luther also writes about the great power and gift of absolution:

This is now a power, against which imperial and royal power are nothing, that an apostle, indeed every disciple of Christ, can pronounce a judgment on the whole world that their sins have been taken away. And such a judgment shall be so powerful and so certain that it is as if Christ himself had pronounced it, as his words here confirm: "As the Father has sent me, so I am sending you. . . ." This is called the apostolic regiment, i. e., a power which does not govern body and soul, money and possessions and that which belongs to life, but instead governs such that you and God hold for sins. In this way the sins of the whole world are laid under the apostles and all the servants of the church, in times of emergency under all Christians.[150]

In this way, Luther often integrates the general sending with the Gospel and the special use of the authority to release and to bind.[151]

---

149 WA 52:267.3ff. (*Öberg's emphasis*).

150 WA 52:269.18ff., 270.29ff.

151 A 1536 sermon on John 20:19ff.: " 'Mitto' etc. 'Et blies sie an dicens' etc. Haec verba bene notanda. Der Herr hat nicht lang kund harren, sed voluit in totum mundum bringen usum und krafft resurrectionis. Ideo ostendit eis etc. ut certo sciant resurrexisse und eylet fluchs cum fructu et krafft resurrectionis. Et significat non pro sua persona resurrexisse. Sed is finis, propter quem resurrexit, et das sols gelten, das ich wil regnum anrichten. 'Sicut pater' etc. et tali potestate et befelh, ut reich anrichten, die Sund weg nemen vel behalten i.e. do potestatem den himel zuschliessen und helle auffschliessen. Ista alia potestas non mundana, sed quae pertinet ad jhenes leben, ubi homines eripiuntur a peccatis vel si non, ut in eis permaneant und inn die helle gestossen. Et mittel. Quomodo? . . . Christus et Apostoli armatura komen, et hodie ministri non cum armis, sed cum verbo, ist odem, qui auditur et ex ore egreditur, et tamen subest tanta potestas remittendi peccata" (WA 41:541.14ff.). WA 41:542.10ff.: "Sequitur: 'Blies' etc. non dicit: accipite, nempt ros, harnisch, strick, schwerd, sed spiritum sanctum, et hoc officium vestrum, ut habeatis officium remittendi et retinendi peccata." The sending and the power of the keys are integrated even in 1540; see WA 49:138.23ff., 139.1ff. This sending and world mission are especially apparent in Lenker 2:396–97 (WA 49:140.24ff.): ". . . give heed to his Word and command when he says: 'I send you,' etc., as if he wanted to say: I must first come to you to announce to you the will of my Father through the Gospel; institute the holy sacraments and absolution. You should not come to me in a different way. But since I cannot be bodily at all places in the whole world, and shall not be visibly present with you always, I will do as my Father hath done. He took a small corner of the earth, namely, the land of Judea, to which he sent me, that I should be a preacher there; I traveled through Galilee and Judea; so much I could accomplish personally; I preached the Gospel to the comfort of

Contemporary Lutheran mission has understood the general sending in John 20:21, but in my experience and the experience of others on mission fields, contemporary Lutheran mission has often failed to see that John 20:23 includes private confession and absolution. However, in these contexts one often uses church discipline without understanding, as did Luther, neither the greater context of the order of repentance nor the goal of returning and helping mistaken fellow Christians to faith in the forgiveness of sins and to a holy life. It is extraordinarily important that world mission should follow Luther by integrating the general sending and the Word and Sacraments with a well thought out, evangelical use of the power of the keys in pastoral care and church discipline. It is especially sorrowful that private confession has such a weak place on the mission field and that this is a development away from original Lutheranism. If one wants to communicate the fullness of original Lutheranism to sister churches in Asia and Africa, one ought to avoid connecting the mission commands only to the preaching of the Word and Baptism (Matthew 28:18ff.; Mark 16:15ff.; Luke 24:45ff.). According to the reformer, the use of the power of the keys in private soul care is one of the signs of the church (*notae ecclesiae*).[152] A sign of the church ought also to be a sign of mission, according to Luther's integration of church and mission that we have reviewed above.

SUMMARY

After this examination and analysis of Luther's exposition of the Gospels with respect to the question of mission, I shall attempt to summarize the main points. The investigation has shown that Luther does not say much concrete about mission work. This depends partly on the fact that Luther is not himself engaged in actual mission work and partly on the fact that he is, above all, an exegete and biblical theologian. He is most concerned about the principle theological factors of the Gospel's expansion from Jerusalem to the ends of the world and to the

---

the poor sinners among the Jewish people, healed the sick and raised the dead etc. This, you will notice, was the work entrusted to him. For this purpose he was sent by the Father . . . . And thus, he says, ye shall also do at all places wherever ye go, and to this purpose I send you, that ye shall run as my messengers through the entire world. And besides you and after you I will ordain others who shall run and preach, as I sent you, even unto the end of the world, and I will continue to be with you that ye may know that it is not you who are accomplishing this, but I through you. From this command we also have the power to comfort the sorrowful consciences and to absolve from sin, and we know that, wherever we exercise this office, not we but Christ himself is doing it."

152 See Öberg, *Himmelrikets nycklar och kyrklig bot i Luthers teologi*, 205–31, 446–585. See also "On the Councils and the Church (1539)," WA 50:631.36ff., about the right use of the power of the keys as one of the *notae ecclesiae*.

end of the age. Among others, the following main themes are emphasized in Luther's exposition of the Gospels.

1. From a salvation history perspective, Luther notices that the invitation to salvation becomes radically universal at the time the new covenant takes over from the old. If God's salvation even during Jesus' earthly life should be preached in principle only for the lost sheep of Israel (Matthew 15:21ff.; 10:5f.), the Son of Man intimates that the outbreak from particularism is near (John 4:21, 23). Soon he will be glorified and a universal-centrifugal Gospel will go out to all peoples. Salvation comes from the Jews, but it is not offered only to them. In the new covenant, which came into effect through Christ's death, resurrection, and ascension and the outpouring of the Spirit, we have a universal invitation to salvation, an invitation offered to all peoples, Jews and Gentiles (Matthew 6:10; 22:1–4; Mark 16:15–16; Luke 14:16–24; John 3:16–17; 12:32; 14:12, 23–31; 20:21).

2. Along with other passages, Luther notices that in the petition "Thy kingdom come" (Matthew 6:10) and in the parables of God's reign (Matthew 13 and parallels), God himself builds the church and guarantees his reign through the Word/Gospel. This harmonizes well with the sketch of Luther's ecclesiology in chapter 2 (pp. 82–84). The church/mission has along with the expansion of God's reign a continuous struggle against Satan and his arsenal of weapons. The church is characterized by weakness and hiddenness in sin and factions. Only through the power and work of the Father, the Son, and the Spirit is world mission possible.

    Luther especially emphasizes how the glorified Christ is given all authority and as such drives God's reign forward through his Spirit, who is active in the preaching of the Word, the Scraments, and private soul care. Christ's ascension is no loss for church and mission. Only after Christ laid the ground for salvation through his life, his death, and his resurrection and then ascended to sit at the right hand of the Father can the adventure of world mission led by Christ himself and the Spirit really begin. This is something foundational for Luther's mission theology. The exalted Christ promises to draw all people to himself in a completely new way (Matthew 28:18; Mark 16:15–16; John 16:12–16; 12:32; 14:12, 23–31; 20:19–23).

3. Through Christ himself, the church possesses express commissions and instructions concerning world mission (Matthew 28:18–20; Mark 16:15–16; Luke 24:45–49; John 20:19–23). This investigation has shown that the so-called Great Commission is not the most important in Luther's exposition of the Gospels. Instead, the other commissions, together with some texts from John 14–16, are decisive for Luther's mission theology. It is a theme of all Luther's commentaries on the commissions that the

church can never exempt itself from Christ's command to take the Gospel to all peoples on earth.

4. The reformer is also concerned with the question of what message the church's mission should preach and offer to the world. He emphasizes that the message must always have Christ, faith in Christ, and confession of Christ as the basis. All mission work rests on the atoning sacrifice of Christ and his resurrection (Luke 24:46; John 3:16; 14:12; 16:8–11). Because Christ has finished his work of salvation, the church should invite all peoples to her King's feast of joy. A herald's cry about salvation of grace for all and about faith in God's Son should be preached in the world. The mission message must not offer a grace and forgiveness tinged with works of the Law.

5. In Luther's missiology, the themes of Law/Gospel and repentance/forgiveness of sins are brought forward repeatedly as the pervasive structure of the message to people. However energetically he emphasizes that the unconditional and radical Gospel is the main theme in the preaching of the church/mission, Luther knows nothing of a "hypergospel" in which the accusing and sin-revealing function of the Word is set aside. At the same time, preaching (the difficult art of rightly distinguishing Law and Gospel) contains a movement from the Law/commandments to the Gospel, in that order (Luke 24:46–47; John 16:8–11). Only the Gospel can create faith and give eternal life.

6. Especially articulated is the thesis that Christ and the Spirit work instrumentally through the Word, the Sacraments, and soul care/private confession. It ought to be observed that Luther considers the preached Word to be the foremost tool of the church/mission. Preaching's "living Word" (*viva vox*) is, for Luther, not only an informative word but also the sword of the Spirit that with God's own authority breaks into the conscience of both Jews and Gentiles. There the living Word creates the heart's sorrow but most of all faith in God's Son. Luther also forcefully emphasizes the place of Baptism in mission work. Naturally the Lord's Supper and the declaration of the forgiveness of sins also belong to the fullness of the means through which Christ creates and maintains faith (Matthew 6:10; Mark 16:15–16; John 10:16; 14:12, 23–31; 16:8–11; 20:19–23).

7. In the material examined above, Luther has indicated that the Word/Gospel is carried to the world by human agents. After Jesus' commissions and the outpouring of the Spirit, the whole church (all Christians, including those called to ordained ministry) becomes engaged in the expansion of God's reign. The tasks of the apostles and their successors in the church/mission are emphasized (Mark 16:15–16; John 14:12; 16:5–11;

20:19–23). The workers in God's reign will receive power and the Holy Spirit will lead them in their preaching and undertakings. Luther remarks especially after the confrontation with the "spiritualist" movements that the mission message must follow and proceed from God's and Christ's Word. The Spirit does not add anything to Christ's Word. Instead, the Spirit proclaims Christ's Word and glorifies God's Son (John 14:23–31; 16:12–14). Luther always integrates the work of the already existing church and the work on the frontiers with the heathen. Of course, mission has its own specific problems, but both the home front and the mission front always have the same single commission and the same opposition from Satan, unbelief, and godlessness. In a striking manner, Luther emphasizes that the work of God is always accompanied by opposition and the cross. As has been shown in chapter 2 (pp. 35–37), the universal struggle between God and Satan is the background to this. It ought to be pointed out that the reformer does not explain specifically how the church should form itself practically for the task of cross-cultural or foreign mission. In this respect, Luther does not present a complete missiology or mission theory in his exposition of the Gospels.

8. In many of the texts that I have examined, it is said in one way or another that mission (grounded in Christ's saving work, in his commissions, and started at the outpouring of the Spirit) continues during Luther's time and will continue until the end of the world and until the end of time. The reformer has in no way indicated that the time of mission is past. The Gospel continues to go forth in the same arching waves throughout the world and calls people to faith in God's Son (Matthew 6:10; 22:9–10; Mark 16:15–16; Luke 14:16–24; 24:45–49; John 10:16; 14:12). Of course, Luther's Bible exposition and preaching usually has Germany and Europe in its field of vision. This examination and analysis has shown, however, that the reformer does not lack an interest in the Christianization of the heathen.

MISSION AND ITS PRINCIPLE TEACHINGS IN LUTHER'S INTERPRETATION OF THE BOOK OF ACTS AND THE EPISTLES

It has been said that the salvation history of the New Testament draws a line of progressive expansion from the single Jesus and the cross, through the calling of the apostles, and forward to world mission.[153] Against the background of what I have already surveyed and analyzed of Luther's interpretation of the Old Testament and

---

153 See Sundkler, *Missionens värld*, 2ff., 8ff. Old Testament history has gone through a "progressive reduction": humanity > the people of Israel > the remnant of Israel > the Single, Messiah-King. Now salvation history is characterized by a "progressive expansion"

the Gospels, we will here investigate how the mission motif comes to expression in the reformer's commentaries and sermons on the Book of Acts and the letters of the New Testament. It is with a certain excitement that one approaches this source material. This excitement depends partly on the fact that Luther here comments on the texts that report the first decades of the apostolic church's work and partly on the fact that the earlier investigations consistently foreshadowed that, for Luther, a definite breakthrough for world mission comes with Christ's ascension, the outpouring of the Holy Spirit, and the beginning of the work of the apostles. Above all, in the foregoing section we have seen how Luther combines his exegetical work with preaching. The apostolic word has something to say to Luther's time and to ours.

Mission Thinking on the Basis of the Book of Acts

When I here first wish to show the place and the content of the mission motif in the reformer's interpretation of Acts, it can be appropriate to start with his forewords to the Book of Acts written in 1533 and 1546. One is taken aback when Luther says that Acts was not written to describe the personal work and lives of the apostles but to give examples of justification by faith. For example, Luther writes:

> Rather it should be noted that by this book St. Luke teaches the whole of Christendom, even to the end of the world, that the true and chief article of Christian doctrine is this: We must all be justified alone by faith in Jesus Christ, without any contribution from the law or help from our works. . . . Therefore he emphasizes so powerfully not only the preaching of the apostles about faith in Christ, how both Gentiles and Jews must thereby be justified without any merit or works, but also the examples and the instances of this teaching, how the Gentiles as well as Jews were justified through the gospel alone, without the law.[154]

In fact, it may seem to us that Luther is a little narrow-minded when he focuses only on Christianity's doctrine of salvation in Acts and not on all the concrete mission work and mission journeys. This same central doctrine applies to all true workers of God's reign in mission, evangelization, and reformation for all times. Luther is not especially interested in the concrete mission work and journeys recorded here and there in Acts. For Luther, what is important in Acts is the doctrine of and the examples of how the Gospel of Christ provides salvation, righteousness in relationship to God, and the gifts of the Holy Spirit to both Jews and

---

from the Single to the many, from the cross < the apostles < the church < humanity. Because now the time of the Spirit has come.

154 LW 35:363 (WADB 6:415.10ff.).

Gentiles. This occurs undeserved, without the works of the Law, only through faith in God's Son. So Luther writes:

> Therefore this book might well be called a commentary [*eine Glosse*] on the epistles of St. Paul. For what Paul teaches and insists upon with words and passages of Scripture, St. Luke here points out and proves with examples and instances to show that it has happened and must happen in the way St. Paul teaches, namely, that no law, no work justifies men, but only faith in Christ. Here, then, in this book you find a beautiful mirror in which you can see that this is true: *Sola fides justificat*, "faith alone justifies."[155]

Luther continues by pointing out how the doctrine of justification by faith is illustrated with many examples in Acts. Luke tells the stories of the conversion of Paul, Cornelius, Sergius, and others; the Jerusalem Council; and the young church's preaching through Peter, Paul, Stephen, and Philip.

Because Luther considers Acts to be a kind of commentary on the letters of Paul, the material in Acts and the Epistles will be addressed in the same chapter. Because of the reformer's strong emphasis on doctrine in this material, one is compelled to give some special attention to what Luther believes is important in the church's/mission's message in the world. This question is considered especially in connection with the letters of the apostles. Furthermore, careful attention is given to whatever Luther has to say about the practical work of mission.

CHRIST'S ASCENSION, THE OUTPOURING OF THE SPIRIT, AND PETER'S MISSION PREACHING

From the reformer's expositions on texts from the Book of Acts—in this case, the Luther source material consists almost exclusively of sermons—first we will see what Luther says about Christ's enthronement at the Father's right hand as he year after year works with the basic text about Christ's ascension in Acts 1:1–11. Luther constantly supports his preaching on Acts 1:1–11 with passages such as Matthew 28:18; Mark 16:19; Luke 24:51; John 16:7, 11; Psalm 110:1ff.; and Ephesians 4:8ff. In the early years of his career, Luther did not emphasize so energetically Christ's lordship and church-building work through the Word and Sacraments,[156] but this theme is articulated in later sermons from 1531, 1542, and 1544. In these later texts, this theme is emphasized powerfully, along with the

---

155 LW 35:364 (WADB 6:415.26ff.).

156 In sermons from 1520 (WA 9:453–59), Luther emphasizes in connection with Christ's ascension the mutual love between the ascended and the true faithful and the importance of keeping the goal of heaven in focus (WA 9:453.14ff., 456.15ff.). Luther emphasizes that Christ continues to be the only head of the church so he might build up his church and through the Spirit give power to the members of Christ's body. Luther

waiting of the disciples in Jerusalem and especially with the sending of the Spirit. It is first with Christ's ascension and the outpouring of the Spirit that the enthroned and active Christ actually begins to build the worldwide church. At the same time, it is said that the Spirit, through the means of grace (the Word, Baptism, the Lord's Supper, and absolution), accomplishes his work to create a happy and willing people. Luther focuses especially on the words in Acts 1:8: "But you will receive power when the Holy Spirit comes on you; and you will be my witnesses in Jerusalem, and in all Judea and Samaria, and to the ends of the earth." The reformer's interest in this verse shows that he possesses a powerful mission vision. Every word and clause of this verse is important for Luther. The work of the Spirit is to establish Christ's reign through the church's preaching of repentance and the Gospel. For this task, witnesses and preachers are needed. The apostles and their followers—including laypeople—will through the Spirit be filled with power and joy and become witnesses in a mission drama that starts in Jerusalem and continues to the end of the world and the end of time. One clearly understands from these sermons that Luther is not at all blind to the continuing direct confrontation with heathenism. Here, as in other passages of the Luther material, one notices that Luther does not want to confuse the public work of the preaching ministry of Word and Sacrament with the important witness of laypeople in their meeting with individual unbelievers.[157] It is also clear that the reformer considers his own struggle to reform the church in Germany as part of this work. Even the Reformation is included in this sending of Christ, this work of the Spirit. Luther does not draw a definitive line of demarcation between mission in heathen lands and reformation/evangelization in Germany.[158]

Thus salvation history in Luther's understanding develops progressively, and Pentecost and the outpouring of the Spirit in Jerusalem constitute a decisive mile-

---

lambastes the neglect of the church hierarchy by saying that Christ's ambassadors ought to present Christ's words and feed Christ's sheep (he refers to John 20:16 and Ephesians 4:8, 11ff., 15f.). See WA 9:457.18ff., 458.4ff., 458:31ff. In these sermons one lacks the emphasis on Christ's lordship through the Gospel. The accent is more on the ambassadors and their work.

157 Cf. *Luther and World Mission*, 88–95.

158 The Spirit and the commissioning are not emphasized especially powerfully in the 1531 sermon for Christ's ascension (WA 34/1:401ff.). However, see WA 34/1:404.5ff., 405.8ff. But in the sermons from 1542 and 1544, these themes are exceedingly central. Here Luther emphasizes how after the ascension, the Spirit through the Gospel—against all enthusiast leanings, markedly bound to the Word and Sacraments—will build a reign characterized by joy and the freedom of faith, not a worldly reign. Luther also notices that the apostles and their followers—including the witness of laypeople—will be ambassadors and witnesses in a mission drama starting in Jerusalem and

stone in that history. It is not without some great expectation, therefore, that one considers Luther's many sermons in connection with Acts 2. With the arrival of the Spirit on Pentecost, the actual start of world mission would begin.

Luther's early sermons on Acts 2 are not especially well thought out. In them, Luther emphasizes, as he does later, the difference between Sinai as the location of the Law and Jerusalem as the location of the Gospel of salvation, but in these earlier sermons, the Spirit is more connected with the problem of sanctification than in the later sermons.[159] Luther's Pentecost sermons become progressively more evangelical and mission oriented as the years go by. In the later sermons, Luther more often connects the mercy of Christ and of God and the sending of the church out into the world with the message of the outpouring of God's Spirit over the disciples.[160]

In the exceedingly copious sermons on Acts 2 from 1529 and onward, Luther emphasizes that the drama of Pentecost and Peter's preaching, as it was promised, touched only the Jews who were gathered in Jerusalem from the Diaspora. World mission would begin with the chosen people (Acts 1:8). The wind, the noise, the tongues of fire, etc., were, however, a God-given manifestation that Pentecost introduced a new epoch in salvation history. In the middle of the Jewish festival of Pentecost—a thanksgiving for harvest, for exodus, and for the giving of the Law at Sinai—the general breakthrough of the Gospel out to the peoples occurs. After all the disappointments, in the middle of all the fears of the disciples, it occurs, and

---

continuing to the end of the world and the end of time. Cf. WA 41:242.13ff., 244.18ff., 244.28ff. About how the Spirit gives birth to the testimony of all and leads the work of the preaching ministry of the Word, Baptism, the Lord's Supper, and absolution, see WA 41:245.16–247.29. See also WA 49:417.17ff. about the fire and power of the Spirit. And about the sending, see WA 49:419.2ff: "Verbum venit ad nos per Apostolos propagatum, ut dicit: 'Eritis testes usque ad finem mundi' [Acts 1:8]. Nos certe particula mundi habitamus, hie im winckel. Ideo triffts uns auch, quicquid illis praedicatum. . . . Loquor de iis, qui audiunt verbum et versiegelt und angestrichen durch Euangelium, Sacramentum, vergebung der sunden und versamlet in Ecclesiam." Cf. WA 41:245.30ff. (on Acts 1:8): "Iam totus mundus vol feur worden, spiritus sanctus ubique suum Euangelium, Tauffe, Sacrament hat lassen aus gehen. . . . Ideo populus non Mosaicus, sed erit sacerdotium et tales, qui offerent froliche opffer i.e. mit trost et libenter praedicabunt de te et propter te patientur. Hoc fiet post tuam victoriam, ubi den streit gewonnen."

159 WA 9:461ff.

160 This is clear already in a 1523 Pentecost sermon. Cf. WA 12:571.9ff. (the Word is the Spirit's way to touch people) and WA 12:572.6ff. (the Spirit teaches about Christ and grace). The Spirit also sanctifies, but Luther notes that this sanctification is only partially completed in this present age; see WA 12:572.25ff., 573.26ff., 574.22ff. Cf. WA 20:393.29ff.

despite all that Luther had said about the church of the patriarchs, the Holy Spirit is poured out and Christ's universally oriented church is founded. The age when God's reign will be offered to all through the Gospel has dawned. Its message is something different than Sinai and the Law. One preaches that the Crucified One is risen and lives. The mission of the church has its start in this first "Christian" Pentecost and continues until Christ's parousia.[161] Now there is no longer any need to fear. Indeed, one is ready to accept martyrdom if only God's salvation can be preached in the entire world. Now the Spirit of God roars and whistles in the hearts of those true to Christ and in the hearts of the apostles, says Luther.[162]

The reformer has spoken about Pentecost's tongues of fire and ecstacy in this way. If one only gives proper weight to the Word/Gospel in the expansion of the church, one does not need to end up in some kind of enthusiast cul-de-sac when one interprets the passage about the fire of the Spirit. God needed through the Spirit to give the apostles courage, boldness, and faith so the work of expanding the church throughout the entire world would succeed.[163] In this context, Luther also points out that the Holy Spirit is a divine person of the Trinity, not only an inner residing fire and power.[164] But the Spirit does reside in the hearts of believers and gives them joy and a new boldness.

The Holy Spirit is the power source of the testimony of all God's people. On the basis of Acts 2:16ff. and Joel 2:28f., Luther extensively describes how the Spirit leads all Christians in their testimony about God's salvation. Sons and daughters, youth and old men, manservants and maidservants share without exception in the Spirit and in the gifts of grace. These gifts will be used in the service of building Christ's reign over the earth. But all prophecies, all visions, and all dreams ought to be tested by God's clear Word and the confession of faith. This people of the Spirit and of faith, that is, the priesthood of all believers, ought not reject the ordained pastors when they preach the Word publicly and administer the sacraments.[165] The Spirit is a Spirit of order, according to the reformer.

---

161 WA 29:348.10ff.; 34/1:458.10ff., 459.3ff.; 37:399.17ff., 403.1ff.; 41:601.6ff.; 49:449ff.; 52:315.12ff. See WA 34/1:460.6ff: "Sic cum semel spiritus sanctus sol ecclesiam Christianam anfahen, must er sich so euserlich erzeygen signo, ut comprehenderetur."

162 WA 29:349.3ff.; 34/1:461.2ff., 462.7ff.; 41:602.2ff., 602.32ff.; 52:315.18ff., 315.28ff. See WA 37:400.7ff: "macht frolich und kecke, Ut Christus promiserat [John 16:7], quod eis vellet mittere spiritum sanctum, qui non terreret, Sed keck machen. Isto die quisque Apostolorum in sonderheit stehet auff et vult die gantze welt fressen."

163 WA 34/1:463.1ff.; 37:400.22ff.; 41:254.25ff.; 52:315.15ff.

164 WA 52:315.38ff., with other passages.

165 WA 29:375f., 377ff.; 37:401.14ff., 401.21ff., 406.3ff., 408.27ff.; 41:255.16ff., 263.26ff., 264.13ff., 267.28ff., 605.15ff.

Luther speaks not only about how, according to Joel 2:28f.; Romans 12:7; 1 Corinthians 12:6ff.; and here in Acts 2:16ff., the Spirit sets the tongues of believers in motion and the priesthood of all believers to work. On the basis of Peter's sermon in Acts 2:14ff., 22ff., 32ff., Luther writes of how Peter, the other apostles, and their followers in the ministry of preaching, supported by the same Holy Spirit, will preach a two-edged word in the world. The apostles' public preaching of the Word/Gospel and their definitions and defense of the fundamentals of the Christian faith are relevant for all peoples on earth in all times. Furthermore, just as the people had gathered in Jerusalem after journeying there from all peoples and were able to hear the enthusiastic testimony in all languages, so the preaching of the church and of mission in all times ought to be characterized by Pentecost, that is, it ought to have an indisputable universal vector.[166] Luther also says something about the structure of Peter's first Pentecost sermon. From his comments on Peter's sermon, one can understand how important the theme of Law/Gospel, repentance/forgiveness of sins is for him. All mission and evangelization must be characterized by a double word, a word that reveals sins to the sinner and a word that preaches the forgiveness of sins.

One notices in Luther's exposition of Acts 2:16ff., 32ff. how powerfully he assigns responsibility for killing God's Messiah to the Jewish leaders, though sometimes he speaks of all people. That humans should be revealed as sinners is so important for Luther because they are in fact sinners in God's eyes. With this punishing word, God's Spirit will drive sinners to regret in their hearts and conscience.[167]

In the middle of Pentecost and for a moment, the Word preaches Law and disaster and grief. But this is not the sum of Peter's preaching and the preaching of later times. Above all, the apostolic word is a preaching about Christ's cross and Christ's resurrection. Its task is to reveal the mystery of Christ, the secret of unconditional grace. The Word and the Spirit will first grant grace and the forgiveness of sins[168] to all those who repent, receive the Gospel, and are baptized in

---

166 WA 29:382ff., 388ff.; 34/1:462.1ff.; 37:401.5ff.

167 WA 29:346.8ff.; 41:602f. Cf. how Luther understands that in the trial against Jesus both Jews and heathen are guilty for the execution of Jesus; see WA 28:323ff. Of course, the reformer says that Christ died according to God's own decision to pay for all sins through his atoning death. Among the many texts about Peter's arousing and punishing word, see WA 29:382.16ff., 383.12ff.; 34/1:346.8ff.; 37:401.11ff.; 41:256.21ff., 257.7ff. About the judgment of the conscience and regret, see, among others, WA 37:401ff.; 41:257ff.

168 Cf. WA 37:399.17ff: "Audivimus hodie et Euangelium et historiam huius frollichs, heiligen fests, in quo beghen et gratias agimus pro maximo beneficio, quod in terris erzeigt und da mit uns verlornen menschen uns lassen offenbaren suum heilig verbum

Christ's name.[169] So the mission message of Pentecost is really the same as has been seen above in connection with Luke 24:47: "and repentance and forgiveness of sins will be preached in his name to all nations, beginning at Jerusalem." Luther notices this connection directly in his work on Peter's Pentecost sermon and Acts 2. The preaching at Pentecost creates both a Pentecost anxiety and a Pentecost joy. The reformer can even say that Peter's Pentecost sermon is a paradigm for all subsequent preaching of mission and church.[170]

In connection with Peter's Pentecost sermon and Acts 2:21, one important theme of the reformer ought to be observed. This recurring theme in Luther's writings is that the Christian daily prays for forgiveness and believes in God's promises of grace. But Luther categorically rejects the idea that without the preaching of the Word one might attain a saving faith by means of mystical prayer or meritorious works. Calling on the Lord is an important part of all living faith, but prayer must be anchored in the preaching of the Word/Gospel. Therefore the reformer integrates the preaching of the Word, calling on the name of the Lord, and faith:

1. Acts 2:21 and Romans 10:13: ". . . everyone who calls on the name of the Lord will be saved."

2. Romans 10:14–15, 17: "How, then, can they call on the one they have not believed in? And how can they believe in the one of whom they have not heard? And how can they hear without someone preaching to them? And how can they preach unless they are sent? . . . Consequently, faith comes from hearing the message, and the message is heard through the word of Christ."

Luther means then that salvation is won through a faith that has been created by preaching the Word/Gospel. It is received not by the one who in some kind of "inwardness" leaves preaching behind, as the enthusiasts do. The Holy Spirit works instrumentally, that is, through the means that God has appointed for the

---

e caelo et non simplex verbum, sed ein unterschiedlich wort gegen dem lege Mosis, quia hoc die caepit Regnum Christi, per Apostolos offenbart coram mundo." Also WA 34/1:463.17ff.: "Wie heist seine predigt, wie lauts? so ut infra in contione Petri: Credo in spiritum sanctum, remissionem peccatorum. Haec est nova doctrina et praedicatio, quae hodierno die e coelo venit, quae praedicari debet. In Regno Christi gilt keine quam remissio peccatorum, Ausser seim reich et antequam dazu kompt, busse et legis praedicatio." Cf. about the word of the cross, resurrection, and the forgiveness of sins in WA 29:346.11ff.; 34/1:465ff.; 37:407f.; 41:604.34ff.

169 WA 29:388.19ff., 390.8ff.; 41:257.22ff., 259.27ff. Luther notes against all spiritualization of Baptism that it communicates the forgiveness of sins and the Holy Spirit.

170 WA 29:388.2ff., 388.25ff.; 41:258.1ff.

communication of the Gospel, grace, and forgiveness.[171] Luther says expressly that the work of God's reign is a *missio corporalis*. It is obvious from this statement that Luther defends an ecclesial Christianity and mission. Wherever Christ and the Spirit work through the means of grace and their servants, salvation can never be reduced to some kind of spiritual inwardness. Luther claims this precisely in connection with the text in Acts 2 about the Holy Spirit and mission. Luther's reasoning about how grace is communicated through the Word and Sacraments in the hands of God's servants shows in a clear way that the reformer does not disregard the human factor in the work of mission. *Missio Dei* takes people into its service. The main accent remains, however, on the church-creating work of the Word and the Sacraments.

Luther in his later comments on Acts 2 also often discusses sanctification. He refers here to John 14:23: "If anyone loves me, he will obey my teaching." Where the Spirit of Pentecost, preaching, and faith exist, there the individual and the church are sanctified. But the reformer rejects any hope of a perfect sanctification within time. Christians in themselves are *peccatores*, and the church in itself is *peccatrix*. But in Christ they are holy.[172]

For Luther's view of mission, the interpretation of the drama in Cornelius's house recorded in Acts 10:34ff. is especially important. Acts 10:44–46 is central: "While Peter was still speaking these words, the Holy Spirit came on all who heard the message. The circumcised believers who had come with Peter were astonished that the gift of the Holy Spirit had been poured out even on the Gentiles. For they heard them speaking in tongues and praising God." This text is the transition from the outpouring of the Spirit on the circumcised to the preaching and outpouring of God's Spirit on uncircumcised heathen. The Jewish Christians were amazed that the heathen spoke in tongues and praised God.

---

171 Cf. the thorough discussions in WA 29:378ff.; 52:318ff. See also WA 41:607.8ff. Luther writes in 1529: "Invocacione nominis domini quae incipit ex auditu verbi, non merito. Paulus hoc verbum tantis laudibus exaltat. Valeant Schwermerii qui hunc locum lacerant 'Fides ex auditu' [Romans 10:17]. Szo sprechen sie: Ja, es ist eyn geystlich horen. Sed ego tuam impietatem aperiam. Si auditus esset spiritualis, sequeretur Praedicatores et Missionem non esse corporalem, sed omnino spiritualem. Apostoli autem in terrarum orbem iverunt et corporaliter praedicaverunt. Illud opus eciam fuit spirituale? Pfui dich, dw unsauber geyst . . . oportet deum mittere praedicatores. Praedicatore fideliter praedicante sequitur auditus verus, sequitur fides . . . . Das ist der rechte steyg gegen hymmel und keyn ander" (WA 29:381.11ff). Observe that Luther here expressly speaks of preaching and mission (*missio corporalis*). Cf. Scherer, *That the Gospel May Be Sincerely Preached*, 11, and his questions about whether Luther has adequately perceived the need to send out people in mission work. See *Luther and World Mission*, 181f.

172 Concerning the Spirit and sanctification, see WA 34/1:464.14ff., 466.6ff., 467.4ff.; 29:389.3ff.; 52:320.7ff.

Luther's few longer commentaries on this text harmonize well with his comments on Acts 2. There is, however, not much here about the Law-Gospel theme because the text does not directly actualize that problem. On the basis of Acts 10:34ff. and 44ff., Luther's focus here is that the Gospel of church/mission from the beginning and through all times must be addressed to all people.[173] Christ has died and is risen for all people. Therefore both Jews and heathen ought to have the opportunity to hear the message about him. The message of the church to the world is a preaching about the Christ who in his life served God and people and through his death on the cross and resurrection won peace for people through his sacrifice of atonement and his victory over Satan, sin, and death.[174] The Gospel of Christ will be preached for all people in all times as long as the world exists—among the Jews, among the heathen, and in Europe. This means that all who believe the Son will receive the forgiveness of sins in his name. No other Gospel may be preached by Christ's church (Galatians 1:8).[175]

Both in his direct commentaries and in his references to this text, Luther makes much of the fact that the oral preaching of Peter (Acts 10:44) proves itself capable to communicate the Holy Spirit to those who listen. This is the same issue of oral preaching and faith that also has been seen in connection with Acts 2:21; Romans 10:14; and Galatians 3:2.[176] Oral preaching (*viva vox*) is a means of grace, according to Luther. It is not only an informing word, it is also the primary instrument of mission, especially in pioneer mission work.

Paul's call and the radical Gospel

The following investigates how the mission idea comes to expression in Luther's comments on some texts in the Book of Acts about the apostle and arch-

---

173 An enlightening example exists in WA 49:362.18ff.: " 'In omni populo.' Er trage schleier oder hut, sive Iudaeus sive gentilis, doctus, indoctus: Crede, sic praedicamus viris, mulieribus . . . knecht, herrn. Qui credit, ist angeneme . . . sive sit in Meissen, Preussen: omnium Deus, Deus unicus omnium Creaturarum et omnes salvat."

174 WA 21:217.18ff.; 49:363.9–364.24.

175 WA 21:218.8ff. See especially WA 49:365.4ff. (both Luther and the apostles are commissioned to preach the cross and the resurrection): "et gentibus haec pax sit praedicanda, cum debeo in hac gentili Civitate et domo praedicare et ipsis gentilibus. Est ergo communis pax et salus etiam gentibus, quae etiam ad hanc pacem pertinent." Concerning Acts 10:43, Luther writes: " 'Omnes', sive Iudaei sive gentiles. Der hat uns weiter das predigampt befolhen, scilicet quod nomen eius. Praedicatio facta est de fide per totum mundum. Woran feilets? Ist gewaltig erschollen in tota Germania, vide, ut dran gleubest . . . . 'In suo nomine.' Non tuo. Er hats durch sein sterben verdienet. . . . per nomen Christi consequor remissionem peccatorum" (WA 49:365.22ff.).

176 Cf. *Luther and World Mission*, 137ff., with 142n103; 205–10.

missionary Paul. One ought first to observe in this connection how important Paul's conversion and apostolate according to Acts 9:1–25 (also 22:3ff.; 26:9ff.) are for Luther. He believes that one ought to preach on Acts 9:1–25 annually. Here are two incomparable examples of two essential facts of theology. First, this pericope shows what humanity in its jealousy for God's Law and the temple can undertake when it lacks the light of faith. Second, this pericope shows how sinners can receive God's grace and accomplish something great in God's reign after they have met Christ. Imprisoned by the Law, one can in God's name become the worst enemy and bloodhound of Christ and Christians. This occurs because natural humanity can never understand that its works mean nothing and that faith means everything in the question of salvation. It is only the Gospel and faith in Christ that can break this captivity to the Law and make humanity useful for the work of God's reign.[177] The fact that Saul/Paul is converted, is given the forgiveness of sins, and is called to be the apostle of the heathen is a great miracle. This persecutor of Christ remains for all times an example for all those who through faith in God's Son want to receive eternal life (1 Timothy 1:12–16).[178]

There is good reason to focus especially on Paul's call to be an apostle and missionary in a mission investigation such as this. The reformer often emphasizes that Paul is called directly by God/Christ as the prophets and the other apostles were called, only in a more dramatic manner. In connection with Paul's call, Luther sometimes expresses the vision of a continuing universal mission. That to which Paul was called is in some respect the church's perennial call. The apostle Paul has, as no one else, made clear that which ought to be preached to the uncircumcised, the heathen. The reformer also notices that the man of violence whom God made to be the apostle of the heathen is *our* apostle, that is, the apostle of the Germans, of the West, and of all non-Jews.[179]

In a January 26, 1546, sermon on Acts 9 delivered just before his death, Luther especially notices the mission idea that is tied to Paul's conversion and the apostolic and mission task among the heathen that he had received from Christ him-

---

177 WA 9:444.14ff., 504.15ff.; 29:45.9ff., 46.19ff., 48.4ff.; 37:267.25ff., 268.6ff.; 41:33.19ff., 34.1ff., 34.22ff., 35.13ff., 36.23ff.; 51:140.30ff., 141.12ff., 143.3ff.; 52:611.30ff., 612.10ff.

178 WA 29:47.14ff., 48.15ff. and, in compressed form, 29:49.11ff.: "2. stuck ist das, quod Sanctus Paulus apostolus et caput inter praedicatores Christianitatis proponitur nobis exemplum ut ipse dicit 'qui in Christum', 'ad vitam aeternam' [1 Timothy 1:16]. Iam in Paulo discimus regnum Christi esse remissionis peccatorum regnum. Ego libenter habeo, quod Sancti fuerunt magni peccatores, ut nos fide firmemur et ut credentibus nobis remittantur peccata nostra." See also WA 37:267.32ff.; 41:37.15ff., 38.19ff.; 51:141.31ff.; 52:615.32ff., 616.26ff.

179 WA 37:268.20ff.; 52:613.3ff., 613.11ff.; 51:136.12ff., 144.30ff. Cf. Luther's commentary on Galatians 1:1, 11ff., about Paul's call direct from God/Christ, WA 40/1:52ff., 126ff.

self. In this sermon, Luther says that on the way to Damascus Paul was called to be the apostle of the heathen and was taught about the Gospel, that is, the true mission message. Paul's call was extraordinary and his apostolic task stretched farther than all others; it stretched to the heathen or to the peoples. Luther rejoices over the fact that Paul is the apostle of the heathen. He is thereby "our apostle," or the great apostle of the Germans, who through Rome communicated the truth of faith to the Western world.[180]

It is impossible to review in detail here those extraordinarily interesting passages about how Paul and the other apostles of Christ communicate the treasure of truth to the church through all times. But this means that in the word of Scripture and the word of preachers faithful to the Bible, Paul, Peter, and ultimately Christ himself speak.[181] The kernel of this inspiring, apostolic Gospel is that sinners receive eternal life through faith in Jesus Christ. It is this holy treasure that was Paul's primary message among the heathen and that must always be sounded among the heathen during Paul's apostolate.[182]

---

180 WA 51:136.12ff: "Denn hie hat unser lieber HERR Christus Jhesus ein solch Mirackel und wunder an dem Paulo geübet und bewisen, da er jn selber in eigener person vom Himel herab zum Apostelampt berüfft und ordinirt . . . . Denn er hat den rechten lehrer hie auff dem wege, da er gen Damascon reyset, selbs gehöret und Studeirt, was er predigen und lehren solte, Und das er zu eim Prediger und lehrer des Euangelij nicht allein den Jüden, sondern und fürnemlich den Heiden beruffen were. Darumb so ist das ein seer schöner och herrlicher beruff gewesen, weit uber der andern Apostel beruff, Denn auch sein beruff sich serner erstreckt hat und weiter gangen ist denn der andern Apostel, das er Predigen solt unter den Heiden. Das sollen wir uns nu frewen und trösten, auch GOTT dancken, der uns Heiden als heute ein solchen herrlichen APOstel Paulum beruffen und gesand hat, wie er selbs dis bezeuget zu Timotheo [1 Timothy 2:7], da er sagt, er sey 'gesezt ein Prediger und Apostel, ein Lerer der Heiden im glauben und in der warheit'. Darumb so ist der liebe Paulus unser Apostel, Wiewol auch andere Apostel alle unsere Apostel sein, denn sie alle zugleich eine lehre von CHRisto empfangen und geleret haben, So ist doch Paulus unser Apostel, denn er ist gen Rom komen, hat da das Euangelium vom glauben in CHRistum Jhesum reichlich gepredigt und gelert, ist auch da entheupt worden, Ob aber S. Petrus hinkomen und zu Rom gewesen sey, das weis ich nicht."

181 WA 51:136.36ff., 137.11ff., 137.38ff., 138.20ff. Cf. *Luther and World Mission*, 282ff.

182 About the kernel in the word of the apostles and Scripture, that which is the true "relic" and treasure, Luther writes: "wie du von Natur ein Sünder seiest, wo du deiner sünden ledig und los werden solt und das ewige leben bekomen, nemlich durch den glauben in Christum . . . das ist allein das rechte Heilthumb und der edle Schatz, wenn ich S. Paulum kan lebendig hören" (WA 51:138.24ff.). WA 51:138.31ff.: "Wenn dein Prediger und Seelsorger leret und predigt, hat S. Pauli schrifft fur jm, so leihet er S. Paulo die zungen und den mund und nimpt sein Wort und saget, wie Paulus: 'Das ist je gewislich war und ein tewer werdes Wort, Das CHRistus Jhesus komen ist in die Welt, die Sünder Selig zu machen [1 Timothy 1:15] . . . leret S. Paulus also Das, Jhesus

The older Luther says this about Paul's preaching and the continuing preaching of the church:

> Thus, Paul is called and ordained. He is also given instructions about the form and manner of his work, how and what he shall preach about Christ, how much he must suffer for the sake of his name. . . . And Christ commands Paul to preach nothing other than what we also preach: namely, faith alone in Christ Jesus, that he is God's Son, that whoever believes in him becomes free from sin and blessed. The whole world will hear, receive, and believe this preaching.[183]

A little further on, he writes:

> For Christ says here: "Listen, Paul. The whole world reels in darkness and delusion. It does not know me. But you will call out and show the way from darkness to light, from the reign of the devil to the reign of God, from death to life. How? By what means shall I accomplish this? By the Word, which you Paul have now heard in my own preaching: namely, that you in my name will preach repentance and forgiveness of sins. And whoever believes in me (that I am truly God's Son) is righteous before God and will receive eternal life."[184]

It is easy to understand from these citations that with a view toward mission Luther unites the question about the content and the structure of the message. Because the entire world suffers in spiritual darkness, a message must go out in which people are called to repentance and faith in God's Son. The doctrine of justification through faith will characterize the message of all the work of God's reign. One may suggest that the above quotations do not especially indicate that the Christianization of the heathen world ought to continue in Luther's time and onward. However, when Luther speaks of that which applies generally to the church of Christ, he includes the Reformation, evangelization, and mission. When I speak of mission in Luther, I refer first to the idea that the church announces the Gospel to those among the peoples who have not yet heard it.

Luther often says that Paul received his mission call on the road to Damascus. He often adds that on the same occasion Paul received from Christ teaching and enlightenment in the Gospel, the same Gospel that Paul would later spread. However, one finds in the source material, among other places in the important *House Postil* of 1544, that Luther assigns much importance to the fact that after Paul's

---

Christus nicht darumb komen sey, die Welt zu richten und zuvordammen, die zuvor allzu sehr gericht und verdampt ist umb jrer Sünden willen, Sondern darumb sey CHRistus komen, die sünder Selig zu machen [John 3:17], welchs er auch seinen Jüngern und Aposteln zu predigen befohlen hab." Cf. WA 51:139.6ff., 139.10ff.

183 WA 51:145.16ff.

184 WA 51:145.33ff.

conversion on the Damascus road, he as a blind man is sent to the obscure Ananias inside the gates of Damascus. In an attack on the enthusiasts, Luther wants to note that Paul's enlightenment, conversion, faith, and apostolic task are also coupled with the Word and Baptism and the Christian congregation. This coupling with the Word and Sacraments of the church is especially relevant concerning personal, saving faith. The colloquy between Jesus and Saul on the Damascus road does not annul the fact that God principally gives his grace instrumentally. Paul was taught both by Jesus and by Ananias. He received first from Christ and then from other Christians the message that he was called to preach, the Gospel for the peoples.[185]

Mission preaching—its tools, audience, content, and method

Paul's mission work is described in Acts 13–28. In connection with the commissioning service in Acts 13:1ff., Luther outlines some general theses about the ministries and charismatic gifts in church/mission. As the congregation in Antioch, so ought every congregation be characterized by a principal parity and unity. This is evident from the fact that the great worker in God's reign, Paul, is named last when the names of the leaders are listed.[186] At the same time, the text in question shows that prophets and teachers have special responsibilities to preach God's Word publicly. So the church always has its public office (*officium publicum*).[187] At

---

185 In a sermon from 1534: " 'Ito,' inquit, 'in Civitatem' etc. [Acts 9:6ff.]. Er wil das predigampt nicht auffheben und jederman etwas sonderlichs machen, Potuisset ei commendare officium de celo, aber er weiset in zum predigtstuel, zum pfarrherr, So wil unser herr Gott nicht einem iderman etwas sonderlichs anrichten. . . . Carolstadius et Marcus [Stübner] weisen die leute jnn winckel, da sollen sie auff unserm herr Gott warten . . . So lest Gott den Teufel er ab fliegen in specie angeli und geschicht jn recht, Paulo hat er nichts sonderlichs angericht und geprediget, qui tamen fuit summus praedicator, Sed dicit: 'vade' etc. weiset in da hin, da sein wort und Tauff ist, Er prediget und Tauffet in nicht auffm feld, Et Paulus obsequitur domini mandato gern, gern, Er weis nicht, wo er hin sol, wer ims sagen sol, Drumb schickt im unser herr Gott Ananiam, qui dicit 'Paule' [Acts 9:19], Prediget jm und leget die hand auff jn, da kompt per verbum Ananiae etc." (WA 37:269.18ff.). WA 37:270.1ff.: "Er mus also sein liecht empfangen von dem kleinen schwebelholtzlin, von dem kleinen Doctorchen Anania, Da sol man hin sehen, horen. Recipit visum. Post per ministerium acquirit intellectum, quid Christus, baptismus sey, und trit auff und ist ein ander man, Als viel er bluts vergossen, ja tausent mal mher, macht er Christen, ut dicam: Ist das nicht ein wunder, das der man also prediget?" Rörer's notes are also carefully given in German in the 1544 *House Postil* (WA 52:614.37–615.31.). Cf. the 1531/1535 commentary on Galatians that, however, discusses this theme a little more weakly (WA 40/1:58ff., 126ff.). See *Luther and World Mission*, 175–77, on Acts 2:21.

186 A 1524 sermon, WA 17/1:510.1ff.

187 WA 17/1:508.10ff., 508.20ff., 509.9ff., 509.16ff. Concerning the functions of the

its side is the priesthood of all believers, in which parents are given a responsibility to teach at home and all Christians in their relationships with other people are given the responsibility to confess the name of Christ and speak God's Word. Thus the special ordained ministries in the congregation are united with the right and call of all Christians to witness, wherever they live and work.[188]

We have previously touched on Paul's call to be Christ's ambassador that took place on the road to Damascus and Paul's meeting with Ananias. The reformer notices that in Acts 13:2f. the Spirit—through the prophecy of a Christian—indicated that Barnabas and Saul/Paul should begin with a concrete ministry. Then after fasting, praying, and the laying on of hands, they were sent out by the congregation in Syrian Antioch on their first missionary journey.[189] Luther once again emphasizes that an external call is necessary for public preaching. An inner prompting alone does not suffice.[190] At the same time, every Christian ought to proclaim Christ in heathen contexts. Luther says hypothetically: "But if I should find myself among the Turks, I would have of course preached for my guests. And

---

prophets and the teachers in the ancient church, see Luther's understanding in WA 17/1:509.8ff., especially 510.11ff.: "Prophetas et doctores. Indicat Lucas honestam fuise eorum conversationem, sunt, qui divites sunt in scriptura per eingeben spiritus sancti, ut possint alios docere, sunt doctores aliorum doctorum, q. d. plures erant hic, qui semper docebant illuminati spiritu sancto, qui interpretabantur etc. Doctores, qui hanc doctrinam et interpretationem susceperunt et aliis impertierunt, et haec ecclesia digna est honore." See also the investigation about spiritual gifts, services, and ordinations in the examination of Paul's letters in *Luther and World Mission*, 292–13.

188 WA 17/1:509.3ff., 509.11ff.: "Tamen homo alteri potest Euangelium praedicare, quia quilibet Christianus baptizatus et credens accipit spiritum sanctum. Hic iam habet potestatem praedicandi, et cuiuslibet Christiani officium est ore confiteri deum et eius verbum fidemque suam, quare Christianus non debet tacere imo verbum dei loqui debet. . . . Parentes sunt schuldig liberos et familiam per proprium os docere. Ibi parentes utuntur officio praedicatoris. Si hoc facit ergo est sacerdos et Episcopus."

189 WA 17/1:508.24ff.: "Supra de vocatione Pauli c. 9. Tempus nondum indicatum fuit, quo incipere deberet, Sed factum est ei ut aliis apostolis in cena, quibus dicebat Christus se predicaturos verbum suum, sed interim iussit expectare, donec acciperent spiritum sanctum. Sic Paulus .1. conversus in via ivit ad illos in Damasco, Iudeos scilicet, postea .2. vocatus, ibi ad gentes missus, hic noster est apostolus." Cf. WA 17/1:509.21ff. Observe how the Spirit is said to speak through a Christian: " 'Segregate' [Acts 13:2]. Hoc dictum est per sanctum virum aliquem. Ut post sequitur de Agabo, qui quanquam Paulo dicit" (WA 17/1:511.1f.). Concerning Acts 13:3, Luther writes: " 'Tunc ieiunabant' etc. Hic fuit mos formandi presbyteros etc. non vocant eum, sed spiritum sanctum, sed confirmant vocationem hanc . . . iterum institui debent sacerdotes, ut coram ecclesia pro eis oraretur eisque commendaretur verbum dei praedicandum" (WA 17/1:511.3ff.).

190 WA 17/1:508.14ff., 509.21ff. Cf. *Luther and World Mission*, 91ff.

if the people gathered, I would do the same because a Christian among them ought to preach Christ's name." Luther is apparently aware that personal testimony has always characterized the meeting of the church/mission with pure heathenism. So the apostle Paul preached for the governor Sergius Paulus in his home on Cypress (Acts 13:7ff.). Jesus' own words in Matthew 10:12 speak of preaching from house to house. Wherever one meets concentrated heathenism, one cannot work only from a public pulpit.[191]

In connection with Paul's meeting with the Jews, and especially with the wizard Bar-Jesus in Paphos (Acts 13:5ff., 8ff.), the reformer says that the Gospel will always be opposed and received by only a few. As is the case with Bar-Jesus, it can be necessary to use harsh words like those that Paul aims at his cunning enemy.[192] But as is evident from Luther's commentaries on Paul's sermon in the synagogue in Pisidian Antioch, the preaching of God's reign in principle builds bridges to its audience (Acts 13:16ff.). It is only when through this bridge-building that the audience had trusted Paul and, thereby, had begun to listen that he began to speak in his mission preaching about the mistakes of the Jews, mistakes in respect to God's salvation and the message of Christ that he was sent to preach. So all preaching must be clothed in a raiment that serves the Gospel. It contains both Law and Gospel, but it must be formed and presented so people listen, understand who they themselves are, and become open to God's salvation.[193]

In this context, Luther also says something about the content and structure of preaching. Paul's preaching in the synagogue in Antioch (Acts 13:16–41) stresses that the promises to the patriarchs had been fulfilled in Jesus Christ. The reformer emphasizes that the Jews then and always refused to accept that God's Messiah would come with something so humble as a teaching about God's grace. It is also evident that preaching is the primary instrument of church/mission in Luther's understanding.[194] The Jews have also not been able to accept the fact that Paul offered God's salvation even to the heathen. Luther says that the Gospel of the church in all times must have both Jews and heathen as its audience.[195]

---

191 WA 17/1:509.24ff.: "homo certus esse debet se vocatum. Si autem essem inter Turcas, certe hospiti meo praedicarem et si conflueret populus, facerem itidem, quia Christianus inter hos eciam debet praedicare nomen Christi. Sic fecerunt apostoli, non illico ascenderunt concionem, non in forum, quia erat mera idolatria. Hic praefectus regionis invitavit eum ad prandium et in domo eius praedicavit [Acts 13:7ff.]. Sic Christus: 'cum intraveritis in domum, dicite ei: pax sit' etc. [Matthew 10:12]."

192 WA 17/1:511.8ff.

193 A 1545 sermon, WA 49:694ff., with much good pastoral advice.

194 WA 49:370.2ff., 374.22ff. See also WA 21:237.26ff.; 22:438.26ff., 439.25ff.

195 WA 49:369.15ff.: "Ista est praedicatio una Pauli, quam fecit Antiochiae in Gretia in Synagoga, ubi congregati Iudaei et Graeci. Ubi enim Iudaei erant inter gentes, habe-

Luther also writes that Paul's sermons were structured as Law and Gospel. It is primarily the Jewish political and religious leaders whom Paul placed under guilt and judgment because they opposed the texts in the Old Testament that clearly spoke of Jesus Christ.[196] But the sermon was above all a word of salvation to Jews and heathen, a message about Christ's cross and resurrection (Acts 13:26, 28, 30, 32ff.). Luther especially notices how the mission message in Antioch was a happy message about Christ's resurrection.[197]

For Luther, preaching is a means of grace, not only of information. Preaching distributes the forgiveness of sins, that is, that which Christ has won through his death and resurrection. Therefore Luther focuses on Acts 13:38–39: "Therefore, my brothers, I want you to know that through Jesus the forgiveness of sins is proclaimed to you. Through him everyone who believes is justified from everything you could not be justified from by the law of Moses." The reformer sees in these words—just as he did in Peter's words in Acts 10:34ff., 43—a kind of summary of the apostolic message to Jews and heathen. Luther says here in no uncertain terms that no one becomes righteous before God through works of the Law. It applies in all times that one Gospel about the forgiveness of sins will be preached for all people on the basis of Christ's death and resurrection. The one who in faith receives this message is promised eternal life. Christ's work, the forgiveness of sins, and faith must always characterize the message of the church. If

---

bant Synagogas, ubi docebant et praedicabant, et ad ipsos multae gentes veniebant. Ita isti Iudaei haben dem Euangelio müssen dienen und Schulen anrichten, ut Apostoli invenirent Iudaeos et Graecos, qui amplexuri essent Euangelium." WA 49:370.12ff.: "Hic 'verbum salutis'. Ist verdrieslich et Iudaeis nicht leidlich nihil mittere quam verbum, quod non solum Iudaeis, sed etiam gentibus. Petrus: omnes, qui credunt. Paulus: filii Abraham et omnes, qui timent Deum. Non ideo aedificaverunt Synagogam, ut gentiles solten inen gleich werden, ut fierent Dei populus ut ipsi. Sed ideo, ut docerent eos, ut essent Domini super eos. Sed Paulus greifft unvernufftig drein und machts, das verbum salutis nicht leiden, quia wil fassen in ein klumpen Iudaeos et gentes." See also the sermon in WA 49:697.9ff., and Cruciger's *Summer Postil*, WA 21:237.10ff. (Lenker 7:204ff.). Cf. WA 22:437.7ff., 438.9ff., 439.12ff.

196 WA 49:372.17–374.4. Cf. also WA 49:695.5–697.5.

197 WA 49:374.4ff.: "Ist inen herrlich gnug gepredigt: 'Euch ist das wort'. Da wird nicht aus. 'Et non occasionem mortis.' 'Hunc excitavit.' 'Und nos' [Acts 13:26, 28, 30, 32]. Alii omnes Apostoli et discipuli et ego et Barnabas apud vos hoc annunciamus, promissionem. Vos estis fratres, quibus Deus. implevit promissionem, quae facta patribus. Promissus eis Messias. . . . Paulus: hic omnes promissiones sunt impletae. Christus mortuus resurrexit." Cf. also a sermon, WA 49:697.6ff., especially 49:699.5ff.: " 'Et nulla causa mortis' [Acts 13:28] Vides Paulum hindringen, scilicet ad resurrectionem. Sed Deus resuscitavit eum. Die predigt ist nicht gantz, ist nur stückweise angezeigt, wird ein schon, lange predigt sein gewest, darauff dringet er. 'Hunc Deus suscitavit' [Acts 13:28]." Cf. WA 49:699.14ff. and 21:237.15ff.

this apostolic foundation is lacking, one is dealing not with a teacher of the church but with a teacher of Satan.[198] Luther emphasizes that no Jew or heathen naturally understands the radical Gospel. It must be preached into human hearts and can be understood and received only through faith.[199]

Church historians have always understood the early church's liberation from the regulations of circumcision and the Law as an important presupposition for the first world mission. In his commentaries, Luther often is occupied with Paul's controversy over circumcision and the Law in connection with his mission among the heathen. Of course, in Luther's understanding the Law has a God-given positive function, that is, to reveal and to awaken humanity to its sinful state (*officium spiritualis legis*). But it is not the way of salvation. In this respect, Luther's often recurring references to the apostolic council in Jerusalem are important (Acts 15:1ff.). To ensure the purity of the doctrine of justification from all legalism, the reformer has thoroughly investigated the false way of the Law and the true way of the Gospel and faith. The demand of the Law-enthusiasts for circumcision and obeying the regulations of the Law of Moses in Paul's time recurs in its own form in every age. True apostolic Christianity constantly struggles against those who seek to mix the Law and works into the doctrine of salvation. Church/mission must, therefore, in its preaching and teaching hold itself to Christ's work as the only ground of faith. Those works that precede faith or follow after it must never be given a place in God's accounting.[200] The radical Gospel of salvation through

---

198 WA 49:375.7ff., 375.19ff., 700.14ff. Cf. Cruciger's *Summer Postil*, Lenker 7:203–4 (WA 21:237.32ff.): "Third, as was true of Peter, Paul does not fail to mention what is of surpassing importance, the use of the historical parts of Scripture and the blessing and benefit accruing to us from that which Scripture proclaims and witnesses; also the method of appropriating its power and blessing. And he concludes with a beautiful utterance of apostolic power, showing how we are to obtain remission of sins and be saved. He says: 'Through this man is proclaimed unto you remission of sins: and by him every one that believeth is justified from all things, from which ye could not be justified by the law of Moses.' This certainly is a powerful passage and so plain it needs no comment, no further explanation. . . . We should note well and remember such clear passages, that we may gain strength and assurance as to the ground of Christian doctrine. Seeing how perfectly, as faithful, truthful and harmonious witnesses, these two apostles agree in their preaching, we are justified in confidently drawing the conclusion that any doctrine at variance with theirs, any teaching concerning the remission of sins and our salvation contrary to theirs, is not of the church, but of the devil's accursed teachers, a doctrine of Satan's own. Gal 1 [:8]." Cf. also WA 22:438.26ff., 439.1ff.

199 WA 22:439.12ff., 439.25ff. Cf. *Luther and World Mission*, 59ff., 170ff., 177ff.

200 "Zwei Sermone auf das. 15. Und 16. Kapitel in der Apostelgeschichte (1524)," WA 15:578ff., 585.28ff. See also WADB 6:141ff. Observe how Luther is led by Peter's words about the heathen having received the Spirit (Acts 10:1ff.) without circumcision and the Law; see WA 15:586.22ff.

faith alone in God's Son must be defended at all costs. As we will see, these ideas are articulated especially in the 1531/1535 *Larger Commentary on Galatians*.[201] Wherever the Law and works take charge in church and mission, Christ and faith are simply lost. Wherever that is the case, church and mission do not exist, according to Luther.

Luther's commentaries on Acts have much to say about mission methodology. Through the Gospel and faith, Christians are liberated from the Law. It is, however, important for Luther to discuss how one ought to use his or her freedom in relation to the weak in faith. The reformer comments on the words of James in Acts 15:19f. that those heathen Christians who have been liberated from the Law and circumcision should nevertheless "abstain from food polluted by idols, from sexual immorality, from the meat of strangled animals and from blood." Sexual immorality was a sin against natural law, but the other regulations were added so as not to offend the Jews and the Jewish Christians. The decision of the apostolic council was that the heathen were basically liberated from the regulations of Moses' Law. Nevertheless, the council decided to command abstinence from "food sacrificed to idols, from blood, from the meat of strangled animals and from sexual immorality" (Acts 15:29). According to Luther, the Christian conscience is actually by faith free from the Law and all its regulations. Still he distinguishes between what natural law forbids (sexual immorality) and those regulations that were accepted voluntarily (that is, the other three regulations). Luther especially emphasizes that one ought not to trouble and weigh down the conscience of the heathen Christians with these latter regulations. However, it may become necessary in a mission context including Jews, Jewish Christians, and heathen Christians for the heathen Christians voluntarily to accept some non-conscience-binding regulations. Faith does not allow itself to be bound by such, but sometimes love must voluntarily accept certain restrictions. The so-called "necessary regulations" are not at all necessary for faith and peace of mind, but they can become important for the sake of love. What is important is not to be a stumbling block for others concerning the Gospel through the exercise of one's own freedom. The Gospel eventually can liberate even such weak Christians from the regulations of Moses.[202] Luther here touches on a special side of contextualization in the work

---

201 See especially on Galatians 2:1, WA 40/1:150–90.

202 WA 15:593ff., especially 15:594.25ff.: "Darumb das Jacob sagt, man sol die drey stucke halten, mus man darauff deuten, das man nicht unruge noch gewissen mache, wie er zuvor sagt, doch die werck halte zu willen der Juden. Denn es hat kein ding die Juden so fast beschweret und geergert als diese. Weil er nu die beschneidung und gesetz hinweg nimpt, ist das ya auch weg genomen, das man wol mag blut und Götzen opffer essen, wie Paulus sagt, und bleibt doch das recht. . . . Denn die Apostel [Acts 15:28f.] lassen das gewissen frey, on das sie eusserliche auffsetze machen und den Juden etwas

of church and mission, that is, regarding with respect those who are weak in faith or those who have not yet fully understood the doctrine of justification through faith without works of the Law.

Luther focuses on the same problem when in 1524 he comments on Acts 16:1–12. He points out that Paul in one context does not circumcise Titus (Galatians 2:3) because in Galatia he was dealing with Jews who had made salvation conditional on the Law and circumcision. According to Acts 16:3, Paul does, however, circumcise Timothy in another context in Lystra. Here the people did not stand so fast by the demands of the Law, but they were uncertain and had a weak faith. In such a situation, Paul could, without making circumcision and the Law conditions for salvation, circumcise Timothy. He compromised so the people there might not be blocked to the Gospel, people who were in the process of more deeply understanding the faith. Thus the apostle wanted to become a Jew for the Jews and weak for the weak (1 Corinthians 9:20).[203] Indeed, the reformer says the following:

> This is just as if I should come among the Jews and preach the Gospel and saw that they were weak. In such a case, I would let myself be circumcised, eat and maintain the food laws, just as they . . . so that I could be with them and do the work of the Gospel. For if I should not adapt myself to their customs, I would be closing the door for me and for my Gospel. Therefore I must adopt their way of being and say something like this: It is true that circumcision has been instituted by God, good and right. But we have a teaching from Christ that nothing else is necessary for salvation except faith in the Savior. And circumcision contributes nothing and in no way helps the conscience before God. . . . (If they nevertheless continued to insist on circumcision), then I must say: Farewell! For this would be to trample too closely on the Gospel and faith and no longer be simple toleration.[204]

Luther's writing here shows that all who are involved in mission work have both the right and the obligation to work carefully and to adapt culturally—as long as one does not come too near to compromising the Gospel and faith. Occasional compromises in a Jewish context have the goal of not offending the weak in faith for the sake of the Gospel. But it must always be clearly understood that circumcision and Jewish practice should not be allowed to make the Gospel condi-

---

nachlassen, das yhn die zeit die Heiden zu liebe und zu dienst hielten." Cf. WA 15:595.26ff., especially 596.24ff.: "da haben die drey beschlossen mit wunderzeichen durch den heiligen geist bestetigt, das das gewissen frey sol sein von allen gesetzen, sol allein Gottes gnade drin sein und regiren, Nichts destoweniger mogen die gesetz zur liebe gehalten werden, das gleich wol das gewissen frey bleibet."

203 WA 15:610ff.

204 WA 15:611.30ff.

tional on works. Compromises that kill the Gospel and faith ought in no way to be allowed. All such compromise should be practiced as a service to the weak and to the Gospel, but it should cease the moment one risks mixing works of the Law into the doctrine of salvation. Luther often says that contact with the regulations of the pope's canon law causes the same problem for evangelical Christians. As soon as something is said to belong to what is necessary for salvation, then that something ought not survive.[205] We will later consider Luther's comprehensive comments on Galatians 2:11ff. in which Paul accuses Peter of hypocrisy at the tables of Antioch. Through his compromises with the Judaizers, Peter bound the consciences of the heathen Christians and risked the truth of the Gospel.[206]

Here we ought to touch on a pair of special problems in Luther's writings about Paul's mission. In chapter 2 (pp. 37–81), I have shown that Luther reckons with a kind of notion or knowledge of God from the testimony of creation (Romans 1:19ff.). The works of the Law also are inextricably written onto the heart of natural humanity (Romans 2:14ff.). Nevertheless, this natural knowledge of God does not lead humanity to true wisdom and worship of God but to an idolatry characterized by the Law and self-righteousness. Luther consistently says that the Word/Gospel is necessary if one will speak of a true knowledge of God and a true faith.[207] This important doctrine is manifest when Luther considers Paul's speech on the Areopagus in Athens (Acts 17:16ff.). Luther emphasizes that God's wisdom and human reason always oppose each other. This antagonism between *sapientia Dei* and *ratio humana* brings to Christians conflicts and the cross. When Christians preach the Gospel, that is, when they reveal God's wisdom, natural humanity automatically opposes such preaching. God's wisdom becomes foolishness for the world.[208] Of course, people possess a God-given natural light for the sake of the civil order,[209] but Paul's meeting with the philosophers in Athens shows that the wise of the world are ignorant fools in regard to God's wisdom.[210] Through the Word, humanity must be enlightened about its sin and dark-

---

205 WA 15:613.32ff. Cf. WA 15:594ff. and the *Larger Commentary on Galatians*, WA 40/1:125f., 146.18ff.

206 WA 40/1:191ff. See *Luther and World Mission*, 227ff.

207 See *Luther and World Mission*, 39ff., 64ff.

208 A 1524 sermon, WA 15:630ff.

209 WA 15:631.33ff., 632.5f.

210 WA 15:631.21ff.: "Summa summarum: Deus satis ostendit hac civitate, quid ratio humana sit. Si non intelligere possumus, videamus hunc textum. Si posset ratio quid efficere, certe Athenis effecisset. Vide in maxima specie richt sichs erger auss quam hurn und buben. Stoici volebant esse sapientissimi et indicarunt se stultissimos esse. Et ideo sivit dominus crescere multos sapientes, ut ostenderet mundo, quam stulti essent sapientes. . . . Ego loquor de rebus spiritualibus: quando videlicet ratio regere hominem vult coram deo, tanto plus peius agit." Cf. WA 15:532.15ff.

ness and be taught to believe in Christ who was crucified for it. God's true wisdom is something that God gives; it is wholly a gift from God.[211] This absoluteness of revelation and the Gospel means that there is always a tension between Christ's church and natural humanity. This tension/conflict can never be resolved nor smoothed over. When God's Word is preached, it will be opposed, and the preachers will carry their own cross. This conflict is at times public, as in Paul's case in the synagogue and town square in Athens.[212]

In Acts 17:18, Paul is called a babbler and an advocate of foreign gods when he preaches about Jesus and the resurrection. Natural humanity's wisdom is poorly equipped to receive God's revelation in Christ and the Gospel. In principle, one ought to preach consistently the Gospel despite opposition. But according to Luther, such opposition and such a hardening for the Gospel can exist among people that preaching becomes only a casting of pearls to swine (Matthew 7:6). Where doors are completely closed, there preachers should leave and preaching should be silent. Wherever one scoffs at the Gospel, there the Word and the Spirit produce no fruit. Some of the seed always falls among thorns and thistles (Matthew 13:7). But it is profitless to sow seed in a field of only thistles, says Luther.[213]

In a 1529 sermon, Luther does not comment on Paul's words about the Athenians' altar and worship in Acts 17:22, but one does otherwise find references to this text.[214]

In the foregoing we often have seen that Luther reckons the Father, the Son, and the Spirit as the operating subject in all mission, evangelization, and reformation. At the same time, we have seen in connection with the Great Commission

---

211 WA 15:632.4ff.: "Sicut et hodie est: qui sunt sapientissimi in rebus terrenis, stultissimi sunt in spiritualibus. Ideo longe separanda regna, quo regnamus et regimur. Nos sapientiam non inveniemus, oportet alium habeamus doctorem, qui dicit nos plenos esse idolatria, sed sinite lucem vestram ingrede tenebras. Si vis sapiens fieri, crede Christum pro te crucifixum et illo tibi [an unreadable word] qui salvet, gubernet. Tandem fit, ut homo nihil patiatur, loquatur, faciat, nisi quod deus in illo. Regnum dei vult solum omnia habere."

212 WA 15:630.13ff., 631.2ff., 631.7f.

213 WA 15:632.23ff. Cf. about hardening, WA 15:632.30ff.: "Sic recipit mundus Euangelium, habet pro salibus. Christus dicit Non proiiciendas margaritas [Matthew 7:6]. Hoc Paulus hic fecit, ubi praedicavit et non acceperunt. Abiit et non diu praedicavit [Acts 15:33]. . . . Sic nobis omnibus inserviendum omnibus et docere omnes. Si vero rident, signum habeo spiritum sanctum non facere hic fructum, et, ubi palam impetitur, item non proiiciendum. In Euangelio 'cadit in spinas' etc. [Matthew 13:7] si solum in spinas, non praedicandum. . . . Ubi quidam sunt, qui libenter audiunt, non cessandum."

214 See *Luther and World Mission*, 46n57, 66n106.

and other texts that Luther in no way denies that the Gospel will be spread through people. God communicates the Gospel through the work of people.

However, this interplay between God and people becomes problematic at times. So Luther wonders a little over the fact that according to Acts 16:16ff. Paul, in all his mission zeal, is hindered by the Spirit to missionize where he personally wanted to do it. When such occurs even in the work of the archmissionary Paul, it is thereby evident that the Father, the Son, and the Spirit always maintain control over the work of mission. As it concerns the church and the Gospel, the reformer believes that God maintains the authority in the church-building work of the Word and Sacraments. About the text in question, Luther points out that with such direct intervention God also can desire to break down pride and the imagined ability of the workers of God's reign. He can close doors in mission work because mission workers should always be reminded of the Lord's place and role in the work. A missionary and evangelist must in everything put God's work and will first. He must give God and the Spirit room to choose the times and ways to go forward with the Gospel in the world. Luther notes that it is not always God's timing when people want to work and go out with the Gospel.[215]

Stephen and Luther's view of mission

Luther's commentaries on Acts 6–7 also provide some insight into his understanding of the work of God's reign. The narrative about the choosing of seven deacons to care for the distribution of necessities to the poor in Jerusalem (Acts 6:1ff.) leads Luther to a double diatribe. First, Luther mourns that the church at large has given the preaching of the Word to uneducated priests (*Pfaffen*). The bishops of the church do not possess the early church's zeal for the preaching of

---

215 WA 15:617.33ff. See especially WA 15:618.27ff.: "Also ists nu darumb geschrieben, das er will abreissen alle vermessenheit, das wir ynn forcht und demut wandeln, das sich niemand rhumen solle: das kan ich odder das habe ich aus guter meinung gethan, Sondern also sage, wie Paulus: Das wil ich thun, wo es gottes wille ist, doch weil es noch nicht zeit ist, wie wol er es gepoten hat, odder vieleicht ein ander ursach yhm furbehalten, mus ich mich nach yhm richten und gehorsam sein, seinem wort folgen, nicht meinem willen, wenn ich auch die gantze welt könd bekeren." WA 15:619.24ff.: "das Paulus verhindert ist, mus man Gott heimstellen, sein will ist gut, aber es ist noch nicht zeit gewesen. Denn er hernach ist hin kommen Act. 18[:18] und hat yhn gepredigt, darnach geschrieben, Als die Epistel zun Galatern." On Luther's struggle with Paul's night vision in Acts 16:9f. (the Macedonian man) and the mission campaign in Macedonia, see WA 15:619.34ff. Luther reviews different texts for and against believing in dreams. He rails against all the myths that have been built up around dreams. Nothing ought to be preached on the basis of dreams. One must keep them between oneself and God. All that does not square with Christian faith (the Creed) must fall to the wayside. Therefore the Word is more important than dreams.

the Word and for prayer. If the apostles consciously had transferred the physical relief work to chosen and trusted laymen to make more time for the Word and for prayer, the later Roman Catholic hierarchy had become completely ensnared in problems of money, possessions, and real estate. Second, Luther mourns the fact that the diaconate had degenerated in the church and had become primarily a liturgical office. Only in hospitals and similar kinds of work could one find traces of the early church's diaconate, which provided physical help to the congregation's poor. Neither the needs of the body nor the soul were served in the church that Luther wanted to reform.[216]

In this connection, Luther comments on the manner in which possessions were owned in common in the early church. The enthusiasts of Luther's time had considered the communal ownership of possessions found in Acts 4:32–5:11 and 6:1ff. as a necessary, divine order of the church. Luther decidedly rejected this notion. Various passages in the New Testament witness the right of Christians to own private property (Luke 3:11; Matthew 5:42; Acts 5:4; 2 Corinthians 8:13). As we have seen, it is a foundational principle for Luther that the Gospel does not necessarily change the existing orders of creation. One has, therefore, the right as a Christian to own private property. But the Word commands us to use our possessions to help our neighbor.[217]

One also observes in the reformer's commentaries that he understands it to be an ideal in the work of God's reign that a pastor and a deacon work side by side in congregations of reasonable and manageable size. Then the people would receive help for the soul through the ministry of preaching and emergency help for the body through the serving hands of the deacon. For Luther, diaconal ministry in the church is important. Only the preaching ministry is more important. If there were enough money, Luther wished to introduce an order of honest, Christian, congregational servants for the management and distribution of the *bona ecclesiae*. With the introduction of such an order, the ministry of preaching could devote itself completely to the preaching of the Word, and the sick and others in need could receive physical help.[218]

In the stories about Stephen in Acts 6–7, one sees, however, that Luther primarily is occupied with the sermon that Stephen preaches in the Spirit against the Jewish focus on the temple and the Law (Acts 6:7ff.; 7:44ff., 48ff.). If the reformer

---

216 WA 9:525.8ff.; 12:692.3ff.; 52:588–92.

217 See especially the dispute with the demand by the enthusiasts for the "communist" ideal of possessions in *House Postil*, WA 52:588.14–590.3.

218 See already in a 1523 sermon, WA 12:693.27ff., and more exhaustively in the 1544 *House Postil*, WA 52:590.4ff., 590.25ff. See especially WA 52:591.4ff.: "Das nun die lieben Apostel so vil vleiss auff diss ambt wenden, so mit ernst betten und die hende den geweleten aufflegen, Solches alles ist ein anzeigen, das dise verwaltung der

in connection with Jesus' words to the Samaritan woman (John 4:21–23) actually rejected all binding of salvation to Jerusalem and the temple,[219] he develops the same theme further in this context. God does not live in houses made by human hands (Acts 7:48ff.). No human finds fellowship with God through the works of the Law (Acts 7:53). However important the tabernacle and the temple were for the Old Testament, after Jesus' sojourn on earth and the Spirit's sending, history had reached the time when God (without making church buildings unnecessary) lived in all the hearts that believe in Jesus Christ. After all, the Creator says: "Heaven is my throne, and the earth is my footstool. Where is the house you will build for me? Where will my resting place be? Has not my hand made all these things, and so they came into being?" (Isaiah 66:1–2; Acts 7:49–50). This radical universalism characterizes God's salvation as well. It is bound neither to Jerusalem nor to the regulations of the Law but only to Jesus Christ and faith in him.[220] God lives in every believer's heart, which, in Luther's words, becomes something of a tabernacle of revelation, an instrument for the expansion of God's salvation. God makes people God's own possession and dwelling and makes them into servants for God's Gospel. At the same time, one sees how Luther puts the accent on the Word and the Sacraments as the bearers of God's presence and salvation.[221]

---

gemeinen Kirchen güter oder des almosens nicht ein schlechte verwaltung sey, Denn was dörffts sonst so eins vleiss und ernsts mit solchen leuten? Wol ist es war, das Predigt ambt ist weit höher unnd mer, Denn dadurch hilfft Gott nit dem leib mit essen und drincken zu disem zeitlichen leben, sonder er hilfft der seel wider sünd unnd ewigen todt, Aber nach dem Predig ambt ist in der Kirchen kein höher ambt denn dise verwaltung, das man mit dem Kirchen gut recht und auffrichtig umbgee, auff. das den armen Christen, die jr narung selb nit schaffen und gewinnen mögen, geholffen werd, das sie nit not leiden." WA 52:591.32ff.: "Derhalb wer es wol von nötten, das in grossen Fürstenthumben und Stetten, ja auch inn einem yeden dorff vil Stephani weren, die solchs diensts mit ernst sich annämen unnd mit den Kirchen gütern recht umbgiengen, die nicht auff jhren nutz und geytz, sonder auff die sähen, denen solche güter von rechts wegen gehörn, als da sind Erstlich, die der Kirchen im wort dienen müssen unnd solches diensts halb jrs eignen thuns nit warten können, Und darnach die armen Christen, welche kranckeit oder ander not halb jr narung nit schaffen mögen. Und zum dritten feine, geschickte, junge knaben, die zum studirn tuglich sind und doch sonst kein hilff haben."

219 See *Luther and World Mission*, 128ff.

220 WA 9:525.31ff.; 10/1.1:247ff., 258.8ff.; 12:693.7ff., 694.10ff., 694.41ff., 696.15ff.; 15:790.26ff., 792.20ff., 793.24ff.; 52:592ff.

221 Concerning believers as the witnesses or "tabernacles of revelation," see WA 12:694.22ff., 697.29ff. See especially WA 12:694.41ff.: "Auffs erst, das man unserm herr gott nicht dienet mit kirchen bawen, dann gott sagt also im Exodo 'Ich wil wonen in euch und in euch wandeln, Ir solt meyn wonung sein, darinn ich wircken und schaffen wil' [Exodus 25:8; 29:45]. Dem tabernackel aber oder der hütten gab er also ein namen,

The Luther source material shows conclusively that Stephen's public testimony or sermon, which was accompanied by miracles and strong opposition, is especially important for the reformer.[222] I have already shown in chapter 2 (pp. 81–95), that the preaching of Stephen, Philip, and Apollos (Acts 6–7; 8:5; 18:24ff.) is considered by Luther as proof for the fact that every Christian in an isolated, non-Christian environment and on the basis of an inner call alone has the right and duty to witness and preach about Christ.[223] Especially in the *Church Postil* (1522), the reformer considers the fact that Stephen, a layperson and deacon, takes it upon himself to preach in the public square. Luther rejects any notion in the Christian tradition that Stephen was the first teacher of the church. Acts 6:1ff. shows that he was not ordained as a pastor but was a layman consecrated as a deacon. He was to serve at the table so the apostles would have enough time for preaching and prayer.[224]

Luther asks himself how Stephen could preach, do miracles, and publicly criticize the Jewish leaders on the square and in the city. In the church of the pope, which with the words *priest* and *church* think only of the priesthood and completely reject the preaching of laypeople, Stephen would have been burned as a heretic, says Luther.[225] The text about Stephen in Acts 6–7 definitely gives to the apostles and to the church's later ministry of preaching the responsibility for public preaching. But Luther emphasizes in 1522, even more powerfully than in his later commentaries, that Acts 6–7 and 1 Corinthians 14:29ff. clearly show that no one may suppress the testimony of laypeople in the public square and at home. Alongside the public ministry's indisputable right to administer the Word and the Sacraments publicly in the church, there is, according to this early sermon from 1522, a great freedom to preach in contact with people.[226] The Luther texts in

---

das es solt heyssen die hütte des zeügniss . . . . Wie wir Christen die tauff haben, nicht das Gott in der tauff wonet, sonder das es ein losung und ein zeichen ist, das da gottes volck ist." Cf. also the *Church Postil* (1522): "God has given no special command in regard to the building of churches, but he has issued his commands in reference to souls—his real and peculiar churches. Paul says concerning them (1 Cor 3, 16–17): 'Ye are a temple [church] of God . . . If any man destroyeth the temple of God, him shall God destroy'" (Lenker 6:198 [WA 10/1.1:253.6ff.; see also WA 10/1.1:252.16ff.]). Cf. the critique against Rome, WA 10/1.1:253ff.

222 *Church Postil* (1522), WA 10/1.1:261ff.; *House Postil* (1544), WA 52:592.10ff., 592.15ff.

223 See *Luther and World Mission*, 94–95.

224 WA 10/1.1:261.10ff., 262.1ff., 263.11ff.

225 WA 10/1.1:263.11ff.

226 Lenker 6:207 (WA 10/1.1:264.3ff.): "The precedent of Stephen holds good. His example gives all men authority to preach wherever they can find hearers, whether it be in a building or at the marketplace. He does not confine the preaching of God's Word to

question are nevertheless somewhat ambiguous because Luther sometimes speaks of preaching even in completely closed contexts. He does not differentiate as in modern usage between preaching (= public in the church) and testimony (= within the private or less public context).

Finally, the reformer claims that Stephen's dispute with the Jews' zeal for the temple (Acts 7:48) and the righteousness of the Law (Acts 7:53) and his preaching of the Gospel of Christ, that is, the way of faith and the forgiveness of sins that results in fellowship with God, necessarily led to a confrontation with the Jews. In the same way, Luther had been confronted by the Roman theologians precisely in his preaching/teaching about justification through faith. The reformer means that all true mission, evangelization, and reformation unavoidably bear with them opposition and the cross. Indeed, sometimes the workers in God's reign must suffer death for the sake of the message about Christ. The radical Gospel about justification through faith in God's Son is always a stumbling block for the natural human who is occupied with works of the Law.[227] But during all times of confrontation, Christ will strengthen his witnesses and give them a spirit of love for their persecutors.[228] The Spirit of the Father will speak through the persecuted.

---

bald pates and long gowns. At the same time he does not interfere with the preaching of the apostles. He attends to the duties of his own office and is readily silent where it is the place of the apostles to preach. True, order must be observed. All cannot speak at once. Paul writes in the fourteenth chapter of First Corinthians that one or two are to be permitted to speak, and that if a revelation be made to a listener the speaker is to keep silence. . . . Acts 15[:4]."

227 WA 9:525.31ff., 526.11ff., 526.24ff. See also *Church Postil,* especially on Acts 7:54–59: "The dispute arose from Stephen's assertion that whatsoever proceeds not from faith does not profit, and that men cannot serve God by the erection of churches, or by works independent of faith in Jesus Christ. Faith alone renders us godly; faith alone builds the temple of God—the believing hearts. The Jews opposed the doctrine of faith, adducing the Law of Moses and the temple at Jerusalem" (Lenker 6:195 [WA 10/1.1:248.16ff.; see also WA 10/1.1:247.7ff.]). Cf. WA 10/1.1:249.18ff., 252.10ff., and especially on Acts 7:53, WA 10/1.1:258.8ff. See also WA 12:692.15ff., 694.35ff., 696.15ff., 696.30ff.; 15:790.26ff., 791.34ff., 792.34ff., 794.29ff.; 52:592.15ff., 593.19ff.

228 WA 9:525.35ff.; 10/1.1:265.4ff., 266.10ff., 267.5ff.; 15:794.32ff., 796.18f. In the *House Postil* (1544), Luther speaks about how Stephen encountered opposition because he spoke about salvation through the forgiveness of sins and against the way of the Law and concentration on the temple. Luther encounters similar opposition in the conflict with the church of the pope. Cf. WA 52:593.19ff., 593.32ff. The reformer points out that Stephen sees Jesus and is strengthened by God's Spirit just before he dies and that the Son and the Spirit stand beside all who suffer for the sake of Jesus' name. See WA 52:594.1ff. with the application to the struggle of the evangelical church, especially WA 52:594.11ff.: "Disen anblick hat Stephanus mit leyblichen augen gesehen, Wir sehen es leyblich nicht, Aber im wort sehen wirs, Got lob, auch. Darumb halten wir an solcher

In Acts 8:1ff., one reads about the persecutions in Jerusalem after the stoning of Stephen. It narrates how the Christians were scattered throughout Judea and Samaria, thereby spreading the message of the Gospel. The deacon Philip (Acts 8:5) preached the Gospel in the capital of Samaria and taught and baptized the Ethiopian eunuch on the way to Gaza (Acts 8:36ff.). It is surprising that Luther supplies no thorough commentary on these events and texts that are otherwise so important for missiology.

With Stephen, Philip, and Apollos as examples, Luther nevertheless has reckoned with a comprehensive work of evangelization on the mission front, which in a situation where there is a lack of ordained preachers can and must be accomplished by those who are laymen. The lack of priests ought not hinder the expansion of the Gospel, even if Luther normally reckons with an ordained congregational ministry.[229] However, whether Stephen and Philip were only deacons is a question discussed today. It seems that they function in some respects as pastors.

SUMMARY

1. Luther sees the Book of Acts as an enfleshed description of the central Christian teaching about justification through faith apart from works of

---

lehr und lassen die Papisten toben, schreyen, liegen, fangen, würgen, wie sie wöllen, das soll uns wenig kümmern. Wie denn Christus verheisset, Sein geyst sol bey uns sein, uns trösten unnd stercken, das wir in jm alle freud unnd trost haben sollen unnd darneben auch unsere sach dermassen an tag bringen, das man muss spüren, das nit wir, sonder der Geyst Gottes redet, Marci am 13. [13:11]."

229 Luther knows much about the early church's mission on the basis of Bible study and other available historical materials. Cf. WA 10/1.1:544ff., 550ff.; 23:581; 25:363.12ff.; 31/2:502.27ff., 502.32ff. Luther briefly touches on the work of Philip and others in Samaria in WA 25:397.31; 31/2:576.25f.; 39/1:240.3ff.; 39/2:303.11ff.; 49:459.17f. One can read more about the temporary measures on the mission front in "Concerning the Ministry (1523)": "Another example is provided by Stephen and Philip, who were ordained only to the service at the tables [Acts 6:5, 6]. Yet the one wrought signs and wonders among the people, disputed with members of the synagogue and refuted the council of the Jews with the word of the Spirit [Acts 6:8ff.], and the other converted Samaritans and traveled to Azotus and Caesarea [Acts 8:5ff., 40]. By what right and authority, I ask? Certainly they were not asked or called by anyone, but they did it on their own initiative and by reason of a common law, since the door was open to them. . . . And the eunuch converted by Philip [Acts 8:36], whom we may reasonably believe remained a Christian, undoubtedly taught the Word of God to many, since he had the command to make known the wonderful deeds of God who called him from darkness into his marvelous light [1 Pet. 2:9]" (LW 40:38 [WA 12:192.8ff.]). Concerning how Stephen, Philip, and Apollos, without being publicly called, nevertheless rightly acted as evangelists and converted and baptized people, see WA 11:412.15ff. (which is partially quoted in *Luther and World Mission*, 94).

the Law. Outside of this central motif, he emphasizes several other important themes.

2. In connection with Acts 1–2 and Acts 10, Luther emphasizes how Christ's ascension and the outpouring of the Spirit are finally decisive for the great drama of world mission. The apostles, their successors, and many lay witnesses are engaged in preaching about and witnessing to Christ's death and resurrection among Jews and Gentiles. Preaching is double-edged (Law and Gospel) but seeks in everything to anchor people in faith in Jesus Christ. Oral preaching and Baptism are the central instruments of mission.

3. In connection with Paul's conversion, the reformer articulates the difference between the way of the Law/works and the true way of faith in Jesus Christ that results in fellowship with God. We also notice that Luther unites Paul's direct meeting with Christ on the way to Damascus and his reception of the Word and Baptism and his sending within the Christian congregation. Mission is connected with the means of grace and the congregation (*missio corporalis*).

4. On the basis of Acts 13–28 and Paul's work, Luther emphasizes that lay witnesses and publicly called pastors of congregations should work side by side in the work of Christ. The message should go out to both Jews and Gentiles. As Paul preaches so should mission preaching focus on Christ's death and resurrection, repentance, conversion, and the forgiveness of sins. On the basis of Acts 15, Luther rejects the way of the Law and works as a means to salvation. Mission preaches a radical Gospel.

5. At the same time, it can become necessary in a mission context with Jews and Jewish Christians for those Christians (who are in reality free from the Law and from rules) to accept certain rules voluntarily (such rules, however, must not be allowed to bind the conscience). These compromises should not, however, be applied to the point at which there is a risk of losing or misunderstanding the radical Gospel.

6. On the basis of Acts 16:6ff., Luther emphasizes that the Father, the Son, and the Spirit maintain the leadership over the mission efforts of human agents. It is not always God's time, even when people are willing to work.

7. According to Luther, Acts 6–7 shows that the diaconate ought to have a given place in the work of church and mission. In such a way those in crisis receive help and the church's pastors and teachers have enough time for prayer and the preaching of the Word.

8. On the basis of the work of Stephen and Philip, Luther indicates that the distinction between lay and ordained ministry can be somewhat fluid when the work on the front lines with unbelievers and heathens lacks ordained pastors.

9. The reformer often emphasizes that the radical Gospel always encounters conflict with the proponents of Law-religion and with the worldly wise. This is because natural human beings cannot understand that God saves on the basis of faith in Christ who died and rose again and without works of the Law.

The Letters of the Apostles and Luther's Mission Thinking

The next section of this book will survey and analyze the reformer's mission thinking on the basis of his interpretation of the New Testament letters, especially Paul's letters. Luther's work with biblical theology is always riddled with references to the letters of the New Testament. Also Luther's lectures and preaching on the letters of the apostles (except during the years 1526–1530) are quite comprehensive. Because the source material is so comprehensive, I am forced to limit myself to that which can reasonably be considered relevant to our theme of the expanding work of God's reign and the foreign mission of the church.

When the reformer interprets and exposits the letters of the New Testament, the mission epoch during the lifetimes of the apostles, the time of the Reformation in Germany and Europe, and the church's work for God's reign in both inner and outer mission generally speaking are all in the same picture. Thus the same message ought to be preached to everyone on our planet. The Word/Gospel is the same to the non-Christians in all parts of the world as it is to European Christendom and to the new heathenism there.

It is well known that especially the apostle Paul meant a great deal to Luther's spiritual and theological development. Because of what we already have seen, that is, that Luther constantly refers to Paul's letters, we know that Paul is important to Luther's ecclesiology and missiology. However, we have noticed in connection with Acts that Luther is not especially interested in the mission praxis and missionary journeys of Paul and the other apostles. In his 1522 and 1546 forewords to his German translation of the New Testament, Luther makes clear that he valued the letters of the apostles, especially Paul's letters, primarily for their doctrine. They instructed the new Christian congregations about creation and the ruling authorities, about sin and grace, about Law and Gospel, and especially about justification through faith in God's Son without works of the Law. Paul had taught how one ought to deal with legalistic and spiritualistic heresies. He had taught about the means of grace and had with parenesis challenged the Christians to a Christian lifestyle. Other New Testament letters—among them the letters of Peter and John's first letter—emphasized justification through faith in Christ at the same time that they drew the consequences of this doctrine for lifestyle. The apostles' teaching on such subjects has been pointing the way for the church and mission in all times.[230] Because Luther considers the letters of the New Testament to be doctrinal, it follows that Luther's commentaries on the letters have much to say about the theology of the work of God's reign.

It is, however, surprising that in his commentaries on the letters Luther does not comment much about the practical mission work of Paul and the other apostles. The comments on the practical aspects of mission work and mission strategy are brief and enclosed in investigations of a doctrinal nature. Indeed, Luther often says nothing about mission method and praxis when he considers texts in which one might otherwise expect some consideration. There are two main reasons for this. First, Luther is not much involved himself in the concrete problems of foreign mission. Second, as a biblical theologian, he is occupied first with biblical exegesis and doctrine. The reformer's main interest is made visible, for example, in the compendium of what is meant by Law, Gospel, sin, grace, the righteousness of faith, flesh, spirit, etc., in the 1522/1546 foreword to Romans and in the comprehensive investigations of the main problems of theology in, for example, the 1531/1535 *Larger Commentary on Galatians*.[231]

In the following, I will first analyze some of Luther's statements that illuminate some important theological issues in the work of God's reign generally and of mission work especially. I will focus here, among other things, on the questions about the Gospel of Christ and the righteousness of faith; Law and Gospel; the message to Jews and Gentiles; apostolic parenesis; mission and the stance toward

---

230 For Romans, see WADB 7:2–27, especially 26.6ff., 27.15ff.; for 1 and 2 Corinthians, see WADB 7:82ff., 138f.; for Galatians, see WADB 7:173ff.; for Ephesians, see WADB 7:190ff.; for Philippians, see WADB 7:210f.; for Colossians, see WADB 7:224ff.; for 1 and 2 Timothy, see WADB 7:298f., 314f.; and for 1–3 John, see WADB 7:326ff. In the 1522 general foreword to the New Testament, Luther mentions those parts of the New Testament that he considers most noble, those that bear Christ. See LW 35:362 (WADB 6:10.29ff.): "In a word St. John's Gospel and his first epistle, St. Paul's epistles, especially Romans, Galatians, and Ephesians, and St. Peter's first epistle are the books that show you Christ and teach you all that is necessary and salvatory for you to know, even if you were never to see or hear any other book or doctrine. Therefore St. James' epistle is really an epistle of straw, compared to these others, for it has nothing of the nature of the gospel about it." In this connection, see Lønning, "Kanon im Kanon," 76ff., 82ff., 96ff. etc., which ought nevertheless to be read with a certain discretion.

231 WADB 7:2–13 and WA 40/1 and 40/2. Inasmuch as Luther's forewords (1522 and 1546) to the apostolic letters are nearly identical, I will in the following usually refer to the text from 1546, which has somewhat better German.

the receivers of the message; the work of God's reign and prayer; and the relationship between mission, the gifts of grace, and ministries.

The Gospel of Christ and the righteousness of faith

In the reformer's thinking about natural religion and in numerous commentaries on the texts of the Old and New Testaments, we already have seen that Luther rejects the righteousness of the Law and works.[232] He presents Christ and faith in him as the only saving righteousness for humanity in relationship with God. We also have seen that in this respect Luther constantly refers to passages in Paul's letters. Therefore we ought to say something about this main pillar of the message of church/mission. It is the center of this salvation that Luther constantly seeks out in his commentaries on the Epistles. With Paul, Luther understands that the church's real treasure consists in the Gospel about the forgiveness of sins and eternal life. This real treasure is succinctly expressed in, among other places, 1 Timothy 1:15: "Here is a trustworthy saying that deserves full acceptance: Christ Jesus came into the world to save sinners." The Gospel is God's proper work and the unique sign of the church. For Luther, the Gospel is a great word of joy to the world.[233]

It is evident from Luther's forewords to the entire New Testamemt and to the separate books that he believes the proper division of Law and Gospel and the preaching of justification through faith in Christ constitute the true message of the main books of the New Testament.[234] In Luther's critical discussion of the Epistle of James, he says that that which is *apostolic* is that which preaches Christ and lays the foundation of faith. Luther says: "Now it is the office of a true apostle to preach of the Passion and resurrection and office of Christ, and to lay the foundation for faith in him, as Christ himself says in John 15[:27], 'You shall bear witness to me.' All the genuine sacred books agree in this, that all of them preach

---

232 See *Luther and World Mission*, 39ff., 64ff., 75ff., 177ff., 184ff.

233 See *Luther and World Mission*, 64–81, with the referred texts in 76n131. Cf. concerning the Gospel as *opus proprium Dei* and as *unica nota ecclesiae*, Öberg, *Himmelrikets nycklar och kyrklig bot i Luthers teologi*, 138f., with the adduced Luther source material and secondary sources.

234 WADB 6:10.9ff.; WA 7:2ff. See the clear analysis in Lønning, "Kanon im Kanon," 82ff., 88ff. About the Christian's freedom from the Law, see Runestam, *Den kristliga friheten hos luther och Melanchton*, 13ff.; and Althaus, *Die Theologie Martin Luthers*, 220ff. Cf. WA 2:447.34ff., 516.35f.; 39/1:219.3ff.; 40/1:114.13ff., 298.13ff. Concerning the Law as a power of depravity, see Bring, *Dualismen hos Luther*, 154ff., 301ff.; Loewenich, *Luther als Ausleger der Synoptiker*, 172ff.; and Haikola, *Studien zu Luther und zum Luthertum*, 49ff.

and inculcate [*treiben*] Christ. . . . Whatever does not teach Christ is not yet apostolic."[235]

The principle distinction between Law (= demand) and Gospel (= gift, promise) and the focus on Christ and faith are, therefore, prominent in Luther's commentaries on the apostolic letters. The distinction between Law and Gospel is the center of the message of church/mission, the message that has the task of leading people to a saving fellowship with God. The Law and circumcision represent a temporary and limited—indeed, actually an impossible—perspective. The promises to Abraham that were given long before the Law on Sinai, the fulfillment of these promises in Jesus Christ, and the new covenant's Gospel about God's Son and faith is the God-given and conclusive way to salvation. This already has been explored in chapter 2 (pp. 64–81). According to Luther, communication of Law and Gospel is the main task of the apostles to the peoples, to the congregations of the early church, and to the church in all times. Among other things, the reformer's commentaries on Romans and Galatians provide evidence for this perspective that Law and Gospel and the message of justification by faith are the cornerstones of the mission message.

Luther's concept of the Law and sin, honed as it was in the struggles with the Roman Catholic Church, implies that the way of the Law to righteousness and salvation is closed. Because the Law demands the commitment both of the heart and of works, humanity is powerless before the Law. All attempts to establish fellowship with God through the Law and works leads to despair and only increase sin. As discussed in chapter 2 (pp. 16–20), sin is primarily unbelief, an aversion to God's will and self-absorption on all levels. Sinful acts are secondary and issue from the unbelieving heart. Sin also places all people under guilt, God's wrath, and judgment.[236]

Against the righteousness of Law and works, Luther powerfully presents the righteousness that is given through the Gospel, grace, and faith in Jesus Christ. God's grace is the same as God's benevolence and favor, through which humanity receives Christ and the Holy Spirit. But faith is a divine work in and with the

---

235 "Foreword to James (1522)," LW 35:396 (WADB 7:384.19–32). Cf. also Christ and Christ's resurrection as the center according to both commentaries on Galatians, WA 2:451–55; 40/1:40ff., 52ff., 64f. See also the fundamental passage in WADB 6:10.29ff. (quoted in *Luther and World Mission*, 197ff., especially 198n230).

236 See the 1546 foreword to Romans, WADB 7:3.20ff.; WA 5:29ff.; 7:27ff. See also the *Larger Commentary on Galatians* (1531/1535), WA 40/1:87f.; 40/2:93f.; and the extensive comments on Galatians 3:22 ("But the Scripture declares that the whole world is a prisoner of sin"), WA 40/1:513ff. Concerning Luther's concept of sin, see Ljunggren, *Synd och skuld i Luthers teologi*, and Öberg, *Himmelrikets nycklar och kyrklig bot i Luthers teologi*, 128f., 213ff.

human subject. It gives the human subject a fast trust in God's grace in Christ and a power for a spontaneous new life in good works and in struggle against the sinful nature.[237]

Luther's commentaries on the Epistles speak with special profundity about the passive righteousness of faith that humanity receives as a gift from God. The active righteousness of the Law and works is another matter altogether.[238] The Law has a positive task, that is, to awaken the hardened, to make sin known, and to force sinful human beings to work for the neighbor. But the Law never gives the Christian saving righteousness before God. Luther energetically makes this point. The reformer speaks in this context about two worlds: the world of active righteousness and the works of the Law and the world of passive righteousness in which one receives God's grace and forgiveness without works of the Law, through faith in God's Son alone. The most difficult art of faith is to distinguish properly between the worldly righteousness of the Law and the heavenly righteousness of faith. In the latter, one does not at all speak of doing something; instead, one speaks only of the perfect righteousness that is given through faith in the Gospel. Pastors and preachers must carefully differentiate and rightly divide Law and

---

237 The foreword to Romans, WADB 7:9.10ff. Cf. LW 35:370–71 (WADB 7:11.6ff., 11.16ff.): "Faith, however, is a divine work in us which changes us and makes us to be born anew of God, John 1[:12–13]. It kills the old Adam and makes us altogether different men, in heart and spirit and mind and powers; and it brings with it the Holy Spirit. O it is a living, busy, active, mighty thing, this faith. It is impossible for it not to be doing good works incessantly. It does not ask whether good works are to be done, but before the question is asked, it has already done them, and is constantly doing them. . . . Faith is a living, daring confidence in God's grace, so sure and certain that the believer would stake his life on it a thousand times. This knowledge of and confidence in God's grace makes men glad and bold and happy in dealing with God and with all creatures." About the freedom from works of the Law and about spontaneous good works, see WADB 7:19.29ff. Cf. the *Larger Commentary on Galatians*, WA 40/1:40ff., 72ff. Concerning the Law-Gospel dialectic and justification through faith, see Harnack, *Luthers Theologie*, 1:401ff., 444ff.; 2:321ff. See also Althaus, *Die Theologie Martin Luthers*, 195ff., 218ff., with references; and Öberg, *Himmelrikets nycklar och kyrklig bot i Luthers teologi*, 138ff.

238 Especially the *Larger Commentary on Galatians*, LW 26:4–5 (WA 40/1:41.15ff.): "But this most excellent righteousness, the righteousness of faith, which God imputes to us through Christ without works, is neither political nor ceremonial nor legal nor works-righteousness but is quite the opposite; it is a merely passive righteousness, while all the others, listed above, are active. For here we work nothing, render nothing to God; we only receive and permit something else to work in us, namely, God. Therefore it is appropriate to call the righteousness of faith or Christian righteousness 'passive.' This is a righteousness hidden in a mystery, which the world does not understand. In fact, Christians themselves do not adequately understand it or grasp it in the midst of their temptations." Cf. WA 40/1:42.26ff. and WADB 7:11.28ff.

Gospel. One ought not confuse the ministry of the letter and of death and the ministry of the Gospel and of the Spirit. If one so confuses, the passive righteousness—that is, the righteousness that is a gift from God—is obliterated.[239] On the basis of Galatians 1:6–9 and other passages, Luther speaks about how false teachers through their gospel that is conditionally tinged with works of the Law easily confuse the newly founded congregations and draw curses on themselves. There is only one Gospel that speaks of Christ and faith as the way to righteousness before God.[240]

With characteristic force, on the basis of Romans 1:17; 3:21ff.; Galatians 2:16; 3:11; and other passages, Luther emphasizes that no one becomes righteous through works of the Law. The righteous will live by faith in Christ and his work of salvation.[241] This way of faith in Christ will be proclaimed for all peoples. The Gospel about Christ, not the preaching of the Law, will characterize mission/preaching among the heathen. This is evident especially in Luther's commentaries on Galatians 1:16:

> *That I might preach Him among the Gentiles.* . . . Here Paul summarizes his whole theology in a few words, as he often does: to preach Christ among the Gentiles. It is as though he were saying: "I refuse to burden the Gentiles with the Law, because I am the apostle and evangelist of the Gentiles, not their lawgiver." Thus he aims all his words against the false apostles. It is as though he were saying: "You Galatians, you have not heard me teach the righteousness of the Law or of works; for this belongs to Moses, not to me, Paul, who am the apostle to the Gentiles. It is my office and ministry to bring you the Gospel and to show you the same revelation that I myself had. Therefore you should not listen to any teacher who teaches the Law. For among the Gentiles not the Law but the Gospel should be preached, not Moses but the Son of God, not the righteousness of works but the righteousness of faith. This is the proclamation that is proper for the Gentiles."[242]

---

239 See the *Larger Commentary on Galatians*, WA 40/1:42–50, and other parts of this important work. I also want to point out Luther's comprehensive sermons on the ministry of the letter/death and the ministry of the new covenant/Spirit, that is, on 2 Corinthians 3:4–11: WA 34/2:162.3ff.; 41:411–38, 655–58; 22:217–31. See also *Church Postil*, WA 10/1.1:491.7–492.17. In the secondary literature, see Wingren, *Luthers lära om kallelsen*, 11ff., on the Law and the earthly kingdom, and 20ff. on the Gospel and the heavenly kingdom. See also Ivarsson, *Predikans uppgift*, 69ff.

240 See the *Larger Commentary on Galatians*, WA 40/1:100–120. On Galatians 2:14–16, see WA 40/1:207–46. On Galatians 2:21, see WA 40/1:300–306. Also see the less well-known 1519 *Commentary on Galatians*, WA 2:487.35–493.18.

241 On Romans 1:17 and Romans 3:21ff., see WADB 7:7.5ff., 7.15ff.; WA 15:18ff.; 54:185.17ff., 186.3ff. On Galatians 2:16 and 3:11, see WA 2:489.6ff., 490.9ff., 491.12ff., 514.37ff.; 40/1:217–64, 420–23.

242 LW 26:73–74 (WA 40/1:142.23, 142.28ff.).

The emphasis is on the thesis that mission among the peoples will be characterized by a radical Gospel, that is, by the preaching of Christ. For Luther, it is not enough to go out with a message. One must in mission go out with the Gospel, to preach Christ and the righteousness of faith. For Luther, this is that by which mission stands or falls, that which makes mission *mission*.

Luther also has expressed what he considers to be central in the mission message on the basis of 1 Peter. He says in the important 1523 writing *1 Peter* that the apostle of the circumcised Jews in this letter does in fact turn toward the heathen in some of the provinces of Asia Minor. These "aliens" are relatively newly converted, believe in Christ, and have sought the fellowship of the Christian Jews. This context is important for understanding the letter.[243] As Luther had earlier emphasized,[244] he also says in 1523 that Peter and all the apostles in the mission of the church teach only one Gospel about God's grace and Christ's work of salvation and that faith in Christ without works of the Law is the only way to righteousness and eternal life. The Gospel is actually nothing written down; it is not a law book nor rules for a blessed spirituality. It is an openly preached message about Christ's substitutionary death of atonement for our sins that without works of the Law is acquired through faith alone. In his Epistle to the heathen, Peter defends this faith in Christ against trust in works of the Law.[245]

---

243 WA 12:261.31ff., 262.2ff.

244 The 1522 foreword to the New Testament, WADB 6:10.9ff.

245 LW 30:3 (WA 12:259.5ff.): "First of all, we must realize that all the apostles teach one and the same doctrine, and that it is incorrect to speak of four evangelists and four gospels; for everything the apostles wrote is one Gospel. And the word 'Gospel' signifies nothing else than a sermon or report concerning the grace and mercy of God merited and acquired through the Lord Jesus Christ with His death. Actually, the Gospel is not what one finds in books and what is written in letters of the alphabet; it is rather an oral sermon and a living Word, a voice that resounds throughout the world and is proclaimed publicly, so that one hears it everywhere. Therefore it is not a book of laws that contains many good teachings, as it has been regarded in the past. It does not tell us to do good works to make us pious, but it announces to us the grace of God bestowed gratis and without our merit, and tells us how Christ took our place, rendered satisfaction for our sins, and destroyed them, and that He makes us pious and saves us through His work." LW 30:3–4 (WA 12:260.4ff., 260.22ff.): "But whenever it deals with Christ as our Savior and states that we are justified and saved through faith in Him without our works, then there is one Word and one Gospel. . . . Accordingly, this Epistle of St. Peter is also one of the noblest books in the New Testament; it is the genuine and pure Gospel. For St. Peter does the same thing that St. Paul and all the evangelists do; he teaches the true faith and tells us that Christ was given to us to take away our sin and to save us, as we shall hear." Cf. on 1 Peter 1:18–19 about the redemption through the blood of the Lamb, WA 12:290.35–292.24. Cf. also on 1 Peter 2:2 about the pure milk for new Christians, WA 12:302.17–306.24, and about Christ as the cornerstone, WA 12:310.10–316.3.

On the basis of 1 Peter 1:3–9, Luther describes salvation as a work of God through Christ, the Gospel, faith, and hope. But the message of this salvation is described more precisely as a preaching about Jesus Christ and about why he suffered death and rose from the dead. In his death, Christ has in our place been subjected to sin, death, and hell. Through his resurrection, he defeats the forces of evil. The Gospel preaching of the cross and of the resurrection, about God's unconditional mercy in Christ, has power to create faith. If one does not preach Christ as dead and risen for us, then one does not preach the Gospel at all.[246] Peter teaches this during the first mission era.

In the commentaries on 1 Peter 1:3–4, Luther especially emphasizes that the message of Christ's resurrection gives new birth to a living hope. This hope of faith and eternity does not exist in the human subject by sight. Instead, under the exigencies of anxiety and struggle, it is rooted fast in the Gospel about Jesus' death and resurrection. The Gospel, faith, new birth, and eternal hope must be anchored in that which God has done in his Son, that is, Christ's death and resurrection. Only through the power of God is one preserved to eternal life. The faith that rests on God and Christ also gives birth to a new lifestyle. It provides a right thinking about justification and a clear view of that which does not communicate Christ and the righteousness of faith. All other faith is only empty talk and fiction.[247] Luther does not discuss the Law-Gospel dialectic further in the commen-

---

246 LW 30:9–10 (WA 12:265.22ff.): "For here St. Peter begins without further ado to tell us what Christ is and what we have acquired through Him. He says that by God's mercy 'we have been born anew to a living hope through the resurrection of Jesus Christ from the dead.' He also says that everything has been given to us by the Father out of pure mercy and without any merit on our part. These are genuinely evangelical words. They must be proclaimed. . . . Therefore one must preach about Jesus Christ that He died and rose from the dead, and why He died and rose again, in order that people may come to faith through such preaching and be saved through faith. This is what it means to preach the genuine Gospel. Preaching of another kind is not the Gospel, no matter who does it." Cf. WA 12:268.28ff. about Christ's death as satisfaction; see also WA 12:266.1ff., 268.4ff., on Christ's resurrection as victory over the forces of evil.

247 See WA 12:267.1ff., 267.28ff., 269.4ff., 270.1ff., 270.27ff., 271.8ff. Briefly in LW 30:14–15 (WA 12:270.4ff., 270.27ff.): "For this is the sequence: Faith follows from the Word, the new birth follows from faith, and from this birth we enter into the hope of looking forward to the blessing with certainty. Therefore Peter has stated here in a truly Christian manner that this must come to pass through faith and not through one's own works. . . . We, however, declare with Peter that faith is a power of God. Where God works faith, man must be born again and become a new creature. Then good works must follow from faith as a matter of course." Cf. WA 12:283.25–285.34 about the exhortation in 1 Peter 1:13 to set hope on grace and on Jesus. Concerning the ground of hope in God's resurrection of Christ, see WA 12:293.24ff. About the new birth through the immortal seed of the Word found in 1 Peter 1:23–25, see WA 12:298.19–300.35.

taries on 1 Peter, but he does give place to the apostolic exhortation that follows on the Gospel and faith. According to Luther, parenesis is not Law but an encouragement and spurring on toward good works. The one who is righteous by faith is stimulated through parenesis to live in congruence with his or her faith.

In summary, one can say that according to Luther the apostles have consistently taught that a radical Gospel will be preached in the new covenant. This Gospel says that the only possibility of salvation is faith in Jesus Christ, his death, and his resurrection. It is a question of an altogether radical Gospel, in which one may not introduce the Law and works if one should preach this message for the peoples. Everything rests on what God/Christ has done and does. Salvation is completely a work of God. As it concerns saving righteousness before God, one may not at all speak of human works and merits. Only where the radical Gospel creates faith and is received in faith does one share in the passive righteousness from God. This righteousness alone is valid for eternal life with God. This is the main doctrine of mission. It will be further explored in the following.

Mission and the preached Gospel

We have now considered the center of the mission message, that is, the proclamation of Jesus Christ and justification through faith in him. From the standpoint of practical mission work, Luther reckons that this message will be communicated primarily through oral preaching.

Not many theologians have written as much as Professor Luther. Nevertheless, he says parenthetically that the Gospel of the new covenant will be spread primarily as a heralded and preached message, that is, as an oral message, about Christ and faith. He thoroughly opposes the idea that the church might be a reign of a book or of reading. Luther scholars have presented texts that show the reformer sees revelation through the Word/Gospel as God's and Christ's continuing work in every time. When the Gospel is preached, then one meets the church as a "mouth house." Through oral preaching, one meets the living Lord who communicates primarily the forgiveness of sins to the hearers. The Gospel is not only a historical, theoretical story about something that happened long ago with Christ. Above all, in oral preaching, one meets the living and risen Christ. Preaching is not only an informative word but also a faith-creating means of grace, which Luther's contemporary Roman Catholic theology did not admit in its emphasis on the seven sacraments as the true means of grace. In the foreword to the 1522 *Church Postil*, Luther writes: "For the preaching of the gospel is nothing else than Christ coming to us."[248]

---

248 LW 35:121 (WA 10/1.1:13.22).

We know, however, that the reformer energetically refuses any declassification of the other means of grace: Baptism, Absolution, and the Lord's Supper. As we already have seen, in the mission context, Luther focuses especially on Baptism. Nevertheless, for Luther evangelization's primary and pioneer instrument is oral preaching, which he calls, among other things, *viva vox* and *mundlich Wort*. At the outset, I want to reject the idea of some theologians that the emphasis on the audible, oral preaching should somehow be a way to escape the authority of the written Word. As few have, the reformer has emphasized that all that is taught and preached by the church must follow the written word of the Bible. The so-called formal principle of the reformer's theology is extraordinarily prominent. It also is not the case that the *viva vox* of preaching is proof that doctrine is irrelevant for the reformer. Of course, oral preaching can oppose a scholastic-legalistic interest in doctrine, but the doctrinal content of faith and life is by no means uninteresting for Luther.[249] When Luther so powerfully emphasizes preaching as the primary tool of mission and evangelization, then it seems to me that in addition to the

---

249 Christ's work of salvation (*historia* or *factum*) is communicated to people through the Word and the Sacraments (*usus historiae* and *usus facti*). Nevertheless, preaching has the central place. See this important theme in Luther's sermons for Christmas, Good Friday, and Easter: WA 17/1:183ff.; 10/1.1:73.12ff.; 11:220.10ff.; 21:40ff.; 52:826.20ff. See also Öberg, *Himmelrikets nycklar och kyrklig bot i Luthers teologi*, 30f. As it concerns the Gospel as an oral and audible word, Luther can decidedly differentiate between the new covenant's oral preaching and the written books of the Old Testament. Cf. *Christmas Postil* (1522), WA 10/1.1:625.19ff., 626.15ff. Therefore Luther scholars have claimed that the church of the reformer is a "mouth house." In my dissertation (*Himmelrikets nycklar och kyrklig bot i Luthers teologi*, 147f.), I have considered many Luther passages with the theme *fides ex auditu, viva vox, vox vocale, mundlich Wort*, etc. The abundance of Luther passages on this subject is enormous and exists throughout Luther's career. But this does not prevent Luther from emphasizing that both the oral and the written Word are important and provide comfort. He emphasizes this especially against the enthusiasts' ideas that the written Word is only paper. See WA 10/1.1:13, 19; 11:82.17; 84.3; 85.16; 25:321.7f.; 34/2:487.1ff., 489.6ff.; 41:412.13ff. In the literature on *viva vox* in Luther, see Prenter (1944), 127ff.; Vajta, *Die Theologie des Gottesdienstes bie Luther*, 139ff.; and Ivarsson, *Predikans uppgift*, 20ff. Other works include Holl, "Luther," 1:291ff.; Ljunggren, *Synd och skuld i Luthers teologi*, 305; Schempp, *Luthers Stellung zur Heiligen Schrift*, 32ff.; and Ebeling, *Evangelische Evangelienauslegung*, 419. In "Luthersk biblesyn," 254ff., Bring has argued that Luther has a more elastic view of the Bible because of his ideas about revelation and *viva vox*. For Östergaard-Nielsen (*Scriptura sacra et viva vox*), the emphasis on the preached Word becomes a key to understanding Luther's view of the Bible, in which the reformer's characteristic obligation to the written Word is questioned. In my work on Luther's view of the Bible (*Bibelsyn och bibeltolkning hos Martin Luther* [2002]), I have investigated such ideas carefully. According to what I have discovered, Luther considers the connection between the living-active God and the sacramental, audible preached Word

theme about the living, active, and present Christ (see above), the following themes are decisive for Luther's position in the question: Christ's command to go out and preach, Christ's example, some of the apostles' words, and the praxis of the early church. Luther's words in the 1522 *Advent Postil* are enlightening:

> Darumb ist die kirch eyn mundhawss, nit eyn fedderhawss; denn sint Christus tzukunfft ist das Euangelium mundlich predigt, das tzuvor, schrifftlich ynn den buchern verporgen lag. Auch sso ist des newen testaments und Euangeli artt, das es mundlich mit lebendiger stym soll gepredigt und getrieben werden. Auch Christus selbs nichts geschriben, auch nitt befolhen hatt tzu schreyben, ssondern mundlich tzu predigen.[250]

The reformer also comments: "The church is not a pen-house but a mouth house." Luther's commentaries on the apostolic letters show that for him oral preaching is the sign of the new covenant and of the Gospel.

Already we have seen several times how central Romans 10:14–15, 17 is for Luther: "How, then, can they call on the one they have not believed in? And how can they believe in the one whom they have not heard? And how can they hear without someone preaching to them? And how can they preach unless they are sent? . . . Consequently, faith comes from hearing the message, and the message is heard through the word of Christ." On the basis of this text, the reformer concludes that audible preaching will be the main instrument of mission and evangelization. The message of preaching is not only an object of knowing, not only guidance for a spirituality of imitation. It is not only a historical and informative word but also a powerfully active, a grace-communicating, a sacramental word. But it does not float in the air freely; it is chained to the work and the word of Christ.[251]

Especially in the commentaries on Galatians, Luther emphasizes that the Holy Spirit and the gift of salvation is received through the preaching of the Gospel. Indeed, listening to preaching in faith is opposed to the false way of works. Paul asks the Galatians: "I would like to learn just one thing from you: Did you receive the Spirit by observing the law, or by believing what you heard?" (Galatians 3:2). To this contraposition of the works of the Law and the hearing of the Gospel in faith in Galatians 3:2, Luther presents parallel texts from the first mission epoch of

---

to be very important. Nevertheless, my studies have also shown that for Luther all preaching must carefully follow the apostolic word without thereby getting lost in intellectualism or a merely historical way of telling stories. Therefore the Scriptures are important for Luther's preaching. This is not contradicted by the theses on *Mundhaus* and *viva vox*. Cf. Prenter (1944), 134.

250 WA 10/1.2:48.5ff.

251 See the sermon on Romans 10:9ff. (WA 10/3:99–101) and the material indicated in *Luther and World Mission*, 175ff., in connection with Acts 2:21. Cf. also on 1 Corinthians 3:5–15, WA 45:389ff.; and on 2 Corinthians 6:1ff., WA 17/2:179.6ff.

the church, among others, Peter's Pentecost sermon in Acts 2, Peter's sermon in the home of Cornelius in Acts 10 (especially v. 44), and Paul's words in Romans 10:13–15. In Luther's understanding, these texts show that the preaching of the primitive church had power to create faith and to grant hearers the gift of the Holy Spirit that on the other hand no work of the Law whatsoever could accomplish. Luther even points out that the Jews took offense at and the apostles were forced to deliberate over the shocking fact that even without circumcision, the Law, sacrifices, etc., and only by listening in faith the heathen shared in the Spirit of the new covenant (Acts 10 and Acts 15). According to Luther, the word of Scripture in general and the experience of the first pioneering time of the Gospel indicate partly that no work of the Law is able to grant the gift of the Holy Spirit; partly that preaching received in faith communicates this gift; and partly that this way to salvation through the Word, faith, and the Spirit is open to all, both Jews and heathen.[252]

Toward the end of Luther's engaging discussion of Galatians 3:2 and the above-named Scripture passages, he writes in the *Larger Commentary on Galatians*:

> The human heart neither understands nor believes that such a great prize as the Holy Spirit can be granted solely through hearing with faith; that it thinks this way: "The forgiveness of sins, deliverance from sin and death, the granting of the Holy Spirit, of righteousness, and of eternal life—this is all something important. Therefore you must do something great to obtain these inestimable gifts." . . . But we must learn by all means that forgiveness of sins, Christ, and the Holy Spirit are granted—and granted freely—only when we hear with faith. Even our huge sins and demerits do not stand in the way.[253]

A little further along, Luther writes:

> Therefore a man becomes a Christian, not by working but by listening. And so anyone who wants to exert himself toward righteousness must first exert himself in listening to the Gospel. Now when he has heard and accepted this, let

---

252 The *Commentary on Galatians* (1519), WA 2:507.27–509.19. See especially: "But the apostle says: 'Not by works but by the hearing of the Word.' [Gal. 3:2] That is, if you endure the Word, then you may have rest from your works and may observe the Lord's Sabbath, in order that you may hear what the Lord your God says to you. Therefore be sure to mark this memorable lesson that Paul has given you. If you want to obtain grace, then see to it that you hear the Word of God attentively or meditate on it diligently. The Word, I say, and only the Word, is the vehicle of God's grace. For what you call works of congruity either are evil or the grace that produces them must already have come. The verdict that the Spirit is received from the hearing of faith stands firm. All those who have received the Spirit have received it in this way" (LW 27:249 [WA 2:509.10ff.]). See especially the *Larger Commentary on Galatians* (1531/1535) with its comprehensive exposition, WA 40/1:328.23–346.22.

253 LW 26:213–14 (WA 40/1:343.22ff.).

him joyfully give thanks to God, and then let him exert himself in good works
that are commanded in the Law.... Therefore if you hear from me that Christ
is the Lamb of God, sacrificed for your sins, see that you really listen to this.
Paul purposely calls it "the hearing of faith" .... He means a Word that you
believe when you hear it, so that the Word is not only the sound of my voice but
is something that is heard by you, penetrates into your heart, and is believed by
you. Then it is truly hearing with faith, through which you receive the Holy
Spirit; and after He has been received, you will also mortify your flesh.[254]

These Luther quotations show that the preaching of the Gospel of grace is a
means of grace. It creates faith and provides the Holy Spirit when it is received by
the heart. Preaching is not only a word of information about grace that is communicated, for example, through the Sacraments. One understands from Luther's
commentaries that the apostolic Gospel's concrete and presenting form in general
ought to be the Gospel message through oral preaching.

In the commentaries on 1 Peter, it is also remarkable how Luther reaffirms that
preaching is the primary instrument of mission and evangelization. The Gospel is
a glad message heralded for all the world, a message about salvation through God's
Son, his death and his resurrection. Already in the introduction to the commentary
on 1 Peter, Luther says: "And the word 'Gospel' signifies nothing else than a sermon
or report concerning the grace and mercy of God merited and acquired through
the Lord Jesus Christ with His death. Actually, the Gospel is not what one finds in
books and what is written in letters of the alphabet; it is rather an oral sermon and
a living Word, a voice that resounds throughout the world."[255] Concerning 1 Peter
1:3–9, he writes this about the central content of preaching: "Therefore one must
preach about Jesus Christ that He died and rose from the dead, and why He died
and rose again, in order that people may come to faith through such preaching and
be saved through faith. This is what it means to preach the genuine gospel."[256] This
quotation shows that Luther nearly identifies the Gospel with oral preaching about
God's grace and mercy in Jesus Christ, his death and resurrection.[257]

---

254 LW 26:214–15 (WA 40/1:345.14ff.).

255 LW 30:3 (WA 12:259.8ff.).

256 LW 30:10 (WA 12:265.30ff.).

257 Concerning the preaching of Christ's death and resurrection, see WA 12:264.8ff.,
268.19ff. Preaching's *viva vox* is emphasized in connection with 1 Peter 1:10–12: "Thus
the books of Moses and the prophets are also Gospel, since they proclaimed and
described in advance what the apostles preached or wrote later about Christ. But there
is a difference. For although both have been put on paper word for word, the Gospel,
or the New Testament, should really not be written but should be expressed with the
living voice which resounds and is heard throughout the world. The fact that it is also
written is superfluous. But the Old Testament is only put in writing. Therefore it is

In the first quotation above, the Gospel is described as "more like an oral preaching and a living word." One must never forget that Luther in his reformation exploited the published word (catechisms, articles, sermon collections) to the highest degree. But the thesis in Luther is nevertheless clear: The church and mission is above all the reign of preaching, listening, and faith. This thesis is important in Luther's missiology.

Nevertheless, Luther expands his description of the Gospel's means and instruments. When it concerns that which makes a person Christian and that which constitutes the central sacrament of the covenant, then the washing of Baptism to new birth always stands side-by-side with the oral *kerygma*. Here, besides the texts already touched on, Galatians 3:26ff. and Titus 3:4f. are wholly decisive for the reformer. Also the Lord's Supper and the power of the keys are emphasized in the work of the Gospel. The enthusiasts forget that atonement must be shared and become *usus facti*. Sometimes Luther speaks expressly of the comfort that the written word (Romans 15:4) and the mutual conversation of the brethren provides. Nevertheless, I can find nothing other than that preaching and Baptism are the main means of mission in Luther. Where he presents a larger arsenal of means of grace, there he probably is most concerned with evangelization in a European context. The Lord's Supper is not a means of breakthrough and mission for Luther. Only the baptized and the taught—even if they are lacking as Christians—those who have learned the elements of the catechism and do not live a careless life, are invited to the Lord's Supper.[258] After all, Luther has always taught that the Lord's Supper is a sacrament of the forgiveness of sins.

---

called 'a letter.' Thus the apostles call it Scripture; for it only pointed to the Christ who was to come. But the Gospel is a living sermon on the Christ who has come" (LW 30:19 [WA 12:275.5ff.]). On the polemic against books, letters, and works against which Luther sets the oral preaching of God's grace and mercy, see WA 12:259.5ff. (see the quotation in *Luther and World Mission*, 203n245).

258 In the *Commentary on 1 Timothy* (1528), Luther comments similarly on 1 Timothy 2:5ff., partly concerning Christ's mediation and partly concerning the preaching of the same in the mission of the church and evangelization. He writes: "Christ has two functions: mediation, or redemption, and a testimony about the forgiveness of sins and mediation. . . . The one is an act; the other, the use of the act. . . . They distinguish between redemption as an actual act and redemption as it is preached. Had Christ been crucified a hundred thousand times and had nothing been said about it, what profit would the act of His being brought to the cross have brought? . . . Therefore to the act also the use of the act must be added, that it may be declared through the Word and that one may hold it by faith and, thus believing may be saved. Paul's intent, then, is this: to the work of redemption belongs the Word of preaching, which does nothing else but impress the work of redemption. 'You have urged this passage beyond measure' " (LW 28:267–68 [WA 26:40.2ff.]). Luther, however, often expands the means of communicating Christ to include Baptism, the Lord's Supper, Absolution, the mutual

The preaching of Law and Gospel

In the previous, we have seen that Luther says that God's Law is holy and tells us about right and wrong. Furthermore, through the Gospel and faith humanity receives saving righteousness. Nevertheless, the reformer claims absolutely that the reception of saving faith and righteousness coheres with the Law-Gospel dialectic

---

consolation of the brethren, and the reading of Scripture. Among these means, however, preaching is central. The Word is important as a component of every means of grace. When the enthusiasts want to apply salvation only to Christ's cross and not connect it to the Word and Sacraments, Luther reacts violently; see WA 26:40.4ff., 40.18ff. and especially LW 28:268–69 (WA 26:40.21ff.): "They say: 'Christ completed the redemption with a single work.' Yes, but He distributes it, applies it, and tells it by testimony. There is a testimony in Baptism. We are baptized into Christ. His Word is present. I am baptized into Christ the Crucified. In Baptism, therefore, there is a use of redemption—an application of its use. In this way the Gospel is the spoken Word, but gives and brings this that Christ is, etc. Thus the Word of God brings out the remission of sins. Therefore there is remission of sins in the Gospel. This one fact—that Christ once, etc.—is divulged and spread in the Word. Thus there is remission of sin in the Sacrament. No one says that Christ is crucified in the Supper and in Baptism, but we say that in the Eucharist His body crucified for us is given to us. . . . They say that neither water nor bread saves us, but Christ crucified. But it profits nothing unless we received in the Word that which in Baptism, in the Sacrament of the Altar, and in the Gospel brings this Christ to me. And wherever the Word of the Gospel is, there is the remission of sins. Therefore, Christ redeemed us once with a single work, but He did not pass out redemption with a single means. He gave it out through the medium of washing in Baptism, through the medium of eating in the Sacrament of the Altar, through the media of comforting the brethren, of reading in the Book, that the fruit of His passion might be spread everywhere. . . . Who will say, then, that remission of sins is not in the Word? So Paul preaches and boasts wonderfully that he is justified by the Word, in which the treasure of our redemption has been enclosed and through which it is offered to us." In "On the Councils and the Churches (1539)," preaching is central (WA 50:269.13ff., 269.28ff.) but is by no means alone among the marks of the holy catholic church (WA 50:630ff.). Cf. also "Confession Concerning Christ's Supper (1528)" (WA 26:505f.); the 1529 LC (*BSLK*, 691ff.); and the 1537 SA (*BSLK*, 449). See also the commentaries on Titus 3:4f. (WA 25:61ff.) and on Galatians 3:26f. (WA 40/1:539ff.). Concerning Luther's estimate of the value of reading the Bible, see, among others, the commentary on Romans 15:4 (WA 10/1.2:70–76) and *Luther and World Mission*, 206–7n249. The following secondary literature ought to be mentioned: the review of the multifaceted arsenal of the means of grace in Ivarsson, *Predikans uppgift*, 38ff. Baptism and the Lord's Supper as means of grace is illuminated by Grönvik, *Die Taufe in der Theologie Martin Luthers*, especially 101ff., 208ff.; and Vajta 1954: 61ff., 157ff. Öberg, *Himmelrikets nycklar och kyrklig bot i Luthers teologi*, illuminates the issue of the power of the keys. See also on Baptism as a means of salvation and "the restrictions" to the Lord's Supper, Öberg, *Himmelrikets nycklar och kyrklig bot i Luthers teologi*, 191ff., 418ff., 428ff.

in the main instrument of mission and evangelization, that is, the preaching of the church. This is an important theme in Luther's missiology.

On the basis of Romans 1–3, the reformer consequently affirms in the foreword to the Epistle (1522/1546) that all evangelical preaching of the apostle must both teach sin as revealed by the Law and explain the righteousness from God through the Gospel. All people who do not live in the Spirit and in faith in Christ are placed under sin and judgment by the apostle in Romans 1–3. The preaching of the Law/commandments will reveal not only individual sins but also above all the opposition of the heart to God and our original sin. This occurs so every person might see and experience his or her guilt before God and seek God's help and grace. Already in Romans 1, the apostle exposes the unbelief and sin of the heathen that causes God's wrath. Despite the fact that they know God exists (Romans 1:19ff.), they not only do not honor God but also drift into a godless lifestyle and idolatry.[259] In Romans 2, Paul considers the Jews and every person as hypocrites with a Law piety and, therefore, under the same wrath and judgment of God. Luther emphasizes that even these hypocrites fall under God's judgment

---

259 The foreword to Romans (1522/1546) shows Luther's real position clearly. He writes concerning chapter 1: "It is right for a preacher of the gospel in the first place by revelation of the law and of sin to rebuke and to constitute as sin everything that is not the living fruit of the Spirit and of faith in Christ, in order that men should be led to know themselves and their own wretchedness, and to become humble and ask for help. This is therefore what St. Paul does. He begins in chapter 1 to rebuke the gross sins and unbelief that are plainly evident. These were, and still are, the sins of the heathen who live without God's grace. He says: Through the gospel there shall be revealed the wrath of God from heaven against all men because of their godless lives and their unrighteousness. For even though they know and daily recognize that there is a God, nevertheless nature itself, without grace, is so bad that it neither thanks nor honors God. Instead it blinds itself, and goes steadily from bad to worse until, after idolatry, it blatantly commits the most shameful sins, along with all the vices, and also allows others to commit them unreprimanded" (LW 35:372 [WADB 7:13.27ff.]). Concerning the question about the Law and Gospel generally in Luther, see Öberg, *Himmelrikets nycklar och kyrklig bot i Luthers teologi*, 138–75, with the adduced and discussed literature. On the basis of a survey of the Luther material in question and with the support of Lau, H. Bornkamm, Ebeling, A. Niebergall, E. Hirsch, Gerhard Heintze, Althaus, and others, I have criticized the Luther interpretation of the old Lund school (Gustaf Aulén and Anders Nygren) in which the Law is described nearly exclusively as a force of evil. In the so-called hyperevangelical understanding of Luther's position, it has been difficult to understand that Luther gives the Law a spiritual and positive task to the extent that it reveals humanity as sinful and disarms any self-reliance. Therefore God's *agape* is taken for granted by the old Lundensians, not, as in Luther, as a wonder of wonders for sinners who are condemned and revealed by the Law/command. Especially Ivarsson (*Predikans uppgift*, 69–112) has corrected the usual picture presented by the Lund school as it concerns Law and Gospel in preaching.

because they oppose God's saving mercy and in their hearts actually hate the Law and are full of lust to judge, of self-assurance, greed, hate, arrogance, etc.[260] The Jews have, of course, God's Word, but few of them believe in the Word. Therefore the apostle finds in Romans 3 that both the Jews and the heathen are under sin, guilt, and judgment. All people are in themselves cut off from God. But the Law and the works of the Law make no one righteous before God. Instead, the Law reveals that humanity is not righteous but sinful. Therefore the apostle follows his teaching on the Law with a teaching on Christ, that is, the only way to righteousness before God. Saving righteousness is a gift from God to a condemned humanity. Without exception all are sinners. Therefore righteousness is given without works and by grace alone to those who believe in Jesus Christ who gave his blood for them, who is the throne of grace, and who grants to humanity God's righteousness or the forgiveness of sins (Romans 3:21–26). The Gospel reveals and provides this righteousness and rejects the Law as a way to salvation. God's righteousness is granted to those who believe in God's Son.[261]

We have seen above that Luther in a quite decided manner asserts that a right preaching will be characterized by the sin-revealing word of Law and the grace-giving word of the Gospel. Preaching ought to reveal humanity's actual situation before God and place all under guilt and judgment so all might seek and live by

---

260 LW 35:372–73 (WADB 7:15.6ff.): "In chapter 2 he extends his rebuke to include those who seem outwardly to be righteous and who commit their sins in secret. Such were the Jews and such are all the hypocrites who without desire or love for the law of God lead decent lives, but at heart hate God's law, and yet are quick to judge other people. This is the nature of all hypocrites, to think of themselves as pure, and yet to be full of covetousness, hatred, pride, and all uncleanness, Matthew 23[:25–28]. These are they who despise God's goodness.... Thus St. Paul, as a true interpreter of the law, leaves no one without sin, but proclaims the wrath of God upon all who would live well simply by nature or their own volition. [*Aus natur oder freiem willem.*] He makes them to be no better than the obvious sinners; indeed, he says they are stubborn and unrepentant." Concerning the concept of sin, see WADB 7:27ff.

261 LW 35:373 (WADB 7:15.17ff.): "In chapter 3 he throws them all together in a heap, and says that one is like the other: they are all sinners before God. Only, the Jews have had the word of God.... [He] proves also by Scripture that all men are sinners, and that by the works of the law nobody is justified, but that the law was given only that sin might be known. Then he begins to teach the right way by which men must be justified and saved. He says: They are all sinners making no boast of God; but they must be justified without merit [of their own] through faith in Christ, who has merited this for us by his blood, and has become for us a mercy-seat by God. God forgives all former sins to demonstrate that we are helped only by his righteousness, which he grants in faith, and which was revealed at that time through the gospel.... Thus the law is upheld by faith, though the works of the law are thereby put down, together with the boasting of them." Cf. WADB 7:9.30ff., 11.28ff.

the righteousness of God, that is, the forgiveness of sins through faith in God's Son. Also in the commentaries on Galatians, especially the comprehensive treatment from 1531/1535, Luther has under the main heading about righteousness through faith in Christ without works of the Law attached investigations of the Law's sin-revealing work and of the Gospel or the forgiveness of sins. Luther is concerned that Gospel preachers will rightly understand the primary and true use of the Law, that which he calls the theological or spiritual use (*usus theologicus seu spiritualis*). Herein the Law has the important task to reveal sin and to terrify the conscience.[262] This can, of course, appear destructive, but the Law performs a necessary service for the Gospel. Unless the Law is allowed to reveal the basic depravity of the human heart, sin, and transgression, the human being is blocked to the Gospel and the forgiveness of sins by a completely ingrown self-righteousness. The preacher of the church must, therefore, also preach Law and the commandments, which show sin and create regret and hunger for God's grace.[263] The

---

262 Cf. *Larger Commentary on the Galatians* (1531/1535), WA 40/1:473–539, with its comprehensive treatments. Concerning the Law's preparatory and interim task in the commentaries on Galatians, see Ljunggren, *Synd och skuld i Luthers teologi*, 308ff.; and Wingren, *Luthers lära om kallelsen*, 70ff. However, Wingren overemphasizes in his work the natural law and the Law as the pressure of existence. He gives smaller place than Luther to the preaching of the Law/command. See also Haikola, *Usus Legis*, 86f.; K. Bornkamm, *Luthers Auslegungen des Galaterbriefs*, 180ff., 346ff.; and Öberg, *Himmelrikets nycklar och kyrklig bot i Luthers teologi*, 169ff.

263 LW 26:309 (WA 40/1:480.32ff.): "The other use of the Law is the theological or spiritual one, which serves to increase transgressions. This is the primary purpose of the Law of Moses, that through it sin might grow and be multiplied, especially in the conscience. Paul discusses this magnificently in Rom. 7. Therefore the true function and the chief and proper use of the Law is to reveal to man his sin, blindness, misery, wickedness, ignorance, hate and contempt of God, death, hell, judgment, and the well-deserved wrath of God." LW 26:310 (WA 40/1:481.26ff.): "Hence this use of the Law is extremely beneficial and very necessary. For if someone is not a murderer, adulterer, or thief, and abstains from external sins, as that Pharisee did (Luke 18:11), he would swear, being possessed by the devil, that he is a righteous man. . . . God cannot soften and humble this man or make him acknowledge his misery and damnation any other way than by the Law. Therefore the proper and absolute use of the Law is to terrify with lightning (as on Mt. Sinai), thunder, and the blare of the trumpet, with a thunderbolt to burn and crush that brute which is called the presumption of righteousness. . . . For as long as the presumption of righteousness remains in a man, there remain immense pride, self-trust, smugness, hate of God, contempt of grace and mercy, ignorance of the promises and of Christ. The proclamation of free grace and the forgiveness of sins does not enter his heart and understanding, because that huge rock and solid wall, namely, the presumption of righteousness by which the heart is itself surrounded, prevents this from happening." Cf. WA 40/1:484.16ff., 484.32ff., and about *lex propter trangressiones* and as "minister and preparation for grace," LW 26:314 (WA 40/1:487.15ff., 488.12).

Law has a temporary and positive task. Luther says with Paul that the Law prepares people for the Gospel and is a schoolmaster leading to Christ (*paidagogos* [Galatians 3:24]). He calls the Law/command *praeparator euangelii* and *paidagogus in Christum* in its sin-revealing work. The Law must destroy the trust in self that blocks humanity from the Gospel. There is no legalism or spiritual terror here; instead, it is God's way to open people for the Gospel. Through the Law, humanity dies to the Law and to self-trust. God decides by God's own Word the proper measure of the sense of sin and regret. Regret is not something we produce by "curling ourselves up." It is a work of God in the human heart when men and women oppose it and taste the Word both as Law and Gospel.

The reformer, however, emphasizes that the work of the Law/command in the conscience is a preparation for something else. The Law is not something with which to play. Isolated from the Gospel, it can, in Luther's understanding, be considered a force of evil. In all his teaching on the Law and the Gospel, the reformer also, therefore, says that the preaching of the Law/command will always be followed by and united with the Gospel about Christ, grace, and the forgiveness of sins. When humanity sees and experiences its situation under sin, God's wrath, and judgment, then the Law has done its work, and the Gospel about the blessed Seed (= Christ) must take over (Galatians 3:19). The Gospel is something completely different than the Law/command. In Christ, the grace of God, forgiveness of sins, and victory over death is preached radically. A right preaching must, therefore, be a movement from Law to Gospel, from the sin-disclosing and anxiety-producing work of the Law to freedom and peace through faith in God's Son. Fundamentally, the Gospel and the Spirit's freedom ought to rule in the conscience of the believers. Just as the Law literally was in force until Christ (Matthew 11:12f.), so it has a place in the repentance and faith of the Christian only until sin is known. Then Christ and grace will be preached and rule in heart and conscience. This is something that applies both when one is first called through the Gospel and thereafter in every Christian's daily repentance in the presence of the Word as Law and Gospel.[264]

---

264 About how the Law isolated from the Gospel produces death, hell, and doubt, see the 1537 SA (*BSLK*, 325). It ought to be observed that the letter of the Law is said to have received its demise with Christ. However, the Law's spiritual use has not been eliminated in the new covenant and the preaching of the same. It will for a time or intermittently touch the conscience, then give place for the Gospel about Christ. One can observe this idea in WA 40/1:491.14ff., 493.11ff., 529.15ff. See especially LW 26:317 (WA 40/1:492.11ff.): "You may understand the duration of the time of the Law either literally or spiritually. . . . In a spiritual sense: The Law must not rule in the conscience any longer than the predetermined time of that Blessed Offspring. Therefore when the Law has disclosed my iniquities to me, has terrified me, and has revealed to me the

Because many Luther scholars have given an uninformed presentation of the Law-Gospel dialectic in Luther, it ought to be emphasized here that by natural knowledge of God humanity knows vaguely, and by no means clearly, sin and the demand of the Law. Especially humanity does not know anything about the Gospel and God's grace; therefore natural human worship of God ends necessarily in self-righteousness and idolatry.[265] For these reasons, Luther argues in the *Larger Commentary on Galatians* that both the Law and the Gospel must be preached. A true preaching of the Law/command reveals that not only the fruit but also the entire tree is rotten. Humanity does not only have sins but also is fundamentally a sinner, *totus peccator*. A rightly preached Gospel, however, promises and grants the forgiveness of sins completely apart from the Law and works, radically and alone through faith in God's Son. Through the Gospel and faith in Christ, humanity is reckoned perfectly righteous, that is, *totus iustus*.[266]

The Smalcald Articles, written by Luther in 1537, are considered to be among the confessional writings in most Lutheran church bodies and will here provide a summary of humanity's conversion and repentance when it receives the preaching of Law and Gospel:

> However, the chief function or power of the law is to make original sin man-ifest and show man to what utter depths his nature has fallen and how corrupt it has become. So the law must tell him that he neither has nor cares for God or that he worships strange gods—something that he would not have believed before without a knowledge of the law. Thus he is terror-stricken and hum-bled, becomes despondent and despairing, anxiously desires help but does not know where to find it, and begins to be alienated from God, to murmur,

---

wrath and judgement of God, so that I begin to blanch and to despair, then the Law has reached the prescribed manner, time, and purpose when it must stop exercising its tyranny. . . . When these terrors and complaints come, it is the time and the hour of the Blessed Offspring. Then let the Law withdraw; for it was indeed added for the sake of disclosing and increasing transgressions, but only until the point when the Offspring would come. . . . Let it surrender its realm to another, that is, to the Blessed Offspring, Christ; He has gracious lips, with which He does not accuse and terrify but speaks bet-ter things than the Law, namely, grace, peace, forgiveness of sins, and victory over sin and death." Concerning the Christian conscience in which the Gospel, Christ, and the freedom of the Gospel ought to rule, see WA 40/1:44.19ff., 46.19ff., 50.24ff., 526.21ff. There is an especially exhaustive passage in WA 40/2:2ff. about Galatians 5:1: "It is for freedom that Christ has set us free. Stand firm, then, and do not let yourselves be burdened again by a yoke of slavery." Cf. also *Luther and World Mission*, 199n234, with the adduced texts and literature.

265 Cf. the comments on Galatians 4:8–9, WA 40/1:600–620. See also the investigation in *Luther and World Mission*, 39–62, 64–81.

266 WA 40/1:223.29ff., 231.21ff., 520.25f.

etc. This is what is meant by Rom. 4:15, "The law brings wrath," and Rom. 5:20, "Law came in to increase the trespass." . . . This function of the law is retained and taught by the New Testament. So Paul says in Rom. 1:18, "The wrath of God is revealed from heaven against all ungodliness and wickedness of men," and in Rom. 3:19, 20, "The whole world may be held accountable to God, for no human being will be justified in his sight." Christ also says in John 16:8, "The Holy Spirit will convince the world of sin." This, then, is the thunderbolt by means of which God with one blow destroys both open sinners and false saints. He allows no one to justify himself. He drives all together into terror and despair. This is the hammer of which Jeremiah speaks, "Is not my word like a hammer which breaks the rock in pieces?" (Jer. 23:29). This is not *activa contritio* (artificial remorse), but *passiva contritio* (true sorrow of the heart, suffering, and pain of death). This is what the beginning of true repentance is like. Here man must hear such a judgement as this: "You are all of no account . . . no matter who you are and no matter how great, wise, mighty, and holy you may think yourselves. Here no one is godly," etc. To this office of the law the New Testament immediately adds the consoling promise of grace in the Gospel. This is to be believed, as Christ says in Mark 1:15, "Repent and believe in the Gospel," which is to say, "Become different, do otherwise, and believe my promise." John, who preceded Christ, is called a preacher of repentance—but for the remission of sins. . . . Christ himself says this in Luke 24:47, "Repentance and the forgiveness of sins should be preached in his name to all nations." But where the law exercises its office alone, without the addition of the Gospel, there is only death and hell, and man must despair like Saul and Judas. As St. Paul says, the law slays through sin. Moreover, the Gospel offers consolation and forgiveness in more ways than one, for with God there is plenteous redemption (as Ps. 130:7 puts it) from the dreadful captivity to sin, and this comes to us through the Word, the sacraments, and the like, as we shall hear.[267]

This text summarizes an often misunderstood and absent preaching task in our time. When contemporary theology under the influence of antinomianism, psychology and psychiatry hides away the necessary, sin-disclosing work of the Law/command, or when it trusts in the natural law or existential anxiety as sufficient background to the preaching of the Gospel, then it does not have Luther on its side. He taught that the Law/command should be preached for some time and reveal sin so all people will experience their true situation before God. But to those who understand their sin, are anxious for it, and taste God's judgment, a radical and unconditional Gospel shall be preached that liberates from the judgment of the Law. For Luther, the Law's spiritual use is actually a bulwark against humanity's ingrown self-righteousness and a bulwark for the Gospel as the for-

---

267 SA III II–III (Tappert, 303–4).

giveness of sins for true sinners. One must through the Law die to the Law as a way of salvation (Galatians 2:19) so salvation will rest on the forgiveness of sins for Christ's sake alone. It ought to be crystal clear that the Law-Gospel dialectic is something important in all preaching to both Jews and heathen in Luther's thought.

ONE SINGLE PEOPLE OF GOD COMPOSED OF JEWS AND GENTILES

Luther's differentiation between the righteousness of the Law/works and the righteousness of faith in Christ has thoroughgoing consequences for his ecclesiology and missiology. Through the Gospel of Christ, any particularism connected with circumcision, the Law, and the chosen people is definitively rescinded. The Gospel as a part of Christ's reign ought to be preached for both Jews and Gentiles, that is, for all people on earth.

In connection with Romans 4:1ff. and Galatians 3:7–20, the reformer emphasizes that even the heathen are included in the blessing that was promised to Abraham and his seed (Genesis 12:3, 7; 17:7; 18:18; 22:18). Through the atoning and sacrificial death of Jesus Christ for all, both Jews and heathen are redeemed from the curse of the Law so both through the Gospel and faith in Christ might receive the Spirit. In Pauline theology, all who are righteous through faith in Jesus Christ are referred to as the children of Abraham. Again those who depend on works of the Law are under the curse whether they are heathen or Jews. Luther says with Paul that this way of the Gospel and faith to righteousness before God that unites all has not been rescinded by the Law that was given long after (430 years) the promises to Abraham. That Law is chiefly a "pedagogue" to Christ.[268] In this way the cornerstone of both Paul's and Luther's doctrine of justification unites all who believe in Christ in one single people. Here mission has its source of total and unreserved universalism.

The commentaries on Galatians 3:25 (compare with the above section about how one receives the Spirit by listening to the Gospel in faith) also say that the Jews and heathen become one single people through the Gospel and faith in Christ. Peter's Pentecost sermon and his sermon in Cornelius's house (Acts 2 and Acts 10, especially 10:44) show also that the Spirit has been poured out on both Jews and heathen. The Spirit was poured out both on the Jews, who were forced to live according to the Law, and on heathen, who lived under no such Law. The Gospel of Christ and faith provides the same salvation and grace to all; therefore

---

268 See the 1546 foreword to Romans (4:1ff., 11ff.), WADB 7:172.2ff.; and the *Larger Commentary on Galatians* (3:7–20), WA 40/1:373–506. See also the exposition of Galatians 3:15–22, WA 41:658–62; 22:232–37. See also, among others, K. Bornkamm, *Luthers Auslegungen des Galaterbriefs*, 278ff., who adduces additional passages.

the people of the new covenant become one people in Christ.[269] Luther summarizes in his commentary on Galatians:

> Therefore in the entire Book of Acts, taken as a whole, nothing is discussed except that Jews as well as Gentiles, righteous men as well as sinners, are to be justified solely by faith in Christ Jesus, without Law or works. This is indicated both by the sermons of Peter, Paul, Stephen, Philip, and others, and by the examples of the Gentiles and Jews. For just as through the Gospel God gave the Holy Spirit to Gentiles who lived without the Law, so He gave the Holy Spirit also to the Jews, not through the Law or through the worship and sacrifices commanded in the Law but solely through the proclamation of faith.[270]

It ought to be observed that in his commentaries on Paul's letters Luther uses the word *heathen* to indicate those who are not circumcised or who do not live under the Law of Moses. With the word *Jews*, he means those who are circumcised and obligated to the Law. The concept of heathens/Jews is, therefore, defined principally in a theological manner on the basis of the Bible's own distinctions. Luther does not speak about the heathen in the contemporary "geographic" sense, which is based more or less on the perspective of the Christian West. The Germans are included, for example, in Paul's apostolate among the uncircumcised heathen, even if they, in the best circumstances, no longer believe and live as heathen. When Luther speaks about the Jews, he is not thinking about race as such but about the Jews as circumcised and living under the Law and its regulations.[271]

On the basis of Galatians 3:13–16, 26–29, the reformer especially emphasizes how the Word about Baptism in and faith in Jesus Christ gathers one single people of God from both Jews and heathen, among whom one can find all categories of people. This one single people of God possess their salvation and their unity in

---

269 WA 40/1:331.19ff. See also the 1522 *Advent Postil* on Romans 15:4–13, WA 10/1.2:63ff., 67ff., 80ff. Here Luther handles the question of how the division between the free/strong and the bound/careful conscience originates. Luther first develops his thesis that the one single faith in Christ will be able to hold together the more liberated and the more strict Christians in one reign, just as in Paul's mission in the early church.

270 LW 26:205 (WA 40/1:332.22ff.).

271 LW 26:130 (WA 40/1:214.30): "15. *We ourselves, who are Jews by birth and not Gentile sinners.* That is: 'We are Jews by nature, namely, by being born into the righteousness of the Law, into Moses, and into circumcision; we bring the Law along with our very birth." LW 26:205 (WA 40/1:333.18ff.): "Therefore when you hear or read the term 'Gentiles' in Acts or anywhere else in the Scriptures, you should know that it is not to be taken in the natural sense but must be taken in a theological sense for those who are without the Law and are not under the Law, as the Jews were." On Galatians 3:28, WA 40/1:542.25ff., and the above investigation of Acts 13:16ff., see *Luther and World Mission*, 183–85.

the fact that Christ, the blessed Seed, redeemed all by becoming the curse and archsinner for all in his atoning death on the cross. The sin and punishment of the entire human race was placed on Jesus Christ. Therefore the way to salvation and unity for all is open through Christ's sacrificial and victorious work. With amazing force, Luther emphasizes how Baptism into Christ is foundational for the salvation and unity of God's people in Christ. Luther often expands the basis of unity to include the "one Father, one Christ, one Spirit, one gospel, one baptism, one faith, one hope" of Ephesians 4:3ff.[272]

On the basis of Galatians 3:14, the reformer speaks about how Christ blesses the peoples by becoming a curse in the place of all people.

> *That in Christ Jesus the blessing of Abraham might come upon the Gentiles.* Paul always has this passage, "In your Offspring," in view, because the blessing promised to Abraham could not come to the nations except through Abraham's Offspring, Christ. How? He Himself had to become a curse, that the promise given to Abraham, "In your Offspring shall all the nations be blessed," [Gen. 22:18] might be fulfilled. What is promised here could not happen in any other way than that Jesus Christ should become a curse, join Himself to the accursed nations, remove the curse from them, and bless them with His blessing.[273]

One ought to observe here that it is the suffering and accursed Christ who unites the Jews and the heathen and grants blessing to the heathen. From a missiological perspective, it is important to notice that the fulfillment of the promise to Abraham is definitely connected to the fact that Jesus Christ became a curse even for the heathen. The promised inclusion of the heathen in the blessed people of God is actualized when Christ becomes a curse even for the heathen. It is thus in Christ and his cross that the wall of division between Jews and heathen is dismantled. Thereby the church's unity is anchored not in human institutions but primarily in Christ and in true participation in him through faith.

If Luther most often anchored saving faith in the preached Gospel in the texts previously analyzed, in connection with Galatians 3:26–27 he focuses on Baptism as a clothing in Christ and as a sacrament of unity based on grace alone:

> He does not say: "You are sons of God because you are circumcised, listen to the Law, and keep its works," as the Jews imagined and as the false apostles taught; but "through faith in Christ Jesus." Therefore the Law does not create sons of God; much less do human traditions. . . . 27. *For as many of you as were*

---

272 See the *Commentary on Galatians* (1519), WA 2:516.5ff., 518.23ff., 530.1ff.; and the *Larger Commentary on Galatians* (1531/1535), WA 40/1:432ff., 453ff., 539ff. Cf. also the sermons on Galatians 3:15ff., WA 22:232ff. and 41:659.1ff., 662.3ff.

273 LW 26:291 (WA 40/1:453.14ff.).

baptized into Christ have put on Christ. Putting on Christ is understood in two ways: according to the Law and according to the Gospel. According to the Law (Rom. 13:14), "Put on the Lord Jesus Christ; that is: Imitate the example and the virtues of Christ. Do and suffer what He did and suffered." . . . But to put on Christ according to the Gospel is a matter, not of imitation but of new birth and a new creation, namely, that I put on Christ Himself, that is, His innocence, righteousness, wisdom, power, salvation, life and Spirit. We were dressed in the leather garment of Adam, which is a deadly garment and the clothing of sin. . . . Paul calls [it] "the old man." He must be put off with all his activities, so that from sons of Adam we may be changed into sons of God (Eph. 4:22 and Col. 3:9). This does not happen by a change of clothing or by any law or works; it happens by the rebirth and renewal that takes place in Baptism.[274]

Wherever people have shared in God's salvation through Christ through the Gospel and Baptism, there all divisions are broken down. God's people composed of Jews and heathen are perfectly united to be one people in Christ and faith. Luther comments on Galatians 3:28:

There is neither Jew nor Greek, there is neither slave nor free, there is neither male nor female. . . . With the words "there is neither Jew," then, Paul vigorously abolishes the Law. For here, where a new man comes into existence in Baptism and where Christ is put on, there is neither Jew nor Greek. Now he is not speaking of the Jew in a metaphysical sense, according to his essence; but by "Jew" he means someone who is a disciple of Moses, who is subject to the laws, who has circumcision, and who observes the form of worship commanded in the Law. Where Christ is put on, he says, there is no Jew any longer, no circumcision, no temple worship, no laws that the Jews keep.[275]

Furthermore, Luther says about the heathen:

With the next words, "nor Greek," Paul also rejects and condemns the wisdom and righteousness of the Gentiles. . . . for we must not imagine that the Gentiles were simply despisers of honesty and religion, but all the nations scattered all over the world have their own laws, worship, and religion, without which the human race cannot be governed—with all these adornments, I say, they amounted to nothing in the sight of God. . . . Then what [is it that amounts to something]? The garment of Christ, which we put on in Baptism.[276]

Concerning "for you are all one in Christ Jesus" (Galatians 3:28), Luther says this vis-à-vis the civil life's necessary social stratification: "In Christ, on the other hand, where there is no Law, there is no distinction among persons at all. There is

---

274 LW 26:351–52 (WA 40/1:539.15ff, 539.33ff.). Luther here adduces Titus 3:5.

275 LW 26:353–54 (WA 40/1:542.13ff.).

276 LW 26:354–55 (WA 40/1:543.12ff.).

neither Jew nor Greek, but all are one; for there is one body, one Spirit, one hope of the calling of all, one and the same Gospel, one faith, one Baptism, one God and Father of all, one Christ, the Lord of all (Eph. 4:4–6)."[277]

As previously pointed out, Luther uses the words *Jew* and *heathen* in a principally theological manner to refer to those who are and are not, respectively, circumcised and obligated to the Law. In the recently cited texts, Luther emphasizes that something completely new is created out of the Jews (with the Law and its regulations) and out of the heathen (with their wisdom and righteousness) through the Gospel of Christ, Baptism, and faith. A new and perfectly united people of God is created in whom all are clothed in Christ through faith. The new Christian people of God exists where one no longer differentiates between the Jews and the heathen. The unity of the parts consists not in a synthesis between the laws/regulations of the Jews and the wisdom of the heathen. Both have laws/morals, but this is not a basis for salvation; instead, something completely new is created through Christ. Thus the reformer speaks of a unity between Jews and heathen—indeed, between all categories of humans—on the basis of Christ's death and resurrection, the Gospel, Baptism, and faith. In this new people of God, circumcision and the Law do not divide people, neither do racial nor other walls that exist between people. Christ has come as Savior for all peoples and for all people and in him the divided people become perfectly united in one single people. Where the Law and works are rescinded as a basis for salvation and where all are sinners in themselves and God's children only on the basis of the Gospel of Christ and faith, there the church of Christ's *communio sanctorum* is built. All have the same poverty in themselves. All have the same single wealth in Christ.

These foundational ideas in Luther's missiology recur in his commentaries on other New Testament Epistles.[278] In his commentary on Zion's precious cornerstone in 1 Peter 2:6, Luther says:

> Besides, the prophet also calls Christ a "Cornerstone." . . . Christ is a Cornerstone because He brought the Gentiles and the Jews, who were mortal enemies, together. Thus the Christian Church was gathered from both. The apostle Paul writes extensively about this (cf. Eph. 2:19–22). The Jews gloried in the

---

277 LW 26:356 (WA 40/1:545.15ff.).

278 WA 12:311.34ff. Cf. WA 12:320.13ff., quoted in *Luther and World Mission*, 223–24n280. Unfortunately, I have been unable to locate in the Luther material any investigation on the unity of the Jews and the heathen in faith in Christ on the basis of Ephesians 2:14–18; 3:6. Cf. how Ephesians 2:16 is used in the struggle between Christ and the condemning Law, WA 40/1:566ff. See, however, the *gloss* on Ephesians 2:14–15, WADB 7:197: "Das Gesetz war die Feindschafft zwischen Heiden und Jüden, Denn da durch wolten die Jüden besser sein. Nu aber on Gesetz allzumal, durch Christum den Geist haben, hat solche Feindschafft ein ende, und ist einer wie der ander."

Law of God, boasted that they were God's people, and despised the Gentiles. But now Christ appeared, deprived the Jews of their glory, and also summoned us Gentiles. Thus He made us both one through one faith and dealt with us in such a manner that we must both confess that we have nothing ourselves but are all sinners, that we must expect piety and heaven from Him alone. . . . Therefore He is the Cornerstone who joins two walls together, the Jews and the Gentiles, so that one building and one house results.[279]

Finally, I want to point out that on the basis of Romans 15:8–9 Luther constantly notes that Christ is the Savior of the Jews, which confirms God's trustworthiness and the promises to the patriarchs. Of course, the Old Testament possesses predictions about how God's salvation will be extended to the heathen peoples, but the heathen do not possess the same oath-sworn promises of God as the people of God, the Jews, do. The salvation of the heathen rests only on an unconditional mercy. Both Jews and heathen receive one and the same salvation in Jesus Christ. By this fact, they become united as one people, the people of the new covenant. The same Christ and the same grace unite the two parties. All the walls of division must fall, and all struggles must cease wherever Christ has united one people.[280]

---

279 LW 30:58 (WA 12:311.34ff.).

280 See "Ennarationes epistolorum et evangeliorum, etc. (1521)," WA 7:485.18ff.; the 1522 *Advent Postil*, WA 10/1.2:86.4ff.; and "Sermon for the 2nd Sunday of Advent (1536)," WA 41:732.26ff. The following provides a good summary: "The Jews, then, have Christ not only through grace in the promise, but also because of the truth of God in fulfilment of his promise. But the gentiles have neither the grace of the promise nor the truth of fulfilment. They have merely the naked, unpromised, unexpected mercy Christ gives to them. There is no promise, and no obligation for fulfilment of the truth of God. Yet, the Scriptures having revealed that the gentiles should obtain Christ, though without promise, hope or expectation, the Scriptures must be fulfilled. Therefore, one people is not favored over the other. But Christ was given to the Jews through divine promise and divine truth, and to the gentiles through pure, unexpected mercy. Since the Scriptures contain a promise to the Jews and a prediction concerning the gentiles, the two peoples have a common bond in Christ. Hence each should receive the other as a participant in the common blessing. The Jews are not to despise the gentiles; because the Scriptures say the gentiles shall praise God for his mercy [Ps. 72:17]. . . . On the other hand, the gentiles should not despise the Jews; for to the latter was Christ promised, and in fulfilment of the promise he became their minister and preacher, making God faithful to his word" (Lenker 6:58–59 [WA 10/1.2:88.14ff.]). Cf. WA 10/1.2:89ff. and, on 1 Peter 2:10, LW 30:66 (WA 12:320.13ff.): "*Once you were no people, but now you are God's people; once you had not received mercy, but now you have received mercy.* This verse is found in Hos. 2:23. St. Paul also quoted it in Rom. 9:25, where he says: 'Those who were not My people I will call My people.' All this points to the fact that Almighty God chose the people of Israel in particular, conferred great honor on them, gave them many prophets, and also performed many miraculous

Thus the church is a new Israel gathered from both Jews and heathen. Following 1 Corinthians 10:18, Luther distinguishes between Israel according to the flesh and the Israel that lives on the basis of God's promises and grace in Christ (= Jews and heathen). He also points out how Paul in Galatians 6:6 wishes peace and mercy on "God's Israel." The recipients of this well-wishing are not those who by blood are connected with Abraham and the other patriarchs but all Jews and heathen who live in faith in God's Son, who is the fulfillment of the promises to Abraham. This is God's Israel according to the spiritual meaning of the new covenant. But this does not mean that Israel according to the flesh disappears from the scene.[281]

It goes without saying that the unity between Jews and heathen on which Luther discourses is a unity based on specifically Christian premises with Jesus of Nazareth as the center of salvation history and as the Messiah of God. Naturally, the Jews cannot admit and experience this unity in Christ as long as they are religiously Jews. If, as according to the preceding analysis, Luther in his missiology has dispensed with all cultural and racial antagonisms, the merely religious antagonism vis-à-vis the Jews remains in the question about who Jesus of Nazareth was and is. I will return to this question in the section on mission among the Jews in chapter 4.

The *hendiadys*—Jews and heathen—that we have been discussing characterizes what we might call Luther's concept of mission. First, with Jews and heathen Luther indicates the whole of humanity, all peoples and tribes. The concept stands for an unabridged universalism in which the heathen are now in Christ offered the same salvation as the people of the old covenant. The prophetic promises to the people of God have now been fulfilled, but the promises of blessing to all people also have begun to be fulfilled in God's mercy. God's salvation applies to all peoples and therefore must be dispensed to all. In one way, the receptors of mission

---

deeds with them because He wanted Christ to become man from this nation. All this took place for the sake of the Child. For this reason they are called God's people in Scripture. But the prophets amplify this and said that this promise should become known and should also concern the Gentiles."

281 See the *Commentary on Galatians* (1519), LW 27:406 (WA 2:615.5ff.): "Paul adds the words 'upon the Israel of God.' He distinguishes this Israel from the Israel after the flesh, just as in 1 Cor. 10:18 he speaks of those who are the Israel of the flesh, not the Israel of God. Therefore peace is upon the Gentiles and Jews, provided that they go by the rule of faith and the spirit." Cf. LW 27:142 (WA 40/2:180.33ff.): " 'The Israel of God are not the physical descendants of Abraham, Isaac, and Israel but those who, with Abraham the believer (3:9), believe in the promises of God now disclosed in Christ, whether they are Jews or Gentiles." See also the discussion of the covenant with Abraham and the spiritual Israel, *Luther and World Mission*, 100ff., 110ff., 118ff.

are one single unity. All people—both Jews and heathen—possess the same need of salvation and are promised the same grace in Jesus Christ.

Second, Luther speaks of both Jews and heathen when he wants to describe more closely the field for mission. He knows well that there is a difference between the two groups. The people of God, Israel, have for a long time had a covenant with the Lord; Israel had read about the Creator and received the Law and the great promises. Now, however, the priority ought to be to spread God's salvation in Christ to the heathen who have not yet been reached by revelation. Therefore in Luther's understanding of mission there is a difference between Jews and heathen as it concerns the context of the Gospel and its audience. Mission work must, as we shall see, be formulated differently in respect to Israel and the heathen.

Third, I want to point out that it is just this vocabulary of the early church that characterizes Luther's understanding of the sending of the church with the Gospel into the world. Seldom does Luther say that there is a difference between domestic mission work in the West and foreign mission among the Jews and the heathen. Luther integrates mission and evangelization. According to Christ and his commands, the Gospel ought to be preached to all peoples, to all who do not possess Christ through faith. One ought also to work to hold the field where the Gospel already is planted. In this way, one integrates and does not separate mission and domestic evangelization/re-Christianization. It is in the one and only Gospel and in the common faith in Christ that we have the foundation that—despite necessary distinctions between the home front and the foreign/cross-cultural front—integrates the work of God's reign in a fundamental unity.

FAITH IN CHRIST, FREEDOM, AND THE WEAK CONSCIENCE

Earlier in our investigation we have seen that Luther periodically has said something about the importance of freedom in questions about customs, laws, seasons, food, etc., as the Gospel expands among the peoples. At the same time that this freedom must continue to be promulgated consistently, love in mission and church work must sometimes adapt and compromise. But it is important that the Gospel and the doctrine of justification through faith without works of the Law is not forgotten in these adaptions and compromises.[282]

Luther does not have a regular commentary on Romans 14, a chapter important in this context, but he often refers to it. His remarks in the 1546 foreword to Romans are a good summary:

> In chapter 14 he teaches that consciences weak in faith are to be led gently, spared, so that we do not use our Christian freedom for doing harm, but for the assistance of the weak. For where that is not done, the result is discord and

---

282 See *Luther and World Mission*, 114ff., 140ff., 186ff.

contempt for the gospel; and the gospel is the all-important thing. Thus it is better to yield a little to the weak in faith, until they grow stronger, than to have the teaching of the gospel come to nothing. And this work is a peculiar work of love, for which there is great need even now, when with the eating of meat and other liberties, men are rudely and roughly—and needlessly—shaking weak consciences, before they know the truth.[283]

This important principle for the work of God's reign is concretized by Luther in many other passages.

In his commentaries on Romans 15:4–13, Luther says a bit about how faith and love conquer, among other things, the differences in regulations, food laws, practices, and uses that exist in a congregation composed of both Jewish and heathen Christians. Paul's encouragement to the Christians in Rome shows that the unity of the congregation ought not be risked because some are free in the question of food and customs while others feel bound in their consciences to follow certain rules. Of course, all such external observances are not at all necessary for salvation, but it may happen that for the sake of those with weak consciences one must restrict his or her freedom. One ought not force those with tender consciences to act against their convictions. One must give the weak time to mature in faith.[284] Those with tender consciences ultimately will by faith discover the difference between human customs and divine commands. Luther wants to emphasize along with Paul that in all mission and evangelization work a violent attack on those weak in faith is not the right method. Love bides its time and does not always show its strength against the weak in faith. One ought not for the sake of

---

283 LW 35:379 (WADB 7:25.26ff.). Cf. WA 17/2:150.25ff.

284 WA 7:481.2ff.: "Institutis autem in fide et bonis moribus adiungit in fine Epistolae praecepta, quibus eos in concordia spiritus confirmet, tollens causas, quae concordiam eorum in fide et moribus possint tollere, quarum sunt duae, prior, quod Iudaei ex usu legis et inolita conscientia infirmiores non poterant vesci carnibus in lege prohibitis et nec omnes caerimonias et ritus legis tam subito omittere, licet essent iam non necessariae. Hos docet a gentibus tolerandos pro tempore, nec propter cibum solvendum fidem et Christianos mores: idem faciendum, si gentilis vel Iudaeus aliquis horreret edere cibos idolis immolatos (ut tunc mos erat), timens se peccare et idolatris consentire, cum tamen liceret quodlibet genus ciborum edere nihilque esset immundum iis qui in Christum credidissent . . . si enim sequerentur firmiores cum eis edendo, iam contra conscientiam faciebant infirmam, quae dictabat non edendum, si omitterent quod videbant alios facere, iam quasi non essent Christiani formidabant, quia non facerent quod alii Christiani. Hos tolerandos docet et coram eis abstinendum etiam a licitis illis cibis, donec usu et ipsi firmati scirent licere." Concerning how Roman canon laws about fasts, ceremonies, etc., bind consciences that are in fact free, see WA 7:481.19ff. Cf. the parallel texts WA 10/1.2:62ff. and 41:732.25ff. Wingren, *Luthers lära om kallelsen*, 105ff., reviews important aspects of the concept of freedom in Luther.

disunity in some external matters break the love and unity of the Christian congregation in Christ and in faith.[285]

Luther recommends a similar way of dealing with things on the basis of 1 Corinthians 8:1ff; 9:38f.; 13:1, 12; 2 Corinthians 6:3; 11:29; and Philippians 2:4. Thus the reformer teaches that there are contexts in the work of God's reign in which an immaturity in the faith of some requires Christians to bind their freedom for a time. True faith respects civil law, but it is not at all a slave to Jewish conventions or to other kinds of regulations. It has, however, clothed itself in love and patience so those who without reason feel bound might have time to mature in faith—and thereby in freedom.[286]

Luther has, however, on the basis of Galatians 2:11–16—in which Paul accuses Peter of hypocrisy at the tables of Antioch and opposes the false way of the Law to the true way of faith to righteousness—with strict consequence taught how the concessions of love ought not be allowed to tread too closely on the doctrine of justification. Peter was guilty of a great transgression when, in a cowardly and opportunistic fashion, he gave in to the Judaizers despite the fact that he clearly understood the doctrine of freedom concerning food, etc. (Galatians 2:12; Acts 11:1ff.). Peter did not eat as he did previously with the heathen. Thereby his

---

285 WA 7:481.30ff.: "Hi omnes rectiora docendi sunt, tolerandi tamen in suis ritibus nec praecipitio a solitis suis opusculis praescindendi, donec paulatim et ipsi discernere possint inter opera dei et hominum, inter praecepta dei et hominum, ne fidei et morum Christianismi comunis hac violentia scindatur concordia, praesertim cum corporalia sint super quibus ita offenduntur et mere humana, potentia suo tempore mutari, fides autem et mores Christiani spiritualia sunt et res dei: quare minora toleranda sunt propter maiora servanda." Cf. WA 41:733.19ff.

286 Concerning 2 Corinthians 6:3, Luther writes in *Lent Postil*: "Two kinds of offense bring the Gospel into disgrace: In one case it is the heathen who are offended, and this because of the fact that some individuals would make the Gospel a means of freedom from temporal restraint, substituting temporal liberty for spiritual. Thus they bring reproach upon the Gospel. . . . In the other case, Christians are offended among themselves. The occasion is the indiscreet exercise of Christian liberty, which offends the weak in faith. Concerning this topic much is said in First Corinthians 8 and Romans 14. Paul here hints at what he speaks of in First Corinthians 10, 32–33: 'Give no occasion of stumbling, either to Jews, or to Greeks, or to the church of God . . .'" (Lenker 7:137 [WA 17/2:181.24ff.]). See also another sermon from 1539, WA 47:667–68 and *Lent Postil* (1525), WA 17/2:145.15ff; WA 17/2:147.15ff., 150.16ff. See Ellwein, *Luthers Epistel-Auslegung*, 2:407f., 424f., with the adduced Luther passages. Love does not consider freedom a right that can ruin the consciences of others. In the first of the 1522 Invocavit Sermons, the reformer teaches about the way of love and patience that those too zealous for reformation in Wittenberg forgot to show those who were not able to so easily leave the Roman Catholic Mass, etc. One must wait for the maturity of faith, then freedom will follow by itself (WA 8:3.5–13.1).

actions endangered the truth of the Gospel because the heathen felt forced to live according to the system of Jewish regulations to be saved.[287]

Commenting on Galatians 2:12, Luther says the following about Peter's freedom to live according to heathen or Jewish observance:

> The Gentiles who had been converted to the faith ate foods prohibited by the Law. When Peter associated with Gentile converts, he, too, ate these foods and drank forbidden wine. He knew that he was doing right when he did this, and he boldly broke the Law along with the Gentiles. Paul says that he did the same thing (1 Cor. 9:20–22): "To the Jews I became as a Jew; to those outside the Law I became as one outside the Law. That is, with the Gentiles I ate and drank like a Gentile and did not keep the Law at all; but with the Jews I lived according to the Law, abstained from pork, etc. For I made an effort to serve and please all men, that I might gain them all." When Peter acted in this same manner, therefore, he did not sin but did well; and he knew that this was permitted. For by this transgression of his he showed, on the one hand, that the Law was not necessary for righteousness; and, on the other hand, he delivered the Gentiles from the observance of the Law.[288]

Thus Peter's principal stance toward customs and regulations of the Law was rightly characterized by a freedom and flexibility to win both Jews and heathen for the Gospel. Thereby he showed that righteousness before God was not conditional on observance of the Law. It is this fundamental understanding that Peter risked

---

287 Cf. the *Commentary on Galatians* (1519), WA 2:483.32–493.18. See especially the more detailed investigation in the *Larger Commentary on Galatians*, WA 40/1:191–246. Among the literature on the conflict in question, see Holl, "Der Streit zwischen Petrus und Paulus," 134–46; Lønning, "Paulus und Petrus," 1–69; and Jensen, "Till spørsmålet om evangelium," 5–22. Luther's commentaries unforgivingly paint a picture of Peter's treachery, sometimes so pointedly that Luther can seem to doubt the apostle's teaching authority; see WA 2:447.18ff., 485.33ff.; 40/1:131f., 132.29ff. Lønning means, then, that Luther dissolves the personal-historical apostolate as a mediator of absolute truth. Only preaching from a Gospel constantly cleansed of human traditions can be absolute. Jensen's critique of Lønning is in general correct, even if a certain exaggeration caused by Luther's severe language ought to have been more appreciated. Luther has said that all apostles have taught the same, true Gospel. Concerning this point, see the *Commentary on Galatians* (1519), WA 2:451.23ff., 454.23ff., 462.8ff., 467.11, 471.35ff., 481.25ff. Cf. the *Larger Commentary on Galatians*, WA 40/1:186.25ff., 189.18ff., and other texts, such as WA 12:362ff.; 20:613.15ff.; 36:526.39ff.; 37:39ff.; 39/1:184.4ff. In "Disputation de potestate concilii (1536)," WA 39/1:194.28f., Luther says this about the controversy in Antioch: "Petrus non docendo, sed simulando peccavit. Cadere autem in vita aliud est, quam errare in fide." So Luther has insisted that Peter taught the truth of the Gospel. Cf. about the apostolate, *Luther and World Mission*, 287ff.

288 LW 26:110 (WA 40/1:198.19ff.).

in his collusion with the Judaizers in Antioch. Luther writes this on Galatians 2:12:

> Here you see Peter's sin. . . . He [Paul] accuses Peter of weakness, not of malice or ignorance. Peter was afraid of the Jews who had come from James, and he fell on account of his fear of them; for he did not want to scandalize them in this way. Thus he was more concerned about the Jews than about the Gentiles and was responsible for endangering Christian freedom and the truth of the Gospel. By drawing back, separating himself, and avoiding foods prohibited by the Law—foods which he had previously eaten—he injected a scruple into the consciences of the faithful, who could draw this conclusion from his actions: "Peter abstains from foods prohibited by the Law. Therefore whoever eats foods prohibited by the Law sins and transgresses the Law, but whoever abstains is righteous and keeps the Law. Otherwise Peter would not have drawn back."[289]

In his comprehensive commentaries on the drama of the tables in Antioch, Luther consistently guards the fundamental freedom from regulations of the Law, the truth of the Gospel, and justification through faith alone. If one gives in to the Law and zealots, then the Gospel of Christ and faith can be experienced as conditional. In the work of God's reign, one ought never pay such a price. If this occurs, the radical Gospel of grace is lost. The Law belongs to the earthly regiment, to the earthly call, and to the sinful nature or the flesh. The Gospel belongs to heaven, to faith, and to the heart.[290]

Luther often comments on the importance of guarding Christian freedom, especially, among other places, in a 1525 sermon on 1 Timothy 1:3–7. Concerning vv. 3–4, Luther emphasizes that one may in a Jewish context, along with the apostles, live according to Jewish customs and laws and in a heathen context live according to their customs and laws. This occurs freely so one might not block the reception of the Gospel. But one must absolutely oppose every attempt to make salvation conditional on the Law and regulations.[291]

---

289 LW 26:110 (WA 40/1:199.19ff.).

290 On Galatians 2:13–16, WA 40/1:203ff. Cf. WA 2:487.35ff.

291 WA 17/1:104.20ff. See especially WA 17/1:106.13ff., 106.30ff.: "Darumb wenn du yemand hörist, der da sagt: so und so mustu thuen, und wil dasselbige thun odder werck auff dein gewissen treiben und gegen Gott stellen, so wisse, das es gewis des teuffels lere ist, und sonder die zwey so weit von einander wie hymel und erden, tag und nacht . . . . Desgleichen sage auch mit andern wercken, so man thuet gegen dem nehisten, Als wenn ich, wo ich bey den Juden wer, mit yhn esse, was sie essen, desgleichen auch mit den heyden, halte mich nach der leut wesen und gesetz und richte mich ynn yhre werck, so halte ich allerley gesetz und habe doch ym gewissen kein gesetz, denn ich die werck nicht thue der meynung, als darzu gezwungen oder dadurch fur Got frum zu werden." Cf. WA 17:107.15ff., 108.12ff. about the apostles' voluntary obser-

In sum, Luther teaches this concerning the stance of both foreign and domestic mission toward immature Christians and those oppressed by the Law: First, those who are free ought not force those bound by their consciences to live against their convictions; instead, they should allow them to mature in faith and thereby in freedom. Second, love's sensitivity and care for the weak in faith ought not be allowed to develop in such a way that those who press the Law, the regulations, and human commands dominate the field. Mission and evangelization sometimes demand accommodations and compromises of love, but one must be careful not thereby to strengthen a legalism that endangers the Gospel and the righteousness of faith.

The work of God's reign, sanctification, and parenesis *

We already have seen in chapter 2 (pp. 64–81) and chapter 3 (pp. 199–205) how energetically Luther emphasizes that humanity becomes righteous before God only through faith in Christ. The communication of this message is the main task of mission and evangelization, and here the reformer builds, above all, on the teaching of Paul. We know, however, that the apostles gave the newly founded congregations a comprehensive ethical teaching about the Christian's personal and social life. Christians were not allowed through an unbridled lifestyle to risk the work of mission. What significance does this apostolic teaching have for Luther?

Did Luther teach something about sanctification? Within Luther scholarship, there are a number of different interpretations of the reformer's teaching on sanctification. On the basis of Kantian philosophy, neo-Protestantism's great representatives—A. Ritschl, W. Herrmann, and Adolf von Harnack—opposed generally and systematically the idea that one should speak of God's/Christ's real-ontic indwelling in faith and in the faithful. The relationship with God was not to be demoted to such a heathen nature religion. It had more to do with the personal-ethical and the will. R. Herrmann, Regin Prenter, and others contributed to this discussion by speaking about nature and person; thereby there was little room left for the idea of a real renewal on the basis of faith and grace. The Christian's life

---

vance of the Law in a Jewish context and the freedom of the heathens from the yoke of the Law (Acts 15:10ff.). Luther also shows how the Gospel of the Reformation must struggle against the new legalism of the enthusiasts.

* *Publisher's Note*: The position of historic, orthodox Lutheranism—and the position of all who regard the Lutheran Confessions as a normative expression of the Lutheran Church and who look to Luther as the foremost teacher of the churches of the Augsburg Confession—is that there is in fact a parenetic use of the Law for Christians. This fact is taught and maintained in the Formula of Concord and does not contradict Luther's own teaching.

under the aspect of sanctification became mostly a constant new beginning, a *semper a novo incipere*.

Against these interpretations of Luther, Axel Gyllenkrok, Manfred Schloen-bach, Paul Althaus, and Wilfried Joest, among others, presented Luther material that spoke of a growth brought about by faith and the Spirit, that is, a real renewal. Furthermore, O. Modalsli and Peter Manns have analyzed incisively Luther's ideas on faith and love, his ideas about justifying faith *per se* (*fides absoluta*), and about the faith that includes good works, love of neighbor, and the struggle against the flesh (*fides concreta* or *fides incarnata*). Later, the Helsinki School under Tuomo Mannermaa—to open a dialogue with the Orthodox theologians in the East and their theosis doctrine (among other reasons)—has shown that Luther reckons both with an inner fellowship of the will and an inner dwelling of God when he speaks of justification and sanctification. In Jesus Christ, *iustificatio* and *inhabitatio Dei* are one and the same. Christ is present in faith both as favor (*favor*) and as gift (*donum*). The Luther phrase *in ipsa fide Christus adest* means that humanity through faith receives Christ for justification and at the same time in him shares divine life. Those who have focused on the sanctification motif in Luther have discovered something important. We only hope that one does not swing over to a new understanding, such as that of Andreas Osiander, in which the Christ *in us* replaces the Christ *for us*, that is, the radical Gospel.[292]

---

292 Among the literature, see especially Gyllenkrok, *Rechtfertigung und Heiligung*, and Schloenbach, *Heiligung als Fortschreiten*. Schloenbach opposes the scholarly contributions of, among others, R. Herrmann, J. Haar, and Regin Prenter, who have difficulty accepting any proposal that Luther spoke of a real renewal among the faithful. Helpful analyses of faith and sanctification in Luther include O. Modalsli, *Das Gericht nach den Werken* (1963), 17–51. Modalsli opposes Holl's thesis that God justifies in an analytical-proleptic judgment by including the sanctification that will be born of a justifying faith (27ff.). See Manns, "*Fides absoluta—fides incarnata*," 1–48. On the basis of the *Larger Commentary on Galatians*, Manns has shown how Luther with·faith *per se* unites a so-called concrete or incarnated faith with the idea that faith forms or gives birth to love. Cf. WA 40/1:228.27ff. Other important interpretations of Luther's position include Althaus, *Die Theologie Martin Luthers*, 195–218; Bring, *Förhållandet mellan tro och gärningar inom luthersk teologi*, 174ff; Bring, *Gesetz und Evangelium*, 46ff.; Joest, *Gesetz und Freiheit*, 57ff., 66ff.; and Ljunggren, *Synd och skuld i Luthers teologi*, 349ff. Among the recent scholarly contributions that emphasize a true renewal on the basis of a real-ontic presence of God-Christ in faith and in the faithful, the following Finnish works by Mannermaa ought to be named: "In ipsa fide Christus adest," "Das Verhältnis von Glaube und Liebe in der Theologie Luthers," "Grundlagenforschung der Theologie Martin Luthers und die Ökumene," and *Der im Glauben gegenwärtige Christus*; as well as Huovinen, "An der Unsterblichkeit teilhaftig," and Peura, "Der Vergöttlichungsgedanke in Luthers Theologie." On the Formula of Concord's dispute with Osiander's view of Christ's indwelling as the basis of justification, see FC SD III (K-W, 562ff.).

For any investigation of Luther's view of apostolic parenesis, it is important to keep in mind that the reformer has in fact understood the importance of speaking of a renewal in the faithful through faith and that it is brought about by the Spirit. Luther teaches as completely decisive that Christ is the only *Eckstein* ("cornerstone") of salvation. Only through faith in Christ can one become righteous before God. But faith alone never remains alone because with faith and grace the Holy Spirit follows, and he gives birth to a new heart and lifestyle. Therefore Luther speaks of faith and love, of justification and God's/Christ's indwelling, about faith in relationship to God and love in relationship to other humans. This is simply a fact, and there is nothing else to expect of the reformer who continues to proclaim his *sola Scriptura*.[293]

The nature of evangelical parenesis. It is one thing to speak of faith and love and another to get them to function. The function of faith and sanctification is opposed by Satan, the world, and the flesh. Luther means that the Christian is drawn into a struggle between God and Satan, spirit and flesh. It is at this juncture that he introduces parenesis, that is, a preaching that will stimulate the Christian to good works and the struggle against the flesh. If the reformer in the context of justification preaches Christ against all works of the Law, so he preaches to the justified about Christ and his example, about faith and the fruit of faith. H. Ivarsson has investigated this issue in a worthwhile doctoral dissertation. Christ is preached as the main theme and foundation of salvation, but the other main theme of love is preached for those who through faith possess Christ. Ivarsson shows that to a high degree the reformer understands parenesis in a different way than the orthodox and pietist theologians. He understands Christ as example and the apostolic pare-

---

293 In *Himmelrikets nycklar och kyrklig bot i Luthers teologi*, 187–96, I have reviewed many passages in Luther on this subject, among others, on faith/love (WA 7:21.18ff.; 15:624.19ff.; 29:31ff.; 34/2:173f.; 36:357.31ff., 416–68); on faith/good works (WA 26:24.10ff.; 32:28.20ff., 96.8ff., 210ff., 318ff.; 34/2:298.16ff.; 40/1:22.13ff.; 40/2:59ff.); on faith toward God/love toward neighbor (WA 7:65.26ff.; 15:626.10ff.; 32:6.35ff.; 34/1:360.12ff.; 36:372.1ff.); on tree/fruit (WA 7:61.26ff.; 15:661.16ff.; 29:496.19ff.; 32:318ff.; 39/1:46.28ff.); and on how works of love confirm the presence of faith (WA 15:624.29ff.; 20:715.15ff.; 32:423.18ff.; 34/2:299.7ff.). "The Freedom of a Christian (1520)" expresses this pregnant relationship between faith and love: "We conclude, therefore, that a Christian lives not in himself, but in Christ and in his neighbor. Otherwise he is not a Christian. He lives in Christ through faith, in his neighbor through love. By faith he is caught up beyond himself into God. By love he descends beneath himself into his neighbor. Yet he always remains in God and in his love" (LW 31:371 translates the Latin version [WA 7:38.6ff.]). The Helsinki School has presented, among others, the following Luther texts about *inhabitio Dei et Christi* in faith and the connection of this indwelling with sanctification: WA 1:29.26ff.; 17/1:438.14ff.; 17/2:74.20ff.; 20:698.12ff.; 21:458.11ff.; 40/1:228.34ff., 283.7ff. About love as the fulfillment of the Law and as a product of faith in Christ, see WA 17/2:98.13ff., 102.27ff.

nesis neither as an accusing/revealing Law (*usus spiritualis legis*) nor as the guidance of the Law for the lifestyle of the faithful (*tertius usus legis*). Luther teaches that parenesis constitutes a continuation of the Gospel, its extension and natural consequence. Parenesis is fundamentally not a preaching of the Law. It springs from and presupposes the Gospel and faith. Christ's example and the apostolic parenesis ought to incite, encourage, and stimulate to good works as a fruit of faith, forgiveness, and the life of the Spirit. Perhaps Ivarsson ought to have more powerfully emphasized that exhortation in Paul and Luther aims both at love of neighbor and at the dying of the sinful nature.[294]

In the beginning of the 1522 *Church Postil*, Luther teaches clearly about what one ought to seek in the Gospel. He points out first that all parts of the New Testament have one single Gospel. But the Gospel contains the following components: (1) the main theme of Christ as gift and (2) the consequent theme of Christ as example. It ought to be emphasized that even parenesis is understood as part of the sum of the Gospel. Luther writes:

> The chief article and foundation of the gospel is that before you take Christ as an example, you accept and recognize him as a gift, as a present that God has given you and that is your own. . . . See, this is what it means to have a proper grasp of the gospel, that is, of the overwhelming goodness of God . . . See, when you lay hold of Christ as a gift which is given you for your very own and have no doubt about it, you are a Christian. Faith redeems you from sin, death, and hell and enables you to overcome all things . . . then the other part follows: that you take him as your example, giving yourself in service to your neighbor just as you see that Christ has given himself for you. . . . Christ as a gift nourishes your faith and makes you a Christian. But Christ as an example exercises your works. These do not make you a Christian. Actually they come forth from you because you have already been made a Christian.[295]

---

294 See Ivarsson, *Predikans uppgift*, 113–63. On the preaching of Christ as "*hewtstuck und grund*" and on preaching about love of neighbor as "*das ander stuck*," see *Christmas Postil*, WA 10/1.1:11.8ff., 75.20ff.; and *Advent Postil*, WA 10/1.2:22.6ff. Concerning the origin of parenesis in the Gospel and its nature as "*reytzen und locken*," see Ivarsson, *Predikans uppgift*, 118ff. Concerning the too weak emphasis on the dying of the sinful nature, see Ivarsson, *Predikans uppgift*, 135ff.

295 "A Brief Instruction on What to Look for and Expect in the Gospels," LW 35:119–20 (WA 10/1.1:11.12–12.20). In the 1522 *Church Postil*, Luther expresses the same theme while preaching on Titus 3:4–7; see WA 10/1.1:95.17ff., 99.20ff., 102.8ff., 107ff., 112ff. Cf. also the 1522/1546 foreword to Romans (WADB 7:17.20ff., 19.17ff.) and *Bondage of the Will* (1525) (WA 18:692f.). It ought to be emphasized that preaching about works or about Christ as example does not mean that one presents the "framework of the Law" in which a Christian ought to live. Love is *per se* the spontaneous fruit of

This extraordinarily pregnant statement about Christ as a gift received in faith and as an example of self-sacrifice and spontaneous love constitutes the blueprint for preaching according to Luther.

The reformer expressly says that preaching about the works of the faithful ought not be understood as the commandments, covenants, and threats of Moses' Law. As Jesus introduced his ethical teaching in the Sermon on the Mount with the Beatitudes (Matthew 5:3–12), so ought preaching's parenesis spring from the Gospel and be a stimulation to, prayer for, and exhortation to good works. Apostolic parenesis does not taste of the threat of the Law. Love says, "I admonish, I request, I beseech."[296]

Some examples of parenesis in Luther. In a 1522 sermon on Romans 13:11–14, Luther notices that there are two parts to apostolic preaching. The first part is a teaching, or *doctrina*, that has the task of enlightening those who do not know and do not believe. The second part that is actualized by the text is a parenesis, or exhortation, that aims to incite, encourage, and inspire to a life in sanctification those who both know and believe.[297]

Luther sings something of a *magnificat* about how the Gospel about Christ leads humanity in all times and moves them from the sleep of unbelief toward the sun and light of salvation, Jesus Christ.[298] This is foundational to a right preaching. Then he reviews Paul's exhortations in Romans. Those who believe and truly know how they ought to live are exhorted and reminded because the enemies—

---

faith, even if it needs to be inspired and preached. See Ivarsson, *Predikans uppgift*, 125ff., who refers to Bring, *Förhållandet mellan tro och gärningar inom luthersk teologi*, and Wingren, *Skapelsen och lagen*, 58f. Ivarsson is cautious about Joest's (*Gesetz und Freiheit*, 74, 132, 154) coupling of the works of faith to the commandments.

296 LW 35:121 (WA 10/1.1:13.15).

297 *Advent Postil* (1522), Lenker 6:9 (WA 10/1.2:1.12ff.): "This epistle lesson treats not of faith, but of its fruits, or works. It teaches how a Christian should conduct himself outwardly in his relations to other men upon earth. But how we should walk in the spirit before God, comes under the head of faith. . . . A close consideration of our passage shows it to be not didactic; rather it is meant to incite, to exhort, urge and arouse souls already aware of their duty. Paul in Romans 12, 7–8 devotes the office of ministry to two things, doctrine and exhortation. The doctrinal part consists in preaching truths not generally known; in instructing and enlightening the people. Exhortation is inciting and urging the duties already well understood. Necessarily both obligations claim the attention of the minister, and hence Paul takes up both." Cf. WA 10/1.2:11.17ff., 15.15ff. One of the merits of Ivarsson's study is that despite the fact that he places the main accent on preaching as the absolving Gospel and a stimulation to faith, he does not one-sidedly overlook the teaching element; see Ivarsson, *Predikans uppgift*, 61ff., with the references.

298 WA 10/1.2:4.14–10.13.

Satan and the flesh—easily make them lazy and careless. According to Luther, to be a Christian means that one is in a vulnerable position, a life in struggle with Satan, the flesh, and spiritual laziness. Parenesis ought to sharpen faith's vigilance and give strength against the forces of evil.[299]

Luther's parenesis is often highly concrete. In Romans 13:13, Paul says, "Let us behave decently, as in the daytime, not in orgies and drunkenness, not in sexual immorality and debauchery, not in dissension and jealousy." With John 3:20–21, Luther says that those who do what is wrong hate and shun the light, while those who live according to the truth come to and live in the light. Many Christians also live so carelessly in regards to goodness, righteousness, and truth that they must hide their works. According to Luther, Christians are drawn into a struggle with Satan, the world, and the flesh, a struggle between unbelief on the one hand and Christ and faith on the other hand. Here there is struggle and pain because the field of battle is the heart and the limbs. For this reason, the war trumpets of exhortation are necessary strengthening signals. But the power for works of the light originates in the Gospel and faith, while all the works of darkness and light-shunning carelessness flow from unbelief.[300]

With incisive and great concretion and on the basis of 1 Thessalonians 5:6; Galatians 5:19–21; and Colossians 3:5–9, Luther exhorts Christians to flee from all the obvious works of darkness, such as revelry, drunkenness, adultery, and sexual immorality. On the basis of Ephesians 4:32 and Galatians 5:20, he encourages them to flee all sins such as hate and divisions. Sin is seen both as harmful for the sinner and for the neighbor.[301]

The parenesis in Romans 13:14 also communicates positively how a Christian ought to clothe himself or herself in Christ through faith. This putting on of Christ is first believing that Christ has died and atoned for sins. But Luther also

---

299 WA 10/1.2:11.23ff., 12.4ff.

300 WA 10/1.2:13.1–14.3. About the function of exhortation in Paul, Luther writes: "Not the works of darkness but the works of light he terms 'armor.' And why 'armor' rather than 'works'? Doubtless to teach that only at the cost of conflicts, pain, labor and danger will the truly watchful and godly life be maintained; for these three powerful enemies, the devil, the world and the flesh, unceasingly oppose us day and night. Hence Job (ch 7,1) regards the life of man on earth as a life of trial and warfare. Now, it is no easy thing to stand always in battle array during the whole of life. Good trumpets and bugles are necessary preaching and exhortation of the sort to enable us valiantly to maintain our position in battle" (Lenker 6:18–19 [WA 10/1.2:12.4ff.]). Lenker 6:19 (WA 10/1.2:12.18ff.): "Now, as already made plain, the word 'light' here carries the thought of 'faith.' The light of faith, in the Gospel day, shines from Christ the Sun into our hearts. The armor of light, then, is simply the works of faith. . . . The 'works of darkness' are, therefore, the 'works of unbelief.' "

301 WA 10/1.2:14.13–15.13.

immediately connects Christ as a gift with Christ as an example and model. On the basis of 1 Corinthians 15:49; Ephesians 4:22–24; Colossians 3:12–15; Philippians 2:1–2, 5–7; Galatians 5:22; and 2 Corinthians 6:1–10, Luther encourages Christians to be sanctified according to Christ's example. He exhorts Christians to lay aside the sinful nature and to put on Christ in truth, righteousness, and holiness. Christians are encouraged as God's holy and beloved people to live in goodness, humility, patience, love, forgiveness, peace, and good works toward one another. A Christian must not live so she or he becomes a stumbling block and an impediment for the Gospel. It is another matter that a decent Christian is often hated by the world without reason.[302] As we see in the commentary on Romans 13:11–14, the accent in parenesis is to a high degree on help and stimulation for the struggle to kill the flesh, that is, the sinful nature in all its aspects. As usual the Scripture passage itself determines where the emphasis in parenesis ought to be. Luther's sermon is, after all, a homily that strives to stick close to the text.

In the 1525 *Lent Postil*, an Epiphany sermon summarizes the message of all the earlier sermons. Luther says that he has preached on faith, love, and the cross/suffering.[303] On the basis of Romans 12:1–5, Luther focuses on the putting to death of the flesh, on love, harmony, and patience. What is the source of this? External and brilliant works that one might find, for example, among the monks are not evidence of this putting to death of the flesh. It is, instead, a work of grace in all layers of the human subject, a sacrifice with and in Christ.[304] Luther says that the apostle uses the exalted word *sacrifice* to exhort the faithful to struggle against the sinful nature because reason, the human heart, and the world are repulsed by any notion of putting to death.[305] It is a putting to death and a spiritual sacrifice

---

302 Luther comments on Romans 13:14: "Christ is 'put on' in two ways. First, we may clothe ourselves with his virtues. This is effected through the faith that relies on the fact of Christ having in his death accomplished all for us. For not our righteousness, but the righteousness of Christ, reconciled us to God and redeemed us from sin. This manner of putting on Christ is treated of in the doctrine concerning faith; it gives Christ to us as a gift and a pledge. . . . Secondly, Christ being our example and pattern, whom we are to follow and copy, clothing ourselves in the virtuous garment of his walk" (Lenker 6:22 [WA 10/1.2:15.15ff.]). On the positive fruits of the Christian life in goodness, love, unity, peace, etc., see WA 10/1.2:15.14–17.21. These ideas are often developed in the *Advent Postil*. Cf. WA 10/1.2:76ff., 80ff., 120ff., 170ff.

303 WA 17/2:5.17f., 9.17ff.

304 WA 17/2:6.11–25. Cf. Lenker 7:12 (WA 17/2:9.21f.): "What more would one, or could one, offer than himself, all he is and all he has?" Cf. WA 17/2:11.32ff.

305 WA 17/2:6.1ff., 7.24ff., 8.1ff., 10.21ff. About the spiritual sacrifice's greatness and about how the world, reason, and the human heart are negative toward this temple service, see WA 17/2:7.3ff., 11.19ff., 13.2ff. Cf. also the exposition of 1 Corinthians 5:6–8 in Cruziger's 1544 *Summer Postil* (WA 21:203–14). Luther preaches extensively that faith

that can occur only in the power of the Spirit because it is a struggle against the entire natural humanity and must occur joyfully, freely, and spontaneously. This putting to death and sacrifice—the sacrificial animal is killed before it is sacrificed—does not occur if one lives under the threat of the Law and fear of punishment or if one seeks wages and honor from God.[306]

Parenesis ought to stimulate a God-pleasing putting to death/sacrifice. With Romans 12:1, Luther emphasizes that parenesis will not be revealed by the Law but will proceed from the Gospel about God's mercy in Christ. Therefore parenesis is not a switch of the Law that beats the Christians but a beckoning, encouraging, and hastening to a new life on the basis of God's good works. Only such an evangelical encouragement begets willing hearts in the struggle against sin and engages such hearts in good works that give God glory and become help for fellow human beings.[307] On the basis of 1 Corinthians 6:19f., the reformer describes this sacrifice and this temple service of faith as something completely theocentric: ". . . we let God alone work in us and we be simply his holy instruments."[308]

Therefore a Christian ought first to exercise faith in trusting the cross of Christ as the source of salvation and grace. Second, Christians ought to practice serving their neighbor in self-sacrifice with the cross of Christ as an example. Christ's sacrifice opposes any notion of self-righteousness. The emerging works of

---

in Christ makes us all participants in atonement's sacrificial Lamb, partly to transform us into a new, sweet dough. Through the power of the Spirit, we ought constantly to work to purge the old sour dough and to live honestly and righteously. A right faith in Christ does not allow itself to live according to the flesh.

306 WA 17/2:6.11ff., 7.25ff., 8.1ff., 10.7ff.

307 On Romans 12:1, Luther says: " 'I beseech you therefore, brethren.' . . . He is preaching to those already godly Christians through faith in the new man; to hearers who are not to be constrained by commandments, but to be admonished. For the object is to secure voluntary renunciation of their old, sinful, Adam-like nature. He who will not cheerfully respond to friendly admonition is no Christian. And he who attempts by the restraints of law to compel the unwilling to renunciation, is no Christian preacher or ruler; he is but a worldly jailer" (Lenker 7:11 [WA 17/2:8.30ff.]). On encouraging/exhorting, see Lenker 7:11–12 (WA 17/2:9.4ff.): " 'By the mercies of God.' A teacher of the Law enforces his restraints through threats and punishments. A preacher of grace persuades and incites by calling attention to the goodness and mercy of God. The latter does not desire works prompted by an unwilling spirit, or service that is not the expression of a cheerful heart. He desires that a joyous, willing spirit shall incite to the service of God. He who cannot, by the gracious and lovely message of God's mercy so lavishly bestowed upon us in Christ, be persuaded in a spirit of love and delight to contribute to the honor of God and the benefit of his neighbor, is worthless to Christianity, and all effort is lost on him."

308 Lenker 7:14 (WA 17/2:11.8f.).

love have fellow humanity as receptor, and they have their source of power in Jesus Christ.[309]

The reformer presents many Bible passages to support and to emphasize the temple service, that is, the putting to death of the sinful nature and the serving of the neighbor.[310] He means that a real renewal occurs when faith and the Spirit are given place.[311] But the necessity of apostolic parenesis witnesses to the fact that complete sanctification is never attained in time. The sinful nature is first cast off completely only on resurrection day.[312]

In the 1522/1546 foreword to Galatians, Luther touches on the fruit of faith and the Spirit in good works.[313] Luther also writes about this quite extensively in the commentaries on Galatians from 1519 and 1531/1535.[314] I will focus my analysis here primarily on the latter commentary, which in an especially clear manner explains sanctification and parenesis. In connection with Galatians 5:6–15, Luther reviews the systematic connection between faith, the Spirit, and renewal and Pauline parenesis. When Paul speaks in Galatians 5:6 of "a faith

---

309 Lenker 7:9 (WA 17/2:7.11ff.): "As I have frequently stated, the suffering and work of Christ is to be viewed in two lights: First, as grace bestowed on us, as a blessing conferred, requiring the exercise of faith on our part and our acceptance of the salvation offered. Second, we are to regard it an example for us to follow; we are to offer up ourselves for our neighbors' benefit and for the honor of God. This offering is the exercise of our love—distributing our works for the benefit of our neighbors. He who so does is a Christian. He becomes one with Christ, and the offering of his body is identical with the offering of Christ's body. This is what Peter calls offering sacrifices acceptable to God by Christ. . . . 1 Peter 2:5."

310 WA 17/2:10ff. refers to the following passages among others: Romans 8:13; Colossians 3:3; Galatians 5:24; 2 Corinthians 10:3; Romans 8:1; 1 Corinthians 6:19f.; Galatians 6:17; 1 Corinthians 3:16.

311 Lenker 7:16 (WA 17/2:13.6ff.): "So shall we be daily changed—renewed in our minds. That is, we come each day to place greater value on the things condemned by human reason—by the world. Daily we prefer to be poor, sick and despised, to be fools and sinners, until ultimately we regard death as better than life, foolishness as more precious than wisdom, shame nobler than honor." Cf. WA 17/2:13.19–29.

312 Lenker 7:17 (WA 17/2:13.30ff.): "Paul, you will observe, does not consider the Christian absolutely free from sin, since he beseeches us to be 'transformed by the renewing of the mind.' [Rom 12:2] Where transformation and renewal are necessary, something of the old and sinful nature must yet remain." See also WA 17/2:13.28f. Cf. WA 21:208–10.

313 WADB 7:173.23ff.

314 WA 2:565–605; 40/2:34–146. Among the literature about faith and works in the commentaries on Galatians, we might name K. Bornkamm, *Luthers Auslegungen des Galaterbriefs*, especially 76ff., 325ff., 316ff., 361ff.; Manns, "*Fides absoluta—fides incarnata*," 1–48; and Modalsli, *Das Gericht nach den Werken*, 39ff.

active in love," the problem is brought into sharp focus. Against the Roman Catholic doctrine of *fides caritate formata*, that is, that only faith formed through love counts before God, Luther says that it is faith that justifies and is active in love. He says:

> ... but [Paul] speaks of "faith working through love." He says that works are done on the basis of faith through love, not that a man is justified through love. ... For Paul's words are clear and plain: "faith *working* through love." ... [H]e attributes the working itself to faith rather than to love. He does not suppose that it is some sort of shapeless and unformed quality; but he declares that it is an effective and active something. ... He does not say: "Love is effective." No, he says: "Faith is effective." He does not say: "Love works." No, he says: "Faith works." He makes love the tool through which faith works. Now who does not know that a tool has its power, movement, and action, not from itself but from the artisan who works with it or uses it? For who would say that an axe gives the power and motion of cutting to a carpenter, or that a ship gives the power and motion of sailing to a sailor? Or, to cite an example used by Isaiah (10:15), who would say: "The saw wields the carpenter, and the staff lifts the hand?"[315]

This citation shows that Luther intensively opposes any notion that faith formed by love (*fides caritate formata*) might replace justifying faith (*fides iustificans*). He also energetically declares that faith is the source of or is active in love. Christ as gift and Christ as example corresponds to this idea. The former is foundational, that is, the source from which the power of discipleship flows.[316]

When the reformer exhorts and says that the human justified by faith will bear the fruits of gratitude in love and good works, then the fellow human in need of

---

315 LW 27:28–29 (*original emphasis*) (WA 40/2:35.24ff.).

316 Observe Luther's words opposing *fides caritate formata*: "Such are the dreams of the scholastics. But where they speak of love, we speak of faith. ... we say in opposition that faith takes hold of Christ and that He is the form that adorns and informs faith as color does the wall. Therefore Christian faith is not an idle quality or an empty husk in the heart" (LW 26:129 [WA 40/1:228.27ff.]). Cf. also the discussion of Bible passages in which faith is spoken of as involving works and how Luther argues against the Catholic doctrine of salvation through a faith formed by love, WA 40/1:224ff. At this point, I want especially to point out Luther's wrestling with Paul's parenesis in love's highest hymn, 1 Corinthians 13:1–13. In connection with this passage, Luther argues against *fides caritate formata*. On the other hand, the text provides Luther with an occasion for extensive comments on how a faith without resulting love and a resulting struggle against the sinful natural is an impossibility. A right faith cannot exist without fruit; instead, right faith proves its substance in love and service to the neighbor. See WA 17/2:161–71; 34/1:162–70; 49:25–29, 351–52. See also Ellwein, *Luthers Epistel-Auslegung*, 2:173ff.

help consistently stands in the center. Luther says this in connection with Galatians 5:6:

> As I have said, therefore, Paul is describing the whole of the Christian life in this passage: inwardly it is faith toward God, and outwardly it is love or works toward one's neighbor. Thus a man is a Christian in a total sense: inwardly through faith in the sight of God, who does not need our works; outwardly in the sight of men, who do not derive any benefit from faith but do derive benefit from works or from our love.[317]

It is clear from this passage that Luther's radicalness concerning the doctrine of justification in no way opposes love and good works toward the neighbor. It is just that person who is justified and free in regard to God whose eyes are opened to the needs of the neighbor. Works are not needed for salvation so they can instead be directed toward the need of the neighbor.

Luther works through this theme especially in connection with Galatians 5:13–14 where he opposes the freedom of the sinful nature to freedom of the Spirit in service to the neighbor. Luther is clearly upset when he describes how people in Germany interpret Christian freedom as a right to do whatever they want, to give themselves over to lust, to exploit others, and to indulge in all kinds of sin.[318] He says:

> . . . the apostle imposes an obligation on Christians through this law about mutual love in order to keep them from abusing their freedom. Therefore the godly should remember that for the sake of Christ they are free in their conscience before God from the curse of the Law, from sin, and from death, but that according to the body they are bound; here each must serve the other through love, in accordance with this commandment of Paul. Therefore let everyone strive to do his duty in his calling and to help his neighbor in whatever way he can. This is what Paul requires of us with the words "through love be servants of one another," which do not permit the saints to run free according to the flesh but subject them to an obligation.[319]

Luther says parenthetically that Christians through faith have consciences freed from the curse of the Law. However, from the outside, humanity appears burdened by the law of love. It is also worth noting how love of neighbor ought to be focused on the tasks of the earthly call or the natural contexts of life. In its service of love, humanity driven by faith and the Spirit is set right in the middle of the tasks of everyday life, not in some special tasks but in the natural.

---

317 LW 27:30 (WA 40/2:37.26ff.).

318 WA 40/2:59ff.

319 LW 27:49–50 (WA 40/2:62.1ff.).

In Galatians 5:14 (cf. Romans 13:9), Luther considers these words, "The entire law is summed up in a single command: 'Love your neighbor as yourself.'" In this verse, Paul focuses on the Golden Rule as love of neighbor.[320] In his extensive review, Luther criticizes the Roman Catholic theologians who define "love" merely as well-meaning or as a condition of the heart, that is, as a conceptual love without concretion and activity. These so-called sophists, as well as the so-called enthusiasts, do not understand what good works are but have bad consciences for trifles about places, times, food, clothing, etc. According to Luther, all this depends on the fact that they have not understood the secret of faith in Christ. "When a tree has been chopped down, its fruit must also perish," says Luther.[321] He also says:

> Therefore the apostle admonishes Christians seriously, after they have heard and accepted the pure doctrine about faith, to practice genuine works as well. . . . This is why faithful preachers must exert themselves as much in urging a love that is unfeigned or in urging truly good works as in teaching true faith. . . . Thus the words "Through love be servants of one another" and "You shall love your neighbor as yourself" are eternal words, which no one can adequately ponder, teach, and practice.[322]

It is obvious, therefore, that preaching about good works is important in mission/evangelization.

Luther points out that the Golden Rule is inscribed on the heart of natural humanity. However, because of the work of the devil, natural humanity's reason is so blinded that it can neither understand what love is nor what good works are. Therefore it must be taught and encouraged to love the neighbor.[323] This love toward the neighbor does not have anything to do with laws, food, drink, religious

---

320 WA 40/2:64–74. Cf. the *Commentary on Galatians* (1519), WA 2:575–82. See also concerning the fulfilling of the Law and the Golden Rule, WA 17/2:98.13ff., 102.27ff. Mannermaa shows how the Christ present in faith is love and produces the love that is the fulfillment of the Law; see "Das Verhältnis von Glaube und Liebe in der Theologie Luthers," 104ff. The humanity of faith loves its neighbor as Christ himself loves the neighbor.

321 LW 27:52.

322 LW 27:54 (WA 40/2:67.33ff.).

323 LW 27:53 (WA 40/2:66.33ff.): "Satan's hatred for truly good works is evident also from this: All men have a certain natural knowledge implanted in their minds (Rom. 2:14–15), by which they know naturally that one should do to others what he wants done to himself (Matt. 7:12). This principle and others like it, which we call the law of nature, are the foundation of human law and of all good works. Nevertheless, human reason is so corrupted and blinded by the malice of the devil that it does not understand this inborn knowledge; or, even if it has been admonished by the Word of God, it deliberately neglects and despises it. So great is the power of Satan!" Cf. concerning this rather reserved estimation of *lex naturae*, WA 40/2:71.22ff. See also *Luther and World Mission*, 32–35, 64–81.

festivals, and external sacrifices of this or that. Love and service to neighbor are exercised wherever one meets people in need of help. Love and service to neighbor are exercised in the trivialities of daily life, in the wear and tear of human relationships, and in the earthly vocation that one is given. Especially Gustaf Wingren has argued that love and service ought to occur in the natural arena of life, in that which is near at hand.[324] The reformer emphasizes that the neighbor is the object of our love and service. Indeed, all fellow humans, even enemies, ought to be served in love. Love does not screen those whom ought to love, but it conquers evil with good and abides all.[325] Finally, Luther summarizes the doctrine about faith and good works with the following words:

> This is why Paul commends love to the Galatians and to all Christians, and exhorts them through love to be servants of one another. It is as though he were saying: "There is no need to burden you with circumcision and the ceremonies of Moses. But above all persevere in the doctrine of faith, which you have received from me. Afterwards, if you want to do good works, I will show you in one word the highest and greatest works, and the way to keep all the laws: Be devoted to one another through love. You will not lack for people to help, for the world is full of people who need the help of others." This is the perfect doctrine of both faith and love. It is also the shortest and the longest kind of theology.[326]

---

324 WA 40/2:70.11ff., 70.24ff. See especially LW 27:57 (WA 40/2:71.32ff.): "The blindness of human reason is so incomprehensible and infinite that it cannot form sound judgments even about life and works, much less about the doctrine of faith. Therefore we must battle unremittingly not only against the opinions of our own heart, on which by nature we would rather depend in the matter of salvation than on the Word of God, but also against the false front and saintly appearance of self-chosen works. Thus we shall learn to praise the works that each man performs in his calling—even though in external appearance they appear to be trivial and contemptible—provided that they have been commanded by God, and, on the other hand, to despise the works that reason decides upon without a commandment from God, regardless of how brilliant, important, great, or saintly they seem to be." Cf. Wingren, *Luthers lära om kallelsen*, 135ff., who presents innumerable texts about works in the given call. See also Nygren, *Den kristna kärlekstanken genom tiderna Eros och agape*, 2:551ff., about "the Christian as a channel of God's down-flowing love."

325 WA 40/2:72ff. See especially LW 27:58 (WA 40/2:72.35ff.): "Thus nothing could be regarded as worthier of love in the whole universe than our neighbor. But such is the amazing craft of the devil that he is able not only to remove this noble object of love from my mind with great skill but even to persuade my heart of the exactly opposite opinion, so that it regards the neighbor as worthy, not of love but of the bitterest hatred." About all types of people, about friends and enemies, and all for whom we can do some good as the object of love, see WA 40/2:73.25ff. Cf. WA 2:77.19ff.

326 LW 27:59 (WA 40/2:74.18ff.).

For Luther, it is important to be precise about the source of love and good works. He says that the Holy Spirit follows justifying faith and that it is the Spirit who produces love and good works. Concerning Galatians 5:7, Luther says: "But when there is sound teaching—which cannot be without results, since it brings the Holy Spirit and His gifts—the life of the devout is strenuous running, even though it may seem to be crawling. . . . what is sorrow, sin, and death in our eyes is joy, righteousness, and life in the eyes of God, for the sake of Christ, through whom we are made perfect."[327]

The Holy Spirit comes with faith in Christ. The Holy Spirit gives birth to a new life in love and good works. But despite the help of the Spirit, Christians are not yet perfect and without sin. The life of the saints produces only the first fruits and has many faults. This coheres with the fact that according to Galatians 5:16–18 a veritable battle rages between the spiritual and sinful natures in the Christian. In this battle, the sinful nature sometimes gets the upper hand. With the use of the word *flesh* or the phrase "sinful nature," Luther does not mean specifically sexual desire but all evil desires and the entire realm of sin that attacks the Christian: unbelief, despair, rejection of God, divisions, pride, hatred, greed, impatience, etc. This realm of the sinful nature constantly struggles against the realm of the Spirit and vice versa. Luther emphasizes that those who have received the down payment of the Spirit will walk in the Spirit and struggle against the sinful nature. At the same time, he argues that believers have real sin in their lives. As long as they hold fast to Christ in faith, they are nevertheless perfectly justified. The reformer's well-known phrase is relevant here: A Christian is at the same time justified and a sinner, *simul iustus et peccator*.[328] The important idea that Christians live in and struggle in the Spirit while opposing the sinful nature and the even more important idea that defeated Christians always remain near Christ in faith are commented on by Luther in the *Larger Commentary on Galatians*:

> With the words "walk by the Spirit" Paul shows how he wants his earlier statements to be understood: "Through love be servants of one another" (5:13) and "Love is the fulfilling of the Law" (Rom. 13:10). It is as though he were saying: "When I command you to love one another, I am requiring of you that you walk by the Spirit. For I know that you will not fulfill the Law. Because sin clings to you as long as you live, it is impossible for you to fulfill the Law. But meanwhile take careful heed that you walk by the Spirit, that is, that by the Spirit you battle against the flesh and follow your spiritual desires." Thus he has not forgotten the matter of justification. For when he commands them to walk by the Spirit, he clearly denies that works justify. . . . ". . . there are two contrary

---

327 LW 27:32 (WA 40/2:40.9ff.).

328 WA 40/2:78–99. Cf. WA 2:583.27–588.20.

guides in you, the Spirit and the flesh. God has stirred up a conflict and fight in your body. For the Spirit struggles against the flesh, and the flesh against the Spirit. All I am requiring of you now—and, for that matter, all that you are able to produce—is that you follow the guidance of the Spirit and resist the guidance of the flesh. Obey the former, and fight against the latter!"[329]

In this parenesis the reformer is concerned that Christians will live a life in the Spirit in a struggle against the sinful nature. At the same time, he energetically emphasizes that believers on earth never become completely free from sin and are never perfected saints, not even through the help of the Holy Spirit. In the struggle of faith/the Spirit against sin/flesh, a Christian will, therefore, always ultimately cling to Christ in faith to receive righteousness before God. Even for those who through the Spirit struggle against the sinful nature, Christ is the only true righteousness.[330]

This does not prevent Luther from extensively investigating what the works of the flesh and the fruit of the Spirit are. He does this in both his commentaries on Galatians and in a manner that follows Paul. In a concrete manner and following Galatians 5:19ff., Luther warns against lazy and careless living according to the sinful nature.[331] One can live so carelessly that salvation is endangered and lost:

> *I warn you, as I warned you before, that those who do such things shall not inherit the kingdom of God.* This is a very harsh but most necessary sentence against the false Christians and smug hypocrites, who boast about the Gospel, faith, and the Spirit but meanwhile go on smugly performing the works of the flesh. Especially the heretics, however, who are puffed up with their opinions about matters that they suppose to be very spiritual, are completely carnal men, possessed by the devil.[332]

---

329 LW 27:65–66 (WA 40/2:81.26ff.).

330 LW 27:71–72 (WA 40/2:90.22ff.): "But we declare it as a certainty that Christ is our principal, complete, and perfect righteousness. If there is nothing on which we can depend, still, as Paul says (1 Cor. 13:13), 'these three abide: faith, hope, love.' Thus we must always believe and love, and we must always take hold of Christ as the Head and Source of our righteousness. 'He who believes in Him will not be put to shame' (Rom. 9:33). In addition, we should take pains to be righteous outwardly as well, that is, not to yield to our flesh, which is always suggesting something evil, but to resist it through the Spirit." Cf. on 1 Corinthians 4:4, WA 10/1.2:139.28–141.3.

331 WA 40/2:100–116. Luther refers also to the comprehensive investigation in the *Commentary on Galatians* (1519), WA 2:588.21–592. Cf. Öberg, *Himmelrikets nycklar och kyrklig bot i Luthers teologi*, 494ff., about the freedom of the flesh and *manifesta opera carnis* in connection with church discipline in Luther. Here I review the relevant literature.

332 LW 27:92 (*original emphasis*) (WA 40/2:116.16ff.).

Similarly, in connection with Galatians 5:22ff.; 6:1ff., Luther describes concretely the fruit of the Spirit in the human heart and the works among fellow Christians and all fellow human beings.[333]

In connection with Galatians 6:15, Luther speaks of a new creation, about a renewal of the mind and lifestyle through the Holy Spirit. This is not only a question of outward works but also of a true change in the heart and life.[334] As we have seen before, and despite all this talk about works, Luther is not writing here about the righteousness that saves us before God.

In Luther's commentaries on the Pastoral Epistles, the meaning of parenesis for the work of church/mission is also apparent. Luther's exposition of 1 Timothy 1:3–7 focuses on the negative parenesis against the old and new teachers of the Law who make salvation dependent on keeping the Law and regulations while at the same time confusing people with fables and genealogies.[335] But the apostle also supplies a positive parenesis in 1 Timothy 1:5: "The goal of this command is love, which comes from a pure heart and a good conscience and a sincere faith." Luther emphasizes here that the uncleanness of the heart is cleansed neither through the Law nor through a heroic power of the will. The basic sanctification of the heart is received through God's grace and forgiveness.[336] Thereby a Christian is free from the Law and its exacting demands and judgments. The one who through faith understands God as graceful and merciful does, however, receive a new heart and a new will that gladly and spontaneously squelches sin and thinks and does what is good.[337] Luther is, however, also on guard here against all notions of full sanctification or sinlessness in the believer. Even Christians have sin, and the Law accuses and troubles their consciences. Therefore through faith they ought always to focus on the Gospel about Christ. Then a continuous blessed exchange occurs in which Christ receives the sin of the believer and in which the believer receives Christ's perfect righteousness.[338] Of course, Paul's rule stands for all times that both faith and love ought to be preached by the church in which the Gospel is presented.[339] We have, thereby, once again entered the right doctrine of preaching about good works.

---

333 WA 40/2:116ff., 135ff. Cf. WA 2:592.22ff. See also the 1525 *Lent Postil* on 2 Corinthians 6:1–10, WA 17/2:178–86. This "Vermahnung und Reizung an die Korinther" cautions against spiritual carelessness while encouraging especially patience, an ordered life, and love in the power of the Spirit.

334 WA 40/2:178ff.

335 A sermon on 1 Timothy 1:3–7, WA 17/1:102ff., 108.23ff.

336 WA 17/1:111.15ff., 112.12ff.

337 WA 17/1:112.22ff.

338 WA 17/1:114.20ff., 115.15ff., 116.15ff.

339 WA 17/1:102.27ff.: "Ich habe bisher offt und viel geleret und gesagt und sag es noch

In connection with 1 Timothy 1:8–10, the reformer emphasizes as usual that the new humanity of faith ought not be forced to love and to do good works because in that case one has sinned against the rule that the source of sanctification is faith and the Holy Spirit. One constructs a way to salvation on the basis of the Law. Love ought not be forced with the switch of the Law. If faith is genuine, good works will follow spontaneously. The likelihood of their absence is similar to the probability that one could stop the sun from shining or the water in a stream from flowing. However, the Law ought to be applied to the sinful nature so one does not do what is evil but is forced to live honestly in outward things toward the world. But only the righteousness of faith in Christ counts as righteousness before God.[340]

---

ymmer dar, das zwey heubstück der Christlichen lere sind, glaube und liebe, wie auch S. Paul allenthalben schreibet und anzeucht, das ich auch nichts anders zu predigen weys." Cf. WA 17/1:103.23ff., 104.11ff.

340 The sermon on 1 Timothy 1:8–10, WA 17/1:121ff., 127.20ff. See especially WA 17/1:128.26ff., 129.15ff.: "Fragistu aber: Wie? sol man denn nicht gute werck thuen und das gesetz halten? Antwort: ja, ja, ja. Das gesetz ist gut, und thuen wol alle, die es hand haben, predigen, treiben und thuen, Warumb sol mans denn thuen? darumb, das man dardurch from werde? Antwort: nein, nein, Man wölle denn so sagen, das man dardurch from für die welt werde, Fur Gott aber mus etwas anders seyn. Wazu ists denn gut odder warumb ist es gegeben? Dazu, das es were, das man nicht böses thue und erzwinge ein eusserliche fromkeit für die welt . . . . Wiltu aber from seyn und hernach rechtschaffene gute werck thuen, so sihe, das du den heiligen geist habist, der dir Christum bringe und ynn dich pflantze und dich ynn yhn, das du ein new mensche werdist, der selb wird dir ein rein hertz, gut gewissen und grundguten glauben schaffen." WA 17/1:130.12ff.: "Das gesetz bleibt wol, aber der gerechte hat so viel, nemlich den heiligen geist und ein rein hertz, damit er thuet alles, was das gesetz haben wil. Nym ein gleichnis: Wenn ein ding gehet, als es gehen sol, darff es niemand treiben, Wenn es thuet, was man haben wil, darff mans nicht heissen, gebieten noch verbieten, Der sonne darff man kein gesetz geben, das sie leüchte und am hymel lauffe, Noch dem wasser, das sie fliesse, Noch dem feüer, das es brenne." Cf. WA 17/1:131.17ff. See also about faith, the indwelling of Christ, and love as the fulfilling of the Law, Mannermaa, "Das Verhältnis von Glaube und Liebe in der Theologie Luthers," 103ff. Concerning the sin that remains in the faithful, about the struggle between flesh and Spirit, and the fact that despite all this Paul encourages and commands, see WA 17/1:132.18–134.25. Luther concludes with these words: "So ist nu Summa summarum: Nach dem geist ist kein gesetz da, nach dem fleisch ist gesetz da, denn das thuet nicht, was es thuen sol, Der geist aber thuet alles" (WA 17/1:134.22ff.). Cf. the Formula of Concord, which says that the newborn Christian spontaneously does God's will without the threat of the Law. This is the fruit of the Spirit. But the Christian also lives with the sinful nature, which needs the discipline and threat of the Law. Also the Law/command prevents "made-up" good works and false worship of God. Concerning this doctrine about the uses of the Law, see FC Ep VI (K-W, 502–3; *BSLK*, 962ff.).

The reformer understands Titus as something of a compendium of what Paul, the apostle to the heathen, wanted to have preached among the peoples. Luther's contemporaries should have learned that both faith in Christ and good works as a consequence of that faith ought to be preached.[341] Concerning the important Baptism pericope Titus 3:4–7, Luther, as a way of introduction, writes about the fundamental necessity of preaching both faith and works. Through Baptism and faith in Christ, we humans receive God's good favor and grace unconditionally. From this unconditional and self-offering love in Christ, we are sanctified, that is, we become channels of the service of love and love of neighbor. The Christian no more requires a reason to love the other than Christ does. In this way Christians become mediators between God and neighbor to communicate the love and care of the Creator. In the commentary on Baptism previously named, the reformer emphasizes both God's abundant grace in Christ and the renewal that without the threat of the Law spontaneously will flow through the Spirit's power and work in the baptized and faithful. A new man is created.[342] A Christian never attains, how-

---

341 *Lectures on Titus* (1527), WA 25:6–69. Luther says: "The Epistle to Titus is short, but it is a kind of epitome and summary of other, wordier epistles. We should be imbued with the attitudes that are taught in it. Paul is the sort of teacher who is engaged most of all in these two topics, either teaching or exhorting. Moreover, he never exhorts in such a way that he fails to mingle didactic, that is, doctrinal, instruction with it. . . . He is a true teacher, one who both teaches and exhorts. By his teaching he sets down what is to be believed by faith, and by his exhortation he sets down what is to be done. Thus by doctrine he builds up faith, by exhortation he builds up life" (LW 29:3 [WA 25:6.8ff.]). Cf. the conclusion, WA 25:69.10ff., and on Titus 3:6–8 about faith in Christ and good works, WA 25:66.8–67.28.

342 The *Church Postil* (1522), Lenker 6:142 (WA 10/1.1:95.17ff.): "This epistle selection inculcates the same principle taught in the conclusion of the Gospel lesson pertaining to contentment, good will and love for our neighbor. The substance of the text is: Why should we be unwilling to do for others what has been done for us by God, of whose blessings we are far less worthy than anyone can be of our help? Since God has been friendly and kindly disposed toward us in bestowing upon us his loving kindness, let us conduct ourselves similarly toward our neighbors, even if they are unworthy, for we too are unworthy." Cf. Lenker 6:145 (WA 10/1.1:99.20ff., especially 100.8ff.): "But the fact is, all Christian doctrines and works, all Christian living, is briefly, clearly and completely comprehended in these two principles, faith and love. They place man as a medium between God and his neighbor, to receive from above and distribute below. Thus the Christian becomes a vessel, or rather a channel, through which the fountain of divine blessings continuously flows to other individuals." Cf. WA 10/1.1:102.8ff. See also Ivarsson, *Predikans uppgift*, 114; and Nygren, *Der kristna kärlekstanken genom tiderna Eros och agape*, 2:548ff., with the adduced texts, among them WA 10/1.2:180.3ff. and 36:180.17ff. At the 1519 Heidelberg Disputation, Luther says this about divine love and so-called natural humanity's love respectively: "28. The love of God does not find, but creates that which is pleasing to it. The love of man comes into

ever, a fully realized, concretized perfection in this lifetime. Perfection must be believed and sought always and only in Christ. Luther says with Titus 3:6 that Christ alone is the foundation of salvation.[343]

The reformer has thoroughly expounded 1 Peter in which the apostle is said to have presented two important themes: (1) salvation by unconditional grace and (2) the good works of love in struggle against the sin that remains. Luther speaks about how the apostle challenges and encourages believers to faith, that is, that Christians ought to trust in the Gospel that has been preached. This is the fundamental teaching of the apostle to the new Christians in his audience. Their entire lives and existence ought to be upheld by one single thing: faith in the Gospel of Christ and grace. They ought always to remind themselves that they are redeemed by Christ's blood and share in Christ's resurrection.[344]

At the same time, on the basis of 1 Peter 4:1ff., Luther reviews how the Scriptures present Christ's suffering in a double manner: "In the first place, as a gift . . . we are redeemed by the blood of Christ, that our sins have been taken away . . . . In the second place, Christ is held up and given to us as an example and a pattern for us to follow, for if we now have Christ as a gift through faith, we should go

---

being through that which is pleasing to it" (LW 31:57 [WA 1:365.2f.]). Cf. the 1521 commentary on the Magnificat, WA 7:547.4–31. From these passages, it is clear that God's love seeks that which is nothing, the poor and the despised, while at the same time establishing and creating something out of this nothing. Human love usually seeks something that is already good and great and having worth. On the basis of such texts, Nygren has one-sidedly focused on the incarnation and seen in a negative light any talk of the transformation that occurs through faith's uniting with Christ; see *Der kristna kärlekstanken genom tiderna Eros och agape*, 2:206ff. Against Nygren on this matter, Mannermaa has aimed a fatal critique. He points out that "die Vergöttlichung bei Luther stets kreuzestheologisch sub contrario verborgen ist" ("Das Verhältnis von Glaube und Liebe in der Theologie Luthers," 33). Nevertheless, Christ is present in faith and leads the Christian into the disposition and work of love. Among other texts, Mannermaa refers to WA 17/1:438.14ff., which speaks clearly against Nygren's thesis. See also on the new creation that is daily renewed through water and the Spirit, WA 10/1.1:112–19. Cf. on Titus 2:11–15, WA 10/1.1:19.10ff.; 23:15ff.; 27:19ff.; 30:15ff.; 37:5ff.; 53:10ff. About Baptism and the daily death-resurrection with Christ, see Stange, "Der Todesgedanke in Luthers Tauflehre"; Gyllenkrok, *Rechtfertigung und Heiligung*, 131ff.; Wingren, *Luthers lära om kallelsen*, 38ff.; Althaus, *Die Theologie Martin Luthers*, 203ff.; Lerfeldt, *Den kristnes kamp*, 176ff.; and Grönvik, *Die Taufe in der Theologie Martin Luthers*, 208ff. See also Öberg, *Himmelrikets nycklar och kyrklig bot i Luthers teologi*, 191ff.

343 WA 10/1.1:121.5ff., 123.15ff., 124.18ff., 126.1ff.

344 *1 Peter* (1523), WA 12:280.27–282.13, 283.25–285.34, 290.35–294.15, etc. About the occasional use of the phrase "challenge to faith" in the commentary, see Ivarsson, *Predikans uppgift*, 131.

forward and do as He does for us. We should imitate Him in our whole life and in all our suffering."[345] Also Luther notices while referring to the Good Samaritan in Luke 10:33ff. that the person of faith never in this lifetime becomes completely pure:

> For we never become perfectly pure while we are living on earth, and everyone still finds evil lust in his body. . . . If we believe, our sin, that is, the wound we have brought from Adam, is bandaged and begins to heal. But in one person this healing is less, and in another person it is more . . . . Therefore if we have these two things, faith and love, we should henceforth devote ourselves to sweeping out sin entirely until we die completely.[346]

Therefore this is the program: Christ, faith, love of neighbor, and struggle against the sinful nature and sin.

In his commentary on 1 Peter, Luther often writes that the church's/mission's preaching of the foundational doctrine of faith in Christ ought to include a challenge and an encouragement to surrender all godless living and live instead for the pleasure of God. Because Christians are never completely free from their sinful nature, they must in sobriety and the power of the Spirit struggle against the old nature and not participate in the desires of the sinful nature nor in the heathen way of life (1 Peter 1:13–14).[347] The Christian is reckoned completely holy and righteous through Baptism and faith in Christ, but this fundamental doctrine ought not lead to spiritual sloth and fleshly freedom. Such libertinism falls under the judgment of God. Christian freedom in faith and conscience is freedom only before God.[348] When God gives the faith of the heart, God himself produces a new mind and lifestyle in the person. One confesses Christ's name in both word and deed so others can be helped to faith. One ought to observe that the sanctified lifestyle is ascribed an evangelizing/missionizing effect. The reformer especially

---

345 LW 30:117 (WA 12:372.11ff, 372.17ff.).

346 LW 30:118 (WA 12:372.32ff., 373.2ff.).

347 WA 12:282.14ff., 286.13ff., 371ff.

348 In connection with 1 Peter 1:15–16, Luther speaks about the fundamental holiness of faith in Christ and Baptism: "For he who is a Christian enters with the Lord Christ into a sharing of all His goods. Now since Christ is holy, he, too, must be holy, or he must deny that Christ is holy. If you have been baptized, you have put on the holy garment, which is Christ, as Paul says (Gal. 3:27)" (LW 30:32 [WA 12:287.21ff.]). About unspiritual libertinism, Luther says: "Now when this is preached, reason comes along and says: 'Ah, if this is true, then I need not do a single good work!' Thus stupid minds seize upon this and change Christian life into carnal liberty. They think they should do what they please. St. Peter confronts these people here, anticipates them, and teaches them that Christian liberty must be exercised solely over against God" (LW 30:32 [WA 12:288.1ff.]).

emphasizes that the works of a Christian ought to be directed to helping and serving the neighbor.[349] When considering the words about the Father "who judges each man's work impartially" (1 Peter 1:17), Luther energetically proclaims the central doctrine of the Reformation: justification by grace alone without works. At the same time, he claims that the doctrine of judgment by works is true but only in a restricted manner.[350] For Luther, the solution to the problem exists in the fact that the Father, on the basis of works, judges whether the human subject had a true or false faith. From the fruit, the Father determines if the tree is good or evil. Works do not justify before God, but they witness to that which is decisive in the question of salvation, that is, faith in Christ. Faith in Christ declares us innocent before the judgment seat, but a true faith can never exist without fruit. Luther summarizes the Christian life as faith and good works.[351] Therefore Christians on

---

349 LW 30:32–33 (WA 12:288.9ff.): "Now when I have given God this honor, then whatever life I live, I live for my neighbor, to serve and help him. The greatest work that comes from faith is this, that I confess Christ with my mouth and, if it has to be, bear testimony with my blood and risk my life. Yet God does not need the work; but I should do it to prove and confess my faith, in order that others, too, may be brought to faith. Then other works will follow. They must all tend to serve my neighbor. All this God must bring about in us. Therefore we should not make up our minds to begin to lead a carnal life and to do what we please."

350 LW 30:34 (WA 12:289.22ff.): "But a question now arises here. Since we say that God saves us solely through faith and without regard to works, why, pray, does St. Peter say that God does not judge according to the person, but that He judges according to the works? Answer: What we have taught, that faith alone justifies before God, is undoubtedly true, since it is so clear from Scripture that it cannot be denied. Now what the apostle says here, that God judges according to the works, is also true. But one should maintain with certainty that where there is no faith, there can be no good works either, and, on the other hand, that there is no faith where there are no good works. Therefore link faith and good works together in such a way that both make up the sum total of the Christian life. As you live, so you will fare. God will judge you according to this." Cf. especially Modalsli, *Das Gericht nach den Werken*, 50ff., 58ff., partly about the difference between *locus iustificationis* and *locus iudicii operum*, partly about Luther's preaching of judgment according to works (Matthew 25:31ff.; 2 Corinthians 5:10ff.), among others, WA 17/2:330.7ff.; WA 32:323.32ff.; 37:128ff.; 40/2:154f.; 45:324ff. Modalsli touches on Luther's understanding of 1 Peter 1:17; see *Das Gericht nach den Werken*, 50. Concerning faith, love, and final judgment, see Althaus, *Die Theologie Martin Luthers*, 372ff., with the references to the Weimar Edition.

351 LW 30:34–35 (WA 12:289.34ff.): "Therefore even though God judges us according to our works, it nevertheless remains true that the works are only the fruits of faith. They are the evidence of our belief or unbelief. Therefore God will judge and convict you on the basis of your works. They show whether you have believed or have not believed, just as one cannot condemn and judge a liar better than from his words. . . . Therefore the only way to understand this is the simplest way, namely, that the works

their pilgrimage of faith never want to give free reign to lusts and in fact always fear not living according to God's good pleasure.[352] The Christian struggles against the sinful nature and its desires. This cannot be restrained by any kind of external asceticism. Sanctification and the struggle against the sinful nature must have its source in the Word/Gospel, in faith and in the Holy Spirit. Then a transformation occurs from the inside out into concrete good works.[353]

As it concerns the concrete content of renewal, Luther assigns great importance to Peter's encouragement to unrestrained sibling love and loving service to all fellow humans, including enemies (1 Peter 1:22). Faith ought not be exercised ascetically but according to the special love for the siblings of the faith. Love ought to be exercised in the congregation and most of all toward every fellow human being. Love is self-sacrificing. It does not seek worth in the one who ought to be loved.[354] Where the truth of faith and unrestrained love have place, there must be laid aside all evil cunning, all gossip, and all slander. Those who have discovered "the Living Stone" will thus be united in faith. As a holy priesthood, they will present themselves as a sacrifice, serve their neighbors, and witness to Christ (1 Peter 2:2, 5, 9).[355]

---

are fruits and signs of faith and that God judges people according to these fruits, which certainly have to follow, in order that one may see publicly where belief or unbelief is in the heart."

352 WA 12:290.12ff.

353 LW 30:40–41 (WA 12:295.24ff.): "But here St. Peter has given a real remedy for this, namely, obedience to the truth in the Spirit [Gal 1:22]. . . . The evil must come out, not go in; for it has grown inside in the flesh and blood, in the marrow and the veins, not outside in the cloth or in the garment. Therefore it is useless to attempt to curb lust with external means. To be sure, one can weaken and mortify the body with fasting and work; but one does not expel evil lust in this way. Faith, however, can subdue and restrain it, so that it gives room to the Spirit. . . . If you want to remain chaste, you must take hold of obedience to the truth in the Spirit; that is, one must not only hear and read the Word of God, but one must take it to heart."

354 LW 30:41–42 (WA 12:296.24ff.): "*For a sincere love of brethren.* To what end should we now lead a chaste life? To be saved by doing so? No, but for the purpose of serving our neighbor. What should I do to check my sin? I must take hold of the obedience to the truth in the Spirit, that is, faith in God's Word. Why do I check sin? To enable me to be of service to others." Cf. WA 12:321.9ff. about love of neighbor. On the unrestrained love of siblings on the basis of one Christ, one Baptism, one faith, etc., see WA 12:297.1ff. Observe how love does not seek worth in its object: "Love, however, is greater than brotherhood; for it extends also to enemies, and particularly to those who are not worthy of love. For just as faith is active where it sees nothing, so love should also not see anything and do its work chiefly where nothing lovable but only aversion and hostility is seen" (LW 30:43 [WA 12:297.31ff.]).

355 WA 12:301.1–302.16, 304–10, 316–20.

Luther has thoroughly commented on Peter's practical exhortations about the obedience of Christians to earthly authorities (1 Peter 2:13–15, 18–20), about the duties of spouses (1 Peter 3:1–7), about patience and good works during suffering (1 Peter 3:13–17), about the struggle against the old sinful nature (1 Peter 4:1–4), about the responsibility of congregational shepherds (1 Peter 5:1–4), etc.[356] Thus Luther unites the major doctrine of parenesis with many concrete challenges in the life situation of Christians and in mission contexts. I will return to this question.

In the texts analyzed above, I often have pointed out that Luther's parenesis includes reproach against godless living that is evidence of unbelief. Sometimes parenesis is close to *usus spiritualis legis*. Generally, Luther's preaching builds in a series: Law, Gospel, and stimulating challenge. The effect of parenesis often depends on the listener's relationship to the Gospel. In some of the challenges about the putting to death of the sinful nature, the reformer inveighs so many harsh judgments and reproaches that at least those slothful in sanctification ought to have experienced the series: Law, Gospel, challenge and at the same time the Law that judges and leads to Christ (*usus spiritualis legis*).[357]

Summary. Parenesis and the doctrine of love and works hold a surprisingly large place in Luther's writings. I have chosen to show this in connection with his commentaries on the Epistles. In the review and the analysis above, we have, however, seen that Luther energetically guards against the possibility that the doctrine of justification through faith in Christ alone might be compromised. One is saved only through faith in Christ.

Nevertheless, grace and faith are not dead things in the justified person. With them, the Holy Spirit and Christ's indwelling follow. These both cause renewal and good works in the life of the Christian. The reformer articulates that this renewal has the crucifixion of the sinful nature and the service of the neighbor in love as its goal. Luther often comments on the self-sacrificing, actual service in daily life as the true place for crucifixion and love of neighbor.

Parenesis aims first at enticing and stimulating these fruits of faith, that is, the struggle against and the putting to death of the sinful nature and love to and care for fellow human beings. Parenesis is not a part of the preaching of the Law, but it has its source in God's/Christ's self-sacrificial love. The reformer understands parenesis as a stimulation to draw out the consequences of faith or to be like Christ in attitude and lifestyle. Thus parenesis stands in service to sanctification, not as the switch of the Law but as a reminder that faith and the Spirit want

---

356 See WA 12:327ff., 334ff., 341ff., 356ff., 371ff.

357 See Ivarsson, *Predikans uppgift*, 134–44, the chapter "Från förmaningen till lagens predikan." See also Joest, *Gesetz und Freiheit*, 131f.

to lead the human subject into renewal. This renewal concerns first the heart and mind, then outer lifestyle. Through the fruits of faith in love and service to the neighbor and through the putting to death of the sinful nature, the believer honors God and serves the neighbor. Sometimes Luther says that a sanctified life is significant for the progress of the Gospel, that is, for evangelization/mission. But these works produced by faith and the Spirit do not attain perfection in this lifetime. Neither are they included in "God's account books," even if they bear witness to that which is decisive *coram Deo,* that is, faith in Christ. I will next consider some important missiological topics in the teaching of the apostles on which Luther has commented.

Mission, Culture, and the Governing Authorities

I have above reviewed the fundamental doctrine of paranesis and supplied many examples of how Luther seeks to stimulate love, good works, and crucifixion of the sinful nature. However, one discovers in the Luther material that some of the passages concern areas and stances that especially have to do with expanding God's reign in mission and evangelization. I will in the following say something about them.

The Gospel of mission does not replace culture and the civil orders. Already in chapter 2, I have touched on the questions about the Creator, the Law, and the worldly regiment.[358] Nevertheless, here I want to consider some texts in which Luther focuses on the questions about how the workers in God's reign ought to relate to the governing authorities, the civil orders, etc., on the mission front and in the work of evangelization.

First, it ought to be emphasized that Luther, on the basis of the central mission text Mark 16:14–20, decidedly rejects the notion that the church in its evangelization should consider it to be its duty to change the sociopolitical life of the mission lands. Life in creation, in the pursuits and orders of this world, pulses as usual when mission reaches a land or a region with the Gospel. The Creator has given all peoples reason and abilities to order civil life. Therefore Peter and Paul both encourage the Christians to consider the existing social orders as reasonable and to obey them (1 Peter 2:13; Romans 13:2).[359]

---

358 See *Luther and World Mission,* 20–21, 25–26, with the referenced literature of, among others, Kinder, Wingren, Törnvall, Lau, Elert, and Olsson.

359 Cruziger's 1544 *Summer Postil*: "On the other hand, Christ's kingdom has nothing to do with the kingdoms of men. He permits them to continue in their own observances. Christ commands that the disciples should preach the Gospel to all creatures. The creatures existed before the Gospel came to them. Governments are instituted, and laws formed, by men, through God-given reason and wisdom. . . . 1 Pet 2, 13 . . . Rom 13,2" (Lenker 3:223 [WA 21:394.24ff.]). Cf. also on 1 Peter 2:11ff. from 1543: "Christ

Luther's exposition of Psalm 117:1 actually contains a policy statement concerning mission's relationship to the sociopolitical reality that missionaries find in their host countries. The reformer says that mission must clearly understand first the distinctive character of God's reign and second the First Article about the Creator, creation, and the Law. He writes that during the time of the apostles only a few understood that Christ's reign was not a legal, spatio-temporal kingdom but an eternal, heavenly reign grounded in the Gospel and faith. Even fewer understood this during the time of the papacy. On the basis of Psalm 117:1; 72:10; and Acts 17:26, therefore, Luther wants to emphasize that the Gospel ought not be spread among the peoples/heathen with the purpose of introducing new political forms, new rights, new customs, and new culture. When they receive the Gospel, both Jews and heathen are allowed freely to continue their old political forms, laws, rights, and customs. Or they may freely change them. When Psalm 117:1 encourages the peoples to praise the Lord, the intention is something much higher than worldly order. The psalm speaks of the Gospel and worship of the living God in faith and praise. Of course, one must abandon idols and godless living, but one can continue with or transform civil laws, rights, and customs according to one's own good pleasure. Thus mission's Gospel of Christ is not aimed at replacing contemporary laws, rights, and lifestyles.[360] Mission does not mean—at any rate, it does not primarily mean—sociopolitical transformation but the planting of faith in Christ through the Gospel.

---

and the apostles do not, in this teaching, design the rejection of external government and human authority—what Peter here terms ordinances of men. No, they permit these to remain as they are; moreover, they enjoin us to submit to and make use of them" (Lenker 7:276 [WA 21:342.10ff.]).

360 "Psalm 117 (1530)," LW 14:14 (WA 31/1:233.19ff.): "This psalm also reveals a peculiarly great mystery, one little known at the time of the apostles and almost faded away under the papacy, namely, that the kingdom of Christ is not a temporal, transitory, earthly kingdom, ruled with laws and regulations, but a spiritual, heavenly, and eternal kingdom that must be ruled without and above all laws, regulations, and outward means. He tells the heathen to remain heathen; He does not ask them . . . to run away from their countries or cities to go to Jerusalem. He does not demand that they give up or abandon their secular laws, customs, and habits to become Jews, just as He does not demand of the Jews that they abandon their laws. . . . Every country and city can observe or change its laws. He does not concern Himself about this. Where laws are retained, they do not hinder His kingdom; for He says: 'Praise the Lord, all you heathen!' " Luther argues, of course, that the heathen must learn to know the true God, be led to faith, and abandon idols (WA 31/1:228.33ff.). Observe that he can translate the Hebrew word *goyim* in Psalm 117:1 as "eine nation oder eins gantzen lands volck." Among other things, he writes: "Let all גּוֹיִם praise the Lord,' that is to say, all nations, countries, peoples; all languages, kingdoms, and principalities, etc." (LW 14:11–12 [WA 31/1:231.13–29]).

Nevertheless, the reformer emphasizes that no land and no place can exist without laws and rights and customs. The earthly regiment must be ruled. One must judge, punish, and protect people and preserve peace and order. The laws of legal states (that is, positive laws) are often changed, but they nevertheless can never be completely avoided in our world.[361]

Whenever the Scriptures speak of kings, lands, and peoples receiving Christ, they assume that these people already possess an earthly regiment and an identity. Their Christianization does not mean that their own regiments, laws, offices, rights, and customs are automatically abandoned. Luther expressly says that the Holy Spirit—through texts such as Psalm 72:10, for example—approves the princes and political leaders of non-Christian lands. God commands all citizens to submit to their leaders. God has created all kings and all peoples and according to Paul in Acts 17:26 divided the earth between them. For Luther, no earthly government of a heathen people is simply a worthless form of the civil law in a chaotic existence. God is an active Creator in the entire world through earthly government, enactment of laws, and the sense of right that is given to people by nature. Therefore mission must honor the earthly government in mission lands.[362] Thus the reformer argues that the Creator is already active through creation/nature and the reasonable plans and work of people whenever the good news of the Gospel reaches the peoples. Therefore he says that the Creator preserves and cares for creation against the destructive work of Satan through civil government and order among all peoples under the sun. In addition to this

---

361 LW 14:14 (WA 31/1:233.31ff., 234.4ff.): "Heathen, however, as I have already said, are people in various countries and cities. Countries and cities cannot maintain themselves without laws, customs, and ordinances with which they govern, judge, punish, protect, and keep the peace. They may change these things on occasion, but they cannot get along without them. Whenever we hear of heathen or kings in Scripture, we must not think only of persons with crowns but of their whole government, with laws, offices, ordinances, customs, usages, and habits by which their kingdoms are maintained and managed."

362 LW 14:14–15 (WA 31/1:234.4ff.): "We read in Ps. 72:10: 'May the kings from the seashore and from the isles render Him tribute.' With such expressions the Holy Spirit confirms the secular laws and government of all countries and calls them 'kings,' giving us to understand that they are to retain their authority, and that everyone is to be obedient and subject to this lord and master. He does not rebuke them for being kings or heathen or nations. He Himself created and established them, and divided up the world for them to rule, as Paul also testifies in Acts 17:26. If He wanted to upbraid or scold them, He would certainly not call them kings, heathen, or nations; in that case He would address them in a different way. Since He does name and confirm them as kings and heathen, we should all the more let them be kings and heathen—that is, nations or worldly authority—and honor them as such."

earthly regiment, steered as it is by laws, offices, and power, God also presides in our world over a spiritual regiment that is primarily undergirded by the Word/Gospel and its servants.[363]

The relation of mission to the civil authorities. Here we will consider some basic elements in the reformer's view of civil authority and the relationship of the work of God's reign to the same. One finds in *Temporal Authority* (1523), among other places, passages in which Luther says that true Christians really ought not need to be ruled by civil orders but that they should spontaneously live justly.[364] Neverthe-less, he argues that all people must be ruled by a civil authority. Those who are not Christians must with force be prevented from doing what is wrong. Christians must be ruled by a civil law because they also continue to live with their own sin-fulness and depravity.[365] Luther also argues that true Christians are barely one in a thousand in any one land. They are dispersed within a crushing majority of non-believers who through Law and power must be forced to live in an orderly manner. Therefore neither any single land nor the entire world can be ruled by the Gospel.[366] Matthew 5:39—which indicates that Christians ought not oppose a violation of their rights—as well as other verses about the freedom of the reign of the Messiah from the Law and the sword (1 Kings 6:7; Psalm 110:3; Isaiah 11:9; 2:4), do not therefore mean that Christians should oppose civil authority and laws. Luther understands such texts to apply only to the inner fellowship of Christians.[367]

---

363 Cf. *Luther and World Mission*, 253–54n359. See the comprehensive sermons from 1522 in WA 10/3:371, 279f. See especially *Temporal Authority* (1523), LW 45:75–129 (WA 11:245–81); and "Whether Soldiers etc. (1526)," WA 19:623–62, especially 624ff. and 628ff. (LW 46:87–137). See also "Sermons on the First Epistle of St. Peter (1523)," WA 12:320ff., and other sermons: WA 21:339ff.; 25:56ff.; 41:60ff.; 47:435ff.; 49:390ff., 716ff. On the connection between the gifts of the Creator, earthly work, and the worldly orders and vocation, see "Psalm 127 (1524)," WA 15:366ff., and "On the Councils of the Church (1539)," WA 50:632.1ff. Cf. Wingren, *Luthers lära om kallelsen*, 19, 33ff.

364 WA 11:249.24–250.20, 251.1ff., 251.32ff., 252.24–253.17, 254.11ff. Cf. *Luther and World Mission*, 257n368.

365 LW 45:90 (WA 11:250.24ff.): ". . . Paul says that the law has been laid down for the sake of the lawless [I Tim. 1:9], that is, so that those who are not Christians may through the law be restrained outwardly from evil deeds, as we shall hear. Now since no one is by nature Christian or righteous, but altogether sinful and wicked, God through the law puts them all under restraint so they dare not willfully implement their wickedness in actual deeds."

366 WA 11:251.12ff., 251.32ff.

367 WA 11:252.24–253.16. Luther concludes: "Whoever would extend the application of these and similar passages to wherever Christ's name is mentioned, would entirely pervert the Scripture; rather, they are spoken only of true Christians, who really do this among themselves" (LW 45:93 [WA 11:253.13ff.]). Cf. "Sermons on the First Epistle of Peter (1523)," WA 12:329.32ff., and "Whether Soldiers, etc.," WA 19:628.30ff.

The reformer energetically defends the place of the earthly regiment and emphasizes its necessity primarily on the basis of Romans 13:1ff.; Titus 3:1ff.; and 1 Peter 2:13ff. In these passages, Paul and Peter, during the first epoch of mission, challenge Christians to obey earthly authority and civil order. Even if sanctified Christians in their internal relationships have no need of the law and the sword, the vast majority of people in the world must be ruled by law and authority. Therefore a Christian motivated by love willingly approaches his or her fellow human beings under the conditions of laws and regulations, serves and honors the ruling authority, promotes its necessary ordering of communal life, pays taxes, etc.[368] Such does not damage faith, but it promotes general order in the land. If Christians pay attention neither to the laws of the state nor to governmental authorities, they are considered revolutionary and enemies of the community. The preaching of the Gospel will be hindered by such behavior. Therefore Christ makes all his own willing servants and shows, by his advice about taxes, the importance of submission to the civil law.[369]

Can a Christian hold secular office? The reformer's answer is a categorical affirmative. Luther points to a list of Old Testament saints who used the worldly regiment/sword. A number of individuals in the New Testament became Chris-

---

368 LW 45:93–94 (WA 11:253.17ff.): "But you say: if Christians then do not need the temporal sword or law, why does Paul say to all Christians in Rom 13 [:1], 'Let all souls be subject to the governing authority,' and St. Peter, 'Be subject to every human ordinance' [I Pet. 2:13], etc., as quoted above? Answer: I have just said that Christians, among themselves and by and for themselves, need no law or sword, since it is neither necessary nor useful for them. Since a true Christian lives and labors on earth not for himself alone but for his neighbor, he does by the very nature of his spirit even what he himself has no need of, but is needful and useful to his neighbor. Because the sword is most beneficial and necessary for the whole world in order to preserve peace, punish sin, and restrain the wicked, the Christian submits most willingly to the rule of the sword, pays his taxes, honors those in authority, serves, helps, and does all he can to assist the governing authority, that it may continue to function and be held in honor and fear. Although he has no need of these things for himself." Cf. WA 19:629.9ff., 630.11ff., 630.14ff.; 50:652.1ff.

369 LW 45:94 (WA 11:253.35ff.): ". . . so he serves the governing authority not because he needs it but for the sake of others, that they may be protected and that the wicked may not become worse. He loses nothing by this; such service in no way harms him, yet it is of great benefit to the world. If he did not so serve he would be acting not as a Christian but even contrary to love; he would also be setting a bad example to others who in like manner would not submit to authority, even though they are not Christians. In this way the gospel would be brought into disrepute, as though it taught insurrection and produced self-willed people unwilling to benefit or serve others, when in fact it makes a Christian the servant of all. Thus in Matthew 17 [:27] Christ paid the half-shekel tax that he might not offend them, although he had no need to do so."

tians without any indication that they were forced to leave their callings as soldiers or government officials.[370]

However, the most important theme in *Temporal Authority* and the other writings is that the apostles have expressly taught that all ruling authorities are of God, and because they are something of God, they may not be despised but shall be obeyed and honored. Here Romans 13:1–7 and 1 Peter 2:13–17 are central.[371] These Bible passages explicitly state that the governing authorities are from God. It is a service to God and a blessing to humanity when the governing authorities punish the wicked and defend law-abiding citizens. A Christian may under no circumstances despise that which is God's work, order, and creation.[372] Therefore a Christian may occupy an office of the state or other civil duties. Luther writes:

---

370 WA 11:255.22–257.15. Luther refers to Genesis 14:15; 1 Samuel 15:33; 1 Chronicles 18:40; Luke 3:14; and Acts 10:48; 8:39; 13:12. Cf. also the Scripture references in WA 11:247.31–248.31 and the discussion in WA 11:271ff. on how a Christian official ought to do his or her job. See also "Whether Soldiers, etc.," WA 19:625ff.

371 LW 45:91 (WA 11:247.21ff.): ". . . and the temporal [government], which restrains the un-Christian and wicked so that—no thanks to them—they are obliged to keep still and to maintain an outward peace. Thus does St. Paul interpret the temporal sword in Romans 13 [:3], when he says it is not a terror to good conduct but to bad. And Peter says it is for the punishment of the wicked [I Pet. 2:14]." See WA 11:251.12ff., 251.18ff., 257.6ff. Cf. "Whether Soldiers, etc. (1526)": "That is the sum and substance of it. The office of the sword is in itself right and is a divine and useful ordinance, which God does not want us to despise, but to fear, honor, and obey, under penalty of punishment, as St. Paul says in Romans 13 [:1–5]. For God has established two kinds of government among men. The one is spiritual; it has no sword, but it has the word, by means of which men are to become good and righteous, so that with this righteousness they may attain eternal life. He administers this righteousness through the word, which he has committed to the preachers. The other kind is worldly government, which works through the sword so that those who do not want to be good and righteous to eternal life may be forced to become good and righteous in the eyes of the world. He administers this righteousness through the sword. . . . Thus God himself is the founder, lord, master, protector, and rewarder of both kinds of righteousness. There is no human ordinance or authority in either, but each is a divine thing entirely" (LW 46:99–100 [WA19:625.20ff., 628.9ff., especially 629.14ff.]). Cf. the *Larger Commentary on Galatians*, WA 40/1:46.19ff., 207ff.; 40/2:123ff. See the sketch in *Luther and World Mission*, 26–30.

372 LW 45:99 (WA 11:257.16ff.): "Moreover, we have the clear and compelling text of St. Paul in Romans 13 [:1], where he says, 'The governing authority has been ordained by God'; and further, 'The governing authority does not bear the sword in vain. It is God's servant for your good, an avenger upon him who does evil' [Rom. 13:4]. Be not so wicked, my friend, as to say, 'A Christian may not do that which is God's own peculiar work, ordinance, and creation.' Else you must also say, 'A Christian must not eat, drink, or be married,' for these are also God's work and ordinance. If it is God's work

In short, since Paul says here that the governing authority is God's servant, we must allow it to be exercised not only by the heathen but by all men. What can be the meaning of the phrase, "It is God's servant," except that governing authority is by its very nature such that through it one may serve God? Now it would be quite un-Christian to say that there is any service of God in which a Christian should not or must not take part, when service of God is actually more characteristic of Christians than of anyone else.... Therefore, you should esteem the sword or governmental authority as highly as the estate of marriage, or husbandry, or any other calling which God has instituted.... For those who punish evil and protect the good are God's servants and workmen.[373]

In conclusion, one might observe how in *Temporal Authority* Luther energetically criticizes the mixing of Christ's regiment through the Word/Gospel and the earthly regiment through laws, power, and authority. When such mixing occurs, chaos and terror result in the church and society. Therefore one must carefully see to it that the princes and government officials rule only in their domain, that is, the worldly regiment and its government. They must not under any circumstances legislate or steer consciences. Likewise, the church's hierarchy ought neither direct nor exercise the authority of the worldly regiment. Luther advises princes and other officials, often after being requested to do so. He does not, however, give detailed orders concerning the way the princes or officials should rule. That would be to confuse the regiments.[374]

It also ought to be observed that Luther understands that the worldly regiment can be misused or used poorly by a king or a prince. The office is good, but the person in the office can be evil or incompetent. In such a situation, however, one does not have the right to revolt or to depose those in power, except in the case of, for example, mental illness.[375] But if the princes—or the bishops dressed in worldly power in church and society—demand their subjects to do something against God's Word and conscience, then one ought not obey them. The prince is

---

and creation, then it is good, so good that everyone can use it in a Christian and salutary way .... [I Tim. 4:4, 3]." Cf. the previous footnote.

373 LW 45:99–100 (WA 11:257.29ff.). Cf. WA 11:260.30ff. See also AC XVI and XXVIII (Tappert, 37–38, 81–94) and the corresponding sections of the Apology (Tappert, 222–24, 281–85). See also the Large Catechism (Tappert, 384ff.).

374 WA 11:258ff., 261ff., with its extensive investigation. Luther gives a lot of advice to the princes who want to be Christian (WA 11:271ff.). This advice concerns primarily general positions, while the written law and above all reason, a sense for the appropriate, etc., ought to give the detailed advice to the princes (WA 11:272.6ff.). A Christian prince's allegiance to God's Word and his will to do it often make it difficult for him to rule (WA 11:273.7ff., 273.25ff.). Cf. WA 19:630ff.

375 WA 11:269.32ff.; 19:632ff., 636ff., 644ff.

not allowed to decide over conscience and faith. One ought to obey God rather than humans (Matthew 22:21; Acts 5:29). Also one can trust that God will set boundaries for tyranny in one way or another.[376]

All the same, Luther is decidedly against any notion that the church/mission ought to engage itself in revolution. Together with Paul and Peter, he strenuously advises obedience to the governing authorities. About those who neglect this apostolic exhortation, the reformer says this:

> If he did not so serve [the governing authority] he would be acting not as a Christian but even contrary to love; he would also be setting a bad example to others who in like manner would not submit to authority, even though they were not Christians. *In this way the gospel would be brought into disrepute, as though it taught insurrection and produced self-willed people unwilling to benefit or serve others.*[377]

The reformer often emphasizes that the position of Christians concerning the governing authorities and civil laws is highly significant for the work of God's reign. When Paul says in 1 Corinthians 6:3 that no Christian ought to live so the ministry of preaching becomes defamed, he emphasizes the risk that the Gospel might become accused, defamed, and hindered in two ways. Some want to be free and oppose the ruling authority and civil order. One makes spiritual freedom in faith into a freedom from the legal governing authority. This arouses wrath among the pagans and their governing powers. On the basis of such a Christian position, the Gospel is accused of teaching chaos. The pagans and other unbelievers become angry because of such behavior, and they become in fact inimical to the Gospel and to Christians. They become closed to God's Word and the Christian faith. In a mission situation, revolution and a false freedom toward the civil law and order close certain people to the Gospel and hinder their conversion to Christ.[378] Luther probably has in mind the peasant revolt in South

---

376 WA 11:261ff., 266.24ff.; 19:636ff.

377 LW 45:94 (WA 11:254.3ff.) (*Öberg's emphasis*).

378 A sermon on 2 Corinthians 6:1–10 in the *Lent Postil* (1525): "Since this is a time of blessing, let us make right use of it, not spending it to no purpose, and let us take serious heed to give offense to none; thus avoiding reproach to our ministry. It is evident from the connection to what kind of offense the apostle has reference; he would not have the Gospel doctrine charged with teaching anything evil. Two kinds of offense bring the Gospel into disgrace: In one case it is the heathen who are offended, and this because of the fact that some individuals would make the Gospel a means of freedom from temporal restraint, substituting temporal liberty for spiritual. Thus they bring reproach upon the Gospel as teaching such doctrine, and make it an object of scandal to the heathen and the worldly people, whereby they are misled and become enemies to the faith and to the Word of God without cause, being the harder to convert since

Germany as he formulates these ideas. But a false freedom also is problematic for the local congregation. Some exercise their freedom in such a manner that those weak in faith become annoyed and troubled. In a number of different passages, therefore, Paul teaches that Christians ought to live in such a way that neither Greek nor Jew nor congregation take offense.[379]

God's Word is a stumbling block (Isaiah 8:14; Romans 9:33) for unbelievers. Therefore one is responsible for living in such a manner that pagans, Jews, princes, and weak Christians are drawn to the Gospel. Christians are responsible for living in such a manner that they are not considered to be a loose and ungovernable people, which may make those non-Christian enemies of the Gospel more closed to the Gospel. It is a serious sin if by such lifestyle choices one hinders the progress of the Gospel among people.[380] All Christians are fellow workers together with

---

they regard Christians as licentious knaves. And the responsibility for this must be placed at the door of those who have given offense in this respect" (Lenker 7:136–37 [WA 17/2:181.19ff.]).

379 Lenker 7:137 (WA 17/2:181.32ff.): "In the other case, Christians are offended among themselves. The occasion is the indiscreet exercise of Christian liberty, which offends the weak in faith. Concerning this topic much is said in First Corinthians 8 and Romans 14. Paul here hints at what he speaks of in First Corinthians 10, 32–33: 'Give no occasion of stumbling, either to Jews, or to Greeks, or to the church of God; even as I also please all men in all things, not seeking mine own profit, but the profit of the many that they may be saved.' He takes up the same subject in Philippians 2, 4, teaching that every man should look on the things of others. Then no offense will be given." Cf. on Romans 14, WADB 7:25.26ff.; on 1 Corinthians 8, WADB 7:87.19ff.; and on Philippians 2:4, WA 27:91ff., especially 94.15ff. See also on 1 Corinthians 10:1–13, WA 41:385ff.; 49:534ff.

380 Lenker 7:137–38 (WA 17/2:182.4ff.): " 'That our ministration [the ministry] be not blamed.' Who can prevent our office being vilified? for the Word of God must be persecuted equally with Christ himself. That the Word of God is reviled by unbelievers ignorant of faith in God is something we cannot prevent. For according to Isaiah 8, 14 and Romans 9, 33, the Gospel is a 'rock of offense.' This is the offense of faith; it will pursue its course and we are not responsible. But for love's offense, offense caused by shortcomings in our works and fruits of faith, the things we are commanded to let shine before men, that, seeing these, they may be allured to the faith—for offense in this respect we cannot disclaim responsibility. It is a sin we certainly must avoid, that the heathen, the Jews, the weak and the rulers of the world may never be able to say: 'Behold the knavery and licentiousness of these people! Surely their doctrine cannot be true.' Otherwise our evil name and fame and the obstacles we place before others will extend to the innocent and holy Word God has given us to apprehend and to proclaim; it must bear our shame and in addition become unfruitful in the offended ones. Grievous is such a sin as this." Cf. Luther's comments on 1 Timothy 2:1ff. about prayer for all people, kings, and the governing authorities, WA 26:33.1–34.29. Christians intercede for peace and calm in the land. A fruit of this peace and calm is that the Gospel, Christian upbringing, and honest lives are given a place in that society (WA 26:34.16ff.).

those who publicly preach the Gospel in the work of church/mission. One ought not hinder the time of the Gospel among people. So Christians must be patient and steadfast in the work of God's reign. They must live honest lives, obey, and bear the cross—all for the sake of the Gospel.[381]

Luther's commentary on Titus 3:1–12 is extremely helpful in this regard. The apostle's parenesis here concerns the Christian's relationship to those outside the Christian fellowship, especially the governing authorities in the society. The Christians must live in such a manner that those outside the fellowship of the church are obligated to give a good testimony to the life of the Christians. This happens when Christians honor the ruling authorities and subordinate themselves to the civil law and do not, as in the Roman Catholic hierarchy, consider themselves to be above the public judicial system (*privilegium fori*). When it is taught that obedience to laws and the general order of the society are God's will, then even the most trivial tasks become a meaningful service to God. The reformer emphasizes that the knowledge that service in civil obedience is God's will (*voluntas Dei*) provides a desire for and a pleasure in work.[382] In this way, even Christian civil leaders are provided with a new courage and a new positive view of the exercise of their office. They know that their work does not harm faith but is instead pleasing to God. Even those who subordinate themselves and obey know that they are acting according to God's will. The reformer emphasizes here the actual obedience to the commands of the governing authorities whether in times of peace or war.[383]

---

381 WA 17/2:179ff., 182.20ff. Cf. WA 47:666.3ff., 668.9ff.

382 *Lectures on Titus and Philemon* (1527), LW 29:71–72 (WA 25:56.9ff.): "Now he also instructs them in the good works which they ought to perform, not to those of their own household but to those on the outside and especially to magistrates. For Christians ought to live in such a way that those who are on the outside are forced to give a good testimony about us . . . . The magistrate ought to be honored in order that he may realize that this doctrine is sound. This is a noteworthy passage which ought to shake up the disobedient clerics so that they are not subject to Christian magistrates in external jurisdiction, even though Paul subjects himself and all Christians to profane magistrates. . . . Therefore all men should be taught to be quick to obey. The reason is that they should be sure they are not obeying men but God. If even a wicked master commands a peasant, he can joyfully carry the wood and be better when he does this than a monk with his works, because all he has to care about is the will of God and what pleases Him. Among the clerics there is no such work. Instead, there is contempt of God, one's own choice, and obedience to the devil." LW 29:72 (WA 25:56.29ff.): "But if a peasant knew that he is serving God, then many would be found who would understand this and would serve willingly. Then one would stir up another and instruct others."

383 About the new positive evaluation of their work by officeholders and ministers who know they are doing something according to God's will: "When they acknowledged

Nevertheless, a Christian cannot obey orders of the governing authorities if they are clearly unrighteous deeds. Paul exhorts the Christians that they ought to be ready for every good work. One can say that in obvious conflict situations Luther allows civil disobedience to a certain degree so God's will may be followed.[384]

Finally, let us consider Luther's exposition of 1 Peter 2:13–15 through the years. After Peter has spoken about the foundation of faith and the stance of Christians toward non-Christians in general, he focuses on their behavior before princes, governing authorities, and masters. Luther notices that the life of Christians in the world ought to be seen from an eschatological horizon. Christians live a double life. They are anchored in the reign of faith in Christ and in the hope of eternal life. At the same time, they live the lives of aliens here in the world and under the conditions and exigencies of the world. They will live the rich life of faith and hope and at the same time live in worldly vocations, undertakings, and all that accompanies life in this world.[385] In this double existence, it is important that they neither, like monks and nuns, separate themselves from the world nor,

---

that the government is a divine ordinance, they acquired a good conscience and administered their office well. Otherwise one is presumptuous and becomes nothing but a tyrant, or he despairs and does nothing. . . . But if he is taught: 'You are in an office which is most pleasing to God, namely, [to protect] widows and orphans, as Rom. 13:3 says, to be a god established in this world (Ps. 82:5),' he can have a good conscience and then can become kind, pious, and firm according to necessity. . . . This Word [Titus 3:1] gives and commends this office, and therefore all the works that are carried on in it are most acceptable to God and holy. A monk cannot say this: 'This is a rule instituted by God.' Therefore he ruins his life. . . . [W]hen you are subject to a ruler, you are subject to Christ, your Lord and God, who for you was obedient even [unto death], as Phil. 2:8 says. Should you not accept this with thanks? You are sure that he is a prince, that his work has been ordained by God, and that my obedience has been ordained by God. Therefore you are subject to him freely . . . . *Submissive,* that is, let them be ready, let them always remain in subjection, let them not stir up sects. [*To be obedient*] *to a command,* so that if any command comes, they obey it. When a command comes from a ruler or a magistrate, I get right to work, whether in peace or in war" (LW 29:72–73 [*original emphasis*] [WA 25:57.3ff., 57.17ff.]).

384 One can, according to Luther, kill in war or as an executioner who follows the command of the prince or the law (WA 25:58.6ff.). But one ought to disobey obviously unrighteous orders: "Likewise, [*to be ready*] *for* [*any honest work*]. He explains what it means to be obedient. I want you to obey the government, but to the extent that it commands you to do good things; for it happens that some men administer the government unjustly. A Christian distinguishes between a good and a bad command of a prince" (LW 29:73 [*original emphasis*] [WA 25:58.12ff.]). Cf. here the sketch in *Luther and World Mission,* 26–30, where more information is given about Luther's view on reacting to the abuse of worldly power.

385 *1 Peter* (1522), WA 12:320ff. Cf. WA 21:339ff.; 41:60ff.; 47:735ff.; 49:390ff.

like the enthusiasts, lose patience and revolt against the society's order and ruling authority.[386]

As aliens and strangers, Christians are encouraged to subordinate themselves to the order of society and to those who govern. It is not only the spiritual regiment that is important. Even the earthly regiment with its laws, power, and sword are given by God.[387] On the one hand, it is a human/worldly order, but it fills a task commanded by God, that is, to set boundaries for the godless and to protect those who do good. God uses the governing authorities and their laws to govern a mostly godless world that without the worldly regiment would simply destroy itself. Unbelievers will be forced to a reasonable righteousness, a civil society. Believers will "for the Lord's sake" (1 Peter 2:13) subordinate themselves to the governing authorities. They ought to be exemplary, law-abiding citizens in the world.[388] By paying fees and taxes, they will in a non-Christian world make dumb all those who from the time of the ancient church have accused the Christians of conspiring to overturn the contemporary societal order.[389]

---

386 The sermon in Cruziger's *Summer Postil,* WA 21:344.14–347.10. Cf. WA 12:328.2ff.; 47:738.14–741.13; 49:392.28ff.

387 LW 30:73–74 (WA 12:328.11ff.): "The Greek for what I have translated into German with *aller menschlicher ordnung,* 'to every human institution,' is χτίσις. The Latin word is *creatura.* . . . 'What the government commands, obey it.' For *schaffen* means 'to command,' and *ordnung* is a creature of man. . . . What God commands, requires, and wants, that is His institution, namely, one's faith. Now there is also a human or secular command, namely, an institution comprising injunctions, as should be true of the external government. To this we should be subject. Therefore you must understand the little words *creatura humana* to mean *Quod creat et condit homo,* 'What man creates and institutes.' " Cf. WA 21:342,.1ff., 345.10ff.; 41:61.32ff.; 47:737.19ff.; 49:393.4ff., 716.3ff.

388 LW 30:74 (WA 12:328.26ff., especially 328.31ff.): "But why should one be subject to the government for God's sake? Because it is God's will that malefactors be punished and that benefactors be protected, in order that in this way unity may remain in the world. Therefore we should further external peace. God wants us to do this. For since we are not all believers but the great majority are unbelievers, God has regulated and ordained matters this way in order that the people of the world might not devour one another. The government should wield the sword and restrain the wicked if they do not want to have peace. Then they have to obey. This He accomplishes through the government, so that in this way the world is ruled well everywhere. Thus you see that if there were not evil people, one would not need a government. Therefore St. Peter adds the words 'to punish those who do wrong and to praise those who do right' [1 Pet 2:14]. Pious people are to be commended for doing what is right. The secular government should praise and honor them, in order that the others may have their conduct as an example. . . . Rom. 13:3." Cf. WA 49:717.1ff.

389 LW 30:74–75 (WA 12:329.16ff.): "*For it is God's will that by doing right you should put*

Luther comments in a similar manner on 1 Peter 2:17–20 concerning obedience and solidarity with princes, lords, and masters. The governing authority will be obeyed even if it is pagan and occasionally tyrannical. But these authorities are only allowed to rule over the earthly life. If the earthly authority seeks to control faith and conscience, then one ought to disobey it even if the cost of this disobedience is life itself.[390] On 1 Peter 2:17, Luther emphasizes that a Christian ought to serve in the given vocation as master or mistress, as servant or maid. Christian faith does not restructure family life nor other elements of everyday life under the earthly regiment. One will find himself or herself in various social classes and tasks; and in those classes and tasks, one must at the same time not forget that he or she is an alien in the world and not flee from the labor and trivialities of life as the monks do.[391] The eschatological perspective is emphasized by Luther in a

---

to silence the ignorance of foolish men [1 Peter 2:15]. . . . [Luther hypothesizes an objection:] 'Since a Christian's faith is sufficient, and works do not make a man pious, why, then, is it necessary to obey the secular authority and pay taxes or tribute?' This must be your reply: 'Although we derive no benefit from this, we should nevertheless do it for God without recompense to stop the mouths of God's enemies, who chide us. Then they cannot charge us with anything and must say that we are pious and obedient people.' Thus one reads of many saints that they went to war under pagan princes, slew the enemy, and were subject and obedient to these princes" (original emphasis). Cf. WA 49:393.11ff., 716.7ff.

390 LW 30:80 (WA 12:334.15ff.): "Fear God. Honor the emperor [1 Pet 2:17]. The apostle does not say that one should esteem lords and kings highly. No, he says that one should honor them even though they are heathen. Christ did this too. So did the prophets, who fell at the feet of the kings of Babylon" (original emphasis). LW 30:80 (WA 12:334.29ff.): "We should be subject to power and do what they order, so long as they do not bind our conscience and so long as they give commands that pertain to external matters only, even though they deal with us as tyrants do. . . . But if they want to encroach on the spiritual rule and want to take our conscience captive where God alone must sit and rule, one should by no means obey them and should sooner let them have one's life. Secular domain and rule do not extend beyond external and physical matters." Cf. also WA 12:335.17ff. about the illegitimacy of the secular domain's attempt to rule over faith and conscience.

391 Lenker 7:276–77 (WA 21:342.37ff.): "So should Christians in all stations of life—lords and ladies, servants and maids—conduct themselves as guests of earth. Let them, in that capacity, eat and drink, make use of clothing and shoes, houses and lands, as long as God wills . . . . Christians should be aware of their citizenship in a better country, that they may rightly adapt themselves to this world. Let them not occupy the present life as if intending to remain in it; nor as do the monks, who flee responsibility, avoiding civil office and trying to run out of the world. For Peter says rather that we are not to escape our fellows and live each for himself, but to remain in our several conditions in life, united with other mortals as God has bound us, and serving one another." Cf. WA 21:343.15ff. and 47:737.20ff.

surprising manner, but he never loses sight of the fact that the Christian's active engagement of and contribution to earthly and natural work is something that the Creator wants and the apostles commanded.[392]

Summary. Luther's writings are extensive and rich in respect to their examination of the relationship between the work of God's reign and the worldly authorities. We have seen how energetically the reformer emphasizes that Christians ought to obey the governing authorities and the civil law. This is also true of non-Christian cultures and pagan governing authorities as long as they are not demanding something against God's will. Partly Luther argues for this teaching about civil obedience and a positive view of engaging society on the basis of creation theology and on the basis of actual apostolic words in which it is said that life in society is something that the Creator has commanded and willed. Partly Luther argues for the civil obedience of Christians out of a desire not to endanger the preaching of the Gospel. From the perspective of both creation and salvation, an earthly regiment needs to exist and needs to be obeyed by believers. One ought not oppose the Creator's left hand and the world's civil government, however deficiently it is practiced by those who rule. One ought not inspire suspicion of the Gospel through an overemphasized freedom and revolution, thereby preventing people from receiving it in faith. At the same time, we have seen that obedience to the authorities and their laws has a limit. A Christian ought not be forced to act against God's commands and will. Evil actions cannot be made good, even by the decision and demand of the ruling authorities. Those authorities ought not involve themselves in that which concerns faith and a conscience bound by God's Word.

MISSION WORK IN GENTLENESS AND FORBEARANCE

It is not only obedience and a positive attitude toward the authorities, their laws, and the civil life that are important for the progress of the Gospel. The general stance of the Christians to those outside of the church is also decisive for mission and evangelization. I will here show how Luther, on the basis of the exhortations of the apostles, stresses that when Christians interact with unbelievers they must do so with gentleness, forbearance, and goodness, whatever they might encounter in the world of unbelief.

In this context, Luther reflects on Philippians 4:5, "Let your gentleness be evident to all." After Paul has written about the joy of faith in Christ and about the

---

392 WA 21:343.19ff., 343.28ff.; 47:738.7ff., 738.16ff., especially 47:739.2ff.: "Si servus. Cur serviam Domino, cum alia vita? Wils lassen stehen, princeps: non defendam subditos. Non sic, sed obedite etc. Haec vita non est Christiana, sed transitoria, et tamen vult Deus, das du dich ehrlich drin haltest. Si etiam mihi hodie moriendum, tamen fatiam, quod est offitii mei, bis in die gruben hinein."

forgiveness of sins, he encourages Christians to be mild, yielding, forbearing, not to insist on their rights, and to follow the example of Christ, thus the Gospel and faith might have more possibilities to spread. Christians ought by their lifestyle to present no reason for disunity and vexation. People ought to be good and gentle toward all—poor and rich, sad and happy. Christian love does not seek its own will but willingly allows the neighbor to get his or her way. This position is also proven by other New Testament texts.[393] The reformer emphasizes that a Christian must show patience, relinquish his or her rights for the good of others and give way, and possess a disposition characterized by love. The apostle exhorts Christians to have this attitude toward all people. He knows that the way of love is opposed to human nature's constant pursuit of power, rights, and its own will.[394]

---

393 *Advent Postil* 1522, WA 10/1.2:173.26–180.33. See especially Lenker 6:96–97 (WA 10/1.2:174.1ff.): "Rejoice always before God, but before men be forbearing. Direct your life so as to do and suffer everything not contrary to the commandments of God, that you may make yourselves universally agreeable. Not only refrain from offending any, but put the best possible construction upon the conduct of others. Aim to be clearly recognized as men indifferent to circumstances, as content whether you be hit or missed, and holding to no privilege at all liable to bring you into conflict or produce discord. With the rich be rich; with the poor, poor. Rejoice with the joyful, weep with the mourning [Rom 12:15]. Finally, be all things to all men [1 Cor 9:22], compelling them to confess you always agreeable, uniformly pleasant to mankind and on a level with everyone. Such is the meaning of the little word employed by the apostle—'epiikia,' equity, clemency, accommodation—and which we cannot better render than by 'moderation' or 'forbearance.' It is the virtue of adapting or accommodating oneself to another; of endorsing that other; of making all equal; of presenting a like attitude toward all men; not setting oneself up as a model and pattern; not desiring mankind to do homage to one, to conform to one's position."

394 Lenker 6:100–101 (WA 10/1.2:177.16ff.): "Now, the illustrations given serve as examples to follow in every instance. As Paul here teaches, let one put himself on an equality with all men, being not content to consider simply his own claims and rights, but the wishes and well-being of others. Paul has here in a single word set aside all rights. If your neighbor's condition really demands that you yield a certain personal right or privilege, and you insist upon that privilege, you act at variance with the principle of love and equality and are indeed blameworthy. . . . Indeed, we further add, in the event of one working you harm or injury, you are to put the best construction upon his act, excusing it in the spirit of that holy martyr who, when all his possessions were taken from him, said, 'Truly, they can never take Christ from me.'" A Christian's stance toward both good and evil people should always look like the love and forbearance of friendship. Lenker 6:101 (WA 10/1.2:178.6ff.): "Each did what pleased his fellow. Each yielded, submitted, suffered, wrought and accepted, just in accordance with this conception of what might profit or please the other, and all voluntarily without constraint . . . [I]n their case was neither law, demand, restraint, nor fear; naught but perfect freedom and good will. Yet all things moved in a harmony the hundredth part of which could not be secured by any laws or restraints." Luther emphasizes that

When Paul says that gentleness ought to be evident to all, he does not mean that one ought to boast or advertise his or her mildness and goodness. One ought not at all think or speak about one's own forbearance. Instead, one ought to practice mildness in actual life, in how one acts in the world. If such should occur, those without faith will have to admit that there is substance to the disposition and works of the Christian. As it says in Matthew 5:16 and 1 Peter 2:12, they will be enticed to praise God for the sake of those who bear Christ.[395] Goodness and the willingness to forbear and to yield to others are part and parcel of Christian discipleship. In addition, these characteristics are extraordinarily important as lifestyle mission. A Christian who is characterized by such a disposition and by such works entices others to the Gospel and faith. Not their own rights, not their own interests and wishes, not the modern self-realization, etc., but the concern to always win someone for Christ ought to permeate and form the life of the Christian, according to Luther. The reformer proves this by attaching to his exposition of Philippians 4:5 a reference to 1 Corinthians 9:20–22:

> To the Jews I became like a Jew, to win the Jews. To those under the law I became like one under the law (though I myself am not under the law), so as to win those under the law. To those not having the law I became like one not having the law (though I am not free from God's law but am under Christ's law), so as to win those not having the law. To the weak I became weak, to win the weak. I have become all things to all men so that by all possible means I might save some.[396]

---

the apostle teaches love, forbearance, and relinquishment of one's own rights toward all sorts of people, that is, poor and rich, friends and enemies, relatives and strangers; see WA 10/1.2:179.21ff. Paul's words oppose human nature to the highest degree; see WA 10/1.2:178.15ff., 180.18ff.

395 Lenker 6:101–2 (WA 10/1.2:179.3f., 179.6ff., 179.21ff.): " 'Let your forbearance be known unto all men.' . . . Paul does not say, boast of and proclaim your forbearance. He says, let it be experimentally known by all men. That is, exercise forbearance in your deeds before men; not think or speak of it, but show it in your conduct. Thus men generally must see and grasp it—must have experience of it. Then no one can do otherwise than admit you are forbearing. Actual experience will defeat every desire to speak of you in any other way. The mouth of the fault-finder will be stopped by the fact that all men know your forbearance. Christ says (Mt 5, 16): 'Even so let your light so shine before men; that they may see your good works, and glorify your Father who is in heaven.' And Peter (1 Pet 2, 12): 'Having your behavior seemly among the Gentiles; that, wherein they speak against you as evil-doers, they may by your good works, which they behold, glorify God in the day of visitation.' "

396 WA 10/1.2:175.5ff.

But especially in this connection, it is important to note that the compromises and concessions undertaken for the sake of saving others must not lead to a compromise of the Gospel, of faith, nor of Christian liberty.[397]

The second chapter of Paul's letter to Titus exhorts Christians to an honest life among people. For example, Titus 2:7–8 says: "In everything set them an example by doing what is good. In your teaching show integrity, seriousness and soundness of speech that cannot be condemned, so that those who oppose you may be ashamed because they have nothing bad to say about us." Luther focuses here on the point that Christians ought to live in such a way that non-Christians have no real reason to accuse them. The Gospel about Christ is always a stumbling block for those who do not believe. But that is all the more reason for Christians to teach about lifestyle in such a way that non-Christians are not repulsed but attracted to the Gospel and become Christians.[398] Luther refers to 1 Corinthians 7:21; Ephesians 6:5f.; and Colossians 3:22f. and encourages servants (Titus 2:9) to please their masters, not to protest against them, nor to use their possessions dishonestly. Simple honesty and faithfulness, in whatever work it might be, ought to be the basic rule for Christians. In all one's work, one ought to serve as if one were serving God himself, says Luther.[399] By such a lifestyle and disposition to serve, Christians will be known as honest people. But they also become, according to Titus 2:9–10, "a decoration of God's doctrine" that many turn to Christ.[400] Even here we

---

397 WA 10/1.2:175.16ff., 175.33ff., 176.6ff.

398 *Lectures on Titus and Philemon* (1527), LW 29:60 (WA 25:48.4ff.): "8. *Sound speech that cannot be censured.* It still causes offense, but because of the truth. I have not said or taught anything, but the Holy Spirit has. It is our aim that your word may be irreproachable. Why is that? That we may be justified by it? No, but so that the heathen are not alienated, but when they see you teaching as I have prescribed, are moved by your doctrine and are converted. If, on the other hand, the doctrine is not sound and they inculcate it, you will have many opponents—heathen with their philosophy, Jews with circumcision and the Law, and wiseacres who will create trouble. Therefore since you are set 'in the midst of a crooked nation' (Phil. 2:15), who are not only offended but look for offenses, conduct yourselves in such a way that they do not find them" (*original emphasis*).

399 WA 25:48.15ff., 49.22ff., 50.7ff.

400 WA 25:50.22ff.: "Sic Paulus: est etiam rhetor, qui unam sententiam varie loquitur, supra verbum dei 'ministerium nostrum' hic 'ut ornent doctrinam'. Eadem sententia, quia si ita sum, ut hic describit, orno verbum. Gentilis nihil potest dicere, si habet Christianum servum, qui per omnia studet placere, cogitur dicere ich hab warlich probum servum. Si est infidelis, dicit: volo cuiuscunque conditionis habere servum quam Christianum. Sic deturpatur doctrina salutaris. . . . Non per bonam vitam tantum glorificatur coram hominibus et tamen ista gloria non fit simpliciter pro verbo, sed ut alii convertantur. Ergo vita bona praestanda, ut convertantur plures non ut

see that the reformer reckons with a lifestyle mission. Only the Gospel can give faith, but a mild and honest life among Christians can open the way for the Gospel.

Luther also considers Titus 3:2 a broader and more general exhortation about the Christians' manner of life, especially toward those outside of the church. Paul exhorts "to slander no one, to be peaceable and considerate, and to show true humility toward all men." Christians ought not abuse nor be rebellious vis-à-vis the authorities or others. Instead of the usual *maledicere et rebellare* of the people, Christians should clothe themselves in gentleness, mildness, and forbearance (Greek: ἐπιείκεια). While referring to, among other passages, 2 Corinthians 10:1ff., 10ff.; Philippians 4:5; and Titus 2:2ff., Luther emphasizes how important mildness and gentleness is when Christians interact with non-Christians.[401] In the context of all the injustice and vulgarity that exists in human society, Christians ought to learn gentleness, forbearance, and not to press the demands of righteousness on unbelievers. Wherever unbelief and darkness reign, which is everywhere, a Christian does not rule like a commissioner of righteousness against all that is evil and wrong. The one who is wise in faith overlooks much and clothes himself or herself in a mild manner and to a certain degree with tolerance in the encounter with unbelievers and open heathenism. Ἐπιείκεια is one of the most important virtues to prevent blocking people for the Gospel.[402] The apostle's

---

salutem consequantur." Cf. WA 25:51.1ff. Concerning God's grace that fosters "a disciplined, righteous and godly life in this present age," see WA 25:51.17–52.13.

401 WA 25:58.20–60.26.

402 LW 29:75–76 (WA 25:59.16ff.): "And earlier in chapter 2, verse 2, he spoke of wisdom, whose virtue it is that a Christian be gentle, flexible, kind and yielding to the evil, the weak, and to all cases of misfortune. In summary, whenever we Christians abide in the world, in the kingdom of the devil, it is necessary that certain things be decided upon; but when what is decided upon is carried out imperfectly, one must be courageous and sing: 'So what!' I will not grieve myself to death, as new rulers sometimes do. One must dissemble a great deal, ignore and not see, which is a necessary virtue. Whoever does not know how to dissemble does not know how to rule; he does not know how to live with people. . . . Therefore this virtue is praised most of all and is the treasure which the Lord entrusts in consequence of epieikeia. A gentle person does not become angry. . . . [*To show perfect*] *courtesy* [*to all men*], that is, this gentle behavior and dissembling. The whole book of Ecclesiastes teaches nothing but epieikeia" (*original emphasis*). LW 29:76 (WA 25:60.1ff.): "Therefore it is a patience toward public evils as well as a patience and tolerance toward private evils. Whoever is able to be gentle in that area, to soften the rigor of the law and of justice, is ἐπιειεχής. Therefore when those who have been placed under magistrates see many things in the public realm which offend us and which ought to be changed, you must, if you want to be a good example to the heathen, put up with them and let them go, even though they trouble and bother you."

exhortation for Christians "to show true humility toward all men" also signifies that this nonjudgmental and mild stance ought to be practiced concretely in relationships with those outside the church.[403] Gentle and humble Christians do not become bogged down or grieve over every evil or vulgar thing they meet. The apostle exhorts us to bear all ill will as others are forced to bear our own envy and malice.[404]

Luther also finds clear indications of the importance of lifestyle for mission in 1 Peter 2:12: "Live such good lives among the pagans that, though they accuse you of doing wrong, they may see your good deeds and glorify God on the day he visits us." The reformer comments on the verse in 1523:

> Look at the excellent sequence St. Peter observes here. He has just taught us [v. 11] what we should do to subdue our flesh with all its evil lusts. Now he also teaches us why this should be done. Why should I subdue my flesh? That I may be saved? No, but in order to maintain good conduct before the world. For good conduct does not make us pious, but we must be pious and believe before we begin to maintain good conduct. But I should not maintain this good conduct in my own interest; I must do so in order that the Gentiles may mend their ways [gebessert] and be attracted [gereytzt] by it, that they may also come to Christ through us, which is a true work of love. They malign and chide us; they regard us as the worst scoundrels. Therefore we should exemplify such fine conduct that they have to say: "Ah, one can find no fault with them!"[405]

The quotation shows that for Luther an exemplary lifestyle does not provide saving righteousness before God. But a good and holy life in the world is extraordinarily important so the pagans will not be inimically inclined when they hear mission preaching. Luther refers also to the positive statement (ca. A.D. 112) of the governor Pliny, who served Caesar Trajan, who writes that no complaint could be lodged against the Christians. It is remarkable that the reformer is aware of this document from the early church. The document and Peter's words teach us clearly that mission meets an unavoidable and undeserved opposition. But it is the good behavior of the Christians among the pagans that leads to the circumstance in

---

403 WA 25:60.8ff.

404 LW 29:77 (WA 25:60.19ff.): "There will be peace only if you are ἐπιειεχής and courteous, if you do not take things personally, if you do not become exercised even when something bad happens to you, if anger does not bite you. Some people pine away with envy, will be consumed with the most evil thoughts, and are their own worst cross.... We should, he says, bear the malicious acts of others. Why? Look behind you. If you see how your envy is tolerated and how those who are compelled to put up with your envy behave, you should act the same way toward that of others."

405 LW 30:72 (WA 12:326.32ff.).

which the protests of the pagans are transformed to spiritual breakthrough and the praise of the pagans to God.[406]

Luther presents similar statements on the basis of 1 Peter 2:15. After the apostle (vv. 13ff.) has taught about how Christians ought to obey all human orders and authorities, he says: "For it is God's will that by doing good you should silence the ignorant talk of foolish men." Christians do not become righteous before God by their good works, but good behavior among those who oppose mission work has its own particular power to open people for the Gospel.[407]

In a 1539/1543 sermon on 1 Peter 2:11–20, the older Luther[408] maintains the importance of the struggle against the lusts of the sinful nature and of righteous Christian behavior for the expansion of the Gospel. Neither Jesus nor the apostles have in the work of God's reign taught that Christians ought to change the given forms of government, laws, and culture. Mission workers and Christians ought, as "guest workers" in the world, gratefully receive and serve all good human orders, faithfully work in their earthly callings, and live honestly among all people.[409] This is always important in the work of church and mission. Luther identifies Jeremiah 29:5ff. and the Babylonian exile as illustrations of this contextualization by God's people and mission in the given sociopolitical situation. Here the people are

---

406 LW 30:72 (WA 12:327.12ff.): "We read that when the emperors reigned and persecuted the Christians, one could find no fault with the Christians except that they worshiped Christ and regarded Him as a god. Thus Pliny writes to the emperor Trajan that he knew no wrong the Christians committed except that they assembled early every morning and sang some hymns of praise, with which they honored their Christ, and that they partook of the Sacrament. Otherwise no one could find any fault with them. Therefore St. Peter now says: You must endure being spoken against as wrongdoers. Consequently, you must maintain such conduct that you harm no one. Then you will cause them to mend their ways. 'On the day of visitation,' that is, you must endure their chiding until it becomes manifest and is revealed how unjustly they have treated you, and they have to glorify God in you." Concerning Pliny's letter (Tert. *Apol.* 2 and Euseb.h.e. III, 33), see the church history books, among others, Christensen and Göransson, *Kyrkohistoria*, 1:57. The information in Pliny's letter led Trajan (ca. A.D. 112) to mitigate the imperial religious policy vis-à-vis the Christians, a mitigation that endured until the Decian persecutions of A.D. 250–251.

407 LW 30:75 (WA 12:329.22ff.): "This must be your reply: 'Although we derive no benefit from this, we should nevertheless do it for God without recompense to stop the mouths of God's enemies, who chide us. Then they cannot charge us with anything and must say that we are pious and obedient people.' Thus one reads of many saints that they went to war under pagan princes, slew the enemy, and were subject and obedient to these princes."

408 A 1539 sermon on 1 Peter 2:11–20, WA 47:735–41. In my analysis, I use Cruziger's somewhat later German text in the 1543 *Summer Postil*, WA 21:339–49.

409 WA 21:342ff. (partially cited in *Luther and World Mission*, 253–54n359).

encouraged to patience, work, sowing and reaping, marriage and childbearing while also praying for those who hold the Jews in exile for seventy years.[410]

The struggle against the sinful nature prevents one from losing the spiritual good. Honest and upright lives also prevent God's name from being blasphemed. Instead, God's name will be praised on the basis of the ordered and peaceful lives of Christians. God's Word and God's name meet with a fundamental and unavoidable opposition among pagans and nonbelievers. Therefore it is necessary that Christians in mission and evangelization live so they give no reason for criticism on the basis of their lifestyles. With their confession and their lives, they ought to praise God (Matthew 5:16) so those who stand outside the church are drawn to the Gospel and faith. Especially in an explicitly pagan context, Peter and Luther exhort Christians to patient service. All ought to be done for the sake of God's Word and God's name.[411]

As a conclusion to this particular question, I want to point out briefly how important it is for mission and evangelization that Christians are generally characterized as good, patient, perseverant, and tolerant in their meeting with pagans and non-Christians. Among other things, this means that Christians ought not act as though they sought justice for themselves or even for justice in general. For the sake of the Gospel, they must clothe themselves in a conciliatory spirit and in a rightly understood gentleness toward all peoples. A behavior that exhibits opposition awakens anger and prevents the expansion of the Gospel. With the apostles, Luther emphasizes that this includes a gentleness and patience toward all people,

---

410 WA 21:344.3ff., 344.14ff.

411 Lenker 7:283–84 (WA 21:348.5ff.): "The apostle assigns two reasons for such self-denial: First, that we may not, through carnal, lustful habits, lose the spiritual and eternal; second, that God's name and the glory we have in Christ may not be slandered among our heathen adversaries, but rather, because of our good works, honored. These are the chief reasons for doing good works. They ought most forcibly to urge us to the performance of our duties." Luther develops how spiritual laziness can lead to the loss of the eternal inheritance, WA 21:348.12ff. Then he continues: "In the second place, God's honor calls for it. God's honor here on earth is affected by our manner of life. We are to avoid giving occasion for our enemies to open their mouths in calumniation of God's name and his Word. Rather must we magnify the name of God by our confession and general conduct, and thus win others, who shall with us confess and honor him. Christ commands (Mt 5, 16): 'Even so let your light shine before men; that they may see your good works, and glorify your Father who is in heaven.' Peter proceeds to enumerate certain good works appropriate to Christians in all stations of life, particularly those Christians under authority, or in a state of servitude—men-servants and maid-servants. In the apostle's day, Christians had to submit to heathen authority—to serve unbelieving masters. Peter admonishes Christians to glorify God by their conduct, patiently bearing the violence and injustice offered, and forbearing to return evil" (Lenker 7:284–85 [WA 21:348.30ff.]).

something that must take shape in concrete living and acting. Such a behavior and such a life make the enemies of the church change their understanding and draws them to the Gospel and the Christian faith. Indeed, Luther believes that an honest lifestyle and the goodness and mildness of Christians help people to glorify God's name and God's Word with church and mission. Especially enticing is goodness, the willingness to forbear with the deficiencies of the lifestyle of the pagans and non-Christians, and the concrete service to the authorities and all people when one evangelizes in an openly pagan context. It ought also to be observed that the reformer who presents the Word/Gospel as the main instrument of mission/evangelization also exhorts to a mission of lifestyle, that is, a lifestyle that does not block people but opens them for and draws them to the Gospel and Christ.

MISSION WORK WITH PRAYER, THANKSGIVING, AND CONFIDENCE

A powerful and prevalent theme in Luther's expositions of the New Testament Epistles is that all work in God's reign must be characterized and surrounded by thanksgiving, prayer, and the confidence of faith that the work in the power of the Father, Son, and the Holy Spirit will win success.

When we analyzed the petition "Thy kingdom come" (Matthew 6:10), we saw that Luther prays for the expansion of the Gospel and faith both in Germany and in the non-Christian world.[412] Luther does not directly comment or preach on the key passages concerning prayer for missions, that is, Ephesians 6:18–20 and Colossians 4:2–3, but the theme appears in connection with other texts. Luther comments on Paul's thanksgiving and prayer for the problematic Corinthian congregation (1 Corinthians 1:4ff.) and applies it to the situation in Germany. Both preachers and laypeople must thank God for the Word/Gospel and pray that it would gain a fast foothold because Satan and his conspirators are always busy. It is one thing to begin believing; it is another to be grounded in faith in Christ and a holy life. Especially the time of breakthrough for mission and reformation must be carried by prayer and thanksgiving.[413]

Luther preaches in a similar manner in 1525 and 1537 on Ephesians 3:14ff. He emphasizes the unspeakable joy for a region blessed by the Gospel and salvation from Satan, sin, and hell through Christ. In the struggle that always exists on the battle lines between the reign of God and the destructive work of the devil, the initial knowledge and faith must, however, be matured and strengthened.[414] Therefore Paul on the mission frontlines and Luther on the Reformation front lines

---

412 See *Luther and World Mission*, 131ff.

413 Sermons on 1 Corinthians 1:4ff., WA 41:696ff.; 49:620ff. See also Ellwein, *Luthers Epistel-Auslegung*, 2:16ff.

414 WA 17/1:430.7ff., 430.31ff.; 45:139.30ff., 140.34ff.

bend their knees and pray to the Father that God's Word and grace might go deeply into the hearts of people so the faith, life, and love of Christians might be improved. Especially preachers ought to pray that the Word would gain strength in a living faith and in service to the neighbor. Nevertheless, Luther underlines that intercession for the work of the reign of God ought to be the practice of all Christians.[415] One ought to pray to God the Father in the name of Jesus Christ. Only in the name of this mediator can we in prayer approach God as our Father.[416]

When the reformer preaches on Ephesians 3:14ff., he is above all concerned that intercession will help new Christians to leave all inconstancy to the Word and faith and to embrace faith and Christ and a sanctified life with all their hearts. Because the opposite result is often the case in mission and evangelization, intercession is important for the apostle. Christians always lack faith, engagement, and strength, but this should not be allowed to create a complaining attitude in us. Instead of complaining, Paul and the Scriptures command us to pray.[417] The strengthening of faith and life does not occur through the Christian's own strength

---

415 WA 17/1:428.28ff. See especially Lenker 8:267–68 (WA 17/1:429.8ff.): "Note how Paul devotes himself to the welfare of the Christian community. He sets an example, to us ministers in particular, of how to effect the good of the people. But we do not rightly heed his example. We imagine it sufficient to hear the Gospel and be able to discourse about it; we stop at the mere knowledge of it; we never avail ourselves of the Gospel's power in the struggles of life. Unquestionably, the trouble is, we do not earnestly pray. We ought constantly to come to God with great longing, entreating him day and night to give the Word power to move men's hearts. David says (Ps 68, 33), 'Lo, he uttereth his voice, a mighty voice.' Not only preachers, but all Christians, should constantly entreat the God who grants knowledge to grant also efficacy; should beseech him that the Word may not pass with the utterance, but may manifest itself in power. . . . Well may we pray, then, as Paul does here. He says, in effect: 'You are well supplied: the Word is richly proclaimed to you—abundantly poured out upon you. But I bend my knees to God, praying that he may add his blessing to the Word and grant you to behold his honor and praise and to be firmly established, that the Word may grow in you and yield fruit.'" Cf. WA 45:139.4ff., 139.24ff.

416 WA 17/1:430.7ff., 430.31ff. Cf. WA 45:139.30ff., 140.34ff.

417 Lenker 8:272 (WA 17/1:433.5ff.): "But what are the blessings for which Paul's prayer entreats? Something more than continuance of the Word with his followers, though it is a great and good gift even to have the Word thoroughly taught: he prays that the heart may taste the Word and that it may be effectual in the life. Thus the apostle contrasts a knowledge of the Word with the power of the Word. Many have the knowledge, but few the impelling and productive power that the results may be as we teach." Cf. WA 45:141.3ff. Concerning the accusations from Rome that the evangelicals who hear so many comforting sermons nevertheless become worse in their lives than they were before, Luther says: "In the first place, considering our unsatisfactory condition and the lack of power with the Word, we have great reason to pray with the earnestness Paul's example teaches. And secondly, though our enemies see little improvement and few

but through the Holy Spirit, as Paul says in Ephesians 3:16.[418] Through the Holy Spirit and faith, Christ becomes known and dwells in the heart (Ephesians 3:17). In grace, then, he rules the faith and life of the Christians. However weak a Christian might be, by faith in Christ he or she has victory over all the forces of destruction.[419] Through the Spirit and faith in God's Son, Christians are grounded in love toward neighbor. Therefore the right intercession always begins first with the strengthening of faith and then its consequences in love and life.[420]

For Luther the attitude that characterizes preachers and Christians in the work of God's reign from the time of the Gospel's breakthrough is important. In connection with Philippians 1:3–11, the reformer calls attention to the fact that thanksgiving and prayer/intercession must constantly engage the ordained and the laypeople during the Gospel's progress out to people. One may thank God for the Gospel one has received by faith. One may pray that the Gospel might gain

---

fruits of the Gospel, it is not theirs to judge. They think we ought to do nothing but work miracles—raising the dead and bordering the Christian's walk with roses, until naught but holiness obtains everywhere. This being the case, where would be the need to pray? . . . But, since Paul and other Scripture authorities command us to pray, a defect somewhere in our strength is indicated. . . . Thus Paul himself acknowledges that the Ephesians were weak" (Lenker 8:273 [WA 17/1:433.15ff.]).

418 WA 17/1:435.7ff.

419 Lenker 8:276 (WA 17/1:436.1ff.): " 'That Christ may dwell in your hearts through faith' [Eph. 3:17]. The Holy Spirit brings Christ into the heart and teaches it to know him. He imparts warmth and courage through faith in Christ. Paul everywhere intimates that no man should presume to approach God otherwise than through Christ, the one Mediator. Now, if Christ dwells in my heart and regulates my entire life, it matters not though my faith be weak. . . . And where he dwells all fullness is, let the individual be weak or strong as God permits. . . . For Christ to dwell in the heart is simply for the heart to know him; in other words, to understand who he is and what we are to expect from him—that he is our Saviour, through whom we may call God our Father and may receive the Spirit who imparts courage to brave all trials." Cf. WA 17/1:437.30ff.

420 Lenker 8:277 (WA 17/1:436.30ff.): "Is it not in faith that we are to be rooted, engrafted and grounded? . . . I reply: Faith, it is true, is the essential thing, but love shows whether or no faith is real and the heart confident and courageous in God. Where one has an unquestioning confidence that God is his Father, necessarily, be his faith never so weak, that faith must find expression in word and deed. He will serve his neighbor in teaching and in extending to him a helping hand. This is what Paul calls being rooted and grounded in love." Lenker 8:278 (WA 17/1:437.5ff.): "So by these two clauses Paul teaches, first, that we should have in our hearts genuine faith toward God; and second, that faith should find expression in loving service to one's neighbor." Cf. on Ephesians 3:19 concerning Christ's love toward us and our love to our neighbor, WA 17/1:438.6ff. Concerning the words about being filled by God's fullness, Luther says we may pray for this, but it will never fully occur in this age (WA 17/1:438.14ff.).

even greater progress and a fast foothold. That which is possessed by faith can be easily lost through Satan's power. Here prayer with thanksgiving is a necessity.[421] Luther says expressly that the work of reformation would never have had such success without prayer and thanksgiving. One ought to work in God's power with prayer and joy.[422] All Christians and especially preachers must be confident that God does not let the work of his reign be in vain or without fruit. With such confidence, the Word and the Sacraments ought to be administered, and wherever they are being used, some will always come to faith. God and Christ work in the work of the church.[423] They continue to work until Christ's parousia. Therefore

---

421 A 1537 sermon, WA 45:198.7ff.: "1. opus Christiani, ut cor, os semper loquatur deo gratias pro bonis, quae dat, et sic erga homines etiam. 2. opus ist das, ut Christiani orent, quoties oro, facio, danckopffer ist en werck gegen Gott. . . . Dixi das danckopffer esse praecipuam partem praedicationis, sic 2. orationis, quae fit ante et post praedicationem. Sicut danck est de donis, quae accepimus, Sic oratio von dem ungluck, des wir gern los weren. . . . Habemus quidem omnia, sed in fide, illic im schawen. Jst noch der alt schalk am hals, lesst uns nicht gern gedencken an die 10 tausent pfund, ideo opus oratione, ut gehen im schwang, non pro nobis paucis, sed omnibus et praecipue Ecclesia, ut cor Christianum gratias agat pro concione Euangelii ut hic Paulus. Ideo simus frolich und singen das Haleluja und bitten, ut inceptum opus, quod dedit concionem Euangelii, ut sui cordis gaudium et lust, das er sehe, quomodo homines susceperint Euangelium, und danckt und preiset und wundscht ut alii accedant, ut gaudium plenum, nicht ein solcher schlinger, qui nihil curet, an homines credant, sed semper cogitat: hilff, lieber vater, un nomen tuum, Regnum, ut diabolus in suo nomine geschendet, sein wil gehindert." Cf. this sermon in Cruziger's 1544 *Summer Postil*, WA 22:352ff., 358ff.

422 WA 45:199.1ff.: "Nostrum Eangelium wer so weit nicht gangen, nisi nostra oratio tam efficax. Haben nun schier 20 jar getobet, et tamen all anschlege zuruck, feilet nicht an weisheit, gewalt et deo, qui est Teufel, et tamen sanctificatur nomen dei et confirmatur eius regnum. Omnia hinc, quod oramus et laudamus. . . . Ideo last uns nur getrost die 2 Christlich ampt treiben: gratias agere et orare etc. et palpamus manibus." Cf. WA 41:459.16ff., 460.3ff.

423 WA 41:460.20ff.: " 'Et bin des inn guter zuversicht' [Philippians 1:6]. Illam trost mus ich haben et omnis praedicator pius, quod non umbsonst predigen. Nos praedicatores et vos Christiani, non wird labor noster verlorn sein, ista est consolatio nostra et vestra. Hic sunt quidam, ob der grosse hauffe tol, toricht etc. tamen, inquit, meum grosser trost, dank gebet, quod scio: is wirds nicht lassen so sthen, sed hin aus furen. . . . Si kundten ausschelen und sondern korn a sprew, libenter, sed non possum. Ideo dico cum Paulo: habeo fiduciam, et kan nicht feylen, quod is, qui incipit praedicare, administrare Sacramentum, non etc. Si papa et alii, feret hin, tamen aliqui, qui credunt, darauff trotzen wir. Ubi praedicatur Euangelium, da mussen sein, qui tam sancti, ut fuerunt in vetere Testamento, alioqui wolten gar stock stil schweigen. Ideo propter illos praedicandum. Et quidam, quos iam baptisamus, audient, quia deus vult apud esse, Christus Matth. 28[:20]. Ideo ubi praedicatur Euangelium, da ist Gott." Cf. WA 45:198.8ff., 198.23ff., 198.36ff., 199.1ff., 199.8ff.

church/mission with its Gospel will—despite the evil work of Satan, the pope, and the enthusiasts and despite the fact that one often does not see much tangible result of all the work—defiantly and courageously seek to win people for the reign of God.[424] Luther bases the confidence in and the unflagging work of the Word and the Sacraments on God's promises in Isaiah 55:10f. As the rain falls from heaven, dampens the earth, and makes it fruitful, so it will be with God's Word. It will not return empty without having accomplished that for which God sent his Word.[425]

Even in connection with Colossians 1:6–12, Luther notes how the apostle Paul, while carrying out his mission work, thanks God in prayer because the addressees in Colosse as true Christians believe the Gospel of Christ, live in communal love, and live with an eternal hope.[426] But the apostle also prays and exhorts the new Christians in the congregation to strive for growth and steadfastness in their Christian faith (Colossians 1:9). This more mature and well-grounded faith is important and God wants to grant it because Satan and the world oppose Christian faith and want to extinguish it. The young shoots growing up from the work of God's reign must accordingly grow in knowledge of God's will and in spiritual wisdom concerning salvation in Christ. They ought to be improved in the skill of recognizing false teaching and in the skill of rightly being able to practice

---

424 WA 41:461.5ff.: "Sed ubi deus templum, ibi Teufel capellen. . . . Das ist ausdermassen fein, quod dicit: 'bis auff' etc. [Philippians 1:6] qui incepit, der wird nicht nachlassen. Et verum, quando Euangelium dat Civitati, sunt homines, qui audiunt et in extremo die apparebunt et dicent: hoc audivimus isto vel isto tempore. Ideo habeo consolationem, quod ego et alii, volo cum Petro, Paulo, Esaia her tretten in illo die, et eorum socii et sol nicht feylen. Quia qui cepit, dedit verbum, baptismum etc. wird nach trucken [= helfen] et hin ausfuren auff jhenen etc. Ideo non setzen datum, sed warten auff. den tag etc. Sicut vos credidistis, ita prophetae et Apostoli. . . . Ob mundus dawider ist, schadet nicht, tamen non debemus deserere hanc consolationem. Et scio vere, quo recht von euch halt, cum credatis in Euangelium und halt von der Tauff." Concerning how God permits entire countries to lose the Gospel because of ingratitude and impenitence, see WA 45:195ff.; 22:352ff.

425 WA 41:461.24ff.: "Cum igitur susceperitis Euangelium, sol als ausgericht werden, quicquid locutus. Sic Paulus freuet et gratias agit, quod habet homines, qui an das heilig Euangelium glauben. Et consolatur non solum doctores, sed etiam auditores, quod, ubicunque Euangelium praedicatur, da mussen heiligen sein. Sic Esaias: meum verbum non redibit vacuum [Isaiah 55:10f.]. Similitudo: Sicut pluvia e celo cadit et feuchtet das land et facit, ut sit fructifera, Sic meum faciet verbum, non redibit vacuum. Ideo anhalten praedicando, quia Esaias et Paulus durr, das nicht an frucht ab ghen. Et sol thun, da zu ichs geschickt hab. . . . Ein wort kans thun, da du ewig durch selig wirst, wenn unser herr Gott kompt und rurt dich 1 mal, tum eternum es genesen."

426 WA 34/2:417.12ff.; 41:463.8ff.; 22:375.11ff.

their faith in their earthly callings and in living to the Lord worthily in sanctifica-tion.[427] On the extremely important growth in faith in Christ, Luther says:

> Paul would gladly have a spiritual knowledge of these things increase in us until we are enriched and filled—wholly assured of their truth. Sublime and glorious knowledge this, the experience of a human heart which, born in sins, boldly and confidently believes that God, in his unfathomable majesty, in his divine heart, has irrevocably purposed—and will for all men to accept and believe it—that he will not impute sin, but will forgive it and be gra-cious, and grant eternal life, for the sake of his beloved Son.[428]

From this we see that growth in the knowledge of justification is that which is more important than anything else for the reformer.

Luther also notices how the apostle wants to teach the Christians and the preachers to "have great endurance and patience" (Colossians 1:11) in their work for God's reign. This is important for Luther because all right work for the Word/Gospel is a human work that receives no thanks. One constantly has to struggle with the manipulations of the sectarians and political powers-that-be.[429]

---

427 WA 34/2:418.10ff.: " 'Non cessamus' [Colossians 1:9]. Das ist die praecipua oratio, ut non tantum audiatis et comprehendatis eius voluntatem, sed ut divites, ja vol und volkomen in hac kunst und erkentnis, quae eius voluntas sit. . . . Ipse optat, ut non solum incipiant, sed reich und vol, 2. ut etiam agnoscant und reichlich gwis werden, quae dei voluntas, quae? Ut Christus: qui videt filium, salvus etc. Hoc etiam hodie praedicavimus. Praecipua dei voluntas, ut agnoscamus illum filium, ut salvemur. . . . Multi quidem habent erkentnis, sed die fülle haben und reichlich sein in hac cogni-tione etc." Cf. WA 41:463.12ff., 464.5ff.; 45:255.20ff. See also Cruziger's *Summer Postil*, WA 22:375.3ff., especially: "Therefore let us learn this truth and with Paul pray for what we and all Christians supremely need—full knowledge of God's will, not a mere beginning; for we are not to imagine a beginning will suffice and to stop there as if we had comprehended it all. Everything is not accomplished in the mere planting; water-ing and cultivation must follow. In this case the watering and cultivating are the Word of God, and prayer against the devil, who day and night labors to suppress spiritual knowledge, to beat down the tender plants wherever he sees them springing up; and also against the world, which promotes only opposition and directs its wisdom and reason to conflicting ends. Did not God protect us and strengthen the knowl-edge of his will, we would soon see the devil's power and the extent of our spiritual understanding" (Lenker 8:362–63 [WA 22:378.3ff.]). See also WA 22:380.36ff.; 34/2:420.5ff.; 41:466.6ff.; 45:256.31ff., 258.13ff. On how to "live a life worthy of the Lord" and to bear "fruit in every good work" (Colossians 1:10), see WA 22:385.36ff.; 34/2:421.1ff.; 41:467.1ff.

428 Lenker 8:361 (WA 22:376.32ff.).

429 WA 34/2:421.5ff.: "Nach der erkentnis und weisheit ist 3. gedultig sein. Omnes, qui pure volunt Euangelium praedicare und halten, vide, wies yhn ghett. Rottae wolten gern das erkentnis, weisheit und verstand, Weltlich oberkeit impedit, ut non praedice-

But the power in and defense of the work of God's reign does not come from any human being but from God. By God's power and despite everything else, great things happen where the Word/Gospel is active.[430] Thanksgiving, prayer, patience, and endurance have their source in the fact that God has had mercy on people and through the Word and Sacraments provided them a share in eternal life.[431]

As a summary, one might say concerning Luther's emphasis on intercession and thanksgiving, on confidence in the progress of the work of God's reign, and on the importance of patience in all work for the Gospel that one ought never forget that the work of the church/mission occurs in a world in which the cosmic struggle and antagonism between God and Satan, the reign of God and the reign of Satan, is a tangible reality. The church and mission have only in God—the Father, the Son, and the Holy Spirit—their guarantee, source, and power. Therefore mission and evangelization must seek power, joy, and endurance where it is available. The church's work in the reign of God can endure and be successful only through prayer and thanksgiving and in the trust that God himself works in the

---

tur, et occidit. Quic hic? Num sollen uns wheren? Non, sed es ist seltzam geredt, Ja böse Text: 'cum patientia et gaudio' [Colossians 1:11]. Quis hoc facit? Ex corde credere in Christum und so treulich dienen, quod officium requirit, und zw lohn nhemen ingratitudinem, contemptum, Tücke, aliquis diceret: Jch lies das predigen etc. . . . Ideo si vis Christianus et credere und treulich dienen, richt dein cor dahin, undanck und hertzeleid zu danck. Ideo opus oratione." Cf. WA 22:386.22ff. and 41:466.11ff.

430 WA 34/2:422.6ff.: "In patientia etc. est haec aurea scientia, das ich mich stercke nicht auff keiser Karols, ferdinand noch auff glerten, sed heist: 'Inn der krafft seiner herlichen macht' [Colossians 1:11]. Sic mus ich das Euangelium predigen, et vos bekennen, quando zun zugen kompt, ut wir her halten. Nemo wird mich schutzen nec keiser etc. Si edifico supra hominem, fal ich billich et omnia zu scheittern, quia est edificatum super macht, quae non sua. Sed mus dahin komen, das gedencke, ut patiens und langmutig und kunne leiden, tragen, harren, uberharren und hin austragen. Auff wen? Est unus, hat macht, quae est herrlich, habes potentem dominum, et qui mit grosser herlickeit ausfuret, quando hora venit, das dir geholffen sol werden, fiet admirabilissime." Cf. WA 22:387.1ff.

431 WA 34/2:424.3ff., 425.2ff.: "Et frolich dazu, et habete guten mut. Quomodo? in eius macht. Das ist mirum: frolich sein in trubsal, tücke und bosheit et gedultig sein et gaudium habere, quomodo? . . . Et 'gratias agentes' [Colossians 1:12], got sey gelobt und gebenedeiet, ego credo etc. et ideo patior. 'Qui tuchtig gemacht', quod sumus erben etc. . . . Mens nequam semper dicit: Tu es peccator et indignus. Ego sol sagen, quod sim Sanctus et rechtschaffen, filius und erbe und gesel omnium Sanctorum in caelo . . . . Non solum da fur halten, quod consors prophetarum, quia oportet credas te baptizatum, te audisse Euangelium, sacramentum et Ecclesia, ergo es gesel und mitgenosse omnium Sanctorum. Petrus quid plus habet quam Christum, baptismum, Sacramentum? . . . Quem ipse dignum facit, est dignus, quomodo? per baptismum, Euangelium, Sacramentum."

work of the church. Help for the enormous task of the expansion of God's reign and the fortress of the Christians against all enemies is God's own power and will to save. The work of God's reign shares in God's power and will through prayer and intercession. Prayer opens the way for God's mighty power in the expansion of the Gospel and the edification of the faith of new Christians. Mission and evangelization are ultimately *missio Dei*, even if they may never exist without human tools.

THE WORK OF GOD'S REIGN, SPIRITUAL GIFTS, MINISTRIES, AND OFFICES

As I have often emphasized above, Luther considers the extension of the Gospel as God's work, *missio Dei*. It is the Father, the Son, and the Spirit who ultimately is the acting subject, the driving power, and the guarantee behind the work of church/mission. The triune God builds the church with the tools of the Word and the Sacraments. If this foundation should be lost, one loses something crucial in Luther's missiology.

Nevertheless, the reformer naturally has never been able to ignore the human instruments, the spiritual gifts, the ministries, and the offices of the church's/mission's extension of the Gospel and faith in Christ. Luther is no speculative theologian. Instead, his thought and work relates both to what the Scriptures say and to the church's actual life in the real world. Even as he emphasizes the divine factor, Luther speaks a good deal about the human factor or those who concretely work for the extension of the Gospel.[432] The issue of spiritual gifts, ministries, and

---

432 Here are a couple examples of the connection between the divine and the human factors in mission. On 2 Corinthians 6:1ff., Luther says: "He calls the Corinthians co-workers, as in First Corinthians 3, 9, where he puts it: 'We are God's fellow-workers; ye are God's husbandry, God's building.' That is, we labor upon you with the external Word—teaching and admonishing; but God, working inwardly through the Spirit, gives the blessing and the success. He permits not our labor with the outward Word to be in vain. . . . The apostle's purpose in praising his co-laborers is to prevent them from despising the external Word . . . . For though God is able to effect everything without the instrumentality of the outward Word, working inwardly by his Spirit, this is by no means his purpose. He uses preachers as fellow-workers, or co-laborers, to accomplish his purpose through the Word when and where he pleases" (*Lent Postil* [1525], Lenker 7:134 [WA 17/2:179.11ff.]). Cf. also WA 45:389ff. Luther also says in an undated sermon on 1 Corinthians 3:4ff.: "Got wenn er die Welt wil frum machen, erwelet er lewtt, den legt er sein bevehl Jn mundt, den sollen sie treyben, Neben dyssem Predig ampt ist Gott darbey und rurt durch das mundtlich wort hewt dyss hercz, morgenn dass hercz, Es sind alle prediger nicht mehr denn die handt, die den weg weyset. Sie thut nicht mehr, sie steht still und lest volgen oder nicht volgen dem Rechten weg. . . . Wenn nun Gott vil Rurenn, dass thut er mit dem wort, sie sindt die lewt nicht, die do sollen yemandt from machen, Gott thut dass allein, Die person soll mann awss den awgen thunn, aber die Lere nicht. Dorumb heyst er sie fleischlich, dass sie die Prediger unter-

offices has been an important and controversial matter for church and mission throughout its history. Reflections on these matters in the different confessions cover a wide range from the most hierarchically structured system (the Roman Catholics and the Orthodox) to a model in which the church's ordained minister and the laypeople have a constructive cooperation (among others, the Lutherans) to a structure in which all Christians are considered to be preachers and mission-aries on the basis of the passages concerning the free use of the spiritual gifts.[433] With respect to the important role of human instruments in the accomplish-ment of mission work, I must here add something to those principles that were briefly sketched in chapter 2 (pp. 81–95).

THE APOSTOLATE AND THE MISSION TASK

For this missiological investigation, it is relevant to examine how Luther defines and considers the contents of the church's highest and most unique office, the apostolate. Especially in the commentary on the greetings of the apostolic let-ters, the reformer has developed his own view of the apostolic office. On the one hand he emphasizes the call of the apostles to the mission task, and on the other hand he emphasizes their authority for doctrine and life in the continuing work of the church/mission.

In the *Commentary on Galatians* (1519), Luther argues on the basis of the Greek that the Latin word *apostolus* ought to be translated as "the one sent out." It ought to be observed how carefully Luther unites the concept of the apostolate with the church's missiological nerve and the extension of the Word/Gospel. The church's highest and most unique office, the apostolate, is connected thus with being sent out or being a missionary. The reformer also emphasizes that the word *apostle* stands for something that is at the same time modest and worthy of rever-ence. The apostolate is an office of serving. In his ministry, the apostle is chained and sold to God/Christ as a servant sent with the Word/Gospel. Luther argues against the way the Roman hierarchy connects the apostolate and the episcopacy and hierarchy with worthiness, honor, and the authority to issue human decrees. An apostle is the humble servant of God and Christ who preaches the Gospel to people. An apostle's honor consists only in this. That which is characteristic of the

---

scheiden der person halben und nicht dess Bawen halben, Da soll man wol acht haben, Also sagt Paulus, Er hab den grundt geleget unther den heyden, Man sehe nur, wass ein Jglicher dorauff bawet . . . Man muss Bawlewt haben, die das werck statlich treiben, Also thut Gott, verschafft Erbeitter zu disem gebewe" (WA 45:390.5ff., 390.11ff.). Then Luther adduces 1 Peter 2:5 and Ephesians 4:13 and says: "Dysser Eckstein Jst Christus, do sindt die arbeiter unnd Bawlewt ungleich Dess hantwergks halben" (WA 45:390.26f.).

433 See Molland, *Kristenhetens kirker og trossamfunn.*

apostle's completely unique office ought also to characterize all servants of the Word after the time of the apostles.[434] Consequently, this means that the apostles and all officeholders have the extension of God's reign as their primary task and ought to do all in humble and high service of Christ. This mission center in Luther's view of the church's ministry ought to be carefully observed.

Even in his 1523 exposition of 1 Peter, Luther powerfully expostulates on the ambassadorial character of the apostolate. An apostle is sent and commanded to preach Jesus Christ. On 1 Peter 1:1, Luther comments:

> St. Peter states that he is an apostle, that is, a messenger. Therefore the word has been correctly translated into German with *Eyn bott* or *zwolffbott,* because of the Twelve. Since it is now understood what the Greek word ἀπόστολος means, I have not translated it into German. But it really denotes a messenger—not one who bears letters, but an emissary who puts forth and takes care of a matter by word of mouth. . . . Thus St. Peter wants to say: I am an apostle of Jesus Christ; that is, Jesus Christ has commanded me to preach about Christ. . . . For he who carries out what Christ has commanded is a messenger of Jesus Christ. If he preaches anything else, he is not a messenger of

---

434 LW 27:163–64 (WA 2:452.6ff.): "For the word 'apostle' has the same meaning as 'one who has been sent.' And, as St. Jerome teaches, the Hebrews have a word which they pronounce 'Sila,' that is, a person to whom, from the act of sending, the name 'Sent' is applied. Thus in John 9:7: 'Go, wash in the pool of Siloam (which means Sent).' . . . [Isaiah 8:6; Genesis 49:10; Hebrews 3:1; and Acts 15:22 are here adduced.] . . . A more important consideration, however, is the fact that 'apostle' is a modest name but at the same time a marvelously awesome and venerable one, a name which expresses equally both remarkable lowliness and loftiness. The lowliness lies in the fact that he is sent, thus bearing witness to his office, his role as servant, his obedience. Furthermore, no one should be impressed by the name as being a title of honor, rely on it, or boast of it. No, by the name of the office he should be drawn at once to Him who does the sending, to Him who authorizes it. From Him one then gains a conception of the majesty and loftiness of·him who has been sent and is a servant, in order that he may be received with reverence, not as in our age, when the terms 'apostleship,' 'episcopate,' and all the rest have begun to be words expressive, not of an office but of prestige and authority. . . . And, as the apostle says in Rom. 10:15: 'How will they preach unless they are sent?' Would that the shepherds and leaders of the Christian people in our day properly weighed these teachings! For who can preach unless he is an apostle? But who is an apostle except one who brings the Word of God? And who can bring the Word of God except one who has listened to God? But the man who brings his own dogmas or those that rest on human laws and decrees, or those of the philosopher—can he be called an apostle?" Cf. the investigation of the concept of the apostle in the 1515–1516 lectures on Romans in WA 56:3ff. Luther notes powerfully that an apostle is chosen and separated (*segregatus*). Cf. the *Larger Commentary on Galatians,* WA 40/1:27–30, about the apostolate, the character of the messenger, and the importance attached to the work of the apostles and all officeholders to preach Christ's Gospel.

Christ. Therefore we should not listen to him. But if he preaches what Christ has commanded, this is no different from hearing Christ Himself in person.[435]

Thus the apostle is a messenger who preaches Christ and is faithful to that which Jesus has commanded. Above all, the apostle uses the spoken word.

On the basis of Titus 1:1, the reformer wrote in 1527 that an apostle is a servant of God and Christ with the office, the call, and the command to proclaim the true Gospel of Christ for the world. The character of the apostle as a servant and the greatness given through Christ and God's Word in this office are also emphasized. Luther also emphasizes that that which characterizes the apostolate as the highest and unique ministry of the church ought also to guide the preaching ministry through the ages. On the basis of God's/Christ's instructions, the first apostles have preached Christ and faith in him. All their successors in the church's ordained ministry ought to follow them as examples.[436] This means that the entire ministry of the church ought to be characterized by its mission of proclaiming Jesus Christ.

---

435 LW 30:5 (WA 12:261.9ff.). Cf. WA 12:259.8ff. The quotation in the main text is a good example of how the *viva vox* does not obviate the need of the written Word. Cf. in *Luther and World Mission*, 205–10.

436 See *Lectures on Titus and Philemon* (1527). Luther writes the following on Titus 1:1: "His first assurance is that he calls himself a minister. Every minister ought to glory in this, that he is an instrument of God through which God teaches, and he ought not doubt that he is teaching the Word of God. Peter says (1 Peter 4:11): 'As one who utters oracles of God.' . . . *An apostle.* Not only do I serve God, but I have an office with which I have been commissioned. This is another kind of certainty. Not only does he know that he serves God and that he speaks the Word of God, but also that he has been sent and commissioned by God and that an obligation to teach has been laid upon him. To know the Word of God and to teach it are two different things. He who has the Word of God does not immediately teach it unless he is called. He should teach as an interloper. Here you see what it means to serve Christ and what sort of kingdom Christ has, namely, a spiritual and an invisible one. His kingdom is not seen; therefore His ministers are those who rule by the Word and who bring the Word. Hence the kingdom of Christ is ruled, and Christ is recognized, solely by the Word" (LW 29:4–5 [*original emphasis*] [WA 25:7.4ff., 7.21ff.]). LW 29:5–6 (WA 25:8.1, 8.6ff., 8.15ff.): "It is not without reason that he adds the word 'an apostle of Jesus Christ,' . . . [b]ut Paul is not the sort of servant that Moses and the prophets were. He brings better things, as he says in 2 Cor. 3:7–11. Therefore he adds 'an apostle of Jesus Christ,' as he also says in 2 Cor. 5:20; and here he adds: 'To proclaim the faith.' . . . *According to faith.* These are extraordinarily outstanding words, and they are full of doctrine. Here one could discuss the sum total of the Christian life. These words contradict false dogmas. . . . Faith is that by which we believe in the Lord Jesus through the word of the apostles" (*original emphasis*). Cf. also the investigation in the *Lectures on 1 Timothy* (1528), WA 26:4ff.

According to Luther the call and the task of the apostles is unique. Especially in the commentaries on Galatians 1–2, Luther emphasizes that all apostles and prophets have been called directly and immediately by God and Christ to their ministry. Even the replacement apostle Matthias and the apostle of the Gentiles had such a call. Thereby the apostles were unique legates and ambassadors, the representatives of God and Christ, who with an indisputable authority were to preach and defend the true Gospel with its center in Christ's death and resurrection.[437] Luther summarizes this theme in the 1531/1535 *Lectures on Galatians*:

> Therefore Paul deals thoroughly with this doctrine of the call of the apostles. Elsewhere he distinguishes between apostleship and other ministries, as in 1 Cor. 12:28ff. and in Eph. 4:11, where he says: "And God has ordained some in the church as apostles, prophets, etc." He puts apostles into first place, so that those may properly be called apostles who have been sent immediately by God Himself without any other person as the means. Thus Matthias was called . . . . Since he was to be an apostle, it was necessary that he be called by God. Thus Paul was called be the apostle to the Gentiles (Rom. 11:13). This is why the apostles are called saints; for they are sure of their calling and doctrine and have remained faithful in their ministry, and no one of them has become an apostate except Judas, because their call is a holy one.[438]

Concerning the fact that the original apostles were called directly by God/Christ, the call to the ministry of the Word after the time of the apostles comes publicly and through people, according to the reformer. Paul called his disciples Timothy and Titus. Later, these called bishops who in their turn called their own successors. But these mediated calls are no less God's calls. The direct calls and teaching of the apostles and their successors' indirect calls are a defense against the self-appointed and illegitimate calls of the false apostles and the enthusiasts.[439]

In connection with the apostolic and postapostolic calling and sending to preach the Gospel, one additional problem ought to be mentioned. As we have often shown above, in Luther's view the apostles were sent out to preach the Gospel in the whole world, even if this mission in the sixteenth century had not been completed. The command given to the apostles remains and is being accomplished until Christ's parousia. According to Luther, the church as a whole continues to have the assignment to spread the Gospel to the end of the world and to the end of

---

437 *Lectures on Galatians* (1519), WA 2:453.13–455.34. Cf. the foreword to Galatians, WADB 7:172.11ff. See especially the *Larger Commentary on Galatians*, WA 40/1:56–65. The central passages are WA 40/1:55.24ff., 57.16ff., 58.17ff.

438 LW 26:19 (WA 40/1:61.28ff.).

439 WA 2:454.3ff.; 40/1:56.27ff., 58.18ff., 59.16ff. Cf. the investigation in *Luther and World Mission*, 91ff.

time. However, after the time of the apostles, no bishop, no pastor, and no individual Christian has been entrusted with mission in the entire world. In this thesis lay a sting against the pope's episcopal claim to lead all of Christianity and its mission/evangelization. But Luther distinguishes his thought even from the enthusiasts who, on the basis of the priesthood of all believers, want to grant freedom to all Christians to preach and lead. In Luther's idea about the regionally exclusive (that is, not universal) aspect of church work, some have tried to argue that Luther was against world mission as such. This is a mistake. Luther's idea here in no way hinders a continuing world mission. Luther simply means that after the time of the apostles, certain workers were to focus on certain regions (1 Peter 5:2; Titus 1:5ff.). In the concrete world in which one lives after the first apostles and in the sixteenth century, one works with mission and evangelization in distinct regions, pastorates, etc.[440] After the time of the apostles, no individual has the right to exercise the apostolate over the entire world, but the church as a whole ought to make sure that the Gospel reaches out to everyone in the entire world. This perspective explains why Luther could, with good conscience and after a public call, invest his life in the Reformation of Germany and Europe. But it does not mean that Luther wished

---

440 Especially helpful in this respect are Luther's comments in "Psalm 82 (1530)," WA 31/1:210.16ff., 210.35ff. Luther says against those preachers sneaking in to preach in evangelical congregations that they ought not be allowed to preach publicly nor to agitate secretly in the homes. The apostles had a general/universal call and went even into the houses of strangers, but after the apostles, every servant of God has his own distinct area in a properly organized congregation. Therefore Luther says: "Since then, however, no one has had this general apostolic command; but every bishop or pastor has had his definite diocese or parish. For this reason St. Peter (1 Peter 5:3) calls them κλήρους, that is, 'parts,' indicating that to each of them a part of the people has been committed, as Paul writes to Titus also (Titus 1:5). No one else, no stranger shall undertake to instruct his parishioners, either publicly or privately, without his knowledge and consent. . . . This rule should be so rigidly enforced that no preacher, however pious or upright, shall take it upon himself either to preach to the people of a papistic or heretical pastor, or to teach them privately, without the knowledge and consent of that pastor. For he has no command to do this, and what is not commanded should be left undone. If we want to perform the duties that are commanded, we have enough to do. It does not help their case to say that all Christians are priests. It is true that all Christians are priests, but not all are pastors" (LW 13:64–65 [WA 31/1:211.3ff.]). The same point of view concerning the distinction between the field of service of the apostles and their successors can be found in the *Larger Commentary on Galatians*, WA 40/1:59–62. Concerning this rather contemporary problem, see Brunotte, *Das geistliche Amt bei Luther*, 99ff.; and Aagaard, "Luthers syn på mission II," 195ff. Luther developed his principles about regional and parish work, among other principles, in connection with his arguments about the papal claims as chief bishop and in his teaching about the power of the keys in confession and the ban. Cf. Öberg, *Himmelrikets nycklar och kyrklig bot i Luthers teologi*, 41ff., 80ff., 368ff., 456ff., 510ff., 561ff., with the references.

that the evangelical church would be locked into a territorial and state church in which one rather soon loses sight of the evangelization of the peoples.

Apostolic teaching and the church's continuing work in mission and evangelization. The apostles are God's/Christ's unique messengers with the Gospel to the whole world. Their successors are, among others, bishops and the parish pastors who have responsibility to see that the apostolic teaching about faith and life in a regionally oriented mission and evangelization be preached throughout the entire world. Consequently, the apostles and their message are important for the church and mission throughout all times.

When the reformer refers to the apostolic Word/Gospel, he means first that which exists in the Gospels and the Epistles of the New Testament, but the apostolic Christ is predicted even by the Old Testament prophets. As it concerns the apostolic letters, Luther naturally has assigned a great significance to those parts of the Bible that go back to one of Christ's apostles. These men had been assigned by the Lord to build the church that Christ had founded. Their words and confession were the first stones laid on the Cornerstone—Christ—and constitute the foundation on which believers of all ages should build. Thus he writes in a pure Latin: "Apostoli sunt primi lapides, supra petram illam unicam, Supra quos, seu confessionem ipsorum, etiam reliqui Sancti aedificentur."[441]

In addition to the demand for a historical connection with the apostles, Luther adds the demand for a biblical, apostolic substance to the content of theology, preaching, and life. Both together constitute apostolic authority so the text in question can guide the church's faith and life through the ages. However, Luther thinks it important to define precisely the center of the apostolic Word/Gospel. The criterion for a true apostolic Gospel is that it with clarity and power preaches Christ as died and risen and that by faith alone in him people are justified before God and receive the forgiveness of sins. I refer here to principles that were adduced in connection with the Epistle of James, among others.[442] The apostolic Gospel's *Christum predigen und treiben* is extremely important for Luther. Those books that prove to be especially "apostolic" in this regard are John's Gospel, 1 John, Romans, Galatians, Ephesians, and 1 Peter.[443] We have above already shown how consciously Luther asserts that precisely that apostolic Gospel with the previously named general criterion ought to be proclaimed by church and mission. On the basis of the Gospel and faith, the apostolic parenesis ought also to stimulate and spur on to love and good deeds.[444]

---

441 WA 38:620.31ff.

442 See *Luther and World Mission*, 198n230, 199ff.

443 See the 1522 general preface to the New Testament, WADB 6:10.7ff.

444 See *Luther and World Mission*, 199ff., 232ff. Both series of lectures on Galatians (1519

In this way, Luther believes that the material content of the apostolic word is extremely important. In addition to this, he also emphasizes the authority of the apostolic word for the church in all times, an emphasis that often is ignored. This theme is evident in the lectures on Galatians both from 1519 and 1531/1535. When Christ immediately called, taught, and gave the mission assignment to the apostles, he made provision that God's Word and the Gospel, not human teaching, would build up the church. The word of the apostles is an important link in the communication of revelation from God/Christ to the church and the world. The apostles received the Holy Spirit to be able to speak correctly the truth of the Gospel.[445] The apostle Paul boasted about the call that he received from God/Christ because he was and wanted to be considered an apostle and an ambassador who communicated to people the Word/Gospel from God/Christ, who had sent him. An apostle is a fully authorized legate. In the apostle's words, God and Christ speak. Therefore Luther says in the 1531/1535 *Larger Commentary on Galatians*:

> In the same way, when Paul commends his calling so highly, he is not arrogantly seeking his own praise, as some people suppose; he is elevating his ministry with a necessary and a holy pride. Thus he says also to the Romans (11:13): "Inasmuch as I am an apostle to the Gentiles, I magnify my ministry." That is to say: "I want men to receive me, not as Paul of Tarsus but as Paul the apostle or ambassador of Jesus Christ." He has to do this to maintain his authority, so that those who hear this may be more attentive and more willing to listen to him. For they are not listening to Paul; but in Paul they are listening to Christ Himself and to God the Father, who sends him forth. Just as

---

and 1531/1535) have the same basic message, that is, that Christ alone and faith alone should be preached. Cf. WA 2:451.16ff., 452.14ff., 455.11ff.; 40/1:33ff., 39ff., 217ff., 328ff., etc.

445 LW 27:165 (WA 2:453.19f., 453.31ff.): "This is by all means a point to be noted, that Christ wanted no one to be made an apostle by men or by the will of men but as the result of a call from Him alone. . . . All these facts aim to make you see with what care Christ has established and fortified His church, lest anyone rashly presume to teach without being sent by Him or by those whom He has sent. For just as the Word of God is the church's first and greatest benefit, so, on the other hand, there is no greater harm by which the church is destroyed than the word of man and the traditions of this world. God alone is true, and every man a liar (Ps. 116:11). . . . [S]o Christ has left behind the Gospel and other writings, in order that the church might be built by means of them, not by human decrees." Concerning how the apostles were given the Holy Spirit to perform their duties correctly, see WA 2:454.24ff.: "Unde ne Apostoli ex seipsis loquerentur, dedit eis spiritum suum, de quo dicit: Non enim vos estis qui loquimini, sed spiritus patris vestri, qui loquitur in vobis [Matthew 10:20], et rursus: Ego dabo vobis os et sapientiam etc. [Luke 21:15]." Cf. WA 40/1:187f.

men should devoutly honor the authority and majesty of God, so they should reverently receive and listen to His messengers, who bring His Word.[446]

These are clear words concerning the apostolic office and the authority of the apostolic Word/Gospel. In his comments on Galatians 2:6–14, Luther nevertheless underlines that one ought not praise or depend on the person or office of the apostles in and of themselves. Instead, one ought to listen to their words through which the Gospel from God/Christ is communicated.[447] Luther says this clearly: "He does not want us to admire and adore the apostolate in the persons of Peter and Paul, but the Christ who speaks in them and the Word of God itself that proceeds from their mouth."[448] Despite all the evaluations/questions about the Epistle of James, Luther often said that the apostles basically teach the same Gospel. It is precisely this one apostolic word and message that is the criterion of their apostolicity. Luther summarizes Galatians 2:7–9 about how James, Cephas, and John extended Paul the right hand of fellowship in this way:

> This is clear proof that all the apostles had the same calling, the same commission, and the same Gospel. Peter did not proclaim a Gospel different from that of the others; nor did he commission the others with their office. But there was parity among them and throughout; for they had all been taught and called by God, that is, both the call and the commission all of the apostles had come wholly and immediately from God.[449]

Luther emphasizes the fact that the same Gospel ought to be preached for all people: "This is clear proof that there is only one and the same Gospel for Gentiles and Jews, monks and laymen, young and old, men and women, etc. There is no partiality; but the Word and its teaching are one and the same for all men, no matter how diverse the mask or social position may be."[450] In fact, in this proposition about the same Gospel—even if it is communicated in different linguistic forms—for all people lay a decisive basis for the integration of church/church theology and mission/mission theology. In Luther's thought, the integration of church and mission rests on a solid foundation, that is, the apostolic Gospel.

It cannot be my task to review the reformer's expansive trust in the single apostolic word. Let me only point to Luther's 1523 commentary on 1 Peter where he states unequivocally that the apostles preached the same Gospel, even if they

---

446 LW 26:16 (WA 40/1:57.16ff.).

447 WA 2:479.22ff., 483.32ff.; 40/1:170–210. Cf. Althaus, *Die Theologie Martin Luthers*, 52ff., who refers to additional passages.

448 LW 26:94 (WA 40/1:173.21ff.).

449 LW 26:102 (WA 40/1:186.25ff.).

450 LW 26:104 (WA 40/1:189.28ff.).

preached with different degrees of clarity on the doctrine of justification.[451] The apostolic word in the Scriptures is the only authority Luther has left to present because he has refused the authority of reason, of the pope, of the councils, etc., in questions about faith and life. Therefore his Bible exposition is permeated by Bible references in which the apostolic Word/Gospel from the Gospels, above all, and the Epistles of the New Testament strengthens the interpretation.[452]

In the university disputations of the 1530s, Luther clearly and systematically formulated his view of the authority of the apostolic word. An apostle does not speak as a private person. He is chosen by God/Christ and given the Holy Spirit for his apostolic office. Therefore he speaks with a God-given authority in questions about faith and life in the church of Christ. One ought to observe the pneumatological motivation for the unique task of the apostolate. Assigned by God and Christ, the apostles present the Christian truth that must always be the guide for the church's teachers and for the decisions of church meetings. The apostles are, according to Luther, the unanimous, infallible, and normative teachers of the church. Indeed, they can be considered to be the church's foundation because the apostolic Word/Gospel is finally the normative and corrective instance of all other authority for Christ's church in all times. According to Luther, the apostles consequently possess a completely unique task and office. All their successors in the offices of the church and all believers are subordinate to the prophetic and apostolic Word/Gospel.[453]

---

451 LW 30:3 (WA 12:259.5): "First of all, we must realize that all the apostles teach one and the same doctrine, and that it is incorrect to speak of four evangelists and four gospels; for everything the apostles wrote is one Gospel." Cf. LW 30:3–4 (WA 12:260.12ff.): "Thus one apostle has recorded the same things that are found in the writings of the other. But those who stress most frequently and above all how nothing but faith in Christ justifies are the best evangelists. Therefore St. Paul's epistles are gospel to a greater degree than the writings of Matthew, Mark, and Luke." Cf. on Titus 1:1, 4, WA 25:6.18ff., 7.21ff., 8.15ff., 15.2ff., 15.7ff. See also WA 45:390.29ff.

452 See Öberg, "Skriften alene—tron alene," 134ff., which includes much evidence for the thesis about the authority of the apostolic word. See also Schempp, *Luthers Stellung zur Heiligen Schrift*, and Pedersen, *Luther som skriftfortolker*, 44ff.

453 It would take too much space to review Luther's strong accent throughout his lifetime on the authority of the apostolic word. It must suffice with some examples from Luther's writings during the university disputations of the 1530s, which cover well the reformer's understanding. The following references show this. In connection with the question about Paul's doctrine of justification, Luther writes: "Paul, that person who is speaking here, is not only a man, as Caesar or someone else, but was chosen and elected by God and given the Holy Spirit so that he could speak powerfully in this manner and glorify God . . . as if he were to say, 'We apostles so determine, so judge, affirm, and certainly conclude, for we have authority in this matter, as apostles of God.' Therefore this assertion is a reliable statement, since the apostles had a command

In connection with the concept of the apostolate, as has often been shown, Luther highlights that the apostolic word in its original form was an oral preaching. The church's Gospel ought still to be offered to people essentially as a preached word.[454] Although we are considering this subject of the authority of the apostolic word, we also must give attention to the fact that Luther considers it positive that the spoken Word has been established in writing. So the church and individual Christians might through all times possess the Word of the apostles and the Gospel as a bulwark against the heresies that constantly emerge, it became necessary for the apostolic message to be codified in writing.[455] According to Luther, a sermon ought always to hold itself to the apostolic word of the Bible.

---

and the Holy Spirit" (LW 34:158 [WA 39/1:88.11ff., 88.20ff.]). Cf. WA 39/1:206.15ff., 207.1ff. Concerning the undeniable authority of the apostles and the prophets in the church, Luther writes: "Nulla autoritas post Christum est Apostolis et Prophetis aequanda. . . . Ideo soli fundamentum Ecclesiae vocantur, qui articulos fidei tradere debebant" (WA 39/1:184.4ff.). WA 39/1:185.5f: "Sed quidquid volunt docere aut statuere, debent autoritatem Apostolorum sequi et afferre." Cf. in full detail WA 39/1:67.20ff. and especially LW 34:113 (WA 39/1:48.1): "59. For we are not all apostles, who by a sure decree of God were sent to us as infallible teachers." Cf. WA 12:550f.; 18:606ff.; 25:14.8ff.; 28:170ff.; 33:577ff.; 36:527ff.; 46:62ff. Concerning church councils and the apostolic word, it is said, "Congregari facile est, Sed in Spiritu sancto congregari non possunt, nisi Apostolorum fundamentum secuti non suas cogitationes, sed fidei analogiam tractarint" (WA 39/1:186.16ff.). Also, "Nemo igitur tenetur credere decretis Ecclesiae repraesentativae, id est, Conciliis, nisi Apostolorum scripturis iudicent et loquantur, quod fit casu" (WA 39/1:187.11ff.). See also what I have written above about the controversies at the tables in Antioch, *Luther and World Mission*, 227ff., especially 228n287, where I am critical of I. Lønning who destroys the teaching authority of the apostolate in his interpretation of Luther.

454 See on preaching as the main instrument in the work of God's reign, *Luther and World Mission*, 205ff.

455 For example, see the *Christmas Postil* (1522), LW 52:206 (WA 10/1.1:627.1ff.): "However, the need to write books was a serious decline and a lack of the Spirit which necessity forced upon us; it is not the manner of the New Testament. For when heretics, false teachers, and all manner of errors arose in the place of pious preachers giving the flock of Christ poison as pasture, then every last thing that could and needed to be done, had to be attempted, so that at least some sheep might be saved from the wolves. So they began to write in order to lead the flock of Christ as much as possible by Scripture into Scripture. They wanted to ensure that the sheep could feed themselves and hence protect themselves against the wolves, if their shepherds failed to feed them or were in danger of becoming wolves too." Cf. my reservations against those who, on the basis of Luther's words about the oral Gospel, want to introduce a Luther who considered the apostolic word to be something moldable. See *Luther and World Mission*, 206–7n249.

Summary. The investigation above has shown that in Luther the missiological motif powerfully determines the apostolic task and thereby the work of all successive preachers. An apostle is a person who has been called directly by God/Christ and has been sent out to extend above all the Gospel of Christ in the world. Consequently, the apostolate and the apostolic offices are missionizing and evangelizing servant offices under God/Christ and under faithfulness to his Word. The center in the apostolic Gospel and the general criterion for apostolic doctrine is that which proclaims Jesus Christ, his death and resurrection.

The apostles are called directly by God/Christ, and each one is given the Holy Spirit so he might rightly formulate the Gospel. These apostles are united in and teach the same Gospel as faithful and infallible teachers in the church. The apostles possess a unique sending, and their teaching that has been received immediately from God/Christ is completely decisive and binding for the servants of the church and mission in all times. When some continue the work of the apostles, especially in the preaching of the Word, they must let themselves be guided by the apostolic word while they energetically hold to the center, that is, the Gospel of Christ.

Other aspects of the spiritual gifts, ministries, and offices. Because we already have touched on the apostolate and mission, I want now to consider what Luther says about other spiritual gifts and ministries on the basis of texts from the church's first mission time, especially Romans 12; 1 Corinthians 12 and 14; Ephesians 4:11–12; and 1 Peter 2:5–9. One finds a veritable breadth in Luther's exposition of these texts because of his encounters with Anabaptists and enthusiasts, which forced him to focus on the Bible's words about the many spiritual gifts, ministries, and offices. The reader ought to observe that it is the material from 1525 and onward that will be analyzed here, though I refer to and compare the earlier and less-prolific material as well.

Luther points out in the 1525 *Lent Postil* how immediately before Paul writes about the spiritual gifts in Romans 12:1–5, he emphasizes that Christians ought not split the unity of the church for the sake of worldly self-promotion. They ought not seek their own glory but the glory of God and Christ by offering themselves as living sacrifices to God, by esteeming highly their brothers and sisters, and by serving one another in love. In his teaching about the church/congregation as the body of Christ with many members in mutual service, the apostle wanted to emphasize the fundamental unity of all Christians and their parity under the Head/Christ. When one first understands this, one can without human conceit about who is higher or lower rightly speak of different gifts, ministries, and offices. The idea about the *corpus Christi* consequently preserves the essential unity of believers by showing that all parts of the body of Christ possess one and the same righteousness through faith in God's Son. Where one is a part of Christ's body by grace alone, there one is satisfied to take one's place and work, there one is prepared to bear, help, and share in the sorrows and joys of fellow Christians. Luther points out that the works-righteousness of Roman Catholicism and the idea that priests, monks, and nuns have a higher spiritual status than normal Christians had torn apart the unity of the church. Where honor and trust in one's own work is given place, there the church as Christ's body is split.[456]

On the basis of Romans 12:1–5, the reformer also emphasizes that in the church/congregation that is characterized and united by faith in Christ there are many members with different spiritual gifts and tasks. Christians are part of one and the same body, but this does not preclude the fact that the spiritual gifts and tasks given by God are different. Not every one has the same gifts and tasks given by God. For the reformer, it is important that one remain in the tasks and calls that one has been given. No one ought, for example, to presumptuously take on himself the ordained office of pastoral ministry. This difference in spiritual gifts and functions that exists only within the basic unity and parity given by grace and faith ought not lead to a division of Christ's body. In the commentaries on Romans 12, the reformer constantly refers to 1 Corinthians 12 and 1 Corinthians 14, as well as to Ephesians 4:11ff., 16. After granting the basic gift of faith, God distributes additional gifts on the basis of undeserved grace and according to the measure of each person's faith. These are gifts of grace, so no one may proudly

---

456 Lenker 7:21 (WA 17/2:32ff., especially 33.14ff.): ". . . and the common faith will be generally prized as the highest and most precious treasure, the result being satisfaction for all men. Paul next adds the simile: 'For even as we have many members in one body, and all the members have not the same office: so we, who are many, are one body in Christ, and severally members one of another.' . . . Paul likens the various gifts to ourselves, the different members of the common body of Christ. It is an apt and beautiful simile, one he makes use of frequently; for instance, 1 Cor 12, 12 and Eph 4, 16." This is later developed thematically: "First, if we examine this simile, we shall find that all the members perform certain functions of the body because they are members of it; and no member has its place through its own efforts or its own merits. It was born a member, before the exercise of the office was possible. It acts by virtue of being a member; it does not become a member by virtue of its action" (Lenker 7:21 [WA 17/2:33.27ff.]). Lenker 7:23 (WA 17/2:35.10f.): "In the second place, the simile teaches that each member of the body is content with the other members, and rejoices in its powers, not being solicitous as to whether any be superior to itself." Lenker 7:24–25 (WA 17/2:36.14f.): "In the third place, according to the simile each member of the body conducts itself in a manner to profit the others—the whole body." Lenker 7:25 (WA 17/2:37.1ff.): "In the fourth place, 'whether one member suffereth, all the members suffer with it; or one member is honored, all the members rejoice with it,' as Paul says. 1 Cor 12, 26." Cf. WA 41:507ff. See also the sketch of the priesthood of all believers and the offices of the church in *Luther and World Mission*, 88ff., with the adduced literature.

boast about his or her own gift. All gifts, tasks, and works that originate in grace and faith ought to be aimed at the physical and spiritual needs of the neighbor—and that is all at which they should be aimed.[457] These gifts have nothing to do with status or glory.

In connection with Romans 12:6–8, Luther tentatively develops his view of different ministries and functions in the Christian congregation. Concerning the gift of prophecy, he says that this sometimes refers to the ability of the apostles and prophets to predict what will happen in the future. But in commentary on Romans 12:6, Luther interprets it as the gift of grace to exposit the Scriptures. Those who have this gift of grace exercise a fundamental work in service to preachers and to individual Christians. Compare here Luther's own role in Reformation Germany where he was a doctor and professor of biblical theology. He sometimes calls himself the prophet of the Germans. The reformer translates Romans 12:6 in this way: "If someone has a prophecy, let it be in accordance with faith." No prophecy may be different from the Scriptures. It must hold itself within the boundaries of the creed and focus on Jesus Christ as the foundation of salvation (1 Corinthians 3:11). The foundational teaching about faith already had been laid in Rome before Paul's arrival. Now it was Paul's task to confirm the church above all in faith in God's Son by means of a right prophecy/Scripture

---

457 WA 17/2:33.14ff., especially Lenker 7:27 (WA 17/2:38.10ff.): " 'Measure of faith' [Rom 12:3] may be understood as implying that God imparts to some more of faith itself; and to others, less. But I presume Paul's thought in employing the expression is that faith brings gifts, which are its chief blessing. These are said to be according to the measure of our faith, and not to the measure of our will or our merit. We have not merited our gifts. Where faith exists, God honors it with certain gifts, apportioned, or committed, according to his will. [Luther adduces 1 Corinthians 12:11 and Ephesians 4:16 here.] . . . The same reason may be assigned for Paul's words, 'Having gifts differing according to the grace that was given to us,' not 'differing according to our merits.' Grace as well as faith brings these noble jewels—our gifts—to each one according to his measure. It excludes in every respect our works and our merits, and directs us to make our works minister only to our neighbors." Cf. WA 41:507.28ff., especially 508.24ff.: "Qui im regiment, ut maneant in eo, in quo beruffen, et quod ir ampt wil haben. Si hoc, so stil, quasi celestis vita. . . . Ideo quisque videat, quod ei datum et commissum et ad quid vocatum und gehe den stand nach, donec deus vult, und nem sich keins anders etc. Petrus: 'allotrioepiscopos' [1 Peter 4:15] i.e. qui inn ein frembd ampt greiffen et nihil faciunt quam se hindern et alios, quod debent facere, lassens anstehen. Econtra. Sind die allerfeindseligsten leut, habent speciem iusticiae. . . . Est quidem eadem in omnibus Christianis fides. Sicut unus Christus, Euangelium, baptismus, ita una fides. In ea equales. Sed illa eadem, mancherley unterscheid der gaben, empter, ut in mundo est discrimen tale. In Vuitenberg gilt als gleich." Cf. WA 41:510.1ff.

exposition.[458] By the way, it is clear that because of his experience with the enthusiast movement Luther is quite standoffish toward the idea of prophecy as prediction of future events.[459]

Romans 12:7b–8a reads: ". . . if it is teaching let him teach; if it is encouraging, let him encourage." While referring to Paul's letters to Timothy, Luther on the one hand points out that teaching refers to the teaching of the ignorant about Christian faith and life and, on the other hand, refers to the exhortation, the guiding, and the disciplining of those who already have been taught so Christians are not overcome by spiritual atrophy.[460]

Generally, it seems that Luther connects the charismatic gifts of prophecy, teaching, and exhortation with the church's pastors and preachers. He does not discuss the question of spontaneous prophecy in the life of the congregation. He apparently knows well that established teachers in the primitive church (Acts 13:1; 15:32) were called prophets. But aren't there New Testament passages that speak about spontaneous prophecy as well?

On the basis of Romans 12:7a, Luther writes about congregational servants or deacons. Their office and service was, according to the reformer, aimed at helping the temporary needs of the poor and widows, among others. The diaconal office also helped the office of preaching because the deacons took care of matters concerning assistance and temporary help so the apostles and teachers had more time to preach, teach, and pray. With some regret, Luther notes that this important way of delegating the work, which helped both the oppressed and the extension of the Gospel, had, through the hierarchialization of the church, ceased to function. The poor are not helped and the pastors are often busy with matters other than the preaching of the Gospel. Consequently, a functioning diaconate would be suitable in the work of God's reign.[461]

---

458 Lenker 7:27–28 (WA 17/2:38.19ff.): " 'Whether prophecy, let us prophesy according to the proportion of our faith.' . . . Prophecy is of two kinds: One is the foretelling of future events, a gift or power possessed by all the prophets under the Old Testament dispensation, and by the apostles; the other is the explanation of the Scriptures. 'Greater is he that prophesieth than he that speaketh with tongues.' 1 Cor 14, 5. Now, the Gospel being the last prophetic message to be delivered previous to the time of the judgment, and to predict the events of that period, I presume Paul has reference here simply to that form of prophecy he mentions in the fourteenth of First Corinthians—explanation of the Scriptures. . . . That reference is to this form, Paul implies in his words, 'Let us prophesy according to the proportion of faith.' Doubtless he means the Christian faith then arising." Cf. WA 41:510.16ff.

459 WA 17/2:39.19ff.; 41:510.31ff.

460 WA 17/2:41.1ff. Cf. on parenesis in *Luther and World Mission*, 232ff.

461 WA 17/2:40.18ff. Cf. *Church Postil* (1522), WA 10/1.1:262.1ff., about the deacon Stephen and the table service. Luther complains that this office in the church that

On the basis of Romans 12:8 (". . . if it is contributing to the needs of others, let him give generously"), Luther describes the gifts that during the time of the apostles were given to the congregational treasury. These gifts were managed by the deacons and were given for the support of the preachers and those in need. However, Luther adds that such giving to the work of the congregation and to the needs of people was neither in the primitive church nor in the sixteenth century regulated by strict laws. What is important is that one gives freely and from the heart without favoring friends or being stingy toward displeasing persons.[462] The words ". . . if it is showing mercy, let him do it cheerfully" (Romans 12:8) refer, according to Luther, to the mercy that Christians generally exercise above and beyond monetary contributions. Here it is a question about all forms of help and good works toward the neighbor. These ought to spring from the desire and joy of giving and helping (adduced here are, among others, Matthew 12:7; Luke 10:37; 2 Corinthians 9:7).[463]

In principle, Luther reckons with one single ecclesial office of the Word and the Sacraments. In his polemic against the Roman ideas about different offices in a hierarchy, he continually sought to show that the biblical words *presbyteros* and *episcopos* refer to the same public exercise of the preaching office. Nevertheless, this does not prevent the church from possessing an office of oversight or a bishop's office without abandoning the fundamental unity of ecclesial office. If this office keeps to the Word and keeps watch over the work of the congregational pastors, it can become the church's defense against heresy, among other things.[464] Luther writes about the episcopal office in connection with Romans 12:8 (". . . if it is leadership, let him govern diligently"). This work of overseeing or leadership is important so all others in their offices and ministries might not neglect that which they were commanded to do. The work of the bishop ought to be characterized by care and love, not by pomp and display of power.[465]

---

was established to meet the needs of the poor had been distorted into a liturgical assistantship. See on Acts 6:1–6, *Luther and World Mission*, 190ff.

462 WA 17/2:41.13ff. Cf. "Ordinance of the Common Chest (1523)," WA 12:11ff. Luther refers directly to the works of love during the time of the apostles; see WA 12:11.12f., 11.17f. Likewise, Luther uses Matthew 25:40 and the *bona ecclesiae* of a later time to motivate the practice of the common chest for the needs of the poor.

463 WA 17/2:43.18ff.

464 See Brunotte, *Das geistliche Amt bei Luther*, 172f. Cf. Öberg, "Den lutherska reformationen och ordinationen," 71ff., about the proposals to the Utraquists in Prague that they ought to begin to ordain pastors and eventually even bishops. An important text is "Concerning the Ministry (1523)," WA 12:193.22–194.20. Cf. Öberg, "Den evangeliska biskopsvigningen," 205ff.

465 Lenker 7:32 (WA 17/2:42.10ff.): "He means those who have oversight of Church offi-

Luther draws our attention to the fact that when Paul lists the ministries/offices, he does not place the episcopal office first among the ministries but last. The ministry of the Word is above all others. Any office of overseeing has only the task of awakening the ministry of the Word, just as a servant might awaken his master. Nevertheless, any office of preaching and any other offices and ministries ought to subordinate themselves to a rightly exercised episcopal office.[466] If the church/congregation is characterized by a serving love and all the believers subordinate their wills to this love, one has a defense against all types of abuse of the gifts of grace, ministries, and offices.[467]

The reformer imposes on all Christians, that is, all with gifts of grace and ministries, an attitude that is important for mission and evangelization, an attitude generally toward all people, even toward unbelievers. Romans 12:14–15 says: "Bless those who persecute you; bless and do not curse. Rejoice with those who rejoice; mourn with those who mourn." On the basis of Acts 8:20f.; Galatians 5:12; 1 Corinthians 16:22; etc., Luther says that the preaching office has the right to judge and prohibit fraud and false teaching.[468] It is another matter that the church's people are directly commanded to bless their persecutors and wish for them everything good. Likewise, they are encouraged to share in every fellow human's joy and sorrow with their whole hearts.[469] Thus Christians become the servants of the whole world and thereby open hearts for the Gospel.[470]

Luther's commentaries on Paul's teaching about the spiritual gifts, ministries/offices, and works of power in 1 Corinthians 12 (while referring to 1 Corinthians 14 and Ephesians 4) harmonize with what he said about Romans 12.

---

cers generally; who take care that teachers be diligent, that deacons and ministers make proper and careful distribution of the finances, and that sinners are reproved and disciplined; in short, who are responsible for the proper execution of all offices. Such are the duties of a bishop. From their office they receive the title of bishops—superintendents and 'Antistrites,' as Paul here terms them; that is, overseers and rulers." Luther refers to 1 Timothy 3:5 and points out the abuse of the bishop's office in the Roman Catholic Church, WA 17/2:42.30ff. On Luther's positive evaluation of a rightly exercised episcopal office of overseeing, see WA 12:390.5ff.; 16:566.21ff.; 30/3:368.4ff.; WABr 8:310.2ff.; WATr 3:642.34ff. (no. 3829).

466 WA 17/2:43.3ff.

467 WA 17/2:44.17ff., 46.8ff.

468 WA 17/2:52.29ff.

469 WA 17/2:51.21ff., 54.12ff. Cf. *Luther and World Mission*, 241ff., 245ff., 267ff.

470 Lenker 7:46 (WA 17/2:54.17ff.): ". . . he speaks here in an unrelated way, of our duty to make ourselves agreeable to all men, to adapt ourselves to their circumstances, whether good or ill, whether or no they are in want. As common servants, we should minister to mankind in their every condition, that we may persuade them to accept the Gospel."

The reformer emphasizes that against the background of the struggles in Corinth the apostle first wanted to impress on the Corinthian Christians an attitude of humility and the fundamental unity of the congregation in Christ and the Spirit. Only after that does Paul discuss the issue of the different charismatic gifts, ministries, etc. One must, among other things, see to it that one does not too easily judge those who have failed in their Christian life or otherwise extinguish Christian love. It is a person's relationship with Jesus Christ that is ultimately decisive (1 Corinthians 12:13). No one who curses Christ speaks in the Spirit, but the one who confesses that "Jesus is Lord" speaks in the Spirit. First, when one has understood and confessed that the Lord Christ through his sacrifice for the sins of all people, and the Spirit, who is poured out on all who believe in God's Son, is the starting point for all in the fellowship, then one can in a fruitful manner and with no un-Christian ostentation speak of the various charismatic gifts and the different ministries/offices in the congregation. Luther points often to how the primitive church in Corinth and the church through all times—in his own time, the schisms caused by, among others, the monastic orders and the enthusiast groups—through Satan's destructive work had lost Christ, the Spirit, and love and is characterized instead by quarrels and divisions. Above all, the situation in Corinth gives Luther the occasion to point out how hyperspiritual enthusiasts and sectarians constantly follow the church as a shadow. In such movements, one is not satisfied with the functions in the church and the earthly callings that God has given to each and every believer. All believe, among other things, that they are called to preach, even if they do not possess any church's—and thereby neither God's—call to the important office of preaching. In a world in which through Satan's work schisms apparently must always occur (1 Corinthians 11:19), the reformer accentuates that Christians are to ". . . test the spirits to see whether they are from God" (1 John 4:1).[471]

Luther also points out that the apostle's words in 1 Corinthians 12:4–6 consciously anchor all spiritual gifts, all ministries/offices, and all works of power in the triune God. Consequently, the triune God is the important and active subject. Luther assigns these different works to the different persons of the Trinity: the Father, the Son, and the Holy Spirit. The charismatic gifts originate from the Spirit, the ministries/offices from the Lord Christ, and the works of power from God the Father. One must constantly hold this theocentric perspective, says Luther, so one does not begin to pride oneself in the gifts, offices, and works of power with which one has been entrusted. Each Christian has received some-

---

471 Cf. sermons through the years, WA 15:603ff.; 34/2:98ff.; 41:391ff., 398ff., 650ff.; 22:170ff. (Cruziger's *Summer Postil*). Ellwein, *Luthers Epistel-Auslegung*, vol. 2, includes a splendid collection of Luther's sermons, etc., on the Corinthian correspondence.

thing, but not all have received the same gifts and functions. That which one has received and which one has been entrusted to manage must be used for the good of others and for the good of the congregation (Romans 12:7). At the same time, the Father, the Son, and the Holy Spirit should get the glory, not the more or less noble human instruments. Only under these preconditions can one in unity build Christ's church.[472] Luther notes that it is a question of plurality and difference as it concerns spiritual gifts, offices, and works of power.[473]

Luther tentatively describes the charismatic gifts worked by the Holy Spirit that are mentioned in 1 Corinthians 12:8f. Those who speak the word of wisdom are not such as those who boast of their own hyperspirituality but those who teach about God and God's will, especially the sum of faith and how one becomes righteous before God. This is the foremost of the spiritual gifts. To speak the word of knowledge means that one teaches Christians about how they in the various tasks of life might act rightly and how they ought to relate to the weak and stiff-necked in faith and life. The charismatic gift of prophecy has to do with the ability to rightly interpret and exposit the Scriptures. Compare this with Luther's words about prophecy in connection with Romans 12:6 above. This powerful charismatic gift lays the foundation for Christian doctrine and overthrows false doctrine. Through it, one meets a double word that through the word of Law threatens the unfaithful and disobedient with God's judgment and that with the Gospel comforts the faithful and weak.[474]

---

472 WA 15:606.11ff.: "Gaben pulchre divisit, spiritualia dona, deinde herrn officia, divisiones operationum deo attribuit. Loquitur vero hic de donis, officiis, virtutibus, quae sunt in Christianismo, Ampter, ut sunt diaconi et Episcopi. De his in epistola ad Ephesios [Ephesians 4:11] virtutes, kreffte, tatten, quando res non in worten stet, sed bricht er haus. . . . Unus est Christus, sed gerit omnia officia nostra: per me praedicat, per alium regit ecclesiam, per tercium infirmos visitat. Nemo habet omnia dona, officia, virtutes, so muss ann eynem ytzlichen Christen sein, das da felt, quare deus ordinavit, ut alter alteri inserviat. Membrum aliquod per se nihil facit . . . et inverecundiora membra sunt maxime necessaria. Sic est in populo Christiano." See also WA 41:396.27ff., 398ff., which is later reworked in Cruziger's *Summer Postil.* Cf. WA 22:181.12ff.

473 Lenker 8:214 (WA 22:183.11ff.): "Paul says of all these, 'There are diversities of gifts, but the same Spirit,' by way of admonishing us against creating sects. The Spirit is equally effective through him whose gifts are few and less significant and through him of remarkable gifts. And as with gifts, so it is with workings and ministrations." Cf. WA 41:396.25ff., 398.25ff., 400.27ff., 651.11ff.

474 Lenker 8:212–13 (WA 22:182.1ff.): "The names and nature of the spiritual gifts, the apostle here specifies. He names wisdom, knowledge, prophecy, power to discern spirits, capacity to speak with tongues and to interpret, extraordinary gifts of faith, and power to work miracles. 'The word of wisdom' is the doctrine which teaches a knowledge of God, revealing his will, counsel and design. It embraces every article of belief

Luther also discusses the works of power—among other things, healings—
that are performed by the Father. Those who receive these gifts are characterized
by a strong faith and a special power of the Spirit so they in Christ's name dare to
do great things, says Luther.[475] But the reformer warns that, according to Matthew
7:22, even false Christians can prophesy and do miracles in the name of Christ.[476]
One sees also that the reformer in the question about works of power (1 Corinthians 12:10) is not especially concerned with such miracles. Yes, God the Father
works such miracles through certain Christians in the church. When Luther
through, for example, Paul's works wants to illustrate the meaning of such miracles, he even names the specific miracles that Paul did. But he emphasizes even
more powerfully how this archmissionary through his preaching converted more
people than the other apostles and produced much fruit for the Gospel. Luther is
always on guard against sensationalism and human glory as it concerns miracles
and works of power. One easily forgets that it is God the Father who works in the
miracles that he equips some Christians to perform.[477]

---

and justification. The world knows nothing of this loftiest, most exalted gift of the
Spirit. . . . The 'word of knowledge' also teaches of the outward life and interests of the
Christian: how we are to conduct ourselves toward all others, making a profitable use
of the Gospel doctrine according as necessity of time and person demands; it teaches
us the wisest course toward the weak and the strong, the timid and the obstinate. . . .
The gift of prophecy is the ability to rightly interpret and explain the Scriptures, and
powerfully to reveal therefrom the doctrine of faith and the overthrow of false doctrine. The gift of prophecy includes, further, the ability to employ the Scriptures for
admonition and reproof, for imparting strength and comfort . . . . Thus did the
prophets with the Word of God, both the Law and the promises." Cf., as it concerns
prophecy, the parallel text from 1524, WA 15:607.13ff., 609.1ff.

475 Lenker 8:213–14 (WA 22:182.21ff.): "Paul is making mention of gifts not common to
all. Only to certain ones are they given, and the gifts in themselves are unlike. 'To
another faith,' he says, 'to another workings of miracles, and to another prophecy.' . . .
Paul is speaking of a particular virtue or power of the Spirit operating in the Church,
whereby certain ones can effect great and glorious things . . . . To work such wonders,
a very strong and sure faith is certainly necessary. An unwavering, vigorous, courageous faith may accomplish a special work in the name and power of Christ." Cf. WA
15:608.16ff.

476 WA 22:182.35ff.

477 Lenker 8:214 (WA 22:183.16ff.): "The term 'workings,' or operations, has reference to
remarkable works of God wrought through certain individuals in an exceptional way.
For instance, he grants to Paul a ministerial office of unusual influence: Paul is permitted to convert more souls than other apostles, to perform more wonders and
accomplish more. He says himself (1 Cor 15, 10) that by the grace of God he labored
more abundantly than all." Cf. the extensive development of the argument in WA
21:408–10.

In this type of missiological study, one question in connection with miracles may not be passed over. The reformer says often throughout his career that miracles were something that God gave especially to the primitive church in its initial encounter with paganism. Consequently, miracles belong above all to the breakthrough time of mission, while they are not as usual nor as important where churches have already been established. As has been discussed previously in chapter 3 (pp. 137–51), in connection with Mark 16:17–18, the enthusiasts demanded that the Lutheran Reformation should establish its authenticity with miracles and signs. For Luther, however, it is the Gospel about Christ and faith that is the unique characteristic of the church's authenticity—though he never denies, for example, the possibility of healing.[478]

When he mentions those who speak words of wisdom and who prophesy, Luther has in view individuals in publicly acknowledged offices of preaching and teaching. Paul says in 1 Corinthians 12:5: "There are different kinds of service, but the same Lord." Luther understands these different kinds of service given by Christ as the ordained offices in the church. In this connection, he reviews extensively the church's different offices. Precisely as in the early church's Corinth, the so-called enthusiasts and Anabaptists during the time of the sixteenth-century Reformation had threatened by their hyperspirituality to dismantle the church's ordained offices. Here Luther does not first speak about ministries in general but about special offices, *officia* or *Ämter*. An office is an ordered, public service to which the church has openly assigned specific tasks of the Word, the Sacraments, and pastoral care to certain people. Luther points out that there were many different offices in the primitive church, for example, apostles, evangelists, and teachers. Even during Luther's time there were different ordered offices, among others, pastors, preachers, and priests. It seems, however, that Luther is not interested in some kind of detailed replica of the primitive church's offices and ministries. The public character—the service to the congregation and the communication of the Word and the Sacraments—characterizes Luther's understanding of the offices, *officia*.[479]

---

478 Cf., for example, WA 23:721.16ff; 21:408.21ff. On the Gospel's way and the concomitant signs according to Mark 16:17–18, see *Luther and World Mission*, 146n113, with the adduced Luther texts.

479 Lenker 8:214–15 (WA 22:183.22ff.): "The meaning of 'administrations' is easily apparent. Office is an ordained and essential feature of every government. It represents various duties imposed and commanded by sovereign authority. It may have reference to the duties enjoined upon a society collectively, in the service of others. There are various offices in the Church; for instance, one individual is an apostle, another an evangelist, another a teacher, as Paul mentions in Ephesians 4, 11. And as he says in First

The reformer emphasizes that such ordered, public offices ought not be exercised by all Christians. Only those who have been properly called by the church to such offices can publicly exercise the office of the Word, the Sacraments, and regular/institutional pastoral care and counseling. The ministries that are given through Christ belong only to certain publicly called people, while the above discussed charismatic gifts and works of power are not distributed only to those with a public call in the church. Indeed, Luther means that these charismatic gifts and works of power ought to support the properly ordered offices, of which the office of preaching is without comparison the highest and most important. In addition to the office of preaching, people are needed who understand and can exposit the Scriptures, know the languages, and have the ability to speak. All ministries of the Word and the Sacraments go back to Christ himself and together with the supporting spiritual gifts and works of power constitute one single divine work and regiment in the congregation.[480]

Corinthians 14, 26 and also hints in this text, the office of one is to read the Scriptures in different languages, of another to interpret and explain. So it was ordained in the Church at that time, and similarly today are ordained certain offices—of pastors, preachers, deacons or priests, their duties being to hear confessions, to administer the Sacrament, and so on." In his sermons on 1 Corinthians 12:1ff. (WA 34/2:98ff. [1531]; 41:391ff., 398ff., 650ff. [1535]), Luther incidentally touches on the questions about spiritual gifts and works of power. Luther focuses here primarily on the church's preaching office and how the opinion that all may take whatever tasks they want has throughout church history created splits and enthusiasm in the church. It is for this reason that the reformer comments on the contemporary relevance of 1 Corinthians 12:1–11. Otherwise, he can even say that the text is not especially necessary for the general population (WA 34/2:98.2). On the public aspect, etc., of the church's offices, see Brunotte, *Das geistliche Amt bei Luther*, 157ff., and the sketch in *Luther and World Mission*, 88ff.

480 Lenker 8:215 (WA 22:183.33ff.): "Not every Christian is obliged, nor is able, to execute such duties; only upon certain ones are they enjoined. 'Administrations' differ from what Paul terms 'workings' and 'gifts.' There have ever been many Christians who, though possessing the Holy Spirit, were not 'administrators;' for instance, virgins and wives—Agnes, Anastasia and others—and martyrs, many of whom wrought miracles and had other gifts. True, both gifts and workings are imparted chiefly for the execution of Christian duties. It is essential here, especially in the superior office of preaching, that the occupant be peculiarly qualified for the place. The preacher must be able to understand and explain the Scriptures and be familiar with the languages. It is necessary to the effectiveness of his labors that he be accompanied by God's operative power. Thus the three—gifts, workings, administrations—are harmonious features of one divine government in the Church; Christ is the Lord, who regulates and maintains the offices, while God works and the Holy Spirit bestows his gifts." Cf. the sermons adduced in the previous note.

The fact that everyone in public, ordered ministries has been given these tasks by the Lord Christ and serves the same single Lord ought also to unify the office bearers, though some of them have greater tasks than others.[481] Also whenever one speaks about the offices that were instituted by Christ and are ordered by the church—above all the office of preaching—one ought continually to focus on the endlessly rich treasures of grace that these ministries communicate through the preaching of the Word, Baptism, Holy Communion, and Absolution. The veritable wealth and nobility of these offices originates in these means of grace, not in the office bearers themselves.[482]

Luther's theology is the origin of both the strong position of the church office and its emphasis on the preaching of the Word in Augsburg Confession V, XIV, and XXVIII. Research has reviewed in detail the reformer's ideas about the relationship between the priesthood of all believers and the public, churchly office of the Word and Sacraments. There is no doubt that Luther in a completely different manner than today's revival-oriented Lutheranism and evangelical Christianity guards the place of the ordered, churchly office in the life of the church. He emphasizes that Christ instituted the office—which by the way is one of the characteristics of the church (*notae ecclesiae*)—and that only those who have been properly installed in the offices by the congregation ought to preach publicly and administer the sacraments.[483] These thoughts are assumed in the exegesis and Bible exposition described above.

In Luther's writings, one finds no extensive commentary or sermon on the texts in 1 Corinthians 14 about speaking in tongues. Sometimes he simply refers to verses in this chapter, but it appears he is not especially interested in speaking in tongues. This probably depends on the fact that when Paul speaks about his own or others' gift to speak in tongues, he always emphasizes that speaking in tongues is a secret language to God, incomprehensible to the congregation (if it is not interpreted) and even more incomprehensible for unbelievers in a mission situation. Besides, on the basis of Acts 2, Luther often understands the texts about speaking in tongues as indicating the significance of linguistic skill for the extension of God's reign. The reformer can say with Paul that speaking in tongues is "a sign, not for believers but for unbelievers" (1 Corinthians 14:22), but he values prophecy much more highly than speaking in tongues. Prophecy teaches and

---

481 Lenker 8:215 (WA 22:184.11ff.), Luther says here, among other places, ". . . an apostle, for instance, is superior to a teacher or expounder, while the office of a baptizer is inferior to that of a preacher."

482 WA 22:185ff. Cf. WA 41:396.30ff.

483 Cf. the investigation in *Luther and World Mission*, 88ff., with the adduced Luther texts and secondary literature.

builds up the congregation and touches the hearts of unbelievers. Prophecy is presented in clear and comprehensible words.[484]

In the years 1520–1523, Luther is quite open to the text 1 Corinthians 14:29ff. about prophecy in the congregation. In this early, antihierarchical period, he is thinking some about spontaneous prophecy during congregational meetings in which prophetic speakers among the Christians would freely be allowed to communicate their message. However, under all conditions, prophecy provides laypeople with the right to intervene in an orderly manner in the congregational worship service with correcting, Bible-anchored words when the ordained office of teaching is preaching false doctrine. First Corinthians 14:26 is decisive for Luther in this connection. First Corinthians 14:30 says, "And if a revelation comes to someone who is sitting down, the first speaker should stop." Even if Luther during this period reckons with an ordained ministry of Word and Sacrament, all Christians have the right and responsibility in emergency situations to correct false doctrine. In the completely hopeless situation in which the Bohemians had found themselves, they were responsible to see that orthodox preachers would be allowed to preach. Here, the reformer's ideas that the priesthood of all believers is the principal and right subject of all means and ministries of grace play a decisive role, as well as the rule that emergency knows no law. In an emergency, the boundary between the authority of the Christian and the authority of the office can be lifted temporarily. This emphasis on the right of emergency is much weaker in the Luther material after about 1525, but Luther never completely abandoned it.[485]

---

484 WA 21:409.23ff. Cf. the 1522 marginal notes on 1 Corinthians 14:22, WADB 7:126: "Durch mancherley zungen werden die unglewbigen zum glawbenn bekert, wie durch andere zeychen und wunder, aber durch weyssagung werden die gleubigen gepessert unnd gesterckt, als durch zeychen, daran sie yhren glawben prufen und erfaren, das er recht sey."

485 In his earlier writings, Luther connects 1 Corinthians 14:26ff. to the priesthood of all believers, sometimes in the context of the right of emergency. Cf. WA 6:411.22ff.; 8:495.37ff.; 11:413.2ff.; 12:192.1ff. Especially important is "That a Christian Assembly (1523)." After he has discussed regulations, public call, and those exceptions that are made in emergency situations, Luther writes: "Indeed, a Christian has so much power that he may and even should make an appearance and teach among Christians— without a call from men—when he becomes aware that there is a lack of teachers, provided he does it in a decent and becoming manner. This was clearly described by St. Paul in I Corinthians 14 [:30], when he says, 'If something is revealed to someone else sitting by, let the first be silent.' Do you see what St. Paul does here? He tells the teacher to be silent and withdraw from the midst of the Christians; and he lets the listener appear, even without a call. All this is done because need knows no command" (LW 39:310 [WA 11:412.33ff.]). In "Concerning the Ministry (1523)," Luther presents approximately the same arguments for the Bohemians in their difficult situation. Even here 1 Corinthians 14:29 is completely decisive for Luther's reasoning that laypeople

After encountering the enthusiasts in the early 1520s, Luther becomes more restrictive in his interpretation of 1 Corinthians 14:29ff. about prophecy in the congregation. Luther encountered a movement that overinterpreted his teachings about the priesthood of all believers, threw suspicion on the work of the ordained ministry, and caused chaos in the evangelical congregations. After 1525, Luther puts prophecy squarely into the hands of the ordained office of preaching and completely rejects any notion that every Christian might have the right to preach at congregational worship services. This is especially clear in "Infiltrating and Clandestine Preachers (1532)." I choose to comment a little bit on this essay because 1 Corinthians 14 is central to the reformer's argument against the infiltration of the so-called clandestine preachers into the domain of churchly office.[486]

Because the unofficial preachers of the enthusiasts made chaos in the congregations and revolution in society, in "Infiltrating and Clandestine Preachers" Luther exhorts both spiritual leaders and civil authorities to stop their activity. The church's ordained, spiritual offices also must react by teaching in such a way that exposes the unofficial preachers. For Luther, it is simply unacceptable—indeed, a destructive work of the devil—that the enthusiasts without a proper call secretly went around and destroyed the congregational work that had been established by the congregational pastor. The fact that they do this secretly, that they make propaganda against evangelical congregations, and that their leaders and unofficial preachers are unable to show who has called and sent them is in and of itself an exposé. Every Christian is responsible to report those who in this way secretly disturb the ordered life of the congregation.[487] Unlike today's rather

---

have the right to correct and teach in emergency situations. Cf. WA 12:171.17ff., 188.20ff., 189.17ff., 190.32ff. In the secondary literature, see especially Brunotte, *Das geistliche Amt bei Luther*, 136n12, 167f.

486 WA 30/3:518–27. Among the other Luther writings that emphasize the institution of the churchly office without questioning the priesthood of all believers, we might name "Psalm 82 (1530)," LW 13:39ff. (WA 31/1:193ff.); and "On the Councils and the Church (1539)," WA 50:631ff. Brunotte, *Das geistliche Amt bei Luther*, 112ff., 118ff., 134ff., shows that the tasks and responsibility of the priesthood of all believers is more emphasized during 1520–1523, the time of the anti-Roman Catholic polemic, while the ordained call and authority of the ordained office is emphasized more in the confrontation with the enthusiasts from 1525 forward. But Luther always believed that the office of the church (that is, the public institution) should hold the pulpit and the altar.

487 LW 40:384–85 (WA 30/3:519.9ff.): "Through the spiritual office, the people must be constantly instructed, emphasizing what has been mentioned previously, so that they admit no infiltrators, considering them truly as sent of the devil, and learning to ask of them, whence do you come? Who has sent you? Who has bidden you to preach to me? Where are your seals and letters of authorization from persons who have sent you?

awkward Lutheranism, Luther is critical of preachers who preach only on the basis of the so-called inner call. Nevertheless, Luther would not have rejected today's recognized district preachers.

If one has a real commission and message from God (one notes here a clear recognition that a legitimate message may exist), then he ought to let himself be tested (cf. 1 Corinthians 14:29) by the pastor and ask for permission to preach publicly. If the pastor still wants to hinder even that which is obviously right, the one who offered himself to be tested is innocent. Nevertheless, principally the pastor is the one who holds the office of the Word, the Sacraments, and regular pastoral care. With this office given by God through the congregation, he ought to oppose Satan and all Satan's unofficial preachers who can point to no proper and public call to the service of the means of grace.[488]

The reformer means that even princes, judges, and other government officials ought to oppose actively these unofficial preachers. Such preachers do not only promulgate false doctrine, they also initiate revolutions that lead to the spilling of blood in the realm. The earthly authorities have the responsibility to enlighten the

---

What signs do you perform to show that God has sent you? Why do you not go to our pastor? Why do you come so furtively to me and crouch as in a corner? Why don't you appear publicly? If you are a child of light, why do you shun the light? With such questions I think you can guard against them easily, for they cannot prove their calling. If we can bring the people to so understand a call, one could control such infiltrators. Also we should teach and urge the people to report such intruders to their pastors, for they are duty bound to do so, if they are Christians and seek salvation. When they do not do so, they abet the emissaries of the devil and these infiltrators in secretly robbing the pastor (indeed God himself) of his ministry, baptism, sacrament of the altar, the care of souls, and his parishioners. Thus they destroy and bring to naught the parish system (ordained of God)." Cf. WA 30/3:518.15ff., 527.10.

488 LW 40:384 (WA 30/3:518.30ff.): "Who is so dull as not to be able to discern that these are messengers of the devil? If they came from God and were honest, they would first of all repair to the parish pastor and deal with him, making clear their call and telling what they believed and asking for his permission to preach publicly. If then the parish pastor would not permit it, they would be blameless before God and could then wipe the dust off their feet, etc. [cf. Luke 10:11]. For to the pastor is committed the pulpit, baptism, the sacrament [of the altar], and he is charged with the care of souls. But now these want to dislodge the pastor secretly, together with all of his authority, without revealing their secret commission. They are indeed regular thieves and murderers of souls, blasphemers, and enemies of Christ and his churches." Cf. LW 40:385 (WA 30/3:519.34ff.): "For, as said, if we emphasize the matter of the call, we can worry the devil. A parish pastor can claim that he possesses the office of the ministry, baptism, the sacrament, the care of souls, and is commissioned, publicly and legally. Therefore the people should go to him for these things. But the alien interlopers and plotters can make no such claim and must confess that they are strangers and graspingly seek what is not theirs. This cannot be of the Holy Spirit, but of an exasperating devil."

public about this evil work. It ought to punish severely those who upset the civil order and peace.[489] Because the unofficial preachers confuse the spiritual and earthly regiments and initiate revolution against the authorities, they must be opposed by earthly-political means.

As we have previously shown, for Luther, ordered congregations and the public call to the office of preaching are always important. That some people without an ordinary call sneak in to preach and administer the sacraments is always something quite dangerous for the church. Luther writes:

> If we did not hold fast to and emphasize the call and commission, there would finally be no church. For just as the infiltrators come among us and want to split and devastate our churches, so afterwards other intruders would invade their churches and divide and devastate them. And there would be no end to the process of intrusion and division, until soon nothing would be left of the church on earth. So indeed is the devil's purpose with such spirits of dissension and intrusion.[490]

Because the enthusiasts and sectarians represent such a danger to the church of Christ, the following demand is relevant for every preacher without exception: Show who has called you and commanded you to preach—or be silent and do not preach![491] The public call is also a source of power and comfort for all those bearing the office because bearing this office is not always easy. Luther himself finds in his own doctorate that was granted publicly for all the world to see and in his office of preaching a comfort against Satan and Satan's crew.[492] Consequently, the public call ought both to hinder sectarianism and be a comforting resource for those who are rightly called.

---

489 WA 30/3:518.12ff., 519.8f., 519.37ff., 520.18ff., 527.10f. Cf. *Luther and World Mission*, 26ff., which discusses civil rule and the Christian's responsibility to obey it. See especially *Luther and World Mission*, 256ff.

490 LW 40:386 (WA 30/3:520.34ff.).

491 LW 40:386 (WA 30/3:521.7ff.): "So we say, either demand proof of a call and commission to preach, or immediately enjoin silence and forbid to preach, for an office is involved—the office of ministry. One cannot hold an office without a commission or a call." Luther here adduces Matthew 25:14; 20:2; Jeremiah 23:21; etc., about the necessary connection between calling/commanding and the office of preaching.

492 WA 30/3:521.28ff. and especially: "I have often said and still say, I would not exchange my doctor's degree for all the world's gold. For I would surely in the long run lose courage and fall into despair if, as these infiltrators, I had undertaken these great and serious matters without call or commission. But God and the whole world bears me testimony that I entered into this work publicly and by virtue of my office as teacher and preacher, and have carried it on hitherto by the grace and help of God" (LW 40:387–88 [WA 30/3:522.2ff.]).

In "Infiltrating and Clandestine Preachers," the reformer completely rejects the idea that 1 Corinthians 14:29ff. grants the office of public preaching to all Christians. Luther is clearly more restrictive than in the texts referred to above from 1520–1523. The verse about prophecy in 1 Corinthians 14:29ff. does not give the people the general task of prophesying/preaching publicly in the church. It is the prophets, that is, those who occupy the ministry as preachers and pastors, who ought to preach and complement each other. The enthusiasts must prove that they are prophets and rightly occupy the office of preaching before they are allowed to preach or criticize the preaching of the pastor. In the worship service, those faithful to Christ ought to listen to those who have been entrusted with the public office of preaching.[493] If the office of preaching would have been granted to any and everybody in the congregation, then Paul would not have been able to reject the woman's right to preach in the church on the basis of the Lord's command.[494]

---

493 LW 40:388 (WA 30/3:522.9ff.): "Undoubtedly some maintain that in I Cor. 14 [:29ff.], St. Paul gave anyone liberty to preach in the congregation, even to bark against the established preacher. For he says, 'If a revelation is made to another sitting by, let the first be silent' [I Cor. 14:30]. The interlopers take this to mean that to whatever church they come they have the right and power to judge the preacher and to proclaim otherwise. But this is far wide of the mark. The interlopers do not rightly regard the text, but read out of it—rather, smuggle into it—what they wish. In this passage Paul is speaking of the prophets, who are to teach, not of the people, who are to listen. For prophets are teachers who have the office of preaching in the churches. Otherwise why should they be called prophets? If the interloper can prove that he is a prophet or a teacher of the church to which he comes, and can show who has authorized him, then let him be heard as St. Paul prescribes. Failing this let him return to the devil who sent him to steal the preacher's office belonging to another in a church to which he belongs neither as a listener nor a pupil, let alone as a prophet and master." Cf. WA 30/3:525.39ff.

494 LW 40:389 (WA 30/3:523.4ff.): "Whoever reads the entire chapter will see clearly that St. Paul is concerned about speaking with tongues, about teaching and preaching in the churches or congregations. He is not commanding the congregation to preach, but is dealing with those who are preachers in the congregations or assemblies. Otherwise he would not be forbidding women to preach since they also are a part of the Christian congregation [I Cor. 14:34f.]. The text shows how it was customary for the prophets to be seated among the people in the churches as the regular parish pastors and preachers, and how the lesson was sung or read by one or two, just as in our days on high festivals it is the custom in some churches for two to sing the Gospel together." Cf. WA 30/3:525.27ff., 525.31ff. Concerning how Luther on the basis of 1 Corinthians 14:34 rejects the possibility of a woman occupying the office of preaching, see WA 30/3:524.10ff., 524.23ff., 522.30ff. See also WA 50:633.12ff. Even in his early writings, Luther argued that a woman is forbidden to preach. Cf. WA 8:197.22ff.; 10/3:170.24ff.; 12:309.14ff. Luther means that the Bible verses about man/woman and creation both in 1 Corinthians 14:34 and 1 Timothy 2:11 forbid a woman to occupy the office of

Luther even points out that Paul in 1 Corinthians 14 expressly differentiates between the people/congregation and the prophets/office bearers who ought to preach for the people and build them up in the Christian faith.[495]

Luther also discusses how the notion that many prophets/office bearers according to 1 Corinthians 14:29ff. speak one after the other has parallels in the history of worship. Even if Paul says that the existing prophets may complement the one who is speaking, for the sake of good order the reformer does not want to remove the pulpit in German congregations. The order that functioned so well against the background of the ordered Jewish worship service and the authoritative leadership of the apostles in the primitive church is in the sixteenth-century worship situation, disturbed as it is by the enthusiasts, simply dangerous. Luther apparently understands the worship order of the primitive church as something that need not be copied in its details in every time. One must manage especially prophecy in a way that serves the Gospel and faith and at the same time hinders a conceited sectarianism.[496]

As we have already seen, in his antitheology of 1532 the reformer wants to guard the peace of the congregations and the firm position of the pastoral office. It is difficult to see how in his Bible interpretation, aimed as it is against the enthusiasts, Luther could have recommended the plurality and dynamic of the primitive church's worship life. We have just seen that to some degree he is conscious of this difficulty. Now we may proceed to a comparison with Luther's earlier texts.

In 1523, Luther comments on 1 Peter 2:5, 9. Here Peter writes about the believers in Christ as if they were a holy and royal priesthood that ought to declare God's great deeds. These important tasks that are commissioned by God himself ought not be concealed by some theories of office and call, according to Luther. This verse refers to the spiritual priesthood of the new covenant. As Christ himself, this priesthood ought to offer itself as a sacrifice to God, witness/preach for all people, and pray for the believers in Christ. Even if not all Christians might step into the pulpit, they must in their interaction with people publicly make known

---

preaching. Concerning Luther and the question of women's ordination, see the following secondary literature: Brunotte, *Das geistliche Amt bei Luther*, 193ff.; Kirsten, "Luther und die Frauenordination," 139ff.; and Brosché, "Luther och kvinnan," 136ff.

495 WA 30/3:525.10ff.

496 WA 30/3:523.15ff., 526.7ff., 526.22ff. See especially LW 40:393 (WA 30/3:527.1ff.): "In the days of the Apostle the custom of prophets sitting alongside each other was possible. For it was a habit of long standing and practiced daily among a well-disciplined people who had inherited from Moses through the Levitical priesthood. It would hardly do to restore the practice among such uncouth, undisciplined, shameless people as ours."

what salvation in Christ signifies. Especially Christians ought to witness about how they have been carried from the darkness of unbelief into God's wonderful light. Testimony about salvation in Christ ought openly to be presented by every Christian, both to those who already believe in Christ and to those who do not yet believe.[497] At the same time Luther in this reverie over the right and responsibility of the priesthood of all believers to witness/preach assigns the pulpit and the public congregational preaching to the office of the church.[498] This is apparent in the commentaries on 1 Peter 4:11 and on Peter's words to the elders about the responsibility of the shepherds for the flock with which they have been entrusted in 1 Peter 5:1ff.[499]

In Ephesians 4:11–12, Paul writes: "It was he who gave some to be apostles, some to be prophets, some to be evangelists, some to be pastors and teachers, to prepare God's people for works of service, so that the body of Christ may be built up." These verses play an important role in modern mission theory. Among other things, one usually speaks about how those who occupy the offices of the church have their most important task in that by their testimonies they strengthen and equip Christians for soul-winning work.

Luther has no extensive commentary on Ephesians 4:11–12, but he often touches on this text in his writings, as we have seen. One ought clearly to understand that Ephesians 4:8, 11 is, for Luther, one of the central texts that support the

---

497 WA 12:306–10, 316–20. See especially LW 30:64–65 (WA 12:318.23ff.): *"That you may declare the wonderful deeds of Him who called you out of darkness into His marvelous light* [1 Peter 2:9]. A priest must be God's messenger and must have a command from God to proclaim His Word. You must, says Peter, exercise the chief function of a priest, that is, to proclaim the wonderful deed God has performed for you to bring you out of darkness into the light. And your preaching should be done in such a way that one brother proclaims the mighty deed of God to the other, how you have been delivered through Him from sin, hell, death, and all misfortune, and have been called to eternal life. Thus you should also teach other people how they, too, come into such light. For you must bend every effort to realize what God has done for you. Then let it be your chief work to proclaim this publicly and to call everyone into the light into which you have been called. Where you find people who do not know this, you should instruct and also teach them as you have learned, namely, how one must be saved through the power and strength of God and come out of darkness into the light" (*original emphasis*).

498 Even if Luther advocates an open testimony/preaching/teaching in the previous note, he also points out how only those rightly called by the congregation ought to preach in the congregational worship service. See WA 12:309.1–23 and briefly in LW 30:55 (WA 12:309.7ff.): "Therefore nobody should come forward of his own accord and preach in the congregation. No, one person must be chosen from the whole group and appointed. If desired, he may be deposed."

499 WA 12:379f., 386ff.

divine institution of the ecclesial offices.[500] At the same time, it is apparent that Ephesians 4 is adduced quite often to elucidate the plurality of the Spirit's gifts in the congregation.[501] In other cases, Luther uses these verses to focus on the ordered offices in the church.[502]

In a sermon as late as 1527, Luther explains Psalm 68:19 with the help of Ephesians 4:11–12. It is clearly apparent that Luther, despite his dispute with the enthusiasts, believes that not only the central work of the preaching office of the Gospel but also the charismatic gifts of all the believers in the church and in Christ ought to build up Christ's body and extend the Gospel among people. The charismatic gifts ought to be aimed first toward the conversion of unbelievers and the extension of faith in all languages and in all the world. It is God's Spirit who equips both laypeople and ordained with charismatic gifts so the Gospel might reach all peoples.[503]

It is interesting to see how, when he focuses on the church's task of worldwide mission, Luther expresses a more dynamic view of the relationship between ordained and laypeople. But perhaps it should be said that Luther's thoughts about the testimony of laypeople and their active cooperation in the work of God's reign did not issue in especially remarkable results in Luther's time or in the following centuries. After Luther's death, the office of the church was placed clearly in the center. Also significant is the fact that Luther nowhere speaks of some kind of special mission office or mission ordination.[504] But that does not mean that he is cool to the Christianization of the peoples.

---

500 "On the Councils and the Church (1539)," WA 50:632.35ff. Cf. Brunotte, *Das geistliche Amt bei Luther*, 106, 127.

501 WA 17/2:33.14ff.; 38:10ff.; 15:606.11ff.

502 WA 22:183.22ff.

503 WA 23:720.23ff.: "Er gibt und reichlich austeilet den Menschen gaben, das ist, Er sendet inen den heiligen Geist und zieret sie mit mancherley gaben, Wie solchs S. Paulus Ephe. iiij [4:11–12] anzeiget, 'Christus', spricht er, 'hat etliche zu Apostel gesetzt, etliche aber zu Propheten, etliche zu Euangelisten, etliche zu Hirten und Lerern, das die Heiligen alle geschickt seien zum werck des Ampts, dadurch der leib Christi erbawet werde' etc. Das ist: er teilet darumb so mancherley gaben aus unter seine Gleubigen, auff das das Euangelium in mancherley sprachen in aller welt gepredigt würde, die ungleubigen bekeret und viel Menschen zum Glauben gebracht, in der gnad und erkentnis wachsen und selig werden. Dazu dienet, das einer die Schrifft auslegen, ein ander die Geister prüfen könne, der dritte mancherley Sprachen wisse und andern auslege und so fortan ij. Cor. xij [:10]."

504 Scherer, *That the Gospel May be Sincerely Preached*, 15 writes: "As for the lay witness, it remained sound evangelical theory and contained a rich promise for the future. In Luther's day, however, the implications of baptism for the witness and service of all believers remained to be worked out. In practice, ministry was identified with calling and roles of clergy. Lutherans had abolished the special missionary orders of Catholi-

Summary. From his exposition of Romans 12:1–5, 1 Corinthians 12, and 1 Corinthians 14, one sees that the reformer energetically emphasizes the fundamental unity and equality of all Christians in the *corpus Christi*. This is for Luther the starting point—among other things in his doctrine of the priesthood of all believers and the offices of the church—when he discusses different gifts, ministries, and works of power. Wherever the fundamental unity and equality in faith in Christ and the Spirit exists, there it ought not be difficult to speak about the plurality and the differences of charismatic gifts and tasks to build up the body of Christ.

Consequently, the reformer speaks about the central gift of faith for all Christians. Then he speaks about the additional gifts or gifts of grace that God freely and differently distributes to all believers. He notices that not all have the same charismatic gifts and ministries in the congregation. However, one ought not boast about those gifts that one has received but use them for the best of the believers and in service to the work of the reign of God. We have seen how Luther often clearly states that the charismatic gifts have been given to expand and to build up the reign of Christ. As it is for us today, the gifts and ministries were something difficult to understand and use for the primitive church.

As it concerns the charismatic gifts and the ministries, one quickly sees that Luther understands the tasks of the prophets and teachers and the words of wisdom and knowledge as tasks and words that normally belong to the domains of the office of preaching. In the many expositions of 1525 and forward, Luther gives little place to the spontaneous exercise of the charismatic gifts. In an earlier period, he emphasized more the plurality and dynamic in the congregation where the Trinity distributes gifts, ministries, and works of power to the faithful.

One also notices how positively Luther values the diaconal work among the poor and oppressed and how he emphasizes the service of all Christians toward the needs of the neighbor. The reformer in no way rejects miracles and works of power in the congregation. These are, however, not as common nor as necessary in the contexts of established churches. They belong primarily to the breakthrough times of the Gospel in mission and evangelization. One probably must admit that Luther discusses speaking in tongues unfairly. But he does not reject this charismatic gift of the primitive church.

---

cism, thereby depriving themselves of the existing means and instruments of evangelization. Luther's own reluctance to recognize any special missionary office, other than the regular calling of parish pastors and the witness of the laity, would return to plague his followers in the ensuing period."

That which remains as the decisive impression of this analysis of the texts is that Luther understands the charismatic gifts and ministries above all as the ability to interpret the Scriptures and teach unbelievers and the people of God. He also guards the place of the ecclesial office as it concerns the message that will be proclaimed publicly and from the pulpit. It is also true that Luther the biblical theologian, in his struggle with the enthusiasts over interpretation of the priesthood of all believers and the scriptural words about the plurality of the charismatic gifts and ministries, loses much of that plurality and dynamic to which the apostolic letters witness. Neither does Luther say that the Reformation ought to duplicate the primitive church's prophecy, miracles, etc. Seen as a whole, one can probably say that the ordered situation to which the Pastoral Epistles witness guides Luther more than the diffuse situation to which 1 Corinthians witnesses. Luther guards the right of the preachers and pastors to administer the means of grace and the leadership in the congregations. All other charismatic gifts and works of power support the ordained offices, of which the office of preaching is the most important. One ought not, however, honor the office in and of itself. Instead, one ought to honor the gifts that the office distributes through the Word and the Sacraments.

However, it ought to be observed that Luther always preserved the right and responsibility of all Christians in fellowship with their brothers and sisters and those outside the fellowship to witness about Christ and faith in him. The extension of the Gospel is not only the task of the pastors but also of the entire gathering of God's people. Luther emphasizes this throughout his life, though it is especially apparent in his writings concerning the conflict with the enthusiasts.

THE MISSION MOTIF IN THE EXPOSITION OF THE EPISTLES

I already have surveyed the Epistle commentaries in which the mission motif is more or less expressed. In these commentaries, however, one seldom finds any comments on the practice of world mission. When he comments on the Epistles, the reformer teaches mostly about the fundamentals of the Christian faith (in Luther's understanding the main teaching of the Epistles) and that is relevant for church/mission in all times. The motif of mission and evangelization is connected generally with the work of God's reign. Often the problems of sixteenth-century Germany and Europe are prominent in these commentaries.

That Luther in his Bible commentaries and homilies focuses on what the texts actually said in the apostolic time and context does not exclude the notion that the mission perspectives and the mission task that are discussed in these texts are relevant for the church and mission in all times and places. We have seen many examples of this above. For Luther, the Scriptures guide the teaching and work of the church for all times. We have especially seen how that which is said about the work of God's reign in the new covenant is relevant as long as the church exists in the world. That which is said about mission and mission responsibility are consequently not merely some opportunities provided by the text to discuss unimportant coincidences. In fact, the letters of the apostles do say something about the new covenant's unavoidable mission and the expansion of God's reign.

The reformer applies the message of the apostolic letters to the time and situation in which he lives. Here it is essentially a question about the Reformation and evangelization in a context in which unbelief and half-heathenism in doctrine and life are prevalent. That he finds that the timeless apostolic teaching is relevant for sixteenth-century Germany and Europe does not mean that Luther has no vision for the Christianization of the peoples. The apostolic letters are relevant for all work in God's reign, even for mission among unbelievers and pagans until Christ's return.

Finally, let me here review some passages in Luther's exposition of the Epistles in which mission among unbelievers is especially prevalent. For example, Luther comments on Romans 15:9–12 in which Paul refers to Psalm 18:50; Deuteronomy 32:43; Psalm 17:1; and Isaiah 11:10. Here it is said that the Gentiles will get to praise God and place their hope in Christ because of the undeserved mercy they share in God's salvation. They have the same God as Israel, and they may praise this God with the chosen people on the basis of undeserved grace. The Jews ought not boast on the basis of the great promises given to them because Christ is given to Jews and Gentiles, strong and weak, high and low.[505] Luther emphasizes that the shoot from Jesse's root will rule over the Gentiles (Romans 15:12) through the Gospel. So one single spiritual realm or Christ's church will grow out into all the world. It is the Gospel and faith in Christ that bears up this realm among all peoples.[506]

The growth of the church is part and parcel of the concrete work of the Gospel. This theme was apparent already in Luther's exposition of the Epistles, especially when he speaks about the oral preaching of the Word and about the evangelistic work of the apostles and their successors. When one carefully examines Luther's choice of words, it is quite apparent that he is thinking even of mis-

---

505 WA 7:486.17ff.; 10/1.2:89.13ff.; 41:734.11ff.

506 On Romans 15:12 (Isaiah 11:10), Luther says: "Christ is the root of Jesse. . . . [O]ut of him grew that beautiful tree, the Christian Church, spreading out into all the world. The root of Jesse is properly delineated when portrayal includes the sufferings of Christ and their fruits. Paul's assertion 'and he that ariseth to rule over the Gentiles' is equivalent to the Hebrew 'that standeth for an ensign to the people.' It shows Christ's government a spiritual one. The Gospel raises him as a standard before the whole world, an ensign to which we must be loyal through faith. We do not see him physically; we behold him only through the ensign, the Gospel. And it is through the Gospel he reigns over men; not in a physical presence" (Lenker 6:61 [WA 10/1.2:91.4f., 91.11ff.]).

sion work among non-Christians in these passages. On 2 Corinthians 5:20, Luther says, for example, that Christ in a wonderful way builds up and maintains his reign. It is not maintained by human wisdom and power. However, Christ sends out his servants into the whole world. Their only weapon is God's Word. They are strengthened and enlightened by the Holy Spirit in their worldwide work to exhort people to be reconciled with God. It is God's Word through the ambassadors that builds up and maintains Christ's universal reign.[507] Rapturously, Luther comments on Galatians 1:16 that it is not the Law but Christ's righteousness that should be preached among the peoples: "This is the proclamation that is proper for the Gentiles."[508]

Luther notes on Ephesians 3:18 that Christ as Lord is active universally both in the natural and the spiritual life.[509] In connection with Ephesians 3:8–10, Luther says that the ascended Lord distributes gifts, ministries, and offices for the work of God's reign. Through his universal reign, the Lord frees people from sin and death until the end of time.[510] On Ephesians 4:11–12 concerning the charismatic gifts and the building up of Christ's body, Luther says: "He distributes so many gifts to believers in order that the Gospel might be preached in various languages throughout the world and in order that unbelievers might repent and many people might be brought to faith, might grow in grace and knowledge, and might become blessed."[511]

On Philippians 1:9, Luther says that the knowledge of the Law that Jews and Turks possess does not contribute toward their salvation. Therefore God has decided that the Son would become a sacrifice of atonement for the sins of humanity. God's desire to save is not satisfied with the atonement alone. God wanted the atonement to be preached for the whole world.[512] This does not only set the church's ordained clergy in motion. According to the commentary on Philippians 1:3, all Christians ought with gratitude to receive the Gospel and work together so other people might come to faith in Christ.[513]

---

507 WA 23:733ff. and WATr 6:78.20ff. (no. 6614).

508 LW 26:74 (WA 40/1:143.12f.).

509 WA 17:437.19ff., especially: ". . . the point where I may be satisfied that wherever I go he is, and that he rules in all places, however long or broad, deep or high, the situation from either a temporal or eternal point of view. No matter how long or wide I measure, I find him everywhere" (Lenker 8:278 [WA 17:437.23ff.]).

510 WA 23:720–25.

511 WA 23:720.28ff.

512 WA 22:376.5ff., 376.19ff.

513 On Philippians 4:13, Luther says this about the true thank offerings of faith, WA 45:196.23ff.: "Vadam et audiam Christum praedicare, honorabo eius verbum et curabo

Especially in the 1523 commentaries on 1 Peter, Luther touches on world mission in many places. We already have seen how he defines the apostolic Gospel as "an oral sermon and a living Word, a voice that resounds throughout the world and is proclaimed publicly, so that one hears it everywhere." The Gospel ought to be "a living voice which resounds and is heard throughout the world."[514]

In connection with 1 Peter 1:9–10, Luther emphasizes in 1523 that God's promise in Genesis 22:18 means that the Gentiles will share in the blessing of Abraham's seed, that is, Christ. On the basis of this promise, the apostles have asserted that the Gospel about Jesus Christ must be carried to all peoples.[515] That even the Gentiles will be offered God's salvation is apparent also in 1 Peter 2:10: "Once you were not a people, but now you are the people of God; once you had not received mercy, but now you have received mercy." In this connection, Luther refers to Hosea 2:23 and Romans 9:25.[516]

First, the reformer understands the work of God's reign in church and mission as a work of the Father, Son, and the Spirit through the Word/Gospel. At the same time, the apostles, their successors, and laypeople are engaged in the expansion of the Gospel among people. The apostles are really messengers of the Gospel as are their successors in the office of preaching. According to the commentary on 1 Peter, all Christians share in the work of God's reign.[517] Therefore the reformer can say: "One must preach about Jesus Christ that He died and rose from the dead, and why He died and rose again, in order that people may come to faith through such preaching and be saved through faith."[518] Indeed, Luther places the responsibility of mission and evangelization on all Christians: "But He permits us to live here in order that we may bring others to faith, just as He brought us."[519]

---

ut audiant alii." Cf. WA 22:352.19ff.: "das wir nicht allein mit mund und worten, sondern von gantzem hertzen, was wir mit leib und leben vermügen, zu lob und preis seiner gnade, Gottes Wort predigen, hören, ehren und fürdern." Cf. the extensive investigation about the right and responsibility of all Christians to work for the extension of the Gospel in "Concerning the Ministry (1525)," WA 12:188ff.

514 LW 30:3, 19 (WA 12:259.11ff., 275.9ff.).

515 WA 12:277.3ff., 277.14ff. Cf. WA 12:284.13ff.

516 WA 12:320.13ff.

517 Cf. WA 12:260.8ff., 261.9ff., 299.25ff., 302.17ff. about the Gospel of Christ and its expansion through the apostles and the office of preaching. On the church's offices and the priesthood of all believers and their corresponding functions in the work of God's kingdom, see WA 12:306–10, 316–20, 360–63. Cf. the investigation in *Luther and World Mission*, 308ff.

518 LW 30:10 (WA 12:265.30ff.).

519 LW 30:11 (WA 12:267.6f.).

The mission perspective shines through even in connection with 1 Peter 3:15–16 where the apostle exhorts the Christians gently to give reason for the Christian hope to all enemies and persecutors. The confession of all Christians takes form in the unavoidable conflict between Christ's realm and Satan's realm. When one wants to substantiate one's hope in Christ, one must present key Bible verses that give reasons for the faith in Christ that one possesses.[520] Luther emphasizes that both laypeople and ordained ought to make this testimony:

> Here we shall have to admit that St. Peter is addressing these words to all Christians, to priests, laymen, men and women, young and old, and in whatever station they are. Therefore it follows from this that every Christian should account for his faith and be able to give a reason and an answer when necessary. . . . Hence if someone tackles you, as if you were a heretic, and asks: "Why do you believe that you are saved through faith?" then reply: "I have God's Word and clear statements of Scripture."[521]

In the primitive church's mission situation, often only one spouse in a marriage accepted the Gospel. Luther comments extensively on this problem in connection with 1 Peter 3:1–2, 7. He especially emphasizes that a Christian woman through subordination and faithful service toward her unbelieving husband can help him to faith. By such an attitude and works, she performs a missionary task. Luther applies the apostle's exhortation here to all marriages where only one partner is a believer.[522] Consequently, there is, just as we have seen in the foregoing material, a mission of lifestyle.

---

520 WA 12:360.1ff., 362.30ff. Both the devil and evil people ought to be given reasons for faith on the basis of God's Word, not on the basis of reason, despite the Vulgate's *rationem reddere* (WA 12:362.10ff.). If someone by saying that Peter, Paul, and even Christ were simply humans does not want to consider the Bible's word to be God's Word, then it is best to be silent before such hardness of heart (WA 12:362.18ff.).

521 LW 30:105 (WA 12:360.3ff., 360.24ff.). Luther here refers to Romans 1: 17; 1 Peter 2:6; Isaiah 28:16; Genesis 12:3; 22:18.

522 On 1 Peter 3:1–2, LW 30:87–88 (*original emphasis*) (WA 12:341.25ff.): "Here St. Peter is speaking primarily of the women who at that time had heathen and unbelieving husbands. On the other hand, he is also speaking of the believing men who had heathen wives. For in those days, when the apostles were proclaiming the Gospel among the Gentiles, it often happened that the one became a Christian and the other did not. Now since at that time wives were commanded to be submissive to their husbands, how much more this should be observed today! Therefore St. Peter wants to say that it is the wife's duty to be submissive to her husband, even though he is a heathen or an unbeliever. And he gives the reason for this. *So that some, though they do not obey the Word, may be won without a word by the behavior of their wives, when they see your reverent and chaste behavior* [1 Peter 3:1–2]. That is, when a husband sees that his wife conducts and adapts herself properly, he may be induced to believe and to regard the Christian estate as

Because of all the arguments that the reformer's ideas about Christ's imminent parousia should have hindered the development of an offensive mission thinking, it can be worth noting what Luther says on the basis of 1 Peter 1:20 with support from 2 Peter 3:8 about the last times, the end of time, and the time of the Gospel or world mission. The reformer emphasizes that God before the creation of the world foreknew and preordained that all would be offered salvation through Christ, God's Lamb. This has, nevertheless, only been revealed in the last days, that is, in the time of the church and of the Gospel between Christ's ascension/the Spirit's sending and Christ's parousia on the Last Day. Luther says parenthetically that on the basis of 1 Peter 1:20 one ought not think that the last time is an especially short time. This last time is, namely, the time of the Gospel of Christ. It is called the last time because after this time no other epoch is coming. No further revelation will be given that can explain God's salvation better than the Gospel of Christ. Luther also says that the Last Day is near. Nevertheless, before the God for whom a day is as one thousand years and one thousand years as a day (2 Peter 3:8), one ought to be careful with human speculations about hour and minute in this question. The important thing is that God's decision for salvation is perfectly finished already today through Christ and the Gospel and that one comes to faith in Christ and the Gospel. God will care for the timing of the parousia. The reformer says that God allows the world to continue for a time so his name, honor, and praise might be carried further among people through the extension of the Gospel. Christ waits to return simply because the mission task has not yet been completed.[523] Consequently, Luther has not been paralyzed for world mis-

---

proper and good. Even though women have no command to preach, yet they should deport themselves in such a way in the matter of gestures and conduct that they induce their husbands to believe, as we read about St. Augustine's mother, who converted her heathen husband before his death. Later she also converted her son Augustine." Cf. WA 12:342.23ff. Observe how the above is balanced by Luther's words that the husband ought to live prudently with and honor his wife (WA 12:345.28–347.25).

523 WA 12:292.10ff., 292.25ff. About the last times as the time of mission, Luther says: "St. Peter calls the era in which we are now living, the period from Christ's ascension to the Last Day, 'the end of the times.' Thus the apostles, the prophets, and Christ Himself also call it the last hour. That does not mean that the Last Day was to come immediately after Christ's ascent into heaven, but the reason is that after this proclamation of the Gospel concerning Christ there will be no other proclamation and that it will not be revealed and set forth better than it has been set forth and revealed. . . . But now no more glorious and no clearer proclamation has come into the world than the Gospel. Therefore this is the last one. All the times have come and gone, but now the Gospel has been revealed to us for the last time. In the second place, the end of the world is not far away so far as time is concerned. St. Peter explains this in 2 Peter 3:8 when he says: 'With the Lord one day is as a thousand years, and a thousand years as one day.'

sion because of Christ's imminent return. On the contrary, he has played down questions about the last times, among other reasons, for the sake of mission work.

The examples that have been presented show that one can find the idea about the extension of the Gospel for all peoples of the earth in Luther's commentaries on the apostolic letters. Of course, this idea about the extension of the Gospel among non-Christians is often wedged between Luther's other discussions about doctrine that is relevant generally for faith and life in Christ's church. But the mission idea is there anyway. When Luther so broadly explains the doctrine about Christ, justification, the Word and the Sacraments, etc., the reader ought to remember that the reformer wants to ensure that the apostolic Gospel is proclaimed and nothing else. He often is extremely critical of the workers who have gone out and proclaimed a false doctrine. It is not important simply to go out. One must proclaim a true Gospel; otherwise, one does not do mission or evangelization, regardless of the zeal with which one does it.

Finally, I want to examine a 1522 sermon on an Epistle text that clearly shows Luther's vision and feeling for world mission. It is the *Church Postil*'s "Christmas Eve Epistle Sermon" in which Luther preaches on Titus 2:11–15. With great power, Luther emphasizes that the church ought to preach Christ for the entire world. After Christ's resurrection, ascension, and the sending of the Spirit, a message about God's grace in Christ will be proclaimed publicly in the entire world.

> The first consideration in this lesson is, Paul teaches what should be the one theme of Titus and every other preacher, namely, Christ. The people are to be taught who Christ is, why he came and what blessings his coming brought us. "The grace of God hath appeared," the apostle says, meaning God's grace is clearly manifest. How was it manifested? By the preaching of the apostles it was proclaimed worldwide. Previous to Christ's resurrection, the grace of God was unrevealed. Christ dwelt only among the Jews and was not yet glorified. But after his ascension he gave to men the Holy Spirit. Concerning the Spirit, he before testified (Jn 16, 14) that the Spirit of truth, whom he should send, would glorify him. The apostle's meaning is: Christ did not come to dwell on earth for his own advantage, but for our good. Therefore he did not retain his goodness and grace within himself. After his ascension he caused them to be proclaimed in public preaching throughout the world—to all men.[524]

He wants to give us this guidance concerning the reckoning of time in order that we may judge according to God's way of looking at it, namely, that 'the end of the times' is already at hand. But the fact that there is still some time left means nothing before God. Salvation has already been revealed and completed; but God permits the world to continue to stand in order that His name may be honored and praised more widely, even though in His own eyes it has already been revealed most perfectly" (LW 30:38 [WA 12:293.1ff.]).

524 Lenker 6:114 (WA 10/1.1:19.10ff.).

Luther then points out that Titus 2:11—which he compares with Mark 16:15; Colossians 1:23; and Psalm 19:5—could be understood in such a way as to mean that the Gospel already had reached the whole world during the time of the apostles. But the reformer will not see the matter so simply. He remarks that Germany was not Christianized until about 800 years after the apostles. He knows that the lands that were discovered at the time of his birth had not yet heard the Gospel about Christ. Because the Bible often uses *pars pro toto,* Titus 2:11 and its parallels need not be understood as if the Gospel had *de facto* reached the whole world during the time of the apostles. It is part and parcel of the nature of the Gospel to go out and to be in motion. It is still on the way in 1522 to those who have not heard it so the command about world mission might be accomplished. Consequently, it is still the time of mission in the world, the time when Christ as Lord and his church will carry the Gospel to all people.

> But you may object, "Surely the words of the apostles did not, in their time, reach the end of the world; for nearly eight hundred years elapsed after the apostolic age before Germany was converted, and also recent discoveries show there are many islands and many countries where no indication of the grace of God appeared before the fifteenth century." I reply: The apostle has reference to the character of the Gospel. It is a message calculated, from the nature of its inception and purpose, to go into all the world. At the time of the apostles it had already entered the greater and better part of the world. . . . Universal proclamation of the Gospel being for the most part accomplished at that time, and its completion being inevitable—as it is today—the Scripture phraseology makes it an accomplished fact. In the Scriptures we frequently meet with what is called "synecdoche" . . . . So the Gospel was in the apostolic day preached to all creatures; for it is a message introduced, designed and ordained to reach all creatures. To illustrate: A prince, having despatched from his residence a message and seeing it started upon the way, might say the message had gone to the appointed place even though it had not yet reached its destination. Similarly, God has sent forth his Gospel to all creatures even though it has not so far reached all.[525]

One sees in the above quotation how Luther describes mission (to use our vocabulary) as the Gospel's way through centuries and lands without ignoring the indispensable human factors. Expansion and seeking those who are not yet Christians is of the very essence of the Gospel

Finally, the reformer does not at all believe that each country or land has only one epoch when the Gospel comes to it. It is worth noting that the commentary above on Titus 2:11–15 says that Germany was converted for the first time in the ninth century. At the same time, we know that Luther understands the Reforma-

---

525 Lenker 6:115–16 (WA 10/1.1:21.14ff.).

tion as a new market of grace and a time when the Gospel is returning to Germany after having been pushed aside in the Middle Ages. The examples of this are legion. Especially interesting are the descriptions about the Gospel's way through the world as a wandering torrential rain (German = *Platzregen)* on the basis of 2 Corinthians 6:1–10. Sixteenth-century Germany has been blessed with such a cloudburst. But the Germans must see to it that this "day of salvation" is not received with ingratitude and spiritual apathy. In that case, the true Gospel would continue on its way away from the ungrateful. Sometimes Luther says in his exhortations that a land could lose the light of Christ forever. But he cannot have meant that because Germany had received the Gospel both in the ninth and the sixteenth centuries. He does not, therefore, only provide examples of how Jews, Greeks, Romans, and Germans through their spiritual sluggishness lost the Gospel. Luther means as well that both the histories of Israel and Germany show that God gives the same people more than one opportunity to receive his grace.[526] This is worth noting because the foremost arch-Lutherans have sometimes been cold to mission/evangelization in post-Christian and secularized lands. A comparative study of the Luther commentaries on Titus 2:11–15 and 2 Corinthians 6:1–10 shows in fact that the reformer does not at all exclude such work of God's reign. We will see later how Luther expressly criticizes Rome for not missionizing among the Turks in formerly Christian regions. This implies the possibility of a new opportunity for those who had lost the Gospel. A new *Platzregen* can come even for those lands in which the Gospel had been pushed aside or completely lost.

SUMMARY

I will now in the following present some important themes from the reformer's exegesis of the Epistles in which the mission perspective is clear.

---

526 On this see Lent Postil, WA 17/2:179ff., especially: "Secondly, Paul shows the danger of neglecting the grace of God. He boldly declares here that the preaching of the Gospel is not an eternal, continuous and permanent mode of instruction, but rather a passing shower, which hastens on. What it strikes, it strikes; what it misses, it misses. It does not return, nor does it stand still. . . . Experience shows that in no part of the world has the Gospel remained pure beyond the length of man's memory. Only so long as its pioneers lived did it stand up and prosper. When they were gone, the light disappeared; factious spirits and false teachers followed immediately" (Lenker 7:134 [WA 17/2:179.28ff.]). However, Luther does not consider the removal of the light or the Gospel as a final and irrevocable darkness. He indicates in connection with Israel how periods with the Word and backsliding have succeeded each other, for example, WA 17/2:180.3ff. He says this even about the already "Christianized" Germany of the ninth century: "So also we now have the pure Gospel. This is a time of grace and salvation and the acceptable day; but should the world continue, this condition, too, will soon pass" (Lenker 7:135 [WA 17/2:180.11ff.]). Cf. also WA 15:31.8ff., 32.4ff., 47.66ff.

1. Luther emphasizes that the message of the new covenant for both Jews and Gentiles should be characterized by a radical Gospel of salvation through faith in God's Son. Saving righteousness is attained not through the Law and works but through faith in Christ's death and resurrection. This does not, however, diminish the importance of the Law-Gospel dialectic in evangelization and mission. The reformer emphasizes that the preaching of an unconditional grace and forgiveness without the least mixing of Law and works is the true and right preaching for the Gentiles.

2. The nucleus of mission and evangelization is clearly maintained when the reformer so powerfully emphasizes that the salvation message of the new covenant should go out into the world as an openly declared oral proclamation of joy. This living word communicates faith and the Holy Spirit to those who listen. It is mission's primary instrument. Baptism is also central in the work of Christianization on the front with unbelief and heathenism.

3. The radical Gospel displaces all the special salvation privileges previously granted to the Jews. Luther emphasizes that the message of the new covenant of one single salvation through faith in the death and resurrection of God's Son creates one single people of God gathered from both Jews and Gentiles. Every category, tribe, etc., of people are subject to guilt and judgment, but every group is offered in Christ the same single salvation and at the same time are united through the cross in the covenant of Christ's reign without barriers. Luther's considerations naturally imply that the Gospel should be taken to both Jews and Gentiles, that is, all people, even during his own lifetime. The mission motif is especially emphasized when the salvation of the Gentiles is said to rest completely on unmotivated mercy (Romans 15:8–9), which is the nucleus of the New Testament's message to all peoples.

4. In his comprehensive accounts of how one in the work of God's reign must go gently forward and for a time spare bound and weak consciences, Luther sometimes touches on the Roman Catholic canon law. Nevertheless, the commentaries speak generally about necessary adjustments in the proclamation of the Gospel among Jews and the heathen. But no obedience to customs and laws is ever allowed to make God's grace conditional.

5. Parenesis is, according to Luther, not a preaching of the Law but an exhortation to inspire and stimulate good works. The reformer's parenesis or teaching on the works of Christians is based on the parenesis of the apostles and is addressed both to the narrower Reformation front and to the

wider mission context in the encounter with open paganism. The mission nerve is exposed when Luther emphasizes the decisive significance of parenesis for spiritual growth among those who have recently received the Gospel and have been baptized. This is true also when he points out that a disorderly life becomes a hindrance for the Gospel and that a holy life has an evangelistic effect. The mission perspective is especially important in connection with parenesis where the workers in God's reign must necessarily have a positive stance (attitude) to culture, the ruling authorities, and the legislative authorities. One should not in any way endanger the spreading of the Gospel among unbelievers and heathen.

6. Although Luther accents so powerfully that the Word/Gospel and Baptism are the primary instruments of mission, he also emphasizes mission/evangelization through lifestyle. All the workers of God's reign and all Christians must allow themselves to bear the stamp of goodness, tolerance, and goodwill to avoid conflicts. All of the workers of God's reign encounter opposition. Therefore all Christians ought to avoid inciting opposition and blocking the ruling authorities and people in general for the Gospel. A life characterized by goodness helps our neighbor and brings the Gospel nearer.

7. When he speaks of mission/evangelization in terms of prayer, thanksgiving, and faith that God wants to work through the workers of God's reign, Luther has all such work, even foreign mission, in his field of vision. Prayer and intercession open doors so the Gospel and faith can spread out and be established.

8. Mission and evangelization are, for the reformer, primarily the work of the Father, the Son, and the Spirit. However, it is easy to recognize in all of Luther's writings that he always reckons with the human factor, that is, that people have different gifts of grace in the work of spreading God's reign. We have seen how energetically Luther emphasizes that the apostolate means both being sent out with the Gospel to the world and that the words of the apostles (the New Testament) are binding for doctrine and life. Both the mission motif and faithfulness to the word of the apostles should then characterize the ministry of all following pastors and bishops. Yes, according to the texts that I have discussed, the whole church is evangelizing and missionizing. As has often been pointed out before, the reformer integrates domestic and foreign work for God's reign.

9. There is no doubt that the younger Luther did, for a time, succeed in expressing the dynamic multiplicity of gifts of grace and tasks for the spreading of God's reign. Later, in the wake of his antitheology against the

"Spiritualists," Luther was more careful to guard the place of the ordained ministry in all such work. This does not mean naturally (compare Roman Catholic mission) that the mission perspective disappears in the older Luther. He always has reckoned that both ordained and laypeople are important in the spreading of the Gospel. The work is God's own work, but it requires both laypeople and pastors in the concrete work.

10. At the end of this survey and analysis, it is clear that Luther's commentaries on the Epistles have a mission perspective. In many and various ways, the reformer expresses that the Gospel about God's salvation must go out to all peoples, both to the Jews and the heathen. He speaks of the importance of both pastors and laypeople in the concrete work of the spreading of the Gospel. Mission is primarily God's work, but it can never come into existence without a human factor. It is also clear that Luther's mission vision is not inhibited by the expectation of Christ's speedy return. This world will continue to exist until the ascended Christ has been able to give God's salvation to all peoples, usually through repeated waves of revival. The reformer has directly contradicted the idea that texts such as Psalm 19:5; Mark 16:15; Colossians 1:23; and Titus 2:11 should indicate that Christ's Great Commission has been fulfilled already during the time of the apostles. For Luther, it is always the time of mission in the world until we see the Son of Man, the driving force of mission through the Word and the Spirit, come in the clouds of heaven.

CHAPTER FOUR

LUTHER AND MISSION PRAXIS

IN THE FOREGOING, WE HAVE SEEN that the reformer has a comprehensive mission thinking or missiology. He integrates reformation (inner mission) and foreign (cross-cultural) mission. He also speaks about how God the Father, the Son, and the Holy Spirit sustains and drives the work of God's reign through the Gospel in the Word and Sacraments, a work that continues in the world until Christ returns. Like rolling waves or rain showers, the Gospel goes out over the world to both Jews and heathen, that is, to all people in the world. According to Luther, it is always the time of mission whenever people exist who do not have the opportunity to encounter the Gospel initially or consistently. Even if Luther powerfully emphasizes *missio Dei*, it never occurs to him that the work of God's reign could proceed without human agents in the concrete work of the Gospel.

In this final chapter, we ask ourselves whether or not Luther can be regarded as possessing a vision for mission outside of the re-Christianization and reformation for which he is famous. Has the reformer been able to take the step from talking about the universality of the Gospel and from his comprehensive mission vision to concrete proposals for a mission among non-Christian peoples? Has he personally become involved in such work? Has he said something about how foreign missions should be constructed? Luther's relation to so-called external (foreign/cross-cultural) mission will be analyzed in this chapter.

In the first part I will show how intensely Luther worked for the sake of the Jews so they would confess Jesus' messiahship, repent, and become Christians. This concerns primarily the Jewish diaspora in Germany and Europe. The reformer also had a vision for the Muslim Turks as they streamed over previously Christian regions in Asia Minor and Southeast Europe. He considered this a mission field as well. Finally, I hope to show how, through his sermons, catechisms, prayers, hymns, etc., Luther inspired a mission vision for his contemporaries and for those who came after him.

LUTHER AND MISSION AMONG THE JEWS

The Jewish diaspora in Germany and Central Europe is the first group of non-Christians with which Luther was ever confronted. Already in his first lectures as a professor, which addressed the Psalms (1513–1515), Luther is thinking about the Jewish faith. Throughout his career, Luther returns in lectures, essays, and sermons to the Jewish faith, the conversion of the Jews, and the right stance Christians should take toward the Jews and their faith. It is undeniable that the Jews, their Mosaic faith, and their conversion to the Christian faith are important questions for the reformer. In the following, I hope above all to concentrate on the zeal Luther exhibits and the apologetics that he presented in his involvement with the Jews and Judaism.

A BRIEF REVIEW OF THE LITERATURE

Luther's stance toward and opinions about the Jews and their faith have given birth to scores of books and longer essays and to hundreds of book chapters and shorter essays. Scholars and other writers from various religious, cultural, political, and linguistic perspectives in this century have discussed the theme "Luther and the Jews/Judaism" as a historical, human, and theological problem. The variety of academic contributions and their divergent interpretations have in the last decades produced a literature with various typical interpretations of Luther's statements about the Jews and the relationship between Christianity and Judaism.[1]

In these various attempts at interpretation, scholars are intensively occupied with whether there is a development or a continuity in Luther's stance toward the Jews and Judaism. The first and most richly represented type of interpretation emphasizes that the reformer changed his stance through the years. As a rule, one demarcates three periods and thereby two noticeable transitions in Luther's stance toward the Jews. During the first phase, which is represented by, among others, the *Lectures on the Psalms* (1513–1515), one notices a certain chilly and

---

1 See Meier, "Zur Interpretation von Luthers Judenschriften," 127–53. See especially Brosseder, *Luthers Stellung zu den Juden*. In all, Brosseder presents 130 different types of interpretation, from Lutheran, Catholic, Barthian, and Jewish perspectives; from legal, philosophical, and political perspectives; and from both professional and amateur historians. Cf. the literature survey in Sucher, *Luthers Stellung zu den Juden*, 125–95.

theoretical/theological conflict vis-à-vis the Jews and their Mosaic faith. A clearly pro-Jewish stance and zeal for mission is represented in the commentary on the *Magnificat* (1521) and above all in the book *That Jesus Christ Was Born a Jew* (1523). From the end of the 1530s and especially in Luther's book *On the Jews and Their Lies* (1543), one, so it is supposed, finds a nearly anti-Semitic position in Luther, who had nearly lost hope about winning Jews for the Christian faith. A second type of interpretation argues—often energetically—that there is a continuity and no development in Luther's stance toward the Jews and their faith. One notices, among other things, that Luther's teaching about Christ and the righteousness of faith creates a religious conflict with Judaism but that the reformer always prayed and hoped that the Jews would receive Christ as the Messiah. A third type of interpretation combines the theses about continuity and development. The continuity would be Luther's articulation of justification through faith in Christ against the Jewish rejection of Jesus' messiahship and their legalistic religion. The development would be that Luther draws different practical/legal consequences on the basis of the *de facto* religious conflict between Judaism and Christianity. One also has sought to clarify which historical and other factors might have produced the previously named transitions. Some scholars in all three types of interpretation have emphasized the continuity in Luther's mission vision vis-à-vis the Jews, while others have completely rejected any notion that the reformer might have hoped to evangelize the Jews.[2]

Early on, great admirers of Luther such as Johann Mathesius and J. G. Walch reacted against certain inappropriate remarks against the Jews made by the aging reformer. At the turn of the century, scholars such as Theodor Kolde, Julius Köstlin, Gustav Kawerau, and Adolf Hausrath observed a certain development by the reformer from an early positive to a later negative stance vis-à-vis the Jews. Luther supposedly had become disappointed by the absence of Jewish conversions and at the same time was affected by personal changes caused by aging.[3]

The source-oriented, scientific research of the problem "Luther and Judaism" was decisively advanced by the historian Reinhold Lewin, who later became a rabbi, and his comprehensive investigation in 1911. He is an expert witness for those who demarcate three periods in Luther's position vis-à-vis the Jews and explains the transitions with psychology. Unfortunately, he pays too little attention to the theological themes that determined Luther's thought.[4] Later W. Walther,

---

2 Cf. the literature in the previous footnote, especially the sketch in Brosseder, *Luthers Stellung zu den Juden*, 35f.

3 See Brosseder, *Luthers Stellung zu den Juden*, 44ff., 67ff.; and Sucher, *Luthers Stellung zu den Juden*, 128ff., 170.

4 Lewin, *Luthers Stellung zu den Juden*. Cohrs generally follows Lewin's theses in his

Werner Elert, and Heinrich Bornkamm wrote of a difference between Luther's approaches in 1523 and 1543. But they explain the change as primarily religiously and/or theologically motivated. Such scholars are loath, however, to completely disregard psychological influences. It is the Jewish stance toward Christ and the Gospel that determined Luther's thought and action. Especially Elert notices a mission theme in Luther's relation to the Jews.[5]

Some well-known scholars did not consider the supposed transitions in Luther's thought as fundamental. Instead, they observed a thoroughgoing continuity in Luther's view of the Jews and Judaism. Walter Holsten means that it is Luther's view of the authority of the Bible (both Old and New Testaments) and his doctrine of justification through faith alone that is the starting point for Luther's assessment of Judaism and for the religious-theological conflict that he experiences between Judaism and Christianity. There is in Luther a consistent theological foundation, though there are developments in the politico-social consequences that he draws during the different periods of his life. He asserts a unity without contradictions. The mission perspective is said to have characterized the young reformer's view of the Jews and Judaism.[6] Erich Vogelsang rejects any notion that Luther had a missionary zeal for the Jews, but even he must reckon that the stance of the Jews toward Jesus' messiahship and the Christian doctrine of justification dominated Luther's thought concerning the Jews. Unfortunately, Vogelsang's analysis is influenced by Nazi ideology.[7] Th. Pauls also agrees with a constant line, that is, the Gospel of Christ, in Luther's meeting with Judaism. He finds a more powerful accent on the degeneration of the character of the Jews in the older Luther and rejects, as per his Nazi-influenced thought, any suggestion

---

foreword to Luther's book *Von den letzten Worten Davids* (1543), but he emphasizes more the biblical/dogmatic themes behind Luther's transitions. The 1928 foreword is in WA 54:16–24.

5 Walther, "Luther und die Juden," 130–33, 146–50, 162–67, 196–99, 213–17, 475–76. Elert, *Morphologie des Luthertums*, 1:345 (English: 395). Bornkamm, "Volk und Rasse bei Martin Luther." As a pro-Nazi theologian, Bornkamm sympathized with Luther's later severe writings against the Jews, but after Hitler's famous speech in the Berlin Sports Arena on November 30, 1933, Bornkamm left Nazism completely.

6 Holsten, "Christentum und nicht-christliche Religion nach der Auffassung Luthers," especially 70–148. Concerning the unity in the diversity, the Jewish writings of 1523 and Luther's problem with Romans 11:25, and the final conversion of the Jews, see Holsten, 117–20. Concerning the conflict regarding the Scriptures and justification, see Holsten, 102ff., 106ff.

7 Vogelsang, *Luthers Kampf gegen die Juden*, 9, 20f., in which it is emphasized that the view of Christ exhibited by the Jews is the decisive factor in Luther's thinking. Cf. also Brosseder, *Luthers Stellung zu den Juden*, 130ff.; and Sucher, *Luthers Stellung zu den Juden*, 173ff.

that Luther was interested in mission among the Jews.[8] It is not part of my task here to present all the Nazi-influenced work on the theme "Luther and the Jews."[9]

The nonideological research on Luther's stance toward the Jews began in earnest after World War II. In an impressive American dissertation from 1949, Armas K. E. Holmio emphasizes that the reformer, after a cold theological relationship to the Jewish question from the commentary on the *Magnificat* (1521), becomes positive to the Jews and is intensely occupied with their conversion. This mission perspective weakens somewhat in the older Luther. Holmio believes the differences between the younger and the older Luther can be reduced to epiphenomena when one has understood that Luther's writings on the Jews are "mission works." Holmio sees with only one eye in his attempt at interpretation, but he sometimes sees quite well with his one eye. His focus on the mission perspective has been a great help in my own research.[10]

Wilhelm Maurer is one of the heavyweights of Reformation scholarship. He has in two careful pieces of scholarship from 1953 and 1968[11] asserted that Luther's position vis-à-vis the Jews can be understood from certain constant theological principles.[12] Alongside these constant theological principles that Luther

---

8 Pauls, *Luther und die Juden*, 3 vols. Through his Nazi-influenced interpretation of Luther, Pauls came to function as a support for Nazi agitation in the Evangelical Church. In the literature, see Brosseder, *Luthers Stellung zu den Juden*, 135ff.

9 See Brosseder, *Luthers Stellung zu den Juden*, 182ff.; and Sucher, *Luthers Stellung zu den Juden*, 137ff.

10 Holmio, *Lutheran Reformation and the Jews*, especially 87f., 125ff. Brosseder, *Luthers Stellung zu den Juden*, 263ff., believes that Holmio overinterprets Luther's writings on the Jews in the direction of "mission epistles." Cf. also Sucher, *Luthers Stellung zu den Juden*, 183f., who is somewhat more positive in his analysis of Holmio.

11 Maurer, *Kirche und Synagoge*, 36–51. Cf. Maurer, "Die Zeit der Reformation," 375–429.

12 Among Luther's consistent theological maxims in his meeting with the Jews and Judaism are the following according to Maurer, *Kirche und Synagoge*, 45f., 89; and Maurer, "Die Zeit der Reformation," 378ff.:

1. Jesus from Nazareth and no one else is the promised Messiah.

2. Humanity is justified with God only through faith in Jesus Christ. The Jews reject and scorn this faith.

3. Therefore the Jews suffer under God's wrath and are dispersed in the world with neither their own land nor a functioning worship of God. They hope in vain for a worldly Messiah. God alone can cease this punishment of the Jews.

4. The Jews can neither through their own power nor through others but only by God be brought to repentance. They become more and more hardened and do not appear to be a people who can be saved. A remnant of the Jews always continues to be won for Christ.

bases on Scripture, there are also developments concerning the practical/legal measures one ought to take vis-à-vis the Jews and their exercise of religion. In the beginning, Luther encourages an inclusive openness. In the older Luther, one finds the so-called severe mercy, that is, a separation of the Jews and Christians as much as possible. Even this does not break up Luther's unified theological judgment of the Jews and Judaism.[13] It is worth noticing that Luther's hope for a mission work for the conversion of the Jews is articulated more powerfully in Maurer's 1953 work than in his 1968 work.[14] Maurer is grieved by the older reformer's inimical stance, his warnings, and his proposals in *On the Jews and Their Lies* (1543). Luther could not maintain his positive stance from *That Christ Was Born a Jew* (1523). Unfortunately, Luther eventually regressed into a medieval, reactionary thought process.[15]

After World War II, many scholars have claimed that the differences in Luther's writings from 1523 and 1543 are real differences. In two essays, Martin Stöhr has suggested that Luther's earlier, friendly invitation to Jews and Gentiles is exchanged for an exclusion of the Jews because Luther does not want to share in the sins of the Jews and their denial of Christ, while at the same time he waits for Christ's imminent return.[16] In 1543 Luther supposedly no longer hoped in the

---

5. In their hardness and their blasphemies against the Christian faith, the Jews prove that theirs is a living religion inimical to Christ. Their understanding of the Scriptures in the Talmud and rabbis is incorrect. Therefore a struggle develops between falsehood and truth in the meeting between Judaism and Christianity.

6. There is, nevertheless, a fundamental solidarity between Jews and Christians concerning guilt, judgment, and grace. Therefore the struggle produced by the religious conflict ought not be carried out with hate and frenzy.

13 Maurer, *Kirche und Synagoge*, 46; and Maurer, "Die Zeit der Reformation," 427f. Cf. also Kupisch, *Das Volk der Geschichte.*

14 Maurer, *Kirche und Synagoge*, 44f., considers Luther's book *That Christ Was Born a Jew* to be a proposal and program for mission among the Jews. But also Luther's later more severe and polemical writings are thought by Maurer to be characterized by an apologetical/missionizing perspective. In "Die Zeit der Reformation," 389, 425, Mauer reduces the mission motif in *That Christ Was Born a Jew* to "eine apologetisch-missionarische Tendenz." In the later writings on the Jews, especially *On the Jews and Their Lies*, Maurer says that the mission perspective has little place. In "Die Zeit der Reformation," Mauer notices partly Luther's thought about the solidarity between Jews and Christians concerning guilt and partly the reformer's occupation with Christology and the right interpretation of the Old Testament prophecies. See Maurer, "Die Zeit der Reformation," 379, 383, 385ff., 394f., concerning this solidarity and 415, 425f., 428, concerning Christology.

15 Maurer, *Kirche und Synagoge*, 45, 48f.; and Maurer, "Die Zeit der Reformation," 403, 407, 409, 416f., 420f.

16 Stöhr, "Luther und die Juden," *Evangelische Theologie*, 157–82. Cf. Stöhr, "Luther und die Juden," 89–108.

power of God's Word to convert the Jews; therefore he proposed a severe handling of them by the authorities.[17] Aarne Siirala also is critical of the notion of a religious-theological continuity as proposed by H. Bornkamm, Holmio, and Maurer. He believes that the differences between the younger and the older Luther's statements have their origin in the inner contradictions of Luther's theology. Thereby he proposes more research concerning the reformer's view of predestination, the Bible as God's Word, and his ecclesiology.[18] Kurt Meier points to the fact that one steps into deep theological problems regardless of whether one perceives a continuity or a discontinuity in Luther's statements about the Jews and their faith.[19] Luther's view of the Jews and Judaism belongs primarily to his doctrine of justification. Meier believes, however, that the older Luther was taken captive by a so-called Bible positivism in which the Bible's statements about the hardness of Israel superceded Luther's understanding of the universality of grace and justification. He reacts negatively to the exclusivity of Luther's "Christ alone" and reacts positively to the soteriological universalism of Vatican II.[20]

In 1972 the Roman Catholic scholar Johannes Brosseder published a bulky and invaluable work with an exhaustive literature review and a shorter analysis of the main problems on the theme "Luther and the Jews." He analyzes primarily *That Christ Was Born a Jew* and *On the Jews and Their Lies* and seeks to clarify the scholarly conflict between Stöhr/Siirala and Holsten/Maurer. He eventually concludes that there is no fundamental theological development between the younger and the older Luther. A decided development in praxis is nevertheless apparent. Brosseder generally accepts Maurer's position. Against Meier, he claims that the change in the older Luther does not depend on Bible positivism and its derivative particularism vis-à-vis the Jews as it concerns the Gospel of Christ. Because Luther's soteriology vis-à-vis all religions is based on faith in Christ alone as the exclusive criterion, a conflict develops with Judaism in its rejection and blasphemy of Christ. Even with the so-called severe mercy (1543), Luther wanted to produce conversions among the Jews while at the same time avoiding sharing in

---

17 Stöhr, "Martin Luther und die Juden," 91ff., 98ff.

18 Siirala, "Luther und die Juden," 427–52. See also Brosseder, *Luthers Stellung zu den Juden*, 281f.

19 Meier, "Zur Interpretation von Luthers Judenschriften," 127–53. Cf. Meier, "Zur Interpretation von Luthers Judenschriften," 144, the discussion concerning the leading proponents of the development hypothesis (Siirala and Stöhr) and of the continuity hypothesis (Maurer and Holsten). Can one so simply differentiate between a theological continuity and a development in the practical/legal consequences? Are not the doctrine of justification and the concrete works better integrated?

20 Meier, "Zur Interpretation von Luthers Judenschriften," 144ff.

the sins of the Jews.[21] Brosseder sees in *That Christ Was Born a Jew* a missiological-apologetical tendency that nevertheless is nearly completely absent in *On the Jews and Their Lies*.[22] The Germanist C. Bernd Sucher has in his work *Luthers Stellung zu den Juden* sought to give a nontheologian's interpretation of Luther's writings.[23] He reacts negatively to the idea of theologians that the reformer's statements must always be determined by his main teachings. This categorizing and periodizing of theses relativizes Luther's words. Instead, one ought to read the texts without theological *Vorverständnis* (presupposition). For Sucher, the concepts *development* and *regression* become important, and he willingly uses psychological arguments to explain the changes in Luther's stance toward the Jews. Sucher finds in the years 1514–1523 a development from the medieval, negative view of the Jews toward a positive, theological reflection and a humanitarian stance toward the Jews who are in this human life together with Christians. Against certain scholars, he has powerfully emphasized the mission perspective in *That Christ Was Born a Jew*.[24]

A regressive period began during the years 1526–1538, which starting in 1543 was powerfully strengthened and resulted in hard judgments against the Jews and in horrid proposals of how to treat them. This regression depended, according to Sucher, on Luther's disappointment with the lack of Jewish conversions and with the fact that some Christians were being tempted to convert to Judaism, plus the increase in Luther's grumpiness caused by his age and illness.[25] Sucher's call *ad fontes* is important for theologians, but to investigate the theme "Luther and the Jews/Judaism" adequately without considering the theological context is impossible.

---

21 Brosseder, *Luthers Stellung zu den Juden*, with the literature review (39–340) and his analysis of the background to and theological motifs in Luther's statements about the Jews and their faith (341–92). Concerning the argument with Meier and about faith in Christ as an exclusive criterion, see Brosseder, *Luthers Stellung zu den Juden*, 382ff., 386ff.

22 Concerning the lack of the mission perspective and the critique against Holmio's exaggerations, see Brosseder, *Luthers Stellung zu den Juden*, 263ff., 354.

23 Sucher, *Luthers Stellung zu den Juden*, with a survey of the source material (32–124), a literature review (125–99), and his own attempt at interpretation (200–291).

24 Sucher, *Luthers Stellung zu den Juden*, 202ff., 238ff.

25 See the summary in Sucher, *Luthers Stellung zu den Juden*, 282–91. Concerning the hard lunges against the Jews from ca. 1543 and the attempt to explain them, see Sucher, *Luthers Stellung zu den Juden*, 261ff., 268ff. Sucher refers to the following historical-psychological studies: Reiter, *Martin Luthers Umwelt, Charakter und Psychose*, and Erikson, *Der junge Martin Luther*.

The subject of Luther and the Jews has engaged many scholars in connection with the 500th anniversary of the reformer's birth in 1483. In a pair of investigations,[26] Heiko A. Oberman has emphasized that Luther's stance toward the Jews must be seen in connection with the medieval view of the Jews and Judaism, as well as the view of his own contemporaries. Furthermore, his stance is determined by the unavoidable front that the newly discovered Gospel about Christ creates against the eschatological and inimical (to God's reign) coalition (that is, the Jews, the papists, the enthusiasts, and eventually the Muslims). That some Christians have gone over to Judaism substantiates that this is a diabolical attack of which the Jews are the foot soldiers. These two main perspectives ought to weigh heavily when one seeks the reasons behind the development in Luther from the friendly stance of 1523 to the severe attitude of 1543. The psychological-medical arguments that others have suggested are not sufficient to explain this development. Walther Bienert has also presented a worthwhile collection of texts on the theme "Luther and the Jews/Judaism." He finds both positive/inclusive and negative/judgmental statements throughout Luther's life as an active theologian. At the same time, says Bienert, the anti-Jewish stance dominates the years 1538–1543. Bienert emphasizes that the reformer's involvement in the German state church system with its Christian monoculture is an important reason for the negative and threatening statements of the older Luther. Luther wishes to preserve religious unity against Jewish propaganda and proselytism. But in the final years, Luther's antagonism is weakened again. Bienert shows that Luther as reformer consistently possessed a more or less articulated desire to win the Jews for the Christian faith. He emphasizes that Luther in his spiritual/dogmatic conflict with Judaism has many anti-Jewish pronouncements but was absolutely not anti-Semitic. Unfortunately, based on his liberal point of view, Bienert depreciates the indispensable dogmatic Christological positions that led to the conflict.[27] After the Luther jubilee, a number of books have contributed to the understanding of the problem of Luther and the Jews/Judaism.[28]

---

26 Oberman, *Wurzeln des Antisemitismus*, and "Luthers Beziehungen zu den Juden." Concerning the relationship of the Gospel to the Jews and others and the inimical coalition, see Oberman, *Wurzeln des Antisemitismus*, 138ff., 140ff. Concerning the younger and the older reformer's stance toward the Jews, see Oberman, *Wurzeln des Antisemitismus*, 145ff., 151ff.

27 Bienert, *Martin Luther und die Juden*. This book contains valuable passages that shed light on the social and theological contexts of Luther's statements.

28 Kremers, *Die Juden und Martin Luther*. In this collection of essays, I want to point especially to the following contributions: Boendermaker, "Luther—ein 'semi-iudaeus'?" 45–57; Ehrlich, "Luther und die Juden," 72–88 (here I use the corresponding essay in *Judaica* 39 [1983]: 131–49); Stöhr, "Martin Luther und die Juden," 89–108;

The above survey of the scholarship shows that research on the question of Luther and the Jews/Judaism is not virgin territory. Some scholars simply have registered what Luther wrote and said during the different periods of his life without seeking to disclose the theological maxims that underlie Luther's statements. This scholarship has taken special interest in psychological explanations of the developments in Luther's position vis-à-vis the Jews and Judaism. Other scholars have primarily concentrated on only those theological maxims that stand behind the reformer's statements and have discovered an inner theological continuity coupled with a development in Luther's thought concerning practical/legal questions. The contributions of the scholarship taken together show that the conflict between Luther and Judaism originates primarily in different ways to answer the question about Jesus' messiahship. Luther's understandings of the Old Testament and of justification also have contributed to the development of the conflict.

My investigation is of a historical/systematic nature in which I seek to give attention to what the texts actually say and at the same time seek which theological and other themes determine the statements. In this way, I want to avoid the methodological one-sidedness that has up to now determined the debate about development or continuity in Luther's stance toward the Jews and their Mosaic faith.

Furthermore, my work seeks to be a contribution to the research into the questions about Luther's mission perspective and the mission method so that such would be illuminated adequately. Because the scholars are so divided about the significance of apology and mission in Luther's encounter with the Jews and their faith, it is not without a certain anticipation that one seeks to investigate their place in Luther's argument and praxis.

LUTHER'S TIME AND THE STEREOTYPES OF JEWS

From the beginning, it ought to be clarified that the late Middle Ages and Luther's own time with its limited social contact between classes and religions possessed a plethora of negative and excluding stereotypes in its description of and propaganda against the Jews, their lifestyle, and their faith. They are described, for example, as parasites and bloodsuckers. The theologians called

---

Heiko A. Oberman, "Die Juden in Luthers Sicht," 136–62 (from the 1983 essay "Luthers Beziehungen zu den Juden"); and Brosseder, "Luther und der Leidensweg der Juden," 109–35. I would also like to point to the following essays from different perpectives: Müller, "Tribut an den Geist seiner Zeit," 305–8; Wallmann, "Luthers Stellung zu den Juden und Islam," 53–56; Maser, "Erbarmen für Luther?" 166–78; Hardt, "Luther," 70–74; Saebø, "Luther og jødene," 641–46; Pfisterer, "Zwischen Polemik und Apologetik," 99–124; and Schreiner, "Jüdische Reaktionen auf die Reformation," 150–65. See also the competent book by Tjernagel, *Martin Luther and the Jewish People.*

them hardened and blind in their hatred of Christ and Christians. The Jewish Talmud was considered a distortion of the Scriptures. Satire and abusive words against the Jews existed everywhere in songs, devotional literature, and Passion plays. Through tracts and wandering monks, an attitude inimical to the Jews was spread among the people through rumors about ritual murder, desecration of the host, poisonings, etc. In this way the Jews came to be considered by the general public as a people obsessed with evil deeds. This, in turn, caused the worldly authorities to interfere. Restrictions were enacted against the exercise of their religion. Jews were forced to live in restricted areas—if they were allowed to live in a town at all. They were constantly expelled for longer or shorter periods of time from princedoms and imperial cities. After a time they were usually allowed to return, at which point the authorities assessed uncountable sums in tribute. Periodically their literature and worship services were forbidden. Indeed, sometimes Jews were executed by action of the authorities or by mob lynchings. Luther knew all this well through his literature studies and through the attitudes of his contemporaries toward and persecution of the Jews.[29]

As we will see, the older Luther was not completely immune to the anti-Jewish propaganda, agitation, and discrimination. He was absolutely not any type of anti-Semite, but in relation to the Jews and Judaism, Luther exhibits two sides: a pastoral, compassionate, and sympathetic side and a strongly critical, irreconcilable, and polemical side. Without a doubt, the older Luther is more negative in his attitude toward the Jews than the younger reformer.

In the analysis of the Luther material, one must, however, give careful attention to which Jews and of what in the exercise of their religion and lifestyle Luther is critical. According to Luther, the patriarchs, prophets, Jesus, and the apostles belong to the Jews. And there have been those among the chosen people who during the previous 1,500 years have believed in Jesus as the God-sent Messiah. But there also are Jews whom the Old Testament describes as enemies to the prophets and who, according to the New Testament and the theologians of the church, rejected Jesus as the Messiah, distorted the Scriptures, and sought to convert baptized Christians to the Jewish faith. Of course, the reformer's statements about these two groups of Jews are completely different. Luther expresses his compassion for the Jews in their diaspora and persecution after the destruction of the temple in A.D. 70. At the same time, he can rage against the fact that in their

---

29 See Degani, "Die Formulierung und Propagierung des jüdischen Stereotyps," 3–44. Degani reviews a mass of literature. See also Maurer, "Die Zeit der Reformation," 363ff.; Sucher, *Luthers Stellung zu den Juden,* 1ff.; Oberman, *Wurzeln des Antisemitismus,* 23ff., 87ff., 125ff., who exhaustively reviews the roots of anti-Semitism and the impact of official legislation; and Bienert, *Martin Luther und die Juden,* 125f., 134ff., 151ff., 157ff.

diaspora they assess usury, economically oppress the poor, and have a more affluent lifestyle while at the same time consistently rejecting the Gospel of Christ and abusing Christ and the Christians. In this way, one must pay attention to the context of Luther's statements and take into account whom he is addressing.

ISRAEL AND GOD'S SALVATION ACCORDING TO THE YOUNG LUTHER

The Dominican theologians in Cologne, among them the converted Jew Johannes Pfefferkorn, had reacted against the fact that the humanist and Hebraicist Johannes Reuchlin opposed Pfefferkorn's proposal to confiscate and burn the Jews' blasphemous books, especially the Talmud. In this way, the Dominicans hoped to produce a general conversion of the Jews. This idea had been proposed earlier. Reuchlin had advocated, instead, a loving relationship to the Jews.

After many twists and turns in the question, Luther gave his requested opinion on the subject to Georg Spalatin in February 1514. Luther does not now think that Reuchlin can be accused of indulgence as it concerns the Christian faith. The theologians in Cologne seek to drive out Beelzebub but not with the finger of God (Luke 11:20). They fight against the Jews for direct blasphemies, but they leave the church's infinitely more blasphemous exercise of religion without critique. Every theologian ought to understand that the Jews' blasphemies against Christ are predicted by Scripture and are a fulfillment of Scripture's words (Matthew 26:54). The theologians of Cologne ought to understand that the Jews will only become more hardened by a book banning. Through such external measures, one cannot change their religion and blasphemies. Here only God can do his work in their hearts because God has placed them under his wrath.[30]

In his 1513–1515 lectures on the Psalms, the reformer writes, among other things, a severe but moderate critique of Jewish biblical commentaries, legalism, and hard-heartedness. He also writes against their rejection of Jesus as the Messiah. Luther is often relentless in his statements that the Jews are the worst enemies of the church who above all reject Jesus as Messiah and his resurrection. It ought to be observed that Luther does not say that the Jews crucified Christ.[31] Luther's

---

30 WABr 1:28f. Cf. especially WABr 1:7.23f., one of the young professor's statements in 1514. Concerning the struggle with the theologians of Cologne, see Lewin, *Luthers Stellung zu den Juden*, 1f.; Maurer, "Die Zeit der Reformation," 378ff.; and Sucher, *Luthers Stellung zu den Juden*, 52ff., who carefully examines the controversy. See also Oberman, *Wurzeln des Antisemitismus*, 23ff., on Johannes Reuchlin, and 40ff., 90ff., on Johannes Pfefferkorn.

31 On Jewish commentaries, WA 3:320.15ff., 492.8ff., 501.5ff., 513.15ff. On Jewish legalism, WA 3:29.26ff., 201.4ff., 201.36f., 172.30ff.; 4:3.29ff., 484.22ff. On Jewish rejection of Jesus as Messiah, WA 3:180.34f., 275.39ff., 515.37ff., 596.35ff.; 4:22.2ff., 22.29ff.

thoughts about the conversion of the Jews before the Reformation breakthrough are quickly replaced in his lectures on the Psalms. Against the idea based on Romans 11:23–26 that all the Jewish people would be saved, Luther believes that Luke 21:32; Malachi 1:4; and Isaiah 10:21 indicate that only a remnant will be saved. Most of the Jews will remain hardened and will never convert. But Luther also can be somewhat open to the possibility of a folk conversion.[32]

Even in the 1515–1516 lectures on Romans, Luther lambastes the Jewish, satanic pride, that is, their trust in election, circumcision, and works of the Law. The Jews understand neither the Old Testament's nor the New Testament's doctrine of justification through faith. It ought to be observed, however, that Luther points out that Jews, Gentiles, and self-righteous Christian hypocrites—among them priests—have the same problem.[33] Something of a mission motif also exists in the commentaries on Romans. Luther marks the difference between Jewish and Christian faith, but at the same time, he learns from the apostle Paul a sorrowful pity for the Jews in their hardening and consequent judgment. Luther emphasizes in connection with Romans 11:1f. that Israel's election stands fast. However, no one ought to count on salvation only on the basis of a blood relation to Abraham and Israel. Salvation is won only by grace and through faith in Christ.[34]

If now God is faithful in God's covenant with Israel, then no one can, on the basis of Romans 9:24–27, assert that all Israel is rejected. A part of Israel—but not the whole people—will believe and be saved before Christ's parousia. Paul refers

---

Concerning Jewish hardness of heart, WA 3:228.5ff., 329.26ff., 583.8ff.; 4:418.31ff., 464.25ff., 468.21f., 468.35ff. I have compiled these references with the help of Maurer, "Die Zeit der Reformation," 379ff.; and Sucher, *Luthers Stellung zu den Juden*, 46f. Concerning Luther's indefensible writings against the Jews, see also Tarald Rasmussen, *Inimici ecclesiae: Das ekklesiologische Feindbild in Luthers "Dictata super Psalterium" (1513–1515) im Horizont der theologischen Tradition*, Studies in Medieval and Reformation Thought 44 (Leiden: Brill, 1989). Rasmussen shows that the Jews are the prototype of God's enemies. Luther's most important argument against the Jews is not the common anti-Semitic complaints about the crucifixion of Jesus. It is worse that they have rejected the resurrected Christ as God's Messiah.

32 WA 3:329.26ff.; 4:468.21ff., 468.32ff. Concerning the commentary on Psalm 73:10–11, see Rasmussen, *Inimici ecclesiae*, 130ff. Concerning Luther's optimism for a folk conversion among the Jews based on Psalm 73:1, see Rasmussen, *Inimici ecclesiae*, 127f.

33 *Gloss*, WA 56:17.19ff., 22.9ff., 22.24ff., 40.26ff., 42.21ff. Cf. *Scholia*, WA 56:200.6ff., 267.9ff., 268.24ff. Concerning Christian hypocrisy, see WA 56:349.18ff., 478.15ff., and especially 436.13ff. Concerning righteousness in Christ alone, see WA 56:22.11ff., 22.24ff., 40.26ff., 42.21ff. See also Maurer, "Die Zeit der Reformation," 382f.; and Bienert, *Martin Luther und die Juden*, 32ff.

34 WA 56:105.13ff., 105.24ff., 428.27ff.

not only to Hosea 2:3 but also to Isaiah 10:22f. The latter passage speaks about salvation for a remnant.[35]

Luther has significant difficulties interpreting Romans 9–11, especially Romans 11:25–26, which includes Paul's revealed secret about Israel's final salvation: "Israel has experienced a hardening in part until the full number of the Gentiles has come in. And so all Israel will be saved . . ." Already in the *Gloss,* Luther has difficulties with the idea that all individuals in Israel will be saved just before Christ's second advent. However, in the *Scholia,* while referring to the church fathers and to a long list of Bible verses (among others Luke 21:23f.; Deuteronomy 4:30f.; Hosea 3:4f.; 5:12), he interprets the text in such a way that the fallen and dispersed Jews among the Gentiles will be saved before Christ's second advent and after the Gentiles had first received the Gospel. As Joseph who had been sold to Egypt was recognized by his father and brothers, so the Jews who rejected the Gospel of Christ will themselves in the diaspora become hungry for God's Word and come to Christ. But they must repent from the way of self-righteousness and come to faith in the forgiveness of sins for the sake of Christ. And a time will come when not merely a remnant of the Jews will be saved. "Now only in part are they saved, but then all shall be," says Luther.[36]

---

35 WA 56:95.19ff., 405.13ff.

36 LW 25:431. *Gloss* on Romans: "*And so all Israel,* all of Israel who are to be saved, *will be saved*" (LW 25:101 [*original emphasis*] [WA 56:113.14f.]). Here Luther is probably speaking about particular Jews, while in the *Scholia* (WA 56:436.25ff.) he speaks generally about the salvation of the Jews. See especially LW 25:429–30 (WA 56:437.18ff., 437.27ff.): "According to this interpretation, therefore, the meaning of the apostle is: 'I want you to understand this mystery, brethren,' that is, 'Do not be proud; it is a holy secret why the Jews fell, a secret which no man knows, namely, that the Jews who are now fallen shall return and be saved, after the Gentiles according to the fullness of their election have entered. They will not remain outside forever, but will return in their own time. . . . (Gen. 37:28) . . . So also the Jews who threw Christ out to the Gentiles, where He now has the position of a ruler, will finally come back to Him, drawn by hunger for the Word, and they will receive Him among the Gentiles. The apostle indicates this when he cites Isaiah in connection with the statement: *And so all Israel will be saved* (v. 26). In our version Isaiah reads thus in chapter 59:20: 'And there shall come a redeemer to Zion, and to them that return from iniquity in Jacob' " (*original emphasis*). LW 25:430–31 (WA 56:438.12, 438.16f., 438.20f., 438.24ff.): "Furthermore, he adds the expression *when I take away their sins* (v. 27) . . . . Therefore he is trying to say: 'This is the testament of the remission of sin,' in which 'He will banish ungodliness from Jacob' . . . . Thus in our time 'a partial blindness has befallen Israel,' but in that future day not a part but all Israel shall be saved. Now only in part are they saved, but then all shall be" (*original emphasis*). Cf. Luther's comments on Romans 11:23ff. (WA 56:133.3ff.). Ehrlich emphasizes how the conflict with the Jews is fundamentally a question of Christology and of the doctrine of justification by faith ("Luther und die Juden," 72f.). See also Jensen, "Luther och Jødene," 80ff.

The apparent idea in the *Gloss* that only the predestined among the Jews will be saved also appears immediately in a so-called *Corollary*. The idea about all Israel being saved is not so simple. One must, according to Luther, remember that "all Israel" includes all God's people of the past, present, and future. In this mystical body, or *massa Iudaeorum*, there are both those who are rejected and some who are chosen/holy. In Romans 11:26, the apostle, according to Luther, uses the figure of speech *pars pro toto,* whereby all Israel as *massa Sancta* is ascribed salvation for the sake of the chosen. Paul expresses himself about the people as a whole, not about all the individuals, among whom one finds many who are impenitent and unholy.[37] It ought to be observed that predestination has a central place in these early texts and that any talk of the salvation of all Israel is a problem also for that reason. Seen as a totality, in his work with Romans (1515–1516), Luther equivocates in his interpretation of Israel's final salvation according to Romans 11:23. Luther stands for a *yes* to Israel—a *yes* with a reservation concerning the separate individual Jews.

For our investigation of mission, it is also worth noting how Luther, with Paul (Romans 9:1–5) in desperation about the Jews' rejection of Jesus Christ, is filled with a compassionate love for the chosen people.[38] In connection with Romans 11:22, Luther cautions the Christians for presumption concerning the Jews. Because in the present state of Christianity many Christians are ignorant of the righteousness of faith, one can in the first place not speak of blessed Christians and cursed Jews. In the second place, those who call the Jews dogs and cursed cannot lead them to repentance. One ought to suffer over their plight and remember Paul's words in Romans 12:14: "[B]less and do not curse," and in 1 Corinthians 4:12: "When we are cursed, we bless; when we are persecuted, we endure it."[39] God

---

37 The *Gloss* has a problem with the idea that all the individual Jews could be saved (WA 56:113.10ff., 113.22ff.). See, however, especially in the *Scholia,* that is, the so-called *Corollary:* "For this entire text has the purpose of persuading his people to return. Therefore in order that the apostle may be understood correctly, we must understand that his remarks extend over the whole mass of the Jewish people and refers to the good among them, both past, present, and future. Although some among them are lost, yet the mass of them must be respected because of the elect. . . . [F]or thus the Jewish people are a 'holy mass' because of the elect, but 'broken branches' because of the lost . . . . Therefore he uses the term 'mass,' so that he may show that he is speaking not of individual people but of the entire race, in which are many unholy people" (LW 25:431 [WA 56:439.6ff.]). Maurer, "Die Zeit der Reformation," 384, speaks of "Antwort in einer eigentümlichen Schwebe" and about "*Spannungszustand*" in the final reference. Cf. Sucher, *Luthers Stellung zu den Juden,* 51f. Maurer writes beautifully. But has Luther not already said that not all the individual Israelites will be saved?

38 WA 56:389.2ff., 389.11ff. Cf. Bienert, *Martin Luther und die Juden,* 34f.

39 WA 56:436.7ff., 436.13ff. See Maurer, "Die Zeit der Reformation," 382f.

has chosen to receive both Jews and Gentiles in an unconditional mercy. Therefore both ought to receive each other in a friendly manner and not fight but instead praise God for salvation.[40]

We have seen that Luther in his commentaries on the Psalms expresses periodically a nearly irreconcilable stance toward the Jews and their faith. He reckons that a remnant of Jews can be saved but not with a general salvation (Romans 11:23ff.) of all individual Jews. In the lectures on Romans (1515–1516), Luther is critical of the Jewish connection of salvation to Israel's election, circumcision, and the Law and their rejection of Christ and the righteousness of faith. But there is a missionary perspective as well. The Jews must repent and believe in Christ. We also have seen that Luther makes more of the promise of a general salvation of Israel before the end of time (Romans 11:25–26). But the matter is still problematic for Luther.

THE MISSION MOTIF AND THE MISSION APPEAL 1519–1523

The source material shows that during the first years after the Reformation breakthrough, Luther expresses himself even more positively concerning the Jews. All harassments of the Jews must cease. All Christians must meet them lovingly and clothe themselves in an inclusive and soul-winning attitude toward the Jews.

The reformer can sometimes link the un-Christian affluence, usury, and oppression of the poor at the hands of the banks and merchants with the Jews. He also can criticize both the papacy and the Jews for their attempt to attain a worldly messianic kingdom.[41] But all this is not decisive for the conflict between Luther and Judaism. Especially Maurer and Oberman have with good justification emphasized that according to the post-breakthrough Luther there is a constant spiritual conflict over Christology between Christian faith and Judaism. Since the

---

40 *Gloss:* "And in all these citations the apostle has settled the contention between Jews and Gentiles, so that they are not in opposition to each other but mutually welcome one another, just as Christ has welcomed them. For not only the Jews, lest they be proud, but also not the Gentiles has He welcomed except out of His pure mercy. Therefore they both have reason to praise God but none for their own contention" (LW 25:122n10 [WA 56:140.16ff.]). Cf. *Scholia*, WA 56:433.24ff., 436.6ff. Cf. also Luther's ideas about the word *heathen* as appropriate for both those "Christians" who are ignorant of faith and those who have never heard the Gospel. See also the reformer's thoughts about one single people of God, consisting of Christ-believing Jews and Gentiles. See *Luther and World Mission*, 61ff., 218ff.

41 "Sermon von dem Wucher (1519)," WA 6:3.20ff., 5.3ff., 5.15ff., 5.32ff. "Treatise on Good Works (1520)," WA 6:262.11f. "To the Christian Nobility, etc. (1520)," WA 6:465.25ff., 466.9ff. "On the Papacy in Rome, etc. (1520)," WA 6:294.35ff., 295.19ff. Cf. WA 1:701.27ff.; 7:505.36ff.; 9:435.5ff. See also Bienert, *Martin Luther und die Juden*, 51ff.

Gospel has come to the light of day, the Jews have been a part of the coalition (that is, the Jews, the pope, the Christian hypocrites, and the enthusiasts) opposing Christ in an eschatological attack on the Gospel, says Oberman. As in earlier writings, it is said, therefore, that the Jews seek their own righteousness through works of the Law, are hardened in their own unbelief, exist under God's wrath, and live dispersed. They stand against Christ and the church and are their enemies. They do not confess Christ's divinity and power to save. The Jews believe that through their own works they can win God's good favor. But through its own fall from faith, the church has a certain solidarity with the fall of the Jews.[42] Both the "Jew" and the "Romanist" get to hear the reformer explain that neither a blood relationship to Abraham nor a connection to Rome have any significance for salvation (Psalm 16:3; Acts 10:34). God's promises and grace to Abraham are not only given to his own descendants, that is, to the Jews. The one blessed in Abraham is Christ and all those who have believed in him throughout the ages. This, his church, will be victorious in the end.[43] Luther is sorry that most of the Jews are hardened and turn their backs on Christ and the church. Without faith in Christ, they exist under God's wrath and are lost.[44]

Early on the young reformer rejected kabbalistic scriptural hermeneutics and especially its magical speculations about God's name. Such does not lead to belief in a graceful God but to unbelief and blasphemy against God. But one ought not burn Jewish books (later, in 1543, Luther held the opposite opinion).[45] In this way,

---

42 *Operationes in Psalmos* (1519–1521), WA 5:363.29f., 449.15ff., 534.20ff., 535.5ff., 538.19ff., 430.8ff.; "Psalm 68," WA 8:22.53ff.; *Church Postil* (1522), WA 10/1.1:259.14ff. Cf. WA 10/1:144.4ff.; 10/1.2:52.27ff.; 10/3:66.28ff., 315.15ff.; 12:148.5ff. See Lewin, *Luthers Stellung zu den Juden*, 4ff.; Maurer, "Die Zeit der Reformation," 385ff.; and Oberman, "Luthers Bezeihungen zu den Juden," 523ff.

43 *Operationes in Psalmos* (1519–1521), WA 5:446.36ff., 447.25f.; *Magnificat* (1521), WA 7:597.28ff., 599.13f., 599.26ff. See Maurer, "Die Zeit der Reformation," 387f.; and Sucher, *Luthers Stellung zu den Juden*, 53f.

44 *Operationes in Psalmos* (1519–1521), WA 5:116.35ff., 281.28f., 534.13ff., 538.10ff. Cf. WA 7:257.27ff.

45 *Galatians* (1519), WA 2:490.34ff. Cf. *Operationes in Psalmos*, WA 5:184.5–187.16. Luther opposes burning Jewish books in "Against Latomus (1521)," WA 8:52.11ff. The Jewish commentaries on Scripture or the tradition (*Kabbala*) had, since the late classical period, often developed into a secret teaching where one, among other things, sought a deeper and mystical meaning in the letters, numbers, and combinations of numbers found in the Old Testament. According to kabbalistic hermenuetics, God's name had $3 \times 72 = 216$ letters of which the letters that appear in the name YHWH are full of great secrets. For Luther, however, it is Christ who says who God is. See Lewin, *Luthers Stellung zu den Juden*, 5f.; and Bienert, *Martin Luther und die Juden*, 42, 162ff. See also Luther's thorough critique in the book *Vom Schem Hamphoras, etc.* (1543), discussed in *Luther and World Mission*, 420–24.

the young reformer presents different criticisms of the Jews, primarily against their hermeneutic and their rejection of Christ and the righteousness of faith.

Nevertheless, the Luther material from 1519–1523 shows an increasingly well-meaning and inviting stance vis-à-vis the Jews. In 1519 Luther can express himself as a protector of the Jews while at the same time reacting against the fact that they do not accept Jesus as the Messiah of God. He is now filled with faith in the authority of the Word and of prayer and opens his arms to Hussites, Turks, Jews, and the heathen.[46] In connection with Psalm 2:4 and Psalm 22:28ff., the young reformer develops both his idea of centrifugal mission and the thesis that Jews and Gentiles will be called to the reign of Christ. United by the Gospel and faith in Christ, they can, under this reign, serve and worship the living God together.[47]

There are, however, things in the church itself that hinder it from converting the Jews. The reformer takes to task both the Passion plays and the Passion sermons that point to the Jews as the only real murderers of Christ. According to Luther, it is the guilt and punishment of all of humanity that crucifies Jesus, and the Jews become only the servants of God's plan of salvation. Also the Christians must understand that it is their own sin that drove Jesus to his death. A sermon about the cross that only and spitefully accuses and abuses the Jews for killing Jesus only superficially treats personal sin and Jesus' suffering. Such preaching is harmful and serves no purpose.[48] Of course, Luther here touches on subjects that

---

46 "Ad aeogcertotem Emserianum M. Lutheri additio (1519)," WA 2:662.5ff., 663.22ff. See especially "Verklärung etlicher Artikel, etc. (1520)," WA 6:82.24ff. Cf. WA 2:136.26ff.; 11:316.1ff.; and especially Luther's commentary on Psalm 14:7 (WA 5:427ff.) and on Psalm 68:9 about the new rain of the new covenant among all peoples ("Eine kurze Form der Zehn gebote, etc. [1520]," WA 8:10.31ff.). Luther even includes intercessions for the Jews (WA 7:226.15ff.). Cf. WA 6:16.22ff. and 10/2:403.5ff.

47 *Operationes in Psalmos*, WA 5:665.27–669.28. See especially WA 5:667.28ff. Cf. a "Sermon on the Good Shepherd (1523)," WA 12:540.1ff. See also WA 2:615.5ff.; 7:485.18ff.; 8:11.2ff.; 12:312.13ff.

48 "A Meditation on Christ's Passion (1519)," LW 42:7 (WA 2:136.3ff.): "Some people meditate on Christ's passion by venting their anger on the Jews. This singing and ranting about wretched Judas satisfies them, for they are in the habit of complaining about other people, of condemning and reproaching their adversaries. That might well be a meditation on the wickedness of Judas and the Jews, but not on the sufferings of Christ." (LW 42:7 [WA 2:136.3ff.]). LW 42:10 (WA 2:138.15ff.): ". . . for the main benefit of Christ's passion is that man sees into his own true self and that he be terrified and crushed by this. . . . You should be terrified even more by the meditation on Christ's passion. For the evildoers, the Jews, whom God has judged and driven out, were only the servants of your sin; you are actually the one who, as was said, by his sin killed and crucified God's Son."

throughout church history have caused much tension between Christians and Jews.

Around 1520 the reformer becomes even more occupied with mission among those groups and colonies of Jews dispersed in Germany and its borderlands. By the word *mission*, I mean here not an organized overseas mission but the fact that the Gospel would be preached for individuals and groups of Jews. I want especially to point out Luther's words in *Operationes in Psalmos* on Psalm 14:7: "Oh, that salvation for Israel would come out of from Zion! When the LORD restores the fortunes of his people, let Jacob rejoice and Israel be glad!" The reformer means that the author of the psalm is writing about Israel's eschatological salvation, that is, the mystery of which Paul speaks in Romans 11:25f. He continues by admitting that he has not quite understood what Paul means.[49] But the promises of the Old and New Testaments stand. Therefore the chosen people must get to hear the Gospel. There is no special way given to them for salvation. If they will be saved, they will be saved through faith in Jesus Christ. Faith and the Spirit are given through preaching and through hearing in faith.[50] Mission is primarily *missio Dei* through the Word/Gospel. It might seem humanly impossible that the Jews would convert, but for God, everything is possible. Therefore in 1520 Luther believes that the Jews will finally receive the Gospel.

> But he (the psalmist) adds "from Zion" in order to show that they (the Jews) or whichever human shall not be given another salvation than that which is Jesus Christ (and) which has been given from Zion and spread thence into all the world. And through this the Jews will be converted to Christ however opposed to Christ they are now. "For nothing is impossible with God" (Luke 1:37). And Romans 11: (23): ". . . for God is able to graft them in again."[51]

Luther reacts decisively against both the pride and the hatred that Christians have for the Jews. When God both will and can engraft the broken branches (the Jews), then just as Paul, Christians must have compassion on them and pray for their salvation. In addition to the reformer's hope in the power of the Word/Gospel, there is also humility and prayer.

> Therefore, the wrath of some Christians (if they are now to be called Christians) must be condemned. They consider themselves to be obedient to God if they persecute the Jews with the greatest hate, wish the greatest evil and with the highest pride and despite scorn them when they complain about the evil of the Jews. With this psalm (14:4–7) and with Paul's profound emotion in

---

49 WA 5:427.19–428.26. Cf. Lewin, *Luthers Stellung zu den Juden*, 6ff.; and Bienert, *Martin Luther und die Juden*, 43ff.

50 We have discussed exactly this point in *Luther and World Mission*, 205–18.

51 WA 5:428.27ff.

Romans 9 (:1ff) one ought to mourn and be in pain for them and constantly pray for them. These [Jew-hating] Christians ought to think about what Paul says in Romans 11:18 "do not boast over those branches."[52]

In Luther's commentary on Psalm 14:7, one sees how Paul's words and the early church's solution to the question of the Jews is much superior to the medieval church's hateful persecution and agitation. His work with the Bible helps the young Luther reject destructive persecutions and stereotypes. God's promises about and his authority to save Israel are decisive for Luther in this question.

The reformer means that the frigidity and hate that many Christians exhibit simply prevents the Jews from hearing the Gospel. One does damage to Christianity and shares in the guilt of Jewish unbelief. It is a godless nominal Christianity that glorifies itself over and tyrannizes the Jews. This hate repulses Jews from Christianity, while the Christians ought to seek to invite the Jews to Chris-tian faith with warmth, love, prayer, and care.[53]

The reformer is interested in mission in these texts. He even wonders who would receive a religion that was forced on them in hate and enmity. If the Christians will be able to win the Jews, then it must (just as in mission to the heathen) occur through a work of the Word and prayer leavened by Christ's love. About his wish for this repentance vis-à-vis the Jews, Luther says:

> Who, I ask, would want to convert to our religion (such a person would have to be most good natured and most patient) when he was handled by us in such a grim and inimical manner and not only in a non-Christian manner but also in a more than deadly manner? If hate against the Jews, the heretics and the Turks ought to characterize the Christians, then we are truly the most Christian of all. If, however, Christians ought to be characterized by Christ's love, then we are without a doubt worse than the Jews, the heretics, and the Turks because no one ought to love Christ more than we. Their unreasonableness resembles that of fools and children who stick out their eyes at the Jews painted on the walls as if they were helping the suffering Christ. Nothing is more damning of those many who complain about Jesus' suffering than that they increase the Jewish opposition to Christ and the hearts of the believers against the Jews. The Gospel, however, works this that God's and Christ's love

---

52 WA 5:428.32ff.

53 WA 5:428.39ff.: "Faciunt autem hoc tyrannide sua impii isti nominetenus christiani non levem iacturam Christiano tum nomini tum populo, ac rei sunt participesque impietatis Iudaicae, quam hoc crudelitatis exemplo velut repellunt a Christianismo, cum eos omni suavitate, patientia, prece, cura debeant attrahere." Cf. Maurer, "Die Zeit der Reformation," 387, who believes that the expression "nominal Christianity" here is used for the first time in a Lutheran context. See also Sucher, *Luthers Stellung zu den Juden*, 54f.

ought to completely and wholly direct us in this question of which those peo-ple do not mention a single word.[54]

Compared with the hate and agitation against the Jews characteristic of late medieval and Reformation times, Luther's 1520 commentaries on the Psalms definitively represent something new.

Luther's commentary on the Magnificat (Luke 1:46–55) was finished at the Wartburg in the summer of 1521. He notices especially Mary's final words about God's mercy "to Abraham and his descendants forever, even as he said to our fathers" (Luke 1:54f.). The promises to the patriarchs in Genesis 12:3; 22:18; and 32:24ff. imply that the whole world lies under guilt. At the same time, God's promise applies to Abraham and all Abraham's descendants—and thereby to Christ and the whole world. Blessing and mercy are promised, therefore, through the Seed/Christ to all people who receive the Gospel in faith. Thereby the great field of Gospel and mission opens. If the word *Israel* first referred only to the Jew-ish people, it has in the new covenant come to mean God's people redeemed and gathered in Christ from both Jews and heathen.[55]

In connection with the Magnificat, the reformer touches on mission among the Jews. He points out that God's promises to the original, earthly Israel are eternal. Israel possesses the promises for salvation through all times to the Last Day. Therefore Luther hopes for the conversion of the Jews. God's sworn, eternal promises give Israel an advantage that the church has often transformed to a dis-advantage. But God neither retracts his promises nor deceives. Therefore one must not treat the Jews in an unfriendly manner. The Gospel is given first to them, and it happens sometimes, despite all, that one among them converts and becomes Christian. None will become a Christian if Jews are treated in the usual manner. Luther also believes that the reluctance of the Germans to receive the Gospel and live truly Christian lives proves that they are not superior to the Jews and heathen. Christians ought not harass the Jews. One must openly and in a friendly manner explain the truth of the Gospel to them. Then they will make their decision and be left in peace.[56] Here Luther speaks of a concrete mission

---

54 WA 5:429.7ff.

55 *Magnificat* (1521), WA 7:597ff. Concerning the Jewish problem in the Magnificat, see Sucher, *Luthers Stellung zu den Juden*, 56; and Bienert, *Martin Luther und die Juden*, 64ff. Cf. also Luther's reflections on the promises to Abraham, in *Luther and World Mission*, 100ff.

56 LW 21:354–55 (WA 7:600.26ff.): "When Mary says, 'His seed forever,' we are to under-stand 'forever' to mean that such grace is to continue to Abraham's seed (that is, the Jews) from that time forth, throughout all time, down to the Last Day. Although the vast majority of them are hardened, yet there are always some, however few, that are converted to Christ and believe in Him. For this promise of God does not lie: the

strategy. It ought to be noted that Luther is not some lackey to the princes in 1521. This book is directed with new and intrepid defiance against the prince.

The 1522 *Church Postil* contains a pair of interesting passages in the sermons for the Feast of Stephen. In the sermon on the Epistle text, Acts 6:8–14 (in fact, primarily on Acts 7:54–59), Luther complains about the hardness of the Jews against the preaching of Christ that Stephen had presented. But Stephen also teaches us how Christians despite this ought to pray and sacrifice all to win Jews for Christ. The Gospel, love, and prayer will win the Jews.[57]

In the sermon on the Gospel for the Feast of Stephen (Matthew 23:34–39), Luther naturally notices the Jews' opposition and violence against the prophets and Jesus and the punishment that will consequently follow. But Luther sees that the pericope concludes with a word of comfort to the Jews, a word that in fact prophesies a final period when Israel may receive the Gospel: "For I tell you, you will not see me again until you say, 'Blessed is he who comes in the name of the Lord'" (Matthew 23:39). Luther says parenthetically that these words are spoken after Palm Sunday and, therefore, constitute one of Jesus' farewell sermons. His

---

promise was made to Abraham and to his seed, not for one year or for a thousand years, but 'for the ages,' that is, from one generation to another, without end. We ought, therefore, not to treat the Jews in so unkindly a spirit, for there are future Christians among them, and they are turning every day. Moreover, they alone, and not we Gentiles, have this promise, that there shall always be Christians among Abraham's seed, who acknowledge the blessed Seed, who knows how or when? As for our cause, it rests upon pure grace, without a promise of God. If we lived Christian lives, and led them with kindness to Christ, there would be the proper response. Who would desire to become a Christian when he sees Christians dealing with men in so unchristian a spirit? Not so, my dear Christians. Tell them the truth in all kindness; if they will not receive it, let them go. How many Christians are there who despise Christ, do not hear His Word, and are worse than Jews or heathen! Yet we leave them in peace and even fall down at their feet and well-nigh adore them as gods." The historian Reinhold Lewin, who later became a rabbi, summarizes his analysis of the Magnificat: "Luther entwirft hiermit ein vollkommen neues Programm. Er stütz sich abermals auf das Bibelwort, aber das Leben hat ihn gelehrt, es mit anderen Augen anzusehen. Die Überzeugung von der Bekehrung der Juden, wenn auch nicht der Judenheit, steht ihm unerschütterlich fest. Gott hat seine Zusage dafür verpfändet" (*Luthers Stellung zu den Juden*, 23). See also Sucher, *Luthers Stellung zu den Juden*, 56ff., who points out that Luther's writing about the Magnificat is even more significant because it was directed toward the landed lord Baron Johann Friedrich of Saxony.

57 *Church Postil*, WA 10/1.1:247ff., on the reaction to Stephen's sermon. Luther emphasizes that the Jews' works-righteousness and hypocrisy opposes the Holy Spirit (WA 10/1.1:259.14ff.). They must be brought to faith in Christ, then they will not struggle with the Law and works but do good spontaneously from faith. See WA 10/1.1:265.3ff. about Stephen's love, prayer, and sacrifice for his enemies.

promises have, therefore, not yet been fulfilled, but they will be. The Jews will be granted a time of grace so at the parousia they can greet Christ as their own Messiah. Therefore one must expect a time when many Jews will convert before Jesus returns. The old, consuming question about the salvation of all Israel receives its most positive and unequivocal answer so far, an answer that Luther bases on many additional Bible passages (Deuteronomy 4:30f.; Hosea 3:4f.; 2 Chronicles 15:2ff.; Romans 11:25f.). God is merciful and faithful to his covenant with the Jews according to the promises he swore to the patriarchs. Despite the continuing stubbornness of the Jews and all the storms around the Diet at Worms, the reformer hopes and prays both for revival among the Jews and for the quick return of Christ.[58]

A powerful apocalyptic sentiment flowed through both the evangelical and the Jewish milieus at the time of the Reformation. Luther's positive stance toward

---

58 *Church Postil*, WA 10/1.1:270ff., about Jesus' words of judgment against a stubborn and unwilling people. Luther writes thus on Matthew 23:39: "Finally comfort is spoken here to the Jews, when the Evangelist adds: 'Verily I say unto you, Ye shall not see me henceforth, till ye shall say, Blessed is he that cometh in the name of the Lord'. Christ spake these words on Tuesday after Palm Sunday, and they form the conclusion and the last words of his preaching upon earth; hence they are not yet fulfilled but they must be fulfilled. . . . Thus it is certain, that the Jews must yet say to Christ, 'Blessed is he that cometh in the name of the Lord.' This very truth Moses proclaimed in Deut. 4, 30–31: 'In the latter days thou shalt return to Jehovah thy God, and hearken unto his voice; for Jehovah thy God is a merciful God; he will not fail thee, neither destroy thee, nor forget the covenant of thy fathers which he sware unto them.' It was also preached in Hos. 3, 4–5: 'The children of Israel shall abide many days without king, and without prince, and without sacrifice, and without pillar, and without ephod or teraphim: afterward shall the children of Israel return, and seek Jehovah their God, and David their king, and shall come with fear unto Jehovah and to his goodness in the latter days.' . . . 2 Chron. 15, 2–5 . . . . This passage cannot be understood as referring to the Jews of the present time: They were never before without princes, without prophets, without priests, and without teachers and the law, St. Paul in Rom. 11, 25–26 agrees with this thought and says: 'A hardening in part hath befallen Israel until the fulness of the Gentiles be come in; and so all Israel shall be saved.' God grant that this time may be near at hand, as we hope it is. Amen" (Lenker 1:237–38 [WA 10/1.1:287.15–289.10]). Concerning the texts about the Jews and the Gospel in the 1522 *Church Postil*, see Bienert, *Martin Luther und die Juden*, 68f. One has discussed the historicity of some of the later information from the 1570s, according to which Luther, after these friendly thoughts to the Jews, was supposed to have met with the Jews in Worms and discussed Isaiah 7:14. In that discussion, one of the Jews was supposed to have been convinced that the word *alma* meant "virgin." Lewin, *Luthers Stellung zu den Juden*, 154; Cohen, "Die Juden und Luther," 39; and Schreiner, "Jüdische Reaktionen auf die Reformation," 153f., believe that there is a true historical background to the story. Bienert, *Martin Luther und die Juden*, 56ff., believes the story is only a legend.

the Jews and his opposition to the contemporary treasons and slanders against the Jews is clearly presented in his 1523 letter to Bernhard Gipher. Gipher had studied in Wittenberg, became a doctor in the Hebrew language, and through Luther's preaching was led to a firmly rooted faith and baptized. In a tender and beautiful letter to "my son in the Lord," Luther complains that as a rule both Christians and Jews agree that it is impossible to convert a Jew to the Christian faith. The reformer will not deny that the Jews are stubborn. Nevertheless, he ascribes the blame for this to the bishops, popes, and monks. They pronounce the most critical words about the Jews while at the same time living shamelessly and preaching mysterious traditions instead of the doctrine of God's Word for the Jews. Christianity becomes everything but impertinent when the preachers of the church bark at their audiences but are unable to show what Christian faith and the Christian life are.[59]

Luther, however, sets his hope on the Gospel as it was rediscovered during the Reformation. The Word/Gospel has power to touch even the hearts of the Jews and lead them to their true Messiah. He also hopes that the Jews converted to Christianity, like Bernhard, will become a mission tool among the Jews in Germany.

> Now that the Gospel's golden light has dawned and shone, there is a realistic hope that many Jews will seriously and faithfully be converted and have their hearts directed toward Christ as you have been raptured and also others who are the remnant of Abraham's seed in order to be saved by grace (Romans 11:5). For he has begun it and he will bring it to completion (Philippians 1:6). He does not allow his word to return empty (Isaiah 55:11). Therefore, I considered it appropriate to send this little book in order to strengthen and establish your faith in Christ whom you have recently come to know through the Gospel. And now for the first time you are baptized in the Spirit and born of God (Matthew 3:11; John 1:13). I should wish that he through your example and work will become generally known to other Jews so that they who were previously set apart will be called and will come to their King David (Romans 8:29f.; Ephesians 1:11).[60]

This important letter shows that Luther's rediscovery of the Gospel is the source of his hope for an era of conversion among the Jews. God's Word and God's faithfulness to the covenant with Israel will accomplish this. At the same time, one sees how this mission among the Jews can never occur without human instruments. The remnant of Abraham's seed that will be saved must be brought to its

---

59 "Luther an den getauften Juden Bernhard (June 1523)," WABr 3:101.1ff., especially 102.17ff. See Ehrlich, "Luther und die Juden," 74f.

60 WABr 3:102.37ff.

true David (Christ) through the Gospel of God as it is preached by humans. When one reads these most recently analyzed texts, the usual thesis that Luther was blind to the mission task must be considered to be either ignorance of or a deliberate falsification of history.

The little book that is sent to the friend and Jew Bernhard is the reformer's important opus *That Christ Was Born a Jew* (1523). For the first time, Luther writes an entire book about the Jews and mission among them. The reformer's indomitable faith in the power of the Gospel also characterizes this book.

In the first section of this work, the reformer must first deal with the false rumors according to which he is accused of playing with heresy, denying the virgin birth, and speaking about Jesus, the seed of Abraham, as if Joseph was his biological father. Christ's true divinity was thought to be in question. Luther was criticized as being too friendly to the Jews. When Luther interprets, among others, Genesis 3:15; 22:18; and Isaiah 7:12, he energetically proclaims the virgin birth, which is decisive for the person and salutary work of Jesus Christ and, thereby, for the salvation of all people. If Christ should save from sin, death, and the power of the Satan, then he must be both true man and true God in one person.[61] The reformer, however, understands the difficulties that the Jews have with the doctrine of the virgin birth and Christ's true divinity. In mission among the Jews, it is important—and Luther follows here the advice of Nicolaus of Lyra—that one first teach them to know the human Jesus. With time they will be able to receive the doctrine about Jesus Christ as true God. For these reasons, in *That Christ Was Born a Jew* the reformer puts aside—temporarily—the most controversial and problematic parts of the Christian faith from the Jewish perspective. He does this because in this book, even in the first Christological section, he has a clear apologetic/missionary goal. Luther's mild tone and friendly stance awakened great enthusiasm among the Jews insofar as they did not perceive Luther's goal to convert them.[62] As a rule, the

---

61 Concerning the first section's comprehensive defense of the virgin birth and Christ as true God and true man, see WA 11:314.3ff., 316.5–325.15. There are pregnant passages in WA 11:316.30ff., 318.3ff. See also Sucher, *Luthers Stellung zu den Juden*, 60. At the Diet of Nürnberg, Archduke Ferdinand, Charles V's brother, accused Luther of Christological heresy. In Central Europe, Nürnberg, Worms, and Prague were the great centers where the Jews, even during all their expulsions, enjoyed a somewhat reliable sanctuary and existed in large numbers. In *That Christ Was Born a Jew*, it is important for Luther to defend himself against the accusations of heresy. He also was challenged to respond. See Lewin, *Luthers Stellung zu den Juden*, 26–36; Holmio, *Lutheran Reformation and the Jews*, 66f.; and Maurer, "Die Zeit der Reformation," 388f. All these authors analyze the themes of this book. Such analysis also can be found in Brosseder, *Luthers Stellung zu den Juden*, 345ff., and "Luther und der Leidensweg der Juden," 121ff., and in a number of other essays by other scholars.

62 Concerning the important rule to first focus on Jesus' humanity, see WA 11:336.14ff.

scholars are united in believing that *That Christ Was Born a Jew* is a mission book.[63] Our continuing analysis of the sources will confirm this.

There is no doubt that Christology, especially Christ's human nature, is important for Luther's 1523 book. Luther must, however, defend himself against

---

Luther is indulgent with the Jews when he temporarily accepts that one interprets the word *alma* in Isaiah 7:14 with the German *Magd* ("young woman") (WA 11:320.21ff., 321.25ff., 322.13ff.). Here he truly believes, however, that *alma* really means a young virgin (WA 11:316.33f., 325.6f.). Cf. also WA 11:71f.; 27:475ff., 480f., 485ff.; 37:54.10ff.; 53:634.6–641.3. In the last passage, that is, from *Vom Schem Hamphoras, etc.* (1543), Luther gives an exhaustive defense of the confession of the virgin birth. He claims that whatever the word *alma* could mean generally, the Old Testament cannot be proven to use the word *alma* except as it refers to virgins. Therefore Isaiah 7:4 and Matthew 1:23 speak about how a virgin became pregnant and delivered a son. The virgin birth is connected also with Jesus' sinlessness and work of salvation. Cf. the words of the Large Catechism: "That is to say, he became man, conceived and born without sin, of the Holy Spirit and the Virgin, that he might become Lord over sin" (LC II 31; Tappert, 414). In the literature, see Maurer, "Die Zeit der Reformation," 389; and Sucher, *Luthers Stellung zu den Juden*, 213ff.

63 Lewin says, among other things, "es ist, es will sein nicht mehr und nicht weniger als eine Missionsschrift" (*Luthers Stellung zu den Juden*, 30). Holsten believes that *That Christ Was Born a Jew* (1523) has "den Charakter einer Missionsschrift an Israel" ("Christentum und nicht-christliche Religion," 120). Holmio (*Lutheran Reformation and the Jews*, 66ff., 89ff.) sees the mission motif clearly in Luther's so-called "mission epistles" to the Jews, especially in *That Christ Was Born a Jew*. Cf. also Cohrs, *Einleitung zu der Schrift "Von den letzten Worten Davids,"* WA 54:24. Elert, *Morphologie des Luthertums*, 1:345 (English: 395); and H. Bornkamm, "Volk und Rasse bei Martin Luther," 15. Among the more recent scholarship that emphasizes the mission motif in *That Christ Was Born a Jew*, one can name especially Sucher, *Luthers Stellung zu den Juden*, 59ff., 241ff. He says: "Hier taucht ganz deutlich ein Missionsgedanke auf, Luthers Wunsch, mit dieser Schrift Juden zum Christentum zu bekehren" (59). Cf. also the essays by Erling, "Martin Luther and the Jews," 73ff.; Ehrlich, "Luther und die Juden," 75ff.; and Pfisterer, "Zwischen Polemik und Apologetik," 103ff. *That Christ Was Born a Jew* inspired a great enthusiasm among the Jews because of Luther's friendly tone and humanitarian presentation. Pfisterer points out that the Jews did not realize at first that the book was a conscious mission book and an attempt to convert them. Schreiner, "Jüdische Reaktionen auf die Reformation," 150, shows how Luther's love of the Old Testament and the Hebrew language and his humanitarian tendencies gave birth to rapture and future hope, not least of all among Jewish leaders. After Luther had presented the less diplomatic writings of the 1540s, the Jews in Frankfurt prayed that Emperor Charles would win the Smalcald War and guarantee the welfare of the Jews. Charles was victorious in 1546. Among those who have deemphasized or denied that *That Christ Was Born a Jew* is a mission book, one ought to name Vogelsang, *Luthers Kampf gegen die Juden*, 21ff. Maurer, *Kirche und Synagoge*, 44f., says, among other things, that the Reformation in 1523 from "eine evangelische Bewegung zur Missionsbewegung werde." He deemphasizes this theme in "Die Zeit der Reformation,"

the accusations that he has taught against Christ's true divinity.[64] At the same time the mission task presents an obligation in the opposite direction. After all the false accusations and painful slanders that the popes, bishops, priests, and monks have pronounced against the Jews, it is necessary to establish that Jesus Christ was born of a virgin and was an actual Jew. This is what Luther wants to prove in the first section of his investigation. Medieval theology had most often placed the main accent on Christ as true God. One had lost something of the Chalcedonian (A.D. 451) emphasis on Jesus' true humanity. To open some Jews for the Gospel and lead them to faith, it is important that Jesus is painted before their eyes as a true human, as a son of Abraham, and as a true Jew.[65] Luther has taken into account that the rabbis have indoctrinated the Jews against the Christ dogma. Toward the end of *That Christ Was Born a Jew*, he says:

> If the Jews should take offense because we confess our Jesus to be a man, and yet true God, we will deal forcefully with that from Scripture in due time. But this is too harsh for a beginning. Let them first be suckled with milk, and begin by recognizing this man Jesus as the true Messiah; after that they may

---

388f. Maurer wants to characterize *That Christ Was Born a Jew* "als eine christologische Studie über die menschliche Natur Jesu . . . die freilich eine apologetisch-missionarische Tendenz gegenüber dem Judentum einwohnt." Brosseder, *Luthers Stellung zu den Juden*, 350ff., follows Maurer's thesis. Indeed, Brosseder is even less open to the idea that this could be a mission book, among other reasons, from his Roman Catholic perspective that mission is folk mission (p. 354). Oberman, "Luthers Beziehungen zu den Juden," 525, says about the time 1519–1523 as a whole: "Ihn bewegt keineswegs ein Anflug von Judenmissionsoptimus . . . . Seine Erwartungen gelten der Wirkung des Wortes auf die Juden, Häretiker und sogar Türken insgesamt . . . Es gilt jetzt aber, den 'Rest' den Zugang zum Wort zu eröffnen." Does he not see the connection between mission and the Word? By overemphasizing Luther's ideas about an eschatological coalition against Christ, Oberman cannot see the mission perspective.

64 WA 11:314.28ff., 315.3ff., 325ff. Maurer, "Die Zeit der Reformation," 388ff.; and Brosseder, *Luthers Stellung zu den Juden*, 350f., believe too one-sidedly that Luther develops certain important elements of classic Christology primarily for his meeting with Judaism. Concerning Luther and Christology, see the references noted above in *Luther and World Mission*, 71–72n118.

65 LW 45:200 (WA 11:314.25ff.): "Therefore, I will cite from Scripture the reasons that move me to believe that Christ was a Jew born of a virgin, that I might perhaps also win some Jews to the Christian faith." After his examination of the texts about the Virgin Mary, about Christ's divinity and humanity, Luther concludes: "This is enough for the present to have sufficiently proved that Mary was a pure maiden, and that Christ was a genuine Jew of Abraham's seed" (LW 45:213 [WA 11:325.6ff.]). Several scholars have considered the fact that Luther, to reach the Jews, wants to temporarily teach them about Jesus the man alone to be a deplorable tactical concession. Cf. Lewin, *Luthers Stellung zu den Juden*, 31, 36; Stöhr, "Luther und die Juden," 168; Cohen, "Die Juden und Luther," 39; and Sucher, *Luthers Stellung zu den Juden*, 216.

drink wine, and learn also that he is true God. For they have been led astray so long and so far that one must deal gently with them, as people who have been all too strongly indoctrinated to believe that God cannot be man.[66]

Luther says, parenthetically, with a strategic mission intent that Jesus is true man, a true son of Abraham, and a true Jew. From this thesis follows that the Jews, if one will for the moment speak of a blood relation, *de facto* stand closer to Jesus than the heathen and Gentile Christians do. God has, thereby, actively shown the Jews greater honor than any Gentile people. God also chose all the patriarchs, the prophets, and the apostles from among the Jews and gave the Old Testament *de facto* to Israel. The Gentiles cannot claim such favor.[67]

This probably must be called a rare friendly gesture toward the Jews and their conception of faith. According to Luther's reasoning, Jesus Christ comes very near the Jews, who are harassed like dogs. If Jesus Christ demonstrably belongs to a certain people, then it is to Israel. The reformer does all he can during this period to break down the many barriers that the church's preaching and stance toward the Jews have built up. The source material shows that Luther has a clear soul-winning tone and missionary purpose. His writings also show that he is neither anti-Semitic nor anti-Jewish. This ought to be observed! I do not want to imply in any way that this is only a question of strategy. One must teach in stages and first seek to find a base from which it might be possible to converse with the Jews. This is pedagogy, not only a hard-boiled strategy.

The other half of the book *That Christ Was Born a Jew* has, as the text shows and as Luther directly expresses, in the first place the goal to explain to the Jews from the Old Testament the Christian motivation for believing in Jesus as the Messiah. Through exegetical and apologetical arguments, Luther wishes to perform this great service to the Jews. He seeks to draw them to faith in the Messiah, whom the Old Testament's true holy Jews knew. The reformer seeks to convince them of

---

66 LW 45:229 (WA 11:336.14ff.).

67 LW 45:201 (WA 11:315.25ff.): "When we are inclined to boast of our position we should remember that we are but Gentiles, while the Jews are of the lineage of Christ. We are aliens and in-laws; they are blood relatives, cousins, and brothers of our Lord. Therefore, if one is to boast of flesh and blood, the Jews are actually nearer to Christ than we are, as St. Paul says in Romans 9 [:5]. God has also demonstrated this by his acts, for to no nation among the Gentiles has he granted so high an honor as he has to the Jews. For from among the Gentiles there have been raised up no patriarchs, no apostles, no prophets, indeed, very few genuine Christians either. And although the gospel has been proclaimed to all the world, yet He committed the Holy Scriptures, that is, the law and the prophets, to no nation except the Jews, as Paul says in Romans 3 [:2] and Psalm 147 [:19–20]." Cf. Luther's awareness that he presents a challenge to his Roman Catholic opponents in his positive pronouncements about the Jews (WA 11:316.1ff.).

the faith in Christ that the patriarchs and the prophets possessed and that is actually identical with, for example, the faith of the apostles. That which the Jews have throughout history understood as something foreign actually belongs to them and was believed by the patriarchs and fathers of the Old Testament. In the second place, Luther wants to equip his fellow workers for mission among the Jews with biblical arguments to win Jews for the Christian faith. The reformer's draft is well thought through and something of a sketch of the content and strategy of a soul-winning mission among the Jews. It is filled with pastoral care and does not exude the hardness that characterizes the earlier and contemporary theologians' attempts to "cast out the devil by means of the devil, and not by the finger of God."[68]

I have not been able in the literature to find any thorough presentation of Luther's exegesis of the Old Testament in which he goes about his own exegetical-apologetic work among the Jews and at the same time equips the evangelical Christians with arguments for mission among the dispersed Jews. Therefore in the following I will, among other things, present something about Luther's argument that Jacob's blessing in Genesis 49:10 and the words about the years/weeks in Daniel 9:24ff. have not been fulfilled within Israel's history but have been fulfilled in the history of Christ and the church.

---

68 LW 45:213 (WA 11:325.16ff.): "While we are on the subject, however, we wish not only to answer the futile liars who publicly malign me in these matters but we would also like to do a service to the Jews on the chance that we might bring some of them back to their own true faith, the one which their fathers held. To this end we will deal with them further, and suggest for the benefit of those who want to work with them a method and some passages from Scripture which they should employ in dealing with them. For many, even of the sophists, have also attempted this; but insofar as they have set about it in their own name, nothing has come of it. For they were trying to cast out the devil by means of the devil, and not by the finger of God [Luke 11:17–20]." Cf. LW 45:200 (WA 11:315.14ff.): "I hope that if one deals in a kindly way with the Jews and instructs them carefully from Holy Scripture, many of them will become genuine Christians and turn again to the faith of their fathers, the prophets and patriarchs." Concerning how Luther considers the Old Testament saints to be true Christians, see *Luther and World Mission*, 99ff. Short commentaries on Luther's Christological interpretation of Genesis 49:10; Daniel 9:24ff.; etc., exist in the following literature: Brosseder, *Luthers Stellung zu den Juden*, 349f.; and Sucher, *Luthers Stellung zu den Juden*, 60f. Erling, "Martin Luther and the Jews," 71ff., is critical of the fact that Luther applies certain passages about afflictions to actual occurrences in Jewish history while at the same time interpreting Genesis 3:15 Christologically. The older Luther would have asked the latter: Shall we have a Christian or a Jewish theology? Luther is a consciously Christian theologian and does not represent any type of panreligious thinking. See Müller, "Tribut an den Gesit seiner Zeit," 306. I will return to this matter later. Maurer, "Die Zeit der Reformation," 389, points out that in his Christological exegesis of the Old Testament's prophecies Luther uses the Dominican Raimundus Martini (d. 1284) and other medieval authorities.

The reformer first argues from Genesis 49:10–12:

> The scepter will not depart from Judah, nor the ruler's staff from between his feet, until he [Shiloh] comes to whom it belongs and the obedience of the nations is his. He will tether his donkey to a vine, his colt to the choicest branch; he will wash his garments in wine, his robes in the blood of grapes. His eyes will be darker than wine, his teeth whiter than milk.

Jewish messianic expectation must be considered vain on the basis of this passage, according to Luther. Here we have an unshakeable, divine promise that must have been fulfilled before the 1,500-year-old diaspora that the Jews now experience. The monarchy was taken away and the prophets disappeared in Judah when Herod became king.[69] Luther identifies Shiloh with the promised Messiah and Christ. The usual refusal of the rabbis to do the same is their big mistake. When the text says that Judah's scepter will not depart until Shiloh-Messiah comes, this ought not be understood as if the Messiah will not possess a scepter. Psalm 2:8; 72:17; and 89:5 give the Messiah the greatest and most glorious kingdom. Also David was promised that his kingdom would remain forever. Because now the Jews are forced to admit that their earthly kingdom has been out of business for 1,500 years, the Shiloh named by Jacob must be Christ. He is of Judah's tribe and David's royal line. Jesus Christ appears when the authority over Judah was passed to the foreigner Herod. Christ took the scepter in a spiritual-messianic reign, has reigned over this kingdom for 1,500 years, and will reign over it forever. Furthermore, the Messiah-Christ has gathered more people to himself than any other king.[70]

---

69 WA 11:326.31ff., 327.15ff., 329.24ff. Luther rejects the Jewish rejoinder that Judah's scepter was taken away during the Babylonian exile. He shows that kings and rulers existed, despite all the historical drama of exile, until Herod became king (WA 11:326.3ff.).

70 LW 45:215 (WA 11:326.23ff., 326.31ff.): "In addition, when Jacob says here that the scepter shall endure until the Messiah comes, it clearly follows that this scepter not only must not perish but also that it must become far more glorious than it ever was previously, before the Messiah's coming. For all the Jews know full well that the Messiah's kingdom will be the greatest and most glorious that has ever been on earth, as we read in Psalms 2, 72, and 89. For the promise is also made to David that his throne shall endure forever [Ps. 89:4, 29, 36–37]. Now the Jews will have to admit that today their scepter has now been nonexistent for fifteen hundred years, not to speak of its having become more glorious. This prophecy can therefore be understood to refer to none other than Jesus Christ our Lord, who is of the tribe of Judah and of the royal lineage of David. He came when the scepter had fallen to Herod, the alien; He has been king these fifteen hundred years, and will remain king on into eternity. For his kingdom has spread to the ends of the earth, as the prophets foretold [Ps. 2:8; 72:8–11]; and the nations have been gathered to him, as Jacob says here [Gen. 49:10]. And there could not possibly be a greater king on earth, whose name would be exalted among more nations, than this Jesus Christ." Cf. WA 11:329.33ff.

Luther believes that Genesis 49:10 clearly describes Christ's reign as a spiritual reign. From David until Shiloh-Christ, the earthly kings of Judah have succeeded one another. When all of them were mortal, none of them could reign eternally. With Jesus Christ, the earthly Davidic regiment was concluded, and he himself took over and reigns alone forever over a spiritual kingdom. Because Shiloh-Christ on the one hand comes from the tribe of Judah and is, thereby, a natural, mortal human, he must die. Because, on the other hand, he is a powerful, immortal, and eternally reigning king, he cannot as the God-man be held by death (*communicatio idiomatum*). Shiloh-Christ goes through death and resurrection to an eternal-spiritual regiment.[71]

Luther knows well that the Jews find it difficult to understand, let alone to accept, this exegesis. He tries to respond to a number of rabbinical rejoinders. Especially detailed is his dispute with the notion that Christ could not have done all the things that Genesis 49:11–12 describes. Particularly interesting is the reformer's argument that the Old Testament here *de facto* uses metaphors that are consistent with Christ's spiritual reign, characterized as it is by the Gospel, the forgiveness of sins, and faith.[72]

However, the Jews cannot understand Luther's reasoning until they accept that the Messiah/Christ came already when the foreigner Herod took over the reins of government in Israel.[73] Luther is also amazed by the fact that the Jews do not understand the consequences of the words in Genesis 49:10 that the peoples or the Gentiles will obey and worship the promised Shiloh. It is a fact that the Gentiles have never in such great numbers or so willingly gathered under a Jewish man and king as they do under Jesus Christ. As a rule, the Gentiles have hated the Jews and refused to submit to them. Now by degrees they submit themselves willingly to this Jew. Mustn't he be the Messiah?[74]

In the reformer's exegetical-apologetic attempt to convince and win the Jews for faith in Jesus of Nazareth as God's Messiah, the commentary on Daniel

---

71 WA 11:327.35ff., 328.9ff.

72 WA 11:327.4ff., 328ff. Luther keenly shows to what absurdities one must resort if one tries to apply Genesis 49:11–12 to the worldly leaders of the Jewish people. Therefore the words must be interpreted metaphorically and Christologically. See also the New Testament interpretation: "So now he lives and reigns, and holds the exalted office of binding his foal to the vine and washing his garments in the red wine; that is, he governs our consciences with the holy gospel, which is a most gracious preachment of God's loving-kindness, the forgiveness of sins, and redemption from death and hell, by which all who from the heart believe it will be comforted, joyous, and, as it were, drowned in God with the overwhelming comfort of his mercy" (LW 45:219–20 [WA 11:330.14ff.]).

73 WA 11:330.20ff.

74 WA 11:330.23ff., 331.3ff., 331.11ff.

9:24–27 is important. To the highest degree, the intended audience here is the Jews, especially their rabbis. Luther says expressly that he will present as evidence that the Messiah must have come 1,500 years ago, that is, that the Messiah must be Jesus. This is because the angel Gabriel, according to the text, says that the Messiah will come after the rebuilding of Jerusalem following the exile in Babylon and before the destruction of Jerusalem in A.D. 70, that is, during the reign of Caesar Titus.[75]

First, Luther disputes the rabbis' interpretation of the text. They say that Daniel 9:24–27 speaks of the Persian king Cyrus who, in Isaiah 45:1, is called "the Anointed." But according to Luther, this king did not accomplish the works named in the text, that is, to separate iniquities and sins and to give forgiveness and an eternal righteousness. How can it be that one and the same Messiah will be stricken before the rebuilding of Jerusalem and come to nothing for a long time afterward (Daniel 9:25–26)? Luther dismisses the Jewish interpretations as mistaken and says that the text in question corresponds to Jesus Christ, who came after the temple had been rebuilt and before the destruction of Jerusalem.[76]

Luther attaches detailed chronological calculations to his argument. He has noted that even the Jewish rabbis agree that the weeks mentioned by the angel Gabriel are year-weeks. If a year-week is seven years, the 70 weeks spoken of in the text must be 490 years. Luther compares the words in Daniel 9:24–27 with the history and lists of monarchs of the Near East. Then he seeks to present as evidence that Jesus of Nazareth must be the Anointed or the Messiah of whom Daniel speaks. First, Luther goes backward from the time Jesus began his public ministry after his baptism in the Jordan, that is, when he began to "reign," preach, and call followers. Moving back 490 years from Jesus is the twentieth and last year of the reign of King Cambyses during the time of the prophet Nehemiah. That is the beginning of 70 year-weeks when the rebuilding of the temple *de facto* first began, Luther points out. Thereafter, it took seven year-weeks (more than 46 years) until the city of Jerusalem was rebuilt under the leadership of Nehemiah.[77]

Then Luther starts with the time Gabriel communicates his message: The Jewish people and Jerusalem have 490 years before the end of their glory and before the Messiah comes who will destroy trespasses, grant forgiveness, reconcile sins, and provide an eternal righteousness. Daniel indicates both the time when Israel will be superceded and something of the quality of the new thing to be given when all the prophecies and visions will be fulfilled through the Messiah.[78]

---

75 WA 11332.4ff. See also WA 15:743.32ff., which discusses Daniel 9:25ff.

76 WA 11:332.21ff., 332.28ff., 333.5ff., 333.13ff.

77 WA 11:333.23–334.13.

78 LW 45:225–26 (WA 11:334.14ff.): "Now Gabriel says [Dan. 9:24], 'Seventy weeks (that

The prophecy in Daniel 9:25–26 has its starting point during the time of Cambyses and Nehemiah. According to the text, there are seven year-weeks (49 years) after that time until the city is rebuilt. Thereafter follow 62 year-weeks (about 441 years) after it has been rebuilt. If one starts with the last year of Cambyses's reign, there are 483 years, according to Luther. But that is one year-week short of 490 years, that is, until the beginning of Jesus' public ministry. Luther says about this—compare with below—that Jesus began his public ministry in the middle of the missing seven-year period. Then it is said (Daniel 9:26a) that he was killed and was granted eternal life while those who killed him are no longer his people.[79]

When Daniel 9:26b speaks of how the city and the sanctuary will be destroyed by the people of the ruler, Luther considers this to be Jerusalem's destruction under Caesar Titus in A.D. 70.

Luther has apparently examined this text and Israel's history in detail. He means that the final year-week spoken of in Daniel 9:27 indicates both Jesus' three-and-a-half years of preaching and the first three-and-a-half years of the apostles' preaching. During this period, the new covenant in Jesus Christ is estab-

---

is, four hundred and ninety years) are determined concerning your people and your city.' This is as if he were to say: Your nation of the Jews and the holy city of Jerusalem have yet four hundred and ninety years to go; then they will both come to an end. As to what shall actually transpire, he says that transgression will be finished and forgiveness sealed and iniquity atoned for and everlasting righteousness brought in, and vision and prophecy fulfilled, that is, that satisfaction will be made for all sins, forgiveness of sins proclaimed, and the righteousness of faith preached, that righteousness which is eternally valid before God. This it is to which all the prophets and the whole of Scripture bear witness, as Paul in Romans 1 [:17] and Peter in Acts 2 [:38–39] testify." Cf. WA 11:333.15ff.

79 LW 45:226–27 (WA 11:334.27ff.): "Next he shows when the period of seventy weeks begins, saying [Dan. 9:25], 'From the going forth of the word to rebuild Jerusalem (that is, at the time of Nehemiah, in the twentieth year of Cambyses), until Messiah the prince (that is, until the baptism of Christ in the Jordan), are seven weeks (that is, forty-nine years, during which Jerusalem was rebuilt in a troubled time, as the book of Nehemiah [2–6] teaches) and sixty-two weeks' (that is, 441 years after Jerusalem was rebuilt). This makes altogether sixty-nine weeks, that is 483 years. There is still lacking one week, that is, seven years, to make the total of seventy weeks, or 490 years. He then shows what is to happen in that selfsame week, saying [Dan. 9:26]: 'And after sixty-two weeks (note that this is after the first seven weeks of troubled rebuilding) Messiah shall be cut off (this did not happen at the beginning of the last week, but right in the middle of it, for Christ preached for three and one-half years, and Gabriel uses the term "cut off," that is, taken from this life into the immortal life through death and his resurrection). And they [who cut him off] shall not be his' (that is, those who crucify him and drive him from this world will no more belong to him and be his people, but he will take unto himself another people)."

lished through the most powerful preaching of the Gospel the world has ever heard. In the middle of this seven-year period, all laws and sacrifices were abolished when Jesus through his death fulfilled all demands for sacrifices.[80]

If the angel Gabriel's message really speaks of year-weeks, a fact the rabbis admit, then Luther's argument to disprove the rabbis is rather convincing. Both the Christians and the Jews reckoned that God spoke through the words of the prophets. And Luther can in his partly metaphorical exposition apply Daniel 9:24–27 to the history of the Persians, Israel, Jesus, and the church. The reformer also points briefly to Haggai 2:10 and Zechariah 8:23, which also witness to the fact that Jesus is the Messiah.[81] The argumentation for Jesus' messiahship from the Old Testament texts (the Jews will not listen, of course, to texts from the New Testament) constitute the anchor of *That Christ Was Born a Jew.* One can, of course, question Luther's hermeneutic and interpretation of these texts from the Old Testament, but in general one can say that the Bible professor in Wittenberg gives honest and thought-out reasons for his faith in Jesus as the Messiah.

The source material shows how energetically the reformer worked with the Old Testament and the rabbinical exegesis of the same to be able to discuss with the Jews and their interpreters of Scripture, to show that the Messiah had come 1,500 years ago in Jesus of Nazareth, to lead some Jews to the Messiah for whom already the patriarchs hoped and in whom they already believed. Furthermore, we have seen how powerfully Luther emphasizes that Jesus is not only true God but also a true man and a real Jew. Indeed, all the patriarchs, prophets, and apostles were Jews. The Jews must first learn to love the human Jesus, then with time they will be led into the doctrine about Jesus as God's Son and true God.

The entire book *That Christ Was Born a Jew* is characterized further by a positive attitude and by love, by a willingness to understand, and by an apologetic-mission nerve. Luther attempts himself or through others to win Jews for Christ. In addition to all this, there is a strong humanitarian element as the basis for Luther's critique of medieval and contemporary anti-Semitism, against the expulsion and discrimination against the Jews in the life of work and human contact. Luther sees anti-Judaism generally as something unacceptable. It hinders the Jews from receiving the Gospel. If one will win them, one must be friendly and loving.

Luther concludes this most positive of his writings vis-à-vis the Jews with the following words:

> Therefore, I would request and advise that one deal gently with them and instruct them from Scripture; then some of them may come along. Instead of

---

80 WA 11:335.12ff., 335.21ff.

81 WA 11:336.6ff.

this we are trying only to drive them by force, slandering them, accusing them of having Christian blood if they don't stink, and I know not what other foolishness. So long as we thus treat them like dogs, how can we expect to work any good among them? Again, when we forbid them to labor and do business and have any human fellowship with us, thereby forcing them into usury, how is that supposed to do them any good? If we really want to help them, we must be guided in our dealings with them not by papal law but by the law of Christian love. We must receive them cordially, and permit them to trade and work with us, that they may have occasion and opportunity to associate with us, hear our Christian teaching, and witness our Christian life. If some of them should prove stiff-necked, what of it? After all, we ourselves are not all good Christians either. Here I will let the matter rest for the present, until I see what I have accomplished. God grant us all his mercy. Amen.[82]

As the quotation shows, Luther is occupied both by the right attitude toward Jews and by a fundamental strategy in mission among the Jews. Here it is a question of a mission both by doctrine and by lifestyle. Neither one by itself is sufficient ground for a successful mission among the Jews. But Christian education and a life of love together will win them for Christ.

Let me finally point out that in *That Christ Was Born a Jew* Luther refrains from referring to the passages in the Bible about God's wrath over Israel, their hardness, etc. As we have seen and shall see later, this is only a temporary restraint designed for the sake of mission. It has, however, surprised me that Luther in this book writes nothing about Romans 9–11, especially Romans 11:25f. about the final salvation of all Israel.[83] He emphasizes primarily an argument exclusively from the Old Testament, which is, the only authority that the Jews will allow.

Hope for the Conversion of the Jews
and a Critical Waiting Period, ca. 1524–1537

The source material concerning Luther's stance toward the Jews and toward their conversion is not as rich in the years 1524–1537 as with the younger or the older Luther. Neither are there many scholars who have taken pains to survey the reformer's position during this period. Maurer notices, among other things, Luther's critique against the banks and usury of the Jews, against the rabbinical exegesis of the Old Testament, and against their hardening toward the Gospel of Christ. During the 1530s, the primary theological-religious conflict hardens, and Luther begins gradually to pour more energy into a literary offensive in the Jewish question.[84] Oberman emphasizes especially how Luther during the 1530s fights

---

82 LW 45:229 (WA 11:336.22ff.).

83 Here against Müller, "Tribut an den Geist seiner Zeit," 307.

84 Maurer, "Die Zeit der Reformation," 391ff., 397ff., who masterfully investigates above all the theological problem in the meeting between Luther and Judaism.

against the eschatological Judaism that he believes to be a member of the Antichrist's coalition (the pope, the Jews, the enthusiasts, and now also the Turks).[85] Sucher has shown that Luther during the entire period 1524–1537 reckons with an epoch of Jewish conversion to Christianity, that he has discussed certain central theological problems he has with the Jews, and that he often praises the Jews for their culture, their promises, and their predecessors. At the same time, he criticizes their arrogance, blasphemies, and their similarities to the pope and the Turks concerning Christ and faith. He also complains about the usury of the Jews, but he is not blind to parallel evils among Christian Germans.[86] Bienert shows how all the previous concessions that Luther had made to the civil life and faith of the Jews come to a head during these years. During the 1530s, there is a dogmatic showdown with and a harder critique against the Jews. Finally, the ecclesitastic-political considerations also play an important role.[87]

In the following, I will give a sketch of the reformer's stance toward the Jews and their Mosaic faith during the period 1524–1537.

If it had been common to blame the Jews for their unrighteousness and usury in business and the handling of capital, Luther blames their greed, lust for interest, and lovelessness primarily in the business life in Germany as a whole with its expanding German and foreign business contacts, monopolies, and loans with interest. The reformer can, on the basis of Deuteronomy 15:1–6, say that the Jews during the time of the old covenant functioned as a God's disciplinary rod among the peoples with the God-given right to take interest on their loans. Because Israel as a gathered nation "ceased" to be God's people and was dispersed, the Jews must now stop taking interest and submit to the business laws of the lands in which they live. Luther is opposed to taking interest as a principle. He thinks it is something non-Christian. At any rate, it is the ruling authority that ought to regulate laws about taking interest.[88]

---

85 Oberman, "Luthers Beziehungen zu den Juden," 525ff., with a too one-sided emphasis on the eschatological themes in Luther. Cf. also Sucher, *Luthers Stellung zu den Juden*, 220ff., on "Jüden-Papisten-Türken."

86 On this, see especially the passage on Luther's *Table Talk* in Sucher, *Luthers Stellung zu den Juden*, 101–21, with the references.

87 Bienert, *Martin Luther und die Juden*, 82ff., 99ff., who provides a mother lode of the Luther texts in question.

88 "Trade and Usury (1524)," WA 15:293ff., 305ff., 310ff. See also a 1524 lecture on Deuteronomy, WA 14:654–57, especially 655.35ff., 656.26ff. Concerning the Jewish diaspora after A.D. 70, see WA 14:656.26ff. See also Sucher, *Luthers Stellung zu den Juden*, 233. Bienert, *Martin Luther und die Juden*, 86f., has not understood the Latin text. According to Sucher, Luther means that God had even 1,500 years earlier given the Jews the right to take interest among the Gentiles and thereby introduced "ein neues und

It is worth noting how powerfully Luther in the middle 1520s articulates the blindness and hardness of the Jews. Luther understands the destruction of Jerusalem as God's punishment because the Jews persecuted and killed the prophets, Jesus, and the apostles. He is sorrowful and has heartache over this people's inflexibility and for the punishment and suffering that was a result of it.[89] Luther's writings from the middle 1520s to the middle 1530s are full of how the Jews oppose the Gospel about Christ and faith, how they blaspheme Christ and the Christians, and how they have become hardened in their unbelief.[90] The matter can be best illuminated by a typical text.

In the 1526 commentary on Psalm 109, the words about the punishment of God's enemies are applied to the Jews and to others who are proud of their denials and sins.[91] God's punishment is severe, especially after the rejection and crucifixion of Jesus. Jerusalem was destroyed, and for 1,500 years the Jews have been homeless, dispersed, and hated wherever they go. All this because they will not receive Christ but instead are his enemies. Satan holds them fast and hardens them so they even call a curse upon themselves (Matthew 27:25).[92]

In Psalm 109:18, we read: "He wore cursing as his garment; it entered his body like water, into his bones like oil." According to Luther, this is said concerning the Jews' incurable hardening. However one might preach and challenge, nothing helps. A decent person always covers his or her body with a shirt or mantle. In the same way, the Jew is clothed in hardening and loves to curse faith in Christ. And the Jew believes that this hardening is right. As when one has drunk water and the body has digested it, so has hardening become one with the nature of the Jews according to Luther. The Jews listen with great eagerness to curses against Christ. As oil or balsam melts into the skin and cannot be taken again

---

positives Verständnis." This is incorrect. Concerning how the Jewish kingdom was definitively crushed by the Romans and how Christ's eternal reign for both Jews and Gentiles replaced it, see the commentary on Matthew 24:15ff. in WA 15:743ff.

89 See a sermon on the end of the Jewish kingdom and the end of the world (Matthew 24:15ff.) in WA 15:745.18ff., 747.13ff. Cf. WA 14:481.36ff. Luther himself was warned of a murder attempt by Jewish medical students and expresses himself on this point to Amsdorf and Spalatin (letters written in 1525, WABr 3:428f., 439f.). See also Sucher, *Luthers Stellung zu den Juden*, 105f.

90 See *Ortsregister*, WA 62:190f., 202f., 195, which lists a mass of passages throughout the Weimar Edition. Maurer, "Die Zeit der Reformation," 392ff., presents many such statements. Cf. also Bienert, *Martin Luther und die Juden*, 88ff.

91 "The Four Psalms of Comfort: 37, 62, 94, 109 (1526)," WA 19:595.10ff., 596.6ff., 596.11ff. See especially on Psalm 109:6–8, WA 19:598.23ff., 599.27ff., 600.22ff. Maurer, "Die Zeit der Reformation," 392ff., thoroughly investigates Luther's view of the Jews' hardening on the basis of Psalm 109.

92 WA 19:601ff. Cf. Bienert, *Martin Luther und die Juden*, 69.

from it, so have the curses and the hardness of the Jews gone deep into their hearts and minds, marrow and bone. And they believe that this balsam secures God's favor.[93] Luther claims to have had bad experience of this rigidness and hardness of the Jews. They speak acidly and spitefully about Christ. They consider faith in and the doctrine about Christ to be curses and fairy tales. Christ is for them an evil rogue who has been crucified or strung up together with other rogues. Those who believe in this strung up (*thola*) rogue are fools. These slanders receive fodder for their hatred from the depravity of Christians and in the poor examples that Christians represent. Thus Luther means that the hardening of the Jews has impressed their hearts and minds so deeply that they simply cannot break free and confess the crucified Jesus to be Lord and God. This hardening is a sign of God's own judgment and wrath.[94]

In this period, Luther sometimes expresses a small hope for the conversion of the Jews.[95] He believes that the denial and the cursing of the doctrine about Jesus' messiahship has gone so deep into their hearts and minds that they are totally closed to Christian preaching. It is clear that Luther in the middle 1520s is more pessimistic than in 1523 when he wrote *That Christ Was Born a Jew*.

At the same time, he never ceases to urge that the Gospel must necessarily be preached for both Jews and Gentiles. In such a way, one single united people will be built, that is, Christ's church.[96] The result of the preaching of the Word ensures

---

93 WA 19:606.20ff., 607.1ff., 607.16, 607.24ff.

94 LW 14:269–70 (WA 19:607.32ff., 608.12ff.): "We see this in our daily contacts with Jews. How stiff and stubborn they are from one generation to the next! They are incredibly venomous and spiteful in their language about Christ. What we believe and teach about Christ they regard as sheer poison and a curse. They suppose that Christ was nothing more than a criminal who, because of His crime, was crucified with other criminals. Whenever they mention Him, therefore, they refer to Him odiously as *Thola*, 'the hanged one.' . . . [I]t is inevitable that they should regard us Christians as the most foolish and filthy people under the sun. . . . What makes it worse is that we Christians are also bad and set a bad example. Thus they are so confirmed in their offense that this curse has penetrated into their bones and marrow and has poisoned them until they cannot escape and come to regard the crucified Jesus as Lord and God. It is always ridiculous to them that we Christians worship a condemned Jewish criminal, as though we worshiped Cain or Absalom as gods. But there they are. The oil has soaked into their bones, and they go on soaking up the water. What a terrible judgment and illustration of divine wrath!" Concerning God's wrath against all the enemies of Christ, especially against the stubborn Jews, see WA 19:609.10ff. on Psalm 109:20. The enemies against Christ sin against the Holy Spirit (WA 19:610.1ff.). Concerning Jesus as *thola*, see Bienert, *Martin Luther und die Juden*, 90, with an examination of Jewish texts.

95 WA 19:608.23ff.

96 See *Ortsregister*, WA 62:177f., with a list of texts, among others, from *Bondage of the*

that at least a remnant of the Jews will be led to conversion and faith. Along with the prophets and the apostles, Luther sets his trust on God's Spirit and the Word, which remain forever and have power to save people.[97] Whether the historical Israel as a whole will be saved before Christ's parousia (Romans 11:25f.) is still a question without an answer for Luther. Luther nearly rejects the thought. But some of Abraham's descendants will be saved through God's saving power.[98]

Does one find in the source material from 1524–1537 the friendly inviting and sympathetic attitude that was so prevalent in the early 1520s? Yes, there are various examples of this, but it becomes successively weaker throughout this period. Luther says often that the Turks, the Jews, the heathen, and the false Christians are of the same sort, that is, people of unbelief and self-righteousness who are the enemies of Christ and faith.[99]

Will (1525): "For shortly before, [Paul] has said: 'The gospel is the power of God for salvation to everyone who has faith, to the Jew first and also to the Greek' [Rom. 1:16]. Here are no obscure or ambiguous words; 'to Jews and Greeks' means that to all men the gospel of the power of God is necessary in order that they may have faith and be saved from the wrath that is revealed" (LW 33:248 [WA 18:757.36ff.]). *Lectures on Isaiah* (1527–1529), WA 25:187.31f.: "Includit enim vocationem gentium. Christus enim coniunxit duos parietes et ex Iudaeis et gentibus unam fecit Ecclesiam." Cf. also WA 15:215.33ff., 447.1, 447.12, and the systematic investigation in *Luther and World Mission*, 218ff.

97 Concerning the conversion of the Jews, see WA 13:637.28ff.; 20:564.1ff.; 23:67.3ff.; 34/1:248.9ff. Luther often says that some of the Jews or a remnant of them will receive the Gospel. See WA 19:608.28ff.; 21:190.27ff.; 25:103.31ff., 211.25ff., 220.32ff., 277.17ff., 280.14ff., 304.23ff. See also *Lectures on Isaiah* (1527–1530), WA 31/2:314.25f., especially on Isaiah 59:21: "*My Spirit and My words shall not depart.* He is saying this of the spiritual coming which will always abide and prevail for the purpose of turning away evil. This is the nature of the covenant, that 'the Spirit and My Word' will endure forever. Thus Paul and the prophet agree. This is Paul's argument: The Gentiles must not despise the Jews, because God can reinstate them, since the Spirit of the Lord and the Word of the Lord will remain in the world, and by them God can reclaim some. As long as the Word remains, God can always save people through the means" (LW 17:307–8 [WA 31/2:498.3ff.]). Cf. WA 31/2:409.31ff., 499.11ff.

98 WA 14:598.36f.; 21:190.12ff., 190.25ff. See especially *Lectures on Isaiah* (1527–1530), WA 31/2:497.6ff., 497.18ff.

99 Cf. *Ortsregister*, WA 62:202f., with, among others, the following examples: "Estate of Marriage (1522)": "You will find plenty of Christians—and indeed the greater part of them—who are worse in their secret unbelief than any Jew, heathen, Turk, or heretic" (LW 45:25 [WA 10/2:283.12ff.]). "On War against the Turk (1529)": "There are entirely too many Turks, Jews, heathen, and non-Christians among us with open false doctrine and with offensive, shameful lives" (LW 46:186 [WA 30/2:131.5f.]). "Sermons on the Gospel of St. John (1538)": "Christians need this comfort, lest they doubt that the Christian Church will remain in the world in the midst of all the unbelievers, Turks,

This eschatological coalition is, however, not only Satan's military troops. They are also the nearest mission field ripe for evangelization. One sees this, among other places, in a writing from 1524 in which the reformer—following the examples of Peter in 1 Peter 3:15f. and Jesus in John 8:46; 18:23—emphasizes the importance of the workers in God's reign clothing themselves in humility toward those who know less spiritually and standing ready to give them reasons to believe. Luther wants to bid farewell to all pride so that he might speak with the poor Jew, heathen, or whomever.[100] It means also that according to 2 Corinthians 6:3 one ought in love to avoid placing any stumbling blocks that might hinder the success of the Gospel among the heathen and Jews.[101]

An example of Luther's desire to win Jews for Christ and the method that will be used to that end is a sermon from 1524 on Matthew 4:1ff. about fasting and the freedom of Christians, etc. Here Luther considers the question of what one might do to convince a Jew that Jesus is God's Son. This is the completely decisive and most conflict-filled religious question in the meeting between Judaism and Christianity. The reformer looks to Paul's pastoral advice in 1 Corinthians 8:13 concerning the question of food and drink for Jews who are bound by their consciences. He remarks that those who are stiff-necked ought to be similarly opposed. But one ought to be more tolerant with the weak who are willing to listen.[102]

These general rules for contact with the weak in faith must be applied by those who seek to win Jews for Christ. One must let the Jews who are stubborn and who do not at all want to hear about Jesus go their own way. But to those who will hear, one ought to give plenty of time and teach by stages and carefully. Because the Jews have difficulty believing that Christ is true God, one ought to set this question on the back burner, which is, of course, nevertheless a necessary part of the Christian confession. First, the inquiring Jew must learn to know the human Jesus and what God has given through him. When he has begun to love Jesus, then can one first speak about Christ as true God. One cannot win Jews if one immediately presses on them the entire dogma of Christ: "true God and true

---

heathen, Jews, heretics, and sects" (LW 24:168 [WA 45:615.1ff.]). Concerning this anti-Christ coalition that in Luther's understanding stormed Christ's reign during the last part of the Reformation, see Oberman, "Luthers Beziehungen zu den Juden," 525ff. See also Sucher, *Luthers Stellung zu den Juden*, 220ff.

100 "Letter to the Princes of Saxony Concerning the Rebellious Spirit (1524)," WA 15:215.33ff.

101 WA 17/2:181.32ff., 182.10ff. Cf. WA 15:611.30ff. Cf. about mission by lifestyle in *Luther and World Mission*, 225ff., 253ff., 266ff.

102 WA 15:444–53. On 1 Corinthians 8:13, see WA 15:446.28ff. The main principle—about an essential freedom of faith in respect to lifestyle and the adaptions one can make for the sake of love—is developed in WA 15:449.16ff.

man." One must meet the Jew where he or she is and as a mission strategy give attention to his or her specific problems. Luther says:

> Therefore, one must in this matter act similarly as when a Jew who has not been poisoned and hardened comes to you, i. e., one whom you want to lead to Christ. Even if it is a necessary article of faith that Christ is God's Son, I want initially to be silent about that and act and teach in such a way that he will first gain a love for the Lord Christ. I would say that he [= Christ] was a person like others sent by God and explain the good things which God has done for humanity through him. When I had succeeded to drive this into his heart so that he burned with and had a love and a desire for Christ, then I would help him further along so that he believed that Christ was God. In this way I would treat him so that I should lead him to faith in Christ. But if he was stiff-necked and unwilling to listen, then I would let him go his way.[103]

As we can see, Luther presents the same mission method that he had presented in *That Christ Was Born a Jew* one year earlier.

In the dreary 1526 commentary on Psalm 109, which I considered above, the reformer has no doubt that some Jews will change their position and receive the Gospel about Christ. But the Jewish people as a whole will remain unconverted, according to Luther, because most of the Jews will not get to hear the Gospel through which the Holy Spirit could draw them to Christ. The Jews in general have been affected by their own schools of thought and their poisonous blasphemies against Christ. Nevertheless, there always will be some individual Jews who exchange Judaism for the Christian faith. Luther says in 1526 that God will in that way continue to be the God of Abraham's physical seed and Paul has a right to say that God does not cast off his own people (Romans 11:2).[104]

Luther expresses a similar conviction in a 1530 letter from castle Coburg in connection with the baptism of an older Jewish girl. Well anchored in the practice of the early church, Luther gives advice about how the baptismal liturgy and ritual ought to be formed. Because Baptism means death and resurrection in Christ, the pastor is encouraged to ensure that the girl is not pretending about her Christian

---

103 WA 15:447.11ff.

104 LW 14:270 (WA 19:608.28ff.): "This does not mean that no Jew may ever come to faith again. Some crumbs must remain, and some individuals must be converted. But Judaism, as we call the Jewish nation, will not be converted. The Gospel, by which the Holy Spirit might find room among them, is not preached among them either. But where they gather in their synagogues, they keep their curse and their poison; they curse Christ, regarding their poison as salvation and their curse as a blessing. Nevertheless, some will occasionally spring up individually from the group, so that God might still remain the God of the seed of Abraham and might not reject them altogether, as St. Paul says in Rom. 11:1–2." Cf. also WA 19:609.33f. See also Sucher, *Luthers Stellung zu den Juden*, 246f.

faith. That is common among the Jews, according to Luther.[105] Toward the conclusion of this letter, the reformer says about this Baptism that he does not doubt that there is still a remnant of the descendants of Abraham (Romans 11:5) that belongs to Christ. If the girl who wants to be baptized is genuine, then Luther wishes her grace and perseverance and greets her lovingly in Christ from the isolation of Coburg. The entire letter is warm and at the same time serious.[106]

Not a lame legalism but an imagination inspired by love ought to characterize the attempts to win both Jews and Gentiles, according to a 1527 writing on Genesis 14: "Love of neighbor ought to characterize all external work so that one does all that love demands and so that all commandments are obeyed by the same. In this way we do all that we can to convert other people and lead them to faith, both Jews and Gentiles. One ought consequently give them as much love and service [i. e., compromise] as one can without endangering the faith."[107]

During the 1530s, there is some movement in Luther's stance toward the Jews and Judaism. It ought to be observed that it was during the same time that there was some movement in the religious politics vis-à-vis the Jews in Saxony. At the Diet of Augsburg in 1530, the Jews were clearly restricted, and Luther had in a so-called *Gutachten* (opinion) pleaded that the Jews would be tolerated in the princedom as long as they did not publicly blaspheme against the Christian faith. Even in 1533–1534, the reformer expressed his opinion that the Jews ought to be tolerated in the princedom but that at the same time they should be avoided. All considered the Jews to be blasphemers, but as long as they did not want to establish their own earthly government or their own church with priests, Luther felt they could be tolerated and easily avoided by the general public. Luther considered the so-called sacramental fanatics (*sacramentarii*), however, to be enemies of the princedom and thought they should not be tolerated because they endangered the public political and religious ordinances in the princedom. In 1536 Prince John Frederick issued an edict that the Jews were not allowed to reside or travel through Saxony without the protection of the prince. The ruling authorities referred to the usury of the Jews in business and bank dealings. Later, Luther would accept these severe restrictions as imposed by the authorities because he saw a sociopolitical

---

105 "Luther to Heinrich Gnesius, Pastor in Jchterschauften," WABr 5:452.1ff., 452.18ff., 452.21f. See also Bienert, *Martin Luther und die Juden*, 94ff.

106 WABr 5:452.23ff.: "non quod dubitem, reliquias Abrahae superesse [Romans 11:5], quae ad Christum pertineant, sed quod hactenus varie illuserunt Iudaei fidem nostram. Hortare igitur, ne fallat se ipsam misera. Si verax fuerit, opto ei gratiam et perseverantiam, meoque nomine dicas illi salutem in Christo et meum charitatis officium. In Domino bene vale. Ex Eremo 9. Iulii 1530. T. Martinus Luther."

107 WA 24:275.23ff.

danger in their *geschäft* (business). At the same time, he is just as hard against the usury that his fellow Germans excercised.[108]

It is uncertain whether social and political factors significantly affected Luther's theological view of the Jews and Judaism. However, before 1536, three Jewish scholars came to Luther to discuss the messianic texts of the Old Testament, though the visitors were not actually interested in discussing those texts but argued completely from rabbinical tradition. Luther could naturally not submit to the rabbinical interpretation of the texts. He wanted in Jesus' name to let such people live, but he did not want to have anything more to do with the Jews.[109] The visitors had touched on the decisive point in the conflict between Luther and Judaism, that is, the question of Jesus' messiahship. Indeed, they had gone so far as to say that they hoped that Christians would convert to Judaism. Luther now realizes that these Jewish scholars possess their own identity and consciousness. They do not want to be only passive and tolerated. They represent an active and living religion and want to win baptized Christians for Judaism.

Scholars have discovered that Judaism during the first half of the sixteenth century was characterized by a surprisingly effective propaganda. After the many expulsions and persecutions of the fifteenth century, hope for the Messiah had become strong. Especially the sack of Rome in 1527 indicated that the Messiah might be near. This expectation of the Messiah was expressed in repentance and faithfulness to the Law, rejection of Christian mission preaching, and work to win Christians for Judaism.[110] The conflict between the Jews and Luther is reflected even in the question about the coming of the Messiah. The Jews expected that the Messiah would finally come and rule the old Israel politically and religiously. On the other hand, Luther expected that the Messiah-Christ would, in his second advent, take care of the new Israel or the church.

Luther sorely experienced the expanding power of Judaism when he learned in the years 1532–1539 that the Jews in Bohemia, Moravia, and Poland had drawn many Christians into Judaism. These converts had been circumcised and gone over to Jewish praxis in life and religious worship. Sometimes it was a matter of entire groups of Christians becoming Jewish.[111]

---

108 See Maurer, "Die Zeit der Reformation," 397; and Oberman, "Luthers Beziehungen zu den Juden," 527f., with references.

109 Maurer, "Die Zeit der Reformation," 398f., who cites WATr 3, no. 3512b; 4, nos. 5026, 4795; and WA 53:461.28ff.; 50:313.5f.

110 Maurer, "Die Zeit der Reformation," 399f.; and Oberman, "Luthers Beziehungen zu den Juden," 527.

111 On this, see Oberman, "Luthers Beziehungen zu den Juden," 527, who in nn87–88 cites sources from, among others, Erasmus of Rotterdam. He refers to other literature as

During the 1530s, Luther spent much time and energy on work with the Christian understanding of the Old Testament, on the doctrine of the Trinity, and on Christology. The activity of the Jews during these years constitutes some of the background for this work. The threat from the Turks and Islam belong here, as well as the types of fanaticism against Christ that the reformer feels he must address. Also, after the Diet of Augsburg, Luther had become more of the theological advisor/supervisor in the German state churches.[112]

Beginning immediately in the lectures on Genesis (1535–1545), Luther warns his students about rabbinical exegesis. Since Jerusalem was destroyed, the Messiah has come. Because the Jews stiff-neckedly refuse to accept Jesus Christ as the fulfillment of the Old Testament promises, it does no good to discuss with them. The Jews ought to be left to themselves. Christian exegesis of the Old Testament is something other than rabbinical exegesis, and it acts as a primary defense against deceitful Jewish exegesis. In the discussion with the Jews about the Old Testament, it is not only a semantic problem. It is a question about the conflict between Judaism and Christianity. According to Luther, the Old Testament ought to be interpreted Christologically.[113] Therefore in the lectures on Genesis, the text about the seed of the woman (Genesis 3:15) and the promises about blessing to Abraham, Isaac, and Jacob (Genesis 22:18; 26:4; 28:14) speak of Christ and the blessing in him to all peoples, first the Jews and then the Gentiles. Furthermore, Genesis 49:10 is interpreted as a prediction of Jesus' advent as the Messiah. He came when the kingdom had *de facto* fallen in Israel. Because Shiloh-Messiah came in Jesus Christ and the Jews reject him and persecute the Gospel, they are no longer truly

---

well. Beginning already at the end of the fifteenth century, the so-called Sabbatarians expanded from the Ukraine and Lithuania as a pan-European movement for the Judaization of Christians.

112 See Maurer, "Die Zeit der Reformation," 400f., whose list of source material I have used; Bienert, *Martin Luther und die Juden*, 99f.; and Oberman, "Luthers Beziehungen zu den Juden," 525ff. Oberman interprets Luther's stance toward the Jews both theologically and generally as psychological (Luther's father died in 1530, and he himself was aging), as real care for the Gospel, and as Luther's concern for the Jewish threat as part of the whole anti-Christ coalition.

113 WA 42:53.14ff., 162.22, 162.40f., 163.36, 597.21ff. Maurer, "Die Zeit der Reformation," 400, writes: "Wir, die wir seit der Aufklärung von historischen Sinn des Alten Testamentes auszugehen gewohnt sind, habe Mühe, den Gegensatz in seiner Tiefe zu erfassen. Für Luther ist die gantze Bible unmittelbares Wort göttlicher Offenbarung und ist diese Offenbarung in allen Schriftaussagen unmittelbar auf Christus bezogen . . . Für den Juden, bei denen Folkstum und Gottesglaube unmittelbar zumsammenträngen, konnten historische Begebenheiten ihrer Volksgeschichte religiöse Bedeutung haben; für Luther was das nur dann der Fall, wenn er ein historisches Faktum in einen christologischen Bezug einordnen vermochte."

God's people. They are under God's wrath, are dispersed, and own no good reputation among people. One ought to observe that Israel's suffering is not connected to the killing of Jesus but to the denial of the fact that the crucified and resurrected Jesus Christ was and is the Messiah of God.[114]

Luther says in the Genesis lectures (1535), with support from tradition, that the Old Testament speaks about the Trinity, about the incarnation, and about the doctrine of the two natures.[115] So the reformer touches on Christian doctrines that the Jews always have rejected and on which the Christian mission to the Jews always has focused.

It ought to be emphasized here that from around 1530 onward Luther energetically teaches about the doctrine of the Trinity and about Christology. In this teaching, he often disputes the theological objections of the Jews and the Muslims. Our contemporary theological milieus would probably be surprised with the comprehensiveness and the conviction of the 1531 Trinity sermon in which Luther relentlessly defends the doctrine of the Trinity. He discusses the Jewish accusations that Christians supposedly preach about one God and nevertheless worship three gods. Luther is pessimistic about whether Jews can truly convert to Christianity.[116] The doctrine of the Trinity is also considered as a subject in and of itself, often as a response to Judaism.[117] After the controversies about the Lord's Supper (from the middle of the 1520s and onward), the reformer worked much on Christology, the doctrine of the two natures, and soteriology. Also in this work, the objections raised by Jews and Muslims are occasionally discussed.[118] In his work on the doctrine of the Trinity and on Christology, Luther claims with the early church that Christianity is an exclusive religion. It is especially emphasized that all is lost wherever Christ is absent.

---

114 See Erling, "Martin Luther and the Jews," 70ff., with the references. Erling is critical of the Christologial interpretation of the Old Testament and the application of the Bible's judgments to Israel.

115 WA 42:8.23ff., 162.22, 162.40f., 163.36, 597.21ff. See Maurer, "Die Zeit der Reformation," 401.

116 WA 34/1:498–504.

117 LC (1529), *BSLK*, 661. "Ein Bekenntnis christlischer Lehre und christlichen Glaubens (1530)," WA 30/3:179.2ff. Cf. SA (1537), *BSLK*, 414f. See also "Die drei Symbola oder Bekenntnis des Glaubens Christi (1538)," particularly its comments against the Jews and the Muslims, WA 50:273.22ff., 281.24ff.

118 A 1525 sermon on Jesus as true God and true man, WA 17/2:237–45; a 1526 sermon on Jerermiah 23:5–8, WA 20:569.25ff.; "Confession Concerning Christ's Supper (1528)," WA 26:500.33ff.; "Ein Bekenntnis christlicher Lehre und christlichen Glaubens (1530)," WA 30/3:178.16–179.12.; SA (1537), *BSLK*, 415f. Cf. also the passages and literature to which I referred in *Luther and World Mission*, 71ff.

After these glimpses of Luther's historical and dogmatic work, I now return to writings specifically about the Jews and Judaism up to 1537. In a 1529 sermon on Easter Eve, the reformer says that the notice above Jesus' cross—"This is the King of the Jews"—has always been a source of Jewish slanders. But because the word *Jew* means "the one who confesses and thanks," those who have faith in Christ are the true Jews.[119] Later, Luther will relentlessly emphasize that the Jews no longer own the right to be called God's people. Instead, the true Israel consists of the mostly uncircumcised Christians.[120] The reformer continues to be critical of the financial transactions of the Jews,[121] but he follows Andreas Osiander and others in not believing the rumors about ritual murder and the desecration of the host among Jews.[122] He does not seek to argue for an anti-Jewish position before the end of the 1530s, but he is increasingly alarmed by the pride of the Jews and their blasphemies against Christ.

At the same time, the reformer expresses some hope that some of the Jews can be led to repentance and faith in Christ. A 1538 *Table Talk* entry records: "I believe, said Doctor Martin Luther, that if they heard our sermons and how we handle and interpret the OT, many of the Jews would be won. But with our disputes, they only become irritated, bitter and stiff-necked. For they are too proud and presumptuous. If a rabbi or two should defect, then a greater defection would begin. They are truly tired of waiting."[123] Luther has had experience of bad discussions with rabbis, but he sets his hope on the preaching of the Gospel and the exegesis of the Old Testament. For Luther it is self-evident that the Jews must turn to and believe in the crucified Jesus and leave their Sabbatarianism.[124]

Luther has always believed that individual Jews can be won for the Christian faith. But during the 1530s, the conflict between Luther and the Jews grows worse. As we have mentioned previously, he saw that Judaism was expanding. An active Jewish propaganda had won some Christians for Judaism. Thus he stands sud-

---

119 WA 29:240ff.

120 From 1530, WA 30/2:224.24ff., 225.6ff.; from 1532, WATr 1:161.2ff. (no. 369). Cf. Bienert, *Martin Luther und die Juden*, 102f.

121 From 1536, WATr 3:369.21–370.21 (no. 3512).

122 See Bienert, *Martin Luther und die Juden*, 105ff., with the adduced source material. See also Oberman, *Wurzeln des Antisemitismus*, 125–34.

123 WATr 6:353.12ff. (no. 7041). Cf. WATr 2:352.1ff. (no. 2184A and B) and 5:532.24ff. (no. 6196). Especially Sucher, *Luthers Stellung zu den Juden*, 101f., has surveyed the place of the mission motif in the *Table Talk*. He ought, however, to have refrained from using Aurifaber's notes, which are uncertain and often three times longer than the parallel Latin notes.

124 WATr 5:530.1ff. (no. 6191).

denly before the request of the political spokesperson for the Jews in Germany, Josel von Rosheim, that the reformer should say a good word to the prince about the Jews so they could travel through the princedom in safety. This was forbidden by an expulsion mandate in 1536.

One may understand from his June 11, 1537, response to Rosheim that Luther experiences the problem as a situation of conflict. His earlier goodwill toward the Jews had been spurned. In the same manner in which he in his earlier writing had sought to protect the Jews against state persecution and the rage of the people, he now wants to help his "good friend" and "dear Josel" with the right to free passage. But there are two reasons he will not appeal to the prince.

1. The Jews had exploited the reformer's earlier goodwill and had been behaving in many ways that the Christians could not accept. Luther must be referring to the pursuit of proselytes, the circumcision of Christians, etc.[125]

2. The Jews and their rabbis had for 1,500 years and in Luther's time raged against and slandered Christ and the Christians. Just as they earlier had opposed the saints and the prophets of the Old Testament, so had the Jews for 1,500 years called Jesus a condemned and executed Jew and rejected his messiahship. This attack on Christ and the Christians was unacceptable to Luther.[126]

The Jews' worldly problems have their ultimate cause in their rejection of Jesus of Nazareth, says Luther. God will not help the Jewish people out of their 1,500-year-old diaspora before they, with the Gentiles, receive the crucified Jesus as Messiah.[127] The prophecy in Daniel 9:24–27 had been fulfilled long ago. They

---

125 WABr 8:89.1ff.: "Dem Fürsichtigen Jesel, Jüden zu Rosheim, meinem guten Freunde. Mein lieber Jesel! Jch wollt wohl gerne gegen meinem gnädigsten Herren für Euch handeln, beide mit Worten und Schriften, wie denn auch mein Schrift der ganzen Jüdischheit gar viel gedienet hat [= *Dass Jesus Christus en geborner Jude* sei 1523]; aber dieweil die Euren solchs meines Diensts so schändlich missbrauchen und solche Ding fürnehmen, die uns Christen von ihnen nicht zu leiden sind, haben sie selbs damit mir genommen alle Forderung, die ich sonsts hätte bei Fürsten und Herrn können tun." The reformer probably means by the previously named "faithless crime" that which Baron Wolf Schlick in Falkenau had experienced of Jewish propaganda and presumptuousness. Luther knew also that the Jews sought to expand their faith, circumcise some Christians, and sought to lay on them Moses' Law. Cf. WATr 3:369.21–370.21 (no. 3512) from 1536; 3:441.20–442.12 (no. 3597) from 1537; and WA 50:312.8ff. Concerning this letter, see especially the investigation in Bienert, *Martin Luther und die Juden*, 110ff.

126 WABr 8:90.34ff., 90.42ff.

127 WABr 8:90.29ff.: "Darumb wolltet ja uns Christen nicht für Narren und Gänse halten, und Euch doch einmal besinnen, dass Euch Gott wollte dermaleins aus dem Elende, nu

wait in vain for their king or Messiah because this messianic text, however one might twist it, clearly shows that Jesus is the promised Messiah.[128]

Luther still hopes to win Jews for Christ through apologetics and preaching. He promises, therefore, to write a book in which he will attempt to lead at least some Jews to their promised Messiah.[129] This book was published first in 1543 with the title *On the Jews and Their Lies*. It ought to be noted that Luther claims that he wants to lead some Jews to the Christ-Messiah through this book.

The mission motif and a conditional goodwill exist in another passage of the letter to Rosheim. Luther says: "For it has been on my heart and it continues to be that one should be friendly toward the Jews so that God would look on them in grace and lead them to their Messiah. And not so that the Jews through my favor and my encouragement would be strengthened in their errors and thereby more evil."[130] Luther still wishes in 1537 that the Jews would be met in a friendly manner so they can be won through God's merciful grace. But his goodwill ought not be misused toward a consolidation of Judaism. Rosheim must finally receive the letter's challenge with goodwill and seek the help of others in the question of free passage. The reformer will gladly for the sake of the Crucified One do all the good he can for the Jews if only they would not exploit his help toward an increased hard-heartedness. Finally, he leaves Rosheim in God's hand.[131]

The letter shows that the reformer stands at a crossroads in his relationship to the Jews. As previously, he is jealous for their salvation and wants to convince them that Jesus is God's Messiah. But he is irritated by their proselytism—of which he was informed already in 1532—and their blasphemy against Christ and the Christians. Religio-political themes also begin to come into the picture. One ought to remember that Luther was as little committed to freedom of religion as his contemporaries. The principle of freedom of religion was developed later in our pluralistic cultures. Because the princedom of Saxony belongs to the *unum corpus Christianum*, Luther cannot accept blasphemy against the princedom's official religion nor propaganda for another religion. The letter to Rosheim portends principles that become decisive during the period 1538–1546.

---

uber funfzehen hundert Jahr lang gewähret, helfen, welches nicht geschehen wird, Jhr nehmet denn Euern Vettern und Herrn, den lieben gekreuzigten Jesum, mit uns Heiden an." I wonder what Luther would have said today when the Jews, without having converted, have *de facto* lived in Palestine for a long time.

128 WABr 8:90.51ff.

129 WABr 8:90.14ff. Cf. Brosseder, *Luthers Stellung zu den Juden*, 356, and WA 50:310.

130 WABr 8:89.9ff.

131 WABr 8:91.56ff.

The Weak Position of Missionary Thought during the Years 1538–1543

Scholars have thoroughly investigated and registered a change in Luther's view of the Jews motivated either by theological or sociopractical considerations, especially during the years 1538–1543.[132] With the question of the mission motif in the center, I will here point out some main themes in the rich source material.

The dispute in *Against the Sabbatarians, etc.* (1538)

Through Baron Wolf Schlick of Falkenau, the reformer already in 1532 had learned that the Jews in "fanatical" Moravia had proselytized Christians. They had misled some Christians into being circumcised. Such proselytes are forced thereafter to keep the Law of Moses. It was especially emphasized that they must keep the Jewish Sabbath. Schlick requests a disputation with the Jews on the basis of the Scriptures.[133] The letter from Luther—it is actually a quickly written little book[134]—had several goals. It will be a dispute with Judaism and an apologetical/missionizing attempt to convince the Jews on the basis of the Old Testament and history that their expectation of the Messiah is mistaken because Jesus is the Messiah of God. Furthermore, Luther claims that Moses' Law and regulations have no eternal relevance. Even the Jewish arguments for circumcision and the Sabbath are addressed.

The reformer does not have a great deal of hope in 1538 that the Jews can be won for the Christian faith. Even if he, as they themselves have requested, seeks to convince them with texts from the Old Testament, they fall back on other authorities, that is, the rabbis and their commentaries. Luther wants nevertheless to

---

132 See the literature review in *Luther and World Mission*, 326–34.

133 LW 47:65 (WA 50:312.8ff.): "You informed me that the Jews are making inroads at various places throughout the country with their venom and their doctrine, and that they have already induced some Christians to let themselves be circumcised and to believe that the Messiah or Christ has not yet appeared, that the law of the Jews must prevail forever, that it must also be adopted by all the Gentiles, etc. Then you inquired of me how these allegations are to be refuted with Holy Scripture. For the time being and until I am at greater leisure, I will convey my advice and opinion briefly in this matter." Cf. WATr 3:441.20ff. (no. 3597) from 1537. See concerning the activity of the so-called Sabbatarians and the pan-European movement to Judaize Christians, in *Luther and World Mission*, 367ff.

134 The "epistle" *Against the Sabbatarians* takes up twenty-five A-4 pages in WA 50:312–37. Among the analyses of this book, see Lewin, *Luthers Stellung zu den Juden*, 67ff.; Maurer. "Die Zeit der Reformation," 404–7; Sucher, *Luthers Stellung zu den Juden*, 63–70; Ehrlich, "Luther und die Juden," 139–42; and Tjernagel, *Martin Luther and the Jewish People*, 47ff.

make an attempt to convince the Jews and strengthen the faith of the Christians.[135]

In the first part of *Against the Sabbatarians*, there is a comprehensive argumentation against the vain waiting of the Jews for a Messiah and an apology for the confession of Christians that Jesus of Nazareth is the Messiah and the Christ. The reformer first considers Lyra's argument that the Jews have, for 1,500 years, been dispersed and without a temple, worship, priesthood, and kingdom, all of which are necessary to live according to the Law and regulations of Moses.[136] Christians must relentlessly ask the Jews which sin they have committed so that Jerusalem and the kingdom lay devastated; the temple, the priesthood, and the temple worship have been out of function; and the regulations of Moses cannot be followed. All that which is now out of function is clearly promised in God's Word and in the covenant with the promises. Because one cannot blame God for exile and evil, the Jews must give a clear answer to the question of which sin or which mistake of the people has caused such retribution from the same God who gave the promises to the Jewish people.[137] Luther thinks that one ought to press the Jews with the questions about the above-named sin, about God's severe punishment during the last 1,500 years, and about the fact that their Messiah has not come. This is one of the most important arguments in Luther's attempt to convince the Jews that they are waiting in vain for another Messiah. If the Jews do not have an answer to the question about God's lengthy discipline, they themselves and their religion, characterized as it is by the Law of Moses, are false.[138] The understanding of the rabbis that the worship of the golden calf initiated God's long wrath and discipline does not hold. Despite this sin, God kept his promises, led the people into the Promised Land, and raised Israel up over all the Gentiles.

---

135 WA 50:313.1ff. In 1539 Luther's close friend Justus Jonas translated *Against the Sabbatrians* into Latin so Luther's ideas could reach other countries. The foreword to the Latin edition is probably more positive and mission oriented than Luther's original book. Jonas shows how the Word lay untouched under the papacy and was distorted by the spiteful handling of the Jews. Because the Gospel has once again opened the Scriptures, one has emphasized Israel's worth, the dramatic history of this people, and the gratitude the Gentiles owe to them. Therefore Gentile Christians are obligated to work for the salvation of the Jews from heresy. Luther is said to have written better than anyone else on this subject in *Against the Sabbatarians*. Jonas translates this work to strengthen the consciences of the Christians and, if possible, so the book might have a greater use among Jews in Italy and the Netherlands, as well as other places. See Lewin, *Luthers Stellung zu den Juden*, 72, and WA 50:310.

136 WA 50:313.12ff. See also Mauer, "Die Zeit der Reformation," 404f.; and Sucher, *Luthers Stellung zu den Juden*, 64ff.

137 WA 50:313.24ff., 313.35ff. See Mauer, "Die Zeit der Reformation," 405f.

138 WA 50:314.14ff.

Neither the sin of the golden calf nor the sin and faithlessness that caused the Babylonian exile for seventy years has been able to force God to withhold the promises. There must be another more serious archsin that is the reason behind God's discipline.[139]

The reformer means that, after all this, the apologetic/missionary argumentation vis-à-vis the Jews and the rabbis must show that the chosen people have hardened themselves to God's salvation, that is, the true Messiah in the new covenant's Jesus Christ. Luther cites Jeremiah 31:31–34 about how God will make a new covenant with the chosen people, another covenant than that made on Sinai, which has been broken by the people. In the new covenant, the Law will be written on their hearts and all will know the Lord because God will forgive sin and transgression. In conversations with the Jews, one ought indefatigably to present the words in Jeremiah 31:31–34 that directly oppose the notion that God should tarry with the Messiah for the sake of nameable, ordinary sins. On the contrary, it is just for the sake of sins and faithlessness that a new covenant has been promised, a covenant in which fellowship with God will rest on the basis of God's forgiveness.[140] But this fact exacerbates the theological conflict between the Jews and the Christians. Either the Jews are lying in their interpretation of Scripture or God is lying in the Word, says Luther. The latter option is naturally impossible. Jeremiah 31:31–34 says clearly that God will not for the sake of sin and faithlessness be hindered from fulfilling the promise about the Messiah.[141]

The reformer goes through a list of examples from the Old Testament that prove the general rule that God has punished the chosen people, allowed them for a shorter or longer time to live in distress or exile—and nevertheless never waited

---

139 WA 50:314.2–315.25.

140 WA 50:315.26ff., 316.1ff. Concerning Luther and Jeremiah 31:31–34, see Lewin, *Luthers Stellung zu den Juden*, 68f.

141 LW 47:70 (WA 50:316.13ff.): "You must base your argument on this passage [Jeremiah 31:31–34] and hold it before the Jews' eyes. For how do these things agree? How do they accord? The Jews say that the Messiah's advent is being impeded because they have not kept God's covenant but have sinned against it. God says, 'No, I will not regard such sin. The fact that they did not keep my covenant will not hinder me. I am prompted to issue a new covenant all the more because they did not keep the old one, in order that such sin might be eternally forgiven and forgotten through the new covenant.' Now it is time to pose the question: Who is lying here? God or the Jew? For they contradict one another. The Jews say, 'Yes,' and God says 'No.' However, the question is quite superfluous, for it is proven that the Jews are lying and that their excuse that the Messiah is delayed because of their sin is worthless. God remains truthful when he declares that he is not stayed by any sin, but that he has held to his promise and the Messiah's coming, and that he still does so, regardless of their sin and their violation of the covenant."

so long to fulfill his promises. He has remained faithfully the God of Abraham, Isaac, and Jacob and has promised to keep David's throne in power in the land. But now God has allowed the people to live in exile and distress for 1,500 years. Because the Jews and their rabbis cannot explain their own dispersion and their abandonment with any particular sin, the promised Messiah must have come. Luther says:

> ... [E]ither the Messiah must have come fifteen hundred years ago, or God must have lied (may God forgive me for speaking so irreverently!) and has not kept his promise. I repeat, either the Messiah must have come fifteen hundred years ago when the throne of David, the kingdom of Judah, the priesthood of Israel, the temple, and Jerusalem were still intact, when the law of Moses and the worship he instituted still endured, and the people were still living under their government in Jerusalem, before all of this had collapsed and been destroyed so miserably; or if not, God has lied. Those Jews who are still in possession of their reason cannot deny this.... The Messiah has come and God's promise has been kept and fulfilled. They, however, did not accept or believe this, but constantly gave God the lie with their own unbelief, etc. Is it any wonder that God's wrath destroyed them together with Jerusalem, temple, law, kingdom, priesthood, and reduced these to ashes, that he scattered them among all the Gentiles, and that he does not cease to afflict them as long as they give the lie to the divine promise and fulfillment and blaspheme them by their unbelief and disobedience? For they should have accepted the new covenant (as promised by Jeremiah) from the Messiah and received him. He was commissioned to teach them properly concerning the throne of David, the priesthood, the law of Moses, the temple, and all things. As Moses writes in Deuteronomy 18 [:15] ...[142]

In the reformer's apologetic/missionary dialogue with Judaism, it is surprising how energetically he attempts to get the Jews to understand that Jesus of Nazareth was and is the promised Messiah. Jesus' messiahship is the cardinal point and nerve in Luther's dispute with the faith of the Jews. If God has previously always held his promises despite repeated sins and falls, would he so basically reject and deceive his own people concerning the general promise about the Messiah?[143]

---

142 LW 47:73–74 (WA 50:318.19ff.). Cf. the entire passage in WA 50:316.28–321.25.

143 LW 47:77–78 (WA 50:322.3ff.): "Why, then, should God forget his promise so woefully in this exile or let it fail of fulfillment or be so hostile to them, since they have no sin which they can name, and yet this promise of the Messiah is the most glorious and the mightiest promise, upon which all other prophecy, promise, and the entire law are built? For the other promises such as those pertaining to Egypt, the wilderness, and Babylon, are to be esteemed very small in comparison with this chief promise of the Messiah. If God kept his less important promises there and then and comforted the people so heartily in lesser exiles; if he specified the time; if he proved himself their

According to Luther, these unavoidable questions about Israel's 1,500 year-long suffering and about the promises for David's eternal throne can be answered if and only if one claims that Jesus is the Messiah and was enthroned in David's place 1,500 years ago. The reformer says:

> The Jews may say what they want about the sins for which they are suffering (for they are lying). God did not promise and pledge an eternal throne to their sin or their righteousness, but to David. . . . This is what David sings in Psalm 89 [:4–52]. However, since David's throne, which God declares is not to be destroyed or fall, has been destroyed now for fifteen hundred years, it is incontrovertible that either the Messiah came fifteen hundred years ago and occupied the throne of his father David, and forever occupies it, or God has become a liar in his most glorious promise because of evil men and disobedient Jews. . . . [T]he Jews are slandering God and deceiving themselves when they accuse God of breaking faith and trust with David because he did not send the Messiah in the manner they would have liked and as they prescribe and imagine him to be.[144]

Luther means that only such arguments can move the reasonable or shake the hardened among the Jews. These Bible arguments are also something of a confession of faith in Christ and a rejection of those who oppose him. Luther means that if the Jews lay such reasons to the side, then one ought to leave them alone as liars.[145] We see from this that *Against the Sabbatarians* has a clear but harsh apologetic/missionary goal.

In the theologically difficult *Against the Sabbatarians*, Luther also teaches the Christians how one ought to respond to the supposition that the Law and regulations of Moses will remain forever and that Gentiles/Gentile Christians must become Jews.[146] The thesis about the eternity of the Law must fall in the first place because the Old Testament and the Jewish tradition *de facto* say that the time of the Law is finished when the Messiah comes. In Deuteronomy 18:15, Moses says that the people will hear the prophet whom God raises up after him. The rabbis themselves teach that their own anointing (= priesthood and kingship) will cease when the Holiest of Holies comes.[147] In the second place, one ought to show

---

faithful God by means of persons and blessings and in every way, and always provided for them—how is it possible, how is it credible, how is it consistent that he would fail to keep, in this terrible, long, and great exile, his glorious promise given to David that his throne should remain established forever, as David exults in his last words [2 Sam 23:5] . . . ?"

144 LW 47:78 (WA 50:322.19ff.).

145 WA 50:322.35ff.–323.7.

146 WA 50:323.8–327.15. See Lewin, *Luthers Stellung zu den Juden*, 69f.; and Maurer, "Die Zeit der Reformation," 406.

147 WA 50:323.9ff.

that the Law has not been in use or practice for 1,500 years because the priesthood, the temple, the kingdom, and temple worship are no longer functioning. The Law and its regulations are tightly connected with these institutions. Because the Jews themselves are *de facto* prevented from keeping the Law, they cannot demand that the Gentiles obey the entire Law.[148] If one speaks about the eternity of the Law and obedience to it, one must in the third place include the entire Law. One does not keep the entire Law through circumcision nor through abstinence from pork or some types of fish.[149]

Because the Law should be replaced by something new with the advent of the Messiah and has *de facto* been out of use since Jesus' time for 1,500 years, the Christians must conclude that Jesus was and is God's Messiah. Through Jesus Christ, the Law of Moses is once and for all superseded; therefore it ought to be required neither of Jews nor Gentiles.[150] That Moses says that some of the laws and regulations that he gave will be held eternally (or *le-olam*) ought not concern us. The Old Testament continually says that the laws and the commands will be in force only as long as the people live in the land.[151] The Old Testament uses both a temporary *le-olam* and a divine-absolute *le-olam*. The absolute eternal is indicated when something near God himself (power, lordship) is said to be both eternal and without end.[152]

Jewish propaganda in Central Europe had emphasized the necessity of circumcision. Against this, the reformer claims that circumcision does not belong to the Law of Moses but was given already to Abraham and his descendants up to the advent of the Messiah. It did not exist before Abraham either. Many Gentiles were converted through the preaching of Joseph in Egypt, through Jonah's preaching in Nineveh, and through Daniel's preaching in Babylon and Persia without being demanded to be circumcised. Therefore it is a human invention and rubbish

---

148 WA 50:323.20–324.10.

149 WA 50:326.16ff., 326.29ff.

150 LW 47:80–81 (WA 50:324.13ff.): "It has been in ruins for fifteen hundred years now and did not survive, and they do not yet know for how long this situation will prevail. We Christians, however, know that it has ceased forever and that it is entirely abrogated through the Messiah, not only among us Gentiles, to whom this law of Moses was never issued and commanded and on whom it never was imposed, but also among the true Jews and posterity of David. For since God himself has let it lapse for these fifteen hundred years, it is reasonable to assume that he pays it no heed and that he is not interested in obedience or service to such a law. . . . Therefore the law of Moses is finished. It does not stand as a law that endures forever; rather it has become a law that is forever abandoned."

151 WA 50:324.27ff., 325.5ff. See Sucher, *Luthers Stellung zu den Juden*, 66f.

152 WA 50:325.32ff., 326.4ff., with many examples from the Old Testament.

when the Jews through the centuries have sought to make the Gentiles into proselytes by circumcising them and laying them under the Law of Moses. Circumcision and Moses' Law apply to the Jews only up to the advent of Jesus Christ.[153]
Luther emphasizes once again that one ought to argue on the basis of Jeremiah
31:31ff. in this connection. That passage speaks of how the old covenant will be
superceded by a new covenant. The old covenant will not remain forever. It also
will not in any way remain in a renovated state; instead, it will be exchanged for
another and a new covenant that does not rest on circumcision and the Law.[154]

The reformer also claims that on the basis of Jesus' own words in Matthew
5:17ff. Jewish scholars without right argue against the Christians' freedom from
the Law. In the first place, they must take Jeremiah 31:31ff. seriously. In the second
place, evidence of the Jesus whom they themselves deny is inadmissable. Furthermore, the continuation of the text shows that Jesus does not speak of circumcision
and the whole Law of Moses but only of the Ten Commandments.[155] The Decalogue is not the same as Moses' Law. It is not given first through Moses and not
only to the Jews. For Luther, the Ten Commandments are an expression of the
moral law or natural law, which from the beginning was given to all people. From
the beginning of creation, it is written on the hearts of all—even if in many ways
it is suppressed and hidden—to reign over all the peoples under the sun.[156] It is
another matter that God proclaims this law that is written in all human hearts
when the old covenant with Israel is established.[157] *Lex naturalis* owns a basic
priority over the Law of Moses, even if it must also be proclaimed by Moses.

---

153 WA 50:327.16–329.3. Summarized in LW 47:87 (WA 50:329.4ff.): "Since circumcision and the law of Moses were not necessary for the kings and heathen in Egypt,
Assyria, Babylon, Persia, and elsewhere who nevertheless believed in the God of Abraham and were saved without circumcision and the law of Moses at the very time when
these were flourishing and when the people had their government in Jerusalem and in
the land, why then should we Gentiles be required to keep a circumcision and a law
which has now ceased and which they themselves cannot keep because they have lost
country, city, government, and all that Moses instituted, without any promise of ever
retrieving them?"

154 WA 50:329, 20ff.

155 WA 50:330.11ff.

156 WA 50:330.28ff., especially: "Thus we and all human beings are obligated to hear his
word, to honor father and mother, to refrain from killing, from adultery, from stealing,
from bearing false witness, from coveting one's neighbor's house or anything else that
is his. All the heathen bear witness to this in their writings, laws, and governments, as
can be clearly seen; but nothing is said therein of circumcision or of the laws Moses
gave to the Jews for the land of Canaan" (LW 47:89–90 [WA 50:331.2ff.]).

157 LW 47:90 (WA 50:331.11ff.): "And later when he wants to set up a special law and
nation apart from all others, as he has been commanded to do, he first introduces God
himself; he is the universal God of all the nations, who gives the universal Ten Com-

Luther emphasizes that the Decalogue proclaimed by Moses has portions and adornments that are addressed only to the Jews. Among these is that which gave this book its title, the commandment about the Sabbath.[158]

This book is actually restrained in its polemic, even if the religious conflict between the parties can sometimes give birth to bitter commentaries.[159]

The missionary and especially the apologetic themes are clearly evident. Luther concludes the first part of the book, which is directed primarily to the Jews, with these words:

> I know the argument is true. Where there are still reasonable Jews, it must move them, and it must even upset the obdurate ones a little, for they cannot bring any substantial evidence against it. But if it does not move them or make them waver, we have nonetheless substantiated our own faith, so that their foul and worthless lies and idle chatter cannot harm us. And if they do not stick to the point of the argument but evade the issue by resorting to other twaddle, as they like to do, let them go their way and you go yours.[160]

In the greeting to Wolf Schlick toward the end of the letter, Luther hopes that he has taught his friend enough so that "you will at least have been supplied with enough material to defend yourself against the Sabbatarians and to preserve the purity of your Christian faith. If you are unable to convert the Jews, then consider that you are no better than all the prophets, who were always slain and persecuted by this base people."[161] We see in this way that Luther continues—but not so optimistically as in 1523—to hope for the conversion of the Jews. He trusts in arguments from the words of the Bible. At the same time, he knows that it is not easy to get Jews to turn toward and believe in Christ. It is also worth noting that here Luther does not at all consider Romans 9–11, especially Romans 11:25–26 about Israel's conversion before the parousia of Christ.

Bienert and Sucher have in their surveys of the *Table Talk* shown how intensively the Jewish question occupies Luther and how he vacillates between sympathy and antipathy toward the Jews in the years 1539–1542.[162] These Jews in 1540

---

mandments—which prior to this had been implanted at creation in the hearts of all men—to this particular people orally as well."

158 WA 50:331.17ff., 331.20ff.

159 WA 50:323.36ff., 324.11ff., 330.9f.

160 LW 47:78 (WA 50:322.35ff.).

161 LW 47:95–96 (WA 50:335.22ff.).

162 Bienert, *Martin Luther und die Juden*, 120–30; and Sucher, *Luthers Stellung zu den Juden*, 103ff. Cf. also Lewin, *Luthers Stellung zu den Juden*, 74ff. Luther accuses the Jews of works-righteousness, expectation of a worldly Messiah, and rejection of Jesus as the Messiah. He criticizes them for their business transactions and—something that is

could consider Luther to be their advocate. However, during the conversations with the three rabbis, things became hot concerning the question of the divinity of Christ. The Jewish missionaries hope that the Christians through their knowledge of the Hebrew Old Testament will become Jews. The reformer hopes that the Jews will become Christians.[163] Luther points out that David and the apostles—who are also Jews—in the Scriptures possess such a depth that no one in the later Gentile Christian church can compare with them.[164] He emphasizes the loftiness of Israel and Jerusalem. He suffers because the temple has been destroyed and because the Jews live in exile and are oppressed by God's wrath. God is silent and does not hear their prayers.[165] The Jews have the blessing that Jesus was first sent to them, then to the Gentiles. Therefore the Jews no longer are the only ones who have the Messiah and the truth.[166]

Luther also can be negative to the faith of the Jews and their slanders. Already Genesis 1:1ff. speaks, among other things through the plural *Elohim*, of the doctrine of the Trinity against all that the Jews say.[167] The Jews trust now in some dead privileges and self-righteousness, but they do not know God's grace and the righteousness of faith in Christ.[168] Nevertheless, Luther can say in connection with the Baptism of a Jew in 1540: "Let him come to me. I am not at all afraid of him. I love the Jews." He rejoices in the confession of the baptismal candidate, but Luther often doubts the honesty of such baptismal candidates and the honesty of the Jews in general.[169] In 1542 the reformer begins to consider for the first time whether the Jews ought to be expelled from the princedom because they call Christ a hung-up

---

new—because they "play under the blanket" with the immigrant invading Turks. The reformer can otherwise speak about Israel's great promises and loftiness. From 1539/1540, Luther is, according to Lewin, pessimistic about the conversion of the Jews, even if he still considers it to be a possibility that Israel can be given a final time of revival as per Romans 11:23ff. Lewin summarizes the situation in the beginning of the 1540s: "nach der Lage der Dinge, nach der Aufeinanderfolge der Phasen, die seine Entwicklung durchlief, kann aus seiner Feder keine Missionsschrift meher fliessen, sein Werk muss eine erbitterte, rücksichtslose Kampfschrift werden" (70).

163 WATr 4:619.20ff. (no. 5026) from 1540. Cf. Sucher, *Luthers Stellung zu den Juden*, 104f.

164 WATr 4:306.26ff. (no. 4225) from 1539.

165 WATr 4:326.21ff. (no. 4466) from 1539. See also WATr 5:235.15ff. (no. 5554a) from 1542/1543.

166 WATr 5:232ff. (no. 5522) from 1543.

167 *Lectures on Genesis* (1534–1545), WA 42:8.21ff., 10.11ff.; 44:13–16.

168 WATr 4:343.23ff. (no. 4493) from 1539.

169 WATr 5:83.1ff. (no. 5354) from 1540. Cf. Lewin, *Luthers Stellung zu den Juden*, 75ff.

rogue (*thola*) and slander Mary as a whore (*haria*).[170] The Jews are hard and stiff-necked, but as before 1543, Luther rejects the idea of killing them.[171]

On the Jews and Their Lies (1543)

I will concentrate in the following on different parts of the comprehensive source material from 1542/1543. Much of what Luther writes in his severe disputes with Judaism and the Jews must be commented on in a summary fashion because I am concentrating on the specific question of mission. Most scholars who have considered the theme "Luther and the Jews" have commented primarily on *On the Jews and Their Lies* (1543). Because Luther unfortunately has been exploited by Nazi propaganda, they also have presented a more or less articulated critique against the most severe passages in the reformer's writings. One has, unfortunately, paid too little attention to the apologetic/missionary center in Luther's writings on the Jews in these years.[172]

On May 18, 1542, Luther had received from the previously mentioned Wolf Schlick a Jewish pamphlet that was an attempt to refute Luther's apologetic in *Against the Sabbatarians*. Because Luther considered this Jewish counterargument to be a distortion of Scripture and an attempt to subvert the ground of the Christian faith and because Schlick expressly requested him to refute this Jewish attack, Luther composed the long-promised dispute with the anti-Christian Jewish propaganda. First, Luther works energetically with the rabbinical literature and with the medieval anti-Jewish books. When one perceives the reformer's ability to handle these subtle materials, it is difficult to come to the conclusion that he suffered from senility. On January 17, 1543, the polemical book *On the Jews and Their Lies*[173] was published, the book that has led many to the conclusion that Luther is the greatest enemy of the Jews.

---

170 WATr 5:166.27ff. (no. 5462) from summer/fall 1542. Cf. WATr 4:619.20f. (no. 5026) from 1540: "They call Christ a hung-up rogue and Mary a whore in the latrine."

171 WATr 5:247.12ff. (no. 5567).

172 One exception is Holmio, *Lutheran Reformation and the Jews*, 131ff. Among others, Stöhr, "Martin Luther und die Juden," 98, has claimed that Luther is only negative toward the Jews. He rejects any notion that Luther might have considered mission among the Jews. See also Brosseder, *Luthers Stellung zu den Juden*, 265, against Holmio. Shorter analyses of *On the Jews and Their Lies* can be found in the following sources: Lewin, *Luthers Stellung zu den Juden*, 81ff.; Maurer, "Die Zeit der Reformation," 407ff., 416ff.; Brosseder, *Luthers Stellung zu den Juden*, 362ff.; Sucher, *Luthers Stellung zu den Juden*, 71ff.; Bienert, *Martin Luther und die Juden*, 130ff.; Ehrlich, "Luther und die Juden," 143ff.; Pfisterer, "Zwischen Polemik und Apologetik," 108ff.; Stöhr, "Martin Luther und die Juden," 100ff.; and Tjernagel, *Martin Luther and the Jewish People*, 50ff.

173 See the foreword in WA 53:412–14, 417.14ff., 552.29ff.

We previously have seen how the aging reformer oscillates between hope and despair concerning the conversion of the Jews to the Christian faith. In *On the Jews and Their Lies,* Luther is nearly out of hope. He apparently had considered not writing the projected book about and against the Jews. When, however, the Jewish propaganda draws and wins confessors of Christ to the Jewish faith, the reformer feels forced to confute such propaganda while at the same time warning Christians about it and to strengthen them against it. The reformer believes that as he stands before the attacks of the Jews, he stands before the power of Satan itself, which no one can oppose without God's Word. God's Word has enough power to reveal the attack of the Jews against the Christian faith. The attempt of the Jews to win Christians to Judaism is an important element behind the dispute in *On the Jews and Their Lies.*[174] Luther is not primarily interested in dialogue with the Jews nor in learning something about the Bible from the Jews. Because Nicolaus of Lyra, Paulus Burgensis, and others have not been able through the centuries to convince the Jews about their mistakes, Luther does not expect with his book to be able to convince and convert them.[175] The reformer is much troubled by the fact

---

174 See the introduction in LW 47:137 (WA 53:417.2ff.): "I had made up my mind to write no more either about the Jews or against them. But since I learned that these miserable and accursed people do not cease to lure to themselves even us, that is, the Christians, I have published this little book, so that I might be found among those who opposed such poisonous activities of the Jews and who warned the Christians to be on their guard against them. I would not have believed that a Christian could be duped by the Jews into taking their exile and wretchedness upon himself. However, the devil is the god of the world, and wherever God's word is absent he has an easy task, not only with the weak but also with the strong. May God help us. Amen." Cf. LW 47:149 (WA 53:427.10ff.): "Our people, however, must be on their guard against them, lest they be misled by this impenitent, accursed people who give God the lie and haughtily despise all the world. For the Jews would like to entice us Christians to their faith, and they do this wherever they can." Cf. WA 53:434.14ff., 449.35ff., 479.24ff.

175 LW 47:137–38 (WA 53:417.20ff.): "It is not my purpose to quarrel with the Jews, nor to learn from them how they interpret or understand Scripture; I know all of that very well already. Much less do I propose to convert the Jews, for that is impossible. These two excellent men, Lyra and Burgensis, together with others, truthfully described the Jews' vile interpretation for us two hundred and one hundred years ago respectively. Indeed they refuted it thoroughly. However, this was no help at all to the Jews, and they have grown steadily worse." Cf. WA 53:419.4ff., 476.5–482.26, 531.35ff. See also Lewin, *Luthers Stellung zu den Juden,* 81f.; and Loewenich, *Luther: Der Mann und das Werk,* 334. Stöhr, "Martin Luther und die Juden," 100, speaks of how the Scripture proofs (WA 53:469, 470, 450) seem directed only toward the goal of strengthening the Christians. I want here to repudiate Stöhr's thesis ("Martin Luther und die Juden," 99f.) that Luther's later writings about the Jews are directed only to Christians, their preachers, and their rulers. For the most part, Brosseder, *Luthers Stellung zu den Juden,* 361f., approves Stöhr's proposal. In Luther's comprehensive investigations, it is quite clear

that the Jews so stiff-neckedly oppose the confession that Jesus is God's Messiah. The words and works of the Christians did not help before; neither do they help now in 1543. Therefore individual Christians ought not discuss too much about the articles of faith. They ought instead only to point to the terrible wrath of God that is revealed by the fact that Jerusalem, the kingdom, the temple, and the priesthood have been destroyed and out of function for nearly 1,500 years— while God is silent and appears to have left the chosen people. This discipline of God that is apparent to all must be allowed to do its work so the Jews will be humbled and understand that the Messiah has already come in Jesus Christ. So far, according to Luther, God's rod has not had enough time to prepare the Jews to believe in Jesus, much less in the Trinity and that God was incarnate in Jesus Christ, etc.[176]

The idea that God continues to discipline the Jews implies, of course, that the Jews will not always oppose and refuse to confess Jesus as the Messiah. Nevertheless, Luther understands the situation in 1543 as nearly hopeless. Therefore Luther gives out his book *On the Jews and Their Lies* primarily to refute the Jews' interpretation of Scripture and to warn and strengthen the Christians of Germany. He writes: "Now, in order to strengthen our faith, we want to deal with a few crass follies of the Jews in their belief and their exegesis of the Scriptures, since they so maliciously revile our faith. If this should move any Jew to reform and repent, so much the better. We are now not talking with the Jews but about the Jews and

---

that the goal of convincing the Jews is relatively important for Luther. In this connection, one ought not forget that one of the decisive themes behind Luther's apologetic/missionary exposition of the Old Testament in *That Christ Was Born a Jew* (1523) was precisely to convince the Jews. In 1543 he uses nearly the entire argument from 1523, though the latter book has a more severe polemical tone and a weaker hope for the conversion of the Jews. I also want to point out that in the 1537 letter to Josel von Rosheim Luther promised the book that became *On the Jews and Their Lies*: "Davon ich, so mir Gott Raum und Zeit gibt, will ein Büchlin schreiben, ob ich etliche künnte aus Eurem väterlichen Stammen der heiligen Patriarchen und Propheten gewinnen, und zu Eurem verheissenen Messia bringen" (WABr 8:90.3ff.).

176 WA 53:418.1–419.3. See especially the conclusion: "In short, as has already been said, do not engage much in debate with Jews about the articles of our faith. From their youth they have been so nurtured with venom and rancor against our Lord that there is no hope until they reach the point where their misery finally makes them pliable and they are forced to confess that the Messiah has come, and that he is our Jesus. Until such a time it is much too early, yes, it is useless to argue with them about how God is triune, how he became man, and how Mary is the mother of God. No human reason nor any human heart will ever grant these things, much less the embittered, venomous, blind heart of the Jews. As has already been said, what God cannot reform with such cruel blows, we will be unable to change with words and works" (LW 47:139 [WA 53:419.4ff.]).

their dealings, so that our Germans, too, might be informed."[177] The quotation shows that, despite everything, Luther entertains a little, secondary hope that some among the Jews might be led to repentance—even through this book. This hope is evident in other parts of the book as well.[178] But it must be admitted that in general the book is a severe and often wretched polemical writing that seeks to prove that the Jewish interpretations of the Bible are an obvious manipulation of the Old Testament and that the Jewish faith is false.

THE FALSE BOASTS OF THE JEWS

In *On the Jews and Their Lies*, the reformer attacks first the idea that the Jews alone are God's people. They boast that they are the only true descendants of the patriarchs, that they have noble blood, and that they are the foremost people on earth, etc.[179] Even if one may say that they are more noble and higher among the peoples, this is irrelevant to God. Genesis 17:14 shows in connection with circumcision that all of Adam's fallen race is condemned unless God comes to help and through the covenant creates something new.[180] From a human perspective, Abraham had noble blood, but he does not boast about this. Instead, he boasts that he has been called through God's Word. He and all the children of Adam were and are dust in and of themselves, but they are called and sanctified through God's Word (Genesis 15:1, 15; 18:27; 3:19).[181] Luther discusses similar arguments on the basis of the stories of Esau and Jacob, Ishmael and Isaac, etc. From the time the children of Cain had been destroyed in the flood, all people are physical descendants of the patriarchs, David, and the prophets.[182] But this physical descent does not help in any way humanity's relationship to God. In Psalm 51:5, David has said that all so-called natural humans are born in sin and subject to God's wrath and judgment. Before God, there is no room to boast. From a strictly human or natural perspective, neither Jews nor Gentiles can be referred to as "God's people."[183]

The reformer cannot, of course, ignore the fact that according to the Old Testament God has chosen from all the fallen children of Adam the Jewish people

---

177 LW 47:140 (WA 53:419.16ff.).

178 See a little hope for the repentance of individual Jews in WA 53:427.18f., 470.29ff., 473.5f., 485.28f. See especially the concluding prayer, WA 53:552.36ff.

179 WA 53:419.22–427.19ff.

180 WA 53:421.15ff., 421.30ff.

181 WA 53:423.11ff., 423.23ff.

182 WA 53:424.6ff., 424.30ff., 425.6ff., 425.20ff., 426.1ff., 426.14ff.

183 WA 53:426.29ff.

and has given them special promises. Luther also speaks often of true Israelites, those who believed the promises and served God in obedience to God's commands. But the prophets, John the Baptist, and Jesus also say that because of their unbelief, sin, and faithlessness Israel has become subject to God's condemnation, the same condemnation that rests over all natural humans. Therefore neither all the Jews nor only the Jews can be referred to as "God's people."[184] Luther wants to emphasize this to strengthen the faith of Christians and to hinder the proselytism of the Jews.[185] He also wants to emphasize that the Jews must abandon their thoughts about their own nobility among all people because such ideas only increase God's anger with them. As a people they probably will not be willing to take this humble path, but individuals can, through God's drawing power, accomplish this. At this point, the idea of a general revival among the Jews based on Romans 11:23ff. apparently has no place in Luther's theology.[186] But an intimation of the mission theme exists here.

The Jews present another type of boasting in their conduct, prayers, and songs. They speak of how God chose them and sanctified them more than other peoples through the covenant of circumcision. Through this, they are supposed to be chosen to be God's people. The Gentiles despise them because of it. Concerning this, Luther says that Genesis 17:9ff., 13, and 18:24ff. clearly show that the commandment about circumcision applied to all in Abraham's house and all his descendants. Thus circumcision was given not only to Israel but also to a whole list of peoples, among others, the Ishmaelites, Edomites, and Midianites. So circumcision provides neither a good reputation nor grace especially to the Jews.[187] The falseness of the Jews' boasting consists even in the fact that Job and his relatives, as well as Naaman from Syria, were not required to be circumcised but were

---

184 WA 53:418.20ff., 419.22ff., 420.17ff. Cf. also how Luther in *On the Jews and Their Lies* often refers to the words of the prophets that the chosen people in their faithfulness are no longer truly God's people (WA 53:441.7–21, 447.5–26, 469.22–30, 495.5ff.).

185 WA 53:427.8ff.

186 LW 47:149 (WA 53:427.14ff.): "If God is to become gracious also to them, the Jews, they must first of all banish such blasphemous prayers and songs, that boast so arrogantly about their lineage, from their synagogues, from their hearts, and from their lips, for such prayers ever increase and sharpen God's wrath toward them. However, they will not do this, nor will they humble themselves abjectly, except for a few individuals whom God draws unto himself particularly and delivers from their terrible ruin." Cf. WATr 5:247.5ff. (no. 5567). In a *Table Talk*, Katie says that John 10:16 opens a possibility for the conversion of the Jews. Luther says that John 10:16 was fulfilled when the Gentiles began to receive the Gospel.

187 For the argument of the Jews, see WA 53:427.20ff., 427.38ff. For Luther's decisive counterarguments, see WA 53:428.10–430.20.

nevertheless considered holy and people of God. The prophets Jonah in Nineveh, Daniel in Babylon and Persia, and Joseph in Egypt converted many through their preaching, especially government leaders. Because the Scriptures do not indicate that circumcision was required in these instances, the Jews and their teachers cannot in their pride despise the uncircumcised and boast that they themselves are alone the people of God.[188]

The reformer also points out how, according to Genesis 10:16 and Jeremiah 4:4; 6:10; and 9:26f., God demands circumcised hearts and ears and punishes disobedience and stiff-neckedness. Also Psalm 5:5–8 shows that God is righteous and graceful but opposes proud sinners. He will in grace have mercy on those who serve him with a proper fear.[189]

When the Scriptures now show on one hand that there has been a people of God who had not been circumcised and on the other that circumcised Jews without the circumcision of the heart do not possess a right relationship to God, then true fellowship with God cannot be based on circumcision. The teachers of the Jews ought to understand that the texts of the Old Testament destroy all boasting based on circumcision as a work. Therefore in the same way as Moses in Genesis 17:11, the teacher of the Christians in Romans 3:1ff. taught that circumcision was given and established so one could hold fast to God's promises, so one could have faith in and obedience to their God.[190] But precisely as the people of the pope have made Baptism, the Lord's Supper, and Absolution an *opus legis* and *opus operatum*, so have the Jews in their depravity lost the purpose of circumcision, its *causa finalis*, that is, the promise connected with the sign. When God's Word— outside of which no one can come into God's presence and live—is left to the side, then one in actuality has no circumcision at all.[191]

The reformer attacks also the third great boast of the Jews: that God has given them Moses' Law on Sinai, has spoken to them and sanctified them among other peoples through the Law.[192] Luther points out, among other things, how this sanctified people followed Korah and did not listen to Moses and the other prophets. Indeed, the Old Testament is full of passages about how the people went astray in their hearts, how they are stiff-necked and disobedient to God (Psalm 95:10; Deuteronomy 31:27; Isaiah 48:4). It does not work either to say that

---

188 WA 53:433.27–434.26. Cf. the discussion of *Against the Sabbatarians*, in *Luther and World Mission*, 373ff.

189 WA 53:430.21–432.23.

190 WA 53:435.15ff.

191 WA 53:435.26ff., 436.26ff., 437.5ff., 437.31ff., 439.12ff.

192 WA 53:439.32–448.36. Cf. the discussion of *Against the Sabbatarians*, in *Luther and World Mission*, 373ff.

God through the prophets criticizes only the godless among the Jews because for nearly 1,500 years the whole people have been punished with exile and wretchedness and their prayers have not been heard.[193]

Luther also emphasizes that it is one thing to have and to know the Law and another to obey it. Israel boasts that it has been sanctified through the Law, to have become God's people and God's bride, but the works of this people of God witness to something else.[194]

Actually Moses and the prophets teach us that the Law is fulfilled only because God forgives transgressions and does not condemn people (Exodus 34:7; Psalm 32:1f., 6; 51:1ff.; 143:7). The Law is fulfilled when the Lord's Suffering Servant silently bears the sin of the guilty (Isaiah 53:3). So the Law strips all boasting from both Jews and Gentiles. Because the path of the Law is impossible (*impossibilitas legis*), humanity has its only point of boasting in God's grace. Therefore Luther warns the Christians against the proud thoughts of the Jews about the Law and its righteousness that only increases God's wrath and judgment upon them.[195]

Luther seeks finally to confute the Jews' fourth boast, that is, that the Lord has granted the land of Canaan, Jerusalem, and the temple to them. After warning Israel about their faithlessness through the prophets, God has shown the whole world through the Babylonians, the Assyrians, and finally the Romans that God cannot tolerate this pride. While God has given his people the land, the city, and the temple, etc., so they might serve him in obedience, the people have misused God's goodness and have brought on themselves exiles and especially God's latest discipline during the past 1,500 years. They have no promises expressed for the future.[196]

The reformer sees in these four boasts a hopeless hardening and something of an obsession. The thoughts of the Jews are always drawn to something external and to the works of the Law. They do not want and cannot see that which some pious Jews had seen through the entire old covenant and that which Paul often describes, that is, that God demands the commitment of the heart to God's will and above all trust in God's forgiveness and mercy.[197]

---

193 WA 53:440.23ff., 441.7ff., 441.22ff., 441.34ff.

194 WA 53:442.29–445.5.

195 WA 53:445.6ff., 445.19ff., 446.1ff., 446.9ff. Cf. *Luther and World Mission*, 86ff.

196 WA 53:446.20–447.19.

197 WA 53:447.20ff., 448.3ff. Brosseder, *Luthers Stellung zu den Juden*, 363ff.; and Bienert, *Martin Luther und die Juden*, 130f., write something about Luther's dispute with the four boasts of the Jews.

The conflict between Jewish and Christian messianic expectation

In his dispute with the boasts of the Jews, Luther has already written about justification's *sola gratia* and *sola fide*. As we saw earlier in the review of the secondary literature, many scholars have argued that the conflict between Luther and the Jews concerns precisely the problem of justification. This subject, in fact, constitutes a decisive tension between Luther and the Jews. But the doctrine of justification in Luther is not only an idea or a formula. In Luther it is connected with God's revelation in the person of Jesus Christ. In the source material that was analyzed above and in Luther's later writings, the question that is, therefore, most prominent in the dispute with the Jews is whether or not, according to the Scriptures, Jesus is God's Messiah. Luther attempts to show that the rabbis oppose *sola scriptura, Christus solus,* and *fides sola.*

With the theme about God's Messiah, we come into the center of the apologetic section of *On the Jews and Their Lies.* Luther stands before the fact that the Jews energetically proclaim that the Messiah has not yet come. He seeks as previously, especially in *That Christ Was Born a Jew*, to prove on the basis of the Old Testament that the promised Messiah had come already 1,500 years ago: Jesus of Nazareth. The reformer means that the Jews and their rabbis oppose the clear words of Scripture and even the Bible expositions of their own people in this question. Paul of Burgos and Antonius Margaritha were baptized Jews. The Jews rebel against the incontrovertible truth that has even been understood by their own people, according to Luther. He sees it as a central task to equip Christians against the Jewish teaching about this center of the Christian faith.[198]

Luther presents a comprehensive examination both of what the Old Testament has to say about the coming Messiah and what he considers to be the horrible interpretations the rabbis have made of those texts. Through a laborious and comprehensive apologetic, Luther seeks to show that many of the promises in the Old Testament have not been fulfilled in the history of the Jewish people but in Christ and his reign.

Here again the comments on Jacob's blessings in Genesis 49:10 are completely decisive: "The scepter will not depart from Judah, nor the ruler's staff from between his feet, until he [Shiloh] comes to whom it belongs." To understand this text correctly, one must, according to the reformer, use a method in which one first focuses on the Hebrew or Chaldaic of the text, then consider history with the

---

198 WA 53:449.1–450.18. Concerning the analysis of the messianic texts in the Old Testament, see Maurer, "Die Zeit der Reformation," 408, 410ff. Brosseder, *Luthers Stellung zu den Juden*, 366ff., only parenthetically considers this Luther theme about the Jewish argumentation against the incontrovertible truth. See also Bienert, *Martin Luther und die Juden*, 139ff.; and Tjernagel, *Martin Luther and the Jewish People*, 55ff.

question of whether or not the text's promise has occurred and continues to occur.[199] Luther claims that the older, true Jews and prophets have interpreted Genesis 49:10 to mean that the Jewish tribe should own its own government until Shiloh, that is, the Messiah, should come. The peoples would connect themselves to him, so both Jews and Gentiles would be obedient to him. Such an interpretation is consistent with the interpretation of Jacob's blessings in Genesis 49:10 by the Christians and by the old, rightly minded Jews.[200] After a thorough examination of both the Hebrew and the Chaldaic version of the text in question, Luther summarizes by claiming that the words are unambiguous and that history has in fact developed according to the words of the text. The tribe of Judah should have its own worldly government until the Messiah would come. It lost its government about 1,500 years ago, and Jesus Christ has founded his own spiritual, messianic government.[201] Therefore the Jews are mistaken in continuing to wait for a Messiah and the Christians are right in their faith in Jesus Christ. The problem is that Jewish scholars will not allow the words of Scripture to be God's Word, says Luther. The Jews and their rabbis are not only mistaken, they also blaspheme against revealed truth and lose both the Scriptures and the Messiah.[202] This is

---

199 Genesis 49:10 is discussed in LW 47:178–92 (WA 53:450.19–462.15). About the method, see LW 47:183 (WA 53:455.18f., 455.21ff.): "Approach the text, both Chaldaean and Hebrew, with this understanding and this thought . . . . And then consult the histories to ascertain whether this has not happened and come to pass in this way and continues to do so. Again you will be compelled to say: It is verily so." Concerning the messianic texts in the Old Testament and the confirmation of history, see also WA 53:546.14–552.28.

200 WA 53:450.33ff.

201 WA 53:456.10ff. Cf. the discussion of *That Christ Was Born a Jew* in *Luther and World Mission*, 349ff.

202 LW 47:192 (WA 53:462.6ff.): "We Christians, however, can greatly strengthen our faith with this statement of Jacob, assuring us that Christ is now present and that he has been present for almost fifteen hundred years—but not, as the devil jeers, as a beggar in Rome; rather, as a ruling Messiah. If this were not so, then God's word and promise would be a lie. If the Jews would only let Holy Scripture be God's word, they would also have to admit that there has been a Messiah since the time of Herod (no matter where), rather than awaiting another. But before doing this, they will rather tear and pervert Scripture until it is no longer Scripture. . . . They have neither Messiah nor Scripture." Luther disputes—often convincingly—the attempts of the rabbis to refute the so-called Christian interpretation of Genesis 49:10. Some suggested, for example, that the sins of the people have hindered God from fulfilling his promises, as if God's promises were conditional (WA 53:460.23ff.). Luther and Christians through the ages have interpreted Shiloh as the Messiah, but the rabbis have "cackled" about the city Shiloh, about the coronation of Jeroboam in Shiloh (which in fact occurred in Shechem), about how Shiloh refers to Nebuchadnezzar as the one sent, about how the

one of the explanations of Luther's severe and often vulgar language. In the book *On the Jews and Their Lies*, Luther constantly returns to the central idea in Genesis 49:10. In this argument, he relies heavily on the late medieval apologetics against the Jews.[203]

Luther finds a second and new argument against the Jews' expectation of the Messiah and for the Christian belief in Jesus as the Messiah in the Old Testament's idea of God's eternal covenant with David and his house. In David's last words, he says: "The Spirit of the LORD spoke through me; his word was on my tongue. The God of Israel spoke, the Rock of Israel said to me .... Is not my house right with God? Has he not made with me an everlasting covenant, arranged and secured in every part?" (2 Samuel 23:32f., 5). In the following analysis, I attach some passages from the *Last Words of David*, which Luther wrote at the same time as *On the Jews and Their Lies*. In the foreword to the former book's thorough exposition of 2 Samuel 23:1–7, Luther emphasizes that the Old Testament is rightly understood only by the one who knows Christ and the New Testament's interpretation of the Old Testament (John 5:46; Luke 21:22; 24:27). He writes: "For that is the all-important point on which everything depends. Whoever does not have or want to have this Man properly and truly who is called Jesus Christ, God's Son, whom we Christians proclaim, must keep his hands off the Bible—that I advise. ... The more he studies, the blinder and more stupid will he grow, be he Jew, Tartar, Turk, Christian, or whatever he wants to call himself."[204] The rabbis possess a great grammatical knowledge, but they cannot understand the message of the Old Testament without Christ: "Furthermore, since the Jews repudiate this Christ, they cannot know or understand what Moses, the prophets, and the psalms are saying, what true faith is, what the Ten Commandments purport, what tradition and story teach and prove."[205] These passages summarize what Luther

---

Messiah would with physical power defeat the Gentiles, etc. (WA 53:456.20ff., 457.31ff., 458.25ff., 459.20ff., 460.14ff., 460.24ff.). When some Jewish commentators gave up on such ideas, they admitted that the Messiah came at the time of Jerusalem's destruction. But he had come secretly and hid himself among the beggars in Rome to await the repentance of the Jews and his open presentation (WA 53:461.5ff.).

203 That Luther draws from this late medieval apologetic and polemic (Nicolaus of Lyra, Raymund Martin, Paul of Burgos, Antonius Margaritha, and Salvagus Porchetus) against the rabbinical interpretation of Scripture is apparent in the following passages: WA 53:449.13f., 451.7ff., 452.21, 457.31ff., 458.25ff., 458.37ff., 459.20ff., 461.21ff. The footnotes in the Weimar Edition indicate which medieval apologists Luther uses. See also Lewin, *Luthers Stellung zu den Juden*, 86; and Bienert, *Martin Luther und die Juden*, 134ff.

204 LW 15:268 (WA 54:29.10ff.).

205 LW 15:269 (WA 54:30.1ff.).

means by the Christological interpretation of the Old Testament and his idea of the unity of the Old Testament and the New Testament—both of which are decisive for him.

First, the reformer points out in *On the Jews and Their Lies* that David claims to speak the words of the Spirit and of God. The words of the prophet in Scripture are God's own words and promises, which of course the Jewish interpreters will not deny.[206] Second, one must observe that the text in question clearly expresses that God will make a covenant with David that will remain forever. When God's and David's house have made this covenant eternal, David's house and government can never cease, all this according to God's Word through the dying prophet.[207] All attempts to place time limitations on the covenant with David are rejected by the reformer. David's house and the tribe of Judah have, of course, been forced into exile and temporarily are near extinction, but its visible government had, through the entire drama of history, maintained its power until the time of Herod.[208]

Here Luther's argumentation nears its climax when he asserts that Jesus is God's Messiah. If the Scriptures say that the covenant between God and the house of David is eternal, then it must also have remained during Herod's time. Indeed, the covenant remains even in Luther's time and forever.[209] The reformer reads the words of King David together with the prophecy of the patriarch Joseph (Genesis 49:10). In Luther's argument, both passages foresee a great epoch when Jesus as God's Messiah becomes the light of both the chosen people and the Gentiles and becomes the eternal Lord. Both texts actually show that the Messiah has already

---

206 WA 53:462.25ff., 463.8ff. Cf. *Last Words of David*, WA 54:34.30ff., about the authority of the prophetic word that derives from the authority of the trinitarian God.

207 LW 47:193 (WA 53:462.36ff.): "Oh, open your ears and listen! My house and God have bound themselves together forever through an oath. This is a covenant, a promise which must exist and endure forever. For it is God's covenant and pledge, which no one shall or can break or hinder." Cf. LW 47:193 (WA 53:463.8ff.): "Well and good, if God is truthful and almighty and spoke these words through David—which no Jew dares to deny—then David's house and government (which are the same thing) must have endured since the time he spoke these words, and must still endure and will endure forever—that is, eternally. Otherwise, God would be a liar. In brief, either we must have David's house or heir, who reigns from the time of David to the present and in eternity, or David died as a flagrant liar to his last day." Cf. WA 54:35.28ff., 38–97, which is an extended investigation on the basis of the Old Testament and to some degree of the New Testament.

208 WA 53:463.24–464.36. Cf. WA 54:39.36ff., 41.37ff., 95.6ff., etc., with extensive argumentation primarily on the basis of the Old Testament against those who want to Judaize and apply 2 Samuel 23:5 to Israel and to the building of the temple.

209 WA 53:465.1ff.

come and that it is precisely through Christ-Messiah that the reign and covenant become eternal. The texts establish the faith of the Christians, but the Jews are hardly convinced by this interpretation.[210] Even 2 Samuel 7:5–12 answers the question of how long David's house will last. Of course, some have attempted to interpret the text so it applies only to Solomon, but the reformer attempts to prove that this is an incorrect interpretation. Other texts, especially Psalm 89:2ff., 19ff., show that Scripture teaches that God's covenant with David and his house is eternal. This confirms the faith of the Christians. It actually convinces the consciences of the Jews, even if they do not want to admit that Jesus is God's Messiah.[211] Luther concludes:

> Now such an eternal house of David is nowhere to be found unless we place the scepter before the Messiah and the Messiah after the scepter, and then join the two together: namely, by asserting that the Messiah appeared when the scepter departed and that David's house was thus preserved forever. In that way God is found truthful and faithful in his word, covenant, and oath. For it is obvious that the scepter of Judah completely collapsed at the time of Herod, but much more so when the Romans destroyed Jerusalem and the scepter of Judah. Now if David's house is eternal and God truthful, then the true King of Judah, the Messiah, must have come at that time. No barking, interpreting, or glossing will change this.[212]

In Luther's apology for the Christian confession of Jesus' messiahship, the commentary on Jeremiah 33:17–26 also can be mentioned. Luther knows that the rabbis and their disciples believe the text is about the Messiah. But he calls them blind, hardened, and liars when they cannot admit that the Messiah is the same Jesus Christ who revealed himself 1,500 years ago. Therefore the reformer writes his apology, partly to strengthen and comfort the Christians, partly to touch the hard hearts of the Jews, even if there is only little hope that they will listen.[213] He summarizes by saying that David's house will reign forever, first through an earthly royal scepter until the Messiah comes, next through the Messiah's even greater glory forever. The eternal-spiritual government has already superceded the earthly when the royal scepter of Judah was destroyed 1,500 years ago. Thereby the Jews' expectation of the Messiah is given a decisive blow according to Luther.

---

210 WA 53:465.12ff.

211 WA 53:466.14ff., 466.27ff., 467.23ff., 468.6ff., 468.28ff. Cf. WA 54:38.20ff.

212 LW 47:199–200 (WA 53:468.16ff.).

213 WA 53:469.8–474.11. As he considers the Jeremiah text, Luther consistently says that the Jews are hopelessly blind and stiff-necked. However, sometimes a little hope that they might move and that they will change shines through. WA 53:470.20f., 470.29ff., 473.5f.

Christians can rejoice again that they have received the Messiah of whom the prophet spoke, that is, David's true Son, Jesus Christ, who will reign forever.[214]

Luther supports his thesis about Jesus as God's Messiah and the universality of God's salvation in him also with Haggai 2:7–10. The prophet speaks of a short time—it is too short to indicate the last 1,500 years of the Jews' distress—then God will send the comfort of the Gentiles, that is, the Messiah, with a message that shakes the entire world, a message about salvation from sin, death, and Satan. In this interpretation, Luther connects with the work of Nicolaus of Lyra and Paulus Burgensis.[215] He delivers an exceedingly polemical argument with the Bible interpretations of the rabbis;[216] with the Jews' deeply rooted hatred for those who say that the Messiah has come in Jesus Christ as the Savior for all peoples;[217] and, because the text speaks of silver and gold, with the Jews' greed for money and usury, which is not suppressed by the ruling authorities.[218] The reformer warns his own people against listening to Jewish anti-Christian propaganda. At the same he does not want to provoke his opponents to more blasphemy against Christ by his argumentation.[219] In his often boorish attacks on the rabbis, Luther does, of course, exactly that.

---

214 LW 47:202–3 (WA 53:470.21ff.): "We quote it because Jeremiah states that David's house will rule forever: first through the scepter up to the time of the Messiah, and after that much more gloriously through the Messiah. So it must be true that David's house has not ceased up to this hour and that it will not cease to eternity. But since the scepter of Judah departed fifteen hundred years ago, the Messiah must have come that long ago, or, as we have said above, 1,468 years ago. All of this is convincingly established by Jeremiah." Cf. WA 53:470.10ff., 472.1ff., 472.21ff., and especially 473.4ff.

215 See WA 53:476.14ff.–480.10 with the review of Lyra's and Burgensis's ideas in the footnotes. See also LW 47:214 (WA 53:480.11ff.): "Thus the verse reads: 'Once again, in a little while, I will shake the heavens and the earth and the sea and the dry land (these are the islands of the sea) and the *chemdath* of all Gentiles shall come'—that is, the Messiah, the Desire of all Gentiles, which we translated into German with the word *Trost* ['consolation']. . . . It would surely not be wrong to translate it with 'the joy and delight of all Gentiles.' In brief, it is the Messiah, who would be the object of displeasure, disgust, and abomination for the unbelieving and hardened Jews, as Isaiah 53 prophesies. The Gentiles, on the other hand, would bid him welcome as their heart's joy, delight, and every wish and desire. For he brings them deliverance from sin, death, devil, hell, and every evil, eternally." Luther compares Haggai 2:7–8 with Jacob's words in Genesis 49:10 (WA 53:479.24f., 483.23f., 485.2f.) and supports his argument with many other texts from the Old Testament. See also the arguments from history that complement the Bible arguments (WA 53:485ff.).

216 WA 53:477.11ff., 478.25ff., 479.2ff., 484.1ff.

217 The root to the conflict with the Jews is primarily the Christian belief that Jesus is the Messiah, even the Messiah of the Gentiles (WA 53:481.6–482.26, 483.19ff., 490ff.).

218 WA 53:482.27ff.

219 WA 53:479.24f., 481.35ff.

Because Luther in his examination of the seventy year-weeks in Daniel 9:24–27 says nothing different from what he had already written in 1523, I do not need to add anything here.[220] Luther is happy that the rabbis, himself, and, among others, Lyra and Burgensis all agree that Daniel 9:24 speaks of year-weeks (one week = seven years), so he can claim that it is a specific period of 490 years until the Messiah comes. He also remarks that there is some agreement that the seventy year-weeks or 490 years was fulfilled during the time of Jerusalem's destruction (Daniel 9:26).[221]

The reformer notes how even Jewish historiography and tradition admit that the Jews for 100 years before the destruction of Jerusalem—indeed, even for some time afterward—were eagerly occupied with the expectation of the chosen Messiah. When Herod, with the help of the Romans, was made king and Judah's scepter was on the way to its fall, the Jews looked for the Messiah. Many took up arms, and thousands of Jews were killed. John the Baptist announced the time of the Messiah, and Jesus himself appeared, preached, and did works of power. The simple people ran to the Messiah in their longing, but the religious and political leaders of the land rejected Jesus as too humble and crucified him. Nevertheless, the people and the leaders reckoned that it was the time of the Messiah and grumbled for forty years against Rome until the Roman leaders under Vespasian defeated the opposition with enormous suffering and flow of blood, took the land, and desolated Jerusalem, the kingdom, the temple, and the priesthood. In their expectation of a political Messiah, the Jews persecuted Christ's young church and during the years A.D. 70 to A.D. 100, Rabbi Akiba preached that the Messiah, according to the Scriptures, must already have come. So bar Kohba was brought forward. It was believed that he carried the scepter of Judah and was greeted as the lord over the Romans and Christians. But the Romans under Hadrian struck back and put a stop to all the enthusiasm. The Jews and their leaders waited for a Messiah especially before A.D. 70, but they rejected the idea that Jesus from Nazareth was God's Messiah, and they searched for a new, powerful Jewish David-figure. They ought to have understood that God's promises had been fulfilled in Jesus Christ, but especially their leaders and teachers were completely blocked to such an idea, claims the church historian Luther.[222]

After the Jews rejected the Christian Messiah and did not receive the Messiah they themselves expected and hoped for, and after they had been defeated by the Romans, they have for 1,400 years done nothing more than attempt to reinterpret

---

220 WA 53:492.7–511.24. Cf. *Luther and World Mission*, 356ff., for a thorough explanation in *That Christ Was Born a Jew.*

221 WA 53:492.23ff., 493.1ff.

222 WA 53:493.18–498.11.

and distort the prophecies of the Old Testament on which the Christians build their faith. It would require more space than our purpose allows to review how Luther argues against their so-called ten lies in their attempt to avoid Daniel 9:24–27. Luther uses severe words in this polemical passage.[223]

The reformer positively claims that Daniel 9:24 clearly predicts both when the Messiah will come and why he will come, that is, to take away sin and to bring righteousness through his death. Daniel's words are an iron wall and a rock that show that the Messiah must come before the seventy weeks or 490 years have elapsed and that the Messiah will suffer death, rise from the dead, and establish the new covenant before the land, the city, and the temple liturgy were desolated. The interpretations of the rabbis oppose the words of Scripture. They are a house of cards built by their hardness, a house that falls to the ground.[224] Daniel 9:24–27 establishes that Jesus was and is God's Messiah, no matter how the Jews lie and gesticulate. Luther is pessimistic. He does not consider it his task to convert those hardened by Satan, of which he considers the rabbis to be the primary examples. He wants primarily to reveal the flimsiness of their so-called house of cards and disclose the truth of Scripture about the Messiah. The one who will not receive and believe makes his own evil decision, means Luther.[225]

The reformer concludes his exegetical-apologetic examination of the Old Testament's predictions of the Messiah with the following words:

> We will limit ourselves for the time being to these four texts—those of Jacob, David, Haggai, and Daniel—wherein we see what a fine job the Jews have done these fifteen hundred years with Scripture, and what a fine job they still do. For their treatment of these texts parallels their treatment of all others, especially those that are in favor of us and our Messiah. These, of course, must be accounted as lies, whereas they themselves cannot err or be mistaken. However, they have not acquired a perfect mastery of the art of lying; they lie so clumsily and ineptly that anyone who is just a little observant can easily detect it.[226]

We have seen above that it is the question about Jesus' messiahship that is the decisive religious conflict in *On the Jews and Their Lies*. For Luther, there exists an

---

223 WA 53:498.12–510.5.

224 WA 53:492.13ff., 493ff., and especially 510.6ff.

225 WA 53:510.18ff. Stöhr, "Martin Luther und die Juden," 105, and Sucher, *Luthers Stellung zu den Juden*, 250f., have unfortunately not observed that Luther is primarily arguing with the rabbis—and their distortion of the Old Testament—when he says it is impossible and not commanded to convert the devil and his own. Their misperception leads them to consider the mission themes in *On the Jews and Their Lies* to be empty, pious wishes of the reformer.

226 LW 47:253 (WA 53:510.31ff.).

unavoidable religious chasm between those who deny and those who confess that Jesus of Nazareth is the Messiah. An icy front grows when the rabbis do everything to argue against Jesus' messiahship and when the Jews in general continue to wait for the Messiah. Luther's argumentation based on the texts of the Old Testament can surely be assailed by modern exegetes. That he, nevertheless, in all this kept an apologetic-missionary goal is a fact. But it ought not to be exaggerated. And it is often drowned in polemic and barking. If in the most missionary book (*That Christ Was Born a Jew*) Luther openly said that he partly wanted to win Jews and partly hoped to equip the Christians for mission among the Jews, so in 1543 it is primarily a question of a disputatious exposé of the Jewish rabbis and of protecting Christians against Jewish apologetics.

We have seen in *That Christ Was Born a Jew* that Luther argues against the rabbis' interpretation of the Old Testament and that he asserts Jesus' messiahship from, among other sources, these texts: Genesis 3:15; 22:18; 26:4; 28:14; 49:10–12; Daniel 9:24–27; Haggai 2:10; and Zechariah 8:23. In *Against the Sabbatarians* and *On the Jews and Their Lies*, the most powerful texts that speak for Jesus' messiahship are Genesis 49:10; 2 Samuel 23:1–7; 7:5–12; Psalm 89:2ff., 19ff.; Jeremiah 31:31–34; 33:17–26; Haggai 2:7–10; and Daniel 9:24–27. Because Luther is disputing with rabbinical interpretation and exegesis, he concentrates on arguments from the Old Testament. We have seen how Luther has sought by means of detailed studies, chronological schemes, and comparisons with the actual historical developments in Israel and the Orient to prove that the Messiah came when Herod became king and before the destruction of Jerusalem in A.D. 70. We have also been able to note that the reformer thought it important to emphasize that the Messiah should rule over a spiritual-eternal kingdom. After he has died and risen, the Christ should give forgiveness and eternal life to all peoples.

Because Luther sees the Bible as a unity and as a whole, he sometimes uses texts from the New Testament as well. Generally he interprets the Old Testament in light of the testimony of the New Testament and under the guidance of undeniable messianic Old Testament texts. He concludes that the messianic texts in the Old Testament cannot be interpreted and understood within the framework of Israel's history alone. The promises in the Old Testament have not been fulfilled definitively within the history of the Jewish people. Instead, they have been fulfilled in Christ and his church. The fulfillment of these promises gives blessing to all peoples, even to the Jews, if they in faith receive the Messiah-Christ of the promises. A consequence of this conclusion is that Luther must consider the rabbinical interpretations of the Old Testament and the faith of the Jews to be false. The Jews deny that the promised Messiah has come in Jesus Christ. According to the reformer, they tread on him through whom God wants to save them and all people. Indeed, they seek to lead Christians away from the only ground and source of faith and the forgiveness of sins to a context characterized by the Law and works. They oppose God's salvation and the way to righteousness with God.

Luther hopes that this program and this apology also will ensure the Christian character of the progressing evangelical research into the Old Testament. He often admits that the rabbis have much insight into the grammar and many of the detailed problems of the Old Testament. But he also believes that they have fundamentally misunderstood and misinterpreted the Old Testament. Therefore Luther polemically lunges against the rabbis' use of the Old Testament. Luther criticizes his friend Sebastian Münster because in his knowledgeable translation of the Old Testament (1534/1535), he allows himself to be too influenced by the opinions of the rabbis. So he warns evangelical Christianity about the Jewish, exclusively historical exegesis and understanding of the Old Testament. The reformer wants to start from the view of the Old Testament possessed by the New Testament and the early church in which the key to understanding the Old Testament is Christ.[227] For Luther, there is much at stake. Either one follows a way in which Christ will be denied or one follows a way in which Christ opens the Scriptures and becomes the only ground to and source of salvation. Luther can absolutely not accept a double accounting in which the historical exegesis produces one result and preaching another.

Because historical-critical research has dominated most of the areas of theological research in our time, there also has been much criticism of Luther's Old Testament hermeneutic. Maurer criticizes Luther's use of historical reason and chronological calculations in the debate about the Messiah. He also questions whether or not the Old Testament's historical side is brushed aside by the reformer's Christological interpretations of the Old Testament.[228] Loewenich means that Luther's Christological interpretation of the messianic texts of the Old Testament cannot be accepted. He openly claims that modern historical and rabbinical exegesis generally agree. Kurt Meier claims that Luther subcribes to a biblical positivism and exclusive claims in the doctrine of justification, so he can see no truth in Judaism and other religions. Bienert also sees a new possibility for a rapprochement because the radical German exegetical and systematic theology has destroyed the doctrines of the Trinity, Christ's divinity, and the virgin birth.

---

227 Cf. Maurer, "Die Zeit der Reformation," 414f. About Luther's relation to Jewish work on the Scriptures, see also Lewin, *Luthers Stellung zu den Juden,* 51ff.

228 Maurer, "Die Zeit der Reformation," 389ff., 410ff. Cf. Stöhr, "Martin Luther und die Juden," 103. He warns against Luther's spiritualizations of the texts and message of the Old Testament when he ignores concrete history. As we have seen, however, the history of Israel and the Orient is important for Luther. This history is nevertheless spiritually significant because it touches the life of Jesus Christ and his eternal-spiritual reign. See also the critique in Erling, "Martin Luther and the Jews," 70ff.

Especially Meier and Bienert believe that the identity of Christian faith has been ripped apart by modern exegesis. Mission among Jews is considered unnecessary and is replaced with dialogue under a panreligious horizon.[229]

I and many others are grateful for the enlightenment into questions about details and context that the historical research of the Old Testament has recently provided. It has, however, for some time surprised me that so many Old Testament exegetes are so preoccupied by the previous and contemporary histories' obvious facts in connection with the messianic texts that they apparently do not or will not see that these texts speak of a Messiah with more than earthly blessings, namely, one with eternal and spiritual blessings. In this way, they distance themselves both from what the texts in fact say or imply about the Messiah and from the classical Christian interpretation of the texts.

Unless the New Testament's use of the Old Testament is to be considered a distortion and if the Old Testament is not to become a dead book that is impossible to use in Christian worship and preaching, then one must reckon with a depth dimension to the Old Testament, just as Jesus, the New Testament, the early

---

229 Loewenich, *Martin Luther: Der Mann und das Werk*, 335 (English: 352), says in his conclusion: "Today we can no longer accept Luther's messianic interpretation that pointed directly to Christ. With the exception of a few passages, the portrayal of the Messiah in the Old Testament does not correspond to our conception of Christ. The historical interpretation of the rabbis is closer to our contemporary understanding than is Luther's Christological exegesis, which admittedly bound him to a tradition that stretched back to the New Testament itself." Meier, "Zur Interpretation von Luthers Judenschriften," 144f., believes that Luther is bound to a so-called biblical positivism and exclusive claims in the doctrine of justification that means that he cannot be open to the truth in Judaism and other religions as Vatican II is. The doctrine of justification is said to be particularistic. Meier apparently does not understand the exclusivity in the New Testament texts about faith in Christ to which he, by the way, does not refer. He also has failed to understand that Luther's doctrine of *iustificatio sola fide* has its foundation and sharpest point in *Christus solus*. Bienert, *Martin Luther und die Juden*, 195–202, criticizes the unnecessary dominance of dogma in Luther's dispute with Judaism. Bienert writes that the doctrines of Christ's divinity and preexistence, about the Trinity, the virgin birth, etc., are antiquated according to many scholars and even according to the contributions of the rabbis. Both Jews and Christians ought to continue the effort to approach one another. Especially Romans 9–11 ought to be an area for continued research by Christians. The 1983 Stockholm Declaration that was the result of a meeting between Jews and Lutherans consists of rejections and regrets for the Luther texts that have become sources for racism and anti-Semitism. Unfortunately, the integrity of Christianity and mission among Jews falls to ground in the conclusion of the document: "Wir bekräftigen Integrität und Würde unserer beiden Glaubensgemeinschaften und lehnen jede organisierte Kampagne zur Bekehrung der Angehörigen des aderen Glaubens ab." The quotation is from *Friede über Israel* (1983), 181, cited in Pfisterer, "Zwischen Polemik und Apologetik," 122.

church, and Luther does. I believe that Luther has understood something important and completely decisive for Christian faith when he claims that God's successive revelation in history is described in the Old Testament and the New Testament taken together and that this history has its center in Jesus Christ. It is only then that one has a Christian understanding of the Old Testament, indeed, an understanding of a Christian theology and identity.[230]

Of course, this led to a religious-theological conflict with Judaism, which also sought to ensure its own identity. But this conflict ought not to have led to the barking and the inhuman proposals concerning the handling of the Jews to which especially the older Luther resorted and that I shall now address.

LUTHER AND JEWISH SLANDERS AGAINST THE CHRISTIAN FAITH

For the first two centuries after the birth of Christ, the Jews persecuted the Christians. In literature, teaching, and interpersonal contact, the Jews and their rabbis often presented nonfactual accusations and slanders against the Christians and the Christian faith, even up to and including the time of the Reformation. Luther is correct that there are no lambs in the continuing conflict between Judaism and Christianity—even if Christians acted worse when they became a majority.

Luther reacts because the Jews and their teachers accuse the Christians of polytheism and defection from monotheism because they confess one God in three persons. The reformer is especially alarmed that the rabbis accuse the Christians of polytheism despite the fact that they know quite well that Christians oppose all forms of polytheism in accordance with Deuteronomy 7:6–8. Furthermore, they say they cannot understand faith in the Holy Trinity. The rabbis judge and insult the Christians concerning matters that they themselves admit they do not understand.[231]

In one passage, Luther deals primarily with the coarse slanders and lies of the Jewish teachers against Jesus Christ, the Virgin Mary, and Christians. He means

---

230 See Ehrlich, "Luther und die Juden," 142f., about how Luther understands the exegesis of the rabbis not only as a blindness but also as an attack on the Christian faith as such. See above all Brosseder, *Luthers Stellung zu den Juden*, 382ff., and his discussion of Kurt Meier's (n211) critique of Luther's doctrine of justification and about the importance of that doctrine to Luther and Christianity. Unfortunately, Brosseder (pp. 387ff.) concludes by remarking that Luther's doctrine of justification ought not be universalized too much.

231 WA 53:539.12–541.5. Cf. *Last Words of David*, WA 54:35ff., in which Luther against, among others, Jews and Turks develops the doctrine of the Trinity. Luther naturally did not mean that any person could fully understand God's being. The doctrine of the Trinity is believed because Scripture teaches it. Cf. *Luther and World Mission*, 460–61.

that the Jews are forced to attack these individuals because they cannot get any-where in their criticism of Christian exegesis and doctrine.[232] The Jewish teachers have called Jesus a wizard and a witness of the devil and have deprived Christians of the name of their Messiah, Jesus (that is, Savior and Helper).[233] They have called Jesus the son of a whore and said that Mary was a heap of dung or a *haria*.[234] This hate and these slanders have even been applied to the Christians who are despised for honoring these wretched individuals (that is, Mary and Jesus) long after they have died. The Jews also pray that God will liberate the chosen people from exile among the Christians. They pray for God to send them the true and powerful Messiah who will destroy the Christians with military might and make Israel the lords of the world.[235]

Luther reacts violently against these slanders of Jesus, Mary, and the Christians and against the Jews' idea that they are captives in the Christian West. It is actually quite the opposite: Everyone wants the Jews to go on their way. That no one wants the Jews to remain in their lands is proven by the fact that the Jews have been dri-ven from France, Spain, and Bohemia and even from Regensburg and Magdeburg in Germany. The Jews are considered a plague and a pest among the peoples

---

232 WA 53:511.25–520.7. Scholars have shown that the Jews in their slanders could be perfectly horrendous. See Maurer, "Die Zeit der Reformation," 409; Oberman, *Wurzeln des Antisemitismus*, 125–34; Bienert, *Martin Luther und die Juden*, 141ff.; and Tjernagel, *Martin Luther and the Jewish People*, 59ff. The footnotes in the Wiemar Edition indicate from which sources Luther draws when he gives examples of Jewish slanders. Among others, the work of Antonius Margaritha, Luther's contemporary and the professor of Hebrew in Vienna, is cited. Margaritha had converted to Christianity from Judaism in 1520 and published his *magnum opus, Der gantze jüdische Glaube*, in 1530.

233 The following are a pair of examples. LW 47:256 (WA 53:513): "In the first place, they defame our Lord Jesus Christ, calling him a sorcerer and a tool of the devil. This they do because they cannot deny his miracles. Thus they imitate their forefathers, who said, 'He casts out demons by Beelzebub, the prince of demons' [Luke 11:15]. They invent many lies about the name of God, the tetragrammaton, saying that our Lord was able to define the name (which they call *Schem Hamphoras*), and whoever is able to do that, they say, is also able to perform all sorts of miracles." See also WA 53:513.20ff., 514.3ff.

234 For the slanders against Jesus' origin, see LW 47:257–58 (WA 53:514.18ff.): "Then they also call Jesus a whore's son, saying that his mother Mary was a whore, who con-ceived him in adultery with a blacksmith. . . . Now they know very well that these lies are inspired by sheer hatred and spite, solely for the purpose of bitterly poisoning the minds of their poor youth and the simple Jews against the person of our Lord, lest they adhere to his doctrine (which they cannot refute)." Concerning the words about Mary as a whore or dung heap and Luther's severe responses, see WA 53:515.9ff., 516.29ff., 517.31ff., 518.9ff.

235 WA 53:519.19ff.

partly because through their usury they oppress and enslave those who work for them and partly because they slander the faith of Christians. Nevertheless, in most of the West, Jews are given freedom to travel, to live and to work with their business and banking ventures, and to continue their religious teaching.[236] The Jewish remarks that Luther reports could easily contribute to anti-Jewish sentiment among his readers.

We remind ourselves that in the early 1520s the reformer intensely hoped for the conversion of the Jews and energetically emphasized that they ought to be met in a friendly spirit and to be given the right to work, which any other citizen in the realm had.[237] In 1543 there is not much left of Luther's hope or friendliness or his defense of the civil rights of the Jews. Apparently because of their usury, their unrepentance, and their slanders against Christianity, the Jews have made themselves impossible even for Luther. They prove themselves to be examples of the darkness and the wrath of God that strikes those who slander Christ and the Christians. The reformer responds with pronouncements against the Jews that are at least as severe as their pronouncements against Christ and the Christians.[238]

It is a mystery how Luther believes he can win Jews for Christianity with fury and wretched vocabulary. However, Luther concludes his discourse on the slanders of the Jews with the following propositions and prayer that God might turn his wrath away from the Jews:

> The wrath of God has overtaken them. I am loath to think of this, and it has not been a pleasant task for me to write this book, being obliged to resort now to anger, now to satire, in order to avert my eyes from the terrible picture which they present. It has pained me to mention their horrible blasphemy concerning our Lord and his dear mother, which we Christians are grieved to hear. I can well understand what St. Paul means in Romans 10 [9:2] when he says that he is saddened as he considers them. . . . O God, heavenly Father, relent and let your wrath over them be sufficient and come to an end, for the sake of your dear Son! Amen.[239]

Thus Luther thinks and prays before his severe practical and legal proposals, which follow immediately thereafter. He has not altogether given up on the Jews. God can still create something new.

---

236 WA 53:520.26–522.19.

237 See *Luther and World Mission*, 345ff., 361ff.

238 WA 53:522.20ff. Concerning Luther's severe writings against the Jews, see the many examples in Lewin, *Luthers Stellung zu den Juden*, 87ff., 93ff.; and Sucher, *Luthers Stellung zu den Juden*, 74–84.

239 LW 47:291–92 (WA 53:541, 541.11ff., 541.22ff.).

The inhuman proposals of the concrete measures to take against the Jews

Luther functioned from about 1530 as the indisputable leader and father of doctrine for the growing Evangelical churches. In this role, he had partly a responsibility to his call as theologian and spiritual leader and partly an advisory function vis-à-vis the electors, who in the German state church system functioned as bishops in emergency. Therefore Luther had, according to what I have written above, sought to teach Jews and strengthen the Christians with his biblical theology of the Messiah. But he is, therefore, also forced to go one step further. He must give some concrete advice to the electors, barons, and magistrates. Luther has also written by request uncountable *Gutachten* (opinions) to ruling authorities on a variety of questions, mostly related to social ethics and religious politics.[240]

In his proposals concerning how the authorities should handle the Jews, the reformer claims that one shares in the lies, curses, and slanders of the Jews just by allowing them to openly and freely continue as they have done up to now. God's wrath burns against the Jews, yet they do not convert. In this predicament, Luther wants to show the Jews a "severe mercy" through these new concrete measures. This is primarily to save some from unbelief and eternal perdition if possible. However, one ought not take revenge on the Jews because God's wrath and revenge has for some time rested on them. This theme about sharing in the sins of others weighs heavily in Luther's proposal (it is, after all, nothing more than a proposal) of concrete measures against the Jews. One even sees that the reformer's outline for severe mercy occurs after prayer, has a goal to save Jews from unbelief, and ought not be considered as an unspiritual revenge.[241] Luther's proposal is also

---

240 See Bienert, *Martin Luther und die Juden*, 115ff., 145ff. Bienert believes that the young reformer's faith in the power of the Gospel and the right of the individual to receive it freely had been entrapped by an absolute Christian state religion that unifies the laws of state and church and lays denial of generally accepted truths of the faith under the punishment of the state. Luther's central theology of the Word and faith has, according to Bienert, not been changed, but in the new politicization of the state church system, Luther sharpens his demand for the adherence of the citizens to the official faith. According to Bienert, one ought therefore to seek the answer to the riddle of Luther's previously unknown severity against the Jews in neither his eruptive nature nor in some postulated senile dementia. There is, as we shall see, much to say for Bienert's thesis, even if the reformer in the *Gutachten* cannot be considered as some sort of lackey to the electors. One also ought to take with a pinch of salt Bienert's idea that Luther became more dogmatic through the years. Here Bienert's own liberal theology plays a trick on him. We will also see that the older Luther has not at all lost his faith in the power of the Gospel. He also never retracted his belief that no one ought to force another to heart belief. In these ways, I am critical of Bienert.

241 LW 47:268 (WA 53:522.29ff.): "What shall we Christians do with this rejected and condemned people, the Jews? Since they live among us, we dare not tolerate their conduct,

motivated by consideration of the usury of the Jews and their banking practices.

Because of the Jews' ignoble slanders, usury, and unwillingness to do honest work, Luther decides that the ruling authorities ought to deport the Jews precisely as is done in other lands.[242] All this despite the fact that the deportation mandate was rescinded in Saxony in 1538.

If now the Jews have the legal right to sojourn in the region of Saxony, the reformer proposes a seven-point program. Above all, this so-called severe mercy involves proposals relevant to the Jews' practice of religion and worship.[243] So the Germans might not share in the slanders and the sins of the Jews, the synagogues ought to be burned down, just as pagan temples were in ancient Israel. Public, false worship of God and slanders against Christ and the Christians ought not be tolerated in Christian lands.[244] One ought also to burn Jewish devotional literature

---

now that we are aware of their lying and reviling and blaspheming. If we do, we become sharers in their lies, cursing, and blasphemy. Thus we cannot extinguish the unquenchable fire of divine wrath, of which the prophets speak, nor can we convert the Jews. With prayer and the fear of God we must practice a sharp mercy to see whether we might save at least a few from the glowing flames. We dare not avenge ourselves. Vengeance a thousand times worse than we could wish them already has them by the throat. I shall give you my sincere advice."

242 LW 47:272 (WA 53:526.9ff.): "But if we are afraid that they might harm us or our wives, children, servants, cattle, etc., if they had to serve and work for us—for it is reasonable to assume that such noble lords of the world and venomous, bitter worms are not accustomed to working and would be very reluctant to humble themselves so deeply before the accursed Goyim—then let us emulate the common sense of other nations such as France, Spain, Bohemia, etc., compute with them how much their usury has extorted from us, divide this amicably, but then eject them forever from the country. For, as we have heard, God's anger with them is so intense that gentle mercy will only tend to make them worse and worse, while sharp mercy will reform them but little. Therefore, in any case, away with them!" Cf. WA 53:538.1ff., 538.7ff., about how the Jews' secret but well-known slanders of the Christian faith can never be squared with anything but deportation.

243 The seven proposals to the ruling authorities can be found in WA 53:523.1–526.16, 536.19–537.17. Nearly all scholars who have considered the theme "Luther and the Jews" have touched on Luther's seven-point program. See *Luther and World Mission*, 326–34, and especially the survey in Maurer, "Die Zeit der Reformation," 416–27.

244 LW 47:268 (WA 53:523.1ff.): "First, to set fire to their synagogues or schools and to bury and cover with dirt whatever will not burn, so that no man will ever again see a stone or cinder of them. This is to be done in honor of our Lord and of Christendom, so that God might see that we are Christians, and do not condone or knowingly tolerate such public lying, cursing, and blaspheming of his Son and of his Christians. For whatever we tolerated in the past unknowingly—and I myself was unaware of it—will be pardoned by God. But if we, now that we are informed, were to protect and shield such a house for the Jews, existing right before our very nose, in which they lie about,

and the Talmud and forbid the rabbis from teaching because Jewish unbelief and slanders are spread by these means. Public Jewish worship with teaching, singing, and prayer that attacks and slanders the Christian faith can continue in their own land but not in Germany. Here we see the general rule in the European religious politics of Luther's time: *cuius regio, eius religio*.[245] In these proposals, both a religious conflict and the state church context speak, a context in which neither religious freedom nor pluralism is accepted. The mission motif is also an element of these proposals. The conversion of the Jews is projected into a hypothetical future after the discipline of the severe mercy has had time to open them for the Gospel.

Luther's proposals to the electors and magistrates affect to the highest degree the human living conditions of the Jews. So they are not able to consider themselves lords in the land, he suggests that they be quarantined in special houses after their own housing has been destroyed. The Jews are really neither nobility nor priests nor merchants; therefore they do not have a given place in the realm. One ought to refuse them the right to free passage if one hopes to avoid sharing in their unrighteous usury.[246] One ought definitely to forbid all their usury and confiscate their cash resources and silver goods that have, in fact, been stolen from the German people.[247] Finally, one ought to give the young Jews hand tools so they can learn to produce their own daily bread through honorable work.[248]

---

blaspheme, curse, vilify, and defame Christ and us (as was heard above), it would be the same as if we were doing all this and even worse ourselves, as we very well know." Cf. WA 53:536.23ff. It is worth noting how Luther (WA 53:523.13ff.) motivates the destruction of synagogues, etc., by referring to what Moses says about the destruction of the cities in which one worships other gods and breaks the law of the land (Deuteronomy 13:13ff.; 4:2; 12:32; cf. 1 Samuel 15:23). In 1521–1522, Luther warned Karlstadt and others about their confiscation and destruction of churches, paintings, and Roman Catholic worship. One ought to preach the Gospel and faith, then right worship would grow out of a right faith without force. In 1543 Luther proposes other-wise.

245 WA 53:523.30ff., 536.29ff., 536.34ff., 537.6ff. Cf. also WA 53:527.32ff., 528.5ff., 528.18ff., the challenges to pastors and other preachers. They must warn their parish members against regular and peaceful interaction with Jews so they are not spiritually damaged by Jewish proselytism. The pastors and preachers must not, however, profusely curse the Jews, and they must absolutely not cause any bodily damage to the Jews. All potential punishments are a matter for the civil authorities.

246 WA 53:523.24ff., 524.6ff.

247 WA 53:524.18–525.30. Luther does not approve of the idea of a moderate usury based on Deuteronomy 23:20. Whatever is said about the right to interest from Gentiles applies only to the Jews who wait for the Messiah in Canaan, not for his contemporary Jews who are dispersed among the peoples. There is a difference between *des Moses Juden* and *des Keisers Juden*. Concerning the theme about usury and how the authorities receive money from usury in exchange for opening their land to the Jews, see WA 53:538.14ff., 538.36.

248 WA 53:525.31ff.

Luther counts on a two-step model. First, one ought to allow the Jews to live in the land while being subject to thoroughgoing restrictions on their religious and social freedom. Luther has little hope that this severe mercy will help them come to their senses. The Jews do not know what they are doing, and as demon-possessed people, they do not want to know, hear, or learn anything. Loving mercy and full religious and social freedom contributes, therefore, only to the solidification of their present positions.

The second step is the only one that will help, according to Luther. If the authorities do not want to or cannot put these restrictions into effect and if the Jews oppose them so that the hoped-for result is not achieved, then the Jews ought to be deported out of the land as an alien element, sent gladly to Israel where they can freely exercise their religious and social life. In such a way, one escapes sharing in God's wrath and condemnation of the Jews by not indulging their sins.[249]

It will be apparent that Luther doubts that it will be possible to accomplish the first step. That which the Jews are forbidden to do publicly, they will continue to do in secret. Therefore deportation is the only real solution—for both Jews and Germans. He writes:

> But what will happen even if we do burn down the Jews' synagogues and forbid them publicly to praise God, to pray, to teach, to utter God's name? They will keep doing it in secret. If we know that they are doing this in secret, it is the same as if they were doing it publicly. For our knowledge of their secret doings and our toleration of them implies that they are not secret after all, and thus our conscience is encumbered with it before God. So let us beware. . . . If we wish to wash our hands of the Jews' blasphemy and not share in their guilt, we have to part company with them. They must be driven from our country. Let them think of their fatherland; then they need no longer wail and lie before God against us that we are holding them captive, nor need we then any longer complain that they are burdening us with their blasphemy and

---

[249] LW 47:292 (WA 53:541.25ff., 541.33ff.): "I wish and I ask that our rulers who have Jewish subjects exercise a sharp mercy toward these wretched people, as suggested above, to see whether this might not help (though it is doubtful). . . . They surely do not know what they are doing; moreover, as people possessed, they do not wish to know it, hear it, or learn it. Therefore it would be wrong to be merciful and confirm them in their conduct. If this does not help we must drive them out like mad dogs, so that we do not become partakers of their abominable blasphemy and all their other vices and thus merit God's wrath and be damned with them. I have done my duty. Now let everyone see to his. I am exonerated." Cf. WA 53:529.18ff., 529.28ff., 530.10ff., 532.1ff., 538.1ff., with, among others, the advice to evangelical pastors.

their usury. This is the most natural and the best course of action, which will safeguard the interest of both parties.[250]

It is remarkable that the scholars have generally made nothing of the fact that Luther in this primarily religious conflict understands deportation of the Jews as the only true solution that can ensure the religious practice of *both* the Christians and the Jews. The scholars have been so occupied by the severe proposals of the first step (above) and the rightful critique of it.

We ought here to see some of the fundamental beliefs that are behind the drastic proposals listed primarily under the first step above. Here there are several themes: First, the reformer believes that one cannot permit open slanders against the Christian faith and an economic oppression of the people through thieving usury. If one does so permit, one shares in the sins of the Jews and falls under God's wrath and condemnation. This is one of Luther's most important and recurring arguments.[251]

Second, Luther argues from the idea of *unum corpus Christianum* and the Germans as a Christian people. In lands where Christianity is publicly and legally recognized as the official religion, public slanders against the Christian faith and against Christians and economic oppression cannot be tolerated. Luther argues here on the basis of the known rule in contemporary European religion politics, that is, that the subjects will swear allegiance to the official religion of the ruling authorities. Those who seek to spread another teaching must be silent or emigrate.[252]

---

250 LW 47:287–88 (WA 53:538.1ff.).

251 WA 53:522.30f., 523.4ff., 524.16f., 528.18ff., 542.1ff., and especially 527.15ff. See Brosseder, *Luthers Stellung zu den Juden*, 371f., who emphasizes the idea of sharing in the sins of the Jews. See also Stöhr, "Martin Luther und die Juden," 101f.

252 LW 47:275 (WA 53:528.18ff.): "We cannot help it that they do not share our belief. It is impossible to force anyone to believe. However, we must avoid confirming them in their wanton lying, slandering, cursing, and defaming. Nor dare we make ourselves partners in their devilish ranting and raving by shielding and protecting them, by giving them food, drink, and shelter, or by other neighborly acts, especially since they boast so proudly and despicably when we do help and serve them that God has ordained them as lords and us as servants." LW 47:276 (WA 53:529.18ff.): "But if the authorities are reluctant to use force and restrain the Jews' devilish wantonness, the latter should, as we said, be expelled from the country and be told to return to their land and their possessions in Jerusalem, where they may lie, curse, blaspheme, defame, murder, steal, rob, practice usury, mock, and indulge in all those infamous abominations which they practice among us, and leave us our government, our country, our life and our property, much more leave our Lord the Messiah, our faith and our church undefiled and uncontaminated with their devilish tyranny and malice. Any privileges that they may plead shall not help them; for no one can grant privileges for practicing

Third, the reformer wants to make certain that one must differentiate between personal, secret unbelief and publicly proclaimed conviction. It cannot be tolerated in an officially Christian land that the Jews publicly in their worship space and before the eyes of all seek to win converts. Nevertheless, the reformer makes it clear that no one can or ought to be forced in matters of faith. The Jews ought to be allowed in their own land and in secret to speak against the New Testament and Christian faith, but they ought not to do it openly or in a way that someone else could know about it in Germany. Neither ought individual Christians be allowed to curse Jews or cause them any harm. It is the ruling authority that ought to take its responsibility vis-à-vis the usury, slanders, and proselytism of the Jews.[253]

---

such abominations. These cancel and abrogate all privileges." Cf. WA 53:523.3ff., 526.31–527.14ff., 532.7ff., 538.1ff. See also Brosseder, *Luthers Stellung zu den Juden*, 368ff., about how unrepentance for heresy (*pertinacitas*) during the Middle Ages cost the heretic his or her life and how Luther considered the Jewish works-righteousness and blasphemy of Jesus to be idolatry. What Luther proposes existed in many earlier and contemporary documents. See especially Bienert, *Martin Luther und die Juden*, 145ff. He emphasizes how Luther was trying to preserve religious unity and that legally Christians didn't need to tolerate public blasphemies against the Christian faith. Luther follows in his proposals much of what was self-evident about Western Christian monoculture in earlier and contemporary history. Hardt, "Luther," 72ff., shows that Luther claimed unity for the religion of the realm in, among other places, the foreword to the Small Catechism. This meant that Jews, Anabaptists, and Roman Catholics were forced to move from Lutheran regions. But if the ruling authority was not Lutheran, Lutherans would usually also move.

253 LW 47:275 (WA 53:528.18ff.): "We cannot help it that they do not share our belief. It is impossible to force anyone to believe. However, we must avoid confirming them in their wanton lying, slandering, cursing, and defaming." LW 47:279 (WA 53:531.34ff.): "Of course, we accord anyone the right not to believe *omissive et privatim* ['by neglect and privately']; this we leave to everyone's conscience. But to parade such unbelief so freely in churches and before our very noses, eyes, and ears, to boast of it, to sing it, teach it, and defend it, to revile and curse the true faith, and in this way lure others to them and hinder our people—that is a far, far diffferent story." LW 47:279 (WA 53:532.8ff.): "It will not do for them to say at this point: 'We Jews care nothing about the New Testament or about the belief of the Christians.' Let them express such sentiments in their own country or secretly. In our country and in our hearing they must suppress these words, or we will have to resort to other measures." Cf. also WA 53:538.1ff. Luther's idea that it is the Christian ruling authority alone who ought to intervene against public slander and usury exists in, among other passages, WA 53:528.1ff., 528.31ff. Aland, "Toleranz und Glaubensfreiheit im 16. Jahrhundert," 76ff., has argued that in *On the Jews and Their Lies* Luther in fact holds up the same rule he had developed in *On Temporal Authority* (1523) (WA 11:261ff.) that the temporal authority may not force or forbid belief as it concerns personal (!) faith convictions. The temporal authority does not rule over the soul, the heart, and faith. The quotations above obviously show that there is a difference between open and secret false teaching in an officially Christian country. See also Hardt, "Luther," 72f.

Fourth, the reformer believes that taking measures with a severe mercy against those Jews who continue to live in Germany ought to function as a healing discipline in which severity and punishment are used for the goal that the Jews eventually will become less hardbound to their unbelief. Luther compares this with the surgeon's severe measures in healing gangrene and with Moses' severity in the desert so the entire people of Israel might not become depraved (Exodus 32:21–29). If the Jews are allowed to develop their religious and social life freely, they will become strengthened in their unbelief and in their heavy-handed and evil business practices.[254] In some ways, Luther considers it a necessity to allow room for God's wrath or at any rate not to hinder its work. Even if he connects this idea to a potential revival among the Jews, his train of thought here can only barely be united with what one generally connects with Luther and what we discovered in *That Christ Was Born a Jew*.

One can only unreservedly regret and reject Luther's seven-point program proposed to the electors for the handling of the Jews, even if it has parallels in Luther's time, even if the Jews were forbidden to live in Norway until 1850. The inhuman proposal does not fit in with what the reformer taught about the mission of the church and evangelization and about human life together. We probably ought to follow the reformer's own advice and bury some meters underground whatever he taught against Scripture. As luck would have it, the ruling authorities did not follow Luther's proposal. Many of Luther's contemporary Protestant theologians did not accept it either.[255] Because the Nazi ideologues did in fact exploit the reformer's later writings as support for the persecution and murder of the Jews, Luther's unfortunate writings have been criticized and rejected from many different points of view.[256]

---

254 WA 53:528.20ff., 528.36ff., and especially 541.27ff. On the severe mercy as a medicine and a help toward the conversion of the Jews, see Stöhr, "Martin Luther und die Juden," 104f. Luther's proposals cannot be considered "mercy." Meier, "Zur Interpretation von Luthers Judenschriften," 144f., has meant that Luther's Scripture principle led him to the point at which he could not succeed at giving the doctrine of justification a reasonable and human application in relationship to the life and faith of the Jews. Luther becomes a particularist vis-à-vis the Jews on the basis of his work with the Bible. Brosseder, *Luthers Stellung zu den Juden*, 382ff., claims, however, under the critical thesis "dass die Universalisierung der Rechtfertigungslehre Luther zu seinen harten Ratschlägen gegen das Judentum verleitet hat." Brosseder (389) points out how Luther's idea that God's wrath as *opus alienum* can also serve God's *opus proprium* could have affected his reactions to the Jews.

255 See Lewin, *Luthers Stellung zu den Juden*, 97ff., 102f.; and Cohrs, *Einleitung zu der Schrift "Von den letzen Worten Davids,"* in WA 54:16ff.

256 See the collection of essays edited by Kremers, *Die Juden und Martin Luther*. See also Müller, "Tribut an den Geist seiner Zeit," 308, with a balanced and clear critique of

There is a great unity now among scholars that Luther never intended to prepare the way for something such as World War II's concentration camps and
Holocaust, an idea that some who have considered the matter only in a shallow
manner have chosen to support.[257] Generally, Luther does not allow the authorities to take revenge on the Jews. It ought to be observed, however, that Luther
reckons a hard punishment from the ruling authorities for murderers, those who
charge usury, and those who publicly blaspheme. But these rules apply just as
much to Germans as to Jews.[258]

In a special section, Luther encourages the evangelical pastors in places with
Jewish populations to consider their responsibility to the ruling authorities. They
ought to teach the electors about their responsibility to God vis-à-vis the Jews.
The authorities must force the Jews to work, forbid them to charge usury, and prevent them from slandering and cursing Christ and the Christians. Because such
transgressions break public law and lead to punishment among German Christians, there is no reason to allow them among the Jews. Their gratitude for being
able to suck the land dry of its resources and for being able to live in wealth is to
curse Christ, the church, the electors, and all German citizens and wish on them
unhappiness and death.[259] If the electors will not force and rein in the Jews, then

---

Luther's relation to medieval and contemporary handling of the Jews. Luther was not
infallible. In his section "Hass ohne Mass" ("Zwischen Polemik und Apologetik,"
106ff.), Pfisterer is critical of the older Luther, whom he accuses of betraying the evangelical vector. Luther regresses to medieval and contemporary anti-Judaism in his
inhuman proposal. Maser, "Erbarmen für Luther?" 166ff., 173ff., means that by claiming that Luther was dependent on the Middle Ages, on his own contemporary time,
and on eschatological fear, etc., Bienert and Oberman have made Luther's late mistakes
into a merely occasional divergence. Maser likens Luther's anti-Judaism to Hitler's;
therefore he misses the mark in his critique.

257 Bienert, *Martin Luther und die Juden*, 129f., 152ff. He says: "Luther wies nicht den Weg
nach 'Auschwitz'. Nie—auch nicht in seinen wütendsten Angriffen auf die Juden bzw.
deren Religion—hat er ein Töten von Juden angeregt oder auch nur gutgeheissen"
(152f.). Cf. also Müller, "Tribut an den Geist seiner Zeit," 308, and the similar severe
critique in Pfisterer, "Zwischen Polemik und Apologetik," 107.

258 LW 47:268 (WA 53:522.34ff.): "With prayer and the fear of God we must practice a
sharp mercy . . . . We dare not avenge ourselves. Vengeance a thousand times worse
than we could wish them already has them by the throat." Cf. also the later statements
against killing the Jews in WATr 5:246.23ff., 247.12ff. (no. 5567). See also WA
53:527.32ff. about the prohibition against allowing Christians to harm Jews. Nevertheless, the eye of the historian sees that according to Luther the electors (!) ought to
punish severely—even with the death penalty—murder, economic oppression, and the
illegal public (!) blasphemy against the Christian faith that may occur even among the
Jews (WA 53:522.7ff., 536.34ff.).

259 WA 53:528.31ff.

the Jews simply must be deported and go to their own country. There they can charge usury and blaspheme and leave German Christianity, its Messiah, faith, and church in peace.[260] Luther is, in fact, fearful that both the ruling authorities and the general population will fail to understand the evil of the Jews, their economic oppression, their unwillingness to hear God's Word, and their horrible slanders against God, Christ, and the Christians. He is worried that the ruling authorities will exercise an undeserved mercy and indulgence that will only strengthen the Jews primarily in their slanders and profiteering. If such occurs, then all the pastors who have been faithful in challenging their people should shake the dust off their feet and say: "We are not guilty of your blood" (see Matthew 10:14).[261] There is not much of a mission perspective in Luther's advice to the pastors and the Christians in this special section.

The reader probably does not recognize Luther the reformer in his proposals to the authorities and in his exhortations to the pastors and laypeople. Scholars have worked intensively in the attempt to understand why the aging Luther attaches these concrete proposals against the profiteering, slandering, and proselytizing Jews to his theological dispute with Judaism. Bienert is probably correct in his supposition that Luther writes this special section as the theologian for the Lutheran state churches in which the evangelical-Lutheran faith is the publicly and legally protected religion and in which other confessions and other religions were not allowed as public and expanding organizations. This goes a long way to explain Luther's program here.

We previously have shown how the propaganda, proselytism, Bible commentaries, and public slanders of the Jews that were well known to Luther caused him great distress. There are also considerations about Luther's eschatological angst and the coalition of the papacy, the enthusiasts, the Jews, and the Turks, considerations that especially Oberman has emphasized. Brosseder's thesis that Luther progressively perceives the exclusivity of the Gospel of Christ vis-à-vis all other faiths and religions is also important here. But the investigation of Luther's relation to Muslims will show that the older Luther thinks that Christ's parousia can occur in 1600 at the earliest. He has always spoken about Christ and faith as the doctrines by which all stands or falls. The distressing choice of words in the books on the Jews from 1542/1543 depends instead primarily on the situation of struggle, but it even implies something of the sickly Luther's elderly "crankiness." I cannot subscribe to the idea that this would have contributed to the contents of his seven-point program, as Sucher has proposed. Luther is not so shallow.[262]

---

260 WA 53:529.18ff.

261 WA 53:529.28ff.

262 See Bienert, *Martin Luther und die Juden*, 115ff., 145ff.; Oberman, "Luthers Beziehun-

Nevertheless, my investigation here has shown that there is a regression in Luther's thinking as compared to the middle 1520s. The differences between the books on the Jews in 1523 and 1543 are especially prominent.

THE POWER OF GOD'S WORD TO CONVERT THE JEWS

We have seen in the foregoing that in *On the Jews and Their Lies* Luther believes that some Jews will become Christians despite all his furious attacks and dreadful proposals and despite the rather small hope for conversion of the Jews. Indeed, even the severe mercy that Luther recommends has the goal of disciplining the Jews to their senses so they will seek Jesus, God's Messiah.[263]

It ought furthermore to be said parenthetically that in the last twenty pages of *On the Jews and Their Lies*, after all the severity and polemic, a section shines through in which Luther even more than earlier sets his ultimate hope on the power of the Word and on the power of the confession of Christ. However the ruling authorities and the people will react to the usury, the slanders against Christian faith, and the proselytism of the Jews, pastors and laypeople must openly proclaim the message of the church about Jesus Christ as God's Messiah. They ought to do this on the basis of the texts of both the Old and New Testaments. The church must preach Jesus' own and the apostles' message and show how it harmonizes with the prophecies of the Old Testament. The turning point (which as far as I understand has not been observed by other scholars) in *On the Jews and Their Lies* is introduced by these words: "That is speaking coarsely about the coarse cursing of the Jews. . . . Let us also speak more subtly and, as Christians, more spiritually about this."[264] Luther wishes to shake off the dreadful polemic. He wants to teach God's Word as a Christian preacher—both to the Christians and to the Jews. The questions in focus are about Christ, the Messiah of the promises, his appearance in history, and the method for the spreading of the Gospel. The last twenty pages of *On the Jews and Their Lies* have much in com-

---

gen zu den Juden," 527ff.; Brosseder, *Luthers Stellung zu den Juden*, 386ff.; and Sucher, *Luthers Stellung zu den Juden*, 268ff.

263 I categorically reject the following assessments of the aging Luther: Lewin, *Luthers Stellung zu den Juden*, 91, that Luther only criticized the Jews and did not have anything positive to say to them. Pfisterer, "Zwischen Polemik und Apologetik," 122f., that Luther pushes away the Jews and no longer thinks about mission among them. Stöhr, "Martin Luther und die Juden," 105f., that God's Word does not have power to affect the Jews and that they can in no way be converted. Holmio, *Lutheran Reformation and the Jews*, 130ff., has, however, written that Luther always believed in the power of the Word and in some kind of mission, even in the depressed situation of the Jews. Holmio does not, however, substantiate this supposition well.

264 LW 47:278 (WA 53:531.8, 531.10f.).

mon with both the material and the tone of *That Christ Was Born a Jew*. But the polemic and severity have a tendency to bubble up between the positive statements. I will concentrate on the positive statements in the following.

The reformer emphasizes that Jesus demanded that people take a stance toward himself and his claims to be the Messiah. He claimed that those who receive him and honor him as God's Son honor God the Father as well. Likewise, those who despise and hate him dishonor God. (See Matthew 10:40; Luke 10:16; John 15:23; 5:23).[265] In this way, the church must punish unrepentant Jews and seek to constrain them to take a stance toward Jesus Christ. Pastors and laypeople ought not in this center of the Christian faith be silent before the stubborn Jews who do not want to recognize the New Testament. The whole Bible is, according to Luther, God's book and God's Word, and its message will be preached even for the Jews, especially in Germany, which is officially a Christian nation.[266]

Furthermore, the reformer claims that Jesus was publicly certified as the Messiah in many ways. In this decisive matter about the Messiah of salvation, God has not acted in secret but has revealed the Messiah to all people. Luther refers to the fact that many passages about the Messiah in the prophets incontrovertibly point to Jesus of Nazareth. Luther points out Jesus' public appearance in history, his cross, and his resurrection from the dead. Furthermore, he describes how the apostles with support from the predictions of the prophets preached the Gospel and did works of power with which they began a 1,500-year-old mission history.[267]

The proclamation of Jesus Christ, his messiahship, and works to the Jews therefore ought to build on three foundations. First, innumerable prophecies (especially Genesis 49:10; Daniel 9:24–27; Haggai 2:7–10; Isaiah 40:3) confirm the fact that Jesus of Nazareth is the Messiah of God.[268] This we have shown earlier.

Second, the New Testament must also be used in the preaching about Christ. The New Testament explains how the prophecies were fulfilled, whether the Jews

---

265 WA 53:531.11ff., 531.21ff.

266 WA 53:531.24ff., 532.7ff., 532.25ff.

267 LW 47:281 (WA 53:533.5ff., 533.15ff.): "This is what God, too, has done. He instated his Son Jesus Christ in Jerusalem in his place and commanded that he be paid homage, according to Psalm 2 [:11–12]: 'Kiss the Son, lest he be angry, and you perish in the way.' Some of the Jews would not hear of this. God bore witness by the various tongues of the apostles and by all sorts of miraculous signs, and cited the statements of the prophets in testimony. However, they did then what they still do now; they were obstinate, and absolutely refused to give ear to it. Then came Master Hans—the Romans—who destroyed Jerusalem, took the villains by the nape of the neck and cast them into the dungeon of exile, which they still inhabit and in which they will remain forever, or until they say, 'We are willing to acknowledge it.' "

268 WA 53:533.15ff.

accept this fact or not. The reformer remarks again that Jesus appeared publicly with his preaching and his miracles, not in a cave somewhere. The stories in the Gospels witness to the fact that the people connected Jesus' preaching and miracles with what they expected would occur when the Messiah appeared.[269] In connection with Zechariah 9:9f., Jesus told the people that he was the polar opposite of what they expected in a Messiah; he was poor and wretched in appearance while at the same time being the salvation-bearing King who, without the help of worldly power, would extend his reign of peace over the whole world. One ought to observe here Luther's original thesis that the expansion of God's reign is in no way linked to earthly means of power. Jesus encouraged the people not to be offended that this poor King rode a donkey and allowed himself to die. This occurred so he could become a guilt offering for the sins of all people. He gave his life for sinners and prayed for them so they through him would become righteous (Daniel 9:26; Isaiah 52:15; 53:4ff.). But Christ's words and miracles could not put a stop to the unrepentance of the Jews nor to their slanders.[270]

Third, one must observe in the work of God's reign that the preaching of the apostolic times, the miracles of the apostles, and the subsequent church and mission history witness to Jesus' messiahship. Timid, uneducated, and nonordained fishermen stepped forward, provided the right interpretation of the prophets, preached, and did miraculous works of power so that both Jews and Gentiles received the Gospel and were prepared to suffer death for the same. So the church for 1,500 years until Luther's time, suffering opposition from worldly enemies, both Jews and Gentiles, preached the Gospel that she had received in Jerusalem. Because no one could silence the preaching of the Gospel, it must be from God.[271]

---

269 LW 47:281–82 (WA 53:533.26ff.): "Shortly thereafter the Messiah himself appeared on the scene, taught, baptized, and performed innumerable great miracles, not secretly but throughout the entire country, prompting many to exclaim, 'This is the Messiah' [John 7:41]. Also [John 7:31]: 'When the Messiah appears, will he do more signs than this man has done?' And they themselves said, 'What are we to do? For this man performs many signs. If we let him go on thus, every one will believe in him' [John 11:47]. When he was on the cross, they said, 'He saved others; he cannot save himself' [Matt. 27:42]. Should God concede that these circumcised saints are ignorant of all this, when they already stand convicted by the four statements cited (Jacob's, Haggai's, Daniel's, and David's), all of which show that the Messiah must have come at that time? Several of their rabbis also declared that he was in the world and was begging in Rome, etc."

270 WA 53:533.36ff., 534.9ff., 534.18ff.

271 LW 47:283 (WA 53:534.30ff.): "After the crucifixion of the King, God first presented the proper signs that this Jesus was the Messiah. Poor, timid, unlearned, unconsecrated fishermen, who did not even have a perfect mastery of their own language, stepped forth and preached in the tongues of the whole world. All the world, heaven

Luther is not, however, especially optimistic about the conversion of the Jews. One constantly sees how stumbling blocks for the Jews bubble up, though he should have spoken better and more pastorally here. He speaks in the passages connected with those just reviewed of how the devil reigns over and hardens the Jews and how those who tolerate their propaganda and proselytism share in their sins, and he repeats the proposal for concrete measures that he had described earlier.[272]

Still the Reformation Gospel works its way forward. Luther articulates the ultimate question about salvation in the passages about the Messiah. He criticizes first the fact that the Jews are counting on an earthly Messiah who will ensure their earthly welfare, make them the lords of the world, and destroy Christians, among others. According to Luther, the Jewish religion has a this-worldly perspective in all its external godliness. Luther perceives in this a similarity between Judaism and Islam.[273] The reformer asks himself then what meaning earthly power, possessions, and wealth can have if one cannot escape death, hell, and God's wrath. He touches on his own intensely personal struggle here, a struggle that was resolved through the Reformation breakthrough and remained relevant to him throughout his entire life. He speaks of the most basic question of human existence, that is, to find a graceful God.[274] If there were a Messiah who could solve the problem of sin, death, and the wrath of God so he no longer needed to fear, then his heart would rejoice and be filled with love. It is just this Messiah whom Christians confess with gratitude to the God of mercy. They have a Messiah who has put all in order and who has reconciled all the damage that Satan caused to humanity from the time of Eden.[275]

---

and earth, is still filled with wonder at this. They interpreted the writings of the prophets with power and correct understanding; in addition they performed such signs and wonders, that their message was accepted throughout the world by Jews and Gentiles. Innumerable people, both young and old, accepted it with such sincerity that they willingly suffered gruesome martyrdom because of it. This message has now endured these fifteen hundred years down to our day, and it will endure to the end of time. If such signs did not move the Jews of that time, what can we expect of these degenerate Jews who haughtily disdain to know anything about this story? Indeed, God, who revealed these things so gloriously to the world, will see to it that they hear us Christians preach and see us keep this message, which we did not invent but heard from Jerusalem fourteen hundred years ago. No enemies, no heathen, and especially no Jews have been able to suppress it, no matter how strongly they opposed it. It would be impossible for such a thing to maintain itself if it were not of God."

272 WA 53:535.21ff., 526.19–537.17, 538ff.

273 WA 53:542.5ff.

274 WA 53:542.22ff.

275 WA 53:543.24ff., 543.32ff.

The reformer shouts out the glee of faith in Jesus Christ who is the resurrection and the life and who leads humanity from death to eternal life (John 11:25; 8:51). When Jews and Turks long for earthly power and wealth, they do not seek such a Messiah. Because they consider themselves pious and holy, they do not fear death. It is only the Christians who in their fear of sin and death have need of a Messiah who is their mediator and their representative to God. They believe that it is only through him that they can approach God.[276] One can compare in this context what was said in chapter 2 about Luther's idea that all non-Christian religions are religions of Law and works.[277] Luther set faith in Christ and his works *pro nobis* against all such religions.[278]

Christians distinguish themselves from Jews and Muslims by the fact that they believe they are saved through Christ without their own holiness. One consequence of this theology is that they clearly reject the notion that earthly power and the sword can liberate them from God's wrath, from sin, death, and the devil. Luther establishes this with some passages from Isaiah (2:2ff.; 11:9; 53:11).[279] When the prophet speaks of "the knowledge of the LORD," it is a question of how one becomes justified before God. Such saving knowledge and righteousness is received only through God's Word, that is, through hearing the preaching of the Gospel and faith in Jesus Christ.[280] This will characterize and undergird mission.

This is clear according to the reformer from all true work of God's reign from the time of the apostles' until the 1500s. The apostles—and after them the bishops, pastors, and other preachers—have worked with their tongues, that is, with the Word. The work of God's reign is constantly carried by the Word when one preaches, baptizes, distributes the Lord's Supper, binds and releases sins, disciplines the wicked, and cares for and leads everyone. The work of mission and

---

276 WA 53:544.12ff.

277 *Luther and World Mission*, 37–81.

278 Cf. *Luther and World Mission*, 55ff., 76ff.

279 WA 53:544.34ff., 545.5ff.

280 LW 47:296–97 (WA 53:545.17ff.): "Similarly sorcery is also practiced upon us poor Goyim in Isaiah 11 [:9]: 'They shall not hurt or destroy in all my holy mountain; for the earth shall be full of the knowledge of the Lord.' We poor blind Goyim cannot conceive of this 'knowledge of the Lord' as a sword, but as the instruction by which one learns to know God; our understanding agrees with Isaiah 2, cited above, which also speaks of the knowledge which the Gentiles shall pursue. For knowledge does not come by the sword, but by teaching and hearing, as we stupid Goyim assume. Likewise Isaiah 53 [:11]: 'By his knowledge shall the righteous one, my servant, make many to be accounted righteous'; that is, by teaching them and by their hearing him and believing in him. What else might 'his knowledge' mean? In brief, the knowledge of the Messiah must come by preaching."

evangelization is undergirded by the fact that God speaks in the Word, and people listen in faith.[281] After all the severe and dreadful words that Luther wrote against the Jews and their rabbis, Luther finds his way back to God's work of building the church through the Gospel. Wherever the Gospel has gone out among the peoples for 1,500 years, external and obvious miracles and the miracle of all miracles, that is, salvation from sin and death, have occurred. The reformer rejoices:

> And consider the miracles. The Roman Empire and the whole world abounded with idols to which the Gentiles adhered; the devil was mighty and defended himself vigorously. All swords were against it, and yet the tongue alone purged the entire world of all these idols without a sword. It also exorcised innumerable devils, raised the dead, healed all types of diseases, and snowed and rained down sheer miracles. Thereafter it swept away all heresy and error, as it still does daily before our eyes. And further—this is the greatest miracle—it forgives and blots out all sin, creates happy, peaceful, patient hearts, devours death, locks the doors of hell and opens the gate of heaven, and gives eternal life. Who can enumerate all the blessings effected by God's word? In brief, it makes all who hear and believe it children of God and heirs of the kingdom of heaven. Do you not call this a kingdom, power, might, dominion, glory? Yes, most certainly, this is a comforting kingdom of the true *chemdath* of all Gentiles.[282]

This is faithful Reformation theology about how the Word/Gospel and faith are what carries forward the work of church and mission. Why have the scholars done nothing with this? Answer: They have been too preoccupied with the unacceptable seven-point program and the reformer's polemic against the Jews.

But Luther has even more to say. It has been too little observed that the reformer concludes his book with a six-page positive explication of the theological-missiological consequences, especially of the central messianic texts: Genesis 49:10; 2 Samuel 23:2, 5f.; Haggai 2:7–10; Daniel 9:24–27.[283] He establishes that

---

281 LW 47:297 (WA 53:545.27ff.): "The proof of this is before your eyes, namely, that the apostles used no spear or sword but solely their tongues. And their example has been followed in all the world now for fifteen hundred years by all the bishops, pastors, and preachers, and is still being followed. Just see whether the pastor wields sword or spear when he enters the church, preaches, baptizes, administers the sacrament, when he retains and remits sin, restrains evildoers, comforts the godly, and teaches, helps, and nurtures everyone's soul. Does he not do all of this exclusively with the tongue or with words? And the congregation, likewise, brings no sword or spear to such ministry, but only its ears." On the spiritual kingdom and the Word/Gospel, see *Luther and World Mission*, 82ff., 90ff.

282 LW 47:297 (WA 53:545.36ff.).

283 Cf. *Luther and World Mission*, 355ff., 389ff., about how Luther as apologist handled these texts.

Genesis 49:10 clearly proves the faith of the Christians that Jesus of Nazareth was and is the Messiah who during the time of Herod, when Judah's scepter was removed, began his reign of peace through the Gospel without the help of earthly power. After Jesus had risen from the dead, the great drama of the church's mission through apostles and bishops began as described in Acts 2:41; 3:11; 4:4; and by the church historian Eusebius. Through the preaching of the Gospel, through miracles and a holy lifestyle, thousands of Jews were called to their promised Messiah. The other apostles also called Gentiles to receive the Messiah-Christ in faith. Without force, these people received the Gospel, left their idols, and stood ready to suffer persecutions and death for and in the power of Jesus' name. Thus both Jews and Gentiles were united through God's mercy to be one single people through mission's Gospel and faith in the Shiloh-Messiah about whom Jacob and the Holy Spirit witness in Genesis 49:10.[284] Haggai 2:7–10 predicts in general the same thing as Genesis 49:10 about the Messiah of God.[285] And the words of 2 Samuel 23:2f. about David's eternal house and faith only make sense if Jesus Christ is the Messiah. Jesus has occupied David's throne and was accepted after his resurrection as King and Messiah by both Jews and Gentiles. Luther emphasizes against all the denials of the Jews to the contrary that all who believe in this Messiah-Christ are the descendants of the children of Israel, the people of God and the seed of Abraham. Because this Son of David and those who believe in him will live forever, David's throne is firmly established.[286] Of course, the Messiah and the salvation of God have come from the Jews, not the Gentiles (John 4:22; Acts 13:17), but in the new covenant, both Jews and Gentiles share in God's salva-

---

284 WA 53:546.22ff., 547.20ff., and the conclusion in 53:548.5ff.

285 WA 53:552.14ff.

286 LW 47:300–301 (WA 53:548.17ff., 548.32ff.): "Likewise the verse regarding the ever-lasting house and throne of David fits no other than this our Messiah, Jesus of Nazareth [II Sam. 23:5]. For subsequent to the rule of the kings from the tribe of Judah and since the days of Herod, we cannot think of any son of David who might have sat on his throne or still occupies it today 'to preserve his throne eternally.' Yet that is what had to take place and still must take place, since God promised it with an oath. But when this Son of David arose from the dead, many, many thousands of children of Israel rallied about him, both in Jerusalem and throughout the world, accepting him as their King and Messiah, as the true Seed of Abraham and of their lineage. These were and still are the house, the kingdom, the throne of David. For they are the descendants of the children of Israel and the seed of Abraham, over whom David was king. . . . We Christians, however, know that he says in John 8 [:56] and in Matthew 22 [:32]: 'Abraham lives.' Also in John 11 [:25]: 'He who believes in me, though he die, yet shall he live.' Thus David's house and throne are firmly established. There is a Son occupying it eternally, who never dies, nor does he ever let die those who are of his kingdom or who accept him in true faith as King." Cf. WA 53:549.4ff.

tion—only by God's fathomless mercy. The new people of God, that is, the church of Christ, which consists of both Jews and Gentiles, have their only foundation in the Messiah-Christ and are constituted through faith in him alone.[287] The seventy so-called year-weeks of Daniel 9:24–27 that are given to the people and the city can only predict the desolation of Israel and Jerusalem and Jesus and his works through which a new people, a new Jerusalem, and a new holiness can be created. This is the end of the Old Testament's temple worship and the repeated sacrifices for reconciliation. The Messiah pays one time for all sins and gives an eternal righteousness.[288] The new people of God is the Christian church, consisting of both Jews and Gentiles who experience that the Old Testament prophecies have been fulfilled in Jesus Christ and who through faith in him own the forgiveness of sins and an eternal righteousness.[289]

Luther says a first *amen* after the positive, Christ-messianic interpretation of these Old Testament prophecies. He then adds some words about how Christians have now received the proper education needed to defend themselves and react against the lies and slanders of the Jews. But this addition is concluded with a prayer for the Jews: "May Christ, our dear Lord, convert them mercifully and preserve us steadfastly and immovably in the knowledge of him, which is eternal life."[290]

The reformer Luther has consistently expressed his anxiety and indignation about the hardening of the Jews concerning the question of Jesus' messiahship. With a terrifying choice of words, he has expressed himself about the rabbinical interpretation of the Old Testament and about the slanders of the Jews. Luther has even proposed a "severe mercy" against the Jews that in our judgment is both inhuman and unacceptable. We have, however, seen that in all his writing about the lies of the Jews he wants to be an apologist who for the sake of the Jews seeks

---

287 WA 53:549.18ff., 549.34ff.

288 WA 53:550.21ff., 550.36ff.

289 LW 47:304 (WA 53:551.13ff.): "The Christian church, composed of Jews and Gentiles, is such a new people and a new Jerusalem. This people knows that sin has been removed entirely by Jesus Christ, that all prophecy has been fulfilled, and eternal righteousness established. For he who believes in him is eternally righteous, and all his sins are forever made of no effect, they are atoned for and forgiven . . . . We no longer hear it said: Whoever offers guilt-offerings or sin-offerings or other offerings in Jerusalem becomes righteous or has atoned for his sin; but now we hear: 'He who believes and is baptized will be saved; but he who does not believe will be condemned' [Mark 16:16], no matter where in the wide world he may be. He need not travel to Jerusalem; no, Jerusalem has to come to him." These themes are also substantiated on the basis of Psalm 40:7–9; Daniel 9:24; Psalm 16:4; Isaiah 33:24; Jeremiah 31:34. See WA 53:551.24ff.

290 LW 47:306 (WA 53:552.36ff.).

to rightly interpret the prophecies of the Old Testament in light of history and of the New Testament. However, he has said that he wants especially to protect the Christians from Jewish propaganda.

The last section of *On the Jews and Their Lies* ultimately signals Luther's fast faith in the power of God's Word. Luther's concluding prayer above shows that he leaves to God and God's Word that which he cannot do himself. This concluding prayer indicates a hope that the Jews will share in God's salvation in Jesus Christ.[291] The prayer summarizes the goal of *On the Jews and Their Lies*: partly that Christ in his mercy might convert the Jews, partly and primarily that the Christians might be upheld in a right faith. This means that Luther's book under the horizon of its severe mercy owns a repressed, but no less true, mission perspective.[292] One ought to notice, however, that Luther does nothing with the verses about the final conversion of the Jews in Romans 11:25ff., despite the fact that he often touches on verses from Romans 9–11.[293]

Vom Schem Hamphoras, etc. (1543)

A couple of months after *On the Jews and Their Lies*, Luther's polemical book *Vom Schem Hamphoras und vom Geschlecht Christi* was published. The entire first polemical section of this opus builds on the eleventh chapter of Salvagus Porcehtus's anti-Jewish work *Victoria adversus impios Hebraeos* (published in Paris in 1529).[294] The scholars generally agree that as a whole this is the most polemical of

---

291 Cf. Luther's prayers that God will have mercy on the Jews in WA 53:541.11ff., 541.22ff., 550.19f. Stöhr, "Martin Luther und die Juden," 104ff.; and Sucher, *Luthers Stellung zu den Juden*, 250f., understand the short and episodic passages about the conversion of the Jews in this concluding prayer as only pious wishes, wishes that Luther did not really mean. I believe that this is an indefensible interpretation of the texts, even if the reformer can sometimes say that the Jews are impossible to convert. God can do everything through the Word/Gospel, according to Luther.

292 Holsten, "Christentum und nicht-christliche Religion," 122, 124ff., notices Luther's concluding prayer but says that the mission perspective is not expressed nearly as strongly in 1543 as in 1523. Maurer, *Kirche und Synagoge*, 45, reckons that there is a mission motif, even under the horizon of the severe mercy of 1543. In Maurer, "Die Zeit der Reformation," 425, this is not emphasized. But Luther has always believed that some Jews will convert to Christianity. Brosseder, *Luthers Stellung zu den Juden*, 376; and Bienert, *Martin Luther und die Juden*, 157, also take Luther's concluding prayer for the conversion of the Jews at face value.

293 For example, WA 53:419.26f., 522.23ff., 541.16ff. See also Brosseder, *Luthers Stellung zu den Juden*, 378f.; Müller, "Tribut an den Geist seiner Zeit," 307f.; and Pfisterer, "Zwischen Polemik und Apologetik," 118, 120.

294 The reformer also uses Lyra and Burgos and *Der gantz Jüdisch glaub* of Antonius Margaritha. See the entire introduction in WA 53:573ff. and the account in Bienert, *Martin Luther und die Juden*, 162ff.

the reformer's writings on the Jews.[295] Jewish mystical and speculative piety used the formula *Schem ha-meporasch* ("the unsayable name"). Luther characterizes the Jewish mystical, magical use and presentation of this formula as a wretched unbelief and as a presentation of letters with sources in the Talmud, the Jewish sow, as Christian tradition would call it.[296]

The reformer says that in all the severities and attacks against the Jews in his previous writings and in this writing he had done nothing wrong because the Jews had slandered God, Christ, and the Christians.[297] In the Jewish mystical calculations of God's name and the 216 letters of Exodus 14:19–21, one is confronted with a demon-possessed use of the Scriptures and with idolatry. The Jews believe in some kind of magic formula, that is, that which is not God. Thus they have drawn God's condemnation on themselves.[298]

In the second and apologetic section of this book, Luther considers the question of whether Mary was really a descendant of David. If such were not the case, the Jews would be right to claim that Jesus was not the Messiah. Because according to Christian faith Jesus was conceived without the help of a man, Joseph's lineage from David has no relevance. Because the genealogies for Jesus in Matthew 1:1–14 and Luke 3:23–38 (inverted) both end with Joseph, the reformer has a real problem on his hands.[299]

First, Luther establishes that Moses (Genesis 3:15 is not directly referred to, but Genesis 49:10 and Deuteronomy 18:15, 18f. are), all the prophets, and even the apostle Paul (Galatians 4:4; Romans 1:3) connect Jesus and Mary to the tribe of Judah and the house of David. One does not need to ground Jesus' lineage to David only on Matthew and Luke.[300] Because the prophets in countless passages certify that the Messiah will come with a new, happy message, his covenant, his book, and his message must be something other than what we find in Moses. The

---

295 Lewin, *Luthers Stellung zu den Juden*, 84ff.; and Sucher, *Luthers Stellung zu den Juden*, 85ff., with an emphasis on Luther's bitter attacks against the Jews and his vulgar language. See also Maurer, "Die Zeit der Reformation," 407ff.; and Bienert, *Martin Luther und die Juden*, 162ff. These latter scholars are more concerned with the theological motifs in the book.

296 See the first section, WA 53:580–609. Concerning the magic with letters and the slander of God's name, see especially WA 53:592.5ff., 600.7ff.

297 WA 53:587ff. and summarized in 53:590.23ff., 590.33ff.

298 WA 53:600–609. See Lewin, *Luthers Stellung zu den Juden*, 84.; Sucher, *Luthers Stellung zu den Juden*, 86ff.; and especially Bienert, *Martin Luther und die Juden*, 162ff., with the enlightening sketch of the background.

299 See the investigation about Christ's lineage, WA 53:610–40. Concerning the problem with Matthew 1:1–14 and Luke 3:23–38, see WA 53:610.1ff.

300 WA 53:611.1–613.2, 622.18ff.

Old and New Testaments are of different species, and the passages of the New Testament are far more important evidence for theological truth than the Old Testament. All this depends naturally on the fact that the Messiah has in fact come. In this case, faith stands against faith. But if the Messiah has already come, then one ought to argue also from the New Testament. Luther means that the Jews have in fact neither the Old nor the New Testament on their side because without the New Testament and the Messiah, one cannot understand the Old Testament either.[301]

Luther understands, however, that the Jews will not listen to this reasoning. He presents, therefore, a long investigation on the genealogies in Matthew and Luke and concludes that both Joseph and Mary are descendants of David. Thereby even the Messiah of the Christians is proven to be of David's lineage despite the fact that Joseph is not the biological father of Jesus.[302]

The reformer has in his analysis of the genealogies consistently claimed that Joseph is only inaccurately called Jesus' father. Thereby he also reenters the debate about an article of faith, that is, the virgin birth, which is problematic for the Jews. He claims decidedly that *alma* in Isaiah 7:14 means "virgin" or an "untouched young woman." Luther supports his claim with other texts from the Old Testament. The pregnancy of the virgin would be a miracle and a great, enlightening sign. Especially the promise about the seed of the woman in Genesis 3:15 (Psalm 22:10–11 is also referred to in this context) proves the virgin birth because otherwise one usually ascribed children only to men.[303] Luther also delivers a violent attack on the rabbis, whom he suspects cheat with the vocalization of the Old Testament texts.[304]

With *Vom Schem Hamphoras*, Luther has chosen above all to expose the rabbis and guard the Christians against Jewish claims that Jesus Christ is not God's Messiah. Luther considers the conversion of the Jews to be just as difficult as converting the devil. As in *On the Jews and Their Lies*, Luther does not direct this book to the Jews but to the Christians. Neither Moses, the prophets, nor Luther can soften their hard-heartedness.[305] Nevertheless, one can see in the introduction to *Vom*

---

301 WA 53:617.14–622.17. On Luther's Christological interpretation of the Old Testament, see *Luther and World Mission*, 97ff., 396ff.

302 WA 53:622.30–629.26. Matthew 1:1 actually already claims that both Jesus and Mary are of David's and Abraham's lineage (WA 53:622.32ff.). An important link in the lineage chain is Matthat, from whose house and lineage both Joseph and Mary come (WA 53:524.11ff., 525.21ff., 525.32ff.). Luther draws up a proper family tree for both Mary and Jesus, WA 53:629.

303 See especially WA 53:634.6–641.3. Cf. also the investigation in *That Christ Was Born a Jew* (1523), WA 11:316.5ff., 317.30ff.

304 Especially WA 53:644ff.

305 See the introduction, WA 53:579.11ff., especially 579.17f., 579.21ff.: "Denn gleich

Schem Hamphoras some little hope that the book might help some individual Jews to believe. Luther continues to reject the notion that all the Jews will be saved. That which he had claimed in his younger years had, by 1543, become something of an illusion. The apostle Paul does not indicate in Romans 11:25f. a general conversion. When one succeeds to convert only a few Germans in "Christian" Saxony, how would it be possible to convert all the Jews who are, as a whole, hardened by the devil, Luther asks.[306] A remnant of the Jews will be saved. But Luther believes that the Jews as a whole and as a people will continue to be under God's wrath, hardened, and dispersed among the peoples "until the times of the Gentiles are fulfilled" (Luke 21:24), that is, until the end of the age. This is a gloomy outlook.[307]

One notices, however, that in *Vom Schem Hamphoras* Luther does not refer with one word to the proposed severe mercy of *On the Jews and Their Lies*. Perhaps he understood that he had gone too far earlier. The reformer nevertheless challenges the electors in the areas with Jewish inhabitants to be careful what they are doing. In their areas, they protect and tolerate people who not only slander Christ but also the divine Majesty with their jokes and their magic.[308] The Jews had been issued the great call to be God's mouth in the world, but they have fallen away in unrepentance. Finally, they crucified Christ and cried out, "Let his blood be on us and on our children!" (Matthew 27:25). It has happened according to their wish.[309]

But to this gloominess, one must add Luther's warm concluding words, prayer, and hope that some Jews will come to know the true God. Luther says after all his fury and at the end of this book: "Such ought to be enjoined on the Hebraicists. Here I will rest the subject and no longer have anything to do with the Jews, neither writing about them nor against them. They have had enough from me. May

---

wie wir müssen leren und schreiben vom Teuffel, Helle, Tod und Sünde, was sie sind und thun . . . Also schreibe ich auch von den Jüden, Denn ein Jüde odder Jüdisch hertz ist so stock, stein, eisen, Teuffel hart, das mit keiner weise zu bewegen ist." Cf. the conclusion in WA 53:648.11ff.

306 WA 53:580.1ff.

307 WA 53:615.8ff.: "Aber weil das newe Testament zeuget, das die Jüden sollen unter alle Heiden zerstrewet, und Jerusalem von den Heiden zutretten werden, 'bis die zeit der Heiden erfüllet sind' (das ist: bis an der Welt ende), wie unser Herr spricht Luce. 21[:24], Denn Christus wird ewig sitzen bleiben und kein ander Messia komen, Darumb mus ich gleuben, das noch etliche und gar wenig hesen [= Reste] von den Jüden uberig bleiben müssen jnn der welt. Aber sollen doch kein eigen herrschafft kriegen, sondern auff ungewissem fusse sitzen" (Psalm 59:11f. and Genesis 4:12 are here adduced).

308 WA 53:605.34ff.

309 WA 53:587.16ff., 587.28ff.

God grant his grace to those who want to repent, grace to learn to know and to praise God, the Father, our Creator, and our Lord Jesus Christ and the Holy Spirit, forever, Amen."[310] Despite all, the door is not completely closed—not for all Jews, at least. Nevertheless, the book is mostly severe and polemical. Thus the mission perspective is scarcely perceptible.

LUTHER'S SWAN SONG ABOUT CHRIST AND THE JEWS (1546)

Despite his illness in the years 1543–1546, Luther was active as a writer and a preacher. He could remark on the Jews' opinion of the doctrine of the Trinity and of the promises to Abraham that even the Gentiles would share in his blessing (Genesis 22:18).[311] Luther even comments on the Jewish question in the final four sermons before his death in 1546.[312] The reformer establishes the Christian faith as an absolute religion. It is not enough that Turks, Gentiles, Jews, or false Christians are monotheists. Because they lack the revelation of God in the Scriptures, they do not share in the true faith in the Father, the Son, and the Spirit. It is primarily this that distinguishes Christianity from the faith of Jews, Turks, and Gentiles, even if these latter reckon with a Creator God, a God of Law and righteousness. Without the word of Scripture about Christ in both the Old and New Testaments, the peoples wander aimlessly in their many shifting ideas about God (Acts 17:21ff.).[313]

In his sermon on Luke 2:22–32, Luther calls the Jews blind blasphemers of God because they ought to understand by the words of the prophets and by a 1,500-year church history where and when the Messiah should have been born.[314] On the parable of the weeds and the wheat in Matthew 13:24–30, the reformer says that one must destroy enthusiastic, papistic, and Jewish heresy not with

---

310 WA 53:648.11ff.

311 *Last Words of David* (1543), WA 54:34.33f., 35.31ff., 75.12ff. Cf. the partly nasty attacks against the Jews' slanders, usury, etc., in 1543, WATr 5:257.11ff. (no. 5576). See Bienert, *Martin Luther und die Juden*, 170f.

312 The ailing Luther gave his last sermons and services in the village where he was born. He mediated between the fighting barons of Mansfeld and could deliver his final four sermons only with difficulty. These were preached January 31, February 2, February 7, and February 15 in Eisleben, the city in which Luther was born October 11, 1483. Luther died three days after the final sermon, that is, February 18, 1546. The sermons that were written down by Mathesius are printed in WA 51:148–96. In the secondary literature, see Weyer, "Die Juden in den Predigten Martin Luthers," 168ff.; Bienert, *Martin Luther und die Juden*, 174ff.; and Oberman, *Wurzeln des Antisemitismus*, 160f.

313 WA 51:149–54, 155.31ff., 156.25ff. Cf. *Luther and World Mission*, 42ff., 49ff., 65ff., 76ff.

314 WA 51:166.1ff., 166.19ff., 166.35ff. Concerning the Jews' pride before the Gentiles and their opposition to Jesus Christ, see WA 53:172.32ff.

physical violence but with God's Word. He says yes to patient work with God's Word and no to all physical means to destroy the forces of evil.[315]

It is especially interesting to us that Luther attaches "an exhortation to the Jews" to these sermons. To be sure, Luther is capable of being bitter toward the Jews in the week before his death, but he is no more severe toward them than he is toward the followers of the pope and toward the enthusiasts. This entire coalition opposes God's decision to save.[316] As always before, he considers the Jews' slanders against Christ, the Virgin Mary, and the Christians as completely unacceptable. Such can neither be tolerated nor accepted in the realm under any circumstances without one sharing in these so-called alien sins. The reformer does not, however, say anything about the burning of synagogues, liturgical books, etc. If the Jews continue their slanders, then toleration and fellowship ought to be broken and the Jews ought to be expelled by the authorities.[317]

This is the first subject in this appendix to Luther's sermons. The reformer also attaches a certain hope and faith in the Messiah of the Christians. It ought to be observed that after the reformer's many twists and turns in the Jewish question, the soon-to-die Luther, under the horizon of this hope, makes room for the mission dimension. He says: "Now we want to handle them in a Christian manner and first offer them the Christian faith so that they will receive the Messiah who is after all their cousin and born of their flesh and blood and the true seed of Abraham, something of which they themselves boast. If you see that they are serious, you ought first to offer them this so that they might turn to the Messiah and let themselves be baptized. If they are not serious, then we do not want to tolerate them."[318]

As he approaches death, Luther continues to own something of the mission perspective that was so clear in the early 1520s. One cannot speak of a mission enthusiasm. The mission motif is now more suppressed by the older Luther's violent reaction against the conscious attempts of the Jews to convert Christians; by his indignation over their usury, blasphemies, and unrepentance; and by his fear that by tolerating them he himself and others would be blamed for the sins of the

---

315 WA 51:175.34ff., 184.4ff., 184.15ff., 184.23ff. Cf. Öberg, *Himmelrikets nycklar och kyrklig bot i Luthers teologi*, 490ff., 494ff., 500ff.

316 LW 51:386 (WA 51:190.12ff.): "This is just the kind of wisdom that Caiaphas had when he was in council with the Jews [John 11:49–50]: You utter fools, you have no heads, you know nothing and understand nothing at all; is it not better that one man should die rather than the whole nation should perish?" Concerning the front against the enthusiasts, etc., see WA 51:190.12ff., 191.29ff., 194.1ff.

317 WA 51:195.20ff., 195.28ff., 195.37ff., 196.4ff., 196.12ff.

318 WA 51:195.10ff.

Jews and, therefore, receive a share of God's wrath against the Jews. But the mission perspective is not completely absent from Luther's "last testament." He says: "But if they repent, leave their usury and receive Christ, so we will gladly call them our brothers."[319] When one speaks of brothers, one is far from the domains of an oppressive racism. There one works in love and with prayer about someone's salvation, there one cannot say (as has been said) that the reformer has given up and left the Jews behind. Luther concludes: "If the Jews want to turn to us and cease their defamations and what they have in fact done against us, we will gladly forgive them. But if not, we ought not tolerate or suffer their presence among us."[320]

Luther's sermons in Eisleben show how powerfully he reacts against all those who oppose the Christ whom he preached until the end of his life. The Jews' slanders and their unyielding rejection of Jesus' messiahship are especially difficult problems for the reformer. If they continue with their public slanders and their usury, then they must be deported. It ought, however, to be emphasized that Luther speaks several times of the "now and not yet" of the Gospel and Christian love, during which the Christians ought to call the Jews to faith in the Messiah and to fellowship in Christ's church. Three days after this last exhortation to the Jews, Luther died (February 18, 1546).

We see from Luther's final sermon that until his death he hoped that some Jews would convert to Christianity. Therefore the Christians must meet them in love and offer them the Gospel about the Messiah who belongs to their own family. If the Jews receive him and cease with their stubborn unrepentance, their usury, and their slanders, then all will be forgiven and the principally religious conflict between Christianity and Judaism will no longer exist. Christianity is, for Luther, the absolute truth. As long as the Jews also consider their religion and their covenant as something absolute, the religious conflict will of course continue.

Short Summary

The following points briefly summarize Luther's general attitude to the Jews, his often polemical apologetics, and his hope and work for their conversion.

1. 1514–1516: Luther has a more chilly relationship with the Jews and Judaism. In the lectures on Romans, he reacts against the legalism of the Jews and their rejection of righteousness of faith in Christ. Some Jews will perhaps be saved, but Luther has problems interpreting what the final number of saved Jews will be according to Romans 11:25–26.

---

319 WA 51:195.25ff., 195.39ff.

320 WA 51:196.14ff.

2. 1519–1523: There is no lack of critique against the Jews' usury, their denial that Jesus is the Messiah, and their trust in their own works. At the same time, a strong belief grows that it should be possible to win some Jews for Christ, especially if it were possible to leave behind the church's old stereotypes that defame the Jews. It involves seeking patiently to convince them from the Old Testament that Jesus is God's Messiah. It means treating them humanly in human life together. Especially in the book *That Christ Was Born a Jew* (1523), the mission perspective and the challenge to mission is prominent. Romans 11:25–26 is no longer problematic.

3. 1524–1537: In this phase, Luther does not handle the question of the Jews comprehensively. He develops and sharpens the old critique against the Jews' usury, their blasphemies against Christ and the Christians, etc. The mission perspective is clearly prominent around 1524–1526, but its strength gives way during the 1530s. The reformer notices the religious stubbornness of the Jews and recognizes from 1532 on that Judaism has its own sustaining power and identity and at the same time seeks to win proselytes among the Christians.

4. 1538–1543: The polemical apologetic dominates these years, while the mission perspective is suppressed. The reformer wants to answer the Jews' blasphemies and above all to reveal the lies of the Jewish rabbis in their interpretations of the Old Testament and its prophecies about Christ. The book *On the Jews and Their Lies* (1543) is especially important in this regard. I have, however, been able to show that Luther, even in this severe opus and in other writings during this period, does to a certain extent work for and pray that God through the Word would convert at least some Jews to faith in the Christ-Messiah. Above all, the conflict between Luther and the Jews consists in whether or not Jesus was God's Messiah and at the same time whether election, circumcision, and the Law or faith in Christ is the way to salvation.

5. 1546: Luther's final sermons do not lack attacks against the Jews' usury, their blasphemies against Christ and the Christians, and their stone-hard opposition to faith in Christ. At the same time, his goodwill for the Jews and his hope and prayers for their conversion also have a certain place.

6. There is a significant difference between the practical and legal consequences in the handling of the Jews to which Luther arrives in 1523 and those to which he arrives in 1543. The reformer's proposal in 1543 that either the public worship of the Jews ought to be abolished or they ought to be exiled from the realm is inhuman and totally unacceptable. It is probably a fact that the order legislated in Saxony for humanitarian rea-

sons, that is, that there could only be one religion in the realm, played an important role in the older Luther's position. It could not be accepted that the Jews blasphemed the Christian faith publicly and sought to win proselytes in an officially Christian land.

7. There are apparent shifts in Luther's attitude toward Judaism and the Jews. The early somewhat chilly stance is relieved by a warm spring in 1519–1523. Then especially around 1530–1537, we meet the critical wait-and-see period. Finally, we get the difficult unreconcilable attacks in 1538–1543 and in 1546 a not insignificant new spring again.

8. For the purposes of our investigation, it is important to draw attention to the fact that through all the shifts and turns, in his many ways of speaking, Luther has always reckoned that at least some of the old covenant's people may finally receive the Gospel of Christ. Especially in his work with the Old Testament, the reformer has worked intensively so that this will occur. Therefore the analysis of Luther's complicated Bible exegesis has been so important for me. It is a part of his mission work vis-à-vis the Jews.

The Apologetic and Missiological Motifs in Luther's Work with Islam

After centuries of successful Christian mission and the establishment of episcopates largely within the boundaries of the Roman Empire, the church experienced a tremendous setback because of the Muslims' mission by the sword and the ensuing Islamicization. After Muhammad's death in A.D. 632, Palestine, Syria, the mighty Sassanids Empire, and Egypt were conquered within ten years. In A.D. 697 Carthage fell, and by A.D. 715 the greater part of Spain was under Muslim control. The Muslims marched north until Charles Martel defeated them in A.D. 732 deep in France at Tours. In principle, the Christians were tolerated as "people of the book," but in practice many went over to the Muslim camp because of discriminatory laws and the pressure of the cultural environment. In this way, many formerly Christian lands became high medieval Islamic cultures.[321]

But the Muslims, or Saracens, were not alone on the scene. Among others, the German Empire (ca. A.D. 950–1050) and the Roman Catholic Empire as a spiritual-temporal superpower (ca. 1050–1270) both acted in such a way that medieval Christian culture was preserved in Europe. Through Roman Catholic mission, all Europe became "Christian." Western Christendom managed to organize mission

---

321 Christensen and Göransson, *Kyrkohistoria*, 1:208–36; Neill, *History of Christian Missions*, 54ff., 112f.

thrusts in Muslim regions in both Asia and Africa. During the twelfth century, the Muslims were forced to retreat into Spain and Portugal. Thomas Aquinas targeted the Saracens when he wrote *Summa contra gentiles* in 1258–1264. When Granada fell in 1492, the Iberian Peninsula again became a Christian region and the starting place for the discovery of new parts of the world. It also became the starting place for Roman Catholic mission in the conquered territories. The high medieval Crusades sent to liberate Jerusalem, among other holy places, from the Muslims became a fiasco and did much to destroy the forward movement of Christ's ambassadors. In this way, Muslims became closed to the Christian message for a long time. Ramon Lull (1235–1315) stands, however, as a brilliant example among the Roman Catholic missionaries to the Muslims. This Franciscan monk wanted only one thing: to convert nonbelievers. He believed that Christianization of the Arab world must build on three main principles:

1. Careful study and knowledge of the languages of the Muslim world. His influence was responsible for the founding of departments to study these languages in the most important universities in Europe.

2. One must have a book with logical arguments that could defend the basic truths of Christianity against the learned scholastics among the Muslims. Apologetics were important in the evangelization of Muslims.

3. Christians must courageously witness to their faith, even if they should for that reason suffer physical abuse and death. According to Islamic law, the death penalty was hazarded for preaching the Gospel in a Muslim land.

Around A.D. 1000, the Eastern Roman Empire and its Orthodox faith became the starting point for mission work among the Slavic peoples. It also was a bulwark against the advances of the Saracens into Southeast Europe. When Constantinople fell in 1453 and the Eastern Roman Empire was crushed, European Christendom, with good reason, feared Muslim expansion into its own regions.[322] Sultan Suleiman II (1520–1466) in Constantinople was more conquest-hungry than was at first believed. In 1522 he conquered the Christian stronghold at Rhodes. The Saracens forced their way forward to the Adriatic Sea and conquered Belgrade in 1521. Soldiers at home from the front, pilgrims, travelers, and many books in the early sixteenth century explained the grim ravages of the Turks. Plans were concocted for a crusade against the Turks, and the realization of this crusade was prepared through income from indulgences and special taxes. The Hungarian army suffered a crushing defeat at Mohacs in 1526. The Turks burned Budapest but retreated quickly.

---

322 Christensen and Göransson, *Kyrkohistoria*, 1:304–93; ; Neill, *Misjon i 2000 är*, 38ff., 70ff., 85ff.

Because Suleiman knew that Ferdinand of Austria was a pretender to the Hungarian crown (his own candidate was Johann Zapolya), it was feared that Suleiman would attempt to crush Ferdinand and thereby strike into Austria. It was during this anxious time that Luther began to write *On War against the Turk* in the summer of 1528. This opus had barely left the press in 1529 when Suleiman marched from Constantinople to the west. He conquered Budapest and with characteristic Ottoman pomp gave the Hungarian crown to his protege Zapolya. Suleiman and his armies marched toward Vienna, attacked the city several times in October 1529, but were forced to retreat. In this situation, Luther wrote his important *Heerpredigt wider den Türken* (*Army Sermon against the Turk*).[323] In 1532 Vienna was again besieged. The Turks were a constant threat.

In what is to follow, I will say something about how Luther reacted to the Turkish threat, especially during the dramatic years 1528–1529. I will also survey and analyze *Vermahnung zum Gebet wider den Türcken* (*Appeal for Prayer against the Turks*) (1541), *Vorlegung des Alcoran Bruder Richardi* (*Brother Richard's Exposition of the Quran*) (1542), and also other source materials that, among other things, illuminate Luther's stance toward the Turks after their occupation of Budapest in the fall of 1541 and their subsequent complete victory over King Ferdinand's armies. Zwingli and Calvin neither became involved nor wrote about the Turkish question. This may depend partly on the fact that the leader of their land, that is, the king of France, was temporarily allied with the Turks. Luther and the Germans, however, were in danger of experiencing an occupation by the Turks and the subsequent Islamicization. Therefore it was impossible for Luther to be silent during the stormy years between 1529 and 1543.[324]

In the following, I will describe how the reformer encourages the emperor and the princes to make the necessary defense against the Turks and how he challenges the entire Western world to repent. However, I want especially to investigate how Luther reckons with the necessity of apologetics and mission at the meeting with the conquering Muslims. Does the source material possibly indicate that Luther himself took steps so the Saracens could be exposed to the Gospel? Has he made any methodological suggestions about how to reach Muslims? Because there is no marked development in the reformer's understanding in the question about Muslims and their Christianization, I will systematize Luther's thought on the subject with the help of certain important questions and main themes.

---

323 About the Turks' conquests and the fear and literary activity that this occasioned, see F. Cohrs and A. Goetze, introduction to *Vom Kriege wider den Türken*, WA 30/2:81–97. See also Pfister, "Reformation, Türken und Islam," 345ff.

324 Wallmann, "Luthers Stellung zu Judentum und Islam," 51ff.

The Turks as Both the Rod of God's Chastisement and as Satan's Evil Tool

In our investigation of Luther and the Jews, we have often come across Luther's idea that the 1,500-year Jewish diaspora should be understood as God's discipline toward repentance for a fallen and unrepentant chosen people who are unresponsive to the Gospel of Christ. It ought, however, to be observed that Luther's idea about the rod of God's chastisement is used with powerful force also against Western Christianity when he seeks to understand the Turks' role and purpose in God's providence of the world. God does not only discipline the Jews but also the Christians for their fallenness, their sins, and their spiritual apathy.[325]

Immediately after the outbreak of the Reformation, Luther suggested that the Turks were God's rod (*virga Dei*). In Thesis 5 of the Heidelberg Disputation (1518), Luther openly laments the church hierarchy because it does nothing but dream about war against the Turks. The hierarchy ought to think more about the spiritual war against sin within Christendom. The Turks are, namely, the rod of God's discipline and affliction. Therefore the leaders of the church only strive against God himself in the Turks when they do not also attack the sin in the church.[326] Expressed as it was in the increasingly threatening situation of Turkish expansion, this opinion does not give the pope and his theologians any peace. When the bull *Exurge Domine* on June 15, 1520, implies that Luther wanted to reject war with the Turks as such,[327] the reformer takes up the question in his

---

325 See here Vielau, *Luther und der Türke*, 17ff.; Lind, *Luthers Stellung zum Kreuz- und Türkenkrieg*, 33ff.; Lamparter, *Luthers Stellung zum Türkenkrieg*, 16ff.; Pfister, "Reformation, Türken und Islam," 374ff.; Vogler, "Luthers Geschichtsauffassung im Spiegel seienes Türkenbildes," 120ff.; Mau, "Luthers Stellung zu den Türken," 1:647f., 656ff. See also Forell, "Luther and the War against the Turks," 259ff.; and Kooiman, "Luthers getuigenes in de oorlogtegen de Turken," 5ff., 17ff.

326 Thesis 5, "Explanation of the Ninety-Five Theses": "Many, however, even the 'big wheels' in the church, now dream of nothing else than war against the Turk. They want to fight, not against iniquities, but against the lash of iniquity and thus they would oppose God who says that through that lash he himself punishes us for our iniquities because we do not punish ourselves for them" (LW 31:92 [WA 1:535.35ff.]). Concerning this thesis and the contemporary Roman Catholic criticism, see Lamparter, *Luthers Stellung zum Türkenkrieg*, 70ff.; and Mau, "Luthers Stellung zu den Türken," 347ff. Mau shows how Luther was uncertain concerning the question about war against the Turks at this time. Luther writes about the pope's ravages against the Gospel, the unrepentance of the people, and the demand for a repentance of the people. See the December 21, 1518, letter to Spalatin (WABr 1:282.3ff., 282.15ff.). Cf. Vielau, *Luther und der Türke*, 17–28, about how Luther emphasizes repentance and prayer and is at the same time restrained in his opinions about the war against the Turks right up to the end of the 1520s.

327 The bull denounces this understanding: "Proeliari adversus Turcas est repugnare Deo

---

response to the bull. In connection with article 34 of the bull, he points out that the failures of attempted war against the Turks indicate that God uses the Turks to chastize Christendom. The power play of the pope and the unrepentant lives of the people have produced God's wrath. Besides, the Germans are financially plundered in the effort to raise funds for the planned war against the Turks. Because the pope is worse than the Turks, people ought not go out to war in the name of the pope. Luther does not reject every war against the Turks. It is, however, critical that before embarking on such a war the people ought to repent of their own sins and win God's grace. It is only then that they will be able to succeed in defending themselves with weapons against the invaders.[328]

This idea that the Turks are God's rod against a godless, blaspheming, and unrepentant people returns in the important essays *On War against the Turk* and *Heerpredigt wider den Türken* (1529). Here Luther says that the Turkish sultan, Suleiman II, does not go to war to defend his own land as an ordained leader; instead, he goes forth to war as an evil plunderer. This is in itself a work of Satan, but at the same time, God uses the evil Turks as a rod to punish Christendom.[329] When the situation develops in this manner, the people must turn away God's wrath and chastisement through repentance. Then *eo ipso* the Turks are disarmed as servants of the devil.[330] God cannot forever tolerate persecution of the true faith and its proponents nor the blasphemies of the pope, bishops, and priests. Indeed, sin, evil, and blasphemy are so overwhelming among Christians, non-Christians, and false Christians that God as the Lord of creation and salvation must discipline the people back to their senses. That's exactly what God is doing through the Turks as his own rod. If the Turks do not exercise this function, someone must do it, as long as Christ does not soon return.[331] In these well-trained Turkish armies,

---

visitanti iniquitates nostras" (WA 30/2:93). About the process of Luther's excommunication, see Öberg, *Himmelrikets nycklar och kyrklig bot i Luthers teologi*, 456ff.

328 WA 7:140.18–141.25, 442.5–443.3.

329 LW 46:170 (WA 30/2:116.9ff.).

330 LW 46:170 (WA 30/2:116.27ff.).

331 *Heerpredigt wider den Türken* (1529), WA 30/2:161.6ff.: "Es haben könige und fürsten, Bischoff und pfaffen bisher das Euangelion veriagt und verfolget, viel bluts vergossen und den dienern Christi alle plag und unglück angelegt und ist die lesterung und schmach auch widder die offentliche erkante warheit, so uber die massen schendlich gros gewest und das volck so über aus böse und mutwillig, das ich hab weissagen müssen, Deudschland müsse ynn kurtz Gott eine torheit bezalen. Dasselbige gehet itzt daher und sehet an, Gott helffe uns und sey uns gnedig, Amen." WA 30/2:180.14ff.: "Aber weil der Türcke gleichwol Gottes rute und eine plage ist über die sunde beide der Christen und unchristen odder falschen Christen . . . weil Deudsch land so vol bosheit und lesterung ist, das zu hoch uber macht ist und yn hymel schreyet, kans nicht anders

the reformer sees above all God's disciplinary rod for the sins of the people and their unrepentance. If the people do not repent, the Turks have powerful allies in the sins of the people and in God's chastising arm. Then the Turks will go from victory to victory like an apocalyptic enemy (*Gog*). According to Luther, God's Word in Ezekiel 7, for example, has predicted that the Turks would be successful.[332]

For Luther, God is not only love. Instead, God is to his core both holy and full of love. He disciplines in holy wrath even those whom he loves. In the pope's church, the reformer has experienced blasphemies and violence against the truth and its proponents. He has seen how certain evangelicals have appropriated the rediscovered Gospel with ingratitude and with a flood of unrighteousness in usury and greed, robbery and distortion of rights, etc. The people despise the preachers who call for repentance. All this causes the reformer to fearfully expect that God is going to come with a harsh discipline to awaken the people. It can come through the violence of the pope's church, through the ravages of pestilence, or through the Turks.[333] God is not driven by lust to destroy, but as the Lord of history, he wants to hold up truth and righteousness and remain God over people and whatever takes place.[334]

---

werden, wo wir uns nicht bessern und ablassen von verfolgung und lesterung des Euangelij, wir müssen herhalten und eine staupe leiden. Wo es der Türcke nicht thut, so mus doch etwas anders thun, Es were denn, das der iüngst tag selbs keme." For more of Luther's opinions about the Turks as God's punishment and rod for a faithless Christianity, see the many examples of all types of Luther's writings in *Ortsregister*, WA 62:346. The Turks are a plague and a catastrophe (WA 62:349f.).

332 About the Turks as a victorious eschatological enemy and as the Antichrist that is prophesied in, for example, Daniel 7:8; 11:36f.; Ezekiel 38:22; Revelation 20:8ff., see WA 30/2:162–73, especially 173.20f.: "hie hörestu das dem Mahometh odder Türcken der sieg widder die Christen und heiligen verkündigt ist." See also *Das XXXVIII. und XXXIX. Capitel Hesechiel vom Gog* (1530), WA 30/2:225.31–226.11, and the column notes, 230.235; and "Sermons on John 1–2 (1537/1538)," WA 46:607.26ff., 609.2ff. *Ortsregister*, WA 62:344, 349, 351, lists hundreds of examples in Luther's sermons, Bible commentaries, and writings wherein the Turks are called the enemies of Christ, the devil himself, and a victorious enemy.

333 *Vermahnung an alle Pfarrherrn* (1539), WA 50:486.7ff., 486.17ff.; *Appeal for Prayer against the Turks* (1541), WA 51:586.2ff., 587.9ff., 589.1ff., 592.13ff. For this theme, see Lamparter, *Luthers Stellung zum Türkenkrieg*, 17ff., 48ff.

334 *Appeal for Prayer against the Turks* (1541), LW 43:219 (WA 51:586.5ff.): "How can he be patient any longer? Ultimately he must rescue and defend truth and justice and punish wickedness and those evil and poisonous blasphemers and tyrants. Otherwise he would forfeit his divinity and would not be regarded as divine by anyone if everyone could continue doing as he pleases and could scorn God and his word and command so complacently and shamefully, treating God like a fool or jumping jack whose commands and warnings are not to be taken seriously. So God has to make us understand that he really means it and is not joking." See also WA 51:594.9ff.

In sixteenth-century Germany, the Turks (and the pope) are not only a rod of discipline in God's hand. Their plundering armies and the faith that they are spreading are in their essence satanic and represent something evil. According to Luther, the papacy constitutes a more terrible evil than the Turks, but both are representatives of the Antichrist.[335] Because the pope attacks primarily Christian doctrine, faith, and conscience while the Muslim Turks attack primarily life and limb, they are called respectively the spirit of Antichrist and the flesh of Antichrist.[336] In this way, the Turkish armies are considered to be not only the rod of God's discipline but also agents of the evil one. Their hordes are said to be filled with devils. In their fight against the empire, Christ's angriest enemy is met.[337] But

---

335 LW 46:180–81 (WA 30/2:125.26–126.20), summarized in LW 46:181 (WA 30/2:126.1f.): "But just as the pope is the Antichrist, so the Turk is the very devil incarnate." Cf. WA 51:599.16ff., especially "Ein Kinderlied, zu singen, wider die zween Ertzfeinde Christi, und seiner heiligen Kirchen, den Bapst und Türcken, etc.," WA 35:467.20ff.:

> Erhalt uns Herr bey deinem Wort
> Und steur des Bapsts und Türcken Mord
> Die Jhesum Christum deinen Son
> Wolten stürtzen von deinem Thron.
> Beweis dein Macht, HERR Jhesu Christ,
> Der du Herr aller Herren bist,
> Beschrim dein arme Christenheit,
> Das sie dich lob in ewigkeit.

> Lord, keep us steadfast in thy Word
> And curb the Turks' and papists' sword
> Who Jesus Christ, thine only Son
> Fain would tumble from off thy throne.
> Proof of thy might, Lord Christ, afford,
> For thou of all the lords art Lord;
> Thine own poor Christendom defend,
> That it may praise thee without end.
> (LW 53:305; cf. *Lutheran Service Book*, 655; *Lutheran Worship*, 334; *Lutheran Book of Worship*, 230)

Many passages about the pope and the Turks as Antichrist are listed in *Ortsregister*, WA 62:342. See also in WA 62:344, 349, those many passages that refer to the Turks as Christ's enemies and as the devil himself.

336 WATr 1:135.14ff. (no. 330): "Ego omnino puto papatum esse Antichristum, aut si quis vult addere Turcam, papa est spiritus Antichristi, et Turca est caro Antichristi. Sie helffen beyde einander wurgen, hic corpore et gladio, ille doctrina et spiritu." Cf. WA 30/2:162.1ff., 162.8ff. Concerning these latter notes and the relevant literature about the Antichrist during the medieval ages and Luther's time, see Vogler, "Luthers Geschichtsauffassung im Spiegel seines Türkenbildes," 132f.

337 *On War against the Turk*, LW 46:174–75, 201–2 (WA 30/2:120.25ff., 144.4ff.). *Heerpredigt wider den Türken* (1529) in connection with Daniel 7:8, WA 30/2:166ff., 169.7ff., 170.9ff., 172.18ff., 179.11ff.

when they have completed their task as one of the worst eschatological menaces in and over the Roman Empire, their time will be up.[338] Then Christ will return on a day that God alone knows.[339]

Here I want to refer back to the sections in chapter 2 about God's providence and people as God's tools in the course of world history.[340] In Luther's understanding of history, the divine and transcendental are united with the course of life, with the works of ordinary people, and with the history of the peoples. People in all social classes and all kinds of work are God's masks (*larva Dei*), and God steers their deeds as the Lord of both the universe and of the smallest thing. Even the history of the peoples and the drama of murky history is undergirded and carried by God's righteousness and love, the so-called providence or play with all that is.[341] God and Satan are in constant battle, but the Almighty can use even the devil

---

338 WA 30/2:171.18ff. and WATr 1:127.11ff. (no. 308); 2:89.1ff. (no. 1405); 5:63.21ff. (no. 5337); 6:354.4ff. (no. 7042). Cf. Vogler, "Luthers Geschichtsauffassung im Spiegel seines Türkenbildes," 122f.

339 WA 30/2:170.29ff. Against his own warnings to the contrary, Luther has, on the basis of the obscure words in Daniel 7:25 and with his starting point at the sack of Constantinople in 1453, sought to say something about the date of Christ's return. Only God knows, but in 1538 (?), Luther reckons that Christ could return in about twenty years: "Jch kan aber diese prophecey: Tempus, duo tempora et dimidium temporis, nicht definieren. Jch wolts gern auff den Turcken ziehen, qui regnare incepit a capta Constantinopli 1453, welchs ist nu 85 jar; wen ich nun tempus rechne secundum aetatem Christi 30 annos, so macht dieser spruch 105 jar, so hat der Turck noch 20 jar zu regiren. Nun, Gott weiss, wie ers machen will. Quomodo suos liberare voluerit, non est nostrum divinare, sed orare et poenitentiam agere" (WATr 3:646.5ff. [no. 3831]). Cf. WATr 3:453.29ff. (no. 904). In the older Luther, we read, however, that 1600 might be an approximate date for Christ's return. See *Luther and World Mission*, 481n505, and the quotation from WA 30/2:224.24ff.

340 See *Luther and World Mission*, 15–32.

341 Concerning this, see first the enlightening essay by Vogler, "Luthers Geschichtsauffassung im Spiegel seienes Türkenbildes," 123ff., which refers to a number of other works. See also Asheim, *Glaube und Erziehung bei Luther*, 118ff., about "Die Erziehung Gottes." Cf. the following enlightening passages: "Das man wol mag sagen, der wellt laufft und sonderlich seyner heyligen wesen sey Gottes mummerey, darunter er sich verbirgt und ynn der wellt so wunderlich regirt und rhumort" (WA 15:373.14ff.). *Lenten Postil* (1525): "Alle creature sind Gottes larven und mumereyen" (WA 17/2:28f.). In the *Larger Commentary on Galatians* (1531/1535): "Thus the magistrate, the emperor, the king, the prince, the consul, the teacher, the preacher, the pupil, the father, the mother, the children, the master, the servant—all these are social positions or external masks" (LW 26:95 [WA 40/1:175.17ff.]). Cf. WATr 1:491.25ff. (no. 972). Concerning God and history, see also "Preface to Galeatius Capella's *History* (1538)," WA 50:384.29–385.35.

and demons to produce something good.[342] It is this wider perspective that undergirds Luther's view that the Turks are at the same time the rod of God's discipline and the eschatological and diabolical instrument of Satan. History is ultimately God's history, and his transcendent power can discipline those whom he loves.

LUTHER EXHORTS THE PEOPLE FIRST TO REPENTANCE AND PRAYER

The reformer taught that God disciplines with the hard rod of the Turks because the people have responded to the Gospel with ingratitude while at the same time living in unrepentance and all types of sin and transgressions. Already at the beginning of the Reformation (1518–1521), Luther prioritized true repentance of the people over crusade against the Turks.[343] In 1524, he is reserved about the war against the Turks planned by the Roman Catholics because this was proposed as a war to preserve the Christian faith while the people continued to be unrepentant.[344] When the Turks closed in on Vienna in 1529, the reformer advised that the first phase of averting the Turkish threat ought to be serious repentance among the people. He exhorts the preachers to preach repentance with power[345] while referring to examples from both the Old and New Testaments.[346] This repentance of the people should be followed by serious prayer for help against the Turks and by steadfast faith in God's promises to answer prayers.[347] Such repentance and prayer defeats Satan and the Turks while at the same time taking the rod out of God's hand.[348] In *Heerpredigt wider den Türken* (1529) and in later passages, Luther emphasizes the same exhortation to repentance in the same way.[349]

We ought to make special mention here of Luther's work *Vermahnung zum Gebet wider den Türken* (*Appeal for Prayer against the Turks*), which was written after the Ottoman Turks' infantry again threatened Vienna and Germany in 1541.[350] Here Luther paints a picture of the spite for the Gospel and the unrepen-

---

342 *Bondage of the Will* (1525), WA 18:782.21ff., 782.30ff., 709.16ff., 709.30ff.

343 For Luther's exhortations to spiritual war through repentance and prayer as the priority in light of the Turkish threat, see Holsten, "Christentum und nicht-christliche Religion," 138f.; Vielau, *Luther und der Türke*, 17ff.; Lind, *Luthers Stellung zum Kreuz- und Türkenkrieg*, 56ff.; Lamparter, *Luthers Stellung zum Türkenkrieg*, 48ff.; Kooiman, "Luthers getuigenes in de oorlogtegen de Turken," 26ff.; and Mau, "Luthers Stellung zu den Türken," 647ff.

344 WA 15:275ff.

345 LW 46:170–71 (WA 30/2:116.26ff., 117.11ff., 117.21ff.).

346 LW 46:173–74 (WA 30/2:118.10ff.).

347 LW 46:173–75 (WA 30/2:118.10ff., 118.22ff., 119.27ff.).

348 LW 46:170–74 (WA 30/2:116.27ff., 120.11ff.).

349 WA 30/2:180.17ff. Cf. WA 30/2:225.25ff. and WA 50:486.12–487.14.

350 In September 1541, Suleiman II had invaded the Hungarian capital, transformed the

tant sinning that continued among all social classes. This has caused God to strike the peoples with the iron rod of the Turks.[351] Then Luther exhorts the people to repent both in heart and in lifestyle. True repentance has both personal and socioethical consequences. If the people repent, then God will hear the prayers of the people and help them withstand.[352] Luther is afraid that because certain people refuse to listen to the appeals for repentance, afflictions will continue to plague the people and affect both the unrepentant and the true Christians. Therefore true Christians ought to pray for God's mercy and try to endure whatever comes.[353] Furthermore, the reformer lays it on the hearts of preachers to encourage all people to pray to God in this dire situation. He even encourages public prayer during worship services to the same end.[354] The Christians will have faith in the power of prayer to hinder the continuing success of the Turkish hordes. They ought not to be gripped by Islamic fatalism in which it is thought that everything has been predestined by an immutable will of God.[355] At any rate, a person ought to live according to God's will in all situations. After one has prayed, equipped himself or herself, and offered resistance, one ought to leave all in God's hands.[356] Repentance and prayer are strong spiritual weapons against the Turks.

---

church into a mosque, and put both the city and the government under Turkish control.

351 WA 51:585–93 in great detail.

352 WA 51:593.15–596.2. See especially LW 43:224–25 (WA 51:594.9ff.): "The Turk, you see, is our 'schoolmaster.' He has to discipline and teach us to fear God and to pray. Otherwise we will do what we have been doing—rot in sin and complacency. If we really want help and guidance, let us repent and change those evil ways which I described before. Princes and rulers are to see that justice prevails in the land. They will have to curb the money-lenders and protect us from the avarice of the nobles, burghers, and peasants. Above all, they will have to honor God's word, support, protect, and further schools and churches, preachers and teachers. The nobles, burghers, and peasants will likewise have to do their part to protect morality and honesty in city and nation. No longer must the rank effrontery of artisans, laborers, and servants be allowed to go unchecked, but should be punished promptly. In short, we have got our instructions in plain and clear German. We all know quite well, thank God, what is proper for every station and rank in life . . . . If we do this, God will hear our prayer and most assuredly help us as he has promised by the prophets and all of Scripture." Cf. WA 51:600.5ff. See also Lamparter, *Luthers Stellung zum Türkenkrieg*, 52ff., concerning, among other things, the concrete fruits of repentance in lifestyle.

353 WA 51:596.3ff., 597.15ff., 600.17ff.

354 WA 51:606–14. Concerning intercession in the church, WA 51:606.15ff., 608.6ff. Cf. also *Vermahnung an die Pfarrherrn in der Superattendenz zu Wittenberg* (1543), WA 53:558–60.

355 WA 51:614.17ff.

356 WA 51:616.15ff., 618.7ff.

The Turks Must Be Met with the Military Might of the Governing Authorities

Luther's emphasis on the repentance of the heart, holy lifestyle, and prayer for mercy led, as we have seen, to the conclusion that a war against the Turks as such ought to be rejected. However, it is clear in Luther's responses to the bulls of 1520 and 1521 that he had reacted negatively only to the kind of war against the Turk that was considered a crusade in the name of the pope. He had not rejected a just war against invaders.[357] During the 1520s, there are many short passages in which Luther supports a war under the leadership of the emperor.[358] Finally, there is an unmistakably clear argument in *On War against the Turk* (1529). Here Luther speaks not only about how the Christian ought to equip himself or herself with a repentant heart, a righteous lifestyle, and prayer. He also encourages Emperor Charles to take responsibility for defending Germany militarily.[359]

Luther says that in his theses of 1518 he had written about the ideas of those times and the eagerness to crusade against the Turks. The reformer had at that time reacted against the confusion of the spiritual and earthly regiments and against the fact that the pope and his hierarchy, while despising the princes, had hunted money using such a crusade as an excuse. Therefore, the emphasis had not been on repentance.[360] In 1529 the reformer especially reacts against the tendency to make the war against the Turks into some kind of religious war in which the soldiers would fight in Christ's name and for the spread of Christ's reign with military might. This is directly opposed to Christ's teaching, according to Luther.

---

357 See especially WA 7:443.19ff. Cf. *Luther and World Mission*, 430ff., with notes.

358 WA 6:419.23ff.; WA 19:604.23ff., 662.9ff. *Ortsregister*, WA 62:350f., shows that during his entire life as a reformer Luther gave his support for a just defensive war against the Turks and under the leadership of the governing authorities.

359 LW 46:184–205 (WA 30/2:129.17–148.29). Concerning the duty of the authorities for defense and war against the Turks, see Vielau, *Luther und der Türke*, 24ff.; Lind, *Luthers Stellung zum Kreuz- und Türkenkrieg*, 61ff.; and Lamparter, *Luthers Stellung zum Türkenkrieg*, 68ff. See also Pfister, "Reformation, Türken und Islam," 348ff.; and Mau, "Luthers Stellung zu den Türken," 649ff.

360 LW 46:162–65 (WA 30/2:108.19–111.12). Luther says this about the situation in 1518: "... no one had taught, no one had heard, and no one knew anything about temporal government, whence it came, what its office and work were, or how it ought to serve God. .... And so it was that at that time the pope and the clergy were all in all and through all, like God in the world [Eph. 4:6], and the temporal rulers were in darkness, oppressed and unknown" (LW 46:163 [WA 46:109.4ff., 109.20ff.]). Concerning the importance of the doctrine of the two regiments for Luther's initial hesitation and later decisiveness against crusade, see Vielau, *Luther und der Türke*, 20ff.; Buchanan, "Luther and the Turks," 146ff., 158ff.; and Kooiman, "Luthers getuigenes in de oorlogtegen de Turken," 29ff.

Christ has come and sent out his Gospel only to save from sin and grant eternal life.[361] That does not mean that a warring prince could not be a Christian or that a Christian could not bear arms in such a prince's army. The point Luther wants to make is that one ought to keep the spiritual and the earthly regiments separate. God has given the worldly authority, not the church, the task to defend the earthly regiment.[362] Against the crusade ideology that was so deeply rooted in the Roman Catholic Church, experience also teaches about war in the name of Christ, the pope, or the church. Such wars have not, for example, been successful in stemming the success of the Turkish armies.[363] In war one should not cry out "Ecclesia, ecclesia: Hie Kirche, Hie Kirche" or storm forward under the banners of the prelates with the crucifix at the point. If a soldier sees such, he ought to retreat and refuse to fight.[364]

---

361 LW 46:165 (WA 30/2:111.13ff.): "They undertook to fight against the Turk in the name of Christ, and taught and incited men to do this, as though our people were an army of Christians against the Turks, who were enemies of Christ. This is absolutely contrary to Christ's doctrine and name. It is against his doctrine because he says that Christians shall not resist evil, fight, or quarrel, nor take revenge or insist on rights [Matt. 5:39]." Cf. LW 46:166 (WA 30/2:112.1ff.). In *Heerpredigt wider den Türken* (1529), the reformer summarizes the theses in the above-cited text and says: "Das man nicht solle widder den Türcken kriegen, als unter der Christen namen noch mit streit angreiffen, als einen feind der Christen . . . . Aber solle nicht streiten als ein Christen odder unter eins Christen namen, Sondern las deinen Welltlichen oberherrn kriegen" (WA 30/2:173.18ff., 173.31f.). Cf. Luther's extremely bitter polemic against the pope's general indulgence for those who volunteer for war against the Turks in *Bulla papae Pauli tertii de indulgentiis contra Turcam, etc.* (WA 50:113–16).

362 LW 46:166 (WA 30/2:112.9ff., 112.14ff.): "I say this not because I would teach that worldly rulers ought not be Christians, or that a Christian cannot bear the sword and serve God in temporal government. . . . But what I want to do is to keep a distinction between the callings and the offices, so that everyone can see to what God has called him and fulfil the duties of his office faithfully and sincerely in the service of God." In LW 46:166 (WA 30/2:112.17ff.), Luther refers to *On Temporal Authority* (1523) (LW 45:81–129 [WA 11:229ff.]) and to *Whether Soldiers, Too, Can Be Saved* (1526) (LW 46:87–137 [WA 19:616ff.]). For the doctrine of the two regiments, see *Luther and World Mission*, 26ff.

363 LW 46:166–67 (WA 30/2:113.1ff., 113.20ff., 114.16ff.). Concerning crusade ideology and its connection with teaching about repentance and the theories about the empire as the *corpus Christianum,* see Lind, *Luthers Stellung zum Kreuz- und Türkenkrieg,* 7ff., 13ff., 25ff. Lind examines Luther's rejection of the so-called holy war or crusade especially from the perspective of the two regiments doctrine; see *Luthers Stellung zum Kreuz- und Türkenkrieg,* 30ff., 41ff. Cf. Buchanan, "Luther and the Turks," 145ff., 150ff.

364 LW 46:168–69 (WA 30/2:115.1ff., especially 115.23ff.).

It is not the church but the emperor and the princes—by virtue of the fact that God has made them defenders of peace and order in their respective lands—who have the duty to meet the Turks with military might. Here they are not acting as defenders of church and faith but exclusively on the basis of God's command to the earthly regiment to defend and secure peace in the kingdom. In practical terms, amid all the rivalry between the princes, Luther exhorts Emperor Charles to defend the realm against the Turks because it is his responsibility.[365] Luther is well enough informed to realize that the Ottoman military has enormous power and potential, which is why the emperor and the princes must hold together, equip themselves, and gather considerable troop strength if they are to have a chance to succeed.[366] Emperor, princes, and soldiers in battle ought to cry out to God for help against the invaders, not fight in the pride of their own strength.[367] Luther often speaks about how the emperor and princes heap sin on themselves when they take too lightly their God-given duty to defend the kingdom against invaders.[368] He has even described the difference between a just, necessary war of defense and an objectionable war of expansion to win new territory and glory.[369] The reformer is concerned not to bait toward war, and he in no way glorifies war. Luther's heart beats for the individual soldiers, some of whom will die and some

---

365 After the Christian has repented and prayed, it is up to the emperor to lead the defense against the Turks: "The second man who ought to fight against the Turk is Emperor Charles, or whoever may be the emperor; for the Turk is attacking his subjects and his empire, and it is his duty, as a regular ruler appointed by God, to defend his own. I repeat it here: I would not urge or bid anyone to fight against the Turk unless the first method, mentioned above, that men had first repented and been reconciled to God, etc., had been followed" (LW 46:184 [WA 30/2:129.17ff.]). Cf. concerning the duty of the emperor and princes also to defend, see LW 46:185–89 (WA 30/2:131.18ff., 132.21ff., 134.15ff., 135.7ff.). See also *Heerpredigt wider den Türken* (1529), WA 30/2:173.18ff., especially 173.31ff.: "Aber solle nicht streiten als ein Christen odder unter eins Christen namen, Sondern las deinen Welltlichen oberherrn kriegen. Unter desselbigen panier und namen soltu reisen als ein welltlicher untersass nach dem leibe, der seinem oberherrn geschworn ist mit leib und gut gehorsam zu sein, das wil Gott von dir haben [Romans 13:1; Titus 3:1]."

366 LW 46:202 (WA 30/2:145ff.). Concerning the enormous power of the Turks according to Luther, see *Ortsregister*, WA 62:338, and Vogler, "Luthers Geschichtsauffassung im Spiegel seines Türkenbildes," 119f.

367 LW 46:191 (WA 30/2:135.15ff., 135.24ff.).

368 *Whether Soldiers, Too, Can Be Saved* (1526), LW 46:87–137 (WA 19:627.3ff.). Cf. *On War against the Turk*, LW 46:186–87 (WA 30/2:132.21ff., 133.7ff., 134.30ff.). See other examples in *Ortsregister*, WA 62:350f.

369 WA 11:272.3ff., 273.34f.; 19:648.1ff., 568.14ff. Cf. Lamparter, *Luthers Stellung zum Türkenkrieg*, 32ff.

of whom will be taken captive. As soldiers in the army of the emperor, they ought to know that they fight under the banner of a just authority. If they die under right repentance and under faith, they will be saved.[370] Those who willingly and out of cowardice submit to the Turks and sabotage the war against them are traitors against the authority placed by God with the emperor. They share in the ravages of the Turks and will soon have the chance to taste the consequences of their choices.[371]

In an examination of Luther and world mission such as this, it is important to be clear about this fact: Luther stands against all forms of holy war and all forms of mission by the sword. He has, as has been shown above, reacted violently against war in the name of Christ and the church, whether such war should be fought under the leadership of the church hierarchy or indirectly through the emperor and princes as the defenders of the Gospel, faith, and the church. For example, in *On Temporal Authority* (1523), Luther had rejected all attempts from the authorities to involve themselves in the affairs of the church, to force consciences in matters of faith, or to try to eliminate heresies with power of violence.[372] He says:

> Heresy can never be restrained by force. One will have to tackle the problem in some other way, for heresy must be opposed and dealt with otherwise than with the sword. Here God's word must do the fighting. If it does not succeed, certainly the temporal power will not succeed either, even if it were to drench the world in blood. . . . Heresy is a spiritual matter which you cannot hack to pieces with iron, consume with fire, or drown in water.[373]

Luther says in another context that the princes ought not set themselves in the place of God, as if faith and the church were dependent on their pleasure and protection. Faith is a rock and a power that is stronger than Satan and death. Faith rests in the Holy Trinity, against whom no one can rise up in presumptuousness.[374] In *On War against the Turk* (1529), Luther remarks that the emperor and the princes should not be regarded as the protectors of Christianity, the Gospel,

---

370 LW 46:184, 191 (WA 30/2:129.35ff., 136.6ff., 136.27ff.) and especially *Heerpredigt wider den Türken* (1529), WA 30/2:173.18ff., 173.29ff., 174.12ff., 174.24ff., 181.3ff., where Luther does everything to comfort those who go out to war under the banner of a just authority.

371 LW 46:193–95 (WA 30/2:137.21–140.23, 182.23ff.).

372 Cf. Aland, "Toleranz und Glaubensfreiheit im 16. Jahrhundert," 77ff., with references, among them passages from *On Temporal Authority* (1523), WA 11:261ff. See also *Luther and World Mission*, 26ff., 253ff.

373 LW 45:114 (WA 11:268.22ff., 268.27ff.).

374 WA 15:278.11ff.

and the faith, the ones who have the responsibility to destroy the faith of the Turks. The protector of the church is God himself, and he alone has power over the mystery of unbelief.[375] Therefore the emperor and the princes ought not commit themselves to holy war against the Turks with the purpose of destroying their false belief and evil lifestyle; instead, they ought to protect the kingdom and its citizens against the invasions of the Saracens. The war against the Turks ought not to have anything to do with religion. It is only the campaign and invasions of their armies that is the reason to meet them with military might. Luther writes: "I do not advise men to wage war against the Turk or the pope because of false belief or evil life, but because of the murder and destruction which he does."[376] In *Heerpredigt wider den Türken* (1529), Luther says "that one ought not wage war against the Turks under the name of Christ nor attack them as enemies of the Christians."[377] Luther could say that the papacy's false teaching and unholy life could be attacked with prayer and God's Word alone.[378] Even concerning Judaism, Luther emphasized the power of the Word and of prayer, but he was willing to draw in the "secular" authorities, as we have seen, when it concerned public blasphemy of the Christian faith. We will see in the following how energetically Luther uses God's Word in the Old and New Testaments against Muhammad, the Qur'an, and Islam. This comprehensive apology is the first step in the meeting with the religion of the Muslims, a preparation or a part of mission for the Muslims.

LUTHER'S APOLOGETIC AGAINST THE RELIGION OF THE MUSLIMS

The reformer has often expressed that something of a new heathenism had spread in the West through the papacy. Here he began his reformation work, which, after some time, also included his controversy with the enthusiasts. Earlier, we also have seen how he thought and reacted in his meeting with German Judaism, which was the first non-Christian religion that he encountered. The other non-Christian religion that Luther and the evangelicals met was Islam, which for Luther was represented by the Turks.

---

375 LW 46:165, 185 (WA 30/2:111.13ff., 130.22ff., 130.31ff.).

376 LW 46:198 (WA 30/2:143.1ff.). Cf. "Sermons on John 1 and 2 (1537/38)," WA 46:606.33ff., 608.1ff. Concerning this subject, see Lamparter, *Luthers Stellung zum Türkenkrieg*, 80ff., and especially the examination of crusade ideology in Lind, *Luthers Stellung zum Kreuz- und Türkenkrieg*, 30ff., 41ff., 61ff. See also Kooiman, "Luthers getuigenes in de oorlogtegen de Turken," 30ff.; and Wallmann, "Luthers Stellung zu Judentum und Islam," 55.

377 WA 30/2:173.18ff.

378 LW 46:198–99 (WA 30/2:143.12ff.).

As we have seen in our investigation of Luther's relationship to the Jews, there exists an inimical alliance that seeks to destroy Christianity and the Reformation in which the Gospel now has began to shine clearly. This coalition consists of the pope and his church, the Jews, the enthusiasts, and finally the Turks. Each in their own way, the members of the alliance share this common feature: They set themselves against the Scriptures and corrupt the doctrine of righteousness through faith in Christ. Against all the partners of this coalition, Luther presents biblical faith and confession, with faith in Jesus at its center as the absolute truth.[379] In the following, I want to point out some of the main themes in Luther's clear apologetic and polemical disputes with Islam. The purpose of this apologetic is partly to describe the faith of the Muslims and partly to comfort and equip the Christians so they are not drawn to that faith if the Turks should invade or if Christians should be taken captive and forced to live among the Muslims.[380] As we shall see, he hopes that at least some Muslims will become Christians.

THE APOLOGIST MUST KNOW THE QUR'AN

When Luther begins his apologetic disputation with the dogma and ethics of Islam, he lacks a complete edition of the Qur'an. In 1529 he complains that though the Turks and a potential invasion are so near, he does not know enough about the faith and life of the Muslims. Scholars had neglected this subject, and they only tease the Germans with lies about the Turks.[381] Luther says, however,

---

379 See Sucher, *Luthers Stellung zu den Juden*, 217–25; and Oberman, "Luthers Beziehungen zu den Juden," 521ff., 527ff., who provides examples. Cf. WA 5:343.1ff.; 12.285.3f.; 19:599.1ff.; 29:612.11ff., 612.17ff.; 37:58.25ff.; 40/1:604.1ff.; 46:129.30ff.; WATr 3:35.2ff., 35.5ff. (no. 2863b). This theme is especially clear in LC II 66: "These three articles of the Creed, therefore, separate and distinguish us Christians from all other people on earth. All who are outside the Christian people, whether heathen, Turks, Jews, or false Christians and hypocrites—even though they believe in and worship only the one, true God—nevertheless do not know what his attitude is toward them. They cannot be confident of his love and blessing, and therefore they remain in eternal wrath and condemnation. For they do not have the LORD Christ, and, besides, they are not illuminated and blessed by the gifts of the Holy Spirit" (K-W, 440 [*BSLK*, 669]). Luther develops this theme in his January 31, 1546, sermon, delivered shortly before his death (WA 46:149.39–151.42).

380 This is expressed clearly in the most important of the writings about the Turks, see LW 46:162, 175 (WA 30/2:108.3ff., 122.25ff.). See also WA 30/2:161.22ff., 190.15ff., 191.30ff., 192.21ff., 206.23ff., 207.23ff.; 51:593.15ff., 622.5ff.; 53:272.30ff.

381 *On War against the Turk*, LW 46:176 (WA 30/2:121.18ff.). Cf. WA 30/2:205.4–15. Many scholars have shown how information about the Turks and Islam was transmitted during the medieval and Reformation ages through poetry, historical research, mission stories, travelogues, and the theological writings of, for example, Peter the Venerable,

that he possesses several passages from the Qur'an that he wishes to translate so the people might learn about the Qur'an and its atrocities. But Luther expresses himself in his apologetics only about things he knows for sure have been written in the Qur'an. Hearsay is not a good foundation for apologetics.[382] Before *Heerpredigt* (1529) was published, Luther worked on a foreword to a new edition of a book by the Dominican Ricoldus de Monte Crucis about the rites and customs of the Turks. It was called *Confutatio Alcorani*. Luther respected this work because it seemed reliable and not written from a negative perspective or with hate. The one who in the attempt to strengthen the faith of others explains only the atrocities and is silent about the positive sides of Islam does a disservice to his or her own purpose.[383] When in February 1542 Luther finally got his hands on a Latin edition of the Qur'an, he published *Confutatio Alcorani* in a free and edited translation with a foreword and his own confutation.[384]

Thomas Aquinas, and Nicholas of Cusa. During the Middle Ages, a large number of works about Islam existed that were often strongly polemical and not well researched. Even the handbook of the Muslims, the Qur'an, was little known in Luther's time. From the writings of the anti-Islamic polemicist John of Damascus and Vicentius Beauvais's *Speculum historale* (ca. 1200), there were spread a mass of fabulous and ill-founded accusations against the Muslims. Furthermore, from the time of John Damascus, it was believed that Muhammad had not been the founder of a new religion but a former Christian who had for some time brought many to faith in Jesus Christ but who later became a heretic and a schismatic. When the papal Curia had supposedly not recognized him, Muhammad built his own sect that spread doctrines of satanic Arianism and polygamy. He was supposedly killed by a pig and eaten by dogs. Muhammad was considered a Christian who had backslid and a corrupter of the Christian faith, even by the reformers. In the polemics against Islam, the Qur'an was generally considered to be satanic. Naturally this made it a difficult book to publish. See Holsten, "Christentum und nicht-christliche Religion," 126f.; Köhler, *Melanchthon und der Islam*, 7–18; Pfister, "Reformation, Türken und Islam," 353ff.; and Mau, "Luthers Stellung zu den Türken," 656–61. These latter two authors show how Luther requested a Latin Qur'an and worked to get such an edition published. See also the foreword to Biblianders's edition of the Qur'an (WA 53:561–68).

382 LW 46:176, 182 (WA 30/2:121.30ff., 127.3ff.).

383 *Vorwort zu dem Libellus de ritu et moribus Turcorum* (1530), WA 30/2:205–8, especially 205.4ff., 205.16ff., 205.25ff. Ricoldus's book is especially important for Luther because the author had lived in an Islamic milieu for 20 years (1280–1300). He learned Arabic and studied the Qur'an thoroughly.

384 *Verlegung des Alcoran Bruder Richardi, Prediger Ordens* (1542), WA 53:272–396. In the foreword (WA 53:272.16ff.), Luther suggests that by reading the Latin Qur'an he has proof that Ricoldus has truly communicated the teaching of the Qur'an. The notes in the Weimar Edition indicate, however, some passages in which Ricoldus had no proof for his arguments.

The fear that some Christians would be led astray by reading the Qur'an made it difficult to publish the Qur'an in Latin. A first edition was published in 1530 in Venice, but it was burned by order of the pope. In 1536 the council in Protestant Basel vetoed the possibility of another Latin edition. But during the mid-1530s in Zurich, Theodor Bibliander—his own time's foremost scholar of Islam, language, and religious history—and the publisher Johann Oporin began to work to publish a Latin Qur'an together with some other writings. These finally were given some invaluable help by Luther, and that Latin edition of the Qur'an was published on January 11, 1543.[385] In Luther's struggle to see that the Qur'an should be published in a language readable by, first, theologians and priests, the humanistic

---

385 Pfister, "Reformation, Türken und Islam," 355f., describes the drama and the many turnabouts in obtaining the approval to publish that edition of the Qur'an. See also Mau, "Luthers Stellung zu den Türken," 659ff. The Latin edition of the Qur'an that was finally published by Bibliander on January 11, 1543, was based on a comparison between Latin and Arabic manuscripts. At first Johann Oporin was most engaged. So the edition might not be censored, it was published with a foreword by Philip Melanchthon, who thoroughly justified the publication of the Qur'an by Oporin. The text of the Qur'an already was printed and the second part of the edition, that is, the anti-Islam apologetic, was on press when the matter was given to the censors and the council in Basel for consideration. The publishers wanted to present the censors and the council with a *fait accompli*. But this dangerous game ended unhappily. The per- mission was being sought while Oporin was receiving support from theologians in Zürich and from Bucer in Strassburg. At the end of August, the council in Basel sentenced Oporin for breaking the law and imprisoned him and confiscated the entire edition of the Qur'an. Oporin was soon after set free.

The enterprise first picked up some speed when Luther came into the picture. In a letter dated October 27, 1542, he writes that it is probably not the competition between different publishers but serious reservations in the Basel council that have caused the censure. However, he could think of no better way to damage the teaching of Muhammad and the Turks than to publish the Qur'an. In that way, the people would really have a chance to read for themselves the scandalous nature of Islamic doctrine. Because the Qur'an exposes its own weaknesses and because the preachers can with that knowledge defend Christian teaching from the Bible and strengthen the believers, he asks the council to release the confiscated version of the Qur'an. Should the council in Basel not be able to repeal its censor, then Luther wants to publish Oporin's version through the agency of the Wittenburgians "auff unser gewissen." Then neither the publishers nor "my beloved mother, the holy Christian church" (WABr 10:161ff. [no. 3802]) should suffer harm.

As a result of Luther's proposal, the Basel council decided to release Oporin's edition of the Latin Qur'an. But there were three conditions: Oporin was not to be named as the publisher; Basel was not to be mentioned as the place of publication; and the Qur'an was not to be sold in Basel. Luther wrote a foreword to that edition of the Qur'an and Bibliander was indicated as the publisher. In this way the Latin Qur'an was published on January 11, 1543, after many turnabouts in a difficult process.

principle *ad fontes* in research is apparent. This is also a good example of the simple honesty appropriate for those who might work with Christian apologetics. One must respect the opposition so much that one studies the other's position concerning faith and life.

Luther writes in the foreword to Bibliander's edition of the Qur'an[386] that the church has from the time of the apostles been forced to struggle against all sorts of distortions of and lies against the Christian truth. In the time of the older Luther, the struggle is against Muhammad, the Jews, the papists, the enthusiasts, and Michael Servet. The reason it has become necessary to publish the Qur'an is that one must first know the enemy before one can confute him or her.[387] Because well-grounded Christians know that the truth is not tolerated by those who deny the word of the prophets and the apostles in the Bible (Isaiah 59:21; John 15:7; Ephesians 2:20), the temptation to backsliding ought not be great among them, even if they hear the word of the Qur'an. Those who are not so well grounded in the Word and in faith will allow themselves anyway to be tempted by and ally themselves with the Jews, the Turks, and the heathen.[388] The church will stand eternally, but the church's teaching and the Gospel about Christ must always be preserved on the foundation of the prophets and the apostles against, among others, the Muslims. Luther says he has worked for this important apologetic by, among other things, reading the writings of Ricoldus. He wants to continue the apologetic work vis-à-vis the Muslims, which is important for him. But for him to be able to write an adequate apology, he has for a long time desired a full edition of the Qur'an. Believers and especially the teachers of the church through their reading of the Qur'an ought to see its incoherence and poison while at the same time become better equipped to refute Muhammad's teaching.[389] We shall see later

---

386 *Vorrede zu Theodor Biblianders Koranausgabe* (1543), WA 53:569–72. Cf. Holl, "Luther und die Mission," 259f.

387 Concerning the church's continuous struggle throughout history and the Reformation's struggle against the inimical coalition, see WA 53:569.3ff., 570.13ff., 570.24ff., 572.9ff.

388 WA 53:570.34ff., 571.18ff.

389 WA 53:571.40ff., with the thesis "Ecclesia Dei est perpetua, ita doctrinam Ecclesiae oportet esse perpetuam" against "figmentum Mahometi." Concerning Luther as an apologist, see especially WA 53:570.24ff: "Ego igitur ut contra Iudaeorum et Papistarum idola scripsi et scribam pro dono mihi concesso, ita et pestiferas Mahometi opiniones confutare coepi et confutabo prolixius. Sed id acturo prodest etiam inspicere ipsum scriptum Mahometi. Ideo optavi, ut viderem integrum Alcorani codicem. Nec dubito quin, cum alij pij et docti legent, magis execraturi sint et errores et nomen Mahometi . . . ita prolato Mahometi libro pij omnes collatis omnibus partibus magis

that a certain mission perspective shines through all Luther's apologetical arguments.

The Muslims as a predicted, eschatological, seductive, and inimical power

I have above[390] in summary fashion indicated that the reformer believes that the Turks stand in a covenant with Satan and are the "flesh" of the Antichrist. Through the former Franciscan brother Johann Hilten, Luther has been led to focus on Daniel 7 in the question about the Turks/Muslims. It ought to be observed that according to Luther the Scriptures say quite clear things about the Turks and their worldly/religious kingdom. Agreeing with the tradition, Luther understands the four beasts in Daniel 7 to be four successive kingdoms: Assyrians/Babylonians, Persians/Medes, the Alexandrian Empire, and finally the Roman Empire, which in Luther's time was still in power. Among the ten horns or kingdoms of the Roman Empire, the prophet sees a little horn (Daniel 7:8) that stands up and slays three of the other ten. Luther interprets this to mean that the Turks—a small but expanding kingdom—already have defeated Egypt, Greece, and Asia Minor. The Scriptures prove that this upstart kingdom will break in and capture other parts of the Roman Empire and rule there.[391]

But according to Daniel 7, Ezekiel 38–39, and Revelation 20:8, it is also a demonic, spiritual power. This is indicated by the words about the humanlike eyes on the little horn. This shows, according to Luther, that the Turks in their religion of reason will blaspheme God and Christ and corrupt the Gospel and Christian doctrine.[392] When the Turks and Islam in their religio-political expansion advance

---

deprehendent insaniam et Diaboli virus et facilius refutare poterunt. Haec me causa movit, ut extare librum optarim." Already in *Vorwort zu den Libellus de ritu et moribus Turcorum* (1530), the same theme is emphasized; see WA 30/2:205.16ff., 206.23ff., 207.23ff. He says: "Itaque pro Apologia quadam Euangelij nostri simul hunc librum edimus" (WA 30/2:207.3f.).

390 See *Luther and World Mission*, 431ff., especially 433nn332 and 434n335. Concerning the Turks as an eschatological, fiendish power, see Vielau, *Luther und der Türke*, 32ff.; Lamparter, *Luthers Stellung zum Türkenkrieg*, 122ff.; Lind, *Luthers Stellung zum Kreuz- und Türkenkrieg*, 47ff.; Forell, "Luther and the War against the Turks," 259f.; Pfister, "Reformation, Türken und Islam," 360ff.; Kooiman, "Luthers getuigenes in de oorlogtegen de Turken," 17ff.; Vogler, "Luthers Geschichtsauffassung im Spiegel seines Türkenbildes," 123ff.; and Mau, "Luthers Stellung zu den Türken," 656ff.

391 *Heerpredigt wider den Turken* (1529), WA 30/2:163.1–172.17. Concerning the accent on the worldly power and conquests of the Turks, see WA 30/2:162.8ff., 166.20ff. On Hilten's significance for Luther's interpretation of Daniel 7, see Mau, "Luthers Stellung zu den Türken," 653. See also Forell, "Luther and the War against the Turks," 259.

392 WA 30/2:168.15ff. Cf. WA 30:223.

toward Central Europe and when the governments of Central Europe go to war with them, one has to contend with a demonic enemy that at its core wants to destroy the Gospel and the Christian faith. It is important, therefore, through repentance and prayer and the Word's spiritual weapons to strike the devil and, with him, the Turks as well. In the conflict with the Turks, one ought not be blind to the fact that one is striving in an eschatological battle with a religio-political enemy that is ultimately the enemy and the persecutor of God and Christ.[393] In the struggle with the Turks and Islam as a demonic power, it is not sufficient to trust in flesh and blood, that is, in military weapons and large armies. Instead, this is an apocalyptic battle. Here caution and the prayer of distress are primary. Unfortunately, the Bible prophesies great victories for "the Turk" until Christ shall cast him down with thunder and lightning at his imminent return.[394]

Luther also points out that Satan, as Gog or the Turks, has a keen sense. The young evangelical church, liberated from all types of heresies, is the true Israel under the banner of the apostolic Gospel. Satan sees that neither the pope nor the emperor and princes have been able to destroy this oasis of the Gospel. Therefore, according to Luther, Satan in the Turks will focus on Luther and the evangelical

---

393 *On War against the Turk* (1529), LW 46:170 (WA 30/2:116.26ff.): "Since the Turk is the rod of the wrath of the Lord our God and the servant of the raging devil, the first thing to be done is to smite the devil, his lord, and take the rod out of God's hand, so that the Turk may be found only, in his own strength, all by himself, without the devil's help and without God's hand. This should be done by Sir Christian, that is, by the pious, holy, precious body of Christians. They are the people who have the arms for this war and they know how to use them. If the Turk's god, the devil, is not beaten first, there is reason to fear that the Turk will not be so easy to beat. Now the devil is a spirit who cannot be beaten with armor, muskets, horses, and men, and God's wrath cannot be allayed by them. [Psalm 33:17f.; 147:10f. are cited here] '[T]he Lord takes pleasure in those who fear him, in those whose hope is in his steadfast love.' Christian weapons and power must do it." (LW 46:170 [WA 30/2:116.26ff.]). *Heerpredigt wider den Türken* (1529) speaks about the Turks as the eschatological Gog from Revelation 20:8 and Ezekiel 38:22 (WA 30/2:171.8ff.). Cf. WA 30/2:172.29ff: "Aber des Mahomets schwerd und reich an yhm selber ist stracks widder Christum gericht, als hette er sonst nichts zu thun und könne sein schwerd nicht besser brauchen, denn das es widder Christum lestert und streitet, wie denn auch sein Alkoran und die that dazu beweisen." Cf. WA 30/2:173.3ff., 173.10ff. In the literature, see especially Lamparter, *Luthers Stellung zum Türkenkrieg*, 21ff., 122ff.; and Pfister, "Reformation, Türken und Islam," 360ff.

394 WA 30/2:166.20ff., 167.18f., 170.14ff., 173.20ff. See also other passages in *Ortsregister* (WA 62:337, 351) and *Hauptregister* (WA 63:401). Concerning how Christ will destroy all the Turks at his imminent return, see WA 30/2:170.29ff., 171.8ff., 171.18ff., 180.23ff., 226.2ff. About caution and prayer, see *Appeal for Prayer against the Turk*, WA 51:597.6ff.

church and thereby on Germany. If Luther's Gospel is the true Gospel, then this will happen. The devil can in no way tolerate the Gospel.[395]

Some Germans wish to become subordinate to Turkish rule. Such individuals betray their governing authorities and share in all the sins of the Turks' life and teaching.[396] The reformer has with terror heard and read that many Christians have backslid and willingly, without force, become Muslims, primarily because of the attractiveness of the outer religiosity that its confessors exhibit. Luther, therefore, encourages these Christians not to deny their Savior who has died for their sake. These Christians are drawn to Islam when they see that the spiritual life of the Roman Catholic priests and monks is only a shadow of the life that is prevalent among the ascetic, contemplative, and miracle-working Muslim priests and monks. But the whole thing is a lie because the Muslims do not know Christ.[397]

Characterized as it is by works of the Law, Roman Catholic Christianity cannot compete with the religion of the Muslims. Luther has often opined that the pope's church, the Jews, and the Muslims possess the same central theme in their religions. They hold forth works and outer spirituality while Christ is held back or denied. In 1530 Luther wrote a foreword to the Dominican Ricoldus's book about the exercise of religion among the Turks. He articulates here what unimaginable magnetic power the cult, the prayers, the asceticism, and the miracles, especially of the Muslim priests and monks, exercise over a Christianity characterized by the Law, in which those Christians see the hollowness and hypocrisy of their own

---

395 *Das XXXVIII. und XXXIX. Capitel Hesechiel vom Gog* (1530), WA 30/2:224.34–225.24, especially 225.11ff., 225.18ff: "Wir sinds, die aus allerley völcker zu samen bracht unter einen herrn Christum, Und sonderlich jtzt, ynn diesen letzten zeiten, sind wir kaum ein wenig durchs Euangelion aus allen yrrigen glauben zu samen bracht, Das merckt der teuffel ym Gog (spricht hie Hesechiel) und wil an uns, das er uns auffreibe . . . . Denn ich kan die gedancken nicht lassen, kans auch den teuffel nicht verwissen, das er mich und mein heufflin nicht fürnemlich solt meinen zu suchen, Wir mussen yhm auch deudsch land heissen, Jst unser Euangelion recht, so feylen mir diese gedancken nicht, Und weis, das der teuffel solchs mus ym synn haben, Denn er wil und kan unser Euangelion nicht leiden, Er risse lieber himel und erden ynn einander, schweige denn, das er nicht solt seinen Gog auff wecken." Cf. Luther's position regarding an indicated Turkish invasion in 1532. Through an imperial messenger, the reformer had learned that Suleiman II was interested in Luther and his movement. The sultan had asked about Luther's age, and when he heard that Luther was 48, he said, "I wish he were younger; he would find me a gracious lord" (LW 46:205n129). When Luther heard this rumor, he made the sign of the cross over himself and said, "Preserve me, God, from this gracious lord!" (WATr 2:508.17ff. [no. 2537b]). Cf. Forrell, "Luther and the War against the Turks," 260.

396 *On War against the Turk*, LW 46:193–95 (WA 30/2:137.20–139.17), which even notes the social atrocities that follow. Cf. WA 30/2:185.3ff.

397 WA 30/2:185.18ff., 185.25ff., 187.1ff.

faith and life.[398] At the same time, Luther wants to publish a book to clarify that the Gospel teaches something different than outer spirituality, an outer spirituality that one finds both among the Catholics and the Turks. What does such outward spirituality help if one does not have faith in Christ?[399] Incidentally, Luther has in many passages complained that Christians have so easily let themselves be drawn to the faith of the Muslims, a faith characterized by works of the Law and often stone hard, and by their impressive and consistent religious lifestyle.[400] The reformer has also understood that Islam appears to be an absolute and missionary religion. The Turks have gone forth in violence and shaken Christendom. But they also come with a religion that is in itself a danger for a watered-down Christianity that does not understand faith in Christ and in all its legalism lacks a reasonable spiritual/ethical lifestyle among its church leaders and the masses.[401]

ISLAM CONTRADICTS THE SCRIPTURE PRINCIPLE

According to Luther, like all the others in the fiendish alliance against the reign of Christ, Muslims oppose the formal or Scripture principle that is charac-

---

398 *Vorwort zu dem Libellus de ritu et moribus Turcorum*, WA 30/2:206.3ff: "Itaque ex hoc libro videmus Turcorum seu Mahomethi religionem caeremonijs, pene dixerim et moribus, esse multo speciosiorem quam nostrorum, etiam religiosorum et omnium clericorum. Nam ea modestia et simplicitas victus, vestitus aedium et omnium rerum, ut hic liber indicat, item ieiunia, et preces, conventus generales vulgi apud nostros non videntur uspiam, imo impossibile est vulgus nostrum ad ea persuaderi. Deinde miracula et monstra abstinentiae et disciplinae in religiosis ipsorum quem non pudefacerent monachorum, sive sit Chartusianus (qui volunt optimi videri) sive Benedictinus? Umbrae sunt nostri religiosi ad illos collati, et vulgus nostrum plane prophanum ad illorum vulgus comparatum. . . . Atque hoc est, quod multi tam facile a Christi Fide deficiunt ad Mahometum et ei tam pertinaciter adhaerent. Ego plane credo nullum Papistam, monachum, clerum aut eorum fide sotium, si inter Turcos triduo agerent, in sua fide mansurum. Loquor de iis, qui serio fidem Papae volunt et optimi inter eos sunt" Concerning how the Turks with devotion gloss over their methods of violence, see WA 30/2:207.11ff.

399 WA 30/2:206.28ff., 207.23ff.

400 LW 46:176f. (WA 30/2:122.25ff.); WA 32:151.20ff.; 34/1:499.12f.; 43:156.32ff.; 45:195.20ff.; 49:390.1ff.; 53:571.18ff.

401 Concerning Islam as an absolute religion, see WA 30/2:170.17f.: "sie gar nicht zweifeln, yhr glaube sey recht und der Christen falsch, als den Got so viel sieg gibt und die Christen also verlesst." WA 57:58.5f.: "Der Turcke wil gehn himmel fharen, wenn ehr den Alchoran helt." Cf. WA 57:61.35–42, 304.22ff: "Post Pontifices Romanos et complices eorum nulla gens est, quae magis superbiat de religione et iusticia quam Turci: Christianos contemnunt tamquam idolatras, se iudicant sanctissimos et sapientissimos." Cf. WA 45:352.30ff.; 53:302.17ff., 374.4ff.

teristic of all genuine Christianity. Turks as well as other non-Christians can from creation and reason know or sense that there is a God and that God demands obedience. But as we have shown in chapter 2, none of these possess a true knowledge of God by nature and apart from the Gospel.[402] Because Muslims do not take the Word of Jesus and of the apostles seriously, they do not know God, God's nature, nor God's will to save in Christ. For them, everything is uncertain.[403] Like the papists, the enthusiasts, and the Jews, the Turks are said to have a faith without foundation in God's Word.[404] They are full of faith, but their faith is imaginary.[405] They have both the Old and New Testaments, but they make a blended mess of the whole thing because they interpret them according to their own reason.[406] Luther can say, "Thus the Turk's faith is a patchwork of Jewish, Christian, and heathen beliefs."[407] For Luther, Islam is in itself a creation of reason and a teaching of humans.[408] Where have God and Scripture decreed what Muhammad has taught? He draws from his own reason and changes the Word of the Gospel. He loses

---

402 See *Luther and World Mission*, 37–81.

403 *Lectures on Genesis* (1535–1545), WA 43:404.7ff., 404.30ff., concerning the fact that the teachings of the Turks and the pope are not based on the Word. They don't want to listen to the word of Scripture. Shortly before his death, Luther criticizes the entire antichrist coalition and says: "Denn Gott kan nicht recht erkant noch angebetet werden denn von denen, die sein Wort haben, dadurch er sich selbs offenbart hat, wie Christus spricht zu dem Samarischen frewlin Joh. iiij [4:22]. 'Jhr wisset nicht, was jr anbetet, Wir aber wissen, was wir anbeten'. Denn on sein Wort kan man weder von seinem Göttlichen wesen noch von seinem willen nichts gewisses sagen noch wissen, Wie das auch die aller weisesten Heiden allezeit selbs bekand haben, das es so hoch, tunckel und tieff verborgen ding umb Gott und sein Regiment sey, das es niemand ergründen noch verstehen künde" (WA 51:150.18ff.; John 1:18 is cited here). Cf. WA 51:151.16ff: "Darumb ob wol Türcken, Juden und alle Heiden, so viel von Gott wissen zusagen, als die Vernunfft aus seinen wercken kan erkennen, das er ein Schöpffer aller dinge ist, und das man jm sol gehorsam sein, etc. . . . So wissen wir doch, das sie noch nicht den rechten Gott haben, Denn sie wollen sein wort nicht hören, so er von jm selb von anfang der Welt her, den heiligen Vetern und Propheten, und zu letzt durch Christum selb und seine Aposteln offenbaret." See WA 51:155.31ff., 156.11ff., concerning how one cannot know God's heart and good works apart from Christ. Concerning the conflict between the Muslims and Luther's *sola scriptura*, see Holsten, "Christentum und nicht-christliche Religion," 127ff.

404 WA 37:175.25ff., 176.23ff.; 44:809.22ff.; 52:499.23ff.

405 WA 30/2:208.9ff.; 43:241.15ff., 241.21ff.; 46:254.1ff.; 47:873.31f.; 52:168.21ff., 168.29ff.

406 WA 20:681.8ff.; 49:648.10ff. Cf. especially LW 46:176f. (WA 30/2:122.25ff.).

407 LW 46:177.

408 WA 32:63.3ff.; 33:119.3ff.; 34/2:152.10ff., 152.17ff.; 47:178.22ff., 328.35ff. See *Ortsregister*, WA 62:345, with another fifty or so references.

Christ as God's Son.[409] Muhammad has studied the Holy Scriptures of the church, but he has not received them as absolute and final truth but has sought to present new teachings. Thus he has, according to Luther, become a liar. Muhammad has above all made Jesus into merely a prophet; he has given Muslims the right to marry more than one wife and at the same time has blessed the mission of the sword of his followers.[410] Muhammad, the Qur'an, and the Turks respect the Old and New Testaments with their patriarchs, prophets, Jesus (as a prophet but not as God's Son), and the Virgin Mary.[411] As the Talmud for the Jews and the teaching authority in Rome subordinate the word of Scripture, so *de facto* the word of the

---

409 *Heerpredigt wider den Türken* (1529), WA 30/2:168.15ff.: "Zum andern hat das horn Menschen augen, das ist, des Mahometh Alkoran odder gesetz damit er regirt, Jnn welchem gesetz ist kein Göttlich auge, sondern eitel menschliche vernunfft on Gottes Wort und geist. Denn sein gesetz leret nichts anders, denn was menschliche witze und ver-nunfft wol leiden kan Und was er ym Euangelio funden hat, das zu schweer und hoch zu gleuben gewest, das hat er ausgethan, sonderlich aber das Christus Gott sey und uns erlöset hat mit seinem todte etc. Das meinet Daniel [7:8] da er des horns auge deutet und spricht: Er wird sich unterstehen gesetz und ordenung zu endern, vernym Gottes ord-nung, als das Euangelion und Christliche lere." Cf. WA 34/1:326.18f.; 40/3:335.12ff., 604.34ff.; 41:268.29ff., 506.10; 52:324.9ff.; 53:394.34ff.

410 Concerning Muhammad's distortion of the word of Scripture, see WA 22:150.23ff.; WA 37:176.15ff.; WA 40/2:390.1f.; WA 45:524.1ff. See especially *On War against the Turk*: "Since, then, Mohammed's Koran is such a great spirit of lies that it leaves almost nothing of Christian truth remaining, how could it have any other result than that it should become a great and mighty murderer, liar, and murderer under the appearance of truth and righteousness? Now just as lies destroy the spiritual order of faith and truth, so murder destroys all temporal order which has been instituted by God" (LW 46:181 [WA 30/2:126.10ff.]). Cf. LW 46:177 (WA 30/2:124.12ff.). See also *Verlegung des Alcoran Bruder Richardi* (1542), WA 53:391.25ff., 391.38ff., 394.9ff., 394.21ff.

411 Muhammad and the Qur'an honor the patriarchs and prophets of the Old Testa-ment (WA 53:284.6, 372.16ff.). But the Jews are said to have falsified the Old Testa-ment (WA 53:286.25ff.) and the Christians the New Testament (WA 53:286.25ff.). Abraham, Isaac, and Jacob were Saracens according to the Qur'an (WA 53:304.16ff., 330.19ff.). The Muslims consider Jesus to be an important prophet but nothing more (WA 20:769.25ff.; 32:262.2ff.; 34/2:152.8f., 152.15ff.; 40/2:259.1f.; 44:808.39f.; 45:296.2ff., 296.21ff., 296.25ff.; 47:60.29ff., 51.9, 51.7ff.). See especially LW 22:18 (WA 46:51.25ff.): "Furthermore, the Turks say that Christ was indeed an excellent prophet and a great man; they exalt Him above David, Isaiah, and all the other prophets. They must admit that Christ was the Word of the Father, and yet they claim that Christ was not so great as their Mohammed." Cf LW 46:176f., 196f. (WA 30/2:122.2ff., 140.29ff.). Occasionally, Muhammad can speak well of Christ and the Gospel (WA 20:769.25ff.; 40/1:82.6ff.; 53:368.8ff., 370.14f., 374.22ff., 374.33ff., 378.24f.). Muhammad holds Mary in honor (WA 53:368.25ff.), but the church has made her into a goddess (WA 53:328.17ff.).

Qur'an as the holiest and absolute revelation will replace the revelation of the Old and New Testaments, despite all its nice words about Jesus, etc.[412]

All this depends on the fact that Muhammad is considered and honored as the prophet above all other prophets. He has communicated God's message to the Arabs and through them to all peoples.[413] Actually the Turks/Muslims consider and honor Muhammad as higher and greater than Christ. They believe that Christ's office has been completed and perfected by the archprophet Muhammad. Not Christ but Muhammad has the honorable place at the right hand of Allah, while Christ has his place on the left hand.[414] Whatever place Muhammad has given to the prophets, Christ, and the Gospel, both the Old and New Testaments have been superceded. That which Jesus teaches concerning, for example, Christian privation is too difficult for common mortals. Therefore God has through Muhammad given a new law in the Qur'an that is possible for normal people to obey. This adapted law has parallels in both the decrees of the pope and

412 The Turks place the Qur'an above the Old and New Testaments and consider it to be categorical truth (WA 6:181.23ff., 181.33f.; 19:600.19ff.; 40/3:604.33ff.). The one who follows the Qur'an is promised heaven (WA 47:58.4ff., 61.35ff.). Luther compares Islam with the Law religion of the Jews and the pope (WA 53:302.17ff.). The Qur'an's absolute authority is described especially in *Verlegung des Alcoran Bruder Richardi*. In all doctrine, Muhammad's word in the Qur'an is understood as the truth (WA 53:286.25ff., 306.6ff., 308.7ff.). Those who doubt this should ask those who have themselves read the Qur'an (WA 53:286.33f.). Concerning Luther's hard criticism, see WA 53:388ff. The legend that Luther is supposed to have said that Muhammad had admitted that only 3,000 to 12,000 words in the Qur'an are true does not have any basis in fact. Cf. WA 53:338n5.

413 In a 1534 sermon, Luther says that, for Muslims, Muhammad is considered the archprophet: "Sed iam venerit Mahomet, verus propheta, is sol populum from machen gladio et zwingen zum glauben. Is habet plures quam Christus" (WA 37:303.16ff.). Cf. WA 46:517.6f.; 49:648.10f, 648.22ff.; 51:88.24; 53:326.27ff., 363.14f.; 53:378.24, 378.35ff., 380.1f.; 54:89.32ff. Muslims believe that God has spoken directly with Muhammad (WA 41:129.3f.). The Turks revere Muhammad (WA 39/2:82.14f.; 41:594.14f.; 52:498.24f., 550.36ff.). He is the seal of all the prophets (WA 53:326.18ff.). He is considered to be a great apostle (WA 53:284.8ff., 286.30f.).

414 *On War against the Turk*: "Therefore the Turks think that their Mohammed is much higher and greater than Christ, for the office of Christ has come to an end and Mohammed's office is still in force" (LW 46:176–77 [WA 30/2:122.13ff.]). *Heerpredigt wider den Türken*, WA 30/2:168.25ff.: "der Mahometh Christum nicht alleine verleucket, sondern auch gantz auffhebt Und gibt für, Er sey uber Christum viel höher und wirdiger für Gott denn alle engel, alle heiligen, alle Creaturn, dazu uber Christum selbs, wie das yn seinem Alkoran klerlich stehet und die Türcken teglich rhümen." Cf. WA 29:612.13ff.; 34/1:413.1ff.; 37:303.13ff.; 46:138.3f., and especially 47:145.28ff. Concerning the idea that Muhammad is on Allah's right hand and Christ on his left, see WA 37:303.23ff.; 51:610.2ff.; 43:294.12f.; WATr 1:450.27ff. (no. 904).

the so-called conciliar and rabbinic interpretation of the Old Testament. Muhammad's and the Muslims' distance from Luther's *sola scriptura* is summarized well in *On War against the Turk*:

> I cannot deny that the Turk esteems the four Gospels as divine and true, as well as the prophets, and that he also speaks very highly of Christ and of his mother. But at the same time, he believes that his Mohammed is superior to Christ and that Christ is not God, as we said above. We Christians acknowledge the Old Testament as divine Scripture, but now that it is fulfilled and is, as St. Peter says in Acts 15 [:10–11], too hard without God's grace, it is abolished and no longer binding upon us. Mohammed treats the gospel the same way. He declares that the gospel is indeed correct, but that it has long since served its purpose and that it is too hard to keep, especially in those points where Christ teaches that one is to leave all for his sake [Matt. 19:29], love God with his whole heart [Matt. 22:37], and the like. This is why God has had to give another new law, one that is not so hard and one which the world can keep. And this law is the Koran.[415]

As can be seen from the above, Luther has sharply reacted against the fact that the Turks or Muslims have so many nice words about the Old and New Testaments, about the patriarchs, the prophets, Christ, and the apostles while at the same time ultimately building their faith on Muhammad's reason-inspired guidance in the Qur'an. On the basis of his own watchword, *sola scriptura*, that is, the word of the prophets and apostles as the ground and criterion for all that ought to be taught in the church about faith and life, Luther must condemn Islam as a religion resting on the ground of reason and as a false religion. The one who ignores or directly rejects the prophetic and apostolic word *eo ipso* rejects Christian truth.[416]

In Luther's apologetics vis-à-vis Islam, this attack on the so-called formal principle is the first main argument. But he has other ways to expose Islam and equip Christians against it as well. That Muhammad connects himself with the

---

415 LW 46:196–97 (WA 30/2:140.29ff.). Cf. WA 34/1:413.1ff., 413.17ff.; WATr 1:450.28ff. (no. 904). Luther compares the Qur'an's law with the decrees of the pope in which laypeople are given milder rules and a higher ethics, or so-called *concilia*, is demanded of priests and monks. See LW 46:197 (WA 30/2:141.19ff., 168.24ff.).

416 Cf. WA 43:404.7ff., 404.30ff.; 51:150.18ff., 151.16ff. See especially *Vorrede zu Theodor Biblianders Koranausgabe*, WA 53:571.1ff.: "quod videlicet impossibile sit ullam religionem ac doctrinam de Dei cultu et invocatione veram esse, quae prorsus abijcit scripta prophetica et apostolica. Una est Ecclesia perpetua inde usque ab Adam, cui se certis et mirandis testimonijs patefecit Deus in hoc ipso verbo, quod tradidit prophetis et Apostolis. Et toties mandat, ut in ea doctrina agnoscatur, et ut omnes aliae opiniones de ipso reijciatur. Ad hanc unam doctrinam nos alligat, sicut clare dicitur Esaiae cap. 59[:21]: 'Hoc est foedus meum, dicit Dominus, Spiritus meus est in te, et verba mea, quae posui in ore tuo, non recedant de ore tuo nec de ore seminis tui in sempiternum'. Et Christus inquit: 'Si manseritis in me, et verba mea manserint in vobis, quicquid

---

Bible of the Christians and at the same time is not prepared to accept its word as the absolute truth supplies Luther with a reason to initiate an apologetic review around the contents of the Christian faith and life.

In the following, I will review Luther's reaction to the content of the Muslims' faith and ethics. As it concerns the former, he relates his description and critique of Islam to the different articles of the Christian creed. Therefore, for the sake of this survey, it can help to organize the reformer's thoughts around these articles.

LUTHER'S REACTION TO THE MUSLIM CONCEPTION OF GOD

For Islam, the idea that Allah is the powerful and sovereign creator and ruler is completely dominant. Even if Allah's will and law with the concomitant concrete rules for the life of the faithful are especially important in Islam, nevertheless one cannot ignore the fact that Muslims believe in some elements of the Christian confession and reject others.

Concerning the conception of God, it must be emphasized that Muslims are decided monotheists. Luther has, among other things, understood that the cornerstone of Islam's confession is: "There is no other God but Allah, and Muhammad is his prophet." They speak constantly about Allah and live in the presence of Allah. His will dominates their faith, and they wish to subordinate themselves to it. Faith in Allah or Islam is considered to be the only true and absolute religion. Because Christians do not praise and pray to Allah, they are considered to be a people of unbelief.[417] Monotheism and the fear of practicing idolatry express

---

petetis, fiet vobis' [John 15:7]. Et Paulus inquit [Ephesians 2:20], Ecclesiam extructam esse super fundamentum Apostolorum et Prophetarum. Constantissimom igitur omnes omnium gentium opiniones de Deo, quae vel ignorant vel reijciunt prophetas et Apostolos, damnandae sunt. Fatetur autem Mahometus se excogitare novam opinionem dissentientem a prophetis et apostolis."

417 Cruziger's *Summer Postil*, WA 22:43.6ff. "Sihe, was der Turck mit seinem Mahmed fur schaden gethan und noch thut, allein mit dem namen und rhum, das er den einigen Gott anbete. Und wie er allein den rechten Gott habe, so sey er mit den seinen allein Gottes Volck auff Erden." Luther often points out how the Muslims, just as the Jews, boast of their faith in one God—often against the Christian faith in the Trinity and the divinity of Christ. See WA 21:510.11ff.; 36:179.22ff.; 43:160.36ff.; 46:601.3ff., 601.15f.; 52:324.7ff.; 53:374.15ff.; 54:48.35ff., 88.6ff., 89.5ff., 89.17ff., 89.33ff., 91.25ff. Concerning the position of the reformers and the Muslims vis-à-vis the First Article of the Apostles' Creed and monotheism, see Vielau, *Luther und der Türke*, 8; and Pfister, "Reformation, Türken und Islam," 358. Concerning the teachings of Muhammad and the Qur'an, see Paret, *Mohammed und der Koran*, 62ff., 136ff., who describes "Der Glaube an den allmächtigen Schöpfergott" on 72ff. Höpfner (editor) compares Christian and Islamic faith in *Christentum und Islam*, vol. 3, *Glaube im Islam*, which includes many enlightening descriptions. Cf. concerning this topic, Raeder, "Islamischer und christlicher Gottesbegriff," 7–25.

themselves in a consistent ban on images.[418] When they storm forth in battle, they cry "Allah, Allah."[419] Luther believes that the Allah that stands behind the political and religious expansion of Islam is simply Satan. Therefore one must first fight the Allah of the Turks with spiritual weapons. Luther demands the repentance of the people and prayer among the Germans before they exploit physical weapons to defend themselves.[420]

But the reformer penetrates to other themes of the Muslim conception of God. Often he remarks that the Muslims emphasize that Allah is the Creator God. He is said to have created heaven, earth, and people. He is near to and leads the Turks and other Muslims. However, they confess the God of creation and Law on the basis of the reflection of their reason on creation, as the Jews and others do. Thus they do not really know God's heart and will because they reject God's revealer, Jesus Christ.[421]

The Muslim must subordinate himself or herself to the power of the Creator God and God's irresistible will. Luther has reacted negatively to this fatalistic view of life. To be sure they become incredibly valiant and courageous in battle when they call out "Allah, Allah" and believe that whatever will be will be. But this remarkable faith in destiny is not Christian. Of course, God's will steers all that happens, Luther says, but this will is a living will, even if it neither can nor ought to be fathomed by humankind. The fatalism of the Muslims has been able to develop primarily because they have not learned to know God in Christ. Among other things, Christians must, in the presence of the Turkish threat and war, learn from God's Word that it helps to pray to God as a living (!) God. Against the Ottoman armies, the Germans ought to defend themselves courageously under the emperor and princes, who have God's commission to defend the empire and its citizens.[422] Faith in God must never develop into a blind faith in fate in which one does not recognize God as a living and active Creator.

---

418 LW 46:183 (WA 30/2:128.22ff.).

419 LW 46:183 (WA 30/2:128.8ff.): "What is more, when the Turks go into battle their only war cry is 'Allah! Allah!' and they shout it till heaven and earth resound." Cf. WA 29:235.3ff.; 49:735.4f., 736.12ff.; 53:298.36ff.

420 LW 49:184 (WA 30/2:129.6ff.). Cf. *Luther and World Mission*, 436ff.

421 See *Ortsregister*, WA 62:345, which refers to many places in the writings of Luther. Cf. WA 10/1:465.4f.; 10/3:386.22ff.; 14:16.8ff.; 21:283.6ff.; 31/2:354.11ff.; 40/2:301.13ff.; 46:27.3ff., 669.1ff., 669.19ff. Luther believes that the Turks believe God's presence with them is conditional on their works; see WA 10/3:153.22ff.; 40/1:603.25ff., 604.16ff.; 53:156.20f., 350.33ff., 392.20ff., 482.20ff., 565.25ff.

422 WA 43:458.25ff.; 44:78.19ff., and especially *Appeal for Prayer against the Turks*, LW 43:235–36 (WA 51:614.17ff.): "Beware of the Turkish, Epicurean philosophy which leads some to say, 'What can I do? What is the use of praying? What does it help to

Especially the Muslim and Jewish denial of the doctrine of the Trinity has forced Luther to make many apologetic and polemical statements. Because Muhammad and the Turks have understood the articles of the Christian faith only from the standpoint of reason, they can't make the math work so that three persons can be one divine being. They react especially against the fact that Christ is said to be truly God and God's Son. Therefore Muslims and Jews accuse the Christians of polytheism and heresy while asserting that they themselves are God's true people. From the Scriptures, Luther shows that there is only one God but that the Father, the Son, and the Spirit are all ascribed divinity and divine works. Even if no human can understand the mystery of the Trinity, it must be asserted and believed because the Bible speaks of the Father, the Son, and the Spirit as three persons in one divinity.[423] Just as we cannot understand how a leaf comes from a

---

worry? If it is predestined, it will happen.' It is the belief of the Turks that no one may die unless his fated hour has come. That is the reason for their fanatical courage and their assurance that what they are doing is right. Yes, of course, it is true: if it is predestined, it will happen. But it has not been given to us to know what is predestined. Much rather, we are forbidden to know what has been predestined. Because I do not know what God has decreed, it is tempting God to push on into unknowable things, and so go to ruin. I am commanded to act on the basis of knowledge. For that reason God has given us his word so that we should know what we are to do and not act on the basis of ignorance. The rest we have to leave to God and hold to our duty, vocation, and office." Cf. WA 51:616.3ff., 616.15ff.

423 Among other passages, see WA 20:335.35ff., 346.32ff.; 29:162.1ff., 162.4ff.; 32:62.18ff.; 34/2:58.4ff.; 40/2:253.33ff. Luther's apology of the doctrine of the Trinity is powerful against accusations of Christian polytheism by the Jews and the Muslims, see WA 46:23.10ff., 415.13ff., 416.1ff., 436.18ff., 437.19ff.; 50:281.20, 281.27; 52:340.23, 341.35. See especially the 1535–1545 lectures on Genesis: "The Jews and the Turks laugh at us and attribute a most impudent lie to us, namely, that we set up a plurality of gods and believe that there are three gods. Therefore they boast that they are the people of God and that they are honored with many brilliant victories and with the wealth of the entire world because they believe in one God . . . . Therefore our hearts must be fortified against these blasphemous utterances and this boast, which, as it appears to reason, is altogether too true and plausible. For it is completely certain that we believe in a God who is completely one and completely simple. But the fact that the Turk does not understand our faith or doctrine properly and does not hear who that one and completely uncompounded God is—this is his own fault, not ours. For we teach and believe not only that there is one God, but that He is completely simple and completely one in His state of being one. We do not separate these three: the Father, the Son, and the Holy Spirit. We do not make separate gods. No, we believe in God who is completely one and completely simple. Is someone going to say: 'But I do not understand these things'? Very well. Nor do you have to understand them. We believe in one God, who nevertheless is wont to speak about Himself and to count Himself in the plural. . . . And we care nothing about those oxen and asses, the Turks and the Jews, who

tree or grass from the ground, no human can understand how it happens "in God's hidden, incomprehensible, inscrutable, and eternal essence."[424] The doctrine of the Trinity is beyond reason and is believed because of the witness of Scripture.

ISLAM DESTROYS CHRISTOLOGY AND THEREBY THE GROUND TO SALVATION

In the foregoing section, we have seen that Islam regards the prophet Muhammad and his words as something higher than the prophet Christ and his words. The fact that Muslims regard Jesus Christ as merely a prophet, at the same time greater than the prophets of the Old Testament and endlessly less significant than Muhammad, does not have consequences only for the authority of Christ's words. It concerns to the highest degree the central task of Christ as God's Son and the Savior in God's decisive act of salvation. When Muhammad and Islam replace Christ's task and work of salvation with a temporary role as prophet, the reformer reacts violently.[425] In *On War against the Turk*, Luther warns his fellow countrymen about what Muhammad says in the Qur'an. Because it concerns dogma, the most repulsive idea is that Jesus is only a prophet:

> In the first place, he greatly praises Christ . . . yet he believes nothing more of Christ than that he is a holy prophet, like Jeremiah or Jonah, and denies that he is God's Son and true God. Furthermore, he does not believe that Christ is the Savior of the world who died for our sins, but that he preached to his own time and completed his work before his death, just like any other prophet. On the other hand, Mohammed highly exalts and praises himself and boasts that he has talked with God and the angels, and that since Christ's office of prophet is now complete, he has been commanded to bring the world to his faith, and if the world is not willing, to compel it or punish it with the sword.[426]

Muhammad is thus in conflict with the Christian faith in Jesus as God's Son and as the Savior of the world. Despite all the words of praise for Christ and the

---

declare that they cannot comprehend this with human reason; for they do not have to either, since such important matters are established on the basis of divine revelation" (LW 5:72–73 [WA 43:478–79]). Cf. the biblical arguments for the doctrine of the Trinity and Christ's divinity in *Last Words of David* (1543), WA 54:4ff., 65ff. Luther emphasizes here each person's divinity in one single deity against the Jews, the Turks, and the heretics (WA 54:67.39–68.20). Concerning the Muslim polemic against the trinitarian doctrine of the Eastern churches, see Holsten, "Polemik der Moslems," 52–60.

424 *On the Jews and Their Lies* (1543), LW 47:290 (WA 53:540.8ff., 540.18f.)

425 WA 10/1.1:465.4ff.; 29:612.11ff.; 32:262.2ff.; 34/2:152.17ff., 152.29ff.; 37:2.26ff.; 40/2:259.22f., 268.1ff.; 44:808.38ff.; 45:296.26ff. Concerning the Christology of the Qur'an, see Höpfner, "Das Jesusbild im Koran," 26–31; and Holsten, "Polemik der Moslems," 44–51.

426 LW 46:176 (WA 30/2:122.2ff.).

Gospel, Muslims nevertheless replace the Scriptures and the Gospel of Christ with the Qur'an and Muhammad.[427]

In a 1537 commentary on John 1:1, Luther writes:

> This text, "And God was the Word," has been tortured by the Jews, the schismatic spirits, and the Turks, all of whom presume to measure and correct it on the basis of their reason . . . . The Turks likewise regard us as stupid geese devoid of reason and understanding, since we do not realize that one family can have no more than one father; and, they aver, it makes even less sense to believe in, and worship, three gods. The Turks do not believe in Christ. Mohammed, with his Turkish faith, raved and ranted against Christ. To be sure, he conceded that Christ was born of a virgin; but the Turks claim that such a thing is no rarity among them. Well, this may happen and be true among them; but with us those virgins who bear children become women. A virgin who gives birth to a child cannot remain a virgin. . . . Furthermore, the Turks say that Christ was indeed an excellent prophet and a great man; they exalt Him above David, Isaiah, and all the other prophets. They must admit that Christ was the Word of the Father, and yet they claim that Christ was not so great as their Mohammed.[428]

Luther means that they make the prophet Muhammad into an idol and Christians ought not follow him.[429] Muhammad is an enemy of Christ. He strives against Christ and is, therefore, an apostle of Satan, the reformer says.[430] Muhammad destroys the foundation of salvation and thereby the Christian faith when he energetically opposes the doctrine that Christ is God's Son and the Savior.[431]

---

427 WA 6:181.24ff., 181.33f.; 43:294.12f.; 45:524.1ff.; 53:252.31ff., 276.16ff. See summarily WA 4:145.38ff. For example, WA 4:148.4ff.: "heben also Christum gentzlichen auff., und der Mahomet solle auch bleiben, bis so lange Gott einen andern Propheten schiecke."

428 LW 22:17–18 (WA 46:551.7ff., 551.15f., 551.25ff.).

429 WA 32:384.35ff.; 45:353.26ff.; 49:48.3ff. See especially *Heerpredigt wider den Türken*, WA 30/2:196.26ff: "Da mustu dich für hüten, das du dich des nicht teilhafftig machest, Gleich wie du seinem lesterlichen abgott und Mahometh nicht must zufallen, ob du gleich unter yhm dienen must."

430 LW 46:177f. (WA 30/2:123.7ff.); WA 30/2:172.19ff., 172.31ff., 189.15ff.; 46:88.24ff., 587.29ff. Concerning Muhammad and the Turks as a tool of the devil, see WA 30/2:173.12ff.; 40/3:709.15ff.; 49:582.12ff.; 53:273.22ff., 278.25ff., 342.8ff., 352.14ff., 389.4ff., 392.21ff., 394.11ff.

431 *On War against the Turk*, LW 46:176–77 (WA 30/2:122.13ff.): "Therefore the Turks think that their Mohammed is much higher and greater than Christ, for the office of Christ has come to an end and Mohammed's office is still in force. From this anyone can easily see that Mohammed is a destroyer of our Lord Christ and his kingdom, and if anyone denies the articles concerning Christ, that he is God's Son, that he died for us

Luther has emphasized that whoever demotes Jesus Christ to the status of mere prophet strives against the dogma of Christ as true God and true human. In innumerable passages, the reformer points out to both students and congregations how the Muslims, like the Jews and the enthusiasts, become annoyed with and stand against the central dogma of the Christian faith, that is, that Jesus is God's Son.[432] Therefore Luther places Muhammad and his followers in the same category as Arius and other trinitarian and Christological heretics who have rejected the true divinity of Christ. Muhammad is believed to have his background in an Arian sect.[433] It pleases the reason of all humans to deny Christ's

---

and still lives and reigns at the right hand of God, what has he left of Christ?" Cf. LW 46:177–78 (WA 30/2:123.9ff.): "Then Christ is no redeemer, savior, or king; there is no forgiveness of sins, no grace, no Holy Ghost. . . . In the article that Christ is beneath Mohammed, and less than he, everything is destroyed." Cf. WA 47:60.29ff. In the literature concerning the Muslim front against the Second Article of faith, see Vielau, *Luther und der Türke,* 8f.; Lamparter, *Luthers Stellung zumTürkenkrieg,* 29ff.; Forell, "Luther and the War against the Turks," 262f.; and Pfister, "Reformation, Türken und Islam," 358f.

432 "Sermon on John 6:41 (1531)," LW 23:82 [WA 33:123.19ff., 123.36ff.): "The Jews, the Turks, and the pope will never reach this conviction, for they are offended by it and resent it. If God had had a book written expressly against Jews, Turks, and other persecutors in defense of this article, it would have been this Gospel of John, which is aimed directly at their wisdom. The Turk looks upon us as nothing but archfools. The Jews and the pope, too, regard us as the greatest dunces for believing that this Person, Christ, is God and man. . . . [T]he Turk does have a rather high regard for Christ, granting that He is a great prophet; but he does not admit that He is the Son of God. Our salvation must rest on the fact that we look to Christ and that in Him we have the bread of life." *Larger Commentary on Galatians* (1531/1535), WA 40/1:27.17ff.: "Cum igitur scriptura dicit Christum in seipso vicisse peccatum, ergo Christus est iusticia quae naturaliter est deus. Hinc sequitur, quod qui negant divinitatem, totum Christianismum negant et fiunt plane Turcae." Cf. innumerable texts: WA 20:345.24ff., 358.33ff., 361.33ff.; 21:512.16ff.; 27:187.16f.; 28:90.12ff.; 30/1:9.26ff.; 30/2:122.25ff.; 31/1:208.14ff.; 33:124.9ff., 156.40ff., 192.22ff., 256.4ff., 428.10ff., 256.39ff., 557.36ff., 612.2ff.; 34:57.7ff., 57.18ff., 149.7ff.; 36:152.12ff., 393.22ff., 393.41ff.; 37:336.11ff.; 38:160.18ff.; 40/1:76.1ff., 441.2f, 441.8ff.; 40/2:302.14ff.; 41:568.29ff., 631.1ff.; 47:113.1ff., 113.32ff.; 49:382.13f., 382.18ff.; 50:246.20ff.; 51:9.4ff.

433 WA 20:681.8ff.; 30/2:207.40; 30/3:561.33ff.; 33:268.15ff., 560.17ff.; 45:31ff., 522.20ff.; 46:417.19f.; 47:113.1ff., 113.32ff.; 49:564.4ff., 564.20ff.; 50:575.1ff.; 53:572.1. Concerning John 1:1, Luther says: "The world cannot tolerate this article. Jews, Turks, Tartars, and heretics oppose it with all their might; they are annoyed and offended by it. They ridicule and taunt us, because, as they say, we Christians are so absurd and foolish as to believe in, and worship, more than one God" (LW 22:17 [WA 46:550.27ff.]). Cf. WA 46:551.7ff., 601.6ff. *Kurzes Bekenntnis vom heiligen Sakrament* (1544), WA 54:160.14ff.: "Denn alle Historien zeugen, Mahmeth sey aus den Arianern,

divinity.[434] Unfortunately, many Christians both before and after Luther's time have not understood that the confession of Jesus as God's Son, including his salutary death and resurrection, is the foundation of grace and forgiveness and the only true weapon against Islam.[435]

Through its rejection of any notion of Jesus Christ as God's Son, Islam seeks to preserve Allah's absolute sovereignty and monotheism. Luther means that when they deny Christ's divinity, Muslims also lose Christ's work of salvation. Muslims admit Christ's miraculous birth through a virgin, but for them that is nothing remarkable.[436] Above all, they do not perceive in the incarnation and his birth of the Virgin Mary that God's eternal Son has become a human who in himself unites two natures and thus continues to be one unique Son, God's true Son. Muslims decidedly deny that Mary has given birth to God's Son.[437] Christ's birth, suffering on the cross, his resurrection, etc., can be accepted as historical facts but not as facts important for existential faith.[438]

Muslims believe in the resurrection of the dead, in judgment, and in eternal life. But for them the forgiveness of sins and eternal life are not dependent on Christ's death on the cross, his resurrection, and his ascension, etc. Christ's cross and resurrection are for Muslims not central to salvation. They do not believe that Christ through his death has atoned for the sins of humans and through the resurrection won eternal life for all who receive him in faith. They lack the right use of the Passion drama (*usus passionis Christi*).[439] Christians confess that Christ has been crucified, dead, and resurrected and sits on the right hand of the Father. But

---

Macedoniern und Nestoriten komen, Jn welchen er auch zeitlich und von anfang gesteckt hat." Muslims sometimes joke that God cannot have a Son because God cannot have a wife (WA 54:48.36ff.).

434 LW 46:177 (WA 30/2:122.25ff.); WA 46:550.27ff., 601.8ff.

435 *Vorwort zu dem Libellus de ritu et moribus Turcorum*, WA 30/2:207.35–208.18, especially 207.36ff.: "nostra summa praesidia et robustissima arma, quae sunt articuli de Christo, Scilicet quod Christus sit filius Dei, mortuus pro nostris peccatis, resuscitatus ad vitam nostram, quod Fide in illum iusti et peccatis remissis salvi sumus etc. Haec sunt tonitrua, quae destruunt non modo Mahomethum, sed et portas inferi. Mahometh enim negat Christum esse filium Dei, Negat ipsum mortuum pro nostris peccatis, Negat ipsum resurrexisse ad vitam nostram."

436 "Sermon (1540)," WA 49:173.4f.: "ut Iudaei, Turcae dicunt non mirum esse, quod virgo gravida sit." Cf. WA 30/2:122.2ff.; 41:630.20ff.; 46:551.16ff.; 49:662.1ff., 662.18ff.; 52:631.14ff.; 53:370.37.

437 "Sermons on John 3 and 4 (1538)," WA 47:51.37ff.; 52:7ff. Cf. WA 41:363.29ff.

438 Cf. WA 10/3:126.13ff.; 34/1:304.15ff.; 37:3.33f.; 38:198.13ff.; 40/1:285.4ff.; 40/3:661.20ff.; 41:567.5ff.; 49:175.30ff., 463.1ff., 463.10ff.

439 WA 31/2:433.28ff.; 40/2:306.35ff.; 46:294.2ff., 294.15ff.

Muslims sometimes say that Jesus was not crucified but that it was another who looked like him. God the Father supposedly took Jesus directly to himself.[440]

Muslims have not been so interested with the various components of the Third Article concerning the Holy Spirit, etc.[441] Luther understands that without an anchoring in Christ's own resurrection, Muslims believe in the resurrection of the dead.[442] They believe in a final judgment in which faithfulness to the teachings of Muhammad and works decide and lead to eternal life.[443] According to Islam, eternal life is like this life, except that after the striving in this life, one is free from all problems. One lives in the happiness of a paradise with, among other things, water-rich gardens, silver chalices filled with wine, the best food, the finest clothing, and many beautiful women. Luther perceives a sensual nerve in Muslim thinking about the heavenly goal.[444]

But whatever they say about Christ's incarnation and the virgin birth, the cross and the resurrection, etc., these soteriological data in Christian faith have no true soteriological significance for Muhammad, the Muslims, and the Turks. In his Christology, Luther persistently repeats the dogma about Christ as true God and true human. Furthermore, he remarks about Christ, "As the person is, so are the works." Therefore the question about Christ's divinity is therefore not simply scholastic sophistry. It touches on all that Christ has done and does for the salvation of humankind through the incarnation, the crucifixion, the resurrection, and the ascension. And in Christian faith, the doctrine of the Holy Spirit touches especially the church, the forgiveness of sins through the means of grace, and the belief in eternal life. Therefore, for Luther, Islam's false teaching about Christ and

---

440 *Verlegung des Alcoran Bruder Richardi*, WA 53:280.26ff., 334.16f., 378.4ff.

441 Concerning Baptism and the Spirit and the confusion concerning the Spirit on the part of the enthusiasts, the pope, the Jews, and the Turks, see WA 46:426f.

442 LW 46:178 (WA 30/2:123.5f.). But Muslims, Jews, and papists do not know how they will come to the resurrection of the dead when they do not believe in Christ. See WA 22:285.30ff.; 41:612.24ff., 612.34f.

443 Cf. *The Licentiate Examination of Heinrich Schmedenstede* (1542), WA 39/2:189.13f.: "31. That is, we are able of our own selves to merit forgiveness of sins and eternal life, as the Turks, Jews, and Tartars believe." Cf. LW 46:178, 184 (WA 30/2:123.2ff., 129.1ff.); WA 30/2:190.15ff.; 36:558.11ff., 558.29ff.; 53:302.17ff. The Turks, therefore, hope in vain for eternal life (WA 41:691.24ff., 691.27ff.). In respect to John 3:13, Luther says that the whole world strives against the fact that Christ is the only ladder to heaven and that justification occurs through faith in Christ. See from 1538, WA 47:59ff., especially 47:58.4ff.: "Als, ein Jude meinet warlich, ehr fhare gehn himmel, wenn ehr sich beschneiden lest und das Gesetz Mosi haltte. Der Turcke wil gehn himmel fharen, wenn ehr den Alchoran heltt. Also hatt der Bapst auch seine leittern und stege gehn Himmel." Cf. concerning John 3:14, WA 47:61.24ff., 61.35ff.

444 WA 42:452.31ff.; 44:743.24ff.; 53:282.11ff., 300.2ff., 322.9ff., 478.16ff.

the Spirit are a deathblow to Christianity as such. In the important essay *On War against the Turk*, Luther summarizes the general direction of his apology against the Turks and Muhammad:

> From this anyone can easily see that Mohammed is a destroyer of our Lord Christ and his kingdom, and if anyone denies the articles concerning Christ, that he is God's Son, that he died for us and still lives and reigns at the right hand of God, what has he left of Christ? Father, Son, Holy Ghost, baptism, the sacrament, gospel, faith, and all Christian doctrine and life are gone, and instead of Christ only Mohammed with his doctrine of works and especially of the sword is left.[445]

Jesus' lowliness and weakness in the incarnation and on the cross and their own human reason prevent Muslims from believing in him as God's Son and Savior.[446]

Justification in Islam and in Luther

In Luther's apologetic work to expose Islam and to edify Christians, it is of the utmost importance for him to show how the Turks, Muhammad, and the Qur'an do not lift up Christ, the Gospel, grace, and faith but present a doctrine in which the Law, works, and self-righteousness are central. Therefore he constantly compares Christian and Islamic soteriology in the same manner as he compares Christian soteriology with that of the pope, the Jews, and the enthusiasts.

By 1542 the reformer has learned that, according to the Qur'an, Allah alone can forgive sins. One ought not to do evil, but if one does, Allah can show grace and mercy.[447] That Luther is so critical of the Qur'an's emphasis on the law and

---

445 LW 46:177 (WA 30/2:122.15ff.). Cf. LW 46:177–78 (WA 30/2:123.7ff.): "What pious Christian heart would not be horrified at this enemy of Christ when he sees that the Turk allows no article of our faith to stand, except the single one about the resurrection of the dead? Then Christ is no redeemer, savior, or king; there is no forgiveness of sins, no grace, no Holy Ghost. Why should I say more? In the article that Christ is beneath Mohammed, and less than he, everything is destroyed." See WA 30/2:161.26ff., 168.24ff. Cf. also WA 30/2:207.33f.; 46:23.10ff., 290.10ff.; 47:112.3ff., 112.19ff., 112.31ff., 113.1ff., 113.11ff., 113.32ff., 179.27ff.; 51:9.4ff.

446 WA 47:210.22ff., 210.33ff.; 43:392.16ff.; 51:4ff., 51.15ff.

447 *Verlegung des Alcoran Bruder Richardi* (1542). See Luther's loose translation of Qur'an 3:129: "Weiter die Engel können (noch keine Creatur) keinen Menschen heiligen, sondern es mus Gott sein, der das, beide durch und on mittel, thu. Und er allein kan sünde vergeben, wie der Alcoran sagt" (WA 53:368.13ff.). In Qur'an 4:110, he has read: "er spricht: 'jr solt nichts böses thun, denn es gefellet Gotte nicht, Thustu es aber, so ist er barmhertzig und gnedig, und wird dirs gern vergeben'" (WA 53:350.2ff.). Raeder, "Islamischer und christlicher Gottesbegriff," 18ff., shows how Allah is both judging and merciful according to the Qur'an. At the same time, Allah reveals himself as mostly a God of the law, a God of blind predestination, a God who demands both works and faith. See Paret, *Mohammed und der Koran*, 63ff., 72ff., concerning how Allah is

works in its soteriology depends on two things: partly on the fact that forgiveness and grace are not central in the Muslim's doctrinal system—which is instead characterized by law, works, and observance—partly on the fact that Muhammad's doctrine of forgiveness is not at all anchored in Jesus Christ as the reconciler and mediator.

The reformer unceasingly asserts that the Muslims/Turks, just as the pope and the Jews, make a Moses of Christ and a Law of the Gospel. For Muslims, true religion is identified with the observance of the Law and the commandments and following the example of, but not having faith in, Christ.[448] The Qur'an as a whole is a book of law that has parallels in the Jewish Talmud and the papal canons and decrees. The rules for life that the Qur'an prescribes can go a long way to encourage good human lifestyle. These rules and laws cannot, however, give an answer to the question about how a person might become righteous before God and cleansed from sin.[449] Because Luther characterizes Islam as a religion of law, it becomes a religion of works and self-righteousness, precisely like the religion of the pope and the Jews. The passages in Luther concerning this are legion.[450] The Turks/Muslims are here on a collision course with the Reformation's so-called

---

thought to be both an all-powerful creator/judge and merciful/good toward human beings. When all is said and done, the God of unconditional grace has no real place in Islam.

448 WA 39/1:420.1ff., 480.15ff.; 49:206.13ff. See especially the 1538 comment on Mark 10:20: "Such people are twofold sinners; they are drowned and dead in sin, and at the same time they give way to the illusion that they are righteous and can keep the Law. The papists, the Turks, the Jews, and all the ungodly are still ensnared in this evil. Turkish, papist, and Jewish belief is: 'No sooner heard than done' " (LW 22:142 [WA 46:660.8ff.]). Cf. WA 46:227.9ff.

449 "Sermons on the Gospel of St. John Chapters 3–4 (1539)," in which Luther expounds on John 3:27–28: " 'A man cannot take anything.' Wherever this does not happen, you are making a hand out of an eye. The pope thought he was handsome, and did this; but when he is compared with the Bridegroom, his beauty vanishes. Therefore no purification avails except that which is provided by the Bridegroom Himself. The canons and decretals may be good, but they are out of place here. The Turk has a good government, and Moses had one too; but all this fades beside Him, as do the councils and canons" (LW 22:438 [WA 47:154.20ff.]). LW 22:440 (WA 47:155.37ff.): "For that matter, all stations are good; so is the Law of Moses, and the Turk also has commendable laws. But if any of this is to be applied to purification, it is the very devil." Cf. WA 47:175.26ff., 175.33ff.; 42:384.10ff.; 52:709.37ff. In the literature concerning the conflict between Luther's doctrine of justification and the Muslim religion of law, see Holsten, "Christentum und nicht-christliche Religion," 130; Vielau, *Luther und der Türke*, 10f.; Lamparter, *Luthers Stellung zum Türkenkrieg*, 29ff.; and Forrell, "Luther and the War against the Turks," 262f.

450 See *Ortsregister*, WA 62:341, 346f., 349, which lists many of these passages.

material principle, that is, justification through faith in Jesus and not through works of the Law.

Muslims believe themselves to be holy and blessed through their own brilliant works and at the same time demote Christ as the only Savior.[451] The soteriology of the Turks, of the pope, and of the Jews is one and the same: Humans are saved through their own works; faith in Christ has no place.[452] Muhammad and the Muslims seek to please God through their own works and their own piety, while the salvation wrought by Christ is not at all in their field of vision.[453] Through his preaching and teaching, Luther holds fast to justification through faith alone in God's Son and without the works of the Law. Righteousness is a gift from God that is received through the Gospel and faith. The Muslims seek to present their own righteousness that in itself is decisive in soteriology.[454] In the question of justification, Luther and Muslims are polar opposites.

The reformer must, therefore, warn the Christians that Muslims deceive themselves and others with a false soteriology and that they thereby destroy the Christian faith.[455] They have not understood the Gospel's teaching about God's uncon-

---

451 *On War against the Turk*, LW 46:183–84 (WA 30/2:129.1f.): "He is also a papist, for he believes that he will become holy and be saved by works. He does not think it a sin to overthrow Christ." *Heerpredigt wider den Türken*, WA 30/2:187.9ff.: "Darumb so mus es falsch sein, Denn der teuffel kan auch ernst sein, saur sehen, viel fasten, falsche wunder thun und die seinen entzücken, Aber Jhesum Christum mag er nicht leiden noch hören. Darumb so wisse, das solche Türckische heiligen des teuffels heiligen sind, die durch yhre eigen grosse wercke wollen frum und selig werden und andern helffen on und ausser dem einigen heilande Jhesu Christo, und verfüren also beide sich selbs und alle andere." Cf. WA 30/2:189ff. and 30/2:206.31ff., 207.25ff.

452 "Sermon on Matthew 24:15ff. (1529)," WA 29:612.11ff: "Turca, Iudaei et Papa sunt in illo errore Christum non esse Salvatorem, quia fides Turcae sthe, quod omnis homo suis operibus et orationibus salutem, et Christus fuerit propheta." Cf. WA 12:285.3ff.; 37:58.25ff.; 46:129.30ff.; 47:148.1ff., 207.8ff., 207.16ff., 207.23ff.

453 See the list of passages in *Ortsregister*, WA 62:349. Cf. WA 28:389.1ff.; 30/2:206.28ff., 289.5ff.; 31/1:269.13f.; 34/1:507.5ff.; 43:158.21ff., 309.23f.; 46:186.8ff. It is understood that the one who keeps the laws in the Qur'an will be saved (WA 20:518.23ff.; 40/1:85.6ff.; 52:709.38ff.).

454 "Sermon (1531)," WA 34:202.19ff.: "Nam Christus vidit hos errores propriae iusticiae . . . Totus mundus, Cayn, Turca, Papa et omnes gentes in hac opinione sunt quaerentes proprias iusticias." WA 39/1:255.7ff.: "Est argumentum papistarum, sophistarum, Turcarum, quod opera mereantur iustitiam et vitam aeternam." Cf. WA 39/1:391.5ff.; 40/1:48.25ff., 48.29ff., 366.18ff.; 40/2:275.19ff., 382.2ff.

455 *On War against the Turk*, LW 46:176–77 (WA 30/2:122.15ff). Cf. WA 30/2:120.28ff., 141.19ff. See also WA 21:323.30ff., 330.9ff.; 25:232.15ff.; 30/2:195.25ff.; 32:9.9ff., 265.10f.; 46:66.8ff.; 47:31.8ff., etc. The Turks seduce a significant part of the world (WA 22:39.20ff.; 49:512.8ff.).

ditional grace and mercy toward sinners. Muslims stand against grace and extinguish the Gospel with their doctrine about Muhammad's laws and human, merit-winning works. Where the Law and works condition the human relationship to God, there is no room for faith in Christ. Faith alone is replaced by the way of performance and works.[456] Even if the pope—amid the church—is the worst Antichrist, Luther doubtless makes the same hard judgment on the Turks/Muslims. The Turks stand against Christ and the doctrine of justification through faith in him.[457]

Luther also evaluates the Muslims' spiritual standing before God. He sees that their hope for salvation rests on the law and works, that they do not understand and instead directly oppose Jesus' work of salvation, the teaching of the Gospel of grace and forgiveness of sins, the doctrine about faith in Christ as the way to salvation, etc. Thereby he must in the first place conclude that Muslims in their religion find themselves outside of Christ.[458] Luther is willing to admit that Muslims know quite a bit about, as they describe him, the man and the prophet Jesus, including even his ascension into heaven. But they do not understand that he is God's Son who through his incarnation, death, and resurrection lays the foundation for the salvation of human beings. So Muslims actually do not know Jesus Christ.[459] As we have seen before, it is precisely faith in Christ that is, according to Luther, Christianity's *differentia specifica*. It constitutes the difference between true Christian faith and heresy/paganism.[460] Thus the reformer is quite decided

---

456 LW 46:177–78 (WA 30/2:123.7ff.); see also WA 30/2:170.15ff., 186.15ff.; 34/1:430.2ff.; 40/1:242.12ff.; 46:349.23ff. Concerning works of the law and self-holiness as the mark of the religion of Muslims, see WA 25:503.13ff.; 29:235.1ff.; 30/2:186.31ff., 187.18ff., 187.26ff., 189.26ff.; 39/1:480.15ff.; 46:660.8ff. The Turks make a Moses of Jesus (WA 46:665.16ff.; 49:292.22f.).

457 WA 3:505.26, 610.19f.; 10/1.1:148.17ff.; 34/2:478.9ff.; 42:389.23ff., 634.17ff., 635.25ff.; 46:678.23ff. *House Postil* (1544) on Matthew 24:24: "kan mans one fahr unterschiden und die falschen Christos auff den Türcken und seinen glauben, Die falschen Propheten aber auff den Bapst und seine lehr deutten. Denn dise zwey Regiment, Baptsts und Türcken, sind on zweyffel der rechte Antichrist, da Daniel, Christus, Paulus, Johannes und ander Apostel vor gewarnet haben" (WA 52:549.29ff.).

458 *Lectures on Genesis* (1535–1545), LW 7:253 (WA 44:487.16ff.): "Such is the kingdom of Christ in every way, and He Himself is such a King; for He has the very best thoughts concerning us . . . . But apart from Christ there can be no discussion or any hope in regard to God. This is the kind of religion the Jews, the Turks, and the papists have." Cf. WA 34/2:125.30ff.; 49:292.18ff., 624.8ff.

459 The Turks can speak about Jesus' crucifixion, resurrection, and ascension, but that is nothing if one lacks a personal faith in him: WA 10/3:126.13ff.; 21:224.35ff.; 32:196.24ff.; 37:3.33f.; 38:198.13ff.; 40/1:285.4f.; 40/3:690.9ff.; 41:64.3ff., 64.12ff.; 45:376.24ff.; 46:227.10ff., 327.2ff., 378.28ff., 760.8ff., 760.15ff.

460 See *Luther and World Mission*, 59ff., 76ff., 443n379, 451n403.

that the Turks/Muslims, though they eagerly pray to Allah and follow the commands and rules of life communicated by Muhammad, do not know the true God.[461] Despite all their wonderful works, they do not know God's heart and works for good that have been revealed by Jesus Christ and his works of salvation that are received through faith alone.[462] Therefore the reformer can say that the Turks are condemned pagans and idolaters.[463] It is not surprising, then, that Luther considers the Muslims to be enemies of the church of Christ and of Christians. The conflict between Luther and Muslims is definitively of a religious nature. Both parties say that they possess an absolute and definitive truth. Both assert that the other party is idolatrous and pagan.[464]

---

461 WA 3:491.5ff., 491.20; 22:73.26ff., 154.7ff., 154.13ff.; 25:503.13ff.; 33:198.12ff.; 39/2:202.14ff.; 41:404.2ff., 489.25ff., 490.4f.; 47:148.5ff., 148.16f., 149.14ff.; 51:611.11ff.; 54:401.7ff., 401.20ff.

462 *Lectures on Isaiah* (1527–1529), WA 25:288.37ff.: " 'Ego sum Dominus.' Respicit Idola. Confutat enim omnes contrarias religiones, ut dicamus: Deus Turcarum, Iudeorum, Papistarum nihil facit. Noster autem Deus facit omnia. Hoc enim vult, cum dicit: Ego sum et nullus mecum." Cf. WA 31/1:404.15ff.; 31/2:168.15–169.4, 190.19ff.; 34/1:262.22ff.; 41:128.7ff., 129.8ff.; 43:347.27ff.

463 WA 30/2:131.1ff., 666.13ff., 666.36f.; 31/2:573.8ff.; 40/1:608.4ff., 608.10f.; 40/3:396.9ff.; 44:560.1f.; 46:449.10f.; 47:482.20ff. See the prayer: "heilige doch deinen namen, beide, jnn uns selbs und jnn aller welt, zerstöre und vertilge die grewel, Abgötterey und Ketzerey des Türcken, des Bapst und aller falschen lerer oder rottengeister" (WA 38:360.15ff.). The reformer can say that the Turks and the papists are condemned because they throw away faith in Christ (WA 31/1:276.6ff.; 40/1:236.17ff.; 43:403.27ff.). The Turks are considered to be heretics (WA 2:406.36ff.; 5:196.1ff.; 16:243.8ff., 555.38ff.; 21:400.31ff.; 43:404.29ff.; 46:413.19ff., etc.). The Turks are said to be pagans because they do not believe in the grace of Christ (WA 6:206.13ff.; 34/1:221.15f.; and *Ortsregister*, WA 62:347). The Turks/Muslims represent the living devil (LW 46:181 [WA 30/2:126.2]; WA 25:214.14; 40/3:714.22; 51:73.5ff., 74.2ff.).

464 See *Ortsregister*, WA 62:343, and *Hauptregister*, WA 63:400. See, among other passages, the central passage in *Heerpredigt wider den Türken*: "Denn er ist dem Christlichen namen feind, den selbigen wolt der teuffel gerne unterdrücken mit dem schwerd des Mahometh, wie er denn auch mit falscher lere bey uns den selbigen unterdruckt, Und wil sich also an unserm Herrn Christo rechen . . . hellts dafür, das kein erger volck auff erden sey, denn die Christen. Darumb nennen uns auch die Türcken nicht anders denn Paganos, das ist heiden, Sich selbs aber halten sie für das heiligste volck auff erden" (WA 30/2:170.5ff.). Cf. *Lectures on Genesis* (1535–1545): "But the Turk does not know what he himself is doing or what is in store for us. He thinks that the Christians have been rejected or cast aside by God, and he takes God's favor and His election for granted and is hardened and obdurate to a greater extent than the devil himself" (LW 4:356 [WA 43:392.33ff.]).

LUTHER'S CRITIQUE OF MUSLIM ETHICS

I will here briefly say something about the reformer's judgment and critique of the ethics of Muhammad and of Islam. In Luther's attempt to warn and to help Christians against the expansion of Islam in Europe, this part of his apologetics occupies quite a significant space. It is often strongly polemical. Some scholars have touched on this subject briefly.[465]

The reformer knows well that Muslim ethics is based on laws and rules that Muhammad himself had communicated. Luther asserts generally that what Muhammad has taught are not God's commands.[466] Therefore when Luther compares them with Scripture, he can call them foolish, unreasonable, scandalous, and full of evil fleshliness.[467] Also, just as the pope, Muhammad has moderated the commands of the Bible so humans are capable of keeping them. Muslims say, therefore, that the Qur'an provides a law that the common person can keep. They praise this law as the only way to salvation because it has replaced the message of the Gospel.[468]

As we have seen, Luther possessed at least some passages of the Qur'an in 1530. The source material shows, however, that through knowledge of the comprehensive contemporary Turkish literature and stories from those who lived among Muslims, he also possessed a broad amount of information about the society, lifestyle, and customs of the Turks/Muslims. When the reformer considers these things, he finds both positive and negative aspects.

Luther asserts positively that the Turks/Muslims in those lands that they have conquered often have an orderly worldly regiment with good laws in which the

---

465 See Lamparter, *Luthers Stellung zum Türkenkrieg*, 27ff., 37ff.; and Holsten, "Christentum und nicht-christliche Religion," 131, 133ff. There are brief observations by Vielau, *Luther und der Türke*, 14ff.; Forell, "Luther and the War against the Turks," 262; Pfister, "Reformation, Türken und Islam," 360; and Mau, "Luthers Stellung zu den Türken," 656. A scholarly sketch of Islam's ethics is provided in Paret, *Mohammed und der Koran*, 136ff. Cf. the essays in Höpfner, *Ethik im Islam*.

466 The laws are revealed through Muhammad (WA 22:148.7ff.; 40/3:605.19f.; 53:292.24f., 292.31ff.), but they are absolutely not from God (WA 51:379.3ff.; 53:286.13ff., 340.31ff., 346.17ff., 378.14ff.).

467 WA 53:316–25.

468 WA 51:379.1ff. Cf. *Verlegung der Alchoran Bruder Richardi*, WA 53:384–88. Luther concludes polemically: "Jsts nu den Menschen not gewest, das die gebot des Euangelij erleichtert, und der Alcoran als ein leichter Gesetz gegeben würde, So möcht einer fur geben, Es were not, das man noch ein leichter Gesetz gebe, welchs die Menschen halten kündten, und also beide, Euangelium, Alcoran, Moses, und zuletzt alle Gesetz weg gethan würden, bis wir theten, was jederman gelüstet" (WA 53:386.36ff.). Cf. *Luther and World Mission*, 450ff., 453n414, 454n415.

citizens are disciplined and orderly and raise their children well. The reformer often remarks that the Turks are decent, honorable, and reasonable people who in their lifestyle are often superior to the wild Germans.[469] Muslims live piously and exercise love toward their fellow human beings.[470] Luther can characterize them as the most honorable, most reasonable, and most religious among human beings, if one measures with the measure of civil righteousness.[471] We already have seen that Muslims—especially the zeal of Muslim priests and monks for prayers, worship services, and a holy life—exercised a strong attraction among the Christians in the occupied territories.[472]

But the reformer also has written many negative passages about the social and personal ethics of the Turks/Muslims. Above all Luther criticizes their military campaigns and murdering. They not only destroy the faith of Christians with false teaching, but they also go forth as highwaymen and kill non-Muslims with support from the command of the Qur'an. In their ravages and mission by the sword, they believe that they accomplish Allah's command and will. In this way, Islam has with might and violence expanded in formerly Christian lands. The religion of the Muslims expands not through preaching and miracles but primarily through the sword, killing, and occupation of constantly new regions followed by Islamicization of those regions. This sword mission strives against the theses of

---

469 "To the Christian Nobility (1520)," LW 44:203 (WA 6:459.24ff.): "It is said that there is no better temporal rule anywhere than among the Turks, who have neither spiritual nor temporal law, but only their Koran. But we must admit that there is no more shameful rule than ours . . . ." It can be expressed in this way: "Turce, Iudei externam vitam meliorem ducunt, quam nos ipsi et praesertim religiosi" (WA 14:63.7f.). See also WA 31/2:464.13f.: "Liber eyn frummen Turcken den eyn bossen Christen"; and WA 29:289.3f: "Sic Turca habet pulchram vitam exepta fornicatione." Cf. WA 39/1:247.30f., 248.9ff.; 41:237.17ff.; 45:708.19ff.; 47:154.26f.; 51:69.29ff. Concerning the fine laws of the Turks, see WA 41:714.29ff.; 47:155.37f. Concerning the friendliness and reasonableness of the Muslims, see WA 30/2:127.19ff. (LW 46:182); 34/1:370.6f.; 49:714.7ff. Cf. the brief comments in Vielau, *Luther und der Türke*, 15f.; Forell, "Luther and the War against the Turks," 262f.; and Mau, "Luthers Stellung zu den Türken," 656.

470 WA 6:6.14ff.; 51:4ff., 51.9ff.; 29:267.12f.; 34/1:370.6ff.; 41:607.21f.

471 *Heerpredigt wider den Türken*, WA 30/2:189.26ff. Cf. WA 47:63.38ff., 175.26f., 724.24f., and especially *Lectures on Genesis* (1535–1545): "The Turks are most honorable people, very wise and very religious. By means of the strictest discipline they are preserving the kingdom which they have acquired through great exertions. Therefore if the people of God were like the Turkish people, nothing more would have to be required. . . . But what else is there among the Turks than the first birth? For reason is born of a woman; and to reason belong wisdom, civil rights, discipline, and laws. About all these people Holy Scripture says that they are lost and condemned before God" (LW 4:345 [WA 43:385.10ff.]).

472 See *Luther and World Mission*, 449ff.

the Scriptures and Luther that the reigning authority ought to work for peace, protect those obedient to the law, and punish the lawless.[473] Luther reacts also against the idea of vengeance[474] and the widespread serfdom among the Muslims.[475]

Luther also criticizes the worldly-spiritual arrogance of the Muslims. Directly against what Paul teaches in Galatians 4:22ff., they assert that they are not at all Hagar's descendants or Ishmaelites. Luther rejects their claims that they are the descendants of Sarah, descendants of the promised son, Isaac, thereby having a family relationship to Abraham. Thereby the so-called Saracens claim to follow the only true religion. They ought, therefore, to be the lords of the world.[476] They find divine legitimation for this pride in, among other things, the fact that the effeminate Christians could never stop the expansion of the masculine Muslims. Allah proves in this way the strength of their faith and life and their right to worldly-spiritual imperialism. Of course, Luther reacts energetically against this, just as he does against the arrogance of the pope, the Jews, and the enthusiasts.[477]

---

473 *On War against the Turk*, LW46:178 (WA 30/2:123.19ff., 123.29ff.): "In the second place, the Turk's Koran or creed teaches him to destroy not only the Christian faith, but also the whole temporal government. His Mohammed, as has been said, commands that ruling is to be done by the sword, and in his Koran the sword is the commonest and noblest work. Thus the Turk is really nothing but a murderer or highwayman, as his deeds show before men's eyes. . . . But never has any kingdom come into being and become so mighty through murder and robbery as that of the Turk; and he murders and robs every day, for robbing and murdering, devouring and destroying more and more of those that are around them, is commanded in their law as a good and divine work; and they do this and think that they are doing God a service." LW 46:179 (WA 30/2:124.12ff.): "Thus when the spirit of lies had taken possession of Mohammed, and the devil had murdered men's souls with his Koran and had destroyed the faith of Christians, he had to go on and take the sword and set about to murder their bodies. The Turkish faith, then, has not made its progress by preaching and the working of miracles, but by the sword and by murder." Cf. LW 46:179–81 (WA 30/2:124.9ff., 126.6ff.). Luther compares how the enthusiasts, the Donatists, and the pope have misused the sword (LW 46:179–81 [WA 30/2:124.20–126.20, 141.15ff.]). He writes about the Turkish religious war—and its success that Daniel 7:8 supposedly predicted—also in *Heerpredigt wider den Türken*, WA 30/2:162.1ff., 166.20ff., and especially 169.5ff. See also *An Appeal for War against the Turk*, WA 51:617.9ff., 617.26ff. Other texts are WA 30/2:207.11ff.; 38:509.19f.; 41:426.26ff.; 46:441.22ff.; 49:712.7ff.

474 *Verlegung des Alcoran Bruder Richardi*, WA 53:308.25ff. Cf. Qur'an 5:49.

475 WA 14:414.15f., 415.8f, 415.33f.; 16:535.6ff.; 24:529.16ff., 529.22f.; 26:229.32ff., 229.41ff.; 28:646.1ff.; 33:657.31ff., 658.11f.; 36:664.7; 46:407.17ff.

476 WA 40/3:659.7ff.; 43:385.18ff., 385.39f., 400.33f.; 44:422.34ff.; 46:468.12f.; WATr 3:418.11ff., 418.29ff. (no. 3571A and B). See also Holsten, "Christentum und nichtchristliche Religion," 131f. Cf. the essay by Moritzen, "Abraham im Koran," 36–43.

477 WA 30/2:191.3ff.; 43:392.16ff. Cf. WA 33:579.37ff.; 40/2:290.1; 42:304.22ff.; 47:802.1ff.; 48:347.7ff.; 49:243.7ff., 243.10ff., 244.20ff., 605.5ff., 605.20ff.

Luther has also characterized the cultic piety and the religious zeal of the Muslims as self-righteous deception. He has heard of the intense religious life of their priests and the Muslims' zeal and discipline when it comes to their worship, prayer hours, and pilgrimages. The deception in all this is that it is not produced by faith in Christ. It is not the amount of fasts, prayers, and penance that is the criterion for genuineness in communal and private life with God. The important thing is that all happens of and in faith in Christ and that all these pious rituals are not considered as a stairway to heaven.[478] It has become a vexation for the Christians that Muslim priests and monks in their asceticism and meditation go into a complete trance. They have also *de facto* performed remarkable miracles. Concerning this, Luther answers that even the devil can fast, be serious, and go into a trance. Indeed, according to the Scriptures (Matthew 24:24; 2 Thessalonians 2:9f.), Satan and false prophets can do miracles. Besides, the miracles of the Muslims occur not in the name of Christ but in Muhammad's name.[479]

Luther knows well that the Muslims in their everyday life are honest, moderate concerning food and clothing, do not drink wine or become drunk, do not swear or curse, and live in submission to the governing authorities. In this respect, they show themselves to be much more disciplined than the Germans. Despite all this good, daily discipline, they lack Christ who ought to characterize the relationship to God and lifestyle. The Scriptures teach moderation concerning food and drink but not sullen self-righteousness as such.[480] Whatever the Muslims

---

478 *Heerpredigt wider den Türcken*, WA 30/2:187.1ff., about the cultic piety of the priests and monks. Concerning the piety of the common Muslim: "Zum andern wirstu auch finden das sie ynn yhren kirchen offt zum gebet zu samen komen und mit solcher zucht, stille und schönen eusserlichen geberden beten, das bey uns ynn unsern kirchen solche zucht und stille auch nirgent zu finden ist. . . . Da drücke aber mal mit dem daumen auff einen finger und dencke an Jhesum Christum, den sie nicht haben noch achten, Denn las sich zieren, stellen, geberden wer do wil und wie er wil, gleubt er nicht an Jhesu Christ, so bistu gewis, das Gott lieber hat Essen und trincken ym glauben, denn fasten on glauben, lieber wenig ordenlich geberde ym glauben, denn viel schöner geberd on glauben, lieber wenig gebet ym glauben, denn viel gebet on glauben" (Luke 7:40ff.; 18:14; Matthew 21:31 are cited; WA 30/2:187.18ff.). Concerning the Muslims' pilgrimages in Muhammad's name, see WA 30/2:188.8ff. Concerning the critique of the cultic piety of the Muslims, see also *Vorwort zu dem Libellus de ritu et moribus Turcorum*, WA 30/2:206ff. See also Vielau, *Luther und der Türke*, 10ff.; Lamparter, *Luthers Stellung zum Türkenkrieg*, 27ff.; and Mau, "Luthers Stellung zu den Türken," 656.

479 See WA 30/2:187.10ff., 188.12ff., 189.7ff., 206.8ff. The miracles of the Turks are not of God: "weil die selbigen nicht ynn Christus namen geschehen, sondern widder Christus namen, ynn Mahomets namen" (WA 30/2:189.15ff.).

480 Concerning the simplicity and discipline of the everyday life of Muslims, see WA 30/2:189.26ff.: "Zum vierden wirstu sehen bey den Türcken nach dem eusserlichen wandel ein dapffer strenge und ehrbarlich wesen: Sie trincken nicht wein, sauffen

might display of piety in worship life and everyday life, they lack both Christ and faith. Therefore Luther often says that Muslims are characterized by self-righteousness and hypocrisy just as the pious Catholics are.[481] Christians must be aware of being deceived by this sham holiness that easily leads to denial of Christ. Christianity is not observance, self-righteous piety, and works, but it is faith in the Gospel of Christ that channels righteousness with God.[482]

The reformer also attacks the hardness and the sensualness of the Muslim view of marriage and sexual life. In a passage in *On War against the Turk*, Luther summarizes his critique:

> The third point is that Mohammed's Koran has no regard for marriage, but permits everyone to take wives as he will. It is customary among the Turks for one man to have ten or twenty wives and to desert or sell any whom he will, so that in Turkey women are held immeasurably cheap and are despised; they are bought and sold like cattle. Although there may be some few who do not take advantage of this law, nevertheless, this is the law and anyone who wants to can follow it. That kind of living is not and cannot be marriage, because none of them takes or has a wife with the intention of staying with her forever, as though the two were one body, as God's word says in Genesis 3 [2:24], "Therefore a man cleaves to his wife and they become one flesh." Thus the marriage of the Turks closely resembles the chaste life soldiers lead with their harlots.[483]

Luther reacts because of Muhammad's and Islam's departure from the nature of marriage that has been revealed in God's Word. They allow the man to take many wives whom afterward he can buy, sell, and exchange whenever he wants. This loose and polygamous system is, according to Luther, contemptuous both of marriage and of women. Later, he also criticizes polygamy and the compulsion and

---

und fressen nicht so, wie wir thun, kleiden sich nicht so leichtfertiglich und frölich, bawen nicht so prechtig, brangen auch nicht so, schweren und fluchen nicht so, haben grossen trefflichen gehorsam, zucht und ehre gegen yhren Keiser und herrn, Und haben yhr regiment eusserlich gefasset und ym schwanck, wie wis gerne haben wolten ynn Deudschen landen." WA 30/2:190.20ff.: "Was hilfft denn solch schön ding, so es ausser und widder Christum ist? Da magst du wol sagen, das sprichwort 'Es ist schön böse' Aber bey uns ist Alber feste, Denn es ist ja besser ynn Christo messig wein trincken und frölich sein, Denn ausser Christo solch trefflich saur ding für geben, das widder Propheten noch Apostel noch Christus selbs hat für gegeben." Cf. WA 30/2:206.3ff.

481 *Heerpredigt wider den Türken*, WA 30/2:186.31ff., 189.7ff., 191.18ff. Cf. WA 25:503.14f.; 29:235.3ff., 235.23f.; 40/2:388.12f., 388.32ff.; 41:703.10ff., 703.18ff.; 45:670.2ff., 673.32ff., 682.36ff.; 47:195.34ff., 642.1ff.

482 WA 30/2:187.15ff., 189.7ff., 189.14ff. See especially *Vorwort zu dem Libellus de ritu et moribus Turcorum*, WA 30/2:206.23ff., 227.23ff.

483 LW 46:181–82 (WA 30/2:126.21ff.).

blind discipline with which Muslim husbands rule over their wives, who must live with the possibility of being cast out and must sometimes have their husband's concubines in the house. According to Luther, among the Muslims and the Turks one really has to do with a scam marriage and a blatant whoredom.[484] When Luther comments on Matthew 19:3–12 (1537), he writes especially about divorce and lifelong, monogamous marriage. Polygamy, the casting out of displeasing wives, and male chauvinism make it so one cannot speak of true marriage but only of the sexually immoral lifestyle among the Turks and the Muslims.[485]

Luther even possesses information that homosexuality occurs among Muslims just as it does among Roman Catholic monks and priests. Because Rome has forbidden priests and monks to marry and because the Turks have broken the ideal of marriage, they have, according to Paul's words in Romans 1:24, 26ff., been given over to all types of sexual sins. Luther sees in this a new Sodom and Gomorrah.[486]

In summary, in his comments about the faith and ethics of the Muslims, the reformer warns the Christians about the nameless destruction that Muhammad's doctrines of faith and life and their cultic piety and everyday life means. They destroy the entire Christian creed, especially faith in God's Son. They destroy the civil government and create strife and destroy divinely ordained monogamous marriage. Islam is a great evil and a crusade of lies, according to the reformer and the apologist Luther.[487] In his apology, Luther seeks to expose the understanding

---

484 Concerning Muhammad's teaching about polygamy, the right to sexual exploitation of women, etc., see the passages in *Hauptregister*, WA 63:402f., 405. See especially *Heerpredigt wider den Türken*: "Und wie wol yhr gesetze zu lesst, das einer mag zwelf fehe weiber haben und dazu Megde odder beyschlefferin wie viel er wil und dennoch aller kinder gleich erben sind, So halten sie doch solche weyber alle ynn grossem zwang und gehorsam, das auch der man für leuten selten mit seiner weib einem redet odder leichtfertiglich bey yhr sitzt odder schertzt. Denn ob wol der man yhm solche weiber lesst vertrawen durch die priester, so behellt er doch das recht und die macht von sich zu lassen welche er wil, nach dem sie verdienet odder er sie lieb hat odder gram wird. Hie mit zwingen sie yhre weiber gewaltiglich Und wie wol solche ehe nicht ein ehe für Gott sondern mehr ein schein ist, denn eine ehe, noch halten sie damit yhre weiber ynn solchem zwang und schönen geberden" (WA 30/2:190.1ff.). See also WA 25:503.1ff.; 30/2:224.4ff.; 38:347.16ff., 347.20ff.; 46:140.22ff., 141.2ff., 143.5ff., 144.20ff.; WATr 5:120.9ff. (no. 5386). In the secondary literature, see Vielau, *Luther und der Türke*, 14f.; Lamparter, *Luthers Stellung zum Türkenkrieg*, 38f.; and Forell, "Luther and the War against the Turks," 264f.

485 "Matthew 18–24 in Predigten ausgelegt (1537–1540)," WA 47:314.4ff., 320.20ff., 322.1ff. Cf. WA 51:620.13ff.

486 *On War against the Turk*, LW 46:198 (WA 30/2:142.11ff.). Cf. WA 30/2:191.25f.

487 LW 46:182 (WA 30/2:127.3ff., 139.1ff.). Cf. WA 30/2:191.25f.

of faith and life according to Muhammad, the Qur'an, and the Muslims. The apology seeks also to defend Christian faith and ethics with the goal that Christians might receive help for their own faith and life.

The Mission Task among Muslims

The Turks were a threat against central Germany during all of Luther's life, chiefly from 1528 to 1543. Especially after the great campaign in Hungary and Austria in 1528/1529 and 1541, the Germans feared a comprehensive invasion. Large portions of the German-Roman Empire's eastern regions and its Christian populations were annexed by the Turks. It was primarily in that situation that Luther worked with his apologetics against the Muslim faith and ethics. He wanted to warn and to equip the churches in their meeting with Islam. Partly he was concerned with defending Christianity and with efforts to "hold the field." Partly Islam was to be exposed as a false religion and the Christians were to be stimulated toward a clear, Christian confession. In these latter themes, there is also the first intimation of a missionary motif. In the early church, for example, apologetics was a part of mission work. In this section, I ask if Luther clearly expressed the idea that Christians must seek to convert Muslims. Did he believe that Christianity in the sixteenth century had a clear responsibility for mission among Muslims? Did he do anything so such mission might occur?

Among the scholars there is no unity concerning this question. Among others, Gustav Warneck, L. Bergman, Manfred Köhler, and H. Lamparter have rejected any attempt to link Luther with true mission among the Turks. They believe that mission is only the work of an organized mission society with a geographic movement to foreign lands.[488] However, other scholars, such as Karl Holl, Werner Elert, Walter Holsten, Hanns Lilje, R. Pfister, and more recently H. Dörries, Volker Stolle, Eugene W. Bunkowske, and this author have noticed mission thinking in Luther's meeting with the Turks. But one has not wanted to exaggerate the reformer's engagement with an organized work to Christianize the Muslims. Likewise, these latter scholars understand the reformer's thoughts concerning the Christianization of the Turks differently than the former scholars.[489] I will here try

---

488 Warneck, *Abriss einer Geschichte der protestantischen Missionen*, 9f., 13f.; Bergman, *Den lutherske Reformation og Missionen*, 63ff.; Köhler, *Melanchthon und der Islam*, 162.; and Lamparter, *Luthers Stellung zum Türkenkrieg*, 83f. Mau, "Luthers Stellung zu den Türken," 655, 657, 659f., ascribes to the reformer little interest for mission among the Turks. Especially Bergman, *Den lutherske Reformation og Missionen*, 66ff., has noted many of the texts that I will shortly review. However, he rejects any talk of mission because Luther does not organize a regular mission society and campaign.

489 Holl, *Luther und die Mission*, 236f.; and Elert, *Morphologie des Luthertums*, 339f. With a certain hesitation to admit that Luther desires mission efforts among the Turks, see

to collect and expound the source material already gathered by the aforementioned scholars so one may obtain a clear picture of how Luther handles the church's responsibility for mission among the Muslims and how his thoughts on that subject are organized.

The above investigation ought to have shown that the Ottoman Turks according to Luther represented both a worldly and a spiritual superpower with unheard-of military potential and with demonic, spiritual power and identity to tempt Christians. A possible mission in those Turkish regions must, therefore, occur in a hazardous religio-political context. No mission can ignore the fact that harshly governed Muslim Turkey and its territories, which were characterized by violent military operations, made organized mission work impossible. Because the Turks' expansion has to a large degree been an anti-Christian holy war, mission among the Muslims has become even more problematic.

Could Luther count on help from the Christian minorities in Turkey and Southeast Europe who lived as something of a struggling martyr group? Luther says often that Satan has decimated the Gospel and that God has abandoned the old Christian Turkey. A spiritual darkness and Satan himself reign over all because the Gospel of Christ, Baptism, Holy Communion, and the ordinary Christian life have no more real place in that empire. As in the church of the pope, Turkey has lost the Gospel because of its faithlessness and speculation.[490]

However, one ought not press such general conclusions too far. Luther knows well that before 1453 Christian Turkey still has some confessing Christians. In those lands that were later occupied by the Ottoman Turks, there were, of course, many struggling Christians—a fact on which scholars generally have not reflected. Thereby a situation existed in which the Greek Orthodox, the Roman Catholic,

---

also Holsten, "Christentum und nicht-christliche Religion," 113f.; Holsten, "Reformation und Mission," 11ff.; Lilje, "Morgenstunden der Mission III," 101f.; and Pfister, "Reformation, Türken und Islam," 364ff. Among the more recent contributions that briefly but decidedly assert that the reformer emphasizes the responsibility to mission among Muslims, see Dörries, "Luther und die Heidenpredigt," 341f.; and Stolle, *Kirche aus allen Völkern*, 57ff., with clear evidence. See also Bunkowske, "Was Luther a Missionary?" 167, 171f.; and Öberg, *Missionsmotivet i bibelutläggning och predikan hos Luther in Misjon*, 61f.

490 WA 31/1:516.20f.; 31/2:516.15ff.; 34/2:150.12ff.; 37:50.28ff., 407.15ff.; 41:43.3ff.; 47:578.19f., 794.25ff.; 49:582.4ff., 583.25ff.; 52:227.29ff. There is a representative text in Luther's 1535 comments on Psalm 110: "Observe how, through Mohammed and the Turks, the devil has subverted and exterminated the Gospel in Greece! They did not lack excellent, learned, sensible, and righteous people, just as they still have many wise, great, and fine people. The damage was done and the area was spiritually ruined and spoiled when Christ stopped preaching there. . . . The same thing happened to Rome and the entire church of the pope" (LW 13:325 [WA 41:188.14ff.]).

and some Protestant Christians were forced *de facto* to live in one or the other regions that the Turks had conquered and that were gradually becoming more Islamicized. When I here focus on the question about Luther and mission among the Turks, it is worth noting how Luther understands that these struggling Christians constitute a resource for mission within the Turkish empire. As long as these Christians are allowed to keep the Word and the Sacraments and use them properly, a remnant of bold confessing laypeople and priests will remain within the Turkish sphere of power. These will advance Christ's reign among the Turks and Muslims. In 1539 the reformer says that he wishes to preach in Turkey.[491]

The question then becomes whether or not the Word, the Lord's Supper, and a functioning worship life are at all permitted within the Turkish empire. We have on the one side seen that Luther understands the pope to be a greater enemy to Christianity than Muhammad and the Turks. The former is the Antichrist's spirit while Muhammad represents the Antichrist's flesh and performs mostly in the outer sphere.[492] On the other side, we have seen that the reformer in his apologetic/polemical work powerfully emphasizes that the Qur'an, Muhammad, and the Turks are simply fatal enemies of and distort Christian faith and ethics.[493] For these reasons, open Christian propaganda within the Ottoman Empire would be punishable by death. If the Christians as a people of the book together with the Jews were permitted some degree of freedom in their private expression of faith, they were not permitted to gather in public meetings. It was forbidden to preach

---

491 *Heerpredigt wider den Türken*, WA 30/2:109.11f., 109.16ff.: "Weil aber das Euangelion und Sacrament von Christo befolhen ynn einem lande bleibt, so sind gewislich ynn dem selbigen lande viel Christen . . . Darümb auch noch ynn der Türckey viel Christen sind Und vielleicht mehr denn sonst ynn einem lande, als die da gefangen sind Und vielleicht Türcken dienen müssen." *Lectures on Isaiah* (1527–1530), LW 17:188 (WA 31/2:408.21ff.): " . . . And even under Duke George, under the tyrant Ferdinand, under the tyrants of the Bavarians, and in Poland and Turkey we will have children belonging to our church. In so fatherly a way the voice of the Gospel carries us and brings grace and forgiveness of sins. It has the gentlest kind of bearing, it forces no one to believe." On John 3:35f. (1539), LW 22:499 (WA 47:205.31ff.): "What a consoling message this would be for the captive Christians in Turkey! They could believe it no matter how furiously the Turk may rant and rave. This was also a source of consolation for the martyrs. . . . Would to God that we could preach this message to our brethren languishing under the tyranny of the pope and the Turk." *Ennartio capitis noni Esaie* (1543/1544), published in 1546, WA 40/3:617.36ff. See also from the beginning of the 1530s, WATr 5:517.22ff. (no. 6161). Cf. WATr 1:456.1ff. (no. 904).

492 See *Luther and World Mission*, 434ff. Luther can sometimes say that the Turks are not as hard on the Gospel as the pope and the enthusiasts. The Turks destroy primarily church buildings and properties, not so much the Gospel and faith. Cf. WA 34/2:553.2ff., 553.9ff., 553.13ff.

493 See *Luther and World Mission*, 434ff., 447ff.

and confess Christ publicly or to criticize Muhammad's doctrines. Luther has as a result come to know that many in the previously so-called Christian lands have become Muslims. Without the Word/Gospel, no one can finally stand against the expanding Islamic religion.[494] It is no easy thing to preserve Christians in Christian faith among the Muslim Turks in the first half of the sixteenth century. Obviously, it is even more difficult to start an expansive Christian mission in a place where one must request the right to public worship and where the practice of the Word and the Sacraments is not permitted. Likewise, the reformer has said much about the necessity and method of mission among the Muslims. The following investigation of the Luther source material will show this.

At an early stage, Luther focuses on the pope's claim of apostolic succession and its relation to universal mission. Thereby Luther speaks of the Christianization of the Turks. In "Resolutio Lutheriana super propositione XIII. de potestate papae (1519)," Luther asks why the pope in his striving for power can at the same time call himself the vicar of Christ in the church and the successor to Peter and can leave great regions without pastoral care and the Gospel:

> Why don't those who think that the word "to take care of" [Latin, *pascere*] applies only to them, go to the Turks? Indeed, why not at least to the Bohemians? . . . Or are there not souls to take care of in Turkey and Bohemia? Or does the pope believe that he has been sent only to those already fed? Why wasn't Peter satisfied to feed only the sheep fed by Christ and instead sought himself in all the world for those whom he could care and teach? Why, I ask, do they claim the right to "take care of" and then don't fulfill that responsibility?[495]

Among all the speeches about crusade against the Turks during the 1520s, in "Bulla coena domini (1522)" the reformer expressly criticizes the pope and his church. They believe that they are able to convert the Turks with military power but do not understand that the Word/Gospel is God's means of church-planting. "But if he had been Christ's vicar, he would have stood up on his feet and gone his way to preach the Gospel for the Turks and to risk his limbs and life for that work. That would have been a Christian way to fight the Turks and help and preserve Christianity."[496]

The reformer rejects, of course, the pope's claim to power, but his reasoning shows that Luther enjoins the mission task among the Turks on the highest leader of his church. If the pope insists on his universal authority, it follows *eo ipso* that he must preach the Gospel among all peoples to expand and to plant the Chris-

---

494 Cf. "Bulla coena Domini (1522)," WA 8:708.3ff. See especially *On War against the Turk*, LW 46:175 (WA 30/2:120.25ff., 121.3ff.).

495 WA 2:225.4ff.

496 WA 8:708.29ff.

tian faith. The quotation possibly indicates also that Luther feels himself trapped behind the Roman Catholic iron curtain and that he sets some hope also on the Roman Catholic mission. Whatever the case may be, we can nevertheless say that the young reformer is occupied with the question about the Christianization of the Turks. That concern shows itself in numerous passages of which some indicate a general hope—compare here the investigations in chapter 3—about the Christianization of the Jews and the heathens.[497] The *Church Postil*'s Epiphany sermon on Matthew 2:1–12 (1522) indicates the possibility for the expansion of Christ's church through the Word/Gospel among Turks, Russians, and Bohemians. The reformer emphasizes that only the Holy Gospel's star leads to Christ and builds Christ's reign among the peoples: "There is only one sure sign whereby you can recognize where Christ and his church are, namely, the star, the holy Gospel; all else is false. But where the Gospel is preached, there this star shines, there Christ certainly is, there you surely find the Church, whether it be in Turkey, Russia, Bohemia, or anywhere else."[498]

But Luther does not only think about a general responsibility to bring the Gospel to the Turks and other peoples. There are a number of passages in which he connects himself with a possible mission preaching among the Turks. If he should reach the Turks, he will preach the Gospel as Paul did among the Gentiles.[499] Nevertheless, during the greater part of the 1520s, Luther is generally more occupied with exposing and criticizing Islam. This is evident from the previous section on Luther's apologetics and polemic concerning the religion of the Muslims.

---

497 See *Luther and World Mission*, 99–199. "Ad aegocerotem Emserianum M. Lutheri additio (1519)," WA 2:663.22ff.: "Volo, opto, oro, gratias ago, gaudeo, guod mea dogmata placent Boemis, atque utinam placerent et Iudaeis et Turcis!" "Verklärung etlicher Artikel (1520)," WA 6:82.25ff.: "Es ist mir aber ym hertzen leytt, das die Behmen nit getrost zu mir kummen und schreyben, ich wolt sie frölich und fruntlich empfangen, dasselb wolt ich auch Juden, Turcken und Heyden." Cf. WA 5:429.9ff.; 6:16.22ff.; 7:226.15ff.; 8:10.18ff., 10.31ff.; 10/2:403.6ff.

498 Lenker 1:443–44 (WA 10/1.1:711.11f.).

499 *Minor Prophets* (1524), WA 13:224.6ff.: "Brevia verba (Jona 1:1), amplissimum officium, Quid noverit nescio . . . credo, consideravit etc. ut si ego Turcis deberem praedicare. Timor humanus corripuit eum, quod noluit etc." "Predigt über Apostelgeschichte 13 (1524)," WA 17/1:509.24ff.: "Si autem essem inter Turcas, certe hospiti meo praedicarem et si conflueret populus, facerem itidem, quia Christianus inter hos eciam debet praedicare nomen Christi, Sic fecerunt apostoli, non illico ascenderunt concionem, non in forum, quia erat mera idolatria. Hic praefectus regionis invitavit eum ad prandium et in domo eius praedicavit. Sic Christus: 'cum intraveritis in domum, dicite ei: pax sit' etc. [Matthew 10:12]."

One would not expect that Luther in the situation characterized by military threat and fear that ruled in 1529 should begin to speak about organized mission work among the warring Turks. But already in *On War against the Turk*, Luther indicates, as he had previously in his challenges to the pope, that the Turks as Christ's spiritual enemies ought to be met and won with the preaching of God's Word, courageous confession, and prayer. The ideology of the Roman Catholic hierarchy about crusade against the Turks is a blasphemy against the Christ who wanted his faithful to wage a spiritual war with spiritual weapons. God's Word and Spirit are the only legitimate spiritual weapons against the Turks and Islam.[500] Luther believes, of course, that he has used the Word/Gospel in the apologetic that I earlier examined and systematized. But he probably believes also that a comprehensive positive work with the Word/Gospel, that is, evangelization, has not yet been accomplished among the Turks. This mission work is not something only for the public preachers of the Word. The reformer knows that many Christians already exist behind the front lines of the Turks. He fears that even more people will be taken captive. Because such captives will not be allowed to openly confess Christ's name and, therefore, will lack the support and nourishment of the preached Word, they will, through the propaganda of the Muslims and their daily ethical examples, be drawn from Christianity to Islam.[501] Luther criticizes those who do not think that it would be disastrous to fall into the hands of the Turks. One ought, according to these optimists, to be able to believe freely as a Christian as long as they submit themselves to the worldly regiment of the Turks. The reformer points out that Turkish religio-politics are not characterized by a true tolerance. Christians in the Turkish empire are not allowed to gather for public worship, they are not allowed to publicly confess Christ's name, and they are not allowed to teach against Muhammad's teaching. Luther asserts that preaching

---

500 *On War against the Turk*, LW 46:165–66 (WA 30/2:111.13–112.8). Concerning the contrast between the views of the Roman Catholic hierarchy and the reformer: "This would be especially so if the pope and the bishops were involved in the war, for they would bring the greatest shame and dishonor to Christ's name because they are called to fight against the devil with the word of God and with prayer, and they would be deserting their calling and office to fight with the sword against flesh and blood. They are not commanded to do this; it is forbidden. O how gladly Christ would receive me at the Last Judgement if, when summoned to the spiritual office to preach and care for souls, I had left it and busied myself with fighting and with the temporal sword! Why should Christ or his people have anything to do with the sword and going to war, and kill men's bodies, when he declared that he has come to save the world, not to kill people [John 3:17]? His work is to deal with the gospel and to redeem men from sin and death by his Spirit to help them from this world to everlasting life" (John 6:15; 18:36; Matthew 26:52 are cited).

501 LW 46:175 (WA 30/2:121.3ff.).

and confession of the Christian truth and especially the name of Christ is an indispensable duty and something the Scriptures lay on the church as a whole and on every Christian. If one is not allowed to publicly preach and confess Christ, then one has to do with a merely illusory religious freedom. A true religious freedom is important both so faith can survive and so faith can be confessed outwardly and expand. It is interesting to see how powerfully the mission idea emerges, even in the commentaries on the difficult situation of the war captives.[502] One cannot, however, avoid asking why Luther could not grant the same religious freedom to the Jews that he now requests for the Christians within the Turkish empire. Here Luther is inconsistent.

The mission perspective in *On War against the Turk* is, however, not especially prominent. That book is primarily occupied with a comprehensive apologetic against Islam and with a restrained challenge to the people to prepare themselves for war against the Turks under the banners of Caesar and with inauspicious prospects. Then Luther leaves the future in God's hands. Whatever might happen in the war against the Turks, Christ will come quickly, and through his return he will give victory to true Christians.[503]

In the reformer's *Heerpredigt wider den Türken* of the same year, Luther teaches and comforts his fellow Germans and the soldiers by describing the Turks as an eschatological enemy that according to, among other sources, Daniel 7 will destroy the empire and attempt to destroy the faith of Christ's reign. It is also emphasized that Christ through his parousia will soon destroy this archenemy. He will together with the angels gather those who die in war and all the faithful to his eternal reign.[504] But one ought not draw the conclusion that soon after the Turks conquer Germany, Christ will come and thus there need not be a mission among the Muslims. At the same time Luther indicates that the Turks will be defeated by Christ's church and the apostolic word's lightning, thunder, and fire. The older Luther writes as a motto in his office: "In 1600 the Turk shall come and destroy all

---

502 LW 36:174–75 (WA 30/2:120.25ff.), especially: "For although some praise the Turk's government because he allows everyone to believe what he will so long as he remains the temporal lord, yet this reputation is not true, for he does not allow Christians to come together in public, and no one can openly confess Christ or preach or teach against Mohammed. What kind of freedom of belief is it when no one is allowed to preach or confess Christ, and yet our salvation depends on that confession, as Paul says in Romans 10 [:9], 'To confess with the lips save,' and Christ has strictly commanded us to confess and teach his gospel" (Matthew 10:32f.; LW 46:175 [WA 30/2:120.29ff.]).

503 LW 46:181, 198 (WA 30/2:126.1ff., 143.29ff.), and especially the conclusion, LW 46:204–5 (WA 30/2:148.26ff.).

504 WA 30/2:161.22ff., 162.15ff., 174.24ff., 177.11ff., 178.19ff., 196.2ff. etc.

of Germany."[505] The thought about Christ's imminent return is powerful in 1529 but gradually fades for some reason. Christ will not come immediately. There is still time for mission among the Turks.

One can understand from *Heerpredigt wider den Türken* that Luther—before the Ottoman armies' success and power—often expresses his fear of Turkish occupation. In such a precarious predicament, can Luther have any hopes for mission among the Turks? A more organized mission work is, of course, impossible. But the reformer is likewise a man of Christ's Gospel, and he has ceaselessly taught that the Gospel ought to be preached for all peoples. Even in this book, the mission motif emerges in connection with those who have been and will be taken captive by the Turks and find themselves living within the borders of the expanding Ottoman Empire. The reformer possesses both written and oral information about how horribly the Turks murder civilians in the moment of conquest, how they without pardon split families, separate children and parents, spouses, etc. Without feeling, they sell the war captives to lifelong service among harsh feudal lords. Also the Christians scattered in the Ottoman Empire are bereft of God's Word and are tempted to backslide through the influence of the Muslim environment.[506]

As Jeremiah writes to the Jews in Babylon (Jeremiah 29:1ff.), so Luther exhorts the present and future captives in Turkey to be patient, to stand fast in their Christian faith, and not to deny or forget Jesus Christ despite all one sees of faith and piety in the Muslims. Luther's fellow Germans are encouraged to pray and meditate on the Lord's Prayer, the Ten Commandments, and the Apostles' Creed before they are captured. Especially one ought to hold fast to the Second Article of the Creed about Christ and his work of salvation against all teachings and examples that can lead astray. The Second Article is what makes us Christians and differentiates Christianity from all other types of faith on earth.[507] Of utmost impor-

---

505 *Das XXXIII. Und XXXIX. Capitel Hesechiel vom Gog* (1530), WA 30/2:224.34ff.: "Gog sol erschlagen werden, Es sind die Christlichen kirchen hin und wider, Unter den Christen sol er darnidder ligen, Aber nicht mit dem schwert sondern mit blix, donner hellisch feur vom himel herab, Denn unser fursten, die lieben Apostel, sind rechte natürliche Israel. So sind wir Christen unter yhrem panier, das ist unter dem Euangelion." Concerning the motto in Luther's office, see Ficker, "Eine Inschrift Luthers im Lutherhause," 65. In the *Table Talk*, Luther can extend the time of grace to 1560. See *Luther and World Mission*, 431ff., 435n339.

506 WA 30/2:184.7–185.9.

507 WA 30/2:185.18–186.34. See especially WA 30/2:186.1ff., 186.15ff.: "So lerne nu, weil du noch raum und stat hast, die zehen gebot, dein vater unser, den glauben und lerne sie wol, sonderlich diesen artickel da wir sagen 'Und an Jhesum Christ seienen einigen Son unsern Herrn . . .' Denn an diesem artickel ligts, von diesem artickel heissen wir Christen und sind auch auff den selbigen durchs Euangelion beruffen, getaufft und ynn die Christenheit gezelet und angenomen und empfahen durch den selbigen den

tance for Luther is that the captives and the serfs remain in the Christian faith. But he adds that those in exile ought to serve their evil, non-Christian lords with patience and faithfulness in accordance with apostolic teaching (1 Corinthians 7:20f.; Colossians 3:22; 1 Peter 2:13, 18). They ought to bear their plight willingly and not run away or commit suicide. The cross so laid and the evil is something that serves toward blessedness. The Bible shows that Jacob, Joseph, the people of Israel, Daniel, Paul, John, Christ, and all his saints have patiently borne similar crosses.[508]

What does this submissive, patient piety serve? The reformer answers that impatience and fleeing from areas ruled by the Turks damage the progress of the Gospel among the Turks/Muslims. Calm service in faith and love, however, adorn the Gospel and the name of Christ. This is a question of mission as a lifestyle that can lead many Muslims to repentance and Christian faith. Luther says:

> With unwillingness and impatience you accomplish nothing more than to anger your lord, whose servant you have become, and make him even more cruel. In this way, you place Christ's doctrine and name in ill repute as if Christians were cruel, faithless, and false people who will not do their service but run away and sneak away as rogues and robbers. . . . If instead you serve faithfully and diligently, they will adore and praise the Gospel and Christ's name so that your master and perhaps many others, however evil they might be, will be forced to say: "Well, then, those Christians are a faithful, obedient, pious, humble, diligent people." And with this you will manage to bring shame on the faith of the Turks and possibly convert some when they see that Christians with humility, patience, diligence, faithfulness, and such are so far superior to the virtues of the Turks. That's what Paul means when he says in Titus 3 [2:10]: "Servants shall in everything adorn and ornament the glory of our Lord."[509]

---

heiligen geist und vergebung der sunden, dazu die aufferstehung von den todten und das ewige leben. . . . Und durch diesen artickel wird unser glaube gesondert von allen andern glauben auff erden, Denn die Jüden haben des nicht, Die Türcken und Sarracener auch nicht, dazu kein Papist noch falscher Christ noch kein ander ungleubiger, sondern allein die rechten Christen. Darumb, wo du ynn die Türkey komest, da du keine prediger noch bücher haben kanst, da erzele bey dir selbs, es sey ym bette odder ynn der erbeit, es sey mit worten odder gedancken, dein Vater unser, den Glauben und die Zehen gebot, und wenn du auff diesen artickel kömpst, so drucke mit dem daumen auff einen finger odder gib dir sonst etwa ein zeichen mit der hand odder fuss . . . . Und bitte mit dem Vater unser, das dich Gott behüte für ergernis und behalte dich rein und feste ynn diesem artickel."

508 WA 30/2:191.21–194.22.

509 WA 30/2:194.23ff. Luther notes that even Christians in Germany must also serve all types of repulsive tyrants (WA 30/2:195.7ff.–196.9). Under the papacy, one must suf-

However, Luther remarks that Christians ought to serve their masters only within the civil domain. No Christian ought to allow himself to be forced out in war against Christians or in any way to work against the Gospel or to persecute Christians. One ought to choose in such cases to endure all types of punishment, including death. No governing authority ought to force a Christian to work against God and God's Word. One must obey God rather than people (Acts 5:29).[510]

In both of Luther's 1529 essays on the Turks, the mission perspective and the challenges to mission among the Turks have a limited place. Besides the preparatory work in his comprehensive apologetic, the preaching of the Word, the confession of the prisoners of war, and the witness through lifestyle shines through as that which ought to be able to call and convert Muslims. Mission among the Turks is thought to be first developed as a lay mission of those taken as prisoners of war in battle with the Turks and of those who have remained behind the front lines and eventually are enslaved. In this way, Luther's opinions about the work of laypeople in mission take concrete form. The priesthood of all believers is important in mission among Muslims. It is worth noting how the central form of missionizing among Muslims is a servantlike, pious lifestyle and clear confession and testimony. Opportunities for mission are widened, of course, when one requests full freedom of religion with the right to publicly confess Christ's name and to gather for public Christian worship within the Ottoman Empire.

Luther does not at all consider the conversion of the Turks impossible. They are not predestined to false belief and hardness. According to *Heerpredigt wider den Türken* and later writings, however, people as a whole (even Luther can doubt) consider the conversion of the Turks to be an impossible illusion. Their stiff-necked persistence with Allah and Islam depends on the fact that they consider all their victories over the Christians as proof that they own heaven's approval, an approval that proves they alone possess the truth. Their categorical

---

fer and tolerate even worse things for the body and the soul. The papacy oppresses above all the true faith in Christ and drives people into the despair of self-righteousness. Among the Turks one suffers primarily physical oppression, but one is not forced directly to deny faith in Christ, though one is tempted to that end. But both the pope and the Turks are archenemies of Christ. "Summa, Wo wir hin komen, da ist der rechte wirt, der teuffel, da heym: Komen wir zum Türcken, so faren wir zum teuffel, Bleiben wir unter dem Bapst, so fallen wir ynn die helle, Eitel teuffel auff beiden seiten und allenthalben." (WA 30/2:195.33). Concerning the lay-oriented mission among the Turks, see Dörries, "Luther und die Heidenpredigt," 338, 340ff.; Holsten, "Reformation und Mission," 12f. Bergman, *Den lutherske Reformation og Missionen*, 66f., does not reckon the witness of prisoners and oppressed Christians among the Turks as mission because that does not involve the sending of missionaries to other lands. Cf. also Warneck, *Abriss einer Geschichte der protestantischen Missionen*, 12ff.

510 WA 30/2:196.20ff., 197.5ff.

persistence with the Qur'an and their rejection of the Holy Scriptures is a major hindrance to their conversion.[511]

The reformer does not allow these disheartening thoughts to get the upper hand. In the lectures on Isaiah (1527–1530), Luther, on the basis of Isaiah 66:9, suddenly remarks on God's universal will to save. The promised salutary Word can come even to the Turks, he says.[512] Yes, just as Luther rightly fell away from the pope and his faith, so it might happen that a Muslim would repent of the faith of the Turks, convert to the Christian faith, and become a blessed apostate, a blessed refugee.[513] Around the dinner table in the beginning of the 1530s, one spoke of how the Gospel existed still in the regions around Budapest and in large parts of Greece. Luther points out how the Turks craftily beset the German-Roman Empire and seek to snare the population with heresy. One ought to pray to God against such evil plans. Luther advocates prayer that the Turks would be converted through the work of faithful preachers.[514] He means that the strife between Jacob and Esau (Genesis 25:22ff.) corresponds to the evangelicals' struggle with the pope and the Turks. Luther emphasizes that both Catholics and Muslims can be saved if they would only repent and be grafted into Jacob's blessing, that is, receive the Gospel and not trust their own good works.[515] Therefore it is the evangelicals who must emphasize the article about justification through faith in Christ. According to Luther, that article has overthrown the papacy. He hopes in his heart

---

511 *Heerpredigt wider den Türken* (1529): "Darüber [that is, the victors] sie so starrig, hart und verstockt werden, das man meinet, es sey unmüglich einen Türcken zu bekeren" (WA 30/2:191.7ff.). On 1 Corinthians 15 (1532): "Whoever refuses to believe that God, Christendom, faith, and the Word are really something will not give ear to instruction or persuasion. All that may be said to him is futile and lost. It is the same as trying to convince a Turk with our faith. He will concede nothing and will reject all your reasons" (LW 28:97 [WA 36:528.32ff.]).

512 LW 17:407 (WA 31/2:577.29ff.): "He is not our husband and head of the family, but He is present by means of the Word, and He sanctifies us while we are in despair. The Word can still get into Turkey." Cf. WA 34/1:439.23f: "Ubi igitur verbum dei est, ibi est ecclesia, Es sey yn der Turkey, Persia odder Hispanien."

513 "Kleine Antwort (1533)," WA 38:146.30ff.

514 WATr 5:517.22ff. (no. 6161): "Dicebant euangelii doctrinam esse in Bassa Buda, in Nieder Ofen, et magna parte Graeciae. Dixit Martinus Lutherus: Turcae conatus est valde subdolus et periculosus contra imperium Romanum, sed nos Deum orabimus, ut ipsius technas confundat, si nos illaqueare studuerit vana spe religionis, ut Deus per pios praedicatores ipsos convertat, sicut per Danielem factum est." Cf. WATr 1:456.1ff. (no. 904).

515 *Lecture on Genesis* (25:23) (1535–1545), WA 43:401.7ff., 401.13ff. Cf. WA 43:400.20ff., 400.33ff.

that it also will succeed in overthrowing Islam before Christ's coming.[516] In Matthew 23:15 Jesus rages against the Jewish pursuit of proselytes who through self-righteousness make the heathen worse than they themselves are. The reformer, however, considers it something praiseworthy in 1538 to convert a Muslim: "Everyone must truly rejoice if someone could lead people from the Turkish faith and from the devil to God, from sin to righteousness. It would truly be the highest and most costly work."[517]

In September 1541, Suleiman II put an end to the succession struggle of regent Johann Zapolya by conquering Hungary. After Zapolya's death, Ferdinand of Austria had hoped to incorporate Hungary into his empire. When the enormous Ottoman armies beset Budapest, they made its main church into a mosque, put Hungary under Turkish command, and completely laid waste those Austrian armies that had attempted to save the Hungarians. It was then that Luther and the Germans were marked as the next possible victims. In this serious situation, it is remarkable that the reformer in the book *An Appeal for Prayer against the Turks* (fall 1541) can focus on the Christians' mission task among the Turks. One ought to carefully teach children the catechism, he says. If they should be captured and taken into Muslim regions, they ought to be spiritually equipped with knowledge of the elements of the catechism and God's Word. Certainly people can become war captives, but God's Word and the faith it produces will never be captive. Because God's ways are indiscernible, no one knows what God in the future might accomplish through the war captives and through the children who have been well instructed. What weren't Joseph in Egypt and Daniel in Babylon able to accomplish?[518] Mission is here markedly *missio Dei*, and no one can predict or

---

516 "Sermon on John 3:14 (1538)," LW 22:337 (WA 47:63.36ff.): "We take such pains to stress this article because it alone has toppled the pope. May God grant that it will yet overthrow the Turk too before the Last Day. It is true that the pope and the Turk have many good and learned men; in fact, the Turks still have many monks. But on this point they all erred; for they were ignorant of this article." (LW 22:337 [WA 47:63.36ff.]). Cf. *Luther and World Mission*, 476n491.

517 WA 47:463.10ff.

518 LW 43:239 (WA 51:621.5ff.): ". . . I strongly urge that the children be taught the catechism. Should they be taken captive in the invasion, they will at least take something of the Christian faith with them. Who knows what God might be able to accomplish through them. Joseph as a seventeen-year-old youth was sold into slavery into Egypt, but he had God's word and knew what he believed. And he converted all Egypt. The same is true of Daniel and his companions." Luther continues: "Those in captivity are simply in captivity. But God's word and faith are not captive, for Christ has not been taken captive. This the preachers should continue to teach and explain. We read, 'How unsearchable are his judgments and how inscrutable are his ways' [Rom. 11:33]. God said to Moses, '. . . you cannot see my face . . . but you shall see my back' [Exod. 33:20, 23]" (LW 43:239 [WA 51:621.14ff.]).

program its development. Nevertheless, Christians ought to prepare themselves to witness and to preach. But the mission task is difficult.

In the work *Vorlegung des Alcoran Bruder Richardi* (1542), Luther is once again pessimistic about the conversion of the Turks. Such a conversion appears to be impossible because they do not listen to God's Word in the Old Testament and the New Testament. Instead, they always fall back to the Qur'an. It is best to let them go with Muhammad and hope that the Christians will be preserved in God's grace and in a true faith.[519]

We have shown above how intensely Luther in the beginning of the 1540s works to see a full Latin Qur'an published.[520] Luther's main interest was to be able to develop a factual and revealing apologetic argument against Muhammad's doctrine on the basis of the Qur'an itself. I have, however, always suspected that the persistence with which Luther fights for a Qur'an accessible to the West was at least partly the result of a missiological motivation. In a letter to the council in Basel (October 20, 1542), one finds that such is the case. Luther says that nothing can so effectively expose the doctrines, fables, and lies of the Qur'an as the Qur'an itself and the apology against it developed by evangelical theologians. Not only that. With the apologists of the early church as his examples, the reformer hopes to warn and to protect the Christians and expose the poison and the wound that Islam gives Christianity so he might be able to heal the wound.[521] Luther prays that the edition of the Qur'an that had been seized by the Basel council might be released to the glory of Christ, to the good of the Christians, to the harm of the Turks, and to the annoyance of the devil. So he says with a clear mission perspective: "But we have in this respect chosen to use your publishers as a help against the apostle of the devil and against Mohammed's scandalous doctrines so that, if God will finally give us grace, this blasphemous persecution would be reduced and not only that we Christians could be armed and preserved against such a poisonous doctrine, but also that some Turks themselves might be converted."[522] We see that the reformer's view of the universality of the Gospel of Christ is vindicated here. Even in a dangerous situation for Western Christians, he wishes that the Turks would be brought to repentance and faith.

The Latin edition of the Qur'an came out on January 11, 1543, in Bibliander's name. One understands from Luther's foreword that the older reformer hopes for a new age for the Gospel in the Ottoman Empire because through their reading of the Qur'an and the attached apology, Christians have become aware of Islam's lies

---

519 WA 53:274.7ff., 276.7ff., 276.16ff.

520 See *Luther and World Mission*, 443–47.

521 WABr 10:162.32ff., 163.74ff.

522 WABr 10:162.54ff.

and the eternal truth of the prophetic-apostolic word. It may happen that God, who earlier through Christian prisoners of war had called some Western military victors to the Gospel, will now through captive servants call some Turks out of their spiritual darkness in the Ottoman Empire. Surely this edition of the Qur'an with its attached apologetic documents can strengthen the Christians in exile so they can more powerfully preach the Gospel. Luther grounds his hope in the belief that Christ's church and Gospel will stand forever.[523]

In a 1544 sermon, Luther rejoices over the possibility that Christians might be considered worthy of suffering for the sake of Christ's name. Under the Turks, preachers have the chance through death to witness to Christ's name and to their faith in him. Even under such conditions, Christ and his cross must be preached.[524] In another sermon from the same year, Luther complains that the enthusiasts have weakened the evangelical front. Had the evangelicals been united, then they could have preached the Gospel even in Turkey.[525]

In conclusion, allow me to quote two *Table Talk* entries noted by Caspar Heydenreich from 1542/1543: "The Turks. I hope dearly to see the day when the Gospel will come to the Turks, as is now a real possibility. It is not so probable that I will see that day. But you might and then you will have to deal with the Turk carefully. Personal facts which they explain about Mohammed don't affect me, but we must attack the doctrine of the Turks. We must look at their

---

[523] *Vorrede zu Theodor Biblianders Koranausgabe*: "Gotthi, Heneti, Franci victores a cap- tivis ad Deum conversi sunt. Ita nunc quoque Deus fortassis aliquos ex Turcis vocabit ex illis tenebris per captivos doctos, aut certe oppressos in Illyrico, in Graecia, in Asia Christianos ineruditos per eos vult confirmari, qui lecto hoc libro firmius propugnare Euangelium poterunt. Magnas confirmationes continent hae antitheses: Ut Ecclesia Dei est perpetua, ita doctrinam Ecclesiae oportet esse perpetuam. At hoc figmentum Mahometi esse novum hic liber testatur. Ecclesia Dei necessario amplectitur Prophetas et Apostolos: at Mahometus horum doctrinam reijcit" (WA 53:571.35ff.). Concerning the necessity that the unbelief of the people might be exposed and that Christ as dead and risen might be proclaimed and confessed, see the powerful words in WA 53:570.13ff., 570.21ff.

[524] "Sermon on 1 Peter 2:21ff. (1544)," WA 49:389.18ff.

[525] "Sermon on Galatians 6:1ff. (1544)," WA 49:563.2ff.: "Si Diabolus non seminasset zizania per Rottenses, potuissemus nos opponere omnibus et wolten brochen haben in Turciam. Sed Diabolus excitavit Zwinglium et Oecolampadium." (WA 49:563.2ff.). WA 49:564.29ff.: "Ach were einigkeit gewesen, hett uns Venedig, Italia und die Turckey nicht starck gnug sollen sein, wir hetten die ler hinein bringen wollen, Denn so wers gangen: Ey es mus ein feine lere sein, do sie eintrechtig leren." Even in a 1545 sermon on 1 Corinthians 15:54ff., Luther can express some hope that the Spirit will be poured out in Turkey besides on the baptized and those who have heard God's Word. Cf. WA 49:763.33ff.

dogma."[526] Here the older reformer expresses his hope of seeing the Gospel's return to Turkey. But he believes it probably will not happen until the next generation. Nevertheless, he sets his trust on the ascended Christ. Luther had earlier taught in his Bible studies that Christ as the Christian worker's Lord and "driving motor" through the Word and the Spirit would bring the Gospel to all peoples. The decisive fact is that Christ lives and is more powerful than Muhammad. The miracle of the Gospel's accessibility to the Turks can occur. Therefore the reformer says:

> The Turks say that Christ in truth has been taken up into heaven. By that very fact they are already defeated. Their Muhammad is dead, but Christ was taken alive into heaven; consequently Christ is greater than Muhammad. God can still do miracles so that they might once again hear the Gospel while the devil only has the power but does not have the knowledge. If a pasha should receive the Gospel, one would see how a hole would be torn among the Turk and his people. So he has many sons? It can easily happen that one of them might receive the Gospel.[527]

Even in this inspiring mission *Table Talk*, one can understand that the expansion of God's reign is God's work. God's way with his Gospel is unsearchable for us humans. We simply cannot know beforehand what God will do to bring the Gospel to the peoples. In the great adventure of mission, God is hidden; we first understand God's works after God has accomplished them. "Well, who knows what God will do? He can, of course, do it. His election is too high for us. He is a wonderful God. We cannot therefore say anything because, as He says: 'My face you shall not see; what I have in mind, you shall not know. You shall see my works [*posteriora*]; when I have done it, will you see it, not before.' Who would have foreseen that Germany would produce such a problem for the pope?"[528]

Summary

I have in this second major division of chapter 4 sought to investigate how Luther thinks that Christians should respond to the expansion of the Ottoman Empire and Islam. I have especially focused on the place of apologetics and the mission motif. Among others, the following points are important to observe.

1. Luther regards the Turks both as the rod of God's discipline against an unrepentant Christianity and as a demonic eschatological enemy of Christians and the Christian faith. Luther believes that according to Daniel 7

---

526 WATr 5:221.1ff. (no. 5536).

527 WATr 5:221.14ff.

528 WATr 5:221.29ff.

and other Bible passages this enemy is promised success against the German-Roman Empire.

2. To stem the military advance of the Ottoman Turks, people of all social classes should first repent of their godless lifestyles. Second, under the rightful governing authorities one ought to defend oneself with physical force. The situation was precarious because Vienna was directly threatened in both 1529 and 1532 and Hungary lay temporarily under Turkish rule.

3. During his entire life, Luther was opposed to religious war or crusades against the Turks/Muslims. One should not fight wars in the name of the church or under the banner of the pope and bishops. One ought not blend the spiritual and temporal regiments. Any war against the Turks ought not aim itself at their faith and lifestyle. The emperor and the princes defend their subjects only against the military machinations of the Turks. The religion of the Muslims must be fought with spiritual weapons, that is, prayer, apologetics (the Word), and mission.

4. The Turks/Muslims are an important part of the eschatological coalition against Christ's reign and the Christian faith. With anxiety, the reformer has observed that many Christians become Muslims when they see the cultic religiosity and everyday discipline of the Muslims. A shallow Roman Catholic Christianity characterized by works-righteousness is not able to withstand Islam in the occupied regions. Because the reformer cannot believe that the devil in the Turks will simply bypass the evangelical church with its true Gospel, he seriously expects the Turks will invade Germany.

5. To equip the Christians against Islam and at the same time expose Muhammad's doctrines about faith and life, Luther develops a comprehensive apologetic for Christianity and against Islam. This attempt to render Islam harmless can be seen as the first step in a mission work. It is worth noting that Luther does not wish to abuse Islam without knowledge but to argue against actual statements in the Qur'an. Therefore he works hard so that, among other things, the Qur'an might be published in Latin.

6. In Luther's coming to terms with the faith of the Turks/Muslims, he latches on first to the fact that the Muslims use both the Old and New Testaments and often have high regard for the patriarchs, the prophets, Jesus, and others. On the other hand, they allow Muhammad and the Qur'an to decide what one ought to believe and how one ought to live. In this way, Islam contradicts the Reformation's *sola scriptura*, that is, that the Old and New Testaments are the authority concerning faith and life. Luther believes that Islam is a religion inspired by reason that, among other things, moderates the Bible's commandments to make it possible for peo-

ple to obey them. It is especially offensive that Muslims esteem Muhammad and his words more highly than Christ and his words.

7. As it concerns the First Article of the Apostles' Creed, Luther has reacted against the Muslims' belief in an all powerful Creator-God, Allah, to whose will and laws they blindly submit. He objects to the Muslims' fatalism, a doctrine that contradicts the Christian belief in a living God. Luther asserts that precisely in their emphasis on monotheism Muslims do not know the true God because they do not know God's revealer, Jesus Christ. The reformer refutes their accusations of Christian tritheism.

8. Muhammad and Islam regard Jesus as a mere prophet. At the same time, Muslims energetically deny that Jesus is God's Son, the Savior and the Mediator between God and people. When they deny his mission as Savior, they tear asunder the whole of Christian faith and become bitter enemies of Christ and the church. For Islam, the birth of Christ, his death on the cross, and his resurrection are much less than the central events of salvation. The conflict between the Christian confession of Christ and the Muslim faith in Allah and his will are definitive.

9. Islam has a lot to say about the Holy Spirit, but it does not reckon with the resurrection, the end of all history, and eternal life. Luther reacts against the Muslim belief that eternal life is conditional on obedience to Muhammad's doctrines and dependent on works. He also reacts against the earthly voluptuousness and the sensual nerve in the Muslim understanding of eternal life.

10. Luther's apologetic is aimed especially against Muslim soteriology. That soteriology is basically grounded in works of the Law and is not in any way anchored in the saving work of Jesus Christ. Islam is characterized as a religion of the law and thus fundamentally contradicts justification through faith in God's Son. Muslims defame the Gospel of unconditional grace and the way of faith in Christ to righteousness before God. The contradictions between Christianity and Islam on the question of justification are so fundamental that Luther regards the Turks/Muslims as heathen and idolaters.

11. The reformer often expresses positive sentiments about the decent, noble, devout, and restrained lifestyle of the Turks. On the other hand, Luther criticizes their violent wars waged in the name of Allah, their pride motivated by success, their religious self-confidence, their self-righteousness in cultic piety, and their polygamous understanding of marriage and the harsh behavior of Muslim men toward women.

12. The mission motif and initiative are important in the foregoing survey and analysis. After Judaism, the Turks' Islamic faith was the second non-Christian religion with which the reformer came in contact. Opportunities for mission were few during the years 1517–1546 because the Turks had already invaded Southeast Europe and were pressing toward Germany. At the same time, this study has shown that Luther understands that Christians have a responsibility to evangelize in their actual meeting with the Turks/Muslims. Luther's doctrines about the universality of the Gospel and that the time of mission endures up until the parousia of Christ come into their own.

13. Thus Turkey and the regions that had been invaded by the Turks should once again be visited by the Gospel. Luther sets a lot of hope on those Christians who remained within the Ottoman Empire. He knows that no power can hinder the Gospel of Christ to bear fruit if only God's people gather to partake of the Word and the Sacraments. However, the Turks/Muslims do not invite such a freedom of and tolerance for the Christian faith. Nevertheless, Luther hopes through the years that God in his power will open the way for the Gospel just as he did during Luther's own battle against the Roman Catholic pope and his system of power.

14. The young reformer's wish for the expansion of the Gospel among the Turks depends partly on the fact that he cannot accept that the pope who ascribes to himself supremacy over all Christianity nevertheless does nothing so the Gospel might come to Turkey and Bohemia. The successor to Peter lacks Peter's own zeal that all people be won for Christ. The pope trusts in crusades while he ought to invest everything in winning the Turks through preaching of the Gospel. In 1524 Luther volunteers himself for possible mission among the Turks.

15. In the writings on the Turkish question in 1529, mission thinking is not so prominent because it was then that Germany was directly threatened by an invasion of the Turks. Nevertheless, Luther sets his hope on prayer, the preaching of the Word, and faithful confession in word and lifestyle of individual Christians. There should be no crusade in the ordinary sense of the word. Instead, God's Word and the Spirit are the legitimate spiritual weapons in the encounter with Muslims. In *On War against the Turk*, the Turks' ban on public Christian worship, confession of Christ, and criticism of Muhammad's doctrines are a big problem for Luther. Still in *Heerpredigt wider den Türken*, Luther hopes that those Christians captured by the Turks and those scattered in the Ottoman Empire might be able to develop a kind of lay mission in which confession of Christ's name is coupled with an

exemplary patient service to the new masters. Luther energetically challenges the evangelical pastors to equip their congregational members with knowledge of the elements of the catechism (especially the relevant truths of the Second Article) in the event that the mission of oral preaching and lifestyle might be temporarily suspended within the Turkish Empire.

16. During the 1530s, the reformer often expresses his hope and prayer that the Gospel might reach the Turks. The one who engages in such work does the most costly of all works. In the writings on the Turkish question in 1529, Luther's expectation of the imminent return of Christ is prominent, but during the years before his death in 1546, he extends considerably the time of the Gospel. Thereby, his expectation of the parousia cannot have been a hindrance to his desire for a more expansive mission.

17. At the beginning of the 1540s, the German lands were for a second time seriously threatened by Turkish invasion. In *An Appeal for Prayer against the Turk*, Luther once again admonishes Christians to prayer and repentance. But even here the mission motif breaks through. The Germans should teach their children the catechism. In the face of God's incomprehensible providence, one cannot know what God will choose to do through these children, especially if they happen to sometime live within the Ottoman Empire. In his work to get the Qur'an published in Latin, the reformer is partially motivated by the hope that preachers and laypeople might be equipped for knowledgeable apologetics against Islam and at the same time for the work of converting Muslims. During Luther's final years, there exists (among all his pessimistic statements to the contrary) clear expressions of how Luther believes that a new spring will bloom for the Gospel in the Turkish Empire. He would have chosen to experience it himself, but it seemed that he would not be blessed with that joy. However, during the continuing drama, his younger friends will get to experience how the ascended Christ will do his work, even in Turkey. This is true even if the expansion of God's reign never lies only in human hands but in the hands of the wonderful God whose work is seen first after it has already been completed. Mission cannot be programmed. It is ultimately *missio Dei*.

THE INCULCATION OF THE MISSION TASK AND THE RESPONSE OF THE FIRST GENERATIONS

In chapter 3, I have surveyed and analyzed the mission perspective, especially in Luther's lectures and sermons on the texts of the Bible. In the first two major divisions of chapter 4, I have shown that Luther was occupied with the work of spreading the Gospel among the Jews and the Turks. In this last section of my study, I want to show how the mission motif during Luther's time and during the latter part of the sixteenth century was imprinted on the Lutherans, above all through the reformer's literary production.[529]

Luther Inculcates the Duty of Mission through His Literary Production

Luther understands his calling as a Bible teacher from a mission perspective. "But perhaps you will say to me, 'Why do you, by your books, teach throughout the world, when you are only preacher in Wittenberg?' . . . [A]s a Doctor in a general free university, I began, at the command of pope and emperor, to do what such a doctor is sworn to do, expounding the Scriptures for all the world and teaching everybody."[530] He has done this even for those who survive him.

Luther's work in translating the Bible has been enormously significant for world mission. He wanted first to serve the Germans, but soon throughout the evangelical world Bibles were produced in the vernacular based on Luther's German translation. The Bible became the main book for Lutheranism. In the world mission of the most recent centuries, Luther's emphasis on the word of Scripture, as well as his translation of the Bible, had a huge significance when missionaries have attempted to produce vernacular Bibles or portions of Scripture.[531]

To give baptized Christians foundational instruction, Luther wrote his Small Catechism in 1529. To provide more thorough instruction, the Large Catechism was produced in the same year. The Small Catechism was written first as a tool to imprint the elements of the Christian faith and Christian life at home, at school,

---

529 Important guidance in this subject is given in the following essays with their adduced Luther texts: Peters, "Luthers weltweiter Missionssinn," 170ff.; Bunkowske, "Was Luther a Missionary?" 167ff.; Elert, *Morphologie des Luthertums*, 1:343ff.; Gensichen, "Missionsgeschichte der neueren Zeit," T 6ff. See also the collection of texts in Stolle, *Kirche aus allen Volker*, 6ff., 43f.

530 "Psalm 82 (1530)," LW 13:66 (WA 31/1:212.6ff., 212.10ff., 212.22ff.). Luther understood his work with Scripture exposition as a divine calling and work (WA 30/2:4ff., 20ff.).

531 Bunkowske, "Was Luther a Missionary?" 168, writes: "As one who has worked with Bible translation in Africa for several decades I can say that the ever spreading circles of the influence of Luther's Bible translation, in which content took precedence over form—cannot be too strongly emphasized. In truth Martin Luther is the father of Bible translations in the vernacular languages throughout the world. At the time of the Reformation only 33 languages of the world had any part of Scripture written in them. By 1982 some portion of the Scripture was available in 1,763 languages; 279 languages had full Bibles, 551 additional languages had New Testaments, and 933 additional languages had a portion of Scripture."

and in the church. It was printed first on posters so one could display them on the walls of the homes and the schools in Germany and other Lutheran countries. According to a passage in the German Mass (1526), the reformer can even connect the catechism with mission: "Catechism means the instruction in which the heathen who want to be Christians are taught and guided in what they should believe, know, do, and leave undone according to the Christian faith."[532] Luther's Small Catechism soon became a standard book for basic Christian instruction in Europe. Its significance for evangelical Lutheran mission to the present day cannot be overestimated.[533]

Even Luther's *Church Postil* (1522) and *House Postil* (1544) have had enormous significance for the realization of the Reformation and for Lutheranism's foothold up to the present day in Europe, the United States, and many mission countries. They have helped preachers both in established domestic churches and on the front lines of mission. The postils have communicated both the right content of an evangelical sermon and the remaining duty for mission.[534] The postils have had enormous significance even for devotions at home, for the prayer houses, and for those groups that during recent centuries have engaged themselves in mission. They have helped to establish the evangelical Lutheran faith in those lands that would become mission senders. The fact that 5,000 foreign students studied the sermons and lectures of Luther and his colleagues in Wittenberg from 1520–1560 contributed to the expansion and consolidation of Lutheranism. The mission dimension that Luther had communicated went forth in this way to his contemporaries and their descendants.[535]

What I have mentioned so far about Luther's literary production has mostly to do with the content of evangelical faith, including the mission perspective. But knowledge of languages has always been important in foreign mission. It is interesting to read what Luther says in the foreword to the German Mass (1526) about worship services in German, Latin, Greek, and Hebrew. Here the mission motif in Luther's school program also is apparent. Youth ought to learn many languages so they can be equipped to go out in a centrifugal mission to foreign countries. In the early church, one did not wait for everyone to come to Jerusalem and learn

---

532 LW 53:64 (WA 19:76.2ff.).

533 Peters, "Luthers weltweiter Missionssinn," 171; and Bunkowske, "Was Luther a Missionary?" 168f.

534 As an example, I would mention that *Det Norske Misjonsselskap* early on motivated an expansive mission in South Africa by referring to a 1522 Ascension sermon, WA 10/3:139.17ff., quoted in *Luther and World Mission*, 145–46. See *Det Norske Misjonsselskap* 1847.8 (1847): 126f.

535 Peters, "Luthers weltweiter Missionssinn," 172f.

Hebrew, but the Spirit gave the apostles power to speak many different languages. The reformer asks himself what God cannot do in the future through these youth equipped with languages. For the sake of mission, Luther hopes for a school curriculum in which knowledge of foreign languages is given a high priority.[536]

Mission was also sung in the evangelical congregations during Luther's time and to the present day. In looking at Luther's thirty-seven hymns (from 1524 on), it is easy to understand that evangelization among non-Christians is important for him. On the basis of Psalm 67, he formulates the following mission hymn:

> Es wollt uns Gott genedig seyn
> und seynen segen geben,
> Seyn andlitz uns mit hellem scheyn
> erleucht zum ewgem leben.
> Das wyr erkennen seyne werck
> und was yhm liebt auff erden,
> *und Jhesus Christus heyl und sterck*
> *bekand den heyden werden*
> *und sie zu Gott bekeren.*
>
> *So dancken Gott und loben dich*
> *die heyden uber alle*
> *Und alle welt die frewe sich*
> *und sing mit grossem schalle,*
> Das du auff erden richter bist
> und lest die sund nicht wallten,
> Deyn wort die hut und weyde ist,
> die alles volck erhallten
> ynn rechter ban zu wallen.
>
> Es dancke Gott und lobe dich
> das volck ynn guten thaten,
> Das land bringt frucht und bessert sich,
> deyn wort ist wol geratten.

---

536 WA 19:74.4ff., especially: "I would rather train such youth and folk who could also be of service to Christ in foreign lands and be able to converse with the natives there, lest we become like the Waldenses in Bohemia, who have so ensconced their faith in their own language that they cannot speak plainly and clearly to anyone, unless he first learns their language. The Holy Spirit did not act like that in the beginning. He did not wait till all the world came to Jerusalem and studied Hebrew, but gave manifold tongues for the office of the ministry, so that the apostles could preach wherever they might go. I prefer to follow this example. It is also reasonable that the young should be trained in many languages; for who knows how God may use them in times to come? For this purpose our schools were founded" (LW 53:63 [WA 19:74.11ff.]). Cf. the connection between school, preaching, and the work for God's reign found in "Kinder zur Schule halten (1530)," WA 30/2:528ff. See also Holl, "Luther und die Mission," 239.

Uns segen vater und der son,
uns segen Gott der heylig geyst,
dem alle welt die ehre thun,
fur yhm sich furchte aller meyst.
Nu sprecht von hertzen Amen."[537]

Would that the Lord would grant us grace,
With blessings rich provide us,
And with clear shining let his face
To life eternal light us;
That we his gracious work may know,
And what is his good pleasure,
And also to the heathen show
Christ's riches without measure
And unto God convert them.

Now let the heathen thank and praise
The Lord with gladsome voices;
Let all the world for joy upraise
A song with mighty noises,
Because thou art earth's judge, O Lord,
And sin no more prevaileth;
Thy word it is both bed and board,
And for all folk availeth
In the right path to keep them.

O let the people praise thy worth,
In all good works increasing;
The land shall plenteous fruit bring forth,
Thy word is rich in blessing.
May we be blest by Father, Son,
Blest also by the Holy Ghost
To whom by all be honor done,
Whom all the world shall fear the most.
Thus heartily say: Amen.[538]

The conversion of non-Christians, faith, and new praise to God/Christ are important in other Luther hymns.[539] For example, the following hymn (hymn 33) is

---

537 WA 35:418.4–419.8 (*Öberg's emphasis*).

538 LW 53:234 (*Öberg's emphasis*). Cf. *Lutheran Service Book*, 823/824; *Lutheran Worship*, 288; *Lutheran Book of Worship*, 335.

539 Cf. Luther's hymn no. 5 (WA 35:425.18ff.) and no. 9 (WA 35:431.17ff.). In hymn 13, Christ is said to be the light and shepherd of both Gentiles and Jews (WA 35:439.15ff.):

based on the commission to baptize and evangelize (Mark 15:15–16; Luke 24:46f.):

> Sein Jünger heisst der Herre Christ,
> Geht hin all Welt zu leren,
> Das sie verlorn in Sünden ist,
> Sich sol zur Busse keren.
> Wer gleubet und sich teuffen lesst,
> Sol dadurch selig werden;
> Ein newgeborner Mensch er heisst,
> Der nicht mehr könne sterben,
> Das Himelreich sol erben."[540]

> Christ to his followers says: Go forth,
> Give to all men acquaintance
> That lost in sin lies the whole earth,
> And must turn to repentance.
> Who trusts and who is baptized, each one
> Is thereby blest for ever;
> Is from that hour a new-born man,
> And thenceforth dying never,
> The kingdom shall inherit.[541]

The reformer also teaches Christians to pray, focusing on the conversion of unbelievers and the heathen. In the Lord's Prayer and other prayers, one ought not only think about the coming of God's reign in his or her own life but also in

---

> Er ist das hell und selig licht
> fur die heyden,
> Zurleuchten, die dich kennen nicht
> und zu weyden,
> Er ist deyns volcks Israel
> der preys, ehr, freud und wonne.

> He is the health and happy light
> Of the heathen,
> To feed them and their eyes make bright
> Thee to see then.
> Of thy folk Israel he is
> The praise, joy, honor, pleasure. (LW 53:248)

Hymns and songs of worship have a missionizing effect. In *Preface to the Babst Hymnal* (1545), the reformer emphasizes that the worship song of the liberated heart has the ability to draw others to faith (WA 35:476.17–477.19).

540 WA 35:469.33ff.

541 LW 53:301. Cf. *Lutheran Service Book*, 406/407; *Lutheran Worship*, 223; *Lutheran Book of Worship*, 79.

the life of family and friends and in the life of the congregation. When one prays "Thy kingdom come," it means: "Dear Father, we ask you first to give us your Word, so that the gospel may be properly preached throughout the world and then that it may also be received in faith and may work and dwell in us."[542] The coming of God's reign is God's own work through the Word/Gospel. One prays that it might come "to us" but also that, "led by the Holy Spirit, [many] may come into the kingdom of grace and become partakers of redemption, so that we may all remain together eternally in this kingdom that has now begun."[543] In *A Simple Way to Pray* (1535), Luther prays: "Dear Lord, God and Father, convert them and defend us. Convert those who are still to become children and members of thy kingdom so that they with us and we with them may serve thee in thy kingdom in true faith and unfeigned love."[544] An intercessor should always have the conversion and salvation of the unbelieving and the peoples in view. We already have seen how often Luther exhorted to prayer for mission among Jews and Muslims. Mission seen from a human perspective is an impossible undertaking. But through his Word, God makes the impossible possible.

How Did the First Generations after Luther Respond to His Mission Perspective?

Finally, I will briefly show that the Lutheranism of the late sixteenth century attempted in certain respects to treat seriously the duty for mission that Luther had in lectures, sermons, and other writings lifted from Scripture. The reformer advocated that the Gospel be taken to the Bohemians, the Russians, and the Turks, among others. As an old man, he expressed the opinion that he himself probably would never come to the Turks but that his younger friends through God's miraculous leading would reach the Muslims with the Gospel.[545]

Werner Elert and H. W. Genischen have factually described the first attempts and concrete mission efforts of the Lutherans after Luther's death in 1546.[546] They write of how the Uracher movement with Primus Truber (1506–1586) and Baron Hans Ungnad von Sonegg (1493–1564) from Würtemberg sought to win the Southern Slavs and the Turks for the Gospel. This occurred, among other ways,

---

542 LC III 54 (K-W, 447).

543 LC III 52 (K-W, 447). See the analysis of the second petition of the Lord's Prayer in *Luther and World Mission*, 131ff.

544 LW 43:195 (WA 38:360.37ff.).

545 See *Luther and World Mission*, 447ff.

546 Elert, *Morphologie des Luthertums*, 1:343ff., and Genischen, "Missionsgeschichte der neueren Zeit," T 6–7. Cf. also Peters, "Luthers weltweiter Missionssinn," 174f.; and Bunkowske, "Was Luther a Missionary?" 171ff.

through the distribution of Bibles and evangelical literature in the language of the Southern Slavs and through personal connections. Thus the course of the Gospel in the Balkan lands was strengthened. Here there existed a significant advance also in mission among Muslims.[547] Stefan Consul from Pinquente translated the Slovenian New Testament to Glagolic. This was considered later by a group of spiritual and worldly authorities, and in their report they expressed the hope that the true Gospel might be carried forward in all of Turkey. In 1561 Ungnad appealed to the German princes for funds for mission work so "the pure doctrine of the divine Word may also be brought to Turkey, since it is to be expected that by this means and in this way almighty God will smite the Turks with the sword of His strength, just as He has exposed and smitten the papacy in its entirety."[548] The Viennese bookseller Ambrosius Fröhlich and the preacher Vlahovic requested that the catechism and other writings be translated into Slavic and Turkish languages. One hoped with such help to reach even the court of the Turkish "emperor."

Money came in from, among other sources, Elector August of Saxony and Duke Christopher of Württemberg, but all 25,000 volumes that were printed in Urach and Tübingen for mission unfortunately came into the hands of counterreformers. Ungnad and the Uracher movement have a place in evangelical mission history. Württemberg proves itself to have a heart for mission among non-Christian peoples when Duke Ludwig in 1583 sends the teacher Valentin Cless to Morocco to learn Arabic and Islam with the goal of missionizing among Muslims.[549] Little became of all the plans for mission in Slavic and Turkish regions, but Luther's followers had understood the signals from the reformer and gropingly sought to realize his thoughts and hopes. It was, however, not easy to reach out with organized mission beyond the iron curtains of the Roman Catholic Church and Islam. First- and second-generation Lutherans often considered mission to be a matter for which the landed gentry (that is, the kings and princes) ought to have the responsibility in the name of the church within the regions over which they ruled. This principle (*cuius regio, eius religio*), propounded as it was especially by Melanchthon, came to limit mission work and to curb mission enthusiasm. The

---

547 It ought to be observed that there were connections between Urach and Zürich according to Genischen, "Missionsgeschichte der neueren Zeit," T 10n30. Cf. how Luther's Elector John Frederick had contact with Hans and Andreas Ungnad in Austria, who reported concerning the situation of the advancing Turks in 1541 (WA 51:577f.).

548 Quotation from Elert, *Morphologie des Luthertums*, 1:344 (English: 394). Cf. *Luther and World Mission*, 483ff.

549 Elert, *Morphologie des Luthertums*, 1:344f.

princes should in their role as house fathers, among other things, be responsible for mission financing.

This we have seen in connection with the aforementioned attempts at mission. It also is reflected in Gustaf Wasa's mission work among the Lapps/Sami of northern Sweden. During Catholic times, the Sami had received some knowledge about the Christian faith through, among others, the Birkarl people who were, however, also cold businessmen and treasure hunters. Although not completely lacking economic and political ulterior motives, King Gustaf was seriously eager for mission among the Sami. Even they were to be converted from idolatry to Christianity. Already in 1525/1526, the Vadstena monk Bengt received royal orders to teach the Sami about "faith in God and what concerns the blessedness of their souls." The priest Michael Agricola was to evangelize the Sami in Torne Lappmark. His situation in a nearly unprecedented non-Christian area was characterized as *vox clamantis in deserto isto vastissimo*. Especially beginning in 1559, Gustaf Wasa ordered mission among the Sami. Nevertheless, mission attempts were generally episodic. From 1606–1607 Karl IX wanted to take the Christianization of Lappmark seriously.[550] Against Warneck and with Elert, we must assert that the mission work led and supported by the state and the state church is true and genuine mission.[551]

It may be that thoughts for mission were somewhat more powerful in Calvin and in those groups wholly or partly influenced by Calvinism. Calvin himself had much in common with Luther's way of thinking about mission, even if his predestination led to a variety of theological problems. Calvin and his church never came into direct contact with the approaching Muslims. In connection with an experimental colony in Brazil where it was planned to set up a reservation for Hugenots, Calvin sent a number of French brothers in the faith. They were to build up "a second Geneva" and undertake mission among the Topimambou Indians. After some dogmatic conflicts with the pro-Catholic leaders in Brazil, this first Protestant attempt at mission overseas ended with three martyrs, a journey home, and a powerful backlash in the Reformed Church against similar mission undertakings.[552] Even Bucer in Strassburg and the Zwinglian Bibliander in Zürich were eager for mission among non-Christians. These were influenced by humanism to consider the religions of the peoples in a more positive light than Luther. Paracelsus stood for another, more charismatic, concept of mission.[553]

---

550 See Öberg, *Mission och evangelisation*, 3ff., with bibliography.

551 Cf. Elert, *Morphologie des Luthertums*, 1:347, against Warneck, *Abriss einer Geschichte der protestantischen Missionen*, 23.

552 Genischen, "Missionsgeschichte der neueren Zeit," T 7f.

553 See Holsten, "Reformation und Mission," 14ff.; Pfister, "Reformation, Türken und Islam," 367ff.

Concerning the missiology of Lutheran orthodoxy, one must sadly certify that during the seventeenth century it came to be encapsulated and paralyzed by the theory that all people on the earth *de facto* had already been introduced to the Gospel. They based this theory on Mark 16:20; Romans 10:18; Psalm 19:4ff.; and Colossians 1:23. The faculty at Wittenberg and Johann Gerhard believed that all peoples had already been Christianized during apostolic times. If the peoples possessed now only remnants or nothing at all of the Christian faith that they once had, it was their own fault. There was no longer any duty to spread God's reign, except the duty resting on the princes who ruled over non-Christian areas (compare with the Sami in Scandinavia) and their colonies.[554]

SUMMARY

I have in this final major division of chapter 4 briefly shown how Luther inculcated the duty for mission in his own contemporaries and for those who became heirs to his theological and spiritual heritage, while at the same time creating a stable ground for evangelical Lutheran mission to the present day. The reformer's Bible translation, catechisms, and sermon collections all have had important roles to play in mission. It is even worth noting how Luther in his school curricula prioritizes teaching in foreign languages, partly for the sake of preparing children for foreign mission. The reformer through his hymns and prayers chose to sing and pray with a fire for mission in the evangelical churches.

Finally, I have pointed out how during the first two generations after Luther, Lutherans did in fact begin missions among the Slavs, the Turks, and the Sami (Lapps). But preorthodoxy and orthodoxy soon squelched mission involvement with the theory that all peoples had heard the Gospel already during the time of the apostles and that, therefore, the peoples themselves were responsible for how they received or did not receive the Gospel. In this way, Lutheran orthodoxy came to distance itself from what Luther taught: that the Gospel must be preached for all peoples until the return of Christ. Some peoples had never heard the Gospel, and others (for example, the Turks) had lost it and needed a new period of evangelization.

---

554 Elert, *Morphologie des Luthertums*, 1:341ff., shows how Philipp Nicolai in his *Commentarii de regno Christi* (1597) exhaustively reviews how all parts of the world and all peoples had received the Gospel and had Christians. Cf. how Lutheran orthodoxy's Johann Gerhard and others could not understand that duty for mission among the peoples rested on the Lutheran Church in the seventeenth century. See Warneck, *Abriss einer Geschichte der protestantischen Missionen*, 26ff.; and J. M. Berentzen, *Teologi og misjon: treck fra protestantismens historie fram till vårt århundre* (Oslo: n.p., 1990).

Bibliography

Aagaard, J. "Kap. Missionstheologie." Pages 225–49 in *Kirchen der Welt*. Vol. XV: *Die evangelisch-lutherische Kirche, Vergangenheit und Gegenwart*. Stuttgart: n.p., 1977.

———. "Luther og laegfolket." Pages 109–22 in *I skal vaere mit folk: Festskrift i anledning af Teologi for Laegfolks 10 aars jubilaeum*. Aarhus: n.p., 1978.

———. "The Lutheran Tradition and Mission Theology." *Ekumenisk Orientering* 38 (1984): 3–10.

———. "Luthers Missionssyn." *Nordisk Missions-Tidsskrift* 2–3 (1969): 114–20.

———. "Luthers syn på kirkens sendelse." *Nordisk Missions-Tidsskrift* 2 (1960): 119–25.

———. "Luthers syn på mission I–II." *Nordisk Missions-Tidsskrift* 3–4 (1967): 131–40, 195–200.

Aland, Kurt. "Toleranz und Glaubensfreiheit im 16. Jahrhundert." Pages 67–90 in *Reformation und Humanismus: Robert Stupperich zum 65. Geburtstag*. Edited by Martin Greschat and J. F. G. Goeters. Witten: Luther Verlag, 1969.

Alpers, Harm. *Die Versöhnung durch Christus: Zur Typologie der Schule von Lund*. Forschungen zur systematischen und ökumenischen Theologie 13. Göttingen: Vandenhoeck & Ruprecht, 1962.

Althaus, Paul. *Communio sanctorum: Die Gemeinde im lutherischen Kirchengedanken*. Vol 1. Forschungen zur Geschichte und Lehre des Protestantismus 1.1. Munich: Christian Kaiser, 1929.

———. "Gottes Gottheit als Sinn der Rechtfertigungslehre Luthers." *Theologische Aufsätze II 1–30. Luther-Jahrbuch: Jahrbuch der Luther-Gesellschaft* (1931): 1–28.

———. *Die Theologie Martin Luthers*. Gütersloh: Gütersloher Verlagshaus Gerd Mohn, 1962.

———. *The Theology of Martin Luther*. Translated by Robert C. Schultz. Philadelphia: Fortress, 1966.

Arnold, Franz X. *Zur Frage des Naturrechts bei Martin Luther: Ein Beitrag zum Problem der natürlichen Theologie auf reformatorischer Grundlage*. Munich: Max Hueber, 1937.

Asheim, Ivar. *Glaube und Erziehung bei Luther: Ein Beitrag zur Geschichte des Verhältnisses von Theologie und Pädagogik*. Pädagogische Forschungen 17. Heidelberg: Quelle & Meyer, 1961.

Aulén, Gustaf. *Christus Victor*. New York: Macmillan, 1969.

———. *Den kristna försoningstanken*. Stockholm: Svenska kyrkans Diakonistyrelsens Bokförlag, 1930.

———. *Till belysning af den lutherska kyrkoidén: Dess historia och dess värde*. Uppsala: Almquist & Wiksell, 1912.

Bandt, Hellmut. *Luthers Lehre vom verborgenen Gott: Eine Untersuchung zu dem offenbarungsgeschichtlichen Ansatz seiner Theologie*. Theologische Arbeiten 8. Berlin: Evangelische Verlagsanstalt, 1958.

Bauer, Karl. *Die Wittenberger Universitätstheologie und die Anfänge der deutschen Reformation*. Tübingen: J. C. B. Mohr, 1928.

Becker, H. " . . . like a traveling rain shower . . . ." *Ekumenisk Orientering* 38 (1984): 1, 27–34.

Beisser, Friedrich. "Mission und Reich Gottes." Pages 43–56 in *Lutherische Beiträge zur Missio Dei*. Veröffentlichungen der Luther-Akademie Ratzeburg 3. Erlangen: Martin Luther Verlag, 1982.

Bergman, L. *Den lutherske Reformation og Missionen*. København: P. Haase & Sons 1936.

———. "Reformationen og Hedningemisjonen." *Nordisk Missions-Tidsskrift* (1923): 13–34, 59–82, 113–41, 189–217.

Bienert, Walther. *Martin Luther und die Juden: Ein Quellenbuch mit zeitgenössischen Illustrationen, mit Einführungen und Erläuterungen*. Frankfurt am Main: Evangelisches Verlagswerk, 1982.

Bizer, E. *Fides ex auditu: Eine Untersuchung über die Entdeckung der Gerechtigkeit Gottes durch Martin Luther*. Neukirchen: Verlag der Buchhandlung des Erziehungsvereins, 1958.

Boendermaker, Johannes P. "Martin Luther—ein 'semi-iudaeus'?" Pages 45–57 in *Die Juden und Martin Luther, Martin Luther und die Juden*. Edited by Heinz Kremers. Neukirchen-Vluyn: Neukirchener Verlag, 1985.

Bornkamm, Heinrich. *Luther und das Alte Testament*. Tübingen: J. C. B. Mohr, 1948.

———. "Volk und Rasse bei Martin Luther." Pages 5–19 in *Volk-Staat-Kirche: Ein Lehrgang der Theol. Fakultät Giessen*. Giessen: n.p., 1933.

Bornkamm, Karin. *Luthers Auslegungen des Galaterbriefs von 1519 und 1531*. Arbeiten zur Kirchengeschichte 35. Berlin: de Gruyter, 1963.

Bring, Ragnar. *Dualismen hos Luther*. Lund: H. Olssons boktryckeri, 1929.

———. *Förhållandet mellan tro och gärningar inom luthersk teologi*. Acta Academiae Aboensis Ser. A. Humaniora IX. Åbo: Åbo Akademi, 1953.

———. *Gesetz und Evangelium und der dritte Gebrauch des Gesetzes in der lutherischen Theologie*. Schriften der Luther-Agricola Gesellschaft in Finland 4. Helsinki: Luther-Agricola Gesellschaft, 1943.

———. "Luthersk bibelsyn." Pages 251–82 in *En bok om Bibeln*. Lund: Gleerup, 1947.

Brosché, Fredrik. "Luther och kvinnan." In *Manssamhällets försvarare—eller skapelsens?* Uppsala: Pro Venitate, 1982.

————. *Luther on Predestination: The Antimony and the Unity between Love and Wrath in Luther's Concept of God*. Acta Universitatis Upsaliensis, Studia doctrinae Christianae Upsaliensis 18. Uppsala: University Press, 1978.

Brosseder, Johannes. "Luther und der Leidensweg der Juden." Pages 109–35 in *Die Juden und Martin Luther, Martin Luther und die Juden*. Edited by Heinz Kremers. Neukirchen-Vluyn: Neukirchener Verlag, 1985.

————. *Luthers Stellung zu den Juden im Spiegel seiner Interpreten*. Beiträge zur ökumenischen Theologie 8. Munich: M. Hueber, 1972.

Brunotte, Wilhelm. *Das geistliche Amt bei Luther*. Berlin: Lutherisches Verlagshaus, 1959.

Buchanan, Harvey. "Luther and the Turks 1519–1529." *Archiv für Reformationsgeschichte* 47.2 (1956): 145–60.

Bunkowske, Eugene W. "Was Luther a Missionary?" *Concordia Theological Quarterly* 49.2 (1985): 161–79.

Christensen, T., and S. Göransson. *Kyrkohistoria*. 2 vols. Stockholm: Läromedelsförlaget (Svenska bokförlaget), 1969.

Cohen, Carl. "Die Juden und Luther." *Archiv für Reformationsgeschichte* 54.1 (1963): 38–51.

Cohrs, F. *Einleitung zu der Schrift "Von den letzen Worten Davids."* WA 54:16–24. Weimar: Hermann Böhlaus Nachfolger, 1928.

Danbolt, E. "Misjon—evangeliets frie løp." *Tidsskrift for Teologi og Kirke* 5 (1934): 242–62.

Degani, Ben-Zion. "Die Formulierung und Propagierung des jüdischen Stereotyps in der Zeit vor der Reformation und sein Einfluss auf den jungen Luther." Pages 3–44 in *Die Juden und Martin Luther, Martin Luther und die Juden*. Edited by Heinz Kremers. Neukirchen-Vluyn: Neukirchener Verlag, 1985.

Dörries, H. "Luther und die Heidenpredigt." Pages 327–46 in *Mission und Theologie*. Edited by Franz Weibe. 1953. Reprint, Göttingen: Reise, 1970.

Drews, P. "Die Anschauungen reformatorischer Theologen über die Heidenmission." *Zeitschrift für praktische Theologie* 19 (1897): 1–26.

Ebeling, Gerhard. "Die Anfänge von Luthers Hermeneutik." *Zeitschrift für Theologie und Kirche* 48 (1951): 172–230.

————. *Evangelische Evangelienauslegung: Eine Untersuchung zu Luthers Hermeneutik*. Forschungen zur Geschichte und Lehre des Protestantismus 10.1. Munich: Christian Kaiser, 1942.

————. *Luther: Einführung in sein Denken*. Tübingen: J. C. B. Mohr, 1964.

————. *Luther: An Introduction to His Thought*. Translated by R. A. Wilson. London: Collins, 1972.

Ehrlich, E. L. "Luther und die Juden." *Judaica* 39 (1983): 131–49.

————. "Luther und die Juden." Pages 72–88 in *Die Juden und Martin Luther, Martin Luther und die Juden*. Edited by Heinz Kremers. Neukirchen-Vluyn: Neukirchener Verlag, 1985.

Elert, Werner. *Morphologie des Luthertums*. Vol. 1. Munich: Verb. Nachdruck, 1953 (1931).

————. *The Structure of Lutheranism*. Translated by Walter A. Hansen. St. Louis: Concordia, 1962.

Ellwein, Eduard, ed. *D. Martin Luthers Epistel-Auslegung.* Vol. 2: *Die Korintherbriefe.* Göttingen: Vandenhoeck & Ruprecht, 1968.

Engeström, Sigfrid von. *Luthers trosbegrepp med särskild hänsyn till församlingens betydelse.* Uppsala Universitetsårskrift 1933.3. Uppsala: Almquist & Wiksells, 1943.

Erikson, Erik H. *Der junge Mann Luther: eine psychoanalytische und historische Studie.* Munich: Szczesny, 1964.

Erling, S. B. "Martin Luther and the Jews, in the Light of His Lectures on Genesis." *Immanuel: Ecumenical Theological Research Fraternity in Israel* (1984): 18, 64–78.

Ficker, J. "Eine Inschrift Luthers im Lutherhause." *Theologische Studien und Kritiken: Zeitschrift dür das ganze Gebiet der Theologie NF* 107 (1936): 65–68.

Forck, Gottfried. *Die Königsherrschaft Jesu Christi bei Luther.* Theologische Arbeiten 12. Berlin: Evangelische Verlagsanstalt, 1959.

Forell, George W. "Luther and the War against the Turks." *Church History* 14 (1945): 256–71.

Forsberg, Juhani. "Abraham als Paradigma der Mission in der Theologie Luthers." Pages 113–20 in *Lutherische Beiträge zur Missio Dei.* Veröffentlichungen der Luther-Akademie Ratzeburg 3. Erlangen: Martin Luther Verlag, 1982.

Frostin, Per. *Politik och hermeneutik: En systematisk studie i Rudolf Bultmanns teologi med särskild hänsyn till hans Luthertolkning.* Studia theologica Lundensia 33. Lund: Gleerup, 1970.

Genischen, H. W. "Missionsgeschichte der neueren Zeit." In *Die Kirche in ihrer Geschichte: Ein Handbuch 4:T.* Edited by Kurt D. Schmidt and Ernst Wolf. 2d ed. Göttingen: Vandenhoeck & Ruprecht, 1969.

Greiner, A. "Finns det et misjonsperspektiv hos Luther?" Translated by D. W. Holter. *Norsk Tidsskrift for Misjon* 38.4 (1984): 240–52.

Grönvik, Lorenz. *Die Taufe in der Theologie Martin Luthers.* Acta Academiae Aboensis Ser. A. Humaniora 36.1. Åbo: Åbo Akademi, 1968.

Gyllenkrok, Axel. *Rechtfertigung und Heiligung in der frühen evangelischen Theologie Luthers.* Uppsala Universitetsårskrift 1952.2. Uppsala: Lundequistska bokhandeln, 1952.

Hägglund, Bengt. *Theologie und Philosophie bei Luther und in der occamistischen Tradition: Luthers Stellung zur Theorie von der doppelten Warhei*t. Lunds universitets årsskrift n.f. 1.51.4 Lund: Gleerup, 1955.

Haikola, Lauri. *Studien zu Luther und zum Luthertum.* Uppsala Universitetsårskrift 1958.2. Uppsala: Lundequistska bokhandeln, 1958.

———. *Usus Legis.* Uppsala Universitetsårskrift 1958.3. Uppsala: Lundequistska bokhandeln, 1958.

Hallencreutz, C. F. "Luther och Olaus Petri om 'missionsbefallningen.'" *Ekumenisk Orientering* 38 (1984): 11–22.

Hardt, T. G. A. "Luther—varken antisemit eller furstelakej." *Nya Väktaren* (1983): 5, 70–74.

Harnack, Theodosius. *Luthers Theologie.* 2 vols. New edition. Munich: Christian Kaiser, 1927.

Headley, John M. *Luther's View of Church History.* Yale Publications in Religion 6. New Haven: Yale University Press, 1963.

Heintze, Gerhard. *Luthers Predigt von Gesetz und Evangelium.* Forschungen zur Geschichte und Lehre des Protestantismus 10.11. Munich: Christian Kaiser, 1958.

Hök, G. "Luthers lära om kyrkans ämbete." Pages 142–79 in *En bok om kyrkans ämbete.* Edited by Hjalmar Lindroth. Stockholm: Svenska kyrkans Diakonistyrelsens Bokförlag, 1951.

Holl, Karl. "Luther." In vol. 1 of *Gesammelte Aufsätze zur Kirchengeschichte.* 7th ed.. Tübingen: J. C. B. Mohr, 1948.

———. "Luther und die Mission." Pages 234–43 in vol. 3 of *Gesammelte Aufsätze zur Kirchengeschichte.* 7th ed. Darmstadt: Wissenschaftliche Buchgesellschaft, 1965.

———. "Luthers Bedeutung für den Fortschrift der Auslegungskunst." Pages 540–82 in vol. 1 of *Gesammelte Aufsätze zur Kirchengeschichte.* 7th ed. Tübingen: J. C. B. Mohr, 1948.

———. "Der Streit zwischen Petrus und Paulus zu Antiochien in seiner Bedeutung für Luthers innere Entwicklung." Pages 134–46 in vol. 3 of *Gesammelte Aufsätze zur Kirchengeschichte.* 7th ed. Darmstadt: Wissenschaftliche Buchgesellschaft, 1965.

Holmio, Armas K. E. *The Lutheran Reformation and the Jews: The Birth of the Protestant Jewish Missions.* Hancock, Mich.: Finnish Lutheran Book Concern, 1949.

Holsten, Walter. "Christentum und nicht-christliche Religion nach der Auffassung Luthers." *Allgemeine Missionstudien* 13 (1932).

———. "Polemik der Moslems gegen die Gottessohnschaft Jesu und das Dogma der Dreieinigkeit." Pages 52–60 in *Glaube im Islam.* Vol. 3 of *Christentum und Islam.* Edited by W. Höpfner. 2d ed. Breklum: n.p., 1978.

———. "Polemik gegen die Gottessohnschaft Jesu." Pages 44–51 in *Glaube im Islam.* Vol. 3 of *Christentum und Islam.* Edited by W. Höpfner. 2d ed. Breklum: n.p., 1978.

———. "Reformation und Mission." *Archiv für Reformationsgeschichte* 44.1 (1953): 1–32.

Höpfner, W. "Das Jesusbild im Koran." In *Glaube im Islam,* vol. 3 of *Christentum und Islam.* Edited by W. Höpfner. 2d ed. Breklum: n.p., 1978.

———, ed. *Ethik im Islam.* Vol. 4 of *Christentum und Islam.* 2d ed. Breklum: n.p., 1978.

———, ed. *Glaube im Islam.* Vol. 3 of *Christentum und Islam.* Breklum: n.p., 1978.

Huovinen, Eero. "An der Unsterblichkeit teilhaftig: Das ökumenische Grundproblem in der Todestheologie Luthers." Pages 130–44 in *Luther in Finnland.* Edited by Miikka Ruokanen. Schriften der Luther-Agricola-Gesellschaft A.23. 2d ed. Helsinki: Luther-Agricola-Gesellschaft, 1986.

Ingebrand, Sigfrid. *Bibeltolkningens problematik: en historisk översikt.* 2d ed. Stockholm: Svenska kyrkans Diakonistyrelsens Bokförlag, 1966.

Iserloh, Erwin, and Gerhard Müller, eds. *Luther und die politische Welt: Wissenshaftliches Symposion in Worms vom 27. bis 29. Oktober 1983.* Historische Forschungen 9. Stuttgart: F. Steiner Verlag Wiesbaden, 1984.

Ivarsson, H. *Predikans uppgift: En typologisk undersökning men särskild hänsyn till reformatorisk och pietistisk predikan.* Lund: Gleerup, 1956.

Jensen, O. "Luther och Jødene." *LTK* (1984): 119, 80, 83.

———. "Till spørsmålet om evangelium, apostolat og embete hos Luther." *Tidsskrift for Teologi og Kirke* (1979): 5–22.

Joest, Wilfried. *Gesetz und Freiheit: Das Problem des Tertius usus legis bei Luther und die neutestamentliche Paranese.* Göttingen: Vandenhoeck & Ruprecht, 1951.

Josefson, Ruben. *Den naturliga teologins problem hos Luther.* Uppsala universitetsårskrift 1943.4. Uppsala: Lundequistska bokhandeln, 1943.

Kinder, Ernst. *Der evangelische Glaube und die Kirche: Grundzüge des evangelisch-lutherischen Kirchenverständnisses.* Berlin: Lutherisches Verlagshaus, 1958.

————. *Geistliches und weltliches Regiment Gottes nach Luther.* Schriftenreihe der Luther-Gesellschaft 12. Weimar: n.p., 1940.

Kirsten, H. "Luther und die Frauenordination." *Lutherischer Rundblick* (1973): 139–48.

Köhler, Manfred. *Melanchthon und der Islam: Ein Beitrag zur Klärung des Verhältnisses zwischen Christentum und Fremdreligionen in der Reformationszeit.* Leipzig: L. Klotz, 1938.

Kooiman, W. J. "Luthers getuigenes in de oorlogtegen de Turken: Een hoofdstuk uit zijn leer der twee rijken." In *Luther en de wereld.* Amsterdam: n.p., 1959.

Köstlin, Julius. *Luthers Theologie: In ihrer geschichtlichen Entwicklung und ihrem inneren Zusammenhange dargestellt.* 2 vols. 2d ed. Stuttgart: J. F. Steinkopf, 1901.

Kremers, Heinz, ed. *Die Juden und Martin Luther, Martin Luther und die Juden: Geschichte, Wirkungsgeschichte, Herausforderung.* Neukirchen-Vluyn: Neukirchener Verlag, 1985.

Kupisch, K. *Das Volk der Geschichte: Randbemerkungen zur Geschichte der Judenfrage.* 2d ed. Berlin: Lettner, 1960.

Lamparter, H. *Luthers Stellung zum Türkenkrieg.* Forschungen zur Geschichte und Lehre des Protestantismus 9.4. Munich: Albert Lempp, 1940.

Latourette, Kenneth Scott. *A History of the Expansion of Christianity.* Vol. 3. 10th ed. Grand Rapids: Zondervan, 1970.

Lau, Franz. *"Äusserliche Ordnung" und "weltlich Ding" in Luthers Theologie.* Studien zur Systematischen Theologie H. 12. Göttingen: n.p., 1933.

————. *Luthers Lehre von den beiden Reichen.* Luthertum 8. Berlin: Lutherisches Verlagshaus, 1953.

Lerfeldt, S. *Den kristnes kamp: Mortificatio carnis, En studie i Luthers teologi.* Copenhagen: G. E. C. Grad, 1949.

Lewin, Reinhold. *Luthers Stellung zu den Juden: Ein Beitrag zur Geschichte der Juden in Deutschland während des Reformationszeitalters.* Neue Studien zur Geschichte der Theologie und der Kirche 10. Aalen: Scientia Verlag, 1973.

Lieberg, Hellmut. *Amt und Ordination bei Luther und Melanchthon.* Forschungen zur Kirchen- und Dogmengeschichte 11. Göttingen: Vandenhoeck & Ruprecht, 1962.

Lienhard, Marc. *Martin Luthers christologisches Zeugnis: Entwicklung und Grundzüge seiner Christologie.* Göttingen: Vandenhoeck & Ruprecht, 1979.

Lilje, Hanns. "Morgenstunden der Mission III: Der missionarische Wille der Reformation." *Evangelische Missionszeitschrift* 3 (1942): 97–102.

Lind, R. *Luthers Stellung zum Kreuz- und Türkenkrieg.* Giessen: Brühl'sche Universitätsdruckerei, 1940.

Ljunggren, Gustaf. *Synd och skuld i Luthers teologi.* Stockholm: Svenska kyrkans Diakonistyrelsens Bokförlag, 1928.

Loewenich, Walther von. *Luther als Ausleger der Synoptiker*. Forschungen zur Geschichte und Lehre des Protestantismus 10.5. Munich: Christian Kaiser, 1954.

———. *Luther und das Johanneische Christentum*. Forschungen zur Geschichte und Lehre des Protestantismus 7.4. Munich: Christian Kaiser, 1935.

———. *Luthers Theologia crucis*. Forschungen zur Geschichte und Lehre des Protestantismus 2.2. 2d ed. Munich: Christian Kaiser, 1933.

———. *Martin Luther: The Man and His Work*. Translated by Lawrence W. Denef. Minneapolis: Augsburg, 1986.

———. *Martin Luther: Der Mann und das Werk*. Munich: List, 1982.

Lohse, Bernhard. *Ratio und Fides: Eine Untersuchung über die ratio in der Theologie Luthers*. Forschungen zur Kirchen- und Dogmengeschichte 8. Göttingen: Vandenhoeck & Ruprecht, 1958.

Lønning, Inge. "Kanon im Kanon." *Zum dogmatischen Grundlagenproblem des neutestamentlichen Kanons*. Forschungen zur Geschichte und Lehre des Protestantismus 10.43. Munich: Christian Kaiser, 1972.

———. "Paulus und Petrus: Gal. 2:11ff als kontroverstheologisches Fundamentalproblem." *Studia theologica* 24.1 (1970): 1–69.

Mannermaa, Tuomo. *Der im Glauben gegenwärtige Christus: Rechtfertigung und Vergottung. Zum ökumenischen Dialog*. Arbeiten zur Geschichte und Theologie des Luthertums n.f. 8. Hannover: Lutherisches Verlagshaus, 1989.

———. "Grundlagenforschung der Theologie Martin Luthers und die Ökumene." Pages 17–35 in *Thesaurus Lutheri*. Edited by Tuomo Mannermaa et al. Schriften der Luther-Agricola-Gesellschaft A.24. Helsinki: Finnische Theologische Literaturgesellschaft, 1987.

———. "In ipsa fide Christus adest." *Der Schnittpunkt zwischen lutherischer und orthodoxer Theologie*. Schriften der Finnischen Gesellschaft für Missiologie und Ökumene 30. Helsinki: Finnische Gesellschaft für Missiologie und Ökumene, 1979.

———. "Das Verhältnis von Glaube und Liebe in der Theologie Luthers." Pages 29–110 in *Luther in Finnland*. Edited by Miikka Ruokanen. Schriften der Luther-Agricola-Gesellschaft A.23. 2d ed. Helsinki: Luther-Agricola-Gesellschaft, 1986.

Manns, Peter. "*Fides absoluta—fides incarnata*: Zur Rechtfertigungslehre Luthers im Grossen Galater-Kommentar." Pages 1–48 in *Vater im Glauben: Studien zur Theologie Martin Luthers: Festgabe zum 65. Geburtstag am 10. März 1988*. Edited by R. Decot and Peter Manns. Veröffentlichungen des Instituts für Europäische Geschichte Mainz, Abteilung für Abendländische Religionsgeschichte 131. Stuttgart: F. Steiner Verlag Wiesbaden, 1988.

———. "Luthers Zwei-Reiche- und Drei Stände-Lehre." Pages 376–96 in *Vater im Glauben: Studien zur Theologie Martin Luthers: Festgabe zum 65. Geburtstag am 10. März 1988*. Edited by R. Decot and Peter Manns. Veröffentlichungen des Instituts für Europäische Geschichte Mainz, Abteilung für Abendländische Religionsgeschichte 131. Stuttgart: F. Steiner Verlag Wiesbaden, 1988.

Maser, P. "Erbarmen für Luther? Zu zwei neuen Büchern über den Reformator und die Juden." *Judaica* 39 (1983): 166–78.

Mau, Rudolf. "Luthers Stellung zu den Türken." Pages 647–62 in vol. 1 and pp. 956–66 in vol. 2 of *Leben und Werk Martin Luthers von 1526 bis 1546*. Edited by Helmar Junghans. Göttingen: Vandenhoeck & Ruprecht, 1983.

Maurer, Wilhelm. *Kirche und Synagoge: Motive und Formen der Auseinandersetzung der Kirche mit dem Judentum im Laufe der Geschicthe*. Franz Delitzsch-Vorlesungen 1951. Stuttgart: Kohlhammer, 1953.

———. "Reformation und Mission." Pages 20–41 in *Ihr werdet meine Zeugen sein Georg F. Vicedom zum 60. Geburtstag*. Nürnberg: Selbstverlag des Bayerische Missions Konferenz, 1963.

———. "Die Zeit der Reformation." Pages 375–429 in vol. 1 of *Kirche und Synagoge: Handbuch zur Geschichte von Christen und Juden*. Darstellung mit Quellen. Edited by Karl Heinrich Rengstorf and Siegfried von Kortzfleisch. Stuttgart: Klett, 1968.

Meier, Kurt. "Zur Interpretation von Luthers Judenschriften." Pages 127–53 in *Kirche und Judentum*. Arbeiten zur Geschichte des Kirchenkampfes, Ergänzungsreihe 7. Göttingen: Vandenhoeck & Ruprecht, 1968.

Molland, E. *Kristenhetens kirker og trossamfunn*. Oslo: Gyldendal, 1976.

Moritzen, N. P. "Abraham im Koran." Pages 36–43 in *Glaube im Islam*. Vol. 3 of *Christentum und Islam*. Edited by W. Höpfner. 2d ed. Breklum: n.p., 1978.

Müller, G. "Tribut an den Geist seiner Zeit: Martin Luthers Stellung zu den Juden." *Evangelische Kommentare* 15 (1983): 305–8.

Myklebust, O. G. *Misjonskunnskap: En innføring*. Oslo: Gyldendal, 1976.

Neill, Stephen. *A History of Christian Missions*. The Pelican History of the Church 6. Middlesex: Penguin, 1964.

———. *Misjon i 2000 år*. Oslo: n.p., 1972.

Nygren, Anders. *Den kristna kärlekstanken genom tiderna Eros och agape*. Vol. 2. 2d ed. Stockholm: Svenska kyrkans Diakonistyrelsens Bokförlag, 1947.

Obendiek, H. *Der Teufel bei Martin Luther: Eine theologische Untersuchung*. Furche-Studien 4. Berlin: n.p., 1931.

Öberg, Ingemar. "Den evangeliska biskopsvigningen i Naumburg 1542." Pages 205–10 in *Så tilholder og formaner jeg deg*. Edited by J. Eriksen and H. Aarflot. Presteforeningens studiebibliotek 21. Oslo: Den Norske kirkes presteforening, 1984.

———. *Himmelrikets nycklar och kyrklig bot i Luthers teologi 1517–1537*. Acta Universitatis Upsaliensis, Studia doctrinae Christianae Upsaliensia 8. Uppsala: University of Uppsala, 1970.

———. ". . . i hans navn skal omvendelse og tilgivelse for syndene forkynnes for alle folkeslag." *Tidsskrift for Teologi og Kirke* 2 (1984): 109–26.

———. "Den lutherska reformationen och ordinationen." Pages 59–87 in *Så tilholder og formaner jeg deg*. Edited by J. Eriksen and H. Aarflot. Presteforeningens studiebibliotek 21. Oslo: Den Norske kirkes presteforening, 1984.

———. *Mission och evangelisation i Gellivare-bygden ca 1740–1770*. Kyrkohist. ark. vid Åbo Akademi 7. Åbo: Åbo Akademi, 1983.

———. "Mission und Heilsgeschichte bei Luther und in den Bekenntnisschriften." Pages 25–42 in *Lutherische Beiträge zur Missio Dei*. Veröffentlichungen der Luther-Akademie Ratzeburg 3. Erlangen: Martin Luther Verlag, 1982.

————. *Missionsmotivet i bibelutläggning och predikan hos Luther in Misjon. En velsignelse til alle folkeslag.* Presteforeningens studiebibliotek 25: 45–68. Oslo: Den Norske kirkes presteforening, 1988.

————. "Skriften alene—tron alene." In *I helige oppdrag: Festskrift ved Misjonshøgskolens 140- årsjubileum og innvielse av fakultetsbygget.* Edited by J. Borgenvik and E. Larsen. Stavanger: n.p. 1983.

Oberman, Heiko A. "Luthers Beziehungen zu den Juden: Ahnen und Geahndete." Pages 519–30 in vol. 1 and pp. 894–904 in vol. 2 of *Leben und Werk Martin Luthers von 1526 bis 1546.* Edited by Helmar Junghans. Göttingen: Vandenhoeck & Ruprecht, 1983.

————. *Wurzeln des Antisemitismus: Christenangst und Judenplage im Zeitalter von Humanismus und Reformation.* Berlin: Severin & Siedler, 1981.

Olsson, Herbert. *Grundproblemet i Luthers socialetik.* Vol. 1. Lund: H. Ohlssons, 1934.

————. "Kyrkans synlighet och fördoldhet enligt Luther." Pages 306–26 in *En bok om kyrkan av svenska teologer.* Stockholm: n.p., 1942.

————. *Schöpfung, Vernunft und Gesetz in Luthers Theologie.* Acta universitatis Upsaliensis, Studia doctrinae Christianae Upsaliensia 10. Uppsala: n.p., 1971.

Östergaard-Nielsen, H. *Scriptura sacra et viva vox: Eine Lutherstudie.* Forschungen zur Geschichte und Lehre des Protestantisumus 10.10. Munich: Christian Kaiser, 1957.

Paret, Rudi. *Mohammed und der Koran: Geschichte und Verkündigung des arabischen Propheten.* Kohlhammer Urban-Taschenbücher 80.32. 3d ed. Stuttgart: Kohlhammer, 1957.

Pauls, Th. *Luther und die Juden.* 3 vols. Eine theologische und religionspädagogische Schriftenreihe, 54, 55, 61. Bonn: G. Scheur, 1939.

Pedersen, Ebbe Thestrup. *Luther som skriftfortolker: En studie i Luthers skriftsyn, hermeneutik og eksegese.* Copenhagen: Nyt Nordisk Forlag Arnold Busck, 1959.

————. "Luthers Laere om Gudserkendelsen." *Dansk teologisk tidsskrift* (1941): 67–97.

————. "Luthers synoptikereksegese." *Praestforeningens Blad* (1955): 705–16.

————. "Schöpfung und Geschichte bei Luther." *Studia theologica* 3.1 (1949): 5–33.

Persson, Per Erik. *Kyrkans ämbete som Kristus-representation: En kritisk analys av nyare ämbetsteologi.* Studia theologica Lundensia 20. Lund: Gleerup, 1961.

————. *Sacra doctrina: En studie till förhållandet mellan ratio och revelatio i Thomas' av Aquino teologi.* Studia theologica Lundensia 15. Lund: Gleerup, 1957.

Peters, P. "Luthers weltweiter Missionssinn." *Lutherischer Rundblick* 1969.17 (1969): 162–75.

Peura, Simo. "Der Vergöttlichungsgedanke in Luthers Theologie 1518–1519." Pages 171–84 in *Thesaurus Lutheri.* Edited by Tuomo Mannermaa et al. Schriften der Luther-Agricola-Gesellschaft A.24. Helsinki: Finnische Theologische Literaturgesellschaft, 1987.

Pfister, R. "Reformation, Türken und Islam." *Zwingliana* 10 (1958): 345–75.

Pfisterer, R. "Zwischen Polemik und Apologetik. Anmerkungen zu Veröffentlichungen über Luthers Stellung zu den Juden." *Tribüne* (1984): 23, 99–124.

Pinomaa, Lennart. *Sieg des Glaubens: Grundlinien der Theologie Luthers.* Edited by Horst Beintker. Göttingen: Vandenhoeck & Ruprecht, 1964.

Pörsti, J. "Luthers syn på evangelisation." *Ekumenisk Orientering* 38 (1984): 23–26.

Prenter, Regin. *Embedets guddommelige indstiftelse og det almindelige praestedømme hos Luther*. Uppsala Universitetsårskrift 12. Uppsala: n.p., 1960.

———. *Spiritus creator: Studier i Luthers theologi*. 2d ed. København: Samlerens Forlag, 1946.

Raeder, S. "Islamischer und christlicher Gottesbegriff." Pages 7–31 in *Glaube und Islam*. Vol. 3 of *Christentum und Islam*. Edited by W. Höpfner. 2d ed. Breklum: n.p., 1978.

Reiter, Paul J. *Martin Luthers Umwelt, Charakter und Psychose, sowie die Bedeutung dieser Faktoren für seine Entwicklung und Lehre: Eine historisch-psychiatrische Studie*. Vol. 1: *Umwelt*. Vol. 2: *Luthers Persönlichkeit, Seelenleben und Krankheiten*. Kopenhagen: Levin & Munksgaard, 1937, 1941.

Rietschel, G. *Lehrbuch der Liturgik*. Vol. 2. 2d ed. neubearbeitete Paul Graff. Göttingen: Vandenhoeck & Ruprecht, 1951.

Runestam, Arvid. *Den kristliga friheten hos Luther och Melanchton*. Stockholm: Svenska kyrkans Diakonistyrelsens Bokförlag, 1917.

Saebø, M. "Luther og jødene." *LKT* 118 (1983): 641–46.

Schäfer, Ernst. *Luther als Kirchenhistoriker: Ein Beitrag zur Geschichte der Wissenschaft*. Gütersloh: C. Bertelsmann, 1897.

Schempp, P. *Luthers Stellung zur Heiligen Schrift*. Forschungen zur Geschichte und Lehre des Protestantismus 2.2. Munich: Christian Kaiser, 1929.

Scherer, James A. *Mission and Unity in Lutheranism*. Philadelphia: Fortress, 1969.

———. *That the Gospel May Be Sincerely Preached throughout the World: A Lutheran Perspective on Mission and Evangelism in the 20th Century*. Lutheran World Federation Report 11–12. Stuttgart: Published on behalf of Lutheran World Federation by Kreuz Verlag Erich Breitsohl, 1982.

Schloenbach, Manfred. *Heiligung als Fortschreiten und Wachstum des Glaubens in Luthers Theologie*. Schriften der Luther-Agricola-Gesellschaft 13. Helsinki: Luther-Agricola-Gesellschaft, 1963.

Schreiner, S. "Jüdische Reaktionen auf die Reformation—einige Anmerkungen." *Judaica* 39 (1983): 150–65.

Seeberg, Erich. *Luthers Theologie: Motive und Ideen*. Vol. 1: *Die Gottesanschauung*. Göttingen: Vandenhoeck & Ruprecht, 1929.

———. *Luthers Theologie: Motive und Ideen*. Vol. 2: *Christus Wirklichheit und Urbild*. Stuttgart: W. Kohlhammer, 1938.

Siirala, Aarne. "Luther und die Juden." *Lutherischen Rundschau* 14 (1964): 427–52.

Skydsgaard, K. E. *Metafysik og tro: En dogmatisk studie i nyere thomisme*. Copenhagen: Nyt Nordisk Förlag Arnold Busck, 1937.

Stange, C. "Der Todesgedanke in Luthers Tauflehre." *Zeitschrift für systematische Theologie* 5 (1927).

Stöhr, Martin. "Luther und die Juden." *Evangelische Theologie* 20.4 (1960): 157–82.

———. "Luther und die Juden." Pages 115–40 in *Christen und Juden*. Edited by Wolf-Dieter Marsch and Karl Thieme. Mainz: Matthias-Grünewald, 1961.

———. "Martin Luther und die Juden." Pages 89–108 in *Die Juden und Martin Luther— Martin Luther und die Juden.* Edited by Heinz Kremers. Neukirchen-Vluyn: Neukirchener Verlag, 1985.

Stolle, Volker. *The Church Comes from All Nations.* Translated by Klaus Detlev Schulz and Daniel Thies. St. Louis: Concordia Academic Press, 2003.

———. *Kirche aus allen Völkern: Luthertexte zur Mission.* Erlangen: Verlag der Ev.-Luth.-Mission (now: Erlanger Verlag für Mission und Ökumene), 1983.

Sucher, C. Bernd. *Luthers Stellung zu den Juden: Eine Interpretation aus germanistischer Sicht.* Bibliotheca humanistica und reformatorica 23. Munich: Nieuwkoop B. de Graaf, 1977.

Sundkler, Bengt. *Missionens värld, Missionskunskap och missionshistoria.* Scand. Univ. Books. Uppsala: Svenska Bokförlaget, 1963.

Tjernagel, Neelak S. *Martin Luther and the Jewish People.* Milwaukee: Northwestern, 1985.

Törnvall, Gustaf. *Andligt och världsligt regemente hos Luther: Studier i Luthers världs- och samhällsbild.* Stockholm: Svenska kyrkans Diakonistyrelsens Bokförlag, 1948.

Vajta, Vilmos. *Die Theologie des Gottesdienstes bei Luther.* Stockholm: Svenska kyrkans Diakonistyrelsens Bokförlag, 1948.

Vielau, H. W. *Luther und der Türke.* Ph.D. diss. Baruth/Mark-Berlin: Särchen, 1936.

Vikström, John. "Mission und Reich Gottes. Erlösung und Reich des Friedens als Glaubensgegenstand und ethische Aufgabe. Ein Beitrag zum aktuellen zwischenkirchlichen Dialog." Pages 57–68 in *Lutherische Beiträge zur Missio Dei.* Veröffentlichungen der Luther-Akademie Ratzeburg 3. Erlangen: Martin Luther Verlag, 1982.

Vogelsang, Erich. *Der angefochtene Christus bei Luther.* Arbeiten zur Kirchengeschichte 21. Berlin: De Gruyter, 1932.

———. *Luthers Kampf gegen die Juden.* Sammlung gemeinverständlicher Vorträge und Schriften aus dem Gebiet der Theologie und Religionsgeschichte 168. Tübingen: J. C. B. Mohr, 1933.

Vogler, Günther. "Luthers Geschichtsauffassung im Spiegel seines Türkenbildes." Pages 118–27 in *450 Jahre Reformation.* Edited by Leo Stern and Max Steinmetz. Berlin: VEB Deutscher Verlag des Wissenschaften, 1967.

Vossberg, Herbert. *Luthers Kritik aller Religion: Eine theologiegeschichtliche Untersuchung zu einem systematischen Hauptproblem.* Leipzig: A. Drichert, 1922.

Wallmann, Johannes. "Luthers Stellung zu Judentum und Islam." *Luther* 57.2 (1986): 49–60.

Walther, W. "Luther und die Juden." *Allgemeine evangelisch-lutherische Kirchenzeitung* 54 (1921): 130–33, 146–50, 162–67, 196–99, 213–17, 475–76.

Warneck, Gustav. *Abriss einer Geschichte der protestantischen Missionen: Von der Reformation bis auf die Gegenwart.* 9th ed. Berlin: M. Warneck, 1910.

Watson, Philip S. *Let God Be God! An Interpretation of the Theology of Martin Luther.* London: Epworth, 1948.

Weyer, Adam. "Die Juden in den Predigten Martin Luthers." Pages 163–70 in *Die Juden und Martin Luther, Martin Luther und die Juden.* Edited by Heinz Kremers. Neukirchen-Vluyn: Neukirchener Verlag, 1985.

Wingren, Gustaf. *Creation and Law*. Translated by Ross McKenzie. Philadelphia: Muhlenberg, 1961.

———. *Luther frigiven: Tema med sex variationer*. Lund: Gleerup, 1970.

———. *Luther on Vocation*. Translated by Carl C. Rasmussen. Philadelphia: Muhlenberg, 1957.

———. "Lutherische Theologie und Weltmission." Pages 73–78 in *Das Lebendige Wort in einer verantwortlichen Kirche: Offizieller Bericht der 2. Vollversammlung des Luth. Weltbundes. Hannover 25.7 bis 3.8.1952*. Hannover: n.p., 1952.

———. *Luthers lära om kallelsen*. 2d ed. Lund: Gleerup, 1948

———. *Skapelsen och lagen*. Lund: Gleerup, 1958

Wolf, Ernst. "Die Christusverkündigung bei Luther." Pages 30–80 in *Peregrinatio: Studien zur reformatorischen Theologie und zum Kirchenproblem*. 1934. Reprint, Munich: Christian Kaiser, 1954.

———. "Martin Luther: Das Evangelium und die Religion." Pages 9–29 in *Peregrinatio: Studien zur reformatorischen Theologie und zum Kirchenproblem*. Reprint, Munich: Christian Kaiser, 1954.

Index